Psychology in Everyday Life

The Science of Behavior and Mental Processing

Revised Preliminary Edition

By Dr. DeAnna Burney

cognella™
San Diego, CA

Bassim Hamadeh, CEO and Publisher
Christopher Foster, General Vice President
Michael Simpson, Vice President of Acquisitions
Jessica Knott, Managing Editor
Jess Busch, Senior Graphic Designer
Kevin Fahey, Cognella Marketing Manager
Zina Craft, Acquisitions Editor
Jamie Giganti, Project Editor
Brian Fahey, Licensing Associate

16 15 14 13 12   1 2 3 4 5

Printed in the United States of America

ISBN: 978-1-60927-509-9

www.cognella.com 800.200.3908

Contents

To my grandparents Shira and Chelsea McKinnie and the late Roberta Smith.

Thank you for modeling the essence of Psychology in life.

TIMELINE OF PSYCHOLOGY: HISTORICAL TO CONTEMPORARY

1879   FIRST PSYCHOLOGY LABORATORY

Wilhelm Wundt opens first experimental laboratory in psychology at the University of Leipzig, Germany. Credited with establishing psychology as an academic discipline, Wundt's students include Emil Kraepelin, James McKeen Cattell, and G. Stanley Hall.

1883   FIRST AMERICAN PSYCHOLOGY LABORATORY

G. Stanley Hall, a student of Wilhelm Wundt, establishes first U.S. experimental psychology laboratory at Johns Hopkins University.

1886   FIRST DOCTORATE IN PSYCHOLOGY

The first doctorate in psychology is given to Joseph Jastrow, a student of G. Stanley Hall at Johns Hopkins University. Jastrow later becomes professor of psychology at the University of Wisconsin and serves as president of the American Psychological Association in 1900.

1888   FIRST PROFESSOR OF PSYCHOLOGY

The academic title "professor of psychology" is given to James McKeen Cattell in 1888, the first use of this designation in the United States. A student of Wilhelm Wundt's, Cattell serves as professor of psychology at University of Pennsylvania and Columbia University.

1892   APA FOUNDED

G. Stanley Hall founds the American Psychological Association (APA) and serves as its first president. He later establishes two key journals in the field: American Journal of Psychology (1887) and Journal of Applied Psychology (1917).

1896   FUNCTIONALISM

Functionalism, an early school of psychology, focuses on the acts and functions of the mind rather than its internal contents. Its most prominent American advocates are William James and John Dewey, whose 1896 article "The Reflex Arc Concept in Psychology" promotes functionalism

PSYCHOANALYSIS

The founder of psychoanalysis, Sigmund Freud, introduces the term in a scholarly paper. Freud's psychoanalytic approach asserts that people are motivated by powerful, unconscious drives and conflicts. He develops an influential therapy based on this assertion, using free association and dream analysis.

STRUCTURALISM

Edward B. Titchener, a leading proponent of structuralism, publishes his Outline of Psychology. Structuralism is the view that all mental experience can be understood as a combination of simple elements or events. This approach focuses on the contents of the mind, contrasting with functionalism.

FIRST PSYCHOLOGY CLINIC

After heading a laboratory at University of Pennsylvania, Lightner Witmer opens world's first psychological clinic to patients, shifting his focus from experimental work to practical application of his findings.

1900   THE INTERPRETATION OF DREAMS

Sigmund Freud introduces his theory of psychoanalysis in The Interpretation of Dreams, the first of 24 books he would write exploring such topics as the unconscious, techniques of free association, and sexuality as a driving force in human psychology.

1901   MANUAL OF EXPERIMENTAL PSYCHOLOGY

With publication of the Manual of Experimental Psychology, Edward Bradford Titchener introduces structuralism to the United States. Structuralism, an approach which seeks to identify the basic elements of consciousness, fades after Titchener's death in 1927.

1904   FIRST WOMAN PRESIDENT OF THE APA

Mary Calkins is elected president of the APA. Calkins, a professor and researcher at Wellesley College, studied with William James at Harvard University, but Harvard denied her a Ph.D. because of her gender.

1905   IQ TESTS DEVELOPED

Using standardized tests, Alfred Binet and Theodore Simon develop a scale of general intelligence on the basis of mental age. Later researchers refine this work into the concept of intelligence quotient; IQ, mental age over physical age. From their beginning, such tests' accuracy and fairness are challenged.

1908   A MIND THAT FOUND ITSELF

Clifford Beers publishes A Mind That Found Itself, detailing his experiences as a patient in 19th-century mental asylums. Calling for more humane treatment of patients and better education about mental illness for the general population, the book inspires the mental hygiene movement in the United States.

1909   PSYCHOANALYSTS VISIT CLARK UNIVERSITY

Sigmund Freud and Carl Jung visit the United States for a Psychoanalysis Symposium at Clark University organized by G. Stanley Hall. At the symposium, Freud gives his only speech in the United States.

1913   BEHAVIORISM

John B. Watson publishes "Psychology as Behavior," launching behaviorism. In contrast to psychoanalysis, behaviorism focuses on observable and measurable behavior.

1917   ARMY INTELLIGENCE TESTS IMPLEMENTED

Standardized intelligence and aptitude tests are administered to two million U. S. soldiers during WWI. Soon after, such tests are used in all U.S. armed forces branches and in many areas of civilian life, including academic and work settings.

1920   FIRST AFRICAN AMERICAN DOCTORATE IN PSYCHOLOGY

Francis Cecil Sumner earns a Ph.D. in psychology under G. Stanley Hall at Clark University. Sumner later serves as chair of the Howard University psychology department.

THE CHILD'S CONCEPTION OF THE WORLD

Swiss psychologist Jean Piaget publishes The Child's Conception of the World, prompting the study of cognition in the developing child.

1921   RORSCHACH TEST CREATED

Swiss psychiatrist Hermann Rorschach devises a personality test based on patients' interpretations of inkblots.

1925   MENNINGER CLINIC FOUNDED

Charles Frederick Menninger and his sons Karl Augustus and William Clair found The Menninger Clinic in Topeka, Kansas. They take a compassionate approach to the treatment of mental illness, emphasizing both psychological and psychiatric disciplines.

1927   FIRST NOBEL PRIZE FOR PSYCHOLOGICAL RESEARCH

1929   ELECTROENCEPHALOGRAM INVENTED

Psychiatrist Hans Berger invents the electroencephalogram and tests it on his son. The device graphs the electrical activity of the brain by means of electrodes attached to the head.

1933   NAZI PERSECUTION OF PSYCHOLOGISTS

After the Nazi party gains control of the government in Germany, scholars and researchers in psychology and psychiatry are persecuted. Many, including Freud, whose books are banned and burned in public rallies, move to Britain or the United States.

1935   ALCOHOLICS ANONYMOUS

Alcoholics Anonymous (AA) is founded by Bob Smith of Akron, Ohio. AA's group meetings format and 12-step program become the model for many other mutual-support therapeutic groups.

GESTALT PSYCHOLOGY

Kurt Koffka, a founder of the movement, publishes Principles of Gestalt Psychology in 1935. Gestalt (German for "whole" or "essence") psychology asserts that psychological phenomena must be viewed not as individual elements but as a coherent whole.

1936   FIRST LOBOTOMY IN THE UNITED STATES

Walter Freeman performs first frontal lobotomy in the United States at George Washington University in Washington, D.C. By 1951, more than 18,000 such operations have been performed. The procedure, intended to relieve severe and debilitating psychosis, is controversial.

1937   THE NEUROTIC PERSONALITY OF OUR TIME

Psychologist Karen Horney publishes The Neurotic Personality of Our Time. Horney goes on to challenge many of Freud's theories, as have many later psychologists and scholars. Specifically, she questions Freud's theories on the Oedipal Complex and castration anxiety.

1938   THE BEHAVIOR OF ORGANISMS

            B.F. Skinner publishes The Behavior of Organisms, introducing the concept of operant
            conditioning. The work draws widespread attention to behaviorism and inspires labora-
            tory research on conditioning.

            ELECTROCONVULSIVE THERAPY BEGUN

            Clifford Beers publishes A Mind That Found Itself, detailing his experiences as a patient
            in 19th-century mental asylums. Calling for more humane treatment of patients and better
            education about mental illness for the general population, the book inspires the mental
            hygiene movement in the United States.

1946   THE PSYCHOANALYTIC TREATMENT OF CHILDREN

            Anna Freud publishes The Psychoanalytic Treatment of Children, introducing basic con-
            cepts in the theory and practice of child psychoanalysis.

            NATIONAL MENTAL HEALTH ACT PASSED

            U.S. President Harry Truman signs the National Mental Health Act, providing generous
            funding for psychiatric education and research for the first time in U.S. history. This act
            leads to the creation in 1949 of the National Institute of Mental Health (NIMH).

1951   FIRST DRUG TO TREAT DEPRESSION

            Studies are published reporting that the drug imipramine may be able to lessen depres-
            sion. Eight years later, the FDA approves its use in the United States under the name
            Tofranil.

1952   THORAZINE TESTED

            The anti-psychotic drug chlorpromazine (known as Thorazine) is tested on a patient in a
            Paris military hospital. Approved for use in the United States in 1954, it becomes widely
            prescribed.

1953   APA ETHICAL STANDARDS

            The American Psychological Association publishes the first edition of Ethical Standards of
            Psychologists. The document undergoes continuous review and is now known as APA's
            Ethical Principles of Psychologists and Code of Conduct.

1954   EPILEPSY AND THE FUNCTIONAL ANATOMY...

In Epilepsy and the Functional Anatomy of the Human Brain, neurosurgeon Wilder G. Penfield publishes results from his study of the neurology of epilepsy. His mapping of the brain's cortex sets a precedent for the brain-imaging techniques that become critical to biopsychology and cognitive neuroscience.

THE NATURE OF PREJUDICE

Social Psychologist Gordon Allport publishes The Nature of Prejudice, which draws on various approaches in psychology to examine prejudice through different lenses. It is widely read by the general public and influential in establishing psychology's usefulness in understanding social issues.

BIOPSYCHOLOGY

In his studies of epilepsy, neuroscientist Wilder G. Penfield begins to uncover the relationship between chemical activity in the brain and psychological phenomena. His findings set the stage for widespread research on the biological role in psychological phenomena.

PSYCHOPHARMACOLOGY

The development of psychoactive drugs in the 1950s and their approval by the FDA initiates a new form of treatment for mental illness. Among the first such drugs is Doriden, also known as Rorer, an anti-anxiety medication approved in 1954.

HUMANISTIC PSYCHOLOGY

In the wake of psychoanalysis and behaviorism, humanistic psychology emerges as the "third force" in psychology. Led by Carl Rogers and Abraham Maslow, who publishes Motivation and Personality in 1954, this approach centers on the conscious mind, free will, human dignity, and the capacity for self-actualization.

1956   COGNITIVE PSYCHOLOGY

Inspired by work in mathematics and other disciplines, psychologists begin to focus on cognitive states and processes. George A. Miller's 1956 article "The Magical Number Seven, Plus or Minus Two" on information processing is an early application of the cognitive approach.

1957   SYNTACTIC STRUCTURES

Noam Chomsky publishes Syntactic Structures, marking a major advancement in the study of linguistics. The book helps spawn the field of psycholinguistics, the psychology of language.

1960   FDA APPROVES LIBRIUM

The FDA approves the use of chlordiazepoxide (known as Librium) for treatment of non-psychotic anxiety in 1960. A similar drug, diazepam (Valium), is approved in 1963.

1963   COMMUNITY MENTAL HEALTH CENTERS ACT PASSED

U.S. President John F. Kennedy calls for and later signs the Community Mental Health Centers Act, which mandates the construction of community facilities instead of large, regional mental hospitals. Congress ends support for the program in 1981, reducing overall funds and folding them into a mental health block-grant program.

1964   FIRST NATIONAL MEDAL OF SCIENCE TO PSYCHOLOGIST

Neal E. Miller receives the National Medal of Science, the highest scientific honor given in the United States, for his studies of motivation and learning. He is the first psychologist to be awarded this honor.

FDA APPROVES LITHIUM

The FDA approves lithium carbonate to treat patients with bipolar mood disorders. It is marketed under the trade names Eskalith, Lithonate, and Lithane.

1973   HOMOSEXUALITY REMOVED FROM DSM

After intense debate, the American Psychiatric Association removes homosexuality from the Diagnostic and Statistical Manual of Mental Disorders (DSM). The widely used reference manual is revised to state that sexual orientation "does not necessarily constitute a psychiatric disorder."

1974   PET SCANNER TESTED

A new brain scanning technique, Positron Emission Tomography (PET), is tested. By tracing chemical markers, PET maps brain function in more detail than earlier techniques.

1976   EVOLUTIONARY PSYCHOLOGY

Richard Dawkins publishes The Selfish Gene, which begins to popularize the idea of evolutionary psychology. This approach applies principles from evolutionary biology to the structure and function of the human brain. It offers new ways of looking at social phenomena such as aggression and sexual behavior.

THE SELFISH GENE

Richard Dawkins publishes The Selfish Gene, a work which shifts focus from the individual animal as the unit of evolution to individual genes themselves. The text popularizes the field of evolutionary psychology, in which knowledge and principles from evolutionary biology are applied in research on human brain structure.

1979   STANDARDIZED IQ TESTS FOUND DISCRIMINATORY

The U.S. District Court finds the use of standardized IQ tests in California public schools illegal. The decision in the case, Larry P. v. Wilson Riles, upholds the plaintiff's position that the tests discriminate against African American students.

1981   AIDS AND HIV FIRST DIAGNOSED

The epidemic of acquired immunodeficiency syndrome (AIDS) and human immunodeficiency virus (HIV) infection presents mental health professionals with challenges ranging from at-risk patients' anxiety and depression to AIDS-related dementia.

1984   INSANITY DEFENSE REFORM ACT PASSED

U.S. Congress revises federal law on the insanity defense, partly in response to the acquittal of John Hinckley, Jr. of charges of attempted assassination after he had shot President Ronald Reagan. The act places burden of proof for the insanity defense on the defendant.

1987   HOMELESS ASSISTANCE ACT PASSED

The Stewart B. McKinney Homeless Assistance Act provides the first federal funds allocated specifically for the homeless population. The act includes provisions for mental health services, and responds, in part, to psychological studies on homelessness and mental disorders.

PROZAC, PAXIL, AND ZOLOFT MADE AVAILABLE

The FDA approves the new anti-depressant medication fluoxetine, (Prozac). The drug, and other similar medications, acts on neurotransmitters, specifically, serotonin. It is widely prescribed and attracts attention and debate.

1990   CULTURAL PSYCHOLOGY

In Acts of Meaning, Four Lectures on Mind and Culture, Jerome Bruner helps formulate cultural psychology, an approach drawing on philosophy, linguistics, and anthropology. Refined and expanded by Hazel Markus and other researchers, cultural psychology focuses on the influences and relationship among mind, cultural community and behavior.

2000   SEQUENCING OF THE HUMAN GENOME

Sixteen public research institutions around the world complete a "working draft" mapping of the human genetic code, providing a research basis for a new understanding of human development and disease. A similar, privately funded, project is currently underway.

DSM ON PDA

The latest revision of the Diagnostic Statistical Manual of Mental Disorders (DSM) is published in a version for personal digital assistants (PDAs). The manual, first published in 1954, outlines prevalence, diagnosis, and treatment of mental disorders.

PSYCHOLOGY: THE STUDY OF MENTAL PROCESSES AND BEHAVIOR

LEARNING OBJECTIVES

After completing Chapter 1, students should be able to:

- Discuss how biology and culture interact to determine behavior.
- Explain the relevance of Jane Elliott's studies of being blue-eyed for our understanding of racism.
- Define *biopsychology*.
- Define *cross-cultural psychology*.
- Discuss the relation of psychology to philosophy.
- Define what is meant by a *scientific paradigm*.
- Discuss the background, assumptions, working metaphors, and methods of the following perspectives in psychology:
     The psychodynamic perspective
     The behaviorist perspective
     The cognitive perspective
     The evolutionary perspective
     The humanistic perspective
     The biological perspective
- Define the *nature-nurture* controversy.
- Describe the mechanisms of *natural selection*.
- Discuss the ways in which the various perspectives in psychology work together or in isolation from each other.
- Discuss the professional areas of psychology
- Identify the professional Associations of Psychology
- Explain the professional ethics of Psychology

PSYCHOLOGY TODAY

The so-called psyche or butterfly is generated from caterpillars which grow on green leaves, chiefly leaves of theraphanus, which some call crambe or cabbage. At first it is less than agrain of millet; it then grows into a small grub; and in three days it is a tiny caterpillar. After this it grows on and on, and becomes quiescent and changes its shape, and is now called a chrysalis. The outer shell is hard, and the chrysalis moves if you touch it. It attaches itself by cobweb-like filaments, and is unfurnished with mouth or any other apparent organ. After a little while the outer covering bursts asunder, and out flies the winged creature that we call the psyche or butterfly.

From Aristotle's History of Animals 551a.1

HOW TO LEARN PSYCHOLOGY

Much of who we are and how we express ourselves is based on our one-to-one correspondence with each other, the socialized world, and the influence of our DNA. This text is designed to give you a general understanding of what psychology is and how it is used to learn about ourselves, learn about others, and how psychology is applied to help improve the lives of people today. The chapters are organized so that you can get a better idea of how psychology works; from basic theories and principles, through research, understanding and explaining results, to the actual application of psychological techniques.

This text is not designed to make you a psychologist or some form of counselor. It is written in a general format so that you can gain a better idea of all of the major concepts in psychology and how psychology is a significant science that impacts every aspect of our daily functioning. If after reading this text, you find a passion for psychology you may consider becoming a major, which then will require you to study the discipline of psychology at a greater level than this text will provide. In Chapter 1, you will learn about the different professions in Psychology and the purpose for each discipline.

INTRODUCTION TO PSYCHOLOGY TODAY

Psychology is in everything. In every aspect of life, psychology plays a significant role in helping people understand who they are, the people around them, and how they fit in the world today. As our world changes, so does the way we as humans experience life. Today, we see increases in health diseases, natural disasters in uncommon geographical regions, changes in the structure of family, economic strain, and use of technology to accomplish a range of simplistic to difficult task. We all use the principles of psychology everyday and probably don't even realize it. When people spank their child for doing something wrong, they are utilizing the learning principle of punishment. When we get nervous right before we have to give that big speech, we are activating our autonomic nervous system. When we talk to ourselves in our heads, telling ourselves to "calm down," "work harder," or "give up," we are utilizing cognitive approaches to change our behaviors and emotions. Yes, Psychology is in everything.

In every issue described above, the discipline of psychology addresses how humans can successfully survive life today. Psychology is a diverse discipline, grounded in science with boundless applications to everyday life. The roles psychologists play in human and ecological relationships is to engage in basic research, develop and test theoretical models exploring human life using research methods involving observation, experimentation and analysis. Other psychologists apply the discipline's scientific knowledge to help people, organizations and communities function better. As psychological research yields new information, whether its improved interventions to treat depression or how humans interact with machines, these findings become part of the discipline's body of knowledge and are applied when working patients and clients, schools, in corporate settings, judicial systems, engineering, medical science, and even in professional sports. So if psychology touches the lives of so many people, the question is what is psychology?

ETYMOLOGY AND RELATED WORDS OF PSYCHOLOGY

In the English language and other modern European languages, "reason", and related words, represent words which have always been used to translate Latin and classical Greek terms in the sense of their philosophical usage. The translation has helped to give clearer meaning of words describing the term *psychology* across different languages. For example, the original Greek term was "λογος" or "*logos,*" the root of the modern English word "logic" but also a word which could mean for example "language" or "explanation" or the ability to understand with meaning. As a philosophical term *logos* was translated in its non-linguistic senses in Latin as ratio. Here, the use of mathematical terminology had its beginning as a necessary component of logical reasoning and processing of quantitative values. The French used the term "raison," which is derived directly from Latin, and this is the direct source of the English word "reason".

Reasoning is the process of critically analyzing concepts for the purpose of gaining a deeper and fuller understanding of a phenomenon. The meaning of the word "reason" in senses such as "human reason" also overlaps to a large extent with "rationality" and the adjective of "reason" in philosophical contexts is normally "rational", rather than "reasoned" or "reasonable". The earliest major philosophers to publish in English, such as Francis Bacon, Thomas Hobbes, and John Locke also routinely wrote in Latin and French, and compared their terms to Greek, treating the words "*logos,*" "*ratio,*" "*raison,*" and "reason" as

interchangeable. Some philosophers such as Thomas Hobbes, for example, also used the word *ratiocination* as a synonym for "reasoning". Later, the word *psychology* was used to understand the reasoning, cognition, and mental processes of humans. Further, the term embraced the use of mathematics as a necessary component of diagnosis and classification of individuals based on their level of functioning cognitively, behaviorally, and socially. The term psychology has its roots in early philosophy, but has experienced further development and change overtime that has transitioned this discipline from philosophy to science.

EARLY PHILOSOPHERS

The statement, expressed by German experimentalist Hermann Ebbinghaus, suggests a key idea about the history of psychology: though psychology is relatively new as a formal academic discipline, scholars have pondered the questions that psychologists ask for thousands of years. According to psychology historian Morton Hunt, an experiment performed by the King of Egypt, as far back as the seventh century B.C., can be considered the first psychology experiment (Hunt, 1993, p. 1). The king wanted to test whether or not Egyptian was the oldest civilization on earth. His idea was that, if children were raised in isolation from infancy and were given no instruction in language of any kind, then the language they spontaneously spoke would be of the original civilization of man—hopefully, Egyptian. The experiment, itself, may have been compromised, the king deserves credit for his idea that thoughts and language come from the mind and his ambition to test such an idea played a significant role in questioning and invetigatin human behavior and functioning.

Typically, historians point to the writings of ancient Greek philosophers, such Socrates, Plato, and Aristotle, as the first significant work to be rich in psychology-related thought. They considered important questions like, what is free will, how does the mind work, and what is the relationship of people to their society. For hundreds of years, philosophers continued to wrestle with these and related questions, and psychology eventually sprouted from the roots of philosophy. Psychology also derived its origins from physiology, another subject that had been studied for thousands of years. In fact, the father of psychology, William Wundt, was originally a professor of physiology.

Greece has given us more philosophy than any other place in the Western World. Greek philosophy as we know it came after the rise and fall of the high culture on Crete, its end now thought to have been hastened by a giant tidal wave due to a major volcanic eruption.

The roots of western psychology can be traced to Greek philosophy. The word psychology itself is derived from the Greek words 'psyche' which means soul and 'logos' which means study. Psychology thus started as a part of philosophy and became an independent discipline much later.

Origins of philosophy comes from the the philosophical underpinnings of three groups (3p's) Philosophy, Physics, and Physiology.

Socrates (460-399bc) • Early philosopher "One thing only I know, and that is I know nothing." • Philosophy begins when one learns to doubt (especially one's cherished beliefs). • There is no real philosophy until the mind begins to examine itself. "Know Thyself" Developed a questioning style that ultimately was called the Socratic Method and included the demand for accurate definitions, clear thinking and exact analysis.

Hippocrates (460bc) • Called the Father of Medicine Developed a new method of inquiry Careful observation and the collection and interpretation of facts. • Method could be incorporated into physical, mental, and emotional reactions of individuals. • Was a major advance over magic, superstition, and supernatural powers. He Pioneered the application of systematic observation to the study of human nature and experience. Was a very knowledgeable physician for his time • Used detailed case histories. • Dissected dead bodies. • Used dream analysis to analyze emotional

disorders.• Developed the Hippocratic oath for physicians. Theory of the Four Humors Humor Symptom 1. Blood Overly enthusiastic or sanguine . 2. Phlegm Slow, sluggish, lethargic, indifferent. 3. Black Bile Depressed, melancholic temperament. 4. Yellow Bile Aggressive, choleric . Ultimately Knowledge was the possession of truth. • But knowledge relied on reasoning Not Sensory Experience. • Brain is the seat of perception

Aristotle (384-322bc) • Disagreed with Hippocrates and taught that all knowledge comes from the senses and through experience. • Taught the Four Laws of Association: Similarity, Contrast, Frequency, and Contiguity.

Plato and Aristotle were among the first philosophers who thought about the mind. Plato believed that body and mind are two separate entities and mind could exist even after death.

Plato • Was a Nativist • believed individuals had innate knowledge that Teach individuals by the Socratic method and bring out innate ideas by asking the right questions. • Everything is in there; all you have to do is ask the right questions. • Believed knowledge existed in two worlds, but he was positive in that education can bring change to the basic nature of the mind.

Aristotle, who was the disciple of Plato, followed the feet of his teacher and believed in the body-mind duality. But he thought that of each of these is the manifestation of the other. He, but, was pessimistic about the role of education in changing the fundamental nature of humans.

Rene Descartes • French philosopher and mathematician, who originated the Cartesian system of coordinates or the coordinate geometry, also believed in the body-mind duality. But he was open enough to consider that there is an uninterrupted transaction between the body and the mind. Descartes (1596–1650) But was also an interactionist • That is, the mind may affect the body and the body could affect the mind. Since the mind could influence the body and vice versa, needed a structure which could be shared by both parts. • For Descartes, this structure was the Pineal Body

Where Are We Now?

Today psychology's focus is concentrated on the scientific aspects that help to explain human behavior and mental processes. Early scientists and philosophers helped to shape the scientific methods used in the study of psychology. First, the definitions of psychology has help to define the essence of this science.

PSYCHOLOGY DEFINED

Psychology is defined as the scientific investigation of mental processes and behavior. It is derived from both Latin and Greek languages as discussed above. It is taken from the root words "psyche" and "ology." Psukhe means breath, life, spirit or soul (a person's mental or moral or emotional nature, or spiritual or immortal elements in a person.), or mind, which is the seat of one's emotion, thoughts, and behavior. The root word "ology" means the study of some phenomenon. Hence, the term psychology means the study of the mind and the life of an individual. It is through our physical senses, cognition or mind, thoughts, and emotions that we experience the fullness of the world and life. Most would also agree they have a "soul" per the second definition above relating to man's mental, moral or emotional nature. We might all have different notions about what these ultimately are, but few would disagree that all mankind possess a soul.

Obviously the definition of psychology has been expanded over the years to fully express the purpose of psychology as a science and that the methods of science are systematically used to investigate and understand the mental processes and behavior of people in our world. From this scientific research, psychologists develop theories of human functioning, often developing new approaches to current knowledge. The cornerstone of psychological knowledge and practice still revolves around the examination and treatment of mental and emotional problems whatever the trigger or area of concern. Be it stress related to the working environment, trauma or shock following a catastrophic life event or the development of a particular form of mental illness such as schizophrenia. Within a multidisciplinary team, the psychologist attempts to offer answers and formulate treatment methods to improve the individual, system, or environment. The goal of psychology is always to understand the life of mankind for the purpose of improving and perfecting their life experiences and functioning. The study of psychology has five basic goals:

Scientific Psychology has five basic goals:

- To Describe
- To Explain
- To Predict
- To Control
- To Change Behavior and Mental Processes

1. Describe: The first goal is to observe behavior and describe, often in minute detail, what was observed as objectively as possible
2. Explain: While descriptions come from observable data, psychologists must go beyond what is obvious and explain their observations. Explaining the functions of behavior often will assist in behavior change.
3. Predict: Once we know what happens, and why it happens, we can begin to speculate what will happen in the future. There's an old saying, which very often holds true: "the best predictor of future behavior is past behavior."
4. Control: Once we know what happens, why it happens and what is likely to happen in the future, we can excerpt control over it.
5. To Change Behavior and Mental Processes: Not only do psychologists attempt to control behavior, they want to do so in a positive manner, they want to improve a person's life by providing skills for coping and improvement.

PSYCHOLOGY: A RESEARCH-BASED SCIENCE

Today, psychologists use more objective scientific methods to understand, explain, and predict human behavior and mental processes. These scientific methods are used in two major areas of psychology: academic psychology and applied psychology. Academic psychology focuses on the study of different sub-topics within psychology including personality psychology, social psychology and developmental psychology. Applied psychology focuses on the use of different psychological principles to solve real world problems. Examples of applied areas of psychology include school psychology, clinical psychology, forensic psychology, ergonomics, and industrial-organization psychology. Many other psychologists work as therapists, helping people overcome mental, behavioral and emotional disorders. Whether applied or academic, psychologists today employ scientific methodology to study the mental and behavioral processes of humans. Psychological studies are highly structured and executed, beginning with a hypothesis that is then empirically evaluated. The results of scientifically based studies are used to expand our theoretical and practical knowledge of some psychological, behavioral, physical, or social phenomenon. Research designed to answer questions about the current state of affairs such as the thoughts, feelings and behaviors of individuals is known as descriptive research. Descriptive research can be qualitative or quantitative in orientation. Qualitative research is descriptive research that is focused on observing and describing events as they occur, with the goal of capturing all of the richness of everyday behavior and with the hope of discovering and understanding phenomena that might have been missed if only more cursory examinations have been made.

In this sense, psychological research is typically used for enhancing the practice of psychology by the following:

- Study development and external factors and the role they play on individuals' mental health
- Study people with specific psychological disorders, symptoms, or characteristics

- Develop tests to measure specific psychological phenomenon
- Develop treatment approaches to improve individuals' mental health

In Chapter 2, you will learn about how research is conducted and the different types of research methods used to gather information within the discipline of Psychology. This will assist in your understanding between real sciences versus pseudoscience.

PSYCHOLOGY VS. PSEUDOSCIENCE

What would a good study of the mind and behavior entail? It would investigate the nature, functioning, and potentials of man's cognitive and behavioral processes. This scientific investigation is based on observable and measurable behavior patterns that follow the standards for scientific research. This would encompass components of research such as theory, hypotheses, assessment, interpretation, and diagnostic conclusions based on data. Finally, the research outcomes would develop techniques for any individual to become aware of best practices to improve life skills and functioning, and also to strengthen and expand their use and control of these functions. It would also investigate the etiology of the problems anyone experiences with their own mind and socio-behavioral functioning. Again, these things can be observed, measured, and intervened based on scientific treatments by psychologists credentialed to examine an individuals mental health functioning based on scientific exploration, investigation, codification and summarizing. The defining feature of a science is that it is based on some theoretical model that is continuously evaluated based on data driven outcomes.

In contrast, pseudoscience is a discipline that does not operate under the standards of scientific investigation. It studies man and phenomenon based limited knowledge, observations, and data. Failing to employ the standardized processes of research has resulted in incorrect theories, faulty observations, eroded results. These are the characteristics of pseudoscience. In science, observations are made, a hypothesis is formed, data are gathered and testing is done, and if the results of testing support the hypothesis, a theory (provisional conclusion) is formulated. If any evidence comes to light that invalidates the conclusion, the conclusion will be amended or even rejected and a replacement theory sought. In pseudoscience, they begin with a solid conclusion (such as 'homeopathy works'), and with little evidence a conclusion is drawn and formulated as valid. Remember, Pseudosciences are practices that masquerade themselves as science but have little or no scientific rigor or cohesion to them. Pseudoscience is often known as fringe-or alternative science which claims to be factual and scientific, yet does not adhere to scientific methodology and principles consistent with the standards for research identified by the The American Educational Research Association (AERA). The most focal of its defects is the lack of the controlled and deduced experiments which provide the foundation of all sciences (i.e., natural and behavioral) and which contribute to their advancement. It can be difficult for the average non-scientist to detect if the processes of science are actual or fictitious. In this case, pseudoscience has many traits that are noticeably different from other substantiated sciences. These qualities are outlined below. It is important to remember that any claimed science that exhibits at least some of these traits is more likely to be pseudoscience. Whilst every feature is not provided here, the most common to every form of pseudoscience is provided. There are Eight Deadly Sins of Pseudoscience.

THE EIGHT DEADLY SINS OF PSEUDOSCIENCE

Popular Culture Ideology

Pseudoscience depends on arbitrary conventions of human culture, rather than on unchanging regularities of nature. Pseudoscientific ideas are sometimes driven by cultural or ideological reasons, but very often are further enhanced by commercialization. A new 'miracle breakthrough' healing device, for example, that is being sold directly to the public, but which has no science references to support it, probably doesn't work. However, scientific breakthroughs will normally have been published in science journals, scrutinized by other scientists, and only announced to the public once scientists have agreed that the scientific breakthrough is indeed genuine. The progress of the acceptance of the idea will be documented by the Center for Disease Control and the Federal Drug Administration for the public knowledge or referenced in the relevant journals for researchers, practitioners, and consumers.

Uses Descriptive Verbose Language

One reason that theories from pseudoscience are vague and untestable is that the language used by the proponents is far too inane and disconnected to a common purpose. This often results in a 'theory' that is so conceptually slippery it becomes difficult to identify what is actually being argued – or how one might test it. Due to their nebulous content, such practices also nearly always hide all sorts of circular reasoning errors. Over-complex words, phrases and over-long sentences are employed in an attempt to 'look' scientific and intelligent. Theories of language need to be able to explain tip-of-the-tongue experiences (where we feel as if what we want to say is just failing to reach our ability to actually say it), slips of the tongue experiences (where we say a related word instead of the one we meant). However, the anecdotal experience of these instances does nothing to explain why and how they actually occur. These experiences are the products of psychological processes; however these products do nothing to explain the underlying processes themselves. Knowing that we have the phenomenal experience of consciousness, does not explain what consciousness is, or how it occurs.

Metaphorical/Analogy Driven Thinking

Metaphors and analogies are essential to science and theory. Complex and more abstract areas of science rely particularly on metaphor and analogy to add clarity to knowledge and to communicate that knowledge. This is perfectly legitimate and indeed, to some extent, unavoidable. In science, analogies and metaphors may emerge as useful ways to think about, describe, and explain objective facts and evidence. For example, psychologists have employed the metaphor of visual selective attention being like a 'spotlight' illuminating the relevant information out there in the world from the surrounding darkness of all that we ignore. In many respects this has proved a very fruitful metaphor guiding thinking in this area of study. The problem here is not the use of analogies or metaphor in scientific thinking, but the clear abuse of them.

Confirmation-Bias (selective evidence)

Pseudoscience deliberately creates mystery where none exists, by omitting crucial information and important details. Anything can be made "mysterious" by omitting what is known about it or presenting completely imaginary details. The "Bermuda Triangle" books are classic examples of this tactic.

Many people report a common perception of thinking about someone—then the phone rings and the caller is the person they were thinking of. Is this strong evidence for a psychic ability between these people? The answer is no. It reflects a selective bias in memory and reason. Although we can remember the instances when this does happen (as they can be striking) we rarely remember the instances when it is not the person we were thinking of. Our memory is biased to place an emphasis on the 'hits' and ignore the 'misses'.

In a similar manner, researchers can sometimes concentrate only on that evidence that is consistent with the argument being developed (the hits) and ignore other evidence that contradicts it (the misses). This is known as the confirmation bias (where we are biased to only notice observations that confirm our assumptions). The confirmation bias relies on a positive biased focus and weighting towards only that evidence which is consistent with the current belief or world-view; and a negative bias to ignore results that challenge the view. It may be impressive to see a

dowser find water in a single trial, but this on its own does not mean dowsing works. When we run tests and see that on many trials the dowser failed to locate water the scant and periodic instances when they are successful no longer looks impressive.

Appellation to Ancient Tradition and Sorcery

Magic, sorcery, witchcraft—these are based on spurious similarity, false analogy, false cause-and-effect connections, etc. That is, inexplicable influences and connections between things are assumed from the beginning—not found by investigation. (If you step on a crack in the sidewalk without saying a magic word, your mother will crack a bone in her body; eating heart-shaped leaves is good for heart ailments; shining red light on the body increases blood production; rams are aggressive so someone born in the sign of the ram is aggressive; fish are "brain food" because the meat of the fish resembles brain tissue, etc.)

Anecdotes as Sufficient Evidence

Although anecdotal evidence has its place in scientific theory: no theory should be solely dependent on anecdotal evidence. Anecdotal evidence is a poor and unreliable source of evidence. One major problem with pseudoscience is that it places a strong and selective emphasis on anecdotes, and anecdotes alone, as support for its claims and theories. In reality, personal anecdotes alone are not a viable argument against data, facts, theory, empirical observation, and objective measurement. Lots of anecdotes do not support a case any more than a few anecdotes do. Furthermore, Pseudoscience attempts to persuade with rhetoric, propaganda, and misrepresentation rather than valid evidence (which presumably does not exist).

Lack of Science Methodology

Pseudoscience is characterized by a complete lack of viable scientific methods applied to study. Even if we were to accept some instances as fact, there is still no clear idea how these phenomena would work or how they could work. There is no clear and plausible proposed mechanism for how apparitions are supposed to be recorded in stone, no clear mechanism for how astrology is supposed to influence human behavior, no clear mechanism for how the mind could survive bodily death or how liquids can hold a memory (as is claimed in homeopathy).

There are many areas of experimental science where mechanisms of action are not well understood – however, under these circumstances there will be some factual and accepted knowledge that provides a framework for thinking. In addition, although a mechanism may not be known, candidate mechanisms will be well specified to a level that guides future experimentation and thinking. What counts in science is the ability for a provisional explanation to feasibly account for the phenomena via a proposed mechanism that is more explicit than any other. An explicit mechanism should also generate clear predictions and these predictions should be testable (and falsifiable). The mechanism should say why the phenomenon occurs, what the principal components are, how it works, and what it does.

In contrast to scientific mechanisms and models, Parapsychology has been actively investigating paranormal and psychic phenomena since the 1940s – and yet despite the decades that have passed, no reliable evidence, or explicit and plausible mechanism has ever been proposed that suggests paranormal phenomena are a real veridical objective event.

Maintains Elusive Evidence

Proponents of pseudoscience often claim that scientific testing is not the best way to test their claim; there is something special about the claim that makes it different to other disciplines. This special pleading is often accompanied by other fallacious reasoning such as scientists being too 'close-minded' to see the truth or that 'science has been wrong before'. Pseudoscience is indifferent to criteria of valid evidence. The emphasis is not on meaningful, controlled, repeatable scientific experiments. Instead it is on unverifiable eyewitness testimony, stories and tall tales, hearsay, rumor, and dubious anecdotes. Genuine scientific literature is either ignored or misinterpreted.

These claims invariably arise because when the pseudoscience is tested by scientists, the claimed results do not occur. One of the hallmarks of science is not only producing results and having those results reviewed by peers and published, but that those results can be reproduced (under controlled conditions) by other scientists independently.

This point is an important one. If something is real it will manifest itself regardless of who's doing the testing or whether the testers believe in it or not. If the phenomenon requires special (i.e. non-scientific) conditions or the testers have to believe in it for it to show up then it's highly likely that the phenomenon is not real and is merely a result of wishful thinking and confounding factors introduced by non-scientific testing. Genuine phenomena will stand up to scrutiny.

SUMMARY OF PSYCHOLOGY TODAY

The defining feature of science is that hypotheses and theories that are put forward must be capable of being tested and shown to be false should they actually be so—this is the scientific criterion of falsifiability. As our examples above show, the tell-tale sign of pseudoscience is that the claims, theories, or products are always pitched in a manner that leads them away from being testable and falsifiable.

Pseudoscience then can be described as theories, methodologies or practices that claim to be scientific but which are presented in such a manner that they cannot be tested or falsified by empirical testing. Table 1 on the next page provides further summarized differences between pure science and pseudoscience.

SCIENCE	PSEUDOSCIENCE
Their findings are expressed primarily through scientific journals that are peer-reviewed and maintain rigorous standards for honesty and accuracy.	The literature is aimed at the general public. There is no review, no standards, no pre-publication verification, no demand for accuracy and precision.
Reproducible results are demanded; experiments must be precisely described so that they can be duplicated exactly or improved upon.	Results cannot be reproduced or verified. Studies, if any, are always so vaguely described that one can't figure out what was done or how it was done.
Failures are searched for and studied closely, because incorrect theories can often make correct predictions by accident, but no correct theory will make incorrect predictions.	Failures are ignored, excused, hidden, lied about, discounted, explained away, rationalized, forgotten, and avoided at all costs.
As time goes on, more and more is learned about the physical processes under study.	No physical phenomena or processes are ever found or studied. No progress is made; nothing concrete is learned.
Convinces by appeal to the evidence, by arguments based upon logical and/or mathematical reasoning, by making the best case the data permit. When new evidence contradicts old ideas, they are abandoned.	Convinces by appeal to faith and belief. Pseudoscience has a strong quasi-religious element: it tries to convert, not to convince. You are to believe in spite of the facts, not because of them. The original idea is never abandoned, whatever the evidence.
Does not advocate or market unproven practices or products.	Generally earns some or all of his living by selling questionable products (such as books, courses, and dietary supplements) and/or pseudoscientific services (such as horoscopes, character readings, spirit messages, and predictions).

Table 1. Contrasts Between Science and Pseudoscience

BOUNDARIES OF PSYCHOLOGY: BIOPSYCHOLOGY AND CULTURE

To further understand psychology, discussion regarding the philosophical roots of psychology is discussed here. First, understand that everything has a root and boundary. As such, psychology has common perspective that further supports its existence, including cultural psychology and biopsychology.

BIOLOGICAL BOUNDARY OF PSYCHOLOGY—MIND BODY CONNECTION

During the 1600s, the famous French philosopher, Rene Descartes, introduced the concept of dualism, which stressed on the fact the body and the mind were basically two separate entities that interacted together to form the normal human experience. Many of the other issues that are still debated by psychologists today, like relative contributions of nature vs. nurture, are deeply rooted in these early philosophical concepts. Even today, most experts in the field of psychology and biology agree that the mind and the body are connected in more complex ways than we can even comprehend. Research constantly shows us that the way we think affects the way we behave, the way we feel, and the way our bodies respond. The opposite is also true, physical illness, physical exhilaration, exercising, insomnia all affect the way we feel and behave, but also the way we think about ourselves and the world. Behavioral neuroscience or biological psychology is a branch of psychology that scientifically studies the impact of the body's neurological workings on behavior and mental processes. It typically investigates at the level of nerves, neurotransmitters, brain circuitry and the basic biological processes that underlie normal and abnormal behavior. Most typically experiments in behavioral neuroscience involve non-human animal models (such as rats and mice, and non-human primates) which have implications

for better understanding of human pathology and therefore contribute to scientific evidence-based practice. In this text, the use of biology will permeate most chapters to further formulate the connection between psychology and biology and demonstrate how psychobiology is necessary in the existence and expression of us.

CULTURAL PSYCHOLOGY

Cultural psychology has its roots in the 1960s and 1970s but became more prominent in the 1980s and 1990s. Richard Shweder, a researcher in the field of culturalism defined "Cultural psychology" as the study of the way cultural traditions and social practices regulate, express, and transform the human psyche, resulting less in psychic unity for humankind than in ethnic divergences in mind, self, and emotion" (1991, p. 72). Cultural Psychology is a field of psychology which assumes the idea that culture and the mind are inseparable, and that psychological theories grounded in one culture are expressed differently when applied to a across various cultures, racial, and ethnic groups. Culture refers to many characteristics of a group of people, including attitudes, behaviors, customs and values that are transmitted from one generation to the next (Matsumoto, 2000). Cultures throughout the world share many similarities, but are marked by considerable differences. For example, while people of all cultures experiences happiness, hunger, sorrow, and pain, how these feelings are expressed varies from one culture to the next.

To further discuss the boundaries of psychology, the concepts of race and ethnicity must be presented. Like culture, humans often categorize themselves in terms of race or ethnicity, sometimes on the basis of differences in appearance. Human racial categories have been based on both ancestry and visible traits,

especially facial features, skull shape, skin color, and hair texture. While there is no scientific and researched consensus conforming a list of the human races, some anthropologists endorse the notion of human "race" using skin color to determine classification. This classification is referred to as the "color terminology for race" and categorizes the following skin tones as a basis of classification: Black (e.g. Sub-Saharan Africa), Red (e.g. Native Americans), Yellow (e.g. East Asians) and White (e.g. Europeans). Along with color terminology for race, culture is a strong influence for determining human differences and similarities. The predominance of genetic variation occurs within racial groups, with only 5 to 15% of total variation occurring between groups. Thus the scientific concept of variation in the human genome is largely incongruent with the cultural concept of ethnicity or race. Ethnic groups are defined by linguistic, cultural, ancestral, national or regional ties. Self-identification with an ethnic group is usually based on kinship and decent. Race and ethnicity are among major factors in social identity giving rise to various forms of cultural variations in foods, clothing, dialect, politics, companionship.

Cultural psychology is that branch of psychology which deals with the study and impact of culture, tradition and social practices on psyche for the unity of humankind. Cultural psychologists generally use either ethnographic or experimental methods (or a combination of both) for collecting data and engaging the practice of scientific research.

CROSS-CULTURAL PSYCHOLOGY

Cultural psychology is distinct from cross-cultural psychology in that the cross-cultural psychologists generally use culture as a means of testing the universality of psychological processes rather than determining how local cultural practices shape psychological processes. Many cross-cultural psychologists choose to focus on one of two approaches: the Etic Approach or Emic Approach of cultural psychology. The Etic Approach focuses on studying how different cultures are similar, and the Emic Approach focuses on studying differences between cultures. For example, whereas a cross-cultural psychologist might ask whether Piaget's stages of development are universal across a variety of cultures, a cultural psychologist would be interested in how the social practices of a particular set of cultures shape the development of cognitive processes in different ways. Cross-cultural psychology is a branch of psychology that looks at how cultural factors influence

human behavior. The International Association of Cross-Cultural Psychology (IACCP) was established in 1972, and this branch of psychology has continued to grow and develop since that time. Today, increasing numbers of psychologists investigate how behavior differs among various cultures throughout the world. Psychologists are only interested in the impact of culture, but also on the impact of the biological influences on the human mind and body.

SUMMARY OF THE BOUNDARIES AND BORDERS OF PSYCHOLOGY

Psychology is the scientific investigation of mental processes and behavior. Understanding a person means practicing and examining the person's biological makeup, psychological experience and functioning, and the cultural and historical moment.

Biopsychology (or behavioral neuroscience) examines the physical basis of psychological phenomena such as motivation, emotion, and stress. Cross-cultural psychology tests psychological hypotheses in different cultures. Biology and culture form the boundaries, or constraints, within which psychological processes operate.

HISTORICAL DEVELOPMENT OF PSYCHOLOGY AND PARADIGMS

WHAT IS A PARADIGM?

A paradigm is a broad system of theoretical assumptions employed by a scientific community to make sense of a domain of experience. Psychology lacks a unified paradigm but has a number of schools of thought, or perspectives, which are broad ways of understanding psychological phenomena. A psychological perspective, like a paradigm, includes theoretical propositions, shared metaphors, and accepted methods of observation. In psychology, paradigms or theoretical perspectives are used to explain the discipline as a science. Evolution and the Nature versus Nurture debates have often been identified as significant parts of Psychologies history and have added to critical debates about the existence of man and the expression of man's abilities.

THEORY OF EVOLUTION AND EVOLUTIONARY PSYCHOLOGY

Charles Darwin's Theory of Evolution is the widely held notion that all life is related and has descended from a common ancestor: the birds and the bananas, the fishes and the flowers are all connected through some genetic process. Darwin's general theory presumes the development of life from non-life and stresses a purely naturalistic descent and development of some animal form overtime. That is, complex creatures evolve from more simplistic ancestors naturally over time. Simply, as random genetic mutations occur within an organism's genetic code, the beneficial mutations are preserved because they aid in the survival of that species. This process is known as "natural selection." Natural selection acts to preserve and accumulate minor advantageous genetic mutations. These beneficial mutations are passed on to the next generation until the mutation further perfects itself through natural selection. Over time, beneficial mutations accumulate and the result is an entirely different organism (not just a variation of the original, but an entirely different creature). Through natural selection, the genetic offspring would inherit the advantages of the gene and pass it on to their offspring. The inferior genetic members of the same species would gradually die out, leaving only the superior genetics being represented among the species. Hence, natural selection also has the function to preserve the best genetic species while neglecting the inferior gene.

While the Theory of Evolution is controversial, the concept of natural selection, survival of the fittest, and adaptation are very much inferred and utilized on different levels in the study of psychology.

For example, psychological adaptations, according to Evolution Psycholgists, might include the abilities to discern kin from non-kin, to identify and prefer healthier mates, to living spaces, and determine friendships. Consistent with the theory of natural selection, evolutionary psychology sees organisms as often in conflict with others of their species, including mates and relatives. Despite this viewpoint, like chimps, humans have subtle and flexible social instincts, allowing them to form extended families, lifelong friendships, and political alliances, (Wright, 1995). In studies testing theoretical predictions, Evolutionary psychologists hold that behaviors or traits that occur universally in all cultures are good candidates for evolutionary adaptations, (Schacter et al. 2007). Evolved psychological adaptations (such as the ability to learn a language) interact with cultural inputs to produce specific behaviors (e.g., the specific language learned). Basic gender differences, such as greater eagerness for sex among men and greater coyness among women (Symons, D., 1979) are explained as sexually dimorphic psychological adaptations that reflect the different reproductive strategies of males and females, (Wright, 1995; Sterelny, Kim. 2009). Evolutionary psychologists contrast their approach to what they term the "Standard Social Science Model,"

according to which the mind is a general-purpose cognition device shaped almost entirely by culture, (Barkow et al. 1992, Encyclopædia Britannica, 2011). What is key in this perspective that the brain is that the brain is adaptable and processes information in response to external and in internal stimuli.

Nature vs. Nature

The nature versus nurture debate is one of the oldest issues in psychology. Nature refers to heredity and genes that are passed on within family lines. Nature is believed to be what determines our basic appearance, temperament, traits, and personality. Research show that temperaments of an infant are influenced more by biology than experiences with their siblings. While many American believe that difficult traits in children are the result of poor parenting and poor peer socialization, difficult traits may be more related to family genetics than environmental influences. Nurture refers to the influence of the environment that is the conditioning of habits and specific behaviors. Both present good arguments to explain the existence and expression of people today. The debate centers on the relative contributions of genetic inheritance and environmental factors to human development. Some philosophers such as Plato and Descartes suggested that certain things are inborn, or that they simply occur naturally regardless of environmental influences. Other well-known thinkers such as John Locke believed in the expression of tabula rasa, which suggests that the mind begins as a blank slate "waiting to be written upon." According to this notion, everything that we are and all of our knowledge is determined by our experience. This suggests that even though genes give us the basic dynamic of our personality, the environment has the power to alter it and make us into the exact opposite of the typical genes expressed within our family line. An example of this phenomenon is expressed below regarding the good and bad apple.

"Bad soil" can alter how something may develop, such as humans. Humans exposed to difficult neighborhoods can impact the growth and development

The Apple Phenomenon

One comparison of how much the environment affects a child's development was done on apples. Apple seeds have certain genes in them, but what they grow into will be the same no matter what and because of those genes in each seed, one may be destined to grow better than others. But if random seeds with different genes were split up into two groups, with different environments, it is likely that the quality of the apple would differ. One group would have all the benefits to help them grow better, such as water, sunlight, good soil, and extra care. The second group of apples, however, would be given bad soil, not enough sunlight and water, and no extra care. These differences in their environment would definitely impact the growth pattern and outcome of the apples. Group one would produce better apples than group two.

of children. We are all perfect examples of the apples because we all from different environments that have influenced the expression of our personalities. Children reared in strict and religious homes tend to demonstrate higher levels of manners and respect for peers and adults. Families that demand high performance levels of achievement cultivate academic discipline in their children. For example, Asian families have higher expectations of their children to perform well in their schoolwork. They are automatically expected to do well and excel academically. For those that do not have the potential for scholastics, they are tracked into factory type jobs to maintain still work ethics. These types of expectations mixed

with environmental supports ultimately may lead to success. The way that Asian children become successful adults, or even less is based on the encouragement and nurturing they receive during their development. This is different from how other children may develop due to lower expected standards and environmental support.

Most scientists base their conclusions about nature and nurture by studying identical twins separated at birth. These twin sets tell us many things about nature vs. nurture. We can compare how they acted in different environments; see how many things they did that were alike, how they score on IQ tests, if they answer many of the questions the same way, and how similar their health records are. (Farber, S. 1981). One current example of are the Lewis and Springer Twins. When they were born, they were both adopted into different families. They first met when they were forty years old found that the similarities between them were extraordinary. Both were named Jim, both got dogs and named them "Toy," they had the same hobbies, jobs, handwriting, weight, appearance, and test results. Because of this, and other similar cases, some scientists believe that genes are the dominant force in creating who we are. (Farber, S. 1981).

In contrast, some scientists however, think that our genes have very little to do with the specific things that we do. Scientists, in their research of the human genome discovered that we only had 30,000 genes. Which they tend to believe is not enough genes to express genetic characteristics. (Clark, et. A., 2000)

The controversy between nature and nurture could affect each of us in many ways. One of the main ways it could change our lives would be if scientists found what triggers diseases like cancer. They could find cures easier if they knew exactly what caused illnesses. Also, from what scientists know now, we can say that many diseases like cancer are a mix of nature and nurture, and that if while we were still infants, we could take out the "nurture," then we would no longer be affected by those diseases. Such research could potentially have an incredibly large impact on our health and lifespan. (Clark et al., 2000)

HISTORICAL DEVELOPMENT AND THEORETICAL PERSPECTIVES

Throughout psychology's history, a number of different paradigms or theoretical perspectives have formed to explain human thought and behavior. A theory is a tested or testable concept that is used to explain a phenomenon, occurrence, or scientific belief. The theory is often shared and supported within a community of scientists that share the same school of thought or view about the concept that is being scientifically researched. These schools of thought often rise to dominance for a period of time and are usurped by some other scientific community that claim to yield a better explanation of the concept of phenomenon being studied. In the case of psychology, this chapter will discuss seven (7) different perspectives of psychology as a discipline. While these schools of thought are sometimes perceived as competing forces, each perspective has contributed to our understanding of psychology. When psychology was first established as a science separate from biology and philosophy, the debate over how to describe and explain the human mind and behavior began. Structuralism and Functionalism were two primary scientific views that began to explain the mental processes and behavior of man.

STRUCTURALISM

The Founder of Experimental Psychology: Wilhelm Wundt

Psychology has a long history as a topic within the fields of philosophy and physiology. It became an independent field of its own through the work of the German Wilhelm Wundt. Wilhelm Wundt (1832-1920): Often called the "father of psychology" for his pioneering research and operation of the first psychological laboratory. He taught the first course in physiological psychology at Heidelberg in 1867. In 1873 he published the first book on psychology Principles of Physiological Psychology, which established psychology as a unique branch of science with its own questions and methods. He was the first one in history to be called a 'psychologist'. Wundt set out purposively to establish a new science. As founder he took it as his right to define the first paradigm in psychology, known as Structuralism. Structuralism had its roots in earlier work in physiology. Scientists there (e.g. Gustav Fechner) had found success in studying sensory perception by manipulating stimuli and having subjects report back their experience. Wundt adopted this general approach for his new science.

Wundt held the belief that there is a connection between sensation and emotion and behavior. His research focused on the study of structuralism or studying the structure of consciousness. Wundt trained subjects to verbally report everything that went through their minds when presented with a stimulus or task. Through introspection that is looking inward into one's own mental contents or process he would study the connection between senses and behavioral reactions. Wundt concluded that the basic elements of consciousness are sensations (such as colors) and feelings. These elements can combine into more meaningful perceptions such as objects or emotions.

One of Wundt's students, Edward B. Tichener, (1867-1927) would subsequently formally establish and name structuralism; although he separated from many of Wundt's ideas, Tichener also studied the structure of consciousness within two schools of thought: Structuralism and Functionalism.

Structuralism can be defined as psychology as the study of the elements of consciousness. The idea is that conscious experience can be broken down into basic conscious elements, much as a physical phenomenon can be viewed as consisting of chemical structures that can in turn be broken down into basic elements. In fact, much of the research conducted in Wundt's laboratory consisted of cataloging these basic conscious elements. In order to reduce a normal conscious experience into basic elements, structuralism relied on a method called introspection. For example, one of Wundt's research assistants might describe an object such as an apple in terms of the basic perceptions it invoked (e.g., "cold", "crisp", and "sweet"). An important principal of introspection is that any given conscious experience must be described in its most basic terms, so that a researcher could not describe some experience or object as itself, such as describing an apple as an apple. Such a mistake is a major introspection faux pas and is referred to as the "stimulus error". Through introspection experiments, Wundt began to catalog a large number of basic conscious elements, which could hypothetically be combined to describe all human experiences. There were limitations to his work.

Limitations

Unlike other schools of psychology, Wundt's methodology had a principal flaw that is not consistent with the main stream views of experimental psychologists today, and this had to do with subject agreement and reliability. By today's scientific standards, the experimental methods used to study the structures of the mind were too subjective—the use of introspection led to a lack of reliability in results.

Other critics argue that structuralism was too concerned with internal behavior, which is not directly observable and cannot be accurately measured. Since psychology often deals with data, it is very important to make sure that multiple observers can agree independently on a phenomenon that is being experienced. This is referred to as reliability. In the contemporary study of sensory and perceptual phenomena, when observers view, touch, or taste some stimulus, researchers go to great lengths to make sure that the observers are not biased or influenced in their report of their experience. Further, agreement among observers in terms of what they are experiencing is a prerequisite for considering the observations as valid. Unfortunately, Wundt's observers were students trained by Wundt, and, in fact, any disagreement was resolved by Wundt. Therefore, reliability or agreement among observers in Wundt's experiments only occurred due to bias induced by training. The use of trained observers, such as those in Wundt's laboratory is diametrically opposed to the current practice of using participants who know as little as possible about the phenomenon being studied in order to decrease bias, and increase objectivity. This is one reason why general psychology students often serve as subjects in psychology experiments.

A second criticism of structuralism, mainly leveled by behaviorists who came some years later, was that structuralist theory dealt primarily with "nonobservable" abstractions. Though participants could report on conscious experiences, these elements of consciousness themselves were thought to be unobservable theoretical constructions. The emphasis then, was on "internal" behavior. Interestingly, structuralism would eventually be vindicated in this internal behavior criticism, in that the cognitive psychologists, one of the most historically recent schools of psychology, have returned to elaborate speculation about internal, nonobservable phenomenon. Further, the basic structuralist notion that conscious experience can be broken down into fundamental elements is also consistent with contemporary research in sensory neuroscience. For example, cells have been identified in visual portions of the brain that respond to basic lines and shapes, and these are eventually combined in subsequent brain areas.

While Wundt's work resulted in some challenges, strengths of his theoretical approach are observed because, Structuralism was the first major school of thought in psychology, which helped to began to form the practices of psychology and Structuralism also strongly influenced the development and implementation experimental psychology.

FUNCTIONALISM

The second paradigm of psychology was 'functionalism'. As its name implies, the primary interest in this approach is in the function of mental processes, including consciousness. Functionalism was the psychological school of thought that followed Structuralism and moved away from focusing on the structure of the mind to a concern with how the conscious is related to behavior. Functionalism formed as a reaction to structuralism and was heavily influenced by the work of William James and the evolutionary theory of Charles Darwin. Functionalists sought to explain the mental processes in a more systematic and scientific method. Rather than focusing on the elements of consciousness, functionalists focused on the purpose of consciousness and behavior. The subject matter of functionalism was based on the study of mental activity (e.g. perception, memory, imagination, feeling, judgment). Mental activity is to be evaluated in terms of how it serves the organism in adapting to its environment.

Functionalism also emphasized individual differences, which had a profound impact on education. As a result, Psychology really flourished in America in the 19th century. William James came out on top as the leading American psychologist during this period and his principles of psychology made him the "Father of American Psychology." Functionalism focused on how the human behavior works towards

Helping people comfortably in their respective environments. Functionalists use methods like direct observation. The functionalists however stressed the fact that consciousness is an ever changing and more continuous process. Although functionalism is no longer considered to be a school of thought, it however did go on to influence the next generation of psychologists.

The functionalists tended to use the term 'function' rather loosely. The term is used in at least two different ways. It can refer to the study of how a mental process operates. This is a major departure from the study of the structure of a mental process, the difference between stopping a train to tear it apart to study its parts (structuralism), and looking at how the systems interact while it is running (functionalism). The term 'function' can also refer to how the mental process functions in the evolution of the species, what adaptive property it provides that would cause it to be selected through evolution. The applied methods of psychology denote that mental acts can be studied through introspection, the use of instruments to record and measure; and objective manifestations of

mind, through the study of its creations and products, and through the study of anatomy and physiology.

Functionalism never really died, it became part of the mainstream of psychology. The importance of looking at process rather than structure is a common attribute of modern psychology. As an individual approach it lacked a clear formulation and inherited the problems of the structuralist reliance on introspection.

Functionalism was a major paradigm shift in the history of American psychology. As an outgrowth of Darwin's evolutionary theory, the functionalist approach focused on the examination of the function and purpose of mind and behavior. Rather than the structures of the mind, functionalism was interested in mental processes and their relation to behavior.

Almost immediately other theories surfaced to vie for dominance in psychology. In response to structuralism, an American perspective emerged under the influence of thinkers such as Charles Darwin and William James.

William James (1842-1910), a Harvard graduate, penned the first psychology textbook in 1890 entitled The Principles of Psychology. In his text, James exclaimed "We know of nothing … which can be in the remotest degree compared with the stream of thought that accompanies the brain's material secretions." "the mind is a stream of consciousness." James believed that knowledge about human psychology could come from many sources, including not only introspection and experimentation, but could also come from studying children, animals, and the mentally ill.

James believed that consciousness exist because it serves a function, and the psychologist job is to understand that function. James was interested in explaining the mind, not just describing the contents of the mind. Darwinism however took a different perspective when describing functionalism.

Darwinism and Functionalism

Charles Darwin's theory of natural selection was tremendously influential on the establishment of functionalism. After his famous voyage on The HMS Beagle, Darwin labored many years to produce the book responsible for a dramatic paradigm shift: The Origin of Species. Darwin's argued that the environment forces a natural selection upon its inhabitants and favors those inhabitants that have adaptive characteristics. The members within a species who have adaptive characteristics pass on this survival component to their offspring while those members without the adaptive characteristics begin to disappear. William James became a major proponent of this changing scientific focus. Other major Functionalists were William James, John Dewey, Harvey Carr, John Angell.

The impact of Functionalism was that it influenced behaviorism and applied psychology and Influenced the educational system, especially with regards to John Dewey's belief that children should learn at the level for which they are developmentally prepared. Following these early foundational beliefs were communities of psychologists that yielded their scientific perspective of psychology. Today, most psychologists have an eclectic outlook on psychology; drawing ideas and theories from different schools rather than holding to any singular outlook. Discussed in the next section are the seven major schools of thought in psychology.

PSYCHOLOGICAL SCHOOLS OF THOUGHT

1. PSYCHODYNAMIC PERSPECTIVE

The psychodynamic perspective originated with Sigmund Freud. Before we can understand this perspective, it is important to understand how Freud described the organization of the mind. According to Freud, the mind can be divided into three parts: Conscious, Unconscious, and Preconscious. The conscious mind includes those things we are aware of, such as day and night, hot and cold. This is the aspect of our mental processing that we can think and talk about rationally. Preconscious is a part of the mind that includes use of memory, which is not always part of consciousness but can be retrieved easily at any time and brought into our awareness. Freud called this ordinary memory the preconsciouness. Unconsciousness is different from consciousness and preconsciousness. The unconscious mind contains a reservoir of feelings, thoughts, urges, and memories that are deliberately held outside of our conscious awareness. Most of the contents of the unconscious are unacceptable or unpleasant, such as feelings of pain, anxiety, or conflict. According to Freud, the unconscious continues to influence our behavior

and experience, even though we are unaware of these underlying influences.

The Incredible Hulk is an example of what could happen in the face of unresolved conflict which often demonstrates itself at points of anger and distress. The words often quoted by Bruce Banner "Don't make me angry, you would not like me when I'm angry" are a great example of unresolved conflict that lies within and can be expressed with or without warning. In most cases, unresolved conflicts are hidden from those who reside within our social circle, but will manifest when some cue sparks the memory of the conflict.

From a psychodynamic perspective, most psychological processes that guide behavior are unconscious, repressed or unconscious impulses, anxieties, and unresolved internal conflicts that are hidden deep in one unconscious due to the anxieties and feelings of discomfort that arise in ones state of awareness of consciousness. Thus, consciousness is like the tip of an iceberg while unconsciousness is submerged out of sight and avoided due to emotional pain associated with unresolved hurt such as child abuse, bullying, domestic violence, rape, and other relational problems experienced in ones environment. This perspective purports that the unconscious is responsible for most thought and behavior in all people and the disorders of the mentally ill. Freud's theory of personality is comprised of three elements. These three elements of personality are the id, the ego and the superego and together they work together and are sometime in conflict which help to create complex human behaviors. More about the Id, Ego, and Superego will be discussed in Chapter 14 Personality. Because a primary aim is to interpret the meanings or motives of human behavior, psychodynamic psychologists have relied primarily on case study methods, although ongoing efforts to apply more rigorous methods to psychodynamic concepts are likely to prove fruitful in integrating these concepts into scientific psychology.

2. BEHAVIORIST PERSPECTIVE

Around 1913, American psychologist John B. Watson founded a new movement that changed the focus of psychology. He believed that in their study of consciousness, both structuralists and functionalist diverged too much from objective science. Internal mental processes should not be studied, because they cannot be observed; instead, Watson advocated that psychology should focus on the study of behavior and thus, his movement became known as behaviorism. As Watson saw it, behavior was not the result of internal mental processes, but rather the result of automatic response to stimuli from the environment. Perhaps the most well known Behaviorist is B. F. Skinner (1904-1990). Skinner followed much of Watson's research and findings, but believed that internal states could influence behavior just as external stimuli. He is considered to be a Radical Behaviorist because of this belief, although nowadays it is believed that both internal and external stimuli influence our behavior. Other major thinkers in Behaviorism are Ivan Pavlov, B.F.Skinner, Edward Thorndike, John B. Watson, and Clark Hull.

Behaviorism essentially holds that all human behavior is learned from one's surrounding context and environment. Behavioral psychology holds the idea that all behaviors are acquired through conditioning. Conditioning occurs through interaction with the environment. According to behaviorism, behavior can be studied in a systematic and observable manner with no consideration of internal mental states.

For many years, these concepts from behavioral theory formed the basis of most of the learning theory applied in child rearing and in classrooms. Parents and teachers still find that, in many instances, individuals do learn when provided with the appropriate blend of stimuli, rewards, negative reinforcement, and punishments. Especially with small children and simpler tasks, behavioral principles are often effective.

Subsequently, some educators began to feel that although stimulus-response does explain many human behaviors and have a legitimate place in instruction; behaviorism alone was insufficient to explain all the phenomena observed in learning situations. Hence the cognitive approach began to gain attention, while the behaviorist theorists went on to explore the possibilities of programmed learning for the computer age. Today, all computer-assisted instruction is solidly planted on the foundation laid by behaviorist researchers.

3. Cognitive Perspective

Cognitive psychology has grown rapidly since the 1950's. A very important event was the publication of Ulric Neisser's book, Cognitive Psychology, in 1967. It gave a new legitimacy to the field and consisted of six chapters on perception and attention and four chapters on language, memory, and thought. Following Neisser's work, another important event was the beginning of the Journal Cognitive Psychology in 1970. This journal has done much to give definition to the field. More recently a new field, called cognitive science, has emerged which attempts to integrate research efforts from psychology, philosophy, linguistics, neuroscience, and artificial intelligence. This field can be dated from the appearance of the journal, Cognitive Science in 1976 (Anderson, 1995).

The cognitive perspective focuses on the way people process, store, and retrieve information. Information processing refers to taking input from the environment and transforming it into meaningful output. This movement is much more objective and calculating than humanism, yet it is very different than behaviorism, as it focuses extensively on mental processes. The main idea of this movement is that humans take in information from their environment through their senses and then process the information mentally. The processing of information involves organizing it, manipulating it, storing it in memory, and relating it to previously stored information. Cognitive theorists apply their ideas to language, memory, learning, dreams, perceptual systems, and mental disorders. Important People in the History of Cognitive Psychology, Gustav Fechner, Wilhelm Wundt, Edward B. Titchener, Hermann Ebbinghaus, William James, Wolfgang Kohler, Edward Tolman, Jean Piajet, Noam Chomsky, David Rumelhart, James McClelland

4. Evolutionary Perspective

The evolutionary perspective argues that many human behavioral proclivities exist because they helped our ancestors survive and produce offspring that would likely survive. Natural selection is the mechanism by which natural forces select traits in organisms that are adaptive in their environmental niche. The basic notion of evolutionary theory is that evolution selects organisms that maximize their reproductive success, defined as the capacity to survive and reproduce and maximize the reproductive success of genetically related individuals. The primary methods are deductive and comparative, although evolutionary psychologists are increasingly relying on experimental methods.

Although the four major perspectives largely developed independently, each has made distinctive contributions, and some areas of integration have occurred, particularly in clinical psychology. The cognitive-behavioral approach accepts many behaviorist principles but emphasizes as well the role of thought processes, such as expectations, in learning. Major thinkers of the Evolutionary Perspective include Charles Darwin, David Buss, Margo Wilson.

5. Humanism

During the 1950s, humanistic psychology began as a reaction to psychoanalysism and behaviorism, which dominated psychology at the time. Psychoanalysis was focused on understanding the unconscious motivations that drove behavior while behaviorism studied the conditioning processes that produced behavior. Humanistic psychology was instead focused on each individual's potential and stressed the importance of growth and self-actualization. The fundamental belief of humanistic psychology was that people are innately good, with mental and social problems resulting from deviations from this natural tendency. In 1962, Abraham Maslow published Toward a Psychology of Being, in which he described humanistic psychology as the "third force" in psychology. The first and second

forces were behaviorism and psychoanalysis respectively.

Each perspective of psychology has contributed to understanding the human mind and behavior. Humanistic psychology added yet another dimension that took a more holistic view of the individual. The concept of the "self" is a central focus for most humanistic psychologists. The followers of this movement considered behaviorism and psychoanalytic theory dehumanizing and they took the name, humanism, for their movement. Instead of behaving as pawns of the environment or the powerful unconscious, humanists believed humans were inherently good and that their own mental processes played an active role in their behavior. Free will, emotions, and a subjective view of experience were important in the humanism movement. Major thinkers of Humanisitic Perspective include, Abraham Maslow, Carl Rodgers, Rolo May.

Maslow's best known contribution to Humanistic psychology is his Hierarchy or Pyramid of Needs. Maslow's Needs Hierarchy is frequently used to sum up the humanistic psychology belief system. The fundamental premise of his hierarchy is that everyone is born with specific needs. If we do not meet those base needs, we are unable to survive and focus upward within the hierarchy. The first stratum consists of physiological needs, or survival needs. Unable to obtain oxygen, sleep, water, and food, all else is irrelevant, see Figure 1.

After we meet these needs, we can shift our focus to the next stratum, the need for security and safety. When pursuing safety needs, we attempt to secure safety in others and yearn to create an environment that protects us, keeping us free from harm. Until these goals are met, it is unlikely that someone would consider higher order needs, and their growth is then stifled.

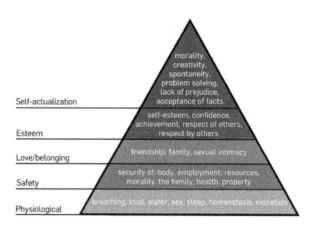

Figure 1. Maslow's Hierarchy of Needs Pyramid

When someone feels safe and secure, we attempt to build friendships and establish a sense of belonging to a greater whole. Maslow's third level of needs, the social needs of belonging and love, focus on our desire to be belong to a group and have a place in a larger whole. Meeting social needs get us one step closer to the top of the triangle -- the fourth level: esteem needs. Those attempting to fulfill esteem needs channel their energy on respect from others, self-esteem, self-respect, and gaining recognition for our accomplishments in life. We push further and further to excel in our careers, to expand our knowledge, and to constantly increase our self-esteem.

The final level in the hierarchy is called the need for self-actualization. Self-actualization refers to a complete understanding of the self. To be self-actualized means to truly know who you are, where you belong in the greater society, and to feel like you are accomplishing all that you are meant to be. It means to no longer feel shame or guilt, or even hate, but to accept the world and see human nature as inherently good. At this stage there is a desire to give back to the world and make ones impact or imprint at a greater capacity.

Given psychology's history, it should come as no surprise to you that there is currently no singe, dominant approach used. Psychology always has been a subject that branches into many issues and approaches. And, for now, it appears poised to continue that way.

The Table below provides a historical account of the discipline of psychology to date.

6. SOCIAL-CULTURAL PERSPECTIVE

Attempts to distinguish universal psychological processes from those that are specific to a particular culture. This perspective investigates how people in different cultures and social environments behave and think. Psychologists study how cultural differences impact an individual's response to their environment. Margaret Meade and Ruth Benedict (anthropologists) were interested in studying the relationship between culture and personality. "They purported that individual psychology is fundamentally shaped by cultural values, ideals, and ways of thinking."Cross cultural Psychology: (Berry et al., 1992, 1997): The study of cross cultural comparisons to determine differences based on cultural factors (race, region, sex). John Berry, Patricia Greenfield, Richard Brislin represent major scientist in this community of researchers.

7. BIOLOGICAL PERSPECTIVE

Biopsychology is a school of thought that focuses on the physical and biological causes of human cognition and behavior. Johannes Muller, Karl Lashley, David Hubel, James Olds, Roger Sperry, Candance Pert, and Torsten Wiesel are some scientists that represent this community. Within this perspective, the focus is on genetics and biological processes in the brain and other parts of the nervous system such as behavior patterns resulting as a matter of brain processes. Two other tenets are studied under this perspective. The first tenet is that all behavior has a physiological origin that is determined by biology. The second tenet is that human cognition and behavior is a function of genetic linkages, hormonal systems, and neurological functions. Although different neural region perform different functions, the neural circuits that underlie psychological events are distributed throughout the brain and cannot be "found" in one location. The biological perspective has a strength in that is uses scientific methods to evaluate hypothetical questions.

Overall, these perspectives yield a view point on the discipline of psychology. While most schools of thought are contrasting, each perspective contains a way of justifying the existence of psychology as a scientific discipline.

Out of the theoretical perspectives discussed, several forms of subdisciplines have formed to study psychology.

PROFESSIONAL AREAS OF PSYCHOLOGY

Psychology is a broad and diverse field. A number of different subfields and specialty areas have emerged. The following are some of the major areas of research and application within psychology:

CLINICAL PSYCHOLOGIST

Clinical Psychologists are trained to focus on the assessment, diagnosis, and treatment of mental disorders. While they often work in medical settings, clinical psychologists are not medical doctors and do not prescribe medications. Clinical psychology represents the largest subfield of psychologists. Specialty areas within clinical psychology include child mental health, adult mental health, learning disabilities, emotional disturbances, substance abuse, geriatrics, and health psychology.

According to the APA Research Office, in 2001 the average salary for a licensed clinical psychologist was $72,000. Of the psychologists surveyed, 65% worked in private practice, 19% worked in medical settings and 2% worked in some other human services setting.

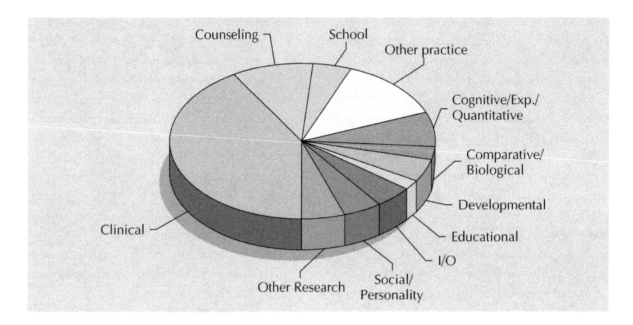

Figure 2. Division of Psychology Subdisciplines

DEVELOPMENTAL PSYCHOLOGIST

Developmental Psychologists are trained psychologist that study human growth and development over the lifespan. Theories often focus on the development of cognitive abilities, morality, social functioning, identity and other life areas.

FORENSIC PSYCHOLOGISTS

Forensic Psychologists are those who study the use of psychological research and principles in the legal and criminal justice system. They often are employed by police departments to assist with investigating crime scenes and perpetrators of criminal behaviors. The popularity of forensic psychology has grown phenomenally in recent years, partly due to sensationalized portrayals of the field in movies and television. Forensic psychologists are often depicted as criminal profilers who are able to almost psychically deduce a killer's next move. In reality, these professionals practice psychology as a science within the criminal justice system and civil courts.

Forensic psychologists are often involved in custody disputes, insurance claims and lawsuits. Some professionals work in family courts and offer psychotherapy services, perform child custody evaluations, investigate reports of child abuse and conduct visitation risk assessments.

Those working in the civil courts often assess competency, provide second opinions, and provide psychotherapy to crime victims. Professionals working in the criminal courts conduct evaluations of mental competency, work with child witnesses, and provide assessment of juvenile and adult offenders.

Salaries within forensic psychology can range greatly depending on the sector of employment, although most entry-level positions for those with a Ph.D. start out between $35,000 and $40,000 annually. Those in private practice who offer consulting services typically earn more.

INDUSTRIAL ORGANIZATIONAL PSYCHOLOGY (I/O)

Industrial and organizational psychologists use psychological research to enhance work performance, select employee, improve product design and enhance usability. Industrial-organizational (I/O) psychology is concerned with the study of workplace behavior. I/O psychologists often apply research to increasing workplace productivity, selecting employees best suited for particular jobs and product testing.

I/O psychology is a diverse field with opportunities in several different areas. Many I/O psychologists work in business in positions dealing with worker productivity, employee training and assessment and human resources. Other I/O psychologists work in research or academic positions. Specific specialty areas in I/O psychology include human-computer interaction and human factors. Consulting opportunities are also available for experienced I/O psychologists.

Typical salaries for I/O psychologists vary considerably depending upon such factors as the type of degree held and type of employer. According to the Society for Industrial (SIOP) and Organizational Psychology:

Starting salary for Master's graduate	$38,750
Starting salary for PhD graduate	$55,000
Median salary	$80,000
University professors	$70,000
Private sector	$100,000

Highest earners—Top 5% of SIOP members earn from $250,000 to several million each year.

There are a number of university programs that offer bachelor's degrees in industrial-organizational psychology. People with a bachelor's degree typically work in human resources, although there are some opportunities in other areas. Those looking for greater job opportunities and higher pay may want to consider continuing their education at the master's level.

There are many opportunities for job candidates with master's degrees in I/O psychology. These psychologists often work in human resources, consulting, government and positions in the private sector. The growing demand for I/O psychologists had led to an increase in the number of universities offering master's degrees in I/O psychology. Those with doctorate degrees in I/O psychology have the highest amount of opportunity and pay.

SCHOOL PSYCHOLOGY

School Psychologist is the branch of psychology that works within the educational system to help children with emotional, social and academic issues. A school psychologist is a type of psychologist that works within the educational system to help children with emotional, social and academic issues. The goal of school psychology is to collaborate with parents, teachers, and students to promote a healthy learning environment that focuses on the needs of children.

School psychology is still a relatively young profession. The National Association of School Psychology (NASP) was established and formally recognized as a doctoral specialty by the American Psychological Association (APA) in 1968. In 2002, U.S. News and World Report named school psychology one of the top ten "hot professions." Many school psychologists in the field are retiring, creating a demand for qualified school psychologists.

School psychologists work with individual students and groups of students to deal with behavioral problems, academic difficulties, disabilities and other issues. They also work with teachers and parents to develop techniques to deal with home and classroom behavior. Other tasks include training students, parents and teachers about how to manage crisis situations and substance abuse problems.

According to the National Association of School Psychology (NASP), there are five major areas where school psychologists provide services: (1) consultation, (2) evaluation, (3) intervention, (4) prevention, and (5) research and planning. School psychologists also act as educators by helping others understand more about child development, behavioral problems and behavior management techniques.

While most work in elementary and secondary schools, there are a number of different areas where school psychologists might find employment. Private clinics, hospitals, state agencies and universities are possible sectors of employment. Some school psychologists also go into private practice and serve as consultants, especially those with a doctoral degree in school psychology.

According to the Occupational Outlook Handbook published by the U.S. Department of Labor, the average salary for a psychologist working in an elementary or secondary school is $58,360. School Psychologists employed by universities as trainers will earn a higher salary than practitioners.

SPORT PSYCHOLOGY

Sport psychology can be traced back to the 1890s, but there was a big revival of interest in it in the late 20th Century. Top athletes emphasize the mental side of the game, both for solving problems and for cultivating states of peak performance. Athletes can identify psychological problems by looking for performance difficulties that tend to increase in pressure situations but not in practice. Some problems involve panicky feelings. An extreme example is "choking" during a game (suddenly losing one's ability to concentrate and perform). The solutions offered to athletes, to enhance performance and prevent problems, typically include relaxation training as well as techniques for concentrating and focusing attention, including visualization and rehearsal. Top athletes also emphasize

the motivation to engage in hard work and endless hours of practice.

Sport psychologists also study the psychology of coaching. The most effective coaches are informative and methodical instructors. They are good mentors and motivators, positive in orientation, willing to acknowledge and reinforce improvements in their athletes. College coaches were generally well aware of their coaching styles, as seen by others; coaches working with younger athletes often were not. Sports psychologists do not earn as much as psychologists with other specialties. The $55,000 average salary for sports psychologists is 83 percent of the average for all practicing psychologists.

The types of psychologists are varied reqiring advanced degree training as a professional. The training for psychologist is outlined by national associations that govern the ethical practices of all psychologists. Types of psychological associations discussed in the next section.

PROFESSIONAL ASSOCIATIONS OF PSYCHOLOGY

Association of Black Psychologists

The ABPsi was formed in the wake of the assassination of Dr. Martin Luther King Jr. and the rise of Black Nationalism Era, (Awodola, Orisade, 2004). The ABPsi intended to create a psychology of the black experience focused on improving the circumstances of black people. The founding psychologists believed that a psychology created mostly by white middle-class men could not explain the situation of people of African descent, and moved to incorporate African Philosophy and cultural experience into the creation of a new understanding of black psychology, (ABPsi).

The founders actively chose to remain independent of the American Psychological Association, decrying that body's complicit role in perpetuating white racism in society. Instead, the ABPsi took a more active stance, seeking "to develop a nation-wide structure for pooling their resources in meeting the challenge of racism and poverty. According to a statement released at their founding in 1968. Ebony Magazine's publication of Toward a Black Psychology by Joseph White in 1970 was a landmark in setting the tone and direction of the emerging field of Black Psychology. By 1974 the ABPsi had established offices in Washington D.C., begun the Journal of Black Psychology, and fully separated from the APA.

American Psychological Association

The American Psychological Association (abbreviated APA) is the largest scientific and professional organization of psychologists in the United States. It is the world's largest association of psychologists with around 150,000 members including scientists, educators, clinicians, consultants and students. The APA has an annual budget of around $115m. The American Psychological Association is occasionally confused with the American Psychiatric Association, (APA).

Mission

The mission of the APA is to advance the creation, communication and application of psychological knowledge to benefit society and improve people's lives. The American Psychological Association aspires to excel as a valuable, effective and influential organization advancing psychology as a science, serving as:

- A uniting force for the discipline
- The major catalyst for the stimulation, growth and dissemination of psychological science and practice
- The primary resource for all psychologists
- The premier innovator in the education, development, and training of psychological scientists, practitioners and educators

- The leading advocate for psychological knowledge and practice informing policy makers and the public to improve public policy and daily living
- A principal leader and global partner promoting psychological knowledge and methods to facilitate the resolution of personal, societal and global challenges in diverse, multicultural and international contexts
- An effective champion of the application of psychology to promote human rights, health, well being and dignity

American Psychiatric Association

The American Psychiatric Association (APA) is the main professional organization of psychiatrists and trainee psychiatrists in the United States. The association publishes various journals and pamphlets, as well as the Diagnostic Statistical Manual of Mental Disorders or DSM. The DSM codifies psychiatric conditions and is used worldwide as a key guide for diagnosing disorders.

APA Theoretical position

The APA reflects and represents mainstream psychiatry in the United States. Reflecting larger trends, the APA members and leaders had been largely psychodynamic in their approaches until recent decades, when the field became more "biopsychosocial."

The DSM is currently intended to be less theoretical than prior editions, having moved away from psychodynamic theories to be more widely accepted, and is proposed to not be committed to a particular theorized etiology for mental disorders. The criteria for many of the mental disorders have been expanded and involve a checklist of so-called 'Feighner Criteria' to try and capture the varying sets of features which would be necessary to diagnose a particular disorder.

Ethics in Psychology

The American Psychological Association's (APA) Ethical Principles of Psychologists and Code of Conduct (hereinafter referred to as the Ethics Code) consist of an Introduction, a Preamble, five General Principles, and specific Ethical Standards. This Ethics Code applies only to psychologists' activities that are part of their scientific, educational, or professional roles as psychologists. Areas covered include but are not limited to the clinical, counseling, and school practice of psychology; research; teaching; supervision of trainees; public service; policy development; social intervention; development of assessment instruments; conducting assessments; educational counseling; organizational consulting; forensic activities; program design and evaluation; and administration. This Ethics Code applies to these activities across a variety of contexts, such as in person, postal, telephone, internet, and other electronic transmissions. These activities shall be distinguished from the purely private conduct of psychologists, which is not within the purview of the Ethics Code.

Membership in the APA commits members and student affiliates to comply with the standards of the APA Ethics Code and to the rules and procedures used to enforce them. Lack of awareness or misunderstanding of an Ethical Standard is not itself a defense to a charge of unethical conduct.

The Ethics Code is intended to provide guidance for psychologists and standards of professional conduct that can be applied by the APA and by other bodies that choose to adopt them. The Ethics Code is not intended to be a basis of civil liability. Whether a psychologist has violated the Ethics Code standards does not by itself determine whether the psychologist is legally liable in a court action, whether a contract is enforceable, or whether other legal consequences occur.

The modifiers used in some of the standards of this Ethics Code (e.g., reasonably, appropriate, potentially) are included in the standards when they would (1) allow professional judgment on the part of psychologists, (2) eliminate injustice or inequality that would occur without the modifier, (3) ensure applicability across the broad range of activities conducted by psychologists, or (4) guard against a set of rigid rules that might be quickly outdated. As used in this Ethics Code, the term reasonable means the prevailing professional judgment of psychologists engaged in similar activities in similar circumstances, given the knowledge the psychologist had or should have had at the time.

In the process of making decisions regarding their professional behavior, psychologists must consider this Ethics Code in addition to applicable laws and psychology board regulations. In applying the Ethics Code to their professional work, psychologists may consider other materials and guidelines that have been adopted or endorsed by scientific and professional psychological organizations and the dictates of their own conscience, as well as consult with others within the field. If this Ethics Code establishes a higher standard of conduct than is required by law, psychologists must meet the higher ethical standard. If psychologists' ethical responsibilities conflict with law, regulations, or other governing legal authority, psychologists make known their commitment to this Ethics Code and take steps to resolve the conflict in a responsible manner in keeping with basic principles of human rights.

CHAPTER 1 SUMMARY

<u>Psychology</u> is defined as the scientific investigation of mental processes and behavior. Psychological processes reflect the influence of biological processes of the cells within the nervous system and the context of cultural beliefs and values.

BIOPSYCHOLOGY

<u>Biopsychology</u> seeks to understand the mind through understanding the biological activity of the brain.

The Mind-Brain problem

- Mental events include memory and emotion.
- Brain processes include the electrical and chemical processes of neurons.

<u>Localization of function</u> refers to the notion that discrete brain regions control discrete aspects of mental functioning. Support for localization of function:

- Electrical stimulation of the brain (Penfield) leads to distinct motor movements.
- Damage to certain brain structures can alter specific mental function.
- Lesions of neural pathways alter behavior in animal studies, e.g. rats with hypothalamic damage overeat to obesity.
- Humans with focal brain damage show evidence of impairment of mental function.
- Broca: Damage to the left front aspect of the brain human language.

Modern imaging techniques (PET, fMRI) have allowed for new ways to examine which brain regions are active during mental activity.

CULTURAL INFLUENCES AND PSYCHOLOGY

<u>Culture</u> refers to the influence of membership in a larger group such as a tribe or nation. A society is not simply the summation of the individuals that make up the society. Rather, culture impacts psychological functioning of individuals within the society.

PHILOSOPHICAL ISSUES OF PSYCHOLOGY

Psychology has inherited a number of issues from philosophy. Modern psychology often views these questions as an interaction between these issues, e.g. the likelihood of developing schizophrenia is an interaction between genetic factors and environmental factors. Examples of the philosophical issues include:

- Nature versus nurture?
     To what extent are psychological processes a function of biological or environmental processes?

- Rationalism versus empiricism?
    This issue asks whether knowledge about the world comes from experience and observation or from logic and reasoning?
- Reason versus emotion?
    This issue asks to what extent are we influenced by emotional processes?
- Continuity versus discontinuity with other animals?
    This issue addresses the question of whether we share a common psychology with animals (continuity).

EARLY PSYCHOLOGICAL SCIENCE

Psychology developed out of philosophy. Psychology distinguished itself from philosophy by its use of experimental methods, instruments and techniques.

- Wilhelm Wundt: Proponent of structuralism. Wundt established the first psychological laboratory. Wundt and his students used the method of introspection to examine mental processes. Wundt sought to define the structure of consciousness.
- William James: Proponent of functionalism. Functionalism argued that consciousness is functional and serves a purpose.

PARADIGMS AND PERSPECTIVES IN PSYCHOLOGY

A paradigm is a system of theoretical assumptions that scientists use to interpret or make sense of their discipline. Paradigm components include:

- Model of the phenomena (e.g. supply and demand).
- Set of shared metaphors (e.g. the mind is like a computer).
- Set of methods used to examine phenomena (microscope for a biologist).

Psychology lacks a unified paradigm. Psychology is organized into perspectives that have models, metaphors, and methods.

PSYCHODYNAMIC PERSPECTIVE

The psychodynamic view posits that conscious and unconscious forces interact to control our thoughts and behaviors. Behavior is viewed as an interplay between thoughts, feelings, and wishes. Some mental events are unconscious. Mental processes can conflict.

- Metaphor for the psychodynamic view: Awareness is like an iceberg: the portion above water is the conscious, the larger bulk below the water is the unconscious.
- Methods: Seek to understand the meanings of the mental life of a client. Speech and dream analyses are examples of these methods.
- Data: Primarily case studies in which a therapist seeks understanding of the thoughts, feelings, and actions of the client.

BEHAVIORIST PERSPECTIVE

The Behaviorist view is that learning plays a role in acquiring and maintaining behaviors. This view considers conditioning in which stimuli are associated: Restaurant is paired with bad news that leads to anxiety. Pairing of novel flavor with illness leads to taste aversion. This view considers conditioning in which behaviors have consequences: Positive consequences are reinforcing. Negative consequences are punishing.

- **Metaphor:** Humans and other animals are mechanistic. We show reflexive responses that can be elicited by external stimuli.
- **Methods:** Behaviorists use the experimental method to consider questions like: What are the relations between stimuli and behaviors?
- **Data:** Behaviorist approach uses quantitative empirical data analyses that can be replicated, e.g. rats running in a maze for food.

COGNITIVE PERSPECTIVE

The Cognitive view focuses on how people process, store, and retrieve information.

- **Metaphor:** The mind is like a computer. The cognitive view seeks to identify inputs, outputs, and to speculate on the mental programs that govern thought.
- **Methods:** Experimental Method Recall of previous material Reaction time
- **Data:** Memory and decision-making.

EVOLUTIONARY PERSPECTIVE

The evolutionary view argues that human behaviors evolved because they helped our ancestors survive and reproduce. Animals and humans share common behaviors. Behaviors are biologically determined. Sociobiology: Natural selection operates on psychological functions as well as physical functions.

- **Metaphor:** "We are all runners in a race, competing for resources…"
- **Methods:** Deductive, some experimental.
- **Data:** The evolutionary perspective may start with a known behavior in a species and attempt to explain it on the basis of evolutionary principles.

MAJOR SUB-DISCIPLINES OF PSYCHOLOGY

Biopsychology	Industrial/Organizational
Developmental	Educational
Social	Health
Clinical	Experimental
School	

PSYCHOLOGY AS A SCIENCE USING RESEARCH METHODS

LEARNING OBJECTIVES

After completing Chapter 2, students should be able to

- Explain the significance of the study by James Pennebaker on emotional expression and health.
- Explain how theories guide research and how in turn, research can confirm or disconfirm theories.
- Define and give an example of a continuous variable and a categorical variable.
- Provide at least three sources of ideas for new research.
- Differentiate between internal and external validity.
- Explain three different measures used to estimate reliability.
- Explain three different measures used to estimate validity
- Explain and define the importance of validity and reliability. What are the most important differences between these terms?
- Discuss the advantages and disadvantages of experimental and descriptive methods. Students should be able to give concrete examples of situations in which various research methods are especially suitable or unsuitable.
- Compare and contrast the case study method, the naturalistic observation approach, and the survey method.
- Explain the relationship between a population and a sample.
- Explain the advantages and disadvantages of a random sample in survey research.
- Define the concept of central tendency.
- How are measures of variability distinct from measures of central tendency?
- Give examples of dependent and independent variables in an experiment.
- Explain what it means to operationalize a variable and be able to give a concrete example of this process.
- Explain the difference between blind and double-blind studies. Indicate in what sorts of situations are blind and double-blind studies necessary?
- Give an example of a confounding variable and explain how it can affect the outcome of a specific study.
- Describe two limitations of the experimental method.
- Explain the significance of the p value for inferential statistics.
- Explain the meaning of a positive correlation coefficient between two variables and explain how this differs from a negative correlation coefficient.
- Explain the difficulty of conducting cross-cultural research.
- Provide an overview of the methods used by Milgram in his studies on obedience.
- Summarize the six points involved in the critical evaluation of a research study.
- Explain the role of deception in psychological research.
- Summarize three of the benefits to humankind that derived from animal research.

PSYCHOLOGY: SCIENTIFIC INVESTIGATION OF MENTAL PROCESSES AND BEHAVIOR

INTRODUCTION

In a very subtle and sometimes direct manner, people make judgments about the intentions, motivations and actions of others on a daily basis. Sometimes these observations are made deliberately and sometimes without much thought. While the everyday judgments we make about human behavior are often subjective, partial, and anecdotal, researchers use the scientific method to study psychology in an objective, unbiased, and systematic way. The results of these studies are often reported in popular media, such as professional journals, books, and news media to assist humans in improving their lives. In order to truly understand how psychologists and other researchers reach these self-enhancing conclusions, one would need to understand the research process that is used to study psychology and the basic steps that are utilized when conducting any type of psychological research. By knowing the steps of the scientific method, you can better understand the process researchers go through to arrive at conclusions about human behavior. This chapter is designed to discuss the scientific method used in psychological research. Upon completion of this chapter, students will know what and how to apply scientific methodology to any life phenomenon.

Introduction to the Scientific Method

Today the term science has come to have two major meanings: First, the term "science" has long been noted as representing bodies of knowledge accumulated in various domains and is used to identify the various sciences, or domains of organized scientific activities. For example, natural sciences are represented by disciplines such as physics, astronomy, chemistry, geology, and biology. The social and behavioral are represented by psychology, economics, education, geography, and sociology. Second, Science is it's fundamentally a method, a process, and a way of thought. These and similar statements are found throughout the literature describing science, with frequent mention, beginning in the 19th century. The most significant point is that science is fundamentally method used to produces the bodies of reliable and valid knowledge in various professional disciplines.

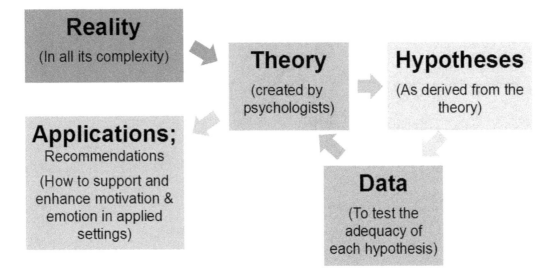

Figure 3. The scientific process for conducting a research

The scientific method is the process by which scientists, collectively and over time, endeavor to construct an accurate (that is, reliable, consistent and non-arbitrary) representation of the world. Recognizing that personal and cultural beliefs influence both our perceptions and our interpretations of natural phenomena, we aim through the use of standard procedures and criteria to minimize those influences when developing a theory. What is imperative is to minimize the influence of bias or prejudice in the researcher when testing a hypothesis or a theory. The goals of psychological studies are to describe, explain, predict and perhaps improve mental processes or behavior. In order to do this, psychologists utilize the scientific method to conduct psychological research. The scientific method is a set of principles and procedures that are used by researchers to develop questions, collect data, and reach conclusions.

Researchers seek not only to describe behaviors and explain why these behaviors occur; they also strive to create research that can be used to predict and even change human behavior. Figure 3. Below depicts the elements involved in scientific research. Figure 3 depicts the scientific process for conducting a research study.

SCIENTIFIC METHODOLOGY PROCEDURAL STEPS

The psychology of science has well-established literatures in most every subfield of psychology, including but not limited to: neuroscience, development, cognition, personality, motivation, social, industrial/organizational, and clinical. The methods of psychology that are applied to the study of scientific thought and behavior range from psychohistorical, psychobiographical, observational, descriptive, correlational, and experimental techniques. The scientific method in psychology is based on six procedural steps that are used to standardize the research process. The steps are listed below.

STEPS IN THE SCIENTIFIC METHOD

Step 1 – Form Testable Hypothesis
Step 2 – Devise a Study and Collect Data
Step 3 – Examine Data and Research Conclusion
Step 4 – Report Finding of Study
Step 5 – Publish findings
Step 6—Build a Theory

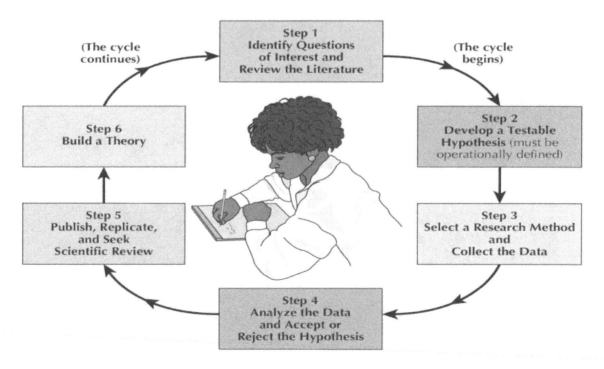

Figure 4. The Steps in Conducting a Psychological Study

2

Before a researcher can begin, they must choose a topic to study. Once an area of interest has been chosen, the researchers must then conduct a thorough review of the existing literature on the subject. This review will provide valuable information about what has already been learned about the topic and what questions remain to be answered. A literature review might involve looking at a considerable amount of written material from both books and academic journals dating back decades. The relevant information collected by the researcher will be presented in the introduction section of the final published results. This background material will also help the research with the first major step in conducting a psychology study—formulating a hypothesis, (see Figure 4).

STEP 1. FORM A TESTABLE HYPOTHESIS

The next step of a psychological investigation is to identify an area of interest and develop a hypothesis that can then be tested. While a hypothesis is often described as a hunch or a guess, it is actually much more specific. A hypothesis can be defined as an educated guess about the relationship between two or more variables. For example, a researcher might be interested in the relationship between study habits and test anxiety. They would then propose a hypothesis about how these two variables are related, such as "test anxiety decreases as a result of effective study habits."

After you have developed some possible hypotheses, it is important to think of ways that you could confirm or disprove each hypothesis through experimentation. In the scientific method, falsifiability is an important part of any valid hypothesis. This does not mean that the hypothesis is false; instead, it suggests that *if* the hypothesis were false, researchers could demonstrate this falsehood.

STEP 2. DEVISE A STUDY AND COLLECT DATA

The third step in a psychology study is to select the research methods that will be used and then collect the

data. The research method a researcher chooses depends largely on exactly what they are studying. There are two basic types of research methods—descriptive research and experimental research.

Descriptive Research Methods

Descriptive research such as case studies, naturalistic observations and surveys are often used when it would be impossible or difficult to conduct an experiment. These methods are best used to describe different aspects of a behavior or psychological phenomenon. Once a researcher has collected data using descriptive methods, a correlational study can then be used to look at how the variables are related.

Experimental Research Methods

Experimental methods are used to demonstrate causal relationships between variables. In an experiment, the researcher systematically manipulates a variable of interest (known as the independent variable) and measures the effect on another variable (known as the dependent variable). Unlike correlational studies, which can only be used to determine if there is a relationship between two variables, experimental methods can be used to determine the actual nature of the relationship. That is to say, if changes in one variable actually *cause* another to change.

STEP 3. EXAMINE DATA AND RESEARCH CONCLUSION

Once a researcher has designed the study and collected the data, it is time to examine this information and draw conclusions about what has been found. Using statistics, researchers can summarize the data, analyze the results, and draw conclusions based on this evidence.

So how does a researcher decide what the results of a study mean? Not only can statistical analysis support (or refute) the researcher's hypothesis; it can also be used to determine if the findings are statistically significant.

When results are said to be statistically significant, it means that it is unlikely that these results are due to chance.

STEPS 4 AND 5. REPORT FINDING OF STUDY AND PUBLISH FINDINGS

The fifth step in a psychology study is to report the findings. This is often done by writing up a description of the study and publishing the article in an academic or professional journal. The results of psychological studies can be seen in peer-reviewed journals such as *Psychological Bulletin*, the *Journal of Social Psychology*, *Developmental Psychology*, and many others.

The structure of a journal article follows a specified format that has been outlined by the American Psychological Association (APA). In these articles, researchers:

- Provide an Abstract, which is a short summary of the research
- Provide a brief history and background on previous research
- Present their hypothesis
- Describe the sample group that is those who participated in the study and how they were selected
- Provide operational definitions for each variable
- Describe the measures and procedures that were used to collect data
- Explain how information collected was analyzed
- Discuss what the results mean
- Discuss the implications of the study and provide recommendations for future research

Why is such a detailed record of a psychological study so important? By clearly explaining the steps and procedures used throughout the study, other researchers can then replicate the results. The editorial process employed by academic and professional journals ensures that each article that is submitted undergoes a thorough peer review, which helps ensure that the study is scientifically sound. Once published, the study becomes another piece of the existing knowledge used to increase our knowledge about the topic of interest.

STEP 6. BUILD A THEORY

If the experiments provide strong support to the literature, it may come to be regarded as a theory or law of nature (more on the concepts of hypothesis and theory below). If the experiment does not support the hypothesis, it must be rejected or modified, *however*. If the scientific results support the hypothesis, then that hyothesis is accepted. What is *key* in the description of the scientific method is to increase its predictive power that is the scientist's ability to affirm the strength of the theory as tested through the process of scientific experimentation. It is often said in science that theories can never be proven; only disproved. There is always the possibility that a new observation or a new experiment will conflict with a long-standing theory. A scientific theory or law represents a hypothesis, or a group of related hypotheses, which has been confirmed through repeated experimental tests. Accepted scientific theories and laws become part of our understanding of the universe and the basis for exploring less well-understood areas of knowledge. Theories are not easily discarded; new discoveries are first assumed to fit into the existing theoretical framework. It is only when, after repeated experimental tests that a new phenomenon cannot be accommodated that scientists seriously question the theory and attempt to modify it. This is a process that must demonstrate strong valid and reliable evidence. When changes in scientific thought and theories occur they potentially will revolutionize our view of the world (Kuhn, 1962). Again, the key force for change in any theoretical framework is the scientific method, and its emphasis on experimentation.

Hypothesis and Hypothesis Testing

As noted earlier, the scientific method requires that a hypothesis be formed to guide the purpose of a research study. A hypothesis is a question (s) or educated guess that is used to guide the scientific experimentation.

Hypotheses are formulated for several reasons. First, to support an existing theoretical framework or give evidence for a need to develop a new theoretical framework which will support a new concept. It is important to remember that hypothses rely on known scientific information. Second, hypotheses are designed to test the ideas of the scientific method. The hypothesis is designed to be tested. Therfore, it should be written simple to enhance its replication by other scientists. Finally, the hypothesis will determine what type of research should be conducted to investigate the topic at hand. When several hypotheses are bind together to yield a support of an idea, a theory is formed to explain that topic or phenomenon. Keep in mind that the predictions must agree with experimental results if we are to believe that it is a valid description of nature. Theories which cannot be tested, because, for instance, they have no observable ramifications (such as, a particle whose characteristics make it unobservable), do not qualify as scientific theories.

We are all familiar with theories which had to be discarded in the face of experimental evidence. In the field of astronomy, the earth-centered description of the planetary orbits was overthrown by the Copernican system, in which the sun was placed at the center of a series of concentric, circular planetary orbits. Later, this theory was modified, as measurements of the planets motions were found to be compatible with elliptical, not circular orbits, and still later planetary motion was found to be derivable from Newton's laws.

Error in experiments has several sources. First, there is error intrinsic to instruments of measurement. Because this type of error has equal probability of producing a measurement higher or lower numerically than the "true" value, it is called random error. Second, there is non-random or systematic error, due to factors which bias the result in one direction. No measurement, and therefore no experiment, can be perfectly precise. At the same time, in science we have standard ways of estimating and in some cases reducing errors. Thus it is important to determine the accuracy of a particular measurement and, when stating quantitative results, to quote the measurement error. A measurement without a quoted error is meaningless. The comparison between experiment and theory is made within the context of experimental errors. Scientists ask, how many standard deviations are the results from the theoretical prediction? Have all sources of systematic and random errors been properly estimated? These questions are asked to explain mistakes or error in research.

Common Mistakes in Applying the Scientific Method

As stated earlier, the scientific method attempts to minimize the influence of the scientist's bias on the outcome of an experiment. That is, when testing a hypothesis or a theory, the scientist may have a preference for one outcome or another, and it is important that this preference not bias the results or their interpretation. There are several common forms of mistakes in research.

1. The most fundamental error is to mistake the hypothesis for an explanation of a phenomenon, without performing experimental tests. Sometimes "common sense" and "logic" tempt us into believing that no test is needed. There are numerous examples of this, dating from the Greek philosophers to the present day.

2. Another common mistake is to ignore or rule out data which do not support the hypothesis. Ideally, the experimenter is open to the possibility that the hypothesis is correct or incorrect. Sometimes, however, a scientist may have a strong belief that the hypothesis is true (or false), or feels internal or external pressure to get a specific result. In that case, there may be a psychological tendency to find "something wrong", such as systematic effects, with data which do not support the scientist's expectations, while data which do agree with those expectations may not be checked as carefully. The lesson is that all data must be handled in the same way.

3. Another common mistake arises from the failure to estimate quantitatively systematic errors (and all errors). There are many examples of discoveries which were missed by experimenters whose data contained a new phenomenon, but who explained it away as a systematic background. Conversely, there are many examples of alleged "new discoveries" which later proved

to be due to systematic errors not accounted for by the "discoverers."

In a field where there is active experimentation and open communication among members of the scientific community, the biases of individuals or groups may cancel out, because experimental tests are repeated by different scientists who may have different biases. In addition, different types of experimental setups have different sources of systematic errors. Over a period spanning a variety of experimental tests (usually at least several years), a consensus develops in the community as to which experimental results have stood the test of time and prove a proposed theory that is suppor ted by reliable and valid data.

SUMMARY

The scientific method is intricately associated with science, the process of human inquiry that pervades the modern era on many levels. While the method appears simple and logical in description, there is perhaps no more complex question than that of knowing how we come to know things. In this introduction, we have emphasized that the scientific method distinguishes science from other forms of explanation because of its requirement of systematic experimentation. We have also tried to point out some of the criteria and practices developed by scientists to reduce the influence of individual or social bias on scientific findings. Further investigations of the scientific method and other aspects of scientific practice may be found in the references listed below.

TYPES OF RESEARCH METHODS

Research is an attempt to achieve systematically and with the support of data the answer to a question, the resolution to a problem, or the greater understanding of a phenomenon.

The goals of psychological research is Describe social behavior, establish a relationship between cause and effect, Develop theories about why people behave the way that they do, and apply effective therapeutic treatments, more successful negotiation tactics, and greater understanding amongst groups of people, (see table 4).

TYPES OF RESEARCH

Quantitative: answer questions about data that can be measured in order to explain and predict and Qualitative: answer questions about nature of phenomena in order to describe phenomena and understand it from the participant's point of view. There are four types of research that are used to study

different phenomenon: Experimental, Descriptive, Correlational, and Biological Research.

1. Experimental Research or Causal Research: When most people think of scientific experimentation, research on cause and effect is most often brought to mind. Experiments on causal relationships investigate the effect of one or more variables on one or more outcome variables. This type of research also determines if one variable causes another variable to occur or change. An example of this type of research would be altering the amount of a treatment and measuring the effect on study participants.

2. Descriptive Research or Naturalistic Research: Descriptive research seeks to depict what already exists in a group or population. An example of this type of research would be an opinion poll to determine which Presidential candidate people plan to vote for in the next election. Descriptive studies do not seek to measure the effect of a variable; they seek only to describe. Descriptive research design is a scientific method

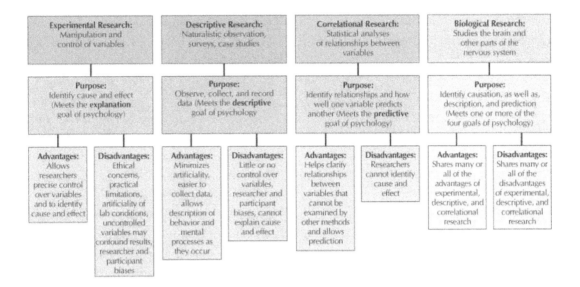

Table 3. Types of Psychological Research

which involves observing and describing the behavior of a subject without influencing it in any way. The subject is being observed in a completely natural and unchanged natural environment. Descriptive research design is a valid method for researching specific subjects and as a precursor to more quantitative studies. While there are some valid concerns about the statistical design limitations that are understood by the researcher, this type of study is an invaluable scientific tool. Whilst the results are always open to question and to different interpretations, there is no doubt that they are preferable to performing no research at all.

3. Correlational or Relational Research: Correlation research investigates the connection between two or more variables is considered relational research. The variables that are compared are generally already present in the group or population. For example, a study that looked at the proportion of males and females that would purchase either a classical CD or a jazz CD would be studying the relationship between gender and music preference.

4. Biological Research: Biological Research examines the brain and other parts of the nervous system. Biological research uses medical science to explain the workings of the biology. Psychologists are interested in biology to further understand and explain the impact of the nervous system and genetics on human behavior. Biological research is instrumental in providing pharmaceutical interventions to improve the health and wellness of humans and various animal species.

Regardless of the type of research that is being used there are specific goals to each type. The goals of scientific psychology is to do the following:

1. T*o Describe*: tells "what" occurred or assign characteristics;
2. T*o Explain*: tells "why" a behavior or mental process occurred;
3. *To Predict*: identifies conditions under which a future behavior or mental process is likely to occur; and
4. *To change behavior and mental processes (Influence or Control)*: which applies to psychological

knowledge to prevent unwanted behavior or to bring about desired goals.

Regardless of the type and goals of research, a research study must have the characteristic design that supports its validity and reliable use. The next section will discuss the characteristics of a good research study.

CHARACTERISTICS OF A GOOD RESEARCH STUDY

A good research study has four basic elements that are used to support its validity. These are described below.

- *Theoretical Framework* – Systematic way of organizing and explaining observations. The research will have a set of hypotheses that flows from the theory or from an important question.
- *Standardized Procedure*—Procedures that is the same for all subjects except where variation is introduced to test a hypothesis.
- *Generalizability* – Sample that is representative of the population. Has procedures (implementation steps) that are relevant to the circumstance (research study) outside the laboratory.
- *Objective Measure*—Measures that are reliable (that produce consistent results. Measures that are valid and reliable

Theoretical Framework

The term *theory* is used with surprising frequency in everyday language. A theory is a systematic way of organizing and explaining observations. It is important to note as you study psychology and other scientific topics, that a theory in science is not the same as the colloquial use of the term. It must be understood based on its true and exact meaning. Throughout the history of psychology, a number of different theories have been proposed to explain and predict various aspects of human behavior and mental processes. Some of these theories have lasted over time and remain accepted today (i.e., cognitive and behavior) while others have

become obsolete and or scientifically understudied, and rejected by other scientific research communities today (structuralism, functionalism).

A theory is a based upon a hypothesis and supported by data based evidence. A theory presents a concept or idea that is testable. In science, a theory is not merely a guess. A theory is a fact-based framework for describing a phenomenon. In psychology, theories are used to provide a model for understanding human thoughts, emotions and behaviors. A psychological theory has two key components: (1) it must describe a behavior and (2) make predictions about future behaviors. The research will have a set of hypotheses that flows from the theory or from an important question. Framework is based on some Theory. A theory systematically organizes and explains observations by including a set of propositions, or statements about the relations among various phenomena. Theory provides a framework for the hypotheses.

As stated above, the hypotheses are a tentative belief about the relationship between two or more variables. A hypothesis is a specific, testable prediction about what you expect to happen in your study. For example, a study designed to look at the relationship between sleep deprivation and test performance might have a hypothesis that states, "This study is designed to assess the hypothesis that sleep deprived persons will perform lower on a test than individuals who are not sleep deprived." Unless you are creating a study that is exploratory in nature, your hypothesis should always explain what you *expect* to happen during the course of your experiment or research. A hypothesis does not have to be right. While the hypothesis predicts what the researchers expect to see, the goal of research is to determine whether this guess is right or wrong

Elements of a Good Hypothesis

When trying to come up with a good hypothesis for your own psychology research or experiments, ask yourself the following questions:

- Is your hypothesis based on your research of a topic?

- Is your hypothesis based on some theoretical framework?
- Can your hypothesis be tested?
- Does you hypothesis include independent and dependent variables?

Before you come up with a specific hypothesis, spend some time conducting a review of the literature conducting a background research on your topic. Once you have completed a literature review, start thinking of potential questions you continue to have about your research topic. Be careful to attend to the discussion section in the journal articles you read and begin to explore, identify, and clearly defined operational variables.

Operationally Defining a Variable

Before conducting a psychology experiment, it is essential to create firm operational definitions for both the independent variable and dependent variable. A variable is something that can be changed, such as a characteristic or value. Variables are generally used in psychology experiments to determine if changes to one thing result in changes to another. Hence, the variable is any phenomenon that can differ, or vary, from one situation to another or from one person to another. Therefore, *a variable can take on different values (quantitative results)*. There are two main types of variables, independent and dependent. However in research we also study other forms of variables such as *extraneous (continuous, categorical, participant and situational and confounding variables.*

The independent variable is the characteristic of a psychology experiment that is manipulated or changed. For example, in an experiment looking at the effects of studying on test scores, studying would be the independent variable. Researchers are trying to determine if changes to the independent variable (studying) result in significant changes to the *dependent variable* (the test results). The *independent variable* is the variable that is controlled and manipulated by the experimenter. For example, in an experiment on the impact of sleep deprivation on test performance, sleep deprivation

would be the independent variable. The result of the sleep deprivation tests would be the *dependent variable.*

The dependent variable is the variable that is being measured in an experiment. For example, in a study on the effects of tutoring on test scores, the dependent variable would be the participants test scores. The *dependent variable* is the variable that is measured by the experimenter. In the previous example, the scores on the test performance measure would be the dependent variable.

In a psychology experiment, researchers are looking at how changes in the independent variable cause changes in the dependent variable.

Extraneous and Confounding Variables, The independent and dependent variables are not the only variables present in many experiments. In some cases, extraneous variables may also play a role. This type of variable is one that may have an impact on the relationship between the independent and dependent variables. The extraneous variables can also be continuous or categorical. **Continuous Variables** represent *c*haracteristics that continue, such as intelligence, temperament, rate recovery. **Categorical Variables** represent a variable comprised of groupings, classifications, or categories. An operational definition describes how the variables are measured and defined within the study.

For example, in the previous description of an experiment on the effects of sleep deprivation on test performance, other factors such as age, gender and academic background may have an impact on the results. These are examples of categorical variables. In such cases, the experimenter will note the values of these extraneous variables so this impact on the results can be controlled for.

There are two other basic types of extraneous variables: *Participant variables* and *Situational Variables*. **Participant Variables:** These extraneous variables are related to individual characteristics of each participant that may impact how he or she responds. These factors can include background differences, mood, anxiety, intelligence, awareness and other characteristics that are unique to each person. These characteristics also represent *continuous variables*.

Situational Variables: These extraneous variables are related to things in the environment that may impact how each participant responds. For example, if a participant is taking a test in a chilly room, the temperature would be considered an extraneous variable. Some participants may not be affected by the cold, but others might be distracted or annoyed by the temperature of the room.

In many cases, extraneous variables are controlled for by the experimenter. In the case of participant variables, the experiment might select participants that are the same in background and temperament to ensure that these factors do not interfere with the results. If, however, a variable cannot be controlled for, it becomes what is known as a **confounding variable**. This type of variable *can* have an impact on the dependent variable, which can make it difficult to determine if the results are due to the influence of the independent variable, the confounding variable or an interaction of the two.

Having consistency and appropriate representation in variables is important to the scientific method. This will assist in researching sample populations that are being studied. Standardization is equally important and will aid in the study being replicated and validated within a theoretical framework.

STANDARDIZATION IN RESEARCH

In order to arrive at legitimate conclusions, it is essential to standard the research procedure. Several steps must occur to secure standardization. First, each participant in each group must receive the same treatment under the same conditions. For example, in our hypothetical study on the effects of sleep deprivation on driving performance, the driving test must be administered to each participant in the same way. The driving course must be the same, the obstacles faced must be the same and the time given must be the same.

Second, it is also essential to ensure that your pool of participants is the same. If the individuals in your control group (those who are not sleep deprived) all happen to be amateur race car drivers while your experimental group (those that are sleep deprived) are all

people who just recently earned their drivers licenses, your experiment will lack standardization. The sample pool must be the same for both the control and experimental group. The sample group must also represent the greater population of people for which the study was originally designed. Standardized procedures will expose participants in the study to the same processes. All subjects are given the same instructions, presented with the same experiment in the same manner, and that all of the data is collected exactly the same or all subjects.

To really demonstrate the validity of a research study, experiments need to be replicated by other researchers with different subjects. To do this, the researchers need to know the exact procedural steps in order to replicate the study. When implementing the standardized procedures, following strict procedural guidelines is very important for generalizability.

GENERALIZABILITY AND TARGET POPULATIONS

Psychological research allows the researcher to study a subset of people to learn about the larger group to whom the research findings (tested hypothesis) are true or false. The research procedures (implementation steps) that are relevant to the circumstance (research study) outside the laboratory must yield results that can be generalized or used to explain the behavior of the greater population. The results of the study is generalized to the greater population as the study's conclusive evidence that can be used to explain a research question based on the _target population_. Three key terms are used to describe subjects that participate in a study:

- Population – a sample
- Sample
- Participants or subjects

A representative sample means the subject group must reflect characteristics of the greater population as a whole. Participants are individuals who participate in a study; also called subjects. A sample is a subset that is representative of the population. In any research study a population of subjects (i.e., humans or animals) must be involved. The subjects must represent a group of people or animals of interest to a researcher from which a sample is drawn. The Sample Group is a subgroup of a population likely to be representative of the population as a whole.

OBJECTIVE MEASURE

Measurement is a part of the scientific process. *Measurement* is the process (rules) for assigning numbers to observations to represent quantities of attributes. *Statistics* is a body of procedures for organizing data, describing variation, and making inferences. Measures that are reliable are those that produce consistent results. Measures that are valid and reliable carefully chosen, systematic and follow standardized procedures for evoking a sample of responses from participants who are members of the sample group. These measurements can be used to assess one or more of their psychological characteristics by comparing their results with those of a representative sample of an appropriate population.

RELIABILITY AND VALIDITY

For a study to be generalizable, it must be reliable and valid. To be valid a study must meet two criteria:

1. **Internal validity** – The extent to which a study methodologically is appropriate
2. **External Validity** – The extent to which the findings of a study can be generalized to situations outside the laboratory.

Sometimes the researcher will experience the Experimenter's Dilemma, which is being faced with the decision to focus on internal versus external validity to best describe the outcomes of the research data. The researcher will need to critically analyze the advantages and disadvantages of choosing the external versus the internal validity, while maintaining the ethics of research and reporting results accurately.

RESEARCH BIASES

There are some aspects of research that can contaminate research results. These poor practices can erode the validity of the study and interfere with accuracy of reporting. These aspects are called research biases and are represented in three main types:

1. Sample Bias: Occurs when differences between groups are present at the beginning of the experiment.
2. Placebo Effect: Involves the influencing of performance due to the subject's belief about the results. In other words, if I believe the new medication will help me feel better, I may feel better even if the new medication is only a sugar pill. This demonstrates the power of the mind to change a person's perceptions of reality.
3. Experimenter Effect (Experimental Bias): The same way a person's belief's can influence his or her perception, so can the belief of the experimenter. If I'm doing an experiment, and really believe my treatment works, or I really want the treatment to work because it will mean big bucks for me, I might behave in a manner that will influence the subject.

Controlling for Biases

When conducting a research study there is a need to control for biases. To control for selection bias, most

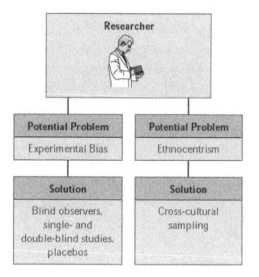

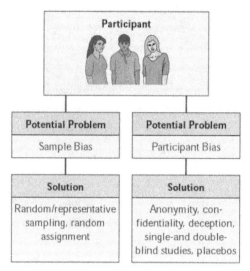

experiments use what's called *Random Assignment*, which means assigning the subjects to each group based on chance rather than human decision. To control for the placebo effect, subjects are often not informed of the purpose of the experiment. This is called a *Blind Study*, because the subjects are blind to the expected results. To control for experimenter biases, the researcher can utilize a *Double Blind Study*, which means that both the experimenter and the subjects are blind to the purpose and anticipated results of the study. When these methods are used and there is reduction in bias, the validity of the study will improve.

VALIDITY

Validity is the extent to which a test measures what it claims to measure. It is vital for a test to be valid in order for the results to be accurately applied and interpreted. Validity isn't determined by a single statistic, but by a body of research that demonstrates the relationship between the test and the behavior it is intended to measure. Whenever a test or other measuring device is used as part of the data collection process, the validity and reliability of that test is important. Just as we would not use a math test to assess verbal skills, we would not want to use a measuring device for research that was not truly measuring what we purport

it to measure. After all, we are relying on the results to show support or a lack of support for our theory and if the data collection methods are erroneous, the data we analyze will also be erroneous.

There are three types of validity: Content Validity, Criterion-related Validity, **Concurrent Validity, Predictive Validity, and** Construct Validity.

Content validity

When a test has content validity, the items on the test represent the entire range of possible items the test should cover. Individual test questions may be drawn from a large pool of items that cover a broad range of topics. Content validity is concerned with a test's ability to include or represent all of the content of a particular construct. To develop a valid test of intelligence, not only must there be questions on math, but also questions on verbal reasoning, analytical ability, and every other aspect of the construct we call intelligence.

Criterion-related Validity

A test is said to have criterion-related validity when the test has demonstrated its effectiveness in predicting criterion or indicators of a construct. There are two different types of criterion validity:

1. **Concurrent Validity.** Concurrent Validity refers to a measurement device's ability to vary directly with a measure of the same construct or indirectly with a measure of an opposite construct. It allows you to show that your test is valid by comparing it with an already valid test. A new test of adult intelligence, for example, would have concurrent validity if it had a high positive correlation with the Wechsler Adult Intelligence Scale since the Wechsler is an accepted measure of the construct we call intelligence. An obvious concern relates to the validity of the test against which you are comparing your test. Some assumptions must be made because there are many who argue the Wechsler scales, for example, are not good measures of intelligence for some culturally diverse populations.

2. **Predictive Validity** occurs when the criterion measures are obtained at a time after the test. Examples of test with predictive validity are career or aptitude tests, which are helpful in determining who is likely to succeed or fail in certain subjects or occupations. In order for a test to be a valid screening device for some future behavior, it must have predictive validity. The SAT is used by college screening committees as one way to predict college grades. The GMAT is used to predict success in business school. And the LSAT is used as a means to predict law school performance. The main concern with these and many other predictive measures is predictive validity does not take into consideration other conditions that surround test taking and assessment such as test anxiety and in class performance. Hence these forms of test should never be used as the sole predictor of someones future performance.

Construct Validity

Construct validity seeks agreement between a theoretical concept and a specific measuring device or procedure. Hence, it is the degree to which an instrument measures the characteristic being investigated; the extent to which the conceptual definitions match the operational definitions. For example, a researcher

inventing a new IQ test might spend a great deal of time attempting to "define" intelligence in order to reach an acceptable level of construct validity.

Construct validity can be broken down into two sub-categories: Convergent validity and discriminate validity. Convergent validity is the actual general agreement among ratings, gathered independently of one another, where measures should be theoretically related. Discriminate validity is the lack of a relationship among measures which theoretically should not be related.

To understand whether a piece of research has construct validity, three steps should be followed. First, the theoretical relationships must be specified. Second, the empirical relationships between the measures of the concepts must be examined. Third, the empirical evidence must be interpreted in terms of how it clarifies the construct validity of the particular measure being tested (Carmines & Zeller, p. 23).

Convergent Validity

Convergent validity is the degree to which an operation is similar to (converges on) other operations that it theoretically should also be similar to. For instance, to show the convergent validity of a test of mathematics skills, the scores on the test can be correlated with scores on other tests that are also designed to measure basic mathematics ability. High correlations between the test scores would be evidence of a convergent validity. Convergent validity shows that the assessment is related to what it should theoretically be related to.

The validity of a measure ought to be gauged by comparing it to measures of the same concept developed through other methods.

Discriminate Validity

Discriminant validity examines the extent to which a measure correlates with measures of attributes that are different from the attribute the measure is intended to assess. If the measures are significantly different, the researcher can then claim uniqueness in their construct.

Overall, the basic difference between convergent and discriminant validity is that convergent validity tests whether constructs that should be related, are related. Discriminant validity tests whether believed unrelated constructs are, in fact, unrelated. It is the degree to which an operation is similar to (converges on) other operations that it theoretically should also be similar to. For instance, to show the convergent validity of a test of mathematics skills, the scores on the test can be correlated with scores on other tests that are also designed to measure basic mathematics ability. High correlations between the test scores would be evidence of a convergent validity.

RELIABILITY

Reliability is the degree to which an instrument measures the same way each time it is used under the same condition with the same subjects. In short, it is the repeatability of your measurement. A measure is considered reliable if a person's score on the same test given twice is similar. It is important to remember that reliability is not measured, it is estimated.

Internal consistency estimates reliability by grouping questions in a questionnaire that measure the same concept. For example, you could write two sets of three questions that measure the same concept (say student attendance in class) and after collecting the responses, run a correlation between those two groups of three questions to determine if your instrument is reliably measuring that concept. One common way of computing correlation values among the questions on your instruments is by using Cronbach's Alpha. The Cronbach's alpha splits all the questions on your instrument every possible way and computes correlation values for them all (we use a computer program for this part). In the end, your computer output generates one number for Cronbach's alpha and like a correlation coefficient, the closer it is to one, the higher the reliability estimate of your instrument. Cronbach's alpha is a less conservative estimate of reliability than test/retest.

The primary difference between test/retest and internal consistency estimates of reliability is that test/retest involves two administrations of the measurement instrument, whereas the internal consistency method involves only one administration of that instrument. There are four types of reliability: Test-Retest Reliability, Inter-rater Reliability, Parallel-Forms Reliability, and Internal Consistency Reliability.

Test-Retest Reliability

Test-retest reliability is when a test is administered twice at two different points in time to the same sample group. This kind of reliability is used to assess the consistency of a test across time. This type of reliability assumes that there will be no change in the quality or construct being measured. Test-retest reliability is best used for things that are stable over time, such as academic knowledge. If the test is reliable, the scores that each student receives on the first administration should be similar to the scores on the second. It would be expected that the relationship between the first and second administration would have a high positive correlation.

One major concern with test-retest reliability is *Practice Effect*. Practice effect is more likely to occur when the two administrations are linked together in time. For example, imagine taking a short 10-question test on good eating habits and then ten minutes later being asked to complete the same test. Most people will remember their responses and when answering the questions again will have the tendency to repeat the same response provided on the first test. This can create an artificially high reliability coefficient as subjects respond from their memory rather than the test itself. When a pre-test and post-test for an experiment is the same, the practice effect can play a role in the results.

Inter-rater Reliability

This type of reliability is assessed by having two or more independent raters score the test. The scores are then compared to determine the consistency of the rater's estimates. One way to test inter-rater reliability is to have each rater assign each test item a score. For example, each rater might score items on a scale from

1 to 10. Next, you would calculate the correlation between the two ratings to determine the level of inter-rater reliability. If the ratings are positively correlated, then it is concluded that the same construct is being measured. It the correlation is low, it is then concluded that the constructs measured are not the same.

Parallel-Forms Reliability

Parallel-forms reliability is gauged by comparing two different tests that were created using the same content. This is accomplished by creating a large pool of test items that measure the same quality and then randomly dividing the items into two separate tests. The two tests should then be administered to the same subjects at the same time. One way to assure that practice effects does not occur is to use a different pre- and posttest. In order for these two tests to be used in this manner, however, they must be parallel or equal in what they measure. To determine parallel forms reliability, a reliability coefficient is calculated on the scores of the two measures taken by the same group of subjects. Once again, we would expect a high and positive correlation is we are to say the two forms are parallel.

Internal Consistency Reliability

This form of reliability is used to judge the consistency of results across items on the same test. Essentially, you are comparing test items that measure the same construct to determine the tests internal consistency. When you see a question that seems very similar to another test question, it may indicate that the two questions are being used to gauge reliability. Because the two questions are similar and designed to measure the same thing, the test taker should answer both questions the same, which would indicate that the test has internal consistency.

CONTROLLING FOR THREATS TO EXPERIMENTS

Understanding how to manipulate variables and control for potential threats to experimental validity can be

Table 4: Controlling for Threats to Internal Validity

Threat to Internal Validity	Controlling Threat
History	Random selection, random assignment
Maturation	Subject matching, randomization
Testing	Control group
Statistical Regression	Omit extreme scores, randomization
Instrumentation	Instrumental consistency, assure alternative form reliability
Selection	Random selection, random assignment
Experimenter Bias	Double blind study
Mortality	Subject matching and omission

the difference between a solid research study and a near meaningless study. Variables are the basis for all of the statistics you will perform on your data. If you choose your variables wisely and make sure to control for as many confounds and threats to experimental validity as possible, your study is much more likely to add to the knowledge base in your area of specialty. Assuring that the measurement devices used are both valid and reliable will also add a lot to significant results. When any of these is called into question, the entire study gets called into question.

External Validity

External validity refers to the generalizability of a study. In other words, can we be reasonable sure that the results of our study consisting of a sample of the population truly represents the entire population? Threats to external validity can result in significant results within a sample group but an inability for this to be generalized to the population at large. Four of these threats are discussed below and summarized in Table 7.2.

Demand Characteristics

Subjects are often provided with cues to the anticipated results of a study. When asked a series of questions about depression, for instance, subjects may become wise to the hypothesis that certain treatments work better in treating mental illness. When subjects become wise to anticipated results (often called a placebo effect), they can begin to exhibit performance that they believe is expected of them. Making sure that subjects are not aware of anticipated outcomes (referred to as a blind study) reduces the possibility of this threat.

Hawthorne Effects

Similar to a placebo, research has found that the mere presence of others watching your performance causes a change in your performance. If this change is significant, can we be reasonably sure that it will also occur when no one is watching? Addressing this issue can be tricky but employing a control group to measure the Hawthorne effect of those not receiving any treatment can be very helpful. In this sense, the control groups are also being observed and will exhibit similar changes in their behavior as the experimental group therefore negating the Hawthorne effect.

Order Effects (or Carryover Effects)

Order effects refer to the order in which treatment is administered and can be a major threat to external validity if multiple treatments are used. If subjects are given medication for two months, therapy for another two months, and no treatment for another two months, it would be possible, and even likely, that the level of depression would be least after the final no treatment phase. Does this mean that no treatment is better than the other two treatments? It likely means that the benefits of the first two treatments have carried over to the last phase, artificially elevating the no treatment success rates.

Treatment Interaction Effects

The term interaction refers to the fact that treatment can affect people differently depending on the subject's characteristics. Potential threats to external validity

Table 5. Controlling for Threats to External Validity

Threat to Internal Validity	Controlling Threat
Demand Characteristics	Blind study, control group
Hawthorne Effect	Control group
Order Effects	Counterbalancing treatment order, multiple groups
Treatment Interaction Effects	Subject matching, naturalistic observation

include the interaction between treatment and any of the following: selection, history, and testing. As an example, assume a group of subjects volunteer for a study on work experience and college grades. One group agrees to find part time work the summer before starting their freshman year and the other group agrees to join a softball leaguer over the summer. The group that agreed to work is likely inherently different than the group that agreed to play softball. The selection itself may have placed higher motivated subjects in one group and lower motivated students in the other. If the work groups earn higher grades in the first semester, can we truly say it was caused by the work experience? It is likely that the motivation caused both the work experience and the higher grades.

Summary

The real difference between reliability and validity is mostly a matter of definition. Reliability estimates the consistency of your measurement, or more simply the degree to which an instrument measures the same way each time it is used in under the same conditions with the same subjects. Validity, on the other hand, involves the degree to which you are measuring what you are supposed to, more simply, the accuracy of your measurement. It is my belief that validity is more important than reliability because if an instrument does not accurately measure what it is supposed to, there is no reason to use it even if it measures consistently (reliably).

STATISTICS

Statistics are all around us. Without statistics we couldn't plan our budgets, pay our taxes, enjoy games to their fullest, evaluate classroom performance, or earn a salary based on wages earned. Statistics are used in everyday life.

Statistics, is the study of data. It includes **descriptive statistics** (the study of methods and tools for collecting data, and mathematical models to describe and interpret data) and **inferential statistics** (the systems and techniques for making probability-based decisions and accurate predictions based on incomplete (sample) data). As its name implies, statistics has its roots in the idea of "the state of things". The word itself comes from the ancient Latin term *statisticum collegium*, meaning "a lecture on the state of affairs". Eventually, this evolved into the Italian word *statista*, meaning "statesman", and the German word *Statistik*, meaning "collection of data involving the State". Gradually, the term came to be used to describe the collection of any sort of data.

The scientific method uses some type of measurement to analyze results, feeding these findings back into theories of what we know about the world. There are two major ways of obtaining data, through measurement and observation. These are generally referred to as quantitative and qualitative measurements.

QUALITATIVE DATA

Qualitative data is a categorical measurement expressed not in terms of numbers, but rather by means of a natural language description. In statistics, it is often used interchangeably with "categorical" data. Although we may have categories, the categories may have a structure to them. When there is not a natural ordering of the categories, we call these **nominal** categories. Examples might be gender, race, religion, or sport.

When the categories may be ordered, these are called **ordinal** variables. **Categorical variables** that judge size (small, medium, large, etc.) are ordinal variables.

Attitudes (strongly disagree, disagree, neutral, agree, strongly agree) are also ordinal variables; however we may not know which value is the best or worst of these issues. Note that the distance between these categories is not something we can measure.

Qualitative research is often regarded as a precursor to quantitative research, in that it is often used to generate possible leads and ideas which can be used to formulate a realistic and testable hypothesis. This hypothesis can then be comprehensively tested and mathematically analyzed, with standard quantitative research methods.

For these reasons, these qualitative methods are often closely allied with survey techniques and individual case studies, as a way to reinforce and evaluate findings over a broader scale.

Qualitative methods are probably the oldest of all scientific techniques, with Ancient Greek philosophers qualitatively observing the world around them and trying to come up with answers which explained what they saw.

The advantages to qualitative techniques are extremely useful when a subject is too complex to be answered by a simple yes or no response. These types of designs are much easier to plan and carry out. They are also useful when budgetary decisions have to be taken into account.

The broader scope covered by these designs ensures that some useful data is always generated, whereas an unproved hypothesis in a quantitative experiment can mean that a lot of time has been wasted. Qualitative research methods are not as dependent upon sample sizes as quantitative methods; a case study, for example, can generate meaningful results with a small sample group.

QUANTITATIVE DATA

Quantitative data is a numerical measurement expressed not by means of a natural language description, but rather in terms of numbers. However, not all numbers are continuous and measurable. For example, security student ID number is a number, but not something that one can add or subtract.

After statistical analysis of the results, a comprehensive answer is reached, and the results can be legitimately discussed and published. Quantitative experiments also filter out external factors, if properly designed, and so the results gained can be seen as real and unbiased.

One disadvantage of Quantitative experiments is that they can be time consuming and to perform. They must be carefully planned to ensure that there is complete randomization and correct designation of control groups and representative samples.

Quantitative studies usually require extensive statistical analysis, which can be difficult, due to most scientists not being statisticians. The field of statistical study is a whole scientific discipline and can be difficult for non-mathematicians

Quantitative research design also tends to generate only proved or unproven results, with there being very little room for grey areas and uncertainty. For the social sciences, education, anthropology and psychology, human nature is a lot more complex than just a simple yes or no response.

The most basic form of statistics is known as descriptive statistics. This branch of statistics lays the foundation for all statistical knowledge and analyses.

Descriptive Statistics

Descriptive statistics are used to describe the basic features of the data in a study. They provide simple summaries about the sample and the measures. Together they form the basis of virtually every quantitative analysis of data.

Descriptive statistics are typically distinguished from inferential statistics. With descriptive statistics you are simply describing what is or what the data shows. With inferential statistics, you are trying to reach conclusions that extend beyond the immediate data alone. For instance, we use inferential statistics to try to infer from the sample data what the population might think. Or, we use inferential statistics to make judgments of the probability that an observed

difference between groups is a dependable one or one that might have happened by chance in this study. Thus, we use inferential statistics to make inferences from our data to more general conditions; we use descriptive statistics simply to describe what's going on in our data. Descriptive statistics provide a powerful summary that may enable comparisons across people or other constructs.

Univariate Analysis

Univariate analysis involves the examination across cases of one variable at a time. There are three major characteristics of a single variable that we tend to look at:

- the distribution
- the central tendency
- the dispersion

In most situations, we would describe all three of these characteristics for each of the variables in our study.

The Distribution. The distribution is a summary of the frequency of individual values or ranges of values for a variable. The simplest distribution would list every value of a variable and the number of persons who had each value. One of the most common ways to describe a single variable is with a ***frequency distribution***. Depending on the particular variable, all of the data values may be represented, or you may group the values into categories first (e.g., with age, price, or temperature variables, it would usually not be sensible to determine the frequencies for each value. Rather, the value is grouped into ranges and the frequencies determined.). Frequency distributions can be depicted in two ways, as a table or as a graph. Table 1 shows an age frequency distribution with five categories of age ranges defined. The same frequency distribution can be depicted in a graph as shown in Figure X. This type of graph is often referred to as a histogram or bar chart.

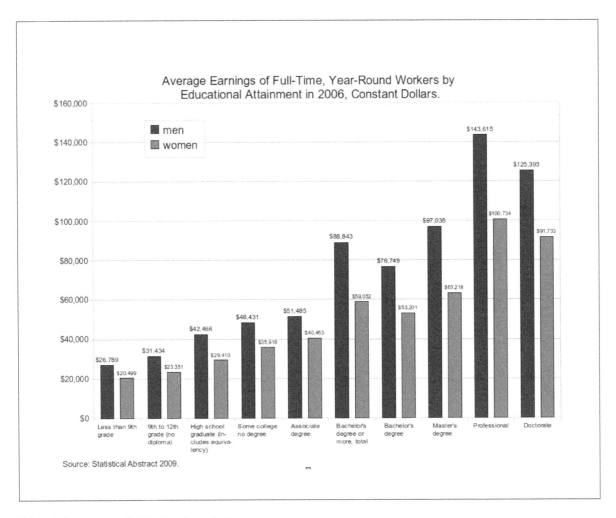

Table 6. Frequency distribution bar chart.

Distributions may also be displayed using percentages. For example, you could use percentages to describe the:

- percentage of people in different income levels
- percentage of people in different age ranges
- percentage of people in different ranges of standardized test scores

In statistics, the term *central tendency* relates to the way in which quantitative data is clustered around some value. A **measure of central tendency** is a way of specifying the central value. In the simplest cases, the measure of central tendency is an average of a set of measurements, the word *average* being variously construed as mean, median, or other measure of location, depending on the context. However, the term is applied to multidimensional data as well as to univariate data and in situations where a transformation of the data values for some or all dimensions would usually be considered necessary. Both "central tendency" and "measure of central tendency" apply to either statistical population or to samples from a population.

Central Tendency. The central tendency of a distribution is an estimate of the "center" of a distribution of values. There are three major types of estimates of central tendency:

- Mean
- Median
- Mode

The *Mean* or average is probably the most commonly used method of describing central tendency. To compute the mean, add up all the values and divide by the number of values. For example, the mean or average quiz score is determined by summing all the scores and dividing by the number of students taking the exam. For example, consider the test score values:

15, 20, 21, 20, 36, 15, 25, 15

The sum of these 8 values is 167, so the mean is 167/8 = 20.875.

The *Median* is the score found at the exact middle of the set of values. One way to compute the median is to list all scores in numerical order, and then locate the score in the center of the sample. For example, if there are 500 scores in the list, score #250 would be the median. If we order the 8 scores shown above, we would get:

15, 15, 15, 20, 20, 21, 25, 36

There are 8 scores and score #4 and #5 represent the halfway point. Since both of these scores are 20, the median is 20. If the two middle scores had different values, you would have to interpolate to determine the median.

The *Mode* is the most frequently occurring value in the set of scores. To determine the mode, you might again order the scores as shown above, and then count each one. The most frequently occurring value is the mode. In our example, the value 15 occurs three times and is the model. In some distributions there is more than one modal value. For instance, in a bimodal distribution there are two values that occur most frequently.

Dispersion. Dispersion refers to the spread of the values around the central tendency. There are two common measures of dispersion, the range and the standard deviation. The range is simply the highest value minus the lowest value. In our example distribution, the high value is 36 and the low is 15, so the range is 36—15 = 21.

The *Standard Deviation* is a more accurate and detailed estimate of dispersion because an outlier can greatly exaggerate the range (as was true in this example where the single outlier value of 36 stands apart from the rest of the values. The Standard Deviation shows the relation that set of scores has to the mean of the sample. The standard deviation allows us to reach some conclusions about specific scores in our distribution. Assuming that the distribution of scores is normal or bell-shaped (or close to it!), the following conclusions can be reached:

- approximately 68% of the scores in the sample fall within one standard deviation of the mean

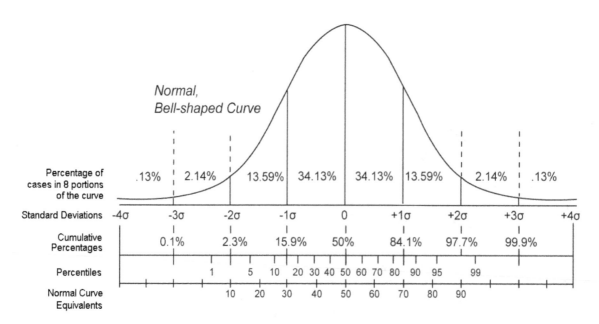

- approximately 95% of the scores in the sample fall within two standard deviations of the mean
- approximately 99% of the scores in the sample fall within three standard deviations of the mean

Data collection is a term used to describe a process of collecting data. The purpose of data collection is to obtain information to keep on record, to make decisions about important issues, to pass information on to others. Primarily, data is collected to provide information regarding a specific topic.

Data collection usually contains the following activity.

1. Pre collection activity – Agree goals, target data, definitions, methods
2. Collection – data collection
3. Present Findings – usually involves some form of sorting analysis and/or presentation.

Prior to any data collection, pre-collection activity is one of the most crucial steps in the process. It serves to obtain baseline data that is used to further strengthen the research design of the study. After pre-collection activity is fully completed, data collection in the field, whether by interviewing or other methods, can be carried out in a structured, systematic and scientific way.

A formal data collection process is necessary as it ensures that data gathered is both defined and accurate and that subsequent decisions based on arguments embodied in the findings are valid. The process provides both a baseline from which to measure from and in certain cases a target on what to improve.

Types of data collection

- 1-By mail questionnaires
- 2-By personal interview.

Other main types of collection include census, sample survey, and administrative by-product and each with their respective advantages and disadvantages. A census refers to data collection about everyone or everything in a group or population and has advantages, such as accuracy and detail and disadvantages, such as cost and time. A sample survey is a data collection method that includes only part of the total population and has advantages, such as cost and time and disadvantages, such as accuracy and detail. Administrative by-product data is collected as a byproduct of an organization's day-to-day operations and has advantages, such as accuracy, time simplicity and disadvantages, such as no flexibility and lack of control.

HUMAN AND ANIMAL RIGHTS IN PSYCHOLOGICAL RESEARCH

ANIMAL RIGHTS IN RESEARCH

A large part of research in physiological psychology is conducted in non-human species. This is done because of two main reasons: 1) our society feels that it is unethical to perform research with invasive procedures in human subjects, and 2) we have an intrinsic interest in the biology of animals (for veterinary reasons as well as for purely academic reasons).

ETHICS IN PSYCHOLOGICAL RESEARCH

We are going through a time of profound change in our understanding of the ethics of applied social research. From the time immediately after World War II until the early 1990s, and even today, there is continuum growing consensus about the key ethical principles that should underlie the research endeavor. Two marker events stand out the most (among many others) as symbolic of this consensus. The Nuremberg War Crimes Trial following World War II brought to public view the ways German scientists had used captive human subjects as subjects in oftentimes gruesome experiments. In the 1950s and 1960s, the Tuskegee Syphilis Study involved the withholding of known effective treatment for syphilis from African-American participants who were infected. Events like these forced the reexamination of ethical standards and the gradual development of a consensus that potential human subjects needed to be protected from being used as 'guinea pigs' in scientific research.

By the 1990s, the dynamics of the situation changed. Cancer patients and persons with AIDS fought publicly with the medical research establishment about the long time needed to get approval for and complete research into potential cures for fatal diseases. In many cases, it is the ethical assumptions of the previous thirty years that drive this 'go-slow' mentality. After all, we would rather risk denying treatment for a while until we achieve enough confidence in a treatment, rather than run the risk of harming innocent people (as in the Nuremberg and Tuskegee events). But now, those who were threatened with fatal illness were saying to the research establishment that they *wanted* to be test subjects, even under experimental conditions of considerable risk. You had several very vocal and articulate patient groups who wanted to be experimented on coming up against an ethical review system that was designed to protect them from being experimented on.

Although the last few years in the ethics of research have been tumultuous ones, it is beginning to appear that a new consensus is evolving that involves the stakeholder groups most affected by a problem participating more actively in the formulation of guidelines for research. While it's not entirely clear, at present, what the new consensus will be, it is almost certain that it will not fall at either extreme: protecting against human experimentation at all costs **vs.** allowing anyone who is willing to be experimented on.

Ethical Issues

There are a number of key phrases that describe the system of ethical protections that the contemporary social and medical research establishment has created to try to protect better the rights of their research participants. The principle of *voluntary participation* requires that people not be coerced into participating in research. This is especially relevant where researchers had previously relied on 'captive audiences' for their subjects (i.e., prisons, universities, mental hospitals). Closely related to the notion of voluntary participation is the requirement of *informed consent*. Essentially, this means that prospective research participants must be fully informed about the procedures and risks involved in research and must give their consent to participate. Ethical standards also require that researchers not put participants in a situation where they might be at *risk of harm* as a result of their participation. Harm can be defined as both physical and psychological. There are two standards that are applied in order to help protect the privacy of research participants. Almost all research guarantees the participant's *confidentiality* -- they are assured that identifying information will not be made available to anyone who is not directly involved in the study. The stricter standard is the principle of *anonymity* which essentially means that the participant will remain anonymous throughout the study -- even to the researchers themselves. Clearly, the anonymity standard is a stronger guarantee of privacy, but it is sometimes difficult to accomplish, especially in situations where participants have to be measured at multiple time points (e.g., a pre-post study).

INSTITUTIONAL REVIEW BOARD

Beginning on April 14, 2003, the Privacy Rule's compliance date for most covered entities, IRBs gained authority to consider, and act upon, requests for a partial or complete waiver or alteration of the Privacy Rule's Authorization requirement for uses and disclosures of PHI for research. Although HHS and FDA Protection of Human Subjects Regulations include protections to help ensure the privacy of subjects and the confidentiality of information, the Privacy Rule supplements these protections by requiring covered entities to implement specific measures to safeguard the privacy of PHI. If certain conditions are met, an IRB may grant a waiver or an alteration of the Authorization requirement for research uses or disclosures of PHI.

Even when clear ethical standards and principles exist, there will be times when the need to do accurate research runs up against the rights of potential participants. To address such needs most institutions and organizations have formulated an *Institutional Review Board (IRB)*, a panel of persons who reviews grant proposals with respect to ethical implications and decides whether additional actions need to be taken to assure the safety and rights of participants. By reviewing proposals for research, IRBs also help to protect both the organization and the researcher against potential legal implications of neglecting to address important ethical issues of participants.

ETHICAL PRINCIPLES OF PSYCHOLOGISTS AND CODE OF CONDUCT

The American Psychological Association's (APA) Ethical Principles of Psychologists and Code of Conduct consist of an Introduction, a Preamble, five General Principles, and specific Ethical Standards. The Preamble and General Principles are used to guide psychologists toward the highest of best practice in psychological practice and research. The Ethical Standards set forth enforceable rules for conduct as psychologists. This Ethics Code applies only to psychologists' activities that are part of their scientific, educational, or professional roles as psychologists. Areas covered include but are not limited to the clinical, counseling, and school practice of psychology; research; teaching; supervision of trainees; public service; policy development; social intervention; development of assessment instruments; conducting assessments; educational counseling; organizational consulting; forensic activities; program design and evaluation; and administration. This Ethics Code applies to these activities across a variety of contexts, such as in person, postal, telephone, internet,

and other electronic transmissions. These activities shall be distinguished from the purely private conduct of psychologists, which is not within the purview of the Ethics Code.

Membership in the APA commits members and student affiliates to comply with the standards of the APA Ethics Code and to the rules and procedures used to enforce them. Lack of awareness or misunderstanding of an Ethical Standard is not itself a defense to a charge of unethical conduct. The Ethics Code is not intended to be a basis of civil liability. Whether a psychologist has violated the Ethics Code standards does not by itself determine whether the psychologist is legally liable in a court action, whether a contract is enforceable, or whether other legal consequences occur.

The modifiers used in some of the standards of this Ethics Code (e.g., reasonably, appropriate, potentially) are included in the standards when they would (1) allow professional judgment on the part of psychologists, (2) eliminate injustice or inequality that would occur without the modifier, (3) ensure applicability across the broad range of activities conducted by psychologists, or (4) guard against a set of rigid rules that might be quickly outdated. As used in this Ethics Code, the term reasonable means the prevailing professional judgment of psychologists engaged in similar activities in similar circumstances, given the knowledge the psychologist had or should have had at the time.

In the process of making decisions regarding their professional behavior, psychologists must consider this Ethics Code in addition to applicable laws and psychology board regulations. In applying the Ethics Code to their professional work, psychologists may consider other materials and guidelines that have been adopted or endorsed by scientific and professional psychological organizations and the dictates of their own conscience, as well as consult with others within the field. If this Ethics Code establishes a higher standard of conduct than is required by law, psychologists must meet the higher ethical standard. Psychologists' ethical responsibilities conflict with law, regulations, or other governing legal authority; psychologists make known their commitment to the Code of Ethics and the basic principles of human rights.

SPECIFIC ETHICAL PRINCIPLES OF PSYCHOLOGISTS AND CODE OF CONDUCT

Standard 1: Resolving Ethical Issues

1.01 Misuse of Psychologists' Work If psychologists learn of misuse or misrepresentation of their work, they take reasonable steps to correct or minimize the misuse or misrepresentation.

1.02 Conflicts Between Ethics and Law, Regulations, or Other Governing Legal Authority If psychologists' ethical responsibilities conflict with law, regulations, or other governing legal authority, psychologists clarify the nature of the conflict, make known their commitment to the Ethics Code, and take reasonable steps to resolve the conflict consistent with the General Principles and Ethical Standards of the Ethics Code. Under no circumstances may this standard be used to justify or defend violating human rights.

1.03 Conflicts Between Ethics and Organizational Demands If the demands of an organization with which psychologists are affiliated or for whom they are working are in conflict with this Ethics Code, psychologists clarify the nature of the conflict, make known their commitment to the Ethics Code, and take reasonable steps to resolve the conflict consistent with the General Principles and Ethical Standards of the Ethics Code. Under no circumstances may this standard be used to justify or defend violating human rights.

1.04 Informal Resolution of Ethical Violations When psychologists believe that there may have been an ethical violation by another psychologist, they attempt to resolve the issue by bringing it to the attention of that individual, if an informal resolution appears appropriate and the intervention does not violate any confidentiality rights that may be involved. (See also Standards 1.02, Conflicts Between Ethics and Law, Regulations, or Other Governing Legal Authority, and 1.03, Conflicts Between Ethics and Organizational Demands.)

1.05 Reporting Ethical Violations If an apparent ethical violation has substantially harmed or is likely to substantially harm a person or organization and is not appropriate for informal resolution under Standard 1.04, Informal Resolution of Ethical Violations, or is not resolved properly in that fashion, psychologists take further action appropriate to the situation. Such action might include referral to state or national committees on professional ethics, to state licensing boards, or to the appropriate institutional authorities. This standard does not apply when an intervention would violate confidentiality rights or when psychologists have been retained to review the work of another psychologist whose professional conduct is in question. (See also Standard 1.02, Conflicts Between Ethics and Law, Regulations, or Other Governing Legal Authority.)

1.06 Cooperating with Ethics Committees Psychologists cooperate in ethics investigations, proceedings, and resulting requirements of the APA or any affiliated state psychological association to which they belong. In doing so, they address any confidentiality issues. Failure to cooperate is itself an ethics violation. However, making a request for deferment of adjudication of an ethics complaint pending the outcome of litigation does not alone constitute noncooperation.

1.07 Improper Complaints Psychologists do not file or encourage the filing of ethics complaints that are made with reckless disregard for or willful ignorance of facts that would disprove the allegation.

1.08 Unfair Discrimination Against Complainants and Respondents Psychologists do not deny persons employment, advancement, admissions to academic or other programs, tenure, or promotion, based solely upon their having made or their being the subject of an ethics complaint. This does not preclude taking action based upon the outcome of such proceedings or considering other appropriate information.

CHAPTER 2 SUMMARY

WHY ARE RESEARCH METHODS IMPORTANT TO THE STUDY OF PSYCHOLOGY?

- Psychologists use scientific methods to carry out research, reducing the problems of hindsight bias and the false consensus effect.
- When carrying out empirical research, psychologists use existing facts and theories to come up with new hypotheses.

WHAT ARE SOME TYPES OF RESEARCH STRATEGIES?

- Experiments, correlational studies, and descriptive studies (naturalistic observation, laboratory observation, case studies, and surveys) are used to conduct different types of research.
- Research can take place in a laboratory or in thefield.
- Data collection may be self-reported or observational.

HOW CAN STATISTICAL METHODS HELP US GATHER AND ANALYZE DATA?

- Descriptive statistics are used to summarize data sets and provide information about measures of central tendency, measures of variability, and frequency distribution.
- Inferential statistics are used to provide information about the statistical significance of data.

HOW CAN WE MINIMIZE BIAS?

- A degree of error is inevitable in any psychological research and is taken into account during statistical analysis.
- Researchers can minimize bias by using representative samples, taking reliable measurements, and avoiding subject and observer expectancy effects.

WHAT ETHICAL ISSUES DO PSYCHOLOGISTS FACE?

- When conducting a study, a psychologist needs to consider three issues: a person's right to privacy, the possibility of harm or discomfort, and the use of deception.
- Researchers must follow the American Psychological Association's code of ethics if they wish to publish their work in APA journals.

Neurological Pathways to Behavior and Mental Processes

Why will this field grow in acceptance? Fisher said there are three reasons.

First, solid research has uncovered clear links between health and behavior. For example, smoking is tied to heart disease, and an overweight and sedentary lifestyle can lead to non-insulin-dependent diabetes.

"The medical field sees those ties and realizes that a patient's health improves when his behavior changes. And changing behavior entails some thorny psychological issues," Fisher said.

The second reason is that as baby boomers age, the number of people with chronic diseases will increase dramatically. Most people start getting chronic diseases, such as hypertension and diabetes, around age 50. Managing the diseases usually involves daily behavior and will become increasingly important, Fisher said.

Third, biological breakthroughs are raising some interesting and troublesome psychological issues. Medical advances such as genetic testing pose a mine field for the mind. How do we handle the discovery of disease-causing genes? Should a woman with a high risk for breast cancer test for the gene? If so, what does she do with the results?

"It's nothing new -- behavioral psychology," Fisher said. "It's always been a part of health care, but its recognition is growing immensely."

GENERAL THOUGHT

In general, biological psychologists study the same issues as academic psychologists, though limited by the need to use nonhuman species. As a result, the bulk of literature in biological psychology deals with mental processes and behaviors that are shared across mammalian species, such as: Sensation and perception; motivation behavior (hunger, thirst, sex); *Control of movement;* Learning and memory; Sleep and biological rhythms; Emotions.

Biological psychology has also had a strong history of contributing to medical disorders including those that fall under the purview of clinical psychology and psychopathology, also known as abnormal psychology. Although animal models for all mental illnesses do not exist, the field has contributed important therapeutic data on a variety of conditions, including those mentioned in this chapter.

INTRODUCTION

Biopsychology is the study of how the brain affects cognitive processes and behavior. Biopsychology is also called neuropsychology and biological psychology. Neuroscience is the study of the structure and function of the brain and nervous system. Psychology is the scientific study of human behavior and cognitive processes, such as memory, perception, and learning. Biopsychology is where the two disciplines of psychology and biology intersect.

The main assumption of biological psychology is that the brain is responsible for the functions of behavior and mental processing. Therefore, behavioral habits and mental processes and illnesses related to and the associated abnormal behavior are caused by abnormal brain functioning such as a chemical imbalance or some genetic disposition. Biological psychology recognizes the role of genetics in behavior since genetics determines the properties of the brain. By using case studies and new technology, biological psychology seeks to define the origins of expressed behavior. Biology and psychology tightly integrate together. This is because the brain is the location of thought or mind, and it is governed by electrochemical properties. These are the same basic principles that underlie all other functions that create life. This means that the actions of the mind are governed by the physical world and since the mind is paramount to the study of psychology, psychology is a viable companion to biology. This chapter will discuss issues concerning the biopsychology and its impact on human behavior and mental processes.

HISTORICAL VIEW OF BIOPSYCHOLOGY

BRIEF HISTORY OF PSYCHOLOGY\BIOLOGY

The works of Avicenna, the medieval Persian physician, was one of the first to recognize the connection between psychology and physiology. The history of biological psychology is a major part of the history of modern scientific psychology. The study of biological psychology can be dated back to Avicenna (980-1037 C.E.), a physician who in *The Canon of Medicine,* recognized and utilized physiological psychology when treating illnesses related to mental health dysfunctions, and developed a system for associating changes in the *pulse* rate with inner

feelings, which is seen as an anticipation of the word association test, (New World Encyclopedia, 2011). Avicenna also gave psychological explanations for certain somatic illnesses, and he always linked the physical and psychological illnesses together. He explained that "humidity" inside the head can contribute to mood disorders, and he recognized that this occurs when the amount of "breath" changes: Happiness increases the breath, which leads to increased moisture inside the brain, but if this moisture goes beyond its limits, the brain would lose control over its rationality and lead to mental disorders, (New World Encyclopedia, 2011).

Ancient Greeks

The **Ancient Greeks** were pioneers of biology and medicine. They were experienced enough with anatomy to hypothesize that behavior and cognition derived from biology rather than spirituality. In particular, Hippocrates proposed that a person's personality is determined by the balance of four bodily fluids, or humors: black bile, yellow bile, blood, and phlegm. Although this idea is not supported by modern evidence, the terms "choleric", "melancholic", "sanguine", and "phlegmatic", which derive from these four fluids, are still popular and are utilized when describing personality traits. Rene Descartes (1596-1650) proposed the idea of mind body dualism, which states that behavior is controlled by the mind or will. This dualistic notion of human behavior suggested at least some components of behavior could be scientifically investigated.

In philosophy, the first issues concerned how to approach what is known as the "mind-body dualism" namely the explanation of the relationship between mental processes and biological states. Historically, *Dualism* is a family of views that attempt to explain the relationship between mind and physical matter. It begins with the claim that mental phenomena are, in some respects, non-physical. In Western Philosophy, some of the earliest discussions of dualist ideas are in the writings of Plato and Aristotle. These two philosophers purported that human "intelligence" could not be explained in physiological terms, (Haque, Amber, 2004). However, the best-known version of dualism is contributed to Rene' Descartes, (Descartes, Rene', 1998), which is expressed in his 1641, *Meditations on First Philosophy*), and holds that the mind is a

non-extended, non-physical substance, (Descartes, Rene', 1998). Descartes was the first to clearly identify the mind with consciousness and self-awareness, and to distinguish this from the brain, which was the seat of intelligence. He maintained that the mind and body though separate, operated in conjunction to carry out the abilities on the human being, (Carlson, Neil, 2007). Some, like Descartes, proposed physical models to explain animal and human behavior. Descartes, for example, suggested that the pineal gland, a midline unpaired structure in the brain of many organisms, was the point of contact between mind and body.

William James

Other philosophers also helped to give birth to psychology, also relating its subject matter to biology. This view, that psychological processes have biological (or physiological) correlates, is the basic assumption of the whole field of biological psychology. One of the earliest textbooks in the new field, *The Principles of Psychology* by William James, (1890), argues that the scientific study of psychology should be grounded in an understanding of biology, (James, William, 1950). William James, like many early psychologists, had considerable training in physiology. The emergence of both psychology and biological psychology as legitimate sciences can be traced from the emergence of physiology from anatomy, particularly neuroanatomy. Physiologists conducted experiments on living organisms, a practice that was distrusted by the dominant anatomists of the eighteenth and nineteenth centuries, (Shepard, G., 1991). The influential work of Claude

Bernard, Charles Bell, and William Harvey helped to convince the scientific community that reliable data could be obtained from living subjects.

Through the years, many people have made contributions to the development of biopsychology. Karl Lashley did experiments that produced his theories of mass action and equipotentiality. Lashley conducted experiments that involved teaching rats a maze and then destroying different parts of the rats' cortex to varying degrees. He found that small cuts to any part of the cortex did not impair the rats' ability to run the maze. His principle of equipotentiality says that all areas of the cortex are involved in memory. When Lashley damaged larger amounts of the cortex, he found that memory is related to the amount of brain tissue destroyed. His principle of mass action describes that the greater the damage, the greater the impairment.

Donald Hebb theorized that the synapses between certain neurons are altered when learning occurs. He called a group of neurons responding to the learning a cell assembly. Hebb theorized that the synapses along this cell assembly are strengthened during the learning process and allows for the retention of the new information.

Other schools of psychology recognize the impact of the brain and biology on psychological processes. Developmental psychology is largely based on the biological processes of growth and development. Piaget thought that all behavior and mental activity is rooted in biological functions. Psychiatry applies knowledge of chemical activity of the brain to describe and treat mental illness. Because mental illness is evident by abnormal behavior and problematic mental activity, psychiatry could be considered applied biopsychology.

THE FIRST PSYCHOLOGY LABORATORY— PHRENOLOGY

Phrenology is the idea that different parts of the brain perform different functions. It was formally proposed by Franz Gall, though others, such as Paul Broca, followed a similar ideology. Gall made the

further claim that the size of the different brain regions corresponded to an individual's relative strengths and

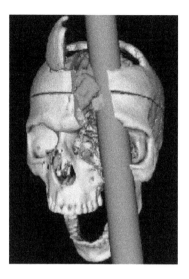

weaknesses, and that the size of brain regions could be detected by analyzing the shape of one's skull. This latter point would be taken by some of Gall's students and turned into a form of divination that led to phrenology's reputation as a parlor trick. However, the idea that the brain is segregated into functional regions remains prominent today.

CONTEMPORARY VIEWS POINTS: LINKS PSYCHOLOGY AND BIOLOGY

For many decades, biopsychology or psychobiology has developed a cross disciplinary approaches to explain the concepts, information, and techniques commonly shared between psychology and biological sciences. During research experimentation, both human and animals are used to get a better understanding of the principles and functionality between biology and psychology. In many cases, humans may serve as experimental subjects in biological psychology experiments; however, a great deal of the experimental literature in biological psychology comes from the study of non-human species, such as rats, mice, and monkeys. Due the scientific study and analytical results from studies performed, a critical assumption has formed in biological psychology, suggesting that organisms share biological and behavioral similarities, enough to permit extrapolations across species. Biological psychology also has paradigmatic and methodological similarities to neuropsychology, which relies heavily on the study of the behavior of humans with nervous system dysfunction (a non-experimentally based biological manipulation). For Example, Biological psychologists may often be interested in measuring some biological variable, such as an anatomical, physiological, or genetic variable, in an attempt to relate it quantitatively or qualitatively to a psychological or behavioral variable, and thus, contribute to evidence based practice.

NEURONS, THE MESSENGERS

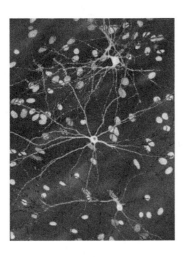

This part of the chapter presents the basic biological processes that are at the root of man's ability to express thoughts, feelings, and actions. The body possesses two systems for coordinating and integrating behavior: the **nervous system** and the **endocrine system**. **The human nervous system** consists of billions of nerve cells also known as *neurons,* plus supporting (neuroglial) cells. The Neuron is a cell in the nervous system and operates as the fundamental unit of the nervous system. The neuron specializes in electrical and chemical communication and helps coordinate all the functions of the body. Cognition and behavior occur due to the connection of multiple neurons communicating with each other at any given time. It is estimated that there are between 10 billion to 100 billion neurons in the brain alone (Stevens, 1979). Lack of neuro activity is the definition of death.

While there are many different kinds of neurons, there are three broad categories which are grouped based on functionality.

1. Neurons that carry messages from the sense organs to the brain or spinal cord are called *Sensory or Afferent neurons. Sensory neurons* are sensitive to various non-neural stimuli. They allow use of the five senses in humans. There are sensory neurons in the skin, muscles, joints, and organs that indicate pressure, temperature, and pain. There are more specialized neurons in the nose and tongue that are sensitive to the molecular shapes we perceive as tastes and smells. Neurons in the inner ear are sensitive to vibration, and provide us with information about sound. And the rods and cones of the retina are sensitive to light, and allow us to see.

2. Neurons that carry messages from the brain or spinal cord to the muscles and glands are called *Motor or Efferent) neurons.*

3. *Interneurons or association neurons* carry messages from one **Motor neurons** are able to stimulate muscle cells throughout the body, including the muscles of the heart, diaphragm, intestines, bladder, and glands. *Interneurons* are the neurons that provide connections between sensory and motor neurons, as well as between themselves. The neurons of the central nervous system, including the brain, are all interneurons.

RESTING MEMBRANE POTENTIAL

When the neuron is at rest, it is called *resting potential*. A neuron at rest has slightly higher levels of negative ions inside the membrane surrounding the cell body than outside, so there is a negative electrical charge inside than outside. This POTENTIAL generally measures about 70 millivolts (with the INSIDE of the membrane negative with respect to the outside). So, the RESTING MEMBRANE POTENTIAL is expressed as -70 mV, and the minus means that the inside is negative relative to (or compared to) the outside. It is called a RESTING potential because it occurs when a membrane is not being stimulated or conducting impulses (in other words, it's resting). At rest, a neuron is in a state of polarization. When an incoming message is strong enough, the electrical charge is changed to action potential. A neural impulse is generated, and the neuron is depolarized. Incoming messages may cause a state of graded potential, which means when combined, may exceed the minimum level of excitation and propel the neuron to fire. After firing, the neuron goes through the absolute refractory period, a state when it will not fire again. Subsequently, the neuron will enter into a relative refractory period, when firing will only occur if the incoming message is much stronger than usual. However, according to the **All-or-None Law**, the impulse sent by a neuron does not vary in strength. **A**ction potentials occur maximally or not at all. Either the threshold potential is reached and an action potential occurs, or it isn't reached and no action potential occurs.

IONS AND MEMBRANE RESTING POTENTIAL

Two ions are responsible for neuron experiencing resting potential, sodium (Na+) and potassium (K+). An unequal distribution of these two ions occurs on the two sides of a nerve cell membrane because carriers actively transport these two ions: sodium from the inside to the outside and potassium from the outside to the inside. As a result of this active transport

mechanism (commonly referred to as the Sodium-Potassium Pump), there is a higher concentration of sodium on the outside than the inside and a higher concentration of potassium on the inside than the outside.

The nerve cell membrane also contains special passageways for these two ions that are commonly referred to as Gates or Channels. Hence, there are both Sodium and Potassium Gates. These gates are the only way that these ions can diffuse through a nerve cell membrane. When the neuron is at rest, all the sodium gates are closed and some of the potassium gates are open. As a result, sodium cannot diffuse through the membrane and will remains mostly outside the membrane. However, some potassium ions are able to diffuse out. A resting neuron differs than a neuron that is at a state of *Action Potential*.

ACTION POTENTIAL OF NEURON

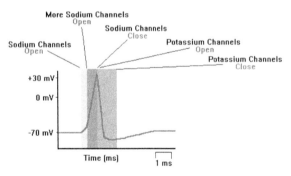

Action Potential is a very rapid change in membrane potential that occurs when a nerve cell membrane is stimulated. Specifically, the membrane potential goes from the resting potential (typically -70 mV) to some positive value (typically about +30 mV) in a very short period of time (just a few milliseconds).

CAUSES OF ACTION POTENTIAL

The stimulus causes the sodium gates (or channels) to open and, because there's more sodium on the outside than the inside of the membrane, sodium then diffuses rapidly into the nerve cell. All these positively-charged sodium's rushing in causes the membrane potential to become positive (the inside of the membrane is now positive relative to the outside). The sodium channels open only briefly, then close again.

The potassium channels then open, and, because there is more potassium inside the membrane than outside, positively-charged potassium ions diffuse out. As these positive ions go out, the inside of the membrane once again becomes negative with respect to the outside.

PATHWAYS OF THE NEURON

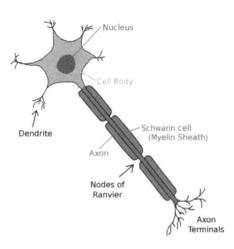

The main portion of the neuron called the cell body is similar to other cells. It contains a nucleus and cytoplasm. Where it is most different from other cells types is that attached to the cell body are long threadlike extensions called dendrites. The Dendrites conducts nerve impulses toward the cell body, the part of a neuron that contains the nucleus and other organelles. In the Greek language, these are known as "trees." In addition, the cell has a long extension known as the axon. The axon conducts nerve impulses away from the cell body. There are three types of neurons: sensory neuron, motor neuron, and interneuron. A sensory neuron takes a message from the receptors in the sense organ to the CNS. A motor neuron sends a message away from the CNS to an effector, a muscle fiber or a gland. An interneuron is always found completely within the CNS and conveys messages between parts of the system. In addition to neurons,

nervous tissue contains glial cells such as the Schwann cells covering the neurons with myelin sheath. These cells maintain the tissue by supporting and protecting the neurons. They also provide nutrients to neurons and help to keep the tissue free of debris. The neurons require a great deal of energy for the maintenance of the ionic imbalance between themselves and their surrounding fluids, which is constantly in flux as a result of the opening and closing of channels through the neuronal membranes. Receptors are parts of the nervous system that sense changes in the internal or external environments. Sensory input can be in many forms, including pressure, taste, sound, light, blood pH, or hormone levels that are converted to a signal and sent to the brain or spinal cord.

MYELINATION CONDUCTION

The myelin sheath (blue) surrounding axons (yellow) is produced by glial cells (Schwann cells in the PNS, oligodendrocytes in the CNS). These cells produce large membranous extensions that ensheath the axons in successive layers that are then compacted by exclusion of cytoplasm (black) to form the myelin sheath. The thickness of the myelin sheath (the number of wraps around the axon) is proportional to the axon's diameter

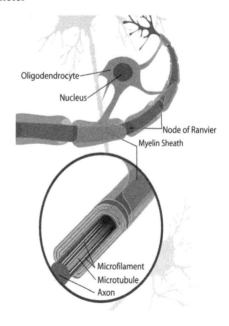

Myelination, the process by which glial cells ensheath the axons of neurons in layers of myelin, ensures the rapid conduction of electrical impulses in the nervous system. The axon is wrapped many times (like a Swiss roll) by these sheet like membrane extensions to form the final myelin sheath, or internodes. Internodes can be as long as 1 mm and are separated from their neighbors by a short gap (the node of Ranvier) of 1 micrometer. The concentration of voltage-dependent sodium channels in the axon membrane at the node, and the high electrical resistance of the multilayered myelin sheath, ensure that action potentials jump from node to node (a process termed "saltatory conduction") (French-Constant 2004).

THE SYNAPSE AND TRANSMISSIONS

The Synpse is the point of impulse transmission between neurons; impulses are transmitted from pre-synaptic neurons to post-synaptic neurons. Synapses usually occur between the axon of a pre-synaptic neuron & a dendrite or cell body of a post-synaptic neuron. At a synapse, the end of the axon is 'swollen' and referred to as an end bulb or synaptic knob. Within the end bulb are found lots of synaptic vesicles (which contain neurotransmitter chemicals) and mitochondria (which provide ATP to make more neurotransmitter). Between the end bulb and the dendrite (or cell body) of the post-synaptic neuron, there is a gap commonly referred to as the synaptic cleft. So, pre- and post-synaptic membranes do not actually come in contact. That means that the impulse cannot be transmitted directly. Rather, the impulse is transmitted by the release of chemicals called chemical transmitters or *neurotransmitters*.

DISCOVERY OF NEUROTRANSMITTERS

In 1921, an Austrian scientist named Otto Loewi discovered the first neurotransmitter by conducting an experiment on frog hearts. In his experiment he used two frog hearts, Heart 1 remained connected to the vagus nerve and placed in a chamber that was filled with saline. This chamber was connected to a second chamber that contained Heart 2. During the experiment, fluid from chamber 1 was allowed to flow into chamber 2. Electrical stimulation of the vagus nerve (which was attached to heart #1) caused Heart 1 to **slow down**. Loewi also observed that after a delay, Heart 2 also slowed down. From this experiment, Loewi hypothesized that electrical stimulation of the vagus nerve released a chemical into the fluid of chamber 1 that flowed into chamber #2. He called this chemical "Vagusstoff," what is known today as the neurotransmitter, **acetylcholine.**

OTTO LOEWI'S EXPERIMENT

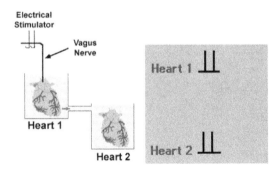

NEUROTRANSMITTER TYPES

There are many types of chemicals that act as neurotransmitter substances, however, each type will fall under major forms of neurotransmitters: Excitatory and Inhibitory. Excitatory—neurotransmitters that make membrane potential less negative (via increased permeability of the membrane to sodium) &, therefore, tend to 'excite' or stimulate the postsynaptic membrane; and the Inhibitory neurotransmitters that make membrane potential more negative (via increased permeability of the membrane to potassium) &, therefore, tend to 'inhibit' (or make less likely) the transmission of an impulse. One example of an inhibitory neurotransmitter is *gamma aminobutyric acid* (GABA; shown below). Medically, GABA has been used to treat both epilepsy and hypertension. Another example of an inhibitory neurotransmitter is beta-endorphin, which results in decreased pain perception by the CNS. Mood is strongly influenced by the neurotransmitter *serotonin*. It is believed that depression results from a shortage of serotonin. It is difficult to treat depression directly with *serotonin* because the chemical has too many other side effects. However, depression can be successfully treated with drugs that act as serotornin neuromodulators. Prozac, the world's top-selling antidepressant, inhibits the reabsorption of serotonin, increasing the amount in the synapse by slowing down its removal Neurotransmitters tend to be small molecules, some are even hormones. Acetycholine is a chemical that affects arousal, attention, memory, motivation, movement. Dopamine is an inbitory neurotransmitter and impacts behavior and emotions, including pleasure. Dopamine has been known to influence schizophrenia and Parkinson's disease. Parkinson's disease has a deficiency of the neurotransmitter dopamine. Progressive death of brain cells increases this deficit, causing tremors, rigidity and unstable posture. L-dopa is a chemical related to dopamine that eases some of the symptoms (by acting as a substitute neurotransmitter) but cannot reverse the progression of the disease. Diseases that affect the function of signal transmission can have serious consequences. Norepinephrine is an excitatory neurotransmitter and affects arousal, wakefulness, learning, memory, and mood. Endorphins are inhibitory neurotransmitters that inhibit pain messages.

Table 7. Major Neurtransmitters and Their Effects

Acetylcholine (ACh)	Generally excitatory	Affects arousal, attention, memory, motivation, movement. Too much: spasms, tremors. Too little: paralysis, torpor.
Dopamine	Inhibitory	Inhibits wide range of behavior and emotions, including pleasure. Implicated in schizophrenia and Parkinson's disease.
Serotonin	Inhibitory	Inhibits virtually all activities. Important for sleep onset, mood, eating behavior.
Norepinephrine	Generally excitatory	Affects arousal, wakefulness, learning, memory, mood.
Endorphins	Inhibitory	Inhibit transmission of pain messages.

THE HUMAN NERVOUS SYSTEM AND NEURAL WORK

The billions of neurons in the brain are connected to neurons throughout the body by trillions of synapses. The nervous system is organized into two parts: the *Central Nervous System*, (CNS) which consists of the brain and the spinal cord, and the *Peripheral Nervous System*,(PNS) which connects the central nervous system to the rest of the body. The **PNS** consists of **sensory neurons** running from stimulus **receptors** that inform the CNS of the stimuli and **motor neurons** running from the CNS to the **muscles and glands** are called **effectors** that are used take action. The **peripheral nervous system** is subdivided into two systems, the **sensory-somatic nervous system** and the **autonomic nervous system.** **The Sensory-Somatic Nervous System** The sensory-somatic system consists of 12 pairs of **cranial nerves** and 31 pairs of **spinal nerves**. Figure X demonstrates the flow of the CNS workings within the human body.

A schematic diagram of the divisions of the nervous system and their various subparts

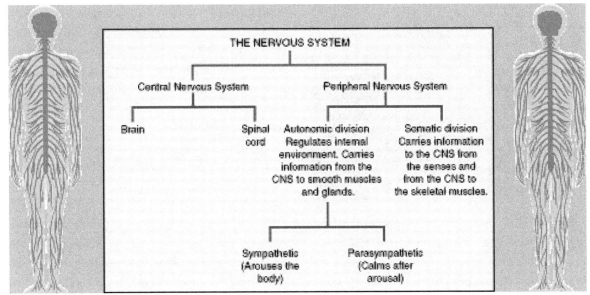

PERIPHERAL NERVOUS SYSTEM

The **Peripheral Nervous System** is divided into two sub-systems. The **Somatic Nervous System** – primary function is to regulate the actions of the skeletal muscles. Often thought of as mediating voluntary activity. The other sub-system, called the **Autonomic Nervous System**, regulates primarily involuntary activity such as heart rate, breathing, blood pressure, and digestion. Although these activities are considered involuntary, they can be altered either through specific events or through changing our perceptions about a specific experience. This system is further broken down into two complimentary systems: Sympathetic and Parasympathetic Nervous Systems. The sympathetic and the parasympathetic nervous system are parts of what is commonly called the autonomic nervous system. These systems work in balance with each other and directly or indirectly affect almost every structure in the body (e.g. heartfrequence, heartcapacity, lumbar function, kidneys, blood vessels, stomach and intestines)

SYMPATHETIC NERVOUS SYSTEM

The *sympathetic* nervous system has an active "pushing" function. The sympathetic nervous system is located to the sympathetic chain, which connects to skin, blood vessels and organs in the body cavity. Nerves of the sympathetic division speed up heart rate, dilate pupils, and relax the bladder. The sympathetic system is also involved in the flight or fight response. This is a response to potential danger or high levels of stress that results in accelerated heart rate and an increase in metabolic rate. The Sympathetic Nervous System ignites to prepare the body to react to danger and stress conditions. There will be an increase in heart rate, increase of blood to the muscles, increase in breathing and at a faster and deeper rate, increase in oxygen and blood flow from the organs so digestion is reduced and the skin gets cold and clammy and rerouted so to speak to the muscles, and your pupils dilate for better vision. In an instant, your body is prepared to either defend or escape. When the body fails to return to a homeostatic state or a condition of allostasis, **allostatic overload** can occur. **Allostasis** is a term that refers to environmental challenges that cause an organism to begin efforts to maintain stability and calm. **Allostatic overload** occurs when the body fails to decrease in the

THE SYMPATHETIC NERVOUS SYSTEM

Sympathetic	**Structure**	**Parasympathetic**
Rate increased	Heart	Rate decreased
Force increased	Heart	Force decreased
Broncial muscle relaxed	Lungs	Broncial muscle contracted
Pupil dilation	Eye	Pupil constriction
Motility reduced	Intestine	Digestion increased
Sphincter closed	Bladder	Sphincter relaxed
Decreased urine secretion	Kidneys	Increased urine secretion

fight or fight response. The body remains in a state of high response. The brain controls the physiological and behavioral coping responses to daily events and stressors. The hippocampal formation expresses high levels of adrenal steroid receptors and is a malleable brain structure that is important for certain types of learning and memory. It is also vulnerable to the effects of stress and trauma. The amygdala mediates physiological and behavioral responses associated with fear. The prefrontal cortex plays an important role in working memory and executive function and is also involved in extinction of learning. All three regions are targets of stress hormones. In animal models, neurons in the hippocampus and prefrontal cortex respond to repeated stress by showing atrophy, whereas neurons in amygdala show a growth response.

PARASYMPATHETIC NERVOUS SYSTEM

This system is slow acting, unlike the sympathetic nervous system. The *Parasympathetic* Division has mainly a relaxing function. The Parasympathetic stimulation causes

- slowing down of the heartbeat (as Loewi demonstrated)
- lowering of blood pressure
- constriction of the pupils
- increased blood flow to the skin and viscera
- peristalsis of the GI tract

The main nerves of the parasympathetic system are the tenth cranial nerves, the **vagus nerves**. They originate in the **medulla oblongata**. Other preganglionic parasympathetic neurons also extend from the brain as well as from the lower tip of the spinal cord. **Acetylcholine (ACh)** is the neurotransmitter at all the pre- and many of the postganglionic neurons of the parasympathetic system.

In short, the parasympathetic system returns the body functions to normal after they have been altered by sympathetic stimulation. In times of danger, the sympathetic system prepares the body for violent activity. The parasympathetic system reverses these changes when the danger is over. Hence the body returns to a state of allostasis or homeostasis.

Overall, these two subsystems work jointly shifting the body to more prepared and more relaxed states. Every time a potentially threatening experience occurs (e.g., someone slams on their breaks in front of you, or a stranger taps you on the shoulder unexpectedly), your body reacts. The constant shifting of control between these two systems keeps your body ready for your current situation.

Although the autonomic nervous system is considered to be involuntary, this is not entirely true. A certain amount of conscious control can be exerted over it as has long been demonstrated by practitioners of Yoga and Zen Buddhism. During their periods of meditation, these people are clearly able to alter a number of autonomic functions including heart rate and the rate of oxygen consumption. These changes are not simply a reflection of decreased physical activity because they exceed the amount of change occurring during sleep or hypnosis.

SUMMARY OF NERVOUS SYSTEM ACTIVITY

In summary, the SNS fosters the release and production of epinephrine and cortisol, as well as glucose and other metabolites in support of mobilization (Porges, 2001; Schore, 1994). The level of SNS response occurs on a continuum, ranging from the local release of norepinephrine, to slightly broader responses associated with a decrease in vagal tone (PNS), to the global response of fight/flight associated with epinephrine secretion, to the stress response and cortisol secretion associated with activation of the HPA axis. SNS activity also promotes attachment behavior between infant and caregiver through dopamine release that fosters engagement, interaction, and exploratory behavior (Schore, 1994). In health, mobilization fosters the body's ability to utilize glucose and is associated with a decreased need for insulin in mobilized tissues, such as skeletal muscles in limbs, which require insulin at rest (Braunwald et al., 2001).

THE ENDOCRINE SYSTEM

ENDOCRINE SYSTEM ANATOMY

The major glands that make up the human endocrine system are the hypothalamus, pituitary, thyroid, parathyroids, adrenals, pineal body, and the reproductive glands, which include the ovaries and testes. The pancreas is also part of this hormone-secreting system, even though it is also associated with the digestive system because it also produces and secretes digestive enzymes.

Although the endocrine glands are the body's main hormone producers, some non-endocrine organs — such as the brain, heart, lungs, kidneys, liver, thymus, skin, and placenta — also produce and release hormones.

The foundations of the endocrine system are the *hormones* and *glands*. As the body's chemical messengers, *hormones* transfer information and instructions from one set of cells to another. Although many different hormones circulate throughout the bloodstream, each one affects only the cells that are genetically programmed to receive and respond to its message. Hormone levels can be influenced by factors such as stress, infection, and changes in the balance of fluid and minerals in blood.

A *gland* is a group of cells that produces and secretes, or gives off, chemicals. A gland selects and removes materials from the blood, processes them, and secretes the finished chemical product for use somewhere in the body. Some types of glands release their secretions in specific areas. For instance, exocrine glands, such as the sweat and salivary glands, release secretions in the skin or inside of the mouth. Endocrine glands, on the other hand, release more than 20 major hormones directly into the bloodstream where they can be transported to cells in other parts of the body.

ENDOCRINE SYSTEM PATHWAYS

Once a hormone is secreted, it travels from the endocrine gland through the bloodstream to target cells designed to receive its message. Along the way to the target cells, special proteins bind to some of the hormones. The special proteins act as carriers that control the amount of hormone that is available to interact with and affect the target cells.

In addition, the target cells have receptors that latch onto only specific hormones, and each hormone has its own receptor, so that each hormone will communicate only with specific target cells that possess receptors for that hormone. When the hormone reaches its target cell, it locks onto the cell's specific receptors and these hormone-receptor combinations transmit chemical instructions to the inner workings of the cell.

When hormone levels reach a certain normal or necessary amount, further secretion is controlled by important body mechanisms to maintain that level of hormone in the blood. This regulation of hormone secretion may involve the hormone itself or another substance in the blood related to the hormone.

For example, if the thyroid gland has secreted adequate amounts of thyroid hormones into the blood, the pituitary gland senses the normal levels of thyroid hormone in the bloodstream and adjusts its release of thyrotropin, the pituitary hormone that stimulates the thyroid gland to produce thyroid hormones.

Although we rarely think about them, the glands of the endocrine system and the hormones they release influence almost every cell, organ, and function of our bodies. The endocrine system is instrumental in regulating mood, growth and development, tissue function, and metabolism, as well as sexual function and reproductive processes.

In general, the endocrine system is in charge of body processes that happen slowly, such as cell growth. Faster processes like breathing and body movement are controlled by the nervous system. But even though the nervous system and endocrine system are separate systems, they often work together to help the body function properly.

THE HYPOTHALAMUS

The hypothalamus, a collection of specialized cells that is located in the lower central part of the brain, is the primary link between the endocrine and nervous systems. Nerve cells in the hypothalamus control the pituitary gland by producing chemicals that either stimulate or suppress hormone secretions from the pituitary.

Although it is no bigger than a pea, the *Pituitary Gland*, located at the base of the brain just beneath the hypothalamus, is considered the most important part of the endocrine system. It's often called the "*master gland*" because it makes hormones that control several other endocrine glands. The production and secretion of pituitary hormones can be influenced by factors such as emotions and seasonal changes. To accomplish this, the hypothalamus relays information sensed by the brain (such as environmental temperature, light exposure patterns, and feelings) to the pituitary.

THE PITUITARY GLAND

The tiny pituitary gland is divided into two parts: the anterior lobe and the posterior lobe. The anterior lobe regulates the activity of the thyroid, adrenals, and

reproductive glands. Among the hormones it produces are:

- **growth hormone**, which stimulates the growth of bone and other body tissues and plays a role in the body's handling of nutrients and minerals
- **prolactin**, which activates milk production in women who are breastfeeding
- **thyrotropin**, which stimulates the thyroid gland to produce thyroid hormones
- **corticotropin**, which stimulates the adrenal gland to produce certain hormones

The pituitary also secretes *endorphins*, chemicals that act on the nervous system to reduce sensitivity to pain. In addition, the pituitary secretes hormones that signal the ovaries and testes to make sex hormones. The pituitary gland also controls ovulation and the menstrual cycle in women.

The posterior lobe of the pituitary releases *antidiuretic hormone*, which helps control body water balance through its effect on the kidneys and urine output; and oxytocin, which triggers the contractions of the uterus that occur during labor.

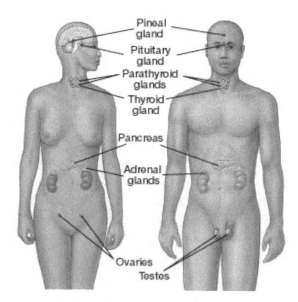

THE THYROID AND PARATHYROIDS

The thyroid, located in the front part of the lower neck, is shaped like a bow tie or butterfly and produces the thyroid hormones thyroxine and triiodothyronine. These hormones control the rate at which cells burn fuels from food to produce energy. As the level of thyroid hormones increases in the bloodstream, so does the speed at which chemical reactions occur in the body.

Thyroid hormones also play a key role in bone growth and the development of the brain and nervous system in children. The production and release of thyroid hormones is controlled by thyrotropin, which is secreted by the pituitary gland.

Attached to the thyroid are four tiny glands that function together called the parathyroids. They release parathyroid hormone, which regulates the level of calcium in the blood with the help of calcitonin, which is produced in the thyroid.

The Adrenal Glands

The body has two triangular adrenal glands, one on top of each kidney. The adrenal glands have two parts, each of which produces a set of hormones and has a different function. The outer part, the adrenal cortex, produces hormones called corticosteroids that influence or regulate salt and water balance in the body, the body's response to stress, metabolism, the immune system, and sexual development and function.

The inner part, the adrenal medulla, produces catecholamines, such as epinephrine. Also called adrenaline, epinephrine increases blood pressure and heart rate when the body experiences stress. (Epinephrine injections are often used to counteract a severe allergic reaction.)

The Pineal Gland and Gonads

The pineal body, also called the pineal gland, is located in the middle of the brain. It secretes melatonin, a hormone that may help regulate the wake-sleep cycle. This gland assists in maintaining regular sleeping patterns which support human immune system.

Gonads and Ovaries

The gonads are the main source of sex hormones. In males, they are located in the scrotum. Male gonads, or testes, secrete hormones called androgens, the most important of which is testosterone. These hormones regulate body changes associated with sexual development, including enlargement of the penis, the growth spurt that occurs during puberty, and the appearance of other male secondary sex characteristics such as deepening of the voice, growth of facial and pubic hair, and the increase in muscle growth and strength. Working with hormones from the pituitary gland, testosterone also supports the production of sperm by the testes.

The female gonads, the ovaries, are located in the pelvis. They produce eggs and secrete the female hormones estrogen and progesterone. Estrogen is involved in the development of female sexual features such as breast growth, the accumulation of body fat around the hips and thighs, and the growth spurt that occurs during puberty. Both estrogen and progesterone are also involved in pregnancy and the regulation of the menstrual cycle.

Pancreas

The pancreas produces (in addition to others) two important hormones, insulin and glucagon. They work together to maintain a steady level of glucose, or sugar, in the blood and to keep the body supplied with fuel to produce and maintain stores of energy.

Health Problems and the Endocrine System

The Endocrine system plays a vital role in maintaining health. Too much or too little of any hormone can be harmful to the body. For example, if the pituitary gland produces too much growth hormone, a child may grow excessively tall. If it produces too little, a child may be abnormally short. Other forms of health problems resulting from hormonal imbalances are discussed below.

Adrenal Insufficiency. This condition is characterized by decreased function of the adrenal cortex and the consequent underproduction of adrenal corticosteroid hormones. The symptoms of adrenal insufficiency may include weakness, fatigue, abdominal pain, nausea, dehydration, and skin changes. Doctors treat adrenal insufficiency by giving replacement corticosteroid hormones.

Cushing syndrome. Excessive amounts of glucocorticoid hormones in the body can lead to Cushing syndrome. In children, it most often results when a child takes large doses of synthetic corticosteroid drugs (such as prednisone) to treat autoimmune diseases such as lupus. If the condition is due to a tumor in the pituitary gland that produces excessive amounts of corticotropin and stimulates the adrenals to overproduce corticosteroids, it's known as Cushing disease. Symptoms may take years to develop and include obesity, growth failure, muscle weakness, easy bruising of the skin, acne, high blood pressure, and psychological changes. Depending on the specific cause, doctors may treat this condition with surgery, radiation therapy, chemotherapy, or drugs that block the production of hormones.

Type 1 diabetes. When the pancreas fails to produce enough insulin, type 1 diabetes (previously known as juvenile diabetes) occurs. Symptoms include excessive thirst, hunger, urination, and weight loss. In children and teens, the condition is usually an autoimmune disorder in which specific immune system cells and antibodies produced by the immune system attack and destroy the cells of the pancreas that produce insulin. The disease can cause long-term complications including kidney problems, nerve damage, blindness, and early coronary heart disease and stroke. To control their blood sugar levels and reduce the risk of developing diabetes complications, kids with this condition need regular injections of insulin.

Type 2 diabetes. Unlike type 1 diabetes, in which the body can't produce normal amounts of insulin, in type 2 diabetes the body is unable to respond to insulin normally. Children and teens with the condition tend to be overweight, and it is believed that excess body fat plays a role in the insulin resistance that characterizes the disease. In fact, the rising prevalence of this type of diabetes in kids has paralleled the dramatically increasing rates of obesity among kids in recent years. The symptoms and possible complications of type 2 diabetes are basically the same as those of type 1. Some kids and teens can control their blood sugar level with dietary changes, exercise, and oral medications, but many will need to take insulin injections like patients with type 1 diabetes.

Growth hormone problems. Too much growth hormone in children who are still growing will make their bones and other body parts grow excessively, resulting in *gigantism.* This rare condition is usually caused by a pituitary tumor and can be treated by removing the tumor. In contrast, when the pituitary gland fails to produce adequate amounts of growth hormone, a child's growth in height is impaired. Hypoglycemia (low blood sugar) may also occur in kids with growth hormone deficiency, particularly in infants and young children with the condition.

Hyperthyroidism. Hyperthyroidism is a condition in which the levels of thyroid hormones in the blood are excessively high. Symptoms may include weight loss, nervousness, tremors, excessive sweating, increased heart rate and blood pressure, protruding eyes, and a swelling in the neck from an enlarged thyroid gland (goiter). In kids the condition is usually caused by Graves' disease, an autoimmune disorder in which specific antibodies produced by the immune system stimulate the thyroid gland to become overactive. The disease may be controlled with medications or by removal or destruction of the thyroid gland through surgery or radiation treatments.

Hypo-thyroidism. Hypothyroidism is a condition in which the levels of thyroid hormones in the blood are abnormally low. Thyroid hormone deficiency slows body processes and may lead to fatigue, a slow heart rate, dry skin, weight gain, constipation, and, in kids, slowing of growth and delayed puberty. Hashimoto's thyroiditis, which results from an autoimmune process that damages the thyroid and blocks thyroid hormone production, is the most common cause of hypothyroidism in kids. Infants can also be born with an absent or underdeveloped thyroid gland, resulting in hypothyroidism. It can be treated with oral thyroid hormone replacement.

Precosious Puberty Body changes associated with puberty may occur at an abnormally young age in some kids if the pituitary hormones that stimulate the gonads to produce sex hormones rise prematurely. An injectable medication is available that can suppress the secretion of these pituitary hormones (known as gonadotropins) and arrest the progression of sexual development in most of these children.

A TOUR THROUGH THE BRAIN

The brain contains more than 90 percent of the body's neurons. Physically, the brain has three more or less distinct areas: the hindbrain, the midbrain, and the forebrain. The *hindbrain* is found in even the most primitive vertebrates. It is made up of the cerebellum, the pons, and the *medulla*. The medulla is a narrow structure nearest the spinal cord; it is the point at which many of the nerves from the left part of the body cross to the right side of the brain and vice versa. The medulla controls such functions as breathing, heart rate, and blood pressure. The *pons*, located just above the medulla, connects the top of the brain to the cerebellum. Chemicals produced in the pons help maintain our sleep-wake cycle. The *cerebellum* is divided into two hemispheres and handles certain reflexes, especially those that have to do with balance. It also coordinates the body's actions. The *midbrain* lies between the hindbrain and forebrain and is crucial for hearing and sight. The *forebrain* is supported by the *brain stem* and buds out above it, drooping somewhat to fit inside the skull. It consists of the *thalamus*, the hypothalamus, and the cerebral cortex. The thalamus relays and translates incoming messages from the sense receptors—except those for smell. The *hypothalamus* governs motivation and emotion and appears to play a role in coordinating the responses of the nervous system in times of stress.

The cerebral hemispheres, located above the thalamus and hypothalamus, represents 80 percent of mass in the brain. The outer covering of the cerebral hemispheres is known as the cerebral cortex. The cerebral hemispheres are the most evolved portion of the brain as they regulate the most complex behavior. Each cerebral hemisphere is divided into four lobes, delineated by deep fissures on the surface of the brain. These four lobes are both physically and functionally distinct. Deep fissures in the cortex separate these areas or lobes. The four lobes are the occipital lobe of the cortex, located at the back of the head, receives and processes visual information. The temporal lobe, located roughly behind the temples, is important to the sense of smell; it also helps us perform complex visual tasks, such as recognizing faces. The parietal lobe, which sits on top of the temporal and occipital lobes, receives sensory information, in the sensory projection areas, from all over the body and figures in spatial abilities. The ability to comprehend language is concentrated in two areas in the parietal and temporal lobes. The frontal lobe is the part of the cerebral cortex responsible for voluntary movement and attention as well as goal-directed behavior, which involves intelligence and executive functioning. The brain starts response messages in the motor projection areas, from which they proceed to the muscles and glands. The frontal lobe may also be linked to emotional temperament or emotional IQ.

BRAIN HEMISPHERES

The two hemispheres of the cerebral cortex are connected by the *corpus callosum*. The two hemispheres

Structure	Location	Functions
Hindbrain		
Medulla	at the top of the spinal cord	controls breathing, heart rate, and blood pressure.
Pons	above the medulla	regulates sensory information and facial expressions.
Cerebellum	at the lower rear	controls movement, coordination, balance, muscle tone, and learning motor skills.
Reticular Formation	a network of nerves extends from the medulla to the cerebrum	monitors the general level of activity in the hindbrain and maintains a state of arousal; essential for the regulation of sleep and wakefulness.
Midbrain above the pons between the hindbrain and forebrain relays sensory information from the spinal cord to the forebrain.		
Pineal Gland	on top of the midbrain behind the thalamus	involved in circadian and circannual rhythms; possibly involves in maturation of sex organs.
Limbic System)		
Thalamus	in the middle of the limbic system	relays incoming information (except smell) to the appropriate part of the brain for further processing.
Hypothatlamus, Pituitary Gland	beneath thalamus	regulates basic biological drives, hormonal levels, sexual behavior, and controls autonomic functions such as hunger, thirst, and body temperature.
Septum	adjacent to hypothalamus	stimulates sexual pleasure
Hippocampus	within the temporal lobe	mediates learning and memory formation.
Amygdala	in front of the hippocampus	responsible for anxiety, emotion, and fear
Basal Ganglia (Striatum)	outside the thalamus	involves in movement, emotions, planning and in integrating sensory information
Cigulate Gyrus	above corpus callosum	concentrates attention on adverse internal stimuli such as pain, contains the feeling of self.
Corpus Callosum	under the cingulate gyrus	is a bundle of nerve fibers linking the cerebral hemispheres, involve in language learning.
Forebrain		
Frontal Lobe	in front of the head	controls voluntary movement, thinking, and feeling.
Prefrontal Cortex	in front of the frontal lobe	inhibits inappropriate actions, forms plans and concepts, helps focus attention, and bestows meaning to perceptions.
Parietal Lobe	in top rear of the head	contains the primary somatosensory area that manages skin sensation.
Occipital Lobe	in the back of the head	contains the visual cortex to manage vision.
Temporal Lobe	on each side of the head above the temples	contains the auditory cortex to manage hearing and speech.

are the left and right. Each hemisphere dominates certain bodily functions. The left side of the hemisphere primarily controls the lpsilateral movement, complex and voluntary movement, verbal memory, ability to apply meaning to memory, visualization of words and letters, auditory production of language, language comprehension, speech, reading, writing, and mathematics. The right side of the hemisphere primarily controls spatial ability (direction, distance, Geometry, and mental rotation of shapes), emotion (expression and language content), musical ability, some memory tasks, visual recognition of faces, recognizing geometric patterns, hearing non-language sounds, sense of touch (tactile patterns), non-verbal memories, and perception of memories.

The right and left hemispheres, work in conjunction although they appear to have some separate functions. One of the best known differences between the two structures is motor control; the right hemisphere controls the left half of the body and the left hemisphere controls the right half of the body. These motor control differences were discovered mainly through the examination of paralysis caused by stokes or other damage to a specific hemisphere.

In 1861 the theory of lateralization of function was expanded with the discovery by Paul Broca of structure in the right hemisphere that controlled speech, this structure is now known as Broca's area Like many other advances in neuroscience this discovery was made possible by an unfortunate stroke victim, who in this case lost his ability to speak. After his death Broca examined his brain and discovered damage in the right hemisphere at this now famous location. This finding was followed soon after by the discovery of an area, also in the right hemisphere, responsible for understanding of written word. This area become known as Wernicke's area named after the man who discovered it by "studying patients with select verbal comprehension deficits," (Piethish, Paul.,XXXX) and comparing these deficits with damages to the brain.

The right hemisphere controls the left side of the body, and the left hemisphere controls the right side. When split-brain patients stare at the "X" in the center of the screen, visual information projected on the right side of the screen goes to the patient's left hemisphere, which controls language. When asked what they see, patients can reply correctly.

When split-brain patients stare at the "X" in the center of the screen, visual information projected on the left side of the screen goes to the patient's right hemisphere, which does not control language. When asked what they see, patients cannot name the object but can pick it out by touch with the left hand.

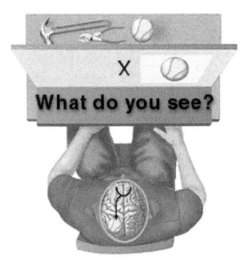

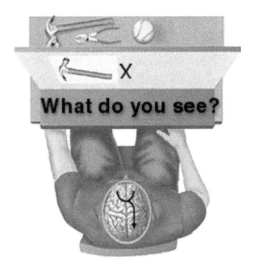

One of the major goals of neuroscience is to be able to understand the relationships between the structures of the nervous system and a person's outward behavior. Often times it is difficult or unethical to directly study the nervous system during a behavior and indirect methods must be used instead. One example of such an indirect method is using a subject's preferred hand to predict which of the two Cerebral Hemispheres is dominant. There are some difficulties with this method of studying lateralization of function but if it can be better understood it could have many practical and theoretical implications for the study of neuroscience.

CEREBRAL LATERALIZATION AND FUNCTIONALITY

There are four methods of cerebral lateralization to study the different functionalities of the left and right hemispheres. This includes the sodium amytal test, the dichotic listening test, and functional brain imaging. Also, the relation between handedness and language lateralization is a method of cerebral lateralization.

In the sodium amytal test, a patient's language abilities are assessed by a neurosurgeon before going into surgery. In the sodium amytal test, sodium amytal is injected into the carotid artery on a side of the neck (Pinel, 2007). The injection anesthetizes the hemisphere on that side for a few minutes, thus allowing the capacities of the other hemisphere to be assessed (Pinel, 2007).

In the dichotic listening test «three pairs of spoken digits are presented through earphones; the digits of each pair are presented simultaneously, one to each ear» (Pinel, 2007, p. 445). For example, a subject might hear the sequence 3, 9, 2 through one ear and at the same time 1, 6, 4 through the other and the subject is then asked to report all of the digits (Pinel, 2007). The test reveals that most people have left-hemisphere dominance because they hear slightly more in the right ear.

In functional brain imaging, while the subject engages in some activity, such as reading, the activity of the brain is monitored by positron emission tomography (PET) or functional magnetic resonance imaging (fMRI) (Pinel, 2007).

The relation between handedness and language lateralization is a method of cerebral lateralization. Studies reveal that «the left hemisphere is dominant for language-related abilities in almost all dextral (right-handed) and in the majority of sinestrals (left-handed); they also indicate that sinestrals are more variable than dextrals with respect to language.

Each method listed above has both benefits and drawbacks. The most important fact to make note of is that even though all four methods are performed for the purpose of discovering which hemisphere is the primary language center, this simply means that one hemisphere has a slight advantage over the other in producing and comprehending language (Pinel, 2007).

THE SPINAL CORD ANATOMY

The Spinal Cord is connected to the brain and is about the diameter of a human finger. From the brain the spinal cord descends down the middle of the back and is surrounded and protected by the bony vertebral column. The spinal cord is surrounded by a clear fluid called Cerebral Spinal Fluid (CSF), that acts as a cushion to protect the delicate nerve tissues against damage from banging against the inside of the vertebrae.

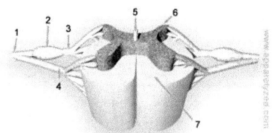

1	Spinal Nerve	5	Central Canal
2	Dorsal Root Ganglion	6	Grey Matter
3	Dorsal Root (Sensory)	7	White Matter
4	Ventral Root (Motor)		

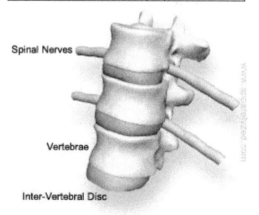

The spinal cord is about 18 inches long and extends from the base of the brain, down the middle of the back, to about the waist. The nerves that lie within the spinal cord are upper motor neurons (UMNs) and their function is to carry the messages back and forth from the brain to the spinal nerves along the spinal tract. The spinal nerves that branch out from the spinal cord to the other parts of the body are called lower motor neurons (LMNs). These spinal nerves exit and enter at each vertebral level and communicate with specific areas of the body. The sensory portions of the LMN carry messages about sensation from the skin and other body parts and organs to the brain. The motor portions of the LMN send messages from the brain to the various body parts to initiate actions such as muscle movement.

Spinal Nerves

Nerves called the spinal nerves or nerve roots come off the spinal cord and pass out through a hole in each of the vertebrae called the Foramen to carry the information from the spinal cord to the rest of the body, and from the body back up to the brain. There are four main groups of spinal nerves which exit different levels of the spinal cord. In descending order down the vertebral column: the nerves are:

Cervical Nerves "C": (nerves in the neck) supply movement and feeling to the arms, neck and upper trunk. The top vertebra is called C-1, the next is C-2,

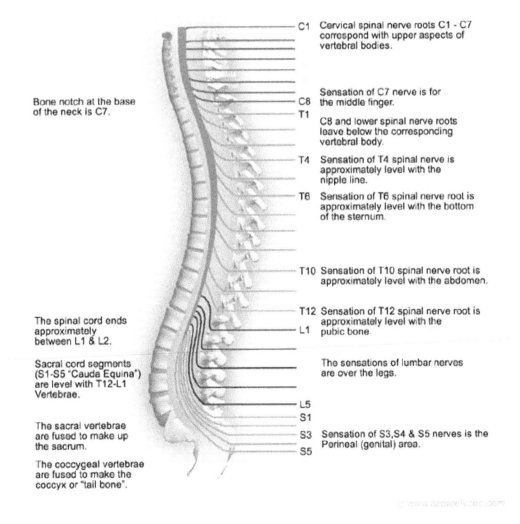

Bone notch at the base of the neck is C7.

The spinal cord ends approximately between L1 & L2.

Sacral cord segments (S1-S5 "Cauda Equina") are level with T12-L1 Vertebrae.

The sacral vertebrae are fused to make up the sacrum.

The coccygeal vertebrae are fused to make the coccyx or "tail bone".

C1   Cervical spinal nerve roots C1 - C7 correspond with upper aspects of vertebral bodies.

C8   Sensation of C7 nerve is for the middle finger.
T1   C8 and lower spinal nerve roots leave below the corresponding vertebral body.

T4   Sensation of T4 spinal nerve is approximately level with the nipple line.

T6   Sensation of T6 spinal nerve root is approximately level with the bottom of the sternum.

T10   Sensation of T10 spinal nerve root is approximately level with the abdomen.

T12   Sensation of T12 spinal nerve root is
L1   approximately level with the pubic bone.

      The sensations of lumbar nerves are over the legs.

L5
S1
S3   Sensation of S3,S4 & S5 nerves is the
      Perineal (genital) area.
S5

Diagram Showing the Relationship Between Spinal Nerve Roots and Vertebrae etc. Cervical SCI's usually cause loss of function in the arms and legs, resulting in quadriplegia.

Thoracic Nerves "T": (nerves in the upper back) supply the trunk and abdomen. The twelve vertebra in the chest are called the Thoracic Vertebra. The first thoracic vertebra, T-1, is the vertebra where the top rib attaches. Injuries in the thoracic region usually affect the chest and the legs and result in paraplegia.

Lumbar Nerves "L" and Sacral Nerves "S": (nerves in the lower back) supply the legs, the bladder, bowel and sexual organs. The vertebra in the lower back between the thoracic vertebra, where the ribs attach, and the pelvis (hip bone), are the Lumbar Vertebra. The sacral vertebra run from the Pelvis to the end of the spinal column. Injuries to the five Lumbar vertebra (L-1 thru L-5) and similarly to the five Sacral Vertebra (S-1 thru S-5) generally result in some loss of functioning in the hips and legs

Spinal Cord Level Numbering System

There are 31 pairs of spinal nerves which branch off from the spinal cord. In the cervical region of the spinal cord, the spinal nerves exit above the vertebrae. A change occurs with the C7 vertebra however, where the C8 spinal nerve exits the vertebra below the C7 vertebra. Therefore, there is an 8th cervical spinal nerve even though there is no 8th cervical vertebra. From the 1st thoracic vertebra downwards, all spinal nerves exit below their equivalent numbered vertebrae.

The spinal nerves which leave the spinal cord are numbered according to the vertebra at which they exit the spinal column. So, the spinal nerve T4, exits the spinal column through the foramen in the 4th thoracic vertebra. The spinal nerve L5 leaves the spinal cord from the conus medullaris, and travels along the cauda equina until it exits the 5th lumbar vertebra.

The level of the spinal cord segments do not relate exactly to the level of the vertebral bodies i.e. damage to the bone at a particular level e.g. L5 vertebrae does not necessarily mean damage to the spinal cord at the same spinal nerve level.

Spinal Cord Injury

Spinal cord injuries usually begin with a blow that fractures or dislocates your vertebrae, the bone disks that make up your spine. Most injuries don't sever your spinal cord. Instead, they cause damage when pieces of vertebrae tear into cord tissue or press down on the nerve parts that carry signals. In a complete spinal cord injury, the cord can't relay messages below the level of the injury. As a result, you are paralyzed below the level of injury. In an incomplete injury, you have some movement and sensation below the injury. A spinal cord injury is a medical emergency. Immediate treatment can reduce long-term effects. Later treatment usually includes medicine and rehabilitation therapy.

Spinal Cord Injury (SCI) is damage to the spinal cord that results in a loss of function such as mobility or feeling. Frequent causes of damage are trauma (car accident, gunshot, falls, etc.) or disease (polio, spina bifida, Friedreich's Ataxia, etc.). The spinal cord does not have to be severed in order for a loss of functioning to occur. In fact, in most people with SCI, the spinal cord is intact, but the damage to it results in loss of functioning. SCI is very different from back injuries such as ruptured disks, spinal stenosis or pinched nerves. A person can "break their back or neck" yet not sustain a spinal cord injury if only the bones around the spinal cord (the vertebrae) are damaged, but the spinal cord is not affected. In these situations, the individual may not experience paralysis after the bones are stabilized.

The effects of SCI

The effects of SCI depend on the type of injury and the level of the injury. SCI can be divided into two types of injury—complete and incomplete. A complete injury means that there is no function below the level of the injury; no sensation and no voluntary movement. Both sides of the body are equally affected. An incomplete injury means that there is some functioning below the primary level of the injury.

A person with an incomplete injury may be able to move one limb more than another, may be able to feel parts of the body that cannot be moved, or may have more functioning on one side of the body than the other. With the advances in acute treatment of SCI, incomplete injuries are becoming more common. The level of injury is very helpful in predicting what parts of the body might be affected by paralysis and loss of function. Remember that in incomplete injuries there will be some variation in these prognoses. Cervical (neck) injuries usually result in quadriplegia.

Injuries above the C-4 level may require a ventilator for the person to breathe. C-5 injuries often result in shoulder and biceps control, but no control at the wrist or hand. C-6 injuries generally yield wrist control, but no hand function. Individuals with C-7 and T-1 injuries can straighten their arms but still may have dexterity problems with the hand and fingers. Injuries at the thoracic level and below result in paraplegia, with the hands not affected. At T-1 to T-8 there is most often control of the hands, but poor trunk control as the result of lack of abdominal muscle control. Lower T-injuries (T-9 to T-12) allow good truck control and good abdominal muscle control. Sitting balance is very good. Lumbar and Sacral injuries yield decreasing control of the hip flexors and legs.

Besides a loss of sensation or motor functioning, individuals with SCI also experience other changes. For example, they may experience dysfunction of the bowel and bladder,. Sexual functioning is frequently with SCI may have their fertility affected, while women's fertility is generally not affected. Very high injuries (C-1, C-2) can result in a loss of many involuntary functions including the ability to breathe, necessitating breathing aids such as mechanical ventilators or diaphragmatic pacemakers. Other effects of SCI may include low blood pressure, inability to regulate blood pressure effectively, reduced control of body temperature, inability to sweat below the level of injury, and chronic pain

Table 8 Symptom(s) of Spinal Cord Injury

Spinal Nerve(s)	Innervated Body Part(s)	Symptom(s) of SCI
C1	Head and Neck	Quadriplegia
C2-C4	Diaphragm	Breathing problem
C5	Deltoids, biceps	No control at wrist or hand
C6	Wrist extenders	No hand function
C7-T1	Triceps, hand	dexterity problems with hand and fingers
T2-T8	Chest muscles	Paraplegia, poor trunk control
T9-T12	Abdominal muscles	Paraplegia
Lumbar and Sacral	Leg muscles, bowel, bladder, sexual organs	Decreasing control of hip flexors and legs, dysfunction of bowel, bladder, and sex

Note: Other effects of SCI may include low blood pressure, inability to regulate blood pressure effectively, reduced control of body temperature, inability to sweat below the level of injury, and chronic pain.

Prevalence Rates of SCI

Approximately 450,000 people live with SCI in the US. There are about 10,000 new SCI's every year; the majority of them (82%) involve males between the ages of 16-30. These injuries result from motor vehicle accidents (36%), violence (28.9%), or falls (21.2%).Quadriplegia is slightly more common than paraplegia.

The *spinal cord* is a complex cable of nerves that connects the brain to most of the rest of the body. It is made up of bundles of long nerve fibers and has two basic functions: to permit some reflex movements and to carry messages to and from the brain. Simple reflexes are controlled by the spinal cord. The message travels from the sense receptors near the skin through the afferent nerve fibers to the spinal cord. In the spinal cord, the messages are relayed through association neurons to the efferent nerve fibers, which carry them to the muscle cells that cause the reflex movement.

Tools for Evaluating the Nervous System

In recent decades science has developed increasingly sophisticated techniques for investigating the brain and nervous system. Among the most important tools are microelectrode techniques; macroelectrode techniques (ERP); structural imaging (CAT scanning, MRI); functional imaging (EEG imaging, MEG, MSI), and tools such as PET scanning that use radioactive energy to map brain activity. Scientists often combine these techniques to study brain activity in unprecedented detail.

An EEG recording of one person's alpha brain waves. Red and violet colors indicate greater alpha-wave activity.

In an EEG, electrodes attached to the scalp are used to create a picture of neural activity in the brain.

The exact function of the terminal nerve in human is still under investigation, which is hampered by its small size and proximity to the olfactory nerve. For mouse and other animals at least, it is connected to the vomeronasal organ (vestige in human), which leads to a pathway for controlling sexual arousal.

Behavior Genetics and Our Human Heritage

Studies of families and twins strongly suggest genetic influences on the development and expression of specific behaviors, but there is no conclusive research demonstrating that genes determine behaviors. Rutter explained the mechanism of genetic influence on behavior—genes affect proteins, and through the effects of these proteins on the functioning of the brain there are resultant effects on behavior. Rutter viewed environmental influences as comparable to genetic influences in that they are strong and pervasive but do not determine behaviors, and studies of environmental effects show that there are individual differences in response. Some individuals are severely affected and others experience few repercussions from environmental factors. This has given rise to the idea of varying degrees of resiliency—that people vary in their relative resistance to the harmful effects of psychosocial adversity—as

well as the premise that genetics may offer protective effects from certain environmental influences.

Jan Strelau, in "The Contribution of Genetics to Psychology Today and in the Decade to Follow" (*European Psychologist*, vol. 6, no. 4, December 2001), asserted that the proportion of phenotypic variance that may be attributed to genetic variance shows that personality traits, including temperament as well as specific behaviors and intelligence, have a heritability ranging from 40% to about 60%, but that it is primarily environmental influences that explain individual differences. He also wrote that genetics influence the environment experienced by individuals, which explains how, for example, children growing up in the same family often experience and interpret their environments differently. This also explains why individuals who share the same genes though living apart show some concordance in selecting or creating similar experiences.

Traditional psychological theory holds that attitudes are learned and most strongly influenced by environment. In "The Heritability of Attitudes: A Study of Twins" (*Journal of Personality and Social Psychology*, vol. 80, no. 6, June 2001), James Olson et al. examined whether there is a genetic basis for attitudes by reviewing earlier studies and conducting original research on monozygotic and dizygotic twins. Olson and his colleagues argued that the premise that attitudes are learned is not incompatible with the idea that biological and genetic factors also influence attitudes. They hypothesized that genes probably influence predispositions or natural inclinations, which then shape environmental experiences in ways that increase the likelihood of the individual developing specific traits and attitudes. For example, children who are small for their age might be teased or taunted by other children more than their larger peers. As a result, these children might develop anxieties about social interaction, with consequences for their personalities such as shyness or low self-esteem discomfort with large groups.

NATURE VS. NURTURE: TWIN AND ADOPTION

Twin and Adoption Studies

More than a century ago, English scientist Sir Francis Galton began to study how genetics influence intelligence. Galton theorized that children inherit their intelligence from their parents. Thus, he believed that genes were responsible for intelligence. In order to test his theory, Galton turned to twin studies.

Twin studies are invaluable to researchers interested in the nature vs. nurture debate. Identical twins have identical genetic compositions. Thus, by studying identical twins who were raised in different environments, scientists can see the impact of genes on development. Also, scientists can study fraternal twins (twins who share only 50 percent of their genes) who were raised in the same environment to determine the impact that the outside environment has on the development of personality. Modern twin studies have shown that almost all of a person's traits are influenced, in part, by genetics. Some characteristics, such as height, are strongly influenced by genetics, while other traits, such as intelligence, are more likely to be affected by outside factors (class, family income, etc.).

Adoption studies can also help scientists determine the roles of nature and nurture in development. Children who are adopted share an environment with their siblings but do not share any genes with them. If adopted children share more characteristics with their adopted families than with their biological parents, a strong argument could be made for the influence of environment on development.

Results of Twin and Adoption Studies

Over the years, a number of twin studies have been conducted. One twin study, known as the Minnesota twin study, examined a set of identical twins that were raised in separate environments. Although the twins did not meet until they were almost 40, they shared many similar characteristics. The only explanation for the similarities was that the twins' genes had strongly guided their development.

In fact, the Minnesota twin study led the researcher to conclude: "[On] multiple measures of personality and temperament, occupational and leisure-time interests and social attitudes, [identical] twins reared apart are about as similar as [identical] twins reared together."

Interestingly, adoption studies have also shown the strong influence of genes (or nature). For instance, the Texas Adoption Project found "little similarity between adopted children and their siblings and greater similarity between adopted children and their biological parents."

The *nature versus nurture* question refers to the interactive role that heredity (nature) and environment (nurture) play in human behavior. Although no contemporary psychologist would take either a pure nature or a pure nurture view of human behavior, the extent to which many traits are influenced by genetics and environment is still debated. The related fields of behavior genetics and evolutionary psychology help psychologists explore the influence of heredity on human behavior.

CHAPTER 3 SUMMARY

NEURONS
A neuron is a cell that specializes in the transfer of information within the nervous system.

THREE CLASSES OF NEURONS
- Sensory: Transmit information from sensory receptors to the brain (also termed afferent).
- Motor: Transmit commands from the brain to the muscles and glands of the body (also termed efferent).
- Interneurons: Interconnect sensory and motor neurons.

COMPONENTS OF THE NEURON
- Dendrites receive information from adjacent cells.
- Cell body of the neuron contains nucleus and cytoplasm.
- Axon is an extension of the cell body.
    - Myelin insulates the nerve cell, speeds up conduction of nerve messages.
    - Terminal buttons of the axon release transmitter into the synapse.

NEURON RESTING POTENTIALS
The membrane of the neuron separates charged ions, producing a voltage potential.
- The ions NA^+ and Cl^- are found outside the membrane, whereas the ion K^+ is found inside the membrane.
- The membrane is slightly permeable to K^+, so that at rest, the inside of the membrane is about -70 millivolts (mV) relative to the outside.
- At rest, very little NA^+ crosses the membrane (entry requires opening of channels through the membrane).

GRADED POTENTIALS

Stimulation of the nerve membrane can open ion channels in the membrane, ions will move into or out of the membrane (depending on which channels open).

- NA^+ ions flowing in will <u>depolarize</u> the membrane (membrane potential moves from -70 mV to say -60 mV.
- K^+ ions flowing out of membrane will <u>hyperpolarize</u> the membrane (-70 mV to say -90 mV).
- These graded potentials are a function of the magnitude of the stimulation of the nerve cell (are graded in size).
- Graded potentials sweep along the nerve cell and degrade with time and distance.

THE ACTION POTENTIAL

If the graded potential passes threshold (often at about –60 mV), then NA+ ions will flow into the cell, thus raising the membrane potential to +40 mV.

- The entry of NA into the cell produces an upward spike of the membrane potential.
- The restoration of the membrane potential back to -70 mV is produced by an opening of channels to K+ ions (that then flow out of the membrane, restoring the membrane potential).
- Once generated, the action potential sweeps along the axon toward the axon terminals.
- The action potential regenerates itself along the membrane (is an all-or-none event).
- The presence of myelin speeds up conduction of the action potential.

DETAILS OF THE SYNAPSE

The synapse is the physical gap that separates the axon terminal from the dendrite.

- The axon terminal is the presynaptic membrane.
- The dendrite is usually the postsynaptic membrane.

<u>Neurotransmitters</u> are chemicals that are stored within <u>vesicles</u> of the presynaptic cell.

- Transmitters are released in response to the action potential sweeping along the presynaptic membrane.
- Transmitter molecules diffuse across the synaptic cleft and bind to postsynaptic receptors.
- Receptor binding either opens or closes ion channels:
    - NA+ channel opening: Depolarizes the membrane.
    - K+ channel opening: Hyperpolarizes the membrane.

ENDOCRINE SYSTEMS

Endocrine glands release hormones into blood stream.

- Have effects at diffuse target sites throughout the body.
- Hormones bind to receptors.

- Hormones can have <u>organizational</u> effects (permanent change in structure and function).
- E.g. androgens permanently lower the voice.
- Hormones can have <u>activational</u> effects (increase a behavior in adulthood).

THE AUTONOMIC NERVOUS SYSTEM (ANS)

Two branches of the ANS:

- <u>Sympathetic</u>: Is the emergency system (fight or flight).
- <u>Parasympathetic</u>: Carries out vegetative functions (e.g. digestion).

The two systems often act in opposition (as in the control of heart rate).

The two systems can also act in concert (as in the control of sexual reflexes).

OVERVIEW OF THE SPINAL CORD

Spinal cord has dorsal and ventral roots (that carry sensory and motor signals to and from the spinal cord).

Cross section of the spinal cord shows an H-shaped structure in the center: this region is gray-colored and consists of cell bodies that project axons.

The outer regions of the spinal cord in cross-section are white in appearance (coloration is due to myelin that surrounds axons).

MIDLINE VIEW OF HUMAN BRAIN

Structures evident in this view include:

- Spinal cord
- Medulla oblongata
- Pons
- Cerebellum
- Pituitary
- Hypothalamus
- Thalamus
- Corpus Callosum

ANATOMY OF THE LIMBIC SYSTEM

- Septal area is involved in pleasure and in relief from pain.
- Amygdala is involved in learning and recognition of fear.
- Hippocampus is involved in memory.
- Patient H.M. shows anterograde amnesia (cannot learn new information).

CEREBRAL CORTEX

The functions of the cerebral cortex include:
- Provides for flexible control of patterns of movement.
- Permits subtle discrimination among complex sensory patterns.
- Makes possible symbolic thinking.
- Symbolic thought is the foundation of human thought and language.

The outer surface of the cortex is organized into:
- Primary areas (visual, auditory, motor)
- Association areas (premotor cortex)

FRONTAL LOBE DAMAGE AND PERSONALITY

The frontal lobes are involved in movement, attention, planning, memory, and personality. The function of the frontal lobes in personality is evident in the case of Phineas Gage:
- Gage suffered frontal lobe damage after an accident involving a dynamite-tamping rod.
- Gage was a railroad supervisor prior to the accident; afterwards, he became childish and irreverent, could not control his impulses, and could not effectively plan.
- Gage lost his job as a result of the brain damage he suffered in this accident.

CEREBRAL LATERALIZATION

The structures of the cortex and sub-cortex appear to specialize in function:
- Hemispheric Specialization
    Left hemisphere is dominant for language, logic, and complex motor behavior.
    Right hemisphere is dominant for non-linguistic functions including recognition of faces, places, and sounds (music).
    The hemispheric specializations are also evident from studies of
    Damage to one hemisphere (Broca's area).
    Split-brain subjects show evidence of hemispheric specialization.
- Gender differences in brain lateralization.
    Issue is whether the brains of males and females may be organized differently and whether such organization might have functional significance.

BEHAVIORAL GENETICS

Behavioral genetics is concerned with the influence of genes on psychological function.
- Genotype: Genetic structure (DNA located on chromosomes).
- Phenotype: Observable psychological (or behavioral) function.

Relatedness is the probability of sharing a gene with parents and others.

Heritability: Quantifies the extent to which variations in a trait across persons can be accounted for by genetic variation.

Studies of twins raised apart suggest heritability coefficients of 0.15 to 0.50 for the traits of:
- Conservatism
- Neuroticism
- Aggressiveness
- Intelligence
- Likelihood of divorce
- Job satisfaction
- Vocational interests

KEY TERMS

THE NEURON
a self-sufficient, specialized cell in the nervous system that receives, integrates, and carries information throughout the body.

- The majority of neurons are located in the brain—approx. 100 billion in the brain, although this is debatable.
- Each neuron receives information, on average, from tens of thousands of other neurons, making it the most complex communications system in creation.

TYPES OF NEURONS
Although most communicate within the central nervous system (CNS—brain & spinal cord), some do get signals from outside the central nervous system. There are three major types of neurons upon which information travels. In addition, the information travels from the Sensory Neurons to the Interneurons, and then finally to the Motor Neurons.

1. Sensory Neurons
bring information from sensory receptors to the central nervous system. Brings information from the eyes, ears, etc., as well as from within the body like the stomach.

2. Interneurons
neurons in the brain and spinal cord that serve as an intermediary between sensory and motor neurons. They carry info around the brain for processing.

3. Motor Neurons
carry the information from the CNS to the appropriate muscles to carry out behaviors.

For example, if you hold your hand over a hot flame, the information about "heat" travels from your hand on the sensory neurons, to the internuerons where it is brought to the appropriate brain region to process the information (now you know it is "hot") and make a decision about a corresponding action (too hot, let's move the hand). The information then travels on the Motor Neurons from the brain to the hand so that your muscles move the hand from the hot flame. See how easy that is?

STRUCTURE OF THE NEURON

1. Soma: the cell body which contains the nucleus, cytoplasm, etc. Everything needed for survival.

> **a. dendrites:** specialized branch-like structures used to receive information from other neurons. The more dendrites a cell has the more neurons it can communicate with.

2. Axon: thin, tail-like fiber that extends from the soma to the terminal buttons. This can range from as small as a red blood cell to 3 ft long.

> **a. axon hillock:** area where the axon connects to the soma.
>
> **b. myelin:** a fatty substance that covers the axon that serves 2 purposes: the myelin forms a sheath (covering) called the myelin sheath that helps the signal travel faster along the neuron (see Nodes of Ranvier below), and it also protects the axon from damage and signals from other neurons. The myelin sheath is not indestructible, but can deteriorate—for example, multiple sclerosis—signals are impeded and don't get to and from the brain properly.
>
> **c. Nodes of Ranvier:** myelin sheath is not an even cover, but there are areas that are covered and others that aren't. The areas w/o myelin are the nodes of Ranvier. The way this helps speed up transmission is that the electrical current/signal jumps from Node of Ranvier to Node of Ranvier instead of traveling down the entire axon.
>
> **d. axon terminal:** area at the end of the neuron where it meets another neuron.

BUT ONE NEURON ALONE IS MEANINGLESS—THEY MUST TALK! They communicate using an electrical signal called the Neural Impulse (sometimes it is combined with chemical signals … you'll see).

1. Frontal: (motor cortex) motor behavior, expressive language, higher level cognitive processes, and orientation to person, place, time, and situation

2. Parietal: (somatosensory Cortex) involved in the processing of touch, pressure, temperature, and pain

3. Occipital: (visual cortex) interpretation of visual information

4. Temporal: (auditory cortex) receptive language (understanding language), as well as memory and emotion

Typically the brain and spinal cord act together, but there are some actions, such as those associated with pain, where the spinal cord acts even before the information enters the brain for processing. The spinal cord consists of the **Brainstem** which is involved in life sustaining functions. Damage to the brainstem is very often fatal. Other parts of the brainstem include the **Medulla Oblongata**, which controls heartbeat, breathing, blood pressure, digestion; **Reticular Activating System** (**Reticular Formation**), involved in arousal and attention, sleep and wakefulness, and control of reflexes; **Pons**—regulates states of arousal, including sleep and dreaming.

Cerebellum: balance, smooth movement, and posture

Thalamus: "central switching station" that relays incoming sensory information (except olfactory) to the brain

Hypothalamus: controls the autonomic nervous system, and therefore maintains the body's homeostasis, which we will discuss later (controls body temperature, metabolism, and appetite. Translates extreme emotions into physical responses.

Limbic System: emotional expression, particularly the emotional component of behavior, memory, and motivation

Amygdala: attaches emotional significance to information and mediates both defensive and aggressive behavior

Hippocampus: involved more in memory, and the transfer of information from short-term to long-term memory

SENSATION AND PERCEPTION: PERCEIVING TODAY'S WORLD

4

LEARNING OBJECTIVES

After completing Chapter 4, students should be able to:

- Explain the relationship between sensation and perception.
- Give examples to support the statement that there is not a one-to-one correspondence between a physical stimulus and our perception of that stimulus.
- Describe how visual perception is an "active" rather than a "passive" process.
- Define the process of transduction and explain how it operates for at least three of the senses.
- Outline the important differences and similarities in transduction as it takes place in the various senses.
- Discuss the process of signal detection for an observer.
- Briefly outline the relation between stimulus intensity and perceived intensity according to:
- Weber's Law.
- Fechner's Law.
- Stevens' Power Law.
- Discuss the process of sensory adaptation as it applies to hearing and to one other sensory system.
- Describe the elements that form the primate visual system.
- Explain the concept of receptive field as it applies to cells in the retina.
- Explain how lateral inhibition shows that visual processing begins in the retina.

- Discuss the role of feature detectors in visual perception.
- Differentiate between the "what" and "where" visual pathways.
- Compare and contrast the two main theories of color vision and explain which gives a better understanding of color vision.
- Contrast the three major properties of sound waves.
- Explain the role of the cochlea in auditory perception.
- Describe how place theory accounts for the detection of high frequency sounds.
- Explain how humans are able to localize the spatial source of a sound.
- Describe the role of smell as part of the sense of taste.
- Describe the information provided by the kinesthetic sense and by the vestibular sense.
- Describe the implications of phantom limbs for our understanding of how the cortex modulates perception.
- Contrast the sensory processes involved in touch, temperature, and pain.
- Discuss the Gestalt principles of form perception.
- Discuss the visual cues that allow for depth perception.
- Explain the two systems that allow for motion perception.
- Give illustrations of shape, size, and color constancy.
- Discuss the impact of culture on illusions in visual perception.
- Compare and contrast bottom-up and top-down processing.

Introduction to Sensation and Perception

Although intimately related, sensation and perception play two complimentary but different roles in how we interpret the world. Sensation refers to the process of sensing the environment through touch, taste, sight, sound, and smell. This information is sent to our brains in raw form where perception comes into play. Perception is the way we interpret these sensations and therefore make sense of everything around us. This chapter will describe various theories related to sensation and perception and explain the important role they play in the field of psychology. Through this chapter it will be explained how senses work and how this information is organized and interpreted for meaning and use on a daily basis.

Sensation

Sensation is the process by which our senses gather information and send it to the brain. The process of receiving information from the outside world, translating it, and transmitting it to the brain is called Sensation. Large amounts of information are constantly being sensed at any one time into our consciousness, (such as room temperature, brightness of the lights, someone talking, a distant train, or the smell of perfume).Consciousness is our state of awareness. With all this information coming into our senses, the majority of our world never gets recognized. We don't notice radio waves, x-rays, or the microscopic parasites crawling on our skin. We don't sense all the odors around us or taste every individual spice in a gourmet dinner. We only sense those elements in our environment that we deliberately attend to based on its importance.

Five Common Features among Senses

- All senses translate physical stimulation into sensory signals.
- All senses have thresholds below which a person does not sense anything despite external stimulation.
- Sensation requires constant decision making, as to determine meaningful and non-meaningful information.
- Sensing the world requires the ability to detect changes in stimulation
- Efficient sensory processing means turning down the volume on information that is redundant , constant messages that have no change.

Therefore how we sense our world is clearly defined by a process of detecting and encoding stimulus energy in the world by our sense organs. Through the process of transduction, the sensation is transformed into an action potential and a neural impulse or message is delivered to the brain. In the brain, the stimulated areas produce what we refer to as *perception*.

Selection Involves:

- Selective attention (filtering out unimportant sensory messages)
- Feature detectors (specialized neurons that respond only to certain sensory information)
- Habituation (brain's tendency to ignore environmental factors that remain constant)

Perception

The process of interpreting information and forming images of the world is called perception. Perception refers to the process of organizing and interpreting sensory information to give it meaning. Three basic perceptual processes are involved in perception which include, *Selection* is attending to some sensory stimuli while ignoring others; *Organization*: assembling information into patterns that help us understand the world; and *Interpretation* is how the brain explains or interprets sensations.

The process of sensation starts with sensory receptors, which are cells found in your sensory organs that are dedicated to receiving the stimulation and transmitting the stimulus information to the afferent nerves that will then take the message to the brain. There are three categories of sensory receptors: photoreception (sight), mechanoreception (touch, hearing, balance), and chemoreception (smell and taste). Psychophysics studies the links between the physical properties of stimuli and a person's experience of them. One important question in psychophysics is how much stimulus is needed for the person to sense and perceive a stimuli? The answer is in the concept of threshold. An absolute threshold is the minimum amount of energy that we can detect 50% of the time. In psychophysics, *noise* is the term used to refer to irrelevant and competing stimuli. When a person senses something without being aware of this sensation, he or she has experienced a subliminal perception. The difference threshold is the smallest difference in stimulation needed to recognize that two stimuli are different from each other 50% of the time. *Signal detection theory* holds that factors such as motivation, expectancy, and urgency of the moment influence sensitivity to sensory stimuli. Our perception of stimuli will be influenced by our selective and transient attention. *The Stroop Effect* and *perceptual set* illustrate some of the variables that shape the process of perception. *Sensory adaptation* happens because we tend to adapt to an average level of stimuli. If the level of stimuli is changed, we will go through a process of *re-adaptation*. As you see there are different dimensions to sensation and perception.

Three Dimensions of Sensation and Perception

To obtain a good understanding of these concepts, it is necessary to understand the dimensions of sensation and perception. There are three dimensions to remember.

1. There is no one-to-one correspondence between physical and psychological reality
2. Sensation and perception are active, not passive
3. Sensory and perceptual processes <u>reflect the impact of adaptive pressures</u> over the course of evolution. Sensation and perception are adaptive.

INFLUENCES ON PERCEPTION

Perception is influenced by a variety of factors, including the intensity and physical dimensions of the stimulus; such activities of the sense organs as effects of preceding stimulation; the subject's past experience; attention factors such as readiness to respond to a stimulus; and motivation and emotional state of the subject.

Understanding Perception

Interpretation in perception involves four major factors:

• Perceptual adaptation
• Perceptual set
• Frame of reference
• Bottom-up vs. top-down processing

Perceptual adaptation is the way the brain adapts to changed environments and changes of stimuli within environments. For example changes in loudness of music, changes in fragrances, and temperature. In each of these examples, perception will change to adapt to threshold differences occurring.

Perceptual set is the readiness to perceive in a particular manner. Perceptual set is often based on expectations, experiences, and cultural influences. This is a person's tendency to develop preconceived ideas and expectations based on their need or desire of the situation.

Frame of reference is a based on ones perception within the context of the situation. Perception or interpretation of a situation is determined on the situation and persons involved within the context of the event. This suggests that an individual's typical manner of perceiving can be altered based on the frame of reference that the typical manner of perceiving. (Under what circumstance did the situation occur).

Bottom-up vs. top-down processing: information either starts with raw sensory data or with thoughts, experiences, expectations, language, and cultural knowledge.

• Negative and positive appraisal

Sensory Adaptation

The last concept refers to stimuli which has become redundant or remains unchanged for an extended period of time. Ever wonder why we notice certain smells or sounds right away and then after a while they fade into the background? Once we adapt to the perfume or the ticking of the clock, we stop recognizing it. This process of becoming less sensitive to unchanging stimulus is referred to as *sensory adaptation*, after all, if it doesn't change, why do we need to constantly sense it? Human beings have five primary senses: sight, sound, smell, taste and touch. When we step into a hot tub filled with water at 102 to 104 degrees Fahrenheit, we initially feel that the water is terribly hot. This is what we sense. When a little time has passed, and our body has adjusted to the hot water, it feels comfortable---even soothing. The temperature has remained constant---this is the experience of sensory adaptation.

Biologically, Sensory Adaptation occurs when sensory receptors change their sensitivity to the stimulus. This phenomenon occurs in all senses, with the possible exception of the sense of pain. For example, during **Dark adaptation**, or adaptation to reduced light intensity, our vision will experience three distinct changes in the visual system:

- Enlargement of the pupil -- takes place immediately. The larger pupil allows more of the available light to enter the eye and stimulate the retina.
- Increased sensitivity of the cones (color receptors) of the eye -- In low levels of illumination, the light-sensitive chemical in the cones increases in concentration. This makes it more likely that molecules of the chemical will be struck by particles of light (photons), initiating a chemical cascade that signals the detection of light by the receptor. Cones become completely dark-adapted within about five to ten minutes, but at best remain unresponsive to the levels of light present at night or in a darkened theater, resulting in a loss of color vision under those conditions.
- Increased sensitivity of the rods (night-vision receptors) of the eye -- As with the cones, the rods contain a light-sensitive chemical whose concentration increases under low light-levels, leading to increased sensitivity. Rods become fully dark-adapted after about 20-30 minutes.

In contrast Light Adaptation as with dark adaptation, involves (a) an immediate change in pupil size (it becomes smaller, admitting less light), (b) a change in the sensitivity of the cones to light (it decreases), and (c) a change in the sensitivity of rods to light (it also decreases). Because the large number of photons entering the eye rapidly destroys any excess light-sensitive chemical, light adaptation takes only a couple of seconds, rather than the many minutes required for dark adaptation.

Other Examples of Sensory Adaptation include, for example, Hearing a loud sound causes a small muscle attached to one of the bones of the inner ear to contract, reducing the transmission of sound vibrations to the inner ear, where the vibrations are detected. (This protective mechanism does not work well for sudden very loud noises such as rifle shots, as the muscle does not have time to contract before the intense vibrations pass through).

STIMULUS TRANSDUCTION

Virtually anything that can excite receptor cells can be a stimulus. Transduction is translating messages for the brain. To be useful to the brain, sensory messages must be translated into neural impulses that the neurons carry and the brain understands. The translation of one form of energy into another is called transduction. Sensory limits determine how strong the messages must be for sensation to take place.

Remember, the brain is not in direct with the outside world. The brain experiences the world through the workings of the senses. The sensory receptor cells have the ability to transduce physical energy into coded neural messages that are sent to the brain (sensation) where they are interpreted (perception).Not all forms of physical energy can become part of perception. Sensory receptor cells are necessary to transduce forms of energy. The stimulus must be strong enough to exceed the sensory threshold in order for stimulus changes to be recognized and perceived.

ABSOLUTE THRESHOLD

The absolute threshold is therefore the point at which a stimulus goes from undetectable to detectable to our senses. The absolute threshold is the point where something becomes noticeable to our senses. It is the softest sound we can hear or the slightest touch we can feel. Anything less than this goes unnoticed. There are three established laws that are discussed below to explain the relationship between stimuli and thresholds: Weber's Law, Fechner's Law, and Stephen's Law.

DIFFERENCE THRESHOLD

Once a stimulus becomes detectable, how do we recognize if this stimulus changes. When we notice the sound of the radio in the other room, how do we notice when it becomes louder. It's conceivable that someone could be turning it up so slightly that the difference is undetectable. The difference threshold is the amount of change needed for us to recognize that a change has occurred. This change is referred to as the **Just Noticeable Difference**. The <u>Difference Threshold</u> (or "Just Noticeable Difference" [JND]) is the minimum amount by which stimulus intensity must be changed in order to produce a noticeable variation in sensory experience.

Weber's Law

Ernst Heinrich Weber (1795-1878) was one of the first people to approach the study of the human response to a physical stimulus in a quantitative fashion. Weber's law expresses a general relationship between a quantity or intensity of something and how much more needs to be added for us to be able to tell that something has been added. Experiments designed to find out such things are called discrimination threshold experiments, because the observer is asked to tell apart, or discriminate between two or more stimuli that vary in minimal increments. The discrimination threshold, then, is the smallest detectable increment above whatever the initial intensity was. The smallest detectable increment typically changes depending on the initial level of stimuli. For instance, if we are trying to discriminate which of two flashes of lights are brighter, the difference between the flashes will be determined based on the flashlight turned on first. This general relationship between the initial intensity of something and the smallest detectable increment is exactly what Weber noticed and formalized into "Weber's Law". The discrimination threshold or the threshold for detecting an increment in the quantity or intensity of something, changes depending on how much there is before we add the increment. Weber's law is a hypothesis explaining how threshold change happens.

Weber's Law can be applied to variety of sensory modalities (brightness, loudness, mass, line length, etc.). The size of the Weber fraction varies across modalities but in most cases tends to be a constant within a specific task modality. Gustav Theodor Fechner (1801–1887) later offered an elaborate theoretical interpretation of Weber's findings, which he called simply **Fechner's law**

FECHNER'S LAW

Fechner's law provides an explanation for Weber's law. Fechner's explanation has two parts. The first part is that two stimuli will be discriminable if they generate a visual response that exceeds some threshold. The second part is that the visual response R to an intensity I is given by the equation R = log( ). I

If you use Fechner's law and graph the reported results, the discrimination threshold for a stimulus will become more intense than shown. Noticeably, the discrimination threshold will be larger. This is consistent with Weber's law, which predicts that the discrimination threshold grows as we increase the base intensity I. Subsequently, Stephens further explained the relationship of thresholds by measuring the intensity in mathematical terms.

STEVENS' POWER LAW

The theory is named after psychophysicist Stanley Smith Stevens (1906–1973). Although the idea of a power law had been suggested by 19th-century researchers, Stevens is credited with reviving the law and publishing a body of psychophysical data to support it in 1957.

The general form of the law is

$$\psi(I) = kI^a,$$

where I is the magnitude of the physical stimulus, $\psi(I)$ is the psychophysical function relating to the subjective magnitude of the sensation evoked by the stimulus, a is an exponent that depends on the type of stimulation and k is a proportionality constant that depends on the type of stimulation and the units used.

Because Stevens fit power functions to data, his method did not provide a direct test of the power law itself. (Luce, 2002), under the condition that respondents' numerical distortion function and the psychophysical functions could be separated, formulated a behavioral condition equivalent to the psychophysical function being a power function. This condition was confirmed for just over half the respondents and the power form was found to be a reasonable approximation for the rest (Steingrimsson & Luce, 2006).

It has also been questioned, particularly in terms of *Signal Detection Theory*, whether any given stimulus is actually associated with a particular and *absolute* perceived intensity?

SIGNAL DETECTION THEORY

Have you ever been in a crowded room with lots of people talking? Situations like that can make it difficult to focus on any particular stimulus, like the conversation we are having with a friend. We are often faced with the daunting task of focusing our attention on certain things while at the same time attempting to ignore the flood of information entering our senses. When we do this, we are making a determination as to what is important to sense and what is background noise. This concept is referred to as signal detection because we attempt to detect what we want to focus on and ignore or minimize everything else. The starting point for signal detection theory is that nearly all reasoning and decision making takes place in the presence of some uncertainty. The *Signal Detection Theory* provides a precise language and graphic notation for analyzing decision making in the presence of uncertainty.

PSYCHOBIOLOGICAL PATHWAYS OF OUR SENSES

Immanuel Kant, a famous philosopher proposed that our knowledge of the outside world depends on our modes of perception. In order to define what is "extrasensory" we need to define what is "sensory." Each of the 5 senses consists of organs with specialized cells that have receptors for specific stimuli. The auditory system is dedicated to one type of mechanoreception, audition. Sound waves vary from each other in frequency and amplitude. Timbre is the perceptual quality of a sound. The skin senses are also dedicated to mechanoreception, specifically to the sensation of touch, temperature, and pain. Touch information goes to the thalamus, which relays information to the corresponding somatosensory areas of the parietal lobes. Pain is the sensation that warns us of damage to our body. The *Gate Control Theory* has been suggested to explain pain perception and acupuncture. Taste and smell are sensations based on chemoreception, thus they are also referred to as the *chemical senses*. Taste buds, which are located on the tongue, respond to sweet, sour, bitter, and salty elements. The olfactory epithelium contains the chemoreceptors for smell. The kinesthetic sense provides information to the brain about movement, posture, and orientation, while the vestibular system provides information about balance and movement. These cells have links to the nervous system and thus to the brain. Sensing is done at primitive levels in the cells and integrated into sensations in the nervous system. Sight is probably the most developed sense in humans, followed closely by hearing.

SENSE OF SIGHT: A COLLABORATION BETWEEN THE EYES AND BRAIN

The Visual System

The visual system is dedicated to photoreception. Light is a form of electromagnetic energy that travels in waves. Light has different wavelengths, the distance from the peak of one wave to the peak of the next wave. We can see light with wavelengths between 400 and 700 nanometers, which is also the range of wavelengths emitted by the sun. The eye has different parts, all specialized in the process of photoreception. The main external structures of the eye include the sclera, iris, pupil, and cornea. Within the eye, the retina records the light information and converts it to neural impulses for processing in the brain. The retina is made up of light-sensitive receptors called *rods* and *cones*, which perform transduction. The fovea is a small area in the center of the retina where vision is at its best. The blind spot lacks receptors since it is where neural impulses exit the eye on the optic nerve. The optic nerve fibers cross and divide at the optic chiasm, resulting in visual information received on the left eye to be processed on the right side of the brain and vice versa. In the visual cortex of the brain there are feature detectors, which are neurons that process specific visual information. In the temporal lobe we process information about the color, form, and texture of the objects we see; in the parietal lobe we process information about the location, movement, and depth of the objects we see. All of this information is processed simultaneously; binding is the process through which it is all integrated into a complete perceptual experience. Objects have color because they reflect only certain wavelengths of light. Three important characteristics of color are hue, saturation, and brightness. Two major theories of color vision are the **trichromatic theory** and the **opponent-process theory**.

Vision: How We See

Both the eye and a camera are instruments that use a lens to focus light onto a light sensitive surface on which the visual image is registered. Light is one small part of the form of energy known as electromagnetic radiation that also includes radio waves and X rays. Light is used in the sensory processes of vision which takes place in the organ of the eye. **Visual Adaptation** is the transition from Dark and Light Adaptation occurs in the rods and cones within the eye. For example, in a lighted room, the rods and cones of the eye are being used frequently, so they are not very sensitive.

When we enter darkness, the rods and cones are not sensitive enough to be stimulated by the low-intensity light and they stop firing almost completely. This gives the receptors a rest so they being regain their sensitivity by making a fresh supply of the chemicals used in light reception.

Nature of Light

Light is energy in the form of electromagnetic radiation. This energy is radiated by processes in the atomic structure of different materials and causes a wide range of effects. The different forms of electromagnetic radiation all share the same properties of transmission although they behave quite differently when they interact with matter. Light is that particular electromagnetic radiation which can be detected by the human sense of sight. The range of electromagnetic radiation to which the eye is sensitive is just a very narrow band in the total spectrum of electromagnetic emissions, as is indicated in the Figure (X) below.

Electromagnetic waves

The transmission of light energy can be described as a wave motion or as 'packets' of energy called photons. The wave motion of light and other electromagnetic waves is the same basic mechanism found in other wave motions such as sea waves, sound waves and earthquakes. All waves can change their direction when subject to the following effects.

- **Reflection** is reversal of direction which occurs at a surface. Examples include mirrors and colored surfaces.
- **Refraction** is deflection that occurs at the boundaries of different materials. For example: prism effects occur at the edge of air and glass, red sunsets are caused by differing layers of the atmosphere.
- **Diffraction** is deflection that occurs at apertures, at edges and in thin layers. Examples include colored patterns in thin layers of oil, and colored spectrums caused by narrow slits.

Figure 9. Total Spectrum of Electromagnetic Waves

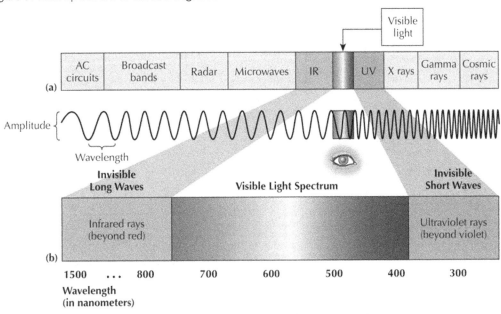

Spectrum of electromagnetic radiation (NASA)

Monochromatic light

Monochromatic light is one particular wavelength and color. If the colors of the spectrum are recombined then white light is again produced. Varying the proportions of the individual colors can produce different qualitiesof 'white' light.

Infrared

Infrared (IR) radiation has wavelengths slightly greater than those of red light and can be felt as heat radiation from the sun and from other heated bodies. Infrared radiation is made use of in radiant heating devices, for detecting patterns of heat emissions, for 'seeing' in the dark, and for communication links.

Ultraviolet

Ultraviolet (UV) radiation has wavelengths slightly less than those of violet light. It is emitted by the sun and also by other objects at high temperature. Ultraviolet radiation helps keep the body healthy but

excessive amounts can damage the skin and the eyes. The composition of the earth's atmosphere normally protects the planet from excessive UV radiation emitted by the sun. Ultraviolet radiation can be used to kill harmful bacteria in kitchens and in hospitals. Certain chemicals can convert UV energy to visible light, and the effect is made use of in fluorescent lamps.

Theory of Color Vision

It has taken psychologists and other scientists more than a hundred years to reach our current understanding of the complex mechanisms of color vision.

There are two major theoretical explanations of how the visual system transduces color.

Young and Helmholz suggested that there are three kinds of cones in the retina that respond mostly to light in either the red, green, or blue range of wavelengths. Their theory is referred to as the **Trichromatic Theory of Color vision. The Opponent-Process Theory** was developed to explain the premise that there are three classes of cone receptors subserving color vision.

Trichromatic Theory of Color Vision

The trichromatic theory of color vision explains how humans are able to view different colors. Years of research have provided information on how the human eye deciphers colors. This theory states that three receptors in the retina of the eye are responsible for the perception of color by the brain. Each receptor is sensitive to a single color: red, green or blue. The combination of these three colors can form any visible color in the spectrum. This theory is more commonly known as the trichromatic theory of color vision. While the trichromatic theory successfully explains how color vision works, it has also been the basis for additional theories that attempt to further explain how the brain receives color images.

Opponent Process Theory

Ewald Hering, the father of the opponent processes theory made some very interesting observations that could not be accounted for by the trichromatic theory. For example, he noted that there are certain pairs of colors one never sees together at the same place and at the same time. For example, one does not see reddish greens or yellowish blues. We do see yellowish greens, bluish reds, yellowish reds, and other blends that match.

Hering also observed that there was a distinct pattern to the color. For example, if one looks at a unique red patch for about a minute and then switches the gaze to a homogeneous white area they will see a greenish patch in the white area.

Hering hypothesized that trichromatic signals from the cones fed into subsequent neural stages and exhibited two major opponent classes of processing. 1. Spectrally opponent processes which were red vs. green and yellow vs. blue. 2. Spectrally non-opponent processes which were black vs. white. This opponent process model lay relatively dormant for many years until a pair of visual scientists working at Eastman Kodak at the time, conceived of a method for quantitatively measuring the opponent processes responses. Leo Hurvich and Dorothea Jameson invented the *hue*

cancellation method to psychophysically evaluate the opponent processing nature of color vision.

Due in large measure to the efforts of Hurvich and Jameson the opponent processes theory attained a central position shared with the trichromatic theory. One very fortuitous scientific event to that also took place in the 1950s was the discovery of electrophysiological responses that emulated opponent processing. Consequently, with the quantitative data provided by the psychophysics and direct neurophysiological responses provided by electrophysiology opponent processing is no longer questioned.

Operation of Vision and Light

The human eye is the last link in the chain of color vision. The human eye has a simple two element lens. The cornea is the front or outer element and the lens is the back or inner element. The amount of light entering the eye is controlled by the iris which lies in between the two. The retina is the light sensitive part of the eye. Its surface is coated with millions of photoreceptors. These photoreceptors sense the light and pass electrical signals indicating its presence through the optic nerve to stimulate the brain. There are two types of photoreceptors, rods and cones. Theretinacontains two types of photoreceptors, rods and cones.

Cone vision

The cones are the light receptors that operate when the eye is adapted to normal levels of light. The retina contains three types of cones, red, yellow, and blue. Each type of cone contains different light sensitive pigments that respond to different wavelengths of light. Red cones are most stimulated by light in the red-yellow spectrum. Green cones are most stimulated by light in the yellow-green spectrum. Blue cones are most stimulated by light in the blue violet spectrum.

The cones are less sensitive to light than rods. Cones are needed for daylight vision and assist in the adaptation needed when experiencing changes in light levels; for example, adjusting to a change like going

THE HERING THEORY OF COLOR VISION

The Opponent Color Theory of the 19th century physiologist Ewald Hering (Hering, 1964; Hurvich, 1981) derived by the analysis of subjective human color vision is in general correct, although the idea of opponent colors was described earlier by Goethe and Schoepenhauer. Certain colors are not perceived together, i.e. they do not mix. We never see bluish-yellows or reddish-greens. The yellow detector is always inactive when the blue detector is active and vice versa. A similar situation occurs for the neurons responding to red or green.

Ewald H. Hering 1834-1918

outdoors to bright levels of light to going indoors to lower levels of light. Like all neurons, the cones fire to produce an electrical impulse on the nerve fiber and then must reset to fire again. The light adaption is thought to occur by adjusting this reset time.

The cones are responsible for all high resolution vision. The eye moves continually to keep the light from the object of interest falling on the fovea centralis where the bulk of the cones reside. The rods are sensitive to very low levels of light but are monochromatic and cannot see color. That's why at very low light levels, humans see things in black and white.

Rod Vision

The rods are responsible for our dark adaption, orscotopic, vision. The rods are incredibly efficient photoreceptors. More than one thousand times as sensitive as the cones, they can reportedly be triggered by individualphoonsunder optimal conditions. The optimum dark-adapted vision is obtained only after a considerable period of darkness, for instance, 30

minutes or longer, because the rod adaption process is much slower than that of the cones.

While the visual acuity or visual resolution is much better with the cones, the rods are better motion sensors…. See the Figure X below.

Anatomy of the Eye

The eye is an almost perfect sphere composed of two fluid filled chambers. Light passes through the clear cornea into the first chamber. At the back of this chamber, the colored iris opens and closes to regulate how much will pass through the pupil into the lens. The lens is held in place by ligaments that attached to the ciliary muscle. Eye has rods and cones. The eye also consists of a transparent lens that focuses light on the retina. The retina is covered with two basic types of light-sensitive cells-rods and cones. The cone cells are sensitive to color and are located in the part of the retina called the fovea, where the light is focused by the lens. The rod cells are not sensitive to color, but have greater sensitivity to light than the cone cells. These cells are located around the fovea and are responsible for peripheral vision and night vision. The eye is connected to the brain through the optic nerve. The point of this connection is called the "blind spot" because it is insensitive to light. Experiments have shown that the back of the brain maps the visual input from the eyes.

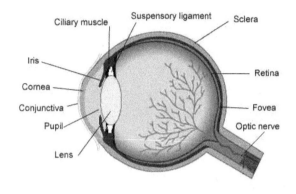

Biological Visual Pathways

Information about the world enters both eyes with a great deal of overlap. Try closing one eye, and you will find that your range of vision in the remaining eye is mainly limited by your nose. The image projected onto your retina can be cut down the middle, with the **fovea** defining the center. Now you have essentially two halves of the retina, a left half and a right half. Generally, the halves are referred to as a **temporal**

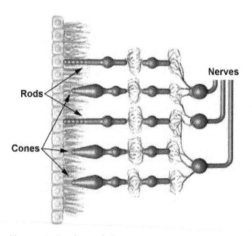

Figure 4. Rods and Cones

half (next to your temple) and a **nasal half** (next to your nose).

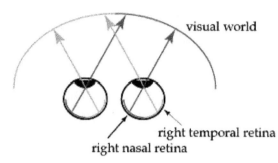

Visual images are inverted as they pass through the lens. Therefore, in your right eye, the nasal retina sees the right half of the world, while the temporal retina sees the left half of the world. Notice also that the right nasal retina and the left temporal retina see pretty much the same thing. If you drew a line through the world at your nose, they would see everything to the right of that line. That field of view is called the **right hemifield**.

So, what you see is divided into right and left hemifields. Each eye gets information from both hemifields. For every object that you can see, both eyes are visualizing the image. This is critical for depth perception. Remember, like the hemifield, the brain works on a crossed wired system as well. The left half of the brain controls the right side of the body, and vice versa. Therefore the left half of the brain is only interested in visual input from the right side of the world. To insure that the brain doesn't get extraneous information, the fibers from the retina sort themselves out to separate right hemifield from left hemifield, Figure 5. below.

The practical consequence of this crossing is that damaging the visual system before the chiasm will affect one eye and perhaps, both hemifields, or damaging the pathway after the chiasm, will damage parts of both eyes, and only one hemifield. This type of damage would restrict the range of vision.

Types of Vision Problems

It's normal for our vision to deteriorate as we age. Here are some very common vision problems that

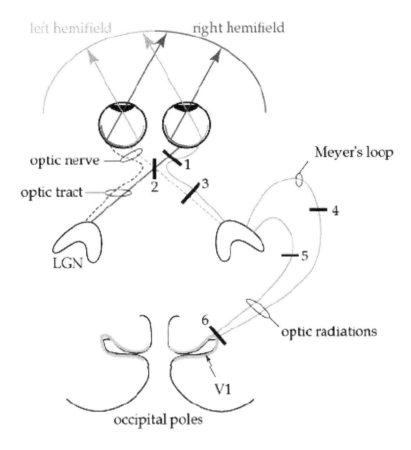

Figure 5. Right and Left Hemified of Vision

can usually be corrected with glasses or contacts. For example, *Farsightedness* occurs when you can see well at a distance, but not close up; *Nearsightedness also* myopia occurs when you can see well close up, but not at a distance.

There are some vision problems that are much more serious than near and far sightedness that can lead to blindness. Consider your family history, past injuries, diet, and other diseases when discovering decreasing eye conditions. For example, if you have a family history of eye disease, you'll have a higher risk of developing vision problems. You may also have other risk factors like previous eye injury, premature birth, diseases that affect the whole body, like diabetes, high blood pressure, heart disease, or AIDS. The only way to determine if you have serious eye problem is by having an eye exam given by an Optometrist (O.D.) or an Ophthalmologist (M.D.). See other conditions below.

- *Glaucoma*. This occurs when the pressure of the fluid inside your eyes damages the fibers in your optic nerve, and causes vision loss. If left untreated, you can lose your eyesight altogether.
- *Cataracts*. A cataract means a 'clouding' of all or part of the normally clear lens within your eye, which results in blurred or distorted vision.
- *Conjunctivis*. This is commonly known as Pink Eye. It is caused by an inflammation of the conjunctiva. This is the thin, transparent layer that lines the inner eyelid and covers the white part of the eye. The inflammation is usually

caused by a virus, and will resolve without any treatment. But, sometimes pink eye is caused by a bacterial infection and will require antibiotics.

- *Eye Floaters.* These may look like small dots or lines moving through your field of vision. They're actually tiny clumps of gel or cells inside the vitreous fluid in the eye. They may be a sign of retinal detachment and you should call your doctor right away.
- *Macular Degeneration.* This results from changes to the macula portion of the retina. The macula is responsible for clear, sharp vision. This condition can cause a blind spot in the middle of your sight line.
- *Retinal Tears and Detachment.* These affect the thin layer of blood vessels that supplies oxygen and nutrients to your retina. Initial symptoms are eye floaters. This condition must be treated immediately. If it isn't, it can lead to permanent vision loss.

Early detection is key to correcting problems with vision deficiencies.

THE HUMAN EAR

Auditory Pathways

The ear is the organ of hearing. The ears are paired sensory organs comprising the **auditory system**, involved in the detection of sound, and the **vestibular system**, involved with maintaining body balance/equilibrium. The ear divides anatomically and functionally into three regions: the **outer ear**, the **middle ear**, and the **inner ear.** All three regions are involved in hearing. Only the inner ear functions in the vestibular system. The outer ear protrudes away from the head and is shaped like a cup to direct sounds toward the tympanic membrane, which transmits vibrations to the inner ear through a series of small bones in the middle ear called the *malleus, incus* and *stapes.* The **outer ear** is composed of the pinna, or ear lobe, and the external auditory canal. Both structures funnel sound

waves towards the ear drum or tympanic membrane allowing it to vibrate. The pinna is also responsible for protecting the ear drum from damage. Modified sweat glands in the ear canal form ear wax. The **middle ear** is an air filled space located in the temporal bone of the skull. Air pressure is equalized in this space via the Eustachian tube which drains into the nasopharynx or the back of the throat and nose. There are three small bones, or ossicles, that are located adjacent to the tympanic membrane. The malleus, incus, and stapes are attached like a chain to the tympanic membrane and convert sound waves that vibrate the membrane into mechanical vibrations of the three bones. The stapes fills the oval window which is the connection to the inner ear. *The inner ear*, or cochlea, is a spiral-shaped chamber covered internally by nerve fibers that react to the vibrations and transmit impulses to the brain via the auditory nerve. **The inner ear has two functions;** the first is hearing and the second is balance. The brain combines the input of our two ears to determine the direction and distance of sounds. **The cochlea** is responsible for hearing, 2) the **semicircular canals** have function associated with balance, and 3) **the vestibule** which connects the two and contains two more balance and equilibrium related structures, the saccule and utricle, (see Figure X. below.

How We Hear—The Auditory System

The human ear can perceive frequencies from 16 cycles per second, which is a very deep bass, to 28,000 cycles per second, which is a very high pitch. Bats and dolphins can detect frequencies higher than 100,000 cycles per second. The human ear can detect pitch changes as small as 3 hundredths of one percent of the original frequency in some frequency ranges. Some people have "perfect pitch", which is the ability to map a tone precisely on the musical scale without reference to an external standard. It is estimated that less than one in ten thousand people have perfect pitch, but speakers of tonal languages like Vietnamese and Mandarin show remarkably precise absolute pitch in reading out lists of words because pitch is an essential feature in conveying the meaning of words in

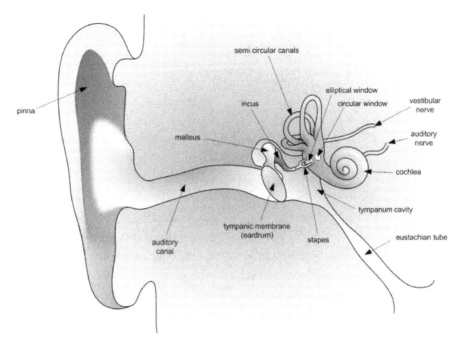

Diagram of outer, middle, and inner ear. The outer ear is labeled in the figure and includes the ear canal. The middle ear includes the eardrum (tympanic membrane) and three tiny bones for hearing. The bones are called the hammer (malleus), anvil (incus), and stirrup (stapes) to reflect their shapes. The middle ear connects to the back of the throat by the Eustachian tube. The inner ear (labyrinth) contains the semicircular canals and vestibule for balance, and the cochlea for hearing.

tone languages. The Eguchi Method teaches perfect pitch to children starting before they are 4 years old. After age 7, the ability to recognize notes does not improve much.

All sounds (music, voice, a mouse-click, etc.) send out vibrations, or sound waves. Sound waves do not travel in a vacuum, but rather require a medium for sound transmission, e.g. air or fluid. What actually travels are alternating successions of increased pressure in the medium, followed by decreased pressure. These vibrations occur at various frequencies, not all of which the human ear can hear. Only those frequencies ranging from 20 to 20,000 Hz (Hz = hertz = cycles/sec) can be perceived or heard by humans.

Range of Human Hearing

The hearing range of the healthy human ear is depicted in Figure 1. This range is bound by the "threshold of hearing" on the bottom and the "threshold of feeling" on top; the boundaries on the left and right represent the lowest and highest frequencies a listener can perceive, respectively. Note that speech occupies only a very small portion of the entire audible range. Even music, with its wide frequency response and dynamic range, does not cover the entire auditory spectrum. To give you a feel for different levels, the sound of a jet taking off 300 feet away measures about 125 dB, average street traffic measures about 85 dB, and sounds in a library measure about 35 dB.

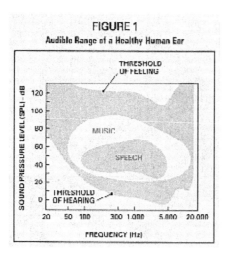

FIGURE 1
Audible Range of a Healthy Human Ear

Sound localization refers to a listener's ability to identify the location or origin of a detected sound in direction and distance. The human auditory system uses several cues for sound source localization, including time- and level-differences between ears, spectral information, timing analysis, correlation analysis, and pattern matching. These cues are also used by animals, but there may be differences in usage, and there are also localization cues which are absent in the human auditory system, such as the effects of ear movements.

How We Balance—The Vestibular System

Balance is a choreographed arrangement that takes sensory information from a variety of organs and integrates it to tell the body where it is in related to gravity and the earth.

Information from the vestibular system of the inner ear (semicircular canals, the saccule and the utricle) is sent to the brainstem, cerebellum, and spinal cord. Potential balance abnormalities do not require conscious input from the cerebrum of the brain. Abnormal vestibular signals cause the body to try to compensate by making adjustments in posture of the trunk and limbs as well as making changes in eye movement to adjust sight input into the brain.

There are three semicircular canals in the inner ear positioned at right angles to each other like a gyroscope. They are able to sense changes in movement of the body. With such changes, endolymph waves within the canals cause hair cells located within their base to move. Position of the head is sensed by hair cells of the utricle and saccule which is stimulated when the head moves and the relationship to gravity changes.

There is a small dense area of nerve fibers called the macule located in each of the saccule and utricle. The macule of the saccule is oriented vertically while the utricle macule is horizontal. Each macule consists of fine hair bundles which are covered by an otolithic membrane that is jelly-like and covered by a blanket of calcium crystals.

The calcium crystals are the structures that ultimately stimulate the position hairs and provoke nerve impulses created by the position changes and transmit that information to the brain stem and cerebellum.

Types and Causes of Hearing Loss

When the ear is exposed to high sound-pressure levels even for short periods of time, the listener experiences a type of hearing loss known as "temporary threshold shift." If you've ever been to a loud rock concert, you know what I'm talking about: When you step outside the arena, everything seems unnaturally quiet. But after awhile, your threshold of hearing returns to a level very close to its original level and you can hear again.

Prolonged exposure to high sound-pressure levels kills the very fine hair cells, progressively impairing hearing. Damage to a few may not cause noticeable impairment, but as more of them are killed off the brain will not be able to compensate for the loss of information. This results in a condition known as "permanent threshold shift." Usually by the time the listener becomes aware of the loss, considerable and irreparable damage has already occurred. The result: a form of sensory-neural hearing loss.

The symptom most common to this kind of impairment is the inability to distinguish between different sounds at normal listening levels – words seem to run together, speech and background noise mesh, and music sounds muffed. While hearing aids and other devices can alleviate some of these problems, full hearing capability can never be restored.

Tinnitus, the ever-present ringing in the ears that I suffer from, is another telltale sign of hearing loss. Depending on the number of damaged hair cells, ringing can vary from mild to severe. Extreme cases require medication and/or sound-making devices, which pump white noise into the ear to mask the ringing.

Aside from damage to your hearing, exposure to high sound-pressure levels also can produce physiological side effects – including disorientation, diarrhea, and chest pains – especially when very low frequencies are prevalent in the music.

People can suffer from **conductive** hearing loss, **sensorineural** hearing loss, or a combination of the two.

Conductive hearing loss occurs when sound waves are physically prevented from reaching the inner ear. These problems can almost always be corrected through medical or surgical treatment (and sometimes take care of themselves on their own). Common causes of conductive hearing loss include:

- **Perforated Eardrum**. The eardrum is like the head of a drum. If it is punctured, it cannot vibrate in time with the vibrational patterns it receives, and so the sound cannot be picked up on the other side by the tiny bones of the middle ear. In time, this condition usually repairs itself. (But see a doctor anyway.)
- **Ear wax buildup** in the ear canal. This can partially block or muffle the sound waves impacting on the eardrum. Wax can easily be removed by a doctor or nurse.
- **Fluid in the middle ear**. This is very common in children. Known as Otitis Media, it is caused by an infection of the middle ear or by a cold when fluid is backed up into the middle ear. (Fluid normally drains through the eustachian tube to the throat .) In either case, fluid fills the middle ear, preventing the tiny bones from vibrating properly and sending the sound impulses onto the inner ear. The problem can be remedied through antibiotics or by surgically installing a tiny tube in the child's ear so the fluid can drain.

- **Abnormal growth of the bones of the middle ear.** As in the condition above, the bones of the middle ear are unable to move properly and cannot transmit the sound. Severe hearing loss can result. Surgery is usually very effective in this situation.

Sensorineural hearing loss occurs when the sensory cells of the inner ear (the hair cells) or the auditory nerve itself are damaged through aging, exposure to loud noise, drug reaction, head injury, or genetic factors. The most common cause is gradual exposure to excessive noise over a number of years or one or more intense exposures. (That's why ear protectors are so important.) Unfortunately, this damage usually cannot be corrected.

TASTE AND SMELL—GUSTATION

Our ability to taste occurs when tiny molecules released by chewing, drinking, or digesting our food stimulates special sensory cells in the mouth and throat. These taste cells, or gustatory cells, are clustered within the taste buds of the tongue and roof of the mouth, and along the lining of the throat. Many of the small bumps on the tip of your tongue contain taste buds. At birth, we have about 10,000 taste buds, but after age 50, we may start to lose them.

When the taste cells are stimulated, they send messages through three specialized taste nerves to the brain, where specific tastes are identified. Each taste cell expresses a receptor, which responds to one of at least five basic taste qualities: sweet, sour, bitter, salty, and umami. Umami, or savory, is the taste we get from glutamate, which is found in chicken broth, meat extracts, and some cheeses. A common misconception is that taste cells that respond to different tastes are found in separate regions of the tongue. In humans, the different types of taste cells are scattered throughout the tongue.

Taste quality is just one aspect of how we experience a certain food. Another chemosensory mechanism, called the common chemical sense, involves thousands of nerve endings, especially on the moist surfaces of the eyes, nose, mouth, and throat. These nerve endings give rise to sensations such as the coolness of mint and the burning or irritation of chili peppers. Other specialized nerves give rise to the sensations of heat, cold, and texture. When we eat, the sensations from the five taste qualities, together with the sensations from the common chemical sense and the sensations of heat, cold, and texture, combine with a food's aroma to produce a perception of flavor. It is flavor that lets us know whether we are eating a pear or an apple.

Our body's ability to sense chemicals is another chemosensory mechanism that contributes to our senses of smell and taste. In this system, thousands of free nerve endings—especially on the moist surfaces of the eyes, nose, mouth, and throat—identify sensations like the sting of ammonia, the coolness of menthol, and the "heat" of chili peppers.

Although our sense of smell is our most primal, it is also very complex. To identify the smell of a rose, the brain analyzes over 300 odor molecules. The average person can discriminate between 4,000 to 10,000 different odor molecules. Much is unknown about exactly how we detect and discriminate between various odors. But researchers have discovered that an odor can only be detected in liquid form.

It is appropriate that we consider taste and smell together because they are so intertwined in our experience that most people are unaware that most of what they call taste is really an olfactory experience. The sensations evoked by a substance put into the mouth are complex and involve much more than taste.

The gustatory system is much simpler than the olfactory system. Four primary taste submodalities are generally recognized: sweet, sour, salty, and bitter. Different regions on the tongue exhibit different maximal sensitivities to the four taste submodalities (Figure 10-1 which also shows the pattern of innervation of the tongue). The tip of the tongue is the most sensitive to sweetness and saltiness. The sensation of sourness is experienced best on the lateral aspects of the tongue, and bitterness is experienced best and perhaps only on the back of the tongue.

The basis for sweet and bitter tastes is not known. Sucrose is a carbohydrate, a disaccharide formed from one molecule each of fructose (a fruit sugar) and glucose. Glucose, fructose, and starch are also carbohydrates. Fructose (grape sugar) is the sweetest; glucose is less sweet than sucrose or fructose; and starch is not sweet at all. Some alcohols are very sweet.

The sensation of bitterness is evoked by many vegetable alkaloids, such as quinine, and by some metallic salts. Some people think that our sensitivity to bitterness may be a protective mechanism because many plant poisons are alkaloids and are bitter.

Summary of Taste

The receptors for taste, called taste buds, are situated chiefly in the tongue, but they are also located in the roof of the mouth and near the pharynx. They are able to detect four basic tastes: salty, sweet, bitter, and sour. The tongue also can detect a sensation called "umami" from taste receptors sensitive to amino acids. Generally, the taste buds close to the tip of the tongue are sensitive to sweet tastes, whereas those in the back of the tongue are sensitive to bitter tastes. The taste buds on top and on the side of the tongue are sensitive to salty and sour tastes. At the base of each taste bud there is a nerve that sends the sensations to the brain. The sense of taste functions in coordination with the sense of smell. The number of taste buds varies substantially from individual to individual, but greater numbers increase sensitivity. Women, in general, have a greater number of taste buds than men. As in the case of color blindness, some people are insensitive to some tastes.

How common are taste disorders?

Many people take the sense of taste for granted, but a taste disorder can have a negative effect on a person's health and quality of life. If you are having a problem with your sense of taste, you are not alone. More than 200,000 people visit a doctor each year for problems with their chemical senses, which include taste and smell. The senses of taste and smell are very

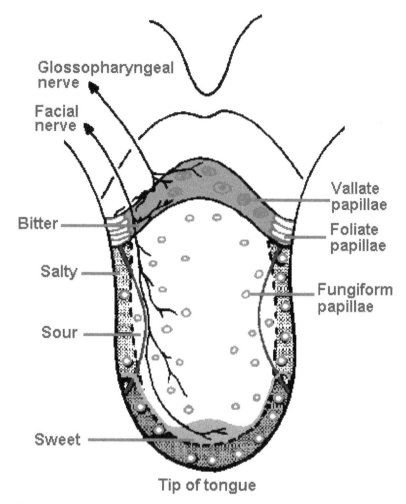

Fig. 10-1. The distribution of gustatory papillae, their innervation, and the regions of maximum sensitivity to different submodalities of taste on the human tongue. (Altner H: Physiology of taste. In Schmidt RF [ed]: Fundamentals of Sensory Physiology. New York, Springer-Verlag, 1978)

closely related. Some people who go to the doctor because they think they have lost their sense of taste are surprised to learn that they have a smell disorder instead.

Many people who think they have a taste disorder actually have a problem with smell. When we chew, aromas are released that activate our sense of smell by way of a special channel that connects the roof of the throat to the nose. If this channel is blocked, such as when our noses are stuffed up by a cold or flu, odors cannot reach sensory cells in the nose that are stimulated by smells. As a result, much of our enjoyment of

flavor is lost. Without smell, foods tend to taste bland and have no flavor.

What are the taste disorders?

The most common taste disorder is phantom taste perception; that is, a lingering, and often unpleasant taste even though you have nothing in your mouth. We also can experience a reduced ability to taste sweet, sour, bitter, salty, and umami, a condition called *hypogensia*. Some people cannot detect any tastes, which is called *ageusia*. True taste loss, however, is rare. As noted above, most often, people are experiencing a loss of smell instead of a loss of taste.

In other disorders of the chemical senses, an odor, a taste, or a flavor may be distorted. *Dygeusia* is a condition in which a foul, salty, rancid, or metallic taste sensation will persist in the mouth. Dysgeusia is sometimes accompanied by burning mouth syndrome, a condition in which a person experiences a painful burning sensation in the mouth. Although it can affect anyone, burning mouth syndrome is most common in middle-aged and older women.

What causes taste disorders?

Some people are born with taste disorders, but most develop them after an injury or illness. Among the causes of taste problems are:

- Upper respiratory and middle ear infections
- Radiation therapy for cancers of the head and neck
- Exposure to certain chemicals, such as insecticides and some medications, including
- some common antibiotics and antihistamines
- Head injury
- Some surgeries to the ear, nose, and throat (e.g., third molar—wisdom tooth—extraction
- and middle ear surgery)
- Poor oral hygiene and dental problems

PATHWAYS TO SMELL: THE ANATOMY OF THE NOSE

The senses of taste and smell are intimately linked to one another. The nose is the organ responsible for the sense of smell. The cavity of the nose is lined with mucous membranes that have smell receptors connected to the olfactory nerve. The smells themselves consist of vapors of various substances. The smell receptors interact with the molecules of these vapors and transmit the sensations to the brain. The nose also has a structure called the *vomeronasal organ* which is suspected of being sensitive to pheromones that

influence the reproductive cycle. The smell receptors are sensitive to seven types of sensations that can be characterized as camphor, musk, flower, mint, ether, acrid, or putrid. The sense of smell is sometimes temporarily lost when a person has a cold. Dogs have a sense of smell that is many times more sensitive than man's.

How does our sense of smell work?

Our sense of smell is part of our chemosensory system, or the chemical senses. Specialized sensory cells, called olfactory sensory neurons, are found in a small patch of tissue high inside the nose. These cells connect directly to the brain. Each olfactory neuron expresses one odor receptor. Microscopic molecules released by substances around us—whether it's coffee brewing or a pine forest—stimulate these receptors. Once the neurons detect the molecules, they send messages to our brain, which identifies the smell. (Because there are more smells in the environment than there are receptors, a given molecule may stimulate a combination of receptors. This response is registered by the brain as a particular smell.)

Smells reach the olfactory sensory neurons by way of two pathways. The first pathway is through your nostrils. The second pathway is through a channel that connects the roof of the throat region to the nose. When we chew our food, aromas are released that access the olfactory sensory neurons through this channel. If the channel is blocked, such as when our noses are stuffed up from a cold or flu, odors cannot reach the sensory cells and much of our ability to enjoy a food's flavor is lost. In this way, our senses of smell and taste work closely together. Without the olfactory sensory neurons, familiar flavors such as chocolate or oranges would be hard to distinguish.

Our sense of smell is also influenced by something called the common chemical sense. This sense involves thousands of nerve endings, especially on the moist surfaces of the eyes, nose, mouth, and throat. These nerve endings help us sense irritating substances such as the tear-inducing power of an onion or the refreshing cool of peppermint.

What are the smell disorders?

People who experiencesmell disordereither have a loss in their ability to smell or changes in the way they perceive odors.Hyposmiais a reduced ability to detect odors.Anosmisis the inability to detect odors at any level. People who experience changes in how they sense odors may notice that familiar odors are distorted or that something that normally smells pleasant now smells foul. Other people may sense an odor that isn't present at all.

What causes smell disorders?

Smell disorders have many causes, with some more obvious than others. Most people who develop a smell disorder have experienced a recent illness or injury. Common causes of smell disorders are:

- Sinus and other upper respiratory infections
- Polyps in the nasal cavities
- smoking
- Frontal head injuries
- Hormonal disturbances
- Dental problems
- Exposure to certain chemicals, such as insecticides and solvents
- Numerous medications, including some common antibiotics and antihistamines
- Radiation associated with the treatment of head and neck cancers
- Aging
- Other health issues that affect the nervous system, such as Parkinson's disease or Alzheimer's disease

Both smell and taste disorders are treated by an Otolaryngolgist, a doctor who specializes in diseases of the ear, nose, throat, head, and neck. Some tests are designed to measure the smallest amount of odor that patients can detect. Another common test consists of a booklet of sheets that contain tiny beads filled with specific odors. Patients are asked to scratch each sheet and identify the odor. An accurate assessment of your smell disorder will include, among other things, a physical examination of your ears, nose, and throat; a review of your health history, such as exposure to toxic chemicals or trauma; and a smell test supervised by a health care professional.

Are smell disorders serious?

Like all of our senses, our sense of smell plays an important part in our lives. The sense of smell often serves as a first warning signal, alerting us to the smoke of a fire, spoiled food, or the odor of a natural gas leak or dangerous fumes.

When smell is impaired, some people change their eating habits. Some may eat too little and lose weight while others may eat too much and gain weight. Food becomes less enjoyable and people may use too much salt to improve the taste. This can be a problem for people with certain medical conditions, such high blood pressure or kidney disease. In severe cases, loss of smell can lead to depression.

Problems with our chemical senses may be a sign of other serious health conditions. A smell disorder can be an early sign of Parkinson's disease, Alzheimer's disease, or multiple sclerosis. It can also accompany or be a sign of obesity, diabetes, hypertension, and malnutrition.

Treatment for Smell Disorders

Many types of smell disorders are curable, and for those that are not, counseling is available to help people adjust to the problem.

Diagnosis by a doctor is important to identify and treat the underlying cause of a potential smell disorder. If your problem is caused by certain medications, talk to your doctor to see if lowering the dosage or changing that medicine may reduce its effect on your sense of smell. Surgery to remove nasal obstructions such as polyps can restore airflow. Some people recover their ability to smell when the illness causing their olfactory problem is resolved. Occasionally, a person may recover his or her sense of smell spontaneously.

The National Institute on Deafness and Other Communication Disorders (NIDCD) supports basic and clinical investigations of smell and taste disorders at institutions across the nation. Some of these studies are conducted at chemosensory research centers, where scientists are making discoveries that help them understand our olfactory system and may lead to new treatments for smell disorders.

Some of the most recent research into our sense of smell is also the most exciting. In 2004, NIDCD grantee Linda B. Buck, Ph.D., together with Richard Axel, M.D., received the Nobel Prize in Physiology or Medicine for their discovery of a family of about 1,000 olfactory receptor genes that encode the receptors found on olfactory sensory neurons—one receptor per neuron. Recent studies on how olfactory sensory neurons recognize odors, aided by new technology, are revealing how our olfactory system detects and identifies the differences between the many chemical compounds that form odors.

Like our sense of taste, our sense of smell can be damaged by certain medicines. However, other medications, especially those prescribed for allergies, may improve the sense of smell. NIDCD-supported scientists are working to find out why this is so in an effort to develop drugs that can help restore a person's sense of smell.

TOUCH

The sense of touch is distributed throughout the body. Nerve endings in the skin and other parts of the body transmit sensations to the brain. Some parts of the body have a larger number of nerve endings and, therefore, are more sensitive. Four kinds of touch sensations can be identified: cold, heat, contact, and pain. Hairs on the skin magnify the sensitivity and act as an early warning system for the body. The fingertips and the sexual organs have the greatest concentration of nerve endings. The sexual organs have "erogenous zones" that when stimulated start a series of endocrine reactions and motor responses resulting in orgasm. Our skin acts as the protective barrier between our internal body systems and the outside world. Its ability to perceive touch sensations gives our brains a wealth

of information about the environment around us, such as temperature, pain, and pressure. Without our sense of touch, it would be very hard to get around in this world! We wouldn't feel our feet hitting the floor when we walked, we wouldn't sense when something sharp cut us, and we wouldn't feel the warm sun on our skin. It is truly amazing how much information we receive about the world through our sense of touch, and although we still don't know all the ins and outs of how the skin perceives touch, what we do know is interesting.

Sense of Touch

The sense of touch is our oldest, most primitive and pervasive sense. It's the first sense we experience in the womb and the last one we lose before death. The organ that is most associated with touch is the skin on the outside of your body. And our skin, which has about 50 touch receptors for every square centimeter and about 5 million sensory cells overall, loves to be touched.

The nerve endings in the skin can detect pressure, pain, and temperature. If you put your hand in a box to search around for something, you can tell when you've found it by feeling the pressure of the object.

WEARING ANATOMY ON THE SKIN

Everyone does not have a tattoo. However, a growing number of people have tattoos that express many ideas, emotions, thoughts, and experiences. There is a great range of art forms, from simple to grandiose. The picture below demonstrates a person who is passionate enough about anatomy to actually have a piece tattoooed to his arm.

The ability to sense pain is a warning device. It warns us to quickly pull our hand away from a hot stove, or not to grab hold of the wrong end of a pair of scissors. The ability to sense temperature is a safety feature too. It reminds us to bundle up when we go out in winter weather, and to stop and cool off after exercising. Your sense of touch allows you to tell the difference between rough and smooth, soft and hard, and wet and dry. Some parts of your skin have more nerve endings that other parts, so some parts are more sensitive to touch than others are. Your fingertips, tongue, and lips have the most nerve endings.

You do not only have skin and sense of touch on the outside of your body! You also have 'skin' and touch sense in the inside of your body. Without skin, people's muscles, bones, and organs would be hanging out all over the place. Skin holds everything together. Skin also protects our bodies, helps keep our bodies at just the right temperature, and allows us to have the sense of touch.

Anatomy of the Skin

While the other four senses (sight, hearing, smell, and taste) are located in specific parts of the body, the sense of touch is found all over. This is because the sense of touch originates in the bottom layer of the skin called the *dermis*. The *dermis* is filled with many tiny nerve endings which give information about the things with which the body comes in contact. They do this by carrying the information to the spinal cord, which sends messages to the brain where the feeling is registered. The skin consists of three layers: Epidermis, Dermis, and Subcutaneous Fat.

Epidermis

The skin is made up of three layers, each with its own important parts. The very top layer is the *epidermis* and is the layer of skin you can see. In Latin, the prefix "epi-" means "upon" or "over." So the epidermis is the layer upon the dermis (the dermis is the second layer of skin). Made of dead skin cells, the epidermis is waterproof and serves as a protective wrap for the underlying skin layers and the rest of the body. It contains melanin, which protects against the sun's harmful rays and also gives skin its color. When you are in the sun, the melanin builds up to increase its protective properties, which also causes the skin to darken. The epidermis also contains very sensitive cells called touch receptors that give the brain a variety of information about the environment the body is in.

The Dermis Is Under the Epidermis

The next layer down is the **dermis** (say:**dur**-mis). The second layer of skin is the*dermis*. The dermis contains hair follicles, sweat glands, sebaceous (oil) glands, blood vessels, nerve endings, and a variety of touch receptors. The nerve endings in your dermis tell you how things feel when you touch them. They work with your brain and nervous system, so that your brain gets the message about what you're touching. Sometimes what you feel is dangerous, so the nerve endings work with your muscles to keep you from getting hurt. The dermis is also full of tiny blood vessels. These keep your skin cells healthy by bringing them the oxygen and nutrients they need and by taking away waste. Its primary function is to sustain and support the epidermis by diffusing nutrients to it and replacing the skin cells that are shed off the upper layer of the epidermis. New cells are formed at the junction between the dermis and epidermis, and they slowly push their way towards the surface of the skin so that they can replace the dead skin cells that are shed. Oil and sweat glands eliminate waste produced at the dermis level of the skin by opening their pores at the surface of the epidermis and releasing the waste.

Subcutaneous Fat

The third and bottom layer of the skin is called the**subcutaneous** (say: sub-kyoo-**tay**-nee-us)**layer**. It is made mostly of fat and helps your body stay warm and absorb shocks, like if you bang into something or fall down. The subcutaneous layer also helps hold your skin to all the tissues underneath it. This layer is where you'll find the start of hair, too. Each hair on your body grows out of a tiny tube in the skin called a**follicle** (say:**fah**-lih-kul). Every follicle has its roots way down in the subcutaneous layer and continues up through the dermis. Hair follicles are all over the body, except on your lips, the palms of your hands, and the soles of your feet. There are more than 100,000 follicles on a person's head. Connected to each follicle in the dermis layer is a tiny sebaceous gland that releases sebum onto the hair. This lightly coats the hair with oil, giving it some shine and a little waterproofing.

Skin Can Warm and Cool You

Your skin can help if you're feeling too hot or too cold. Your blood vessels, hair, and sweat glands cooperate to keep your body at just the right temperature. If you were to run around in the heat, you could get overheated. If you play outside when it's cold, your inner temperature could drop. Either way, your skin can help. Your body is pretty smart. It knows how to keep your temperature right around 98.6° Fahrenheit (37° Celsius) to keep you and your cells healthy. Your skin can respond to messages sent out by your**hypothalamus**(say: hy-po-**thal**-uh-mus), the brain's inner thermometer. If you've been running around on a hot day, your blood vessels get the signal from the hypothalamus to release some of your body's heat. They do this by bringing warm blood closer to the surface of your skin. That's why you sometimes get a red face when you run around. To cool you down, sweat glands also swing into action by making lots of sweat to release body heat into the air. The hotter you are, the more sweat your glands make! Once the sweat hits the air, it evaporates (this means that it changes from a liquid to a vapor) off your skin, and you cool down. What about when you're ice-skating or sledding? When you're cold, your blood vessels keep your body from losing heat by narrowing as much as possible and keeping the warm blood away from the skin's surface. You might notice tiny bumps on your skin. Most kids call these**goosebumps**, but the fancy name for them is the**pilomotor**(say:**py**-lo-mo-ter)

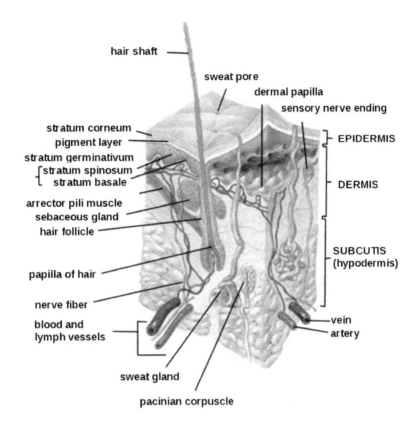

hair shaft

sweat pore
dermal papilla
sensory nerve ending

stratum corneum
pigment layer
stratum germinativum
stratum spinosum
stratum basale

EPIDERMIS

DERMIS

arrector pili muscle
sebaceous gland
hair follicle

SUBCUTIS
(hypodermis)

papilla of hair

nerve fiber

blood and
lymph vessels

vein
artery

sweat gland

pacinian corpuscle

reflex. The reflex makes special tiny muscles called the **erector pili** (say: ee-**rek**-tur**pie**-lie) muscles pull on your hairs so they stand up very straight.

Somatosensory System: The Ability to Sense Touch

Our sense of touch is controlled by a huge network of nerve endings and touch receptors in the skin known as the *somatosensory system*. This system is responsible for all the sensations we feel—cold, hot, smooth, rough, pressure, tickle, itch, pain, vibrations, and more. Within the somatosensory system, there are four main types of receptors: mechanoreceptors, thermoreceptors, pain receptors, and proprioceptors.

It is important to understand how they adapt to a change in stimulus (anything that touches the skin and causes sensations such as hot, cold, pressure, tickle, etc). A touch receptor is considered *rapidly adapting* if it responds to a change in stimulus very quickly. Basically this means that it can sense right away when the skin is touching an object and when it stops touching that object. However, rapidly adapting

receptors can't sense the continuation and duration of a stimulus touching the skin (how long the skin is touching an object). These receptors best sense vibrations occurring on or within the skin. A touch receptor is considered *slowly adapting* if it does not respond to a change in stimulus very quickly. These receptors are very good at sensing the continuous pressure of an object touching or indenting the skin but are not very good at sensing when the stimulus started or ended.

1. Mechanoreceptors: These receptors perceive sensations such as pressure, vibrations, and texture. There are four known types of mechanoreceptors whose only function is to perceive indentions and vibrations of the skin: Merkel's disks, Meissner's corpuscles, Ruffini's corpuscles, and Pacinian corpuscles.

The most sensitive mechanoreceptors, Merkel's disks and Meissner's corpuscles, are found in the very top layers of the dermis and epidermis and are generally found in non-hairy skin such as the palms, lips, tongue, soles of feet, fingertips, eyelids, and the face. Merkel's disks are slowly adapting receptors and Meissner's corpuscles are rapidly adapting receptors

Table 9. Skin Anatomy and Functions

epidermis	The epidermis is the thin outer layer of the skin and consists of three parts: • stratum corneum (horny layer) This layer consists of fully mature keratinocytes which contain fibrous proteins (keratins). The outermost layer is continuously shed. The stratum corneum prevents the entry of most foreign substances as well as the loss of fluid from the body. • keratinocytes (squamous cells) This layer, just beneath the stratum corneum, contains living keratinocytes (squamous cells), which mature and form the stratum corneum. • basal layer The basal layer is the deepest layer of the epidermis, containing basal cells. Basal cells continually divide, forming new keratinocytes that replace the cells that are shed from the skin's surface. The epidermis also contains melanocytes, which are cells that produce melanin(skin pigment).
dermis	Thedermisis the middle layer of the skin. The dermis contains the following: • blood vessels • lymph vessels • hair follicles • sweat glands • collagen bundles • fibroblasts • nerves The dermis is held together by a protein calledcollagen, made by fibroblasts. This layer also contains pain and touch receptors.
subcutis	Thesubcutisis the deepest layer of skin. The subcutis, consisting of a network of collagen and fat cells, helps conserve the body's heat and protects the body from injury by acting as a shock absorber.

so your skin can perceive both when you are touching something and how long the object is touching the skin. Your brain gets an enormous amount of information about the texture of objects through your fingertips because the ridges that make up your fingerprints are full of these sensitive mechanoreceptors.

Located deeper in the dermis and along joints, tendons, and muscles are Ruffini's corpuscles and Pacinian corpuscles. These mechanoreceptors can feel sensations such as vibrations traveling down bones and tendons, rotational movement of limbs, and the stretching of skin. This greatly aids your ability to do physical activities such as walking and playing ball.

2.Thermoreceptors: As their name suggests, these receptors perceive sensations related to the temperature of objects the skin feels. They are found in the

dermis layer of the skin. There are two basic categories of thermoreceptors: hot and cold receptors.

*Cold receptors*start to perceive cold sensations when the surface of the skin drops below 95° F. They are most stimulated when the surface of the skin is at77° F and are no longer stimulated when the surface of the skin drops below 41° F. This is why your feet or hands start to go numb when they are submerged in icy water for a long period of time.

*Hot receptors*start to perceive hot sensations when the surface of the skin rises above 86° F and are most stimulated at 113° F. But beyond 113° F, pain receptors take over to avoid damage being done to the skin and underlying tissues.

Thermoreceptors are found all over the body, but cold receptors are found in greater density than heat receptors. The highest concentration of thermoreceptors can be found in the face and ears (hence why your nose and ears always get colder faster than the rest of your body on a chilly winter day).

3.Pain receptors: The scientific term is nocireceptor. "Noci-" in Latin means "injurious" or "hurt" which is a good clue that these receptors detect pain or stimuli that can or does cause damage to the skin and other tissues of the body. There are over three million pain receptors throughout the body, found in skin, muscles, bones, blood vessels, and some organs. They can detect pain that is caused by mechanical stimuli (cut or scrape), thermal stimuli (burn), or chemical stimuli (poison from an insect sting).

These receptors cause a feeling of sharp pain to encourage you to quickly move away from a harmful stimulus such as a broken piece of glass or a hot stove stop. They also have receptors that cause a dull pain in an area that has been injured to encourage you not to use or touch that limb or body part until the damaged area has healed. While it is never fun to activate these receptors that cause pain, they play an important part in keeping the body safe from serious injury or damage by sending these early warning signals to the brain.

4.Proprioceptors: In Latin, the word "proprius" means "one's own" and is used in the name of these receptors because they sense the position of the different parts of the body in relation to each other and the surrounding environment. Proprioceptors are found in tendons, muscles, and joint capsules. This location in the body allows these special cells to detect changes in muscle length and muscle tension. Without proprioceptors, we would not be able to do fundamental things such as feeding or clothing ourselves.

While many receptors have specific functions to help us perceive different touch sensations, almost never are just one type active at any one time. When drinking from a freshly opened can of soda, your hand can perceive many different sensations just by holding it. Thermoreceptors are sensing that the can is much colder than the surrounding air, while the mechanoreceptors in your fingers are feeling the smoothness of the can and the small fluttering sensations inside the can caused by the carbon dioxide bubbles rising to the surface of the soda. Mechanoreceptors located deeper in your hand can sense that your hand is stretching around the can, that pressure is being exerted to hold the can, and that your hand is grasping the can. Proprioceptors are also sensing the hand stretching as well as how the hand and fingers are holding the can in relation to each other and the rest of the body. Even with all this going on, your somatosensory system is probably sending even more information to the brain than what was just described.

NERVE SIGNALS: MAKING SENSE OF IT ALL

Of course, none of the sensations felt by the somatosensory system would make any difference if these sensations could not reach the brain. The nervous system of the body takes up this important task. Neurons (which are specialized nerve cells that are the smallest unit of the nervous system) receive and transmit messages with other neurons so that messages can be sent to and from the brain. This allows the brain to communicate with the body. When your hand touches an object, the mechanoreceptors in the skin are activated, and they start a chain of events by signaling to the nearest neuron that they touched something. This neuron then transmits this message to the next neuron which gets passed on to the next neuron and on it goes until the message is sent to the brain. Now the brain can process what your hand touched and send messages back to your hand via this same pathway to let the hand know if the brain wants more information about the object it is touching or if the hand should stop touching it.

SCIENTIFIC FACTS

What's the largest organ of your body? You may be surprised to find out it is your skin. The skin makes up about 15% of your body weight—if you weigh 100 pounds, 15 of those pounds come from your skin. Measured in surface area, the skin averages 20 square feet in adults.

Skin is constantly renewing itself, which is a good thing since you shed 50 million skin cells every day—that's about 30,000 to 40,000 skin cells every minute.

Pain Tolerance

There are two steps to feeling pain. First is the biological step, for example, the pricking of skin or a headache coming on. These sensations signal the brain that the body is experiencing trouble. The second step is the brain's perception of the pain.

"Pain is both a biochemical and neurological transmission of an unpleasant sensation and an emotional experience," Doris Cope, MD, an anesthesiologist who leads the Pain Medicine Program at the University of Pittsburgh Medical Center, stated that "Chronic pain actually changes the way the spinal cord, nerves, and brain process unpleasant stimuli causing hypersensitization, but the brain and emotions can moderate or intensify the pain." Past experiences and trauma, Cope says, influence a person's sensitivity to pain.

Managing pain and people's perceptions to their symptoms is a big challenge in a country where more than 76 million people report having pain lasting more than 24 hours, according to the American Pain Foundation. Persistent pain was reported by:

- 30% of adults aged 45 to 64
- 25% of adults aged 20 to 44
- 21% of adults aged 65 and older

More women than men report pain (27.1% compared with 24.4%), although whether women actually tolerate pain better than men remains up for scientific debate.

Pain Rising

Pain produces a significant emotional, physical, and economical toll in the U.S. Chronic pain results in health care expenses and lost income and lost productivity estimated to cost $100 billion every year.

Pain may be on the rise in the U.S. because age and excessive weight contribute to pain and discomfort. Americans are living longer into old age, and two-thirds of the population is either overweight or obese.

The most common type of chronic pain in the U.S. is back pain; the most common acute pain being musculoskeletal pain from sports injuries, says Martin Grabois, MD, professor and chair of the department of physical medicine and rehabilitation at Baylor College of Medicine in Houston.

Perception is influenced by a variety of factors, including the intensity and physical dimensions of the stimulus; such activities of the sense organs as effects of preceding stimulation; the subject's past experience; attention factors such as readiness to respond to a stimulus; and motivation and emotional state of the individual.

Psychology accounts for aspects of tolerance that genetics cannot: "mind over matter." There is

SCIENCE IN THE NEWS

When a person loses an arm or a leg in an accident, they not only lose that limb, they also lose all the touch sensations that were received through that limb. Many amputees (people who have lost a limb) receive prosthetic (artificial) limbs to help regain some of the function and mobility they had before they lost the limb. However, conventional prosthetic limbs couldn't let the person feel when he grabbed hold of an object or when her foot touched the ground, making it a struggle for most amputees to successfully use a prosthetic limb for everyday purposes.

But scientists are making leaps and bounds in helping people regain mobility and sensation after losing a limb. The goal is to someday give amputees prosthetic limbs that will allow them to use only nerve signals from the brain to control the prosthetic limb, and have the limb send touch information back to the brain to make control over the limb a little easier. That someday is getting closer.

Claudia Mitchell, a former US marine who lost her arm in a motorcycle accident, is one of the most recent people to receive such an advanced prosthetic limb. Her new limb has been connected to the motor and sensory nerves in her chest that once controlled her real limb and now controls her new arm. While it is still limited in what it can feel and do, this new limb allows Claudia to feel touch and heat, and she can perform conventional tasks (such as folding laundry and cutting up vegetables) four times faster than she could with a regular prosthetic limb.

a possibility that two people can tolerate the same amount of pain, but that one voices their felt pain more readily than someone else. This could arguably be because one person is mentally stronger than the other. One person might feel an unbearable amount of pain, but stays quiet, does not medicate, goes on with his/her day, etc, while another person, under the same physical stress, manifests his/her pain in moaning, pill-popping, crying, being bed-ridden, etc. Maybe that person that seems stronger has conditioned him-/herself to suppress such manifestations of pain, or maybe he/she has been conditioned by society, so that this idea of "mind over matter" is actually cultural (i.e. feeling pain is a sign of weakness, and in some cultures, weakness is looked down upon more severely than in others). This conscious suppression of reactions to pain must then involve the I-function, an aspect of the nervous system in which the genetic explanation would not be involved. But, obviously, this cannot be the only explanation for the wide ranges of pain tolerance seen across humanity. The research is quite convincing, but does not take into account the genetic explanation for pain tolerance, just as the

genetic explanation does not take into account this theory. So, it leads this student to wonder to what extent pain tolerance is genetic and to what extent is it psychological? Furthermore, is anything else involved in a person's tolerance level for painful? And in fact, this student has found some research that suggests gender has something to do with it.

Researchers have found that estrogen can act as a natural painkiller. Higher estrogen levels result in a higher pain tolerance, and lower estrogenlevels cause effectively lower pain tolerance in subjects. Granted, the study was done only in women, but it is curious that hormones can affect how one deals with pain. Though this student did not find any research that inspected estrogen levels in males, or levels of male-specific hormones like testosterone, the studies examined here open yet another door through which pain tolerance may pass. Now, one can question whether these significant changes in pain tolerance are due to estrogen levels specifically, or to hormone levels in general. Furthermore, estrogen levels change with menstruation so that a woman's pain tolerance would, theoretically, also vacillate with changes in the body.

So, though genetics and psychology may play a part, a woman's pain tolerance is not constant, but is subject to manipulations by hormones.

IN SUMMARY

The study of sensation and perception is one of the oldest specialties in psychology. The earliest psychologists studied sensory inputs to the nervous system as a first step in understanding how we built up our experience of the world. *Psychophysics* is the study of how physical energy like light or sound is converted to psychological sensations. We will discuss psychophysics briefly in this chapter. College courses with titles like Sensation and Perception give a more thorough introduction to the topic.

Information from the environment is analyzed by sensory systems operating in conjunction with the brain. We will take a look at sense organs like the eye and the ear and how specialized sensory receptors convert physical energy into nerve impulses within the nervous system.

RESEARCH PERSPECTIVE ON PAIN

The psychological research done on this topic operates under the understanding that pain can be manifested in negative emotions, such as anxiety, depression and anger, to name a few. These researchers argue that these negative emotional responses to pain stimuli can be counterbalanced by positive emotional responses; in one very compelling study, the positive emotional responses were produced by sexual fantasies. The subject was told to immerse his/her arm in ice water until he/she could no longer bear the pain. Then, the subjects were separated into three groups: one group was instructed to envision a neutral fantasy (e.g. walking); another group was instructed to envision a sexual fantasy, and the third group was not given any specific instructions. Then, each group underwent the same submersion task as before. Interestingly, those subjects that were asked to think of a sexual fantasy while experiencing pain "handled pain better and experienced less pain [than the subjects under other conditions]. They also were less anxious and depressed, and less angry." In general, the subjects under the sexual fantasy condition were able to endure the pain for longer. The pleasant emotions produced by the thought of a sexual fantasy counteract the unpleasant thoughts that are a result of pain. The implications of this are that if a person enduring a painful experience imagines something that evokes in them positive emotions, they are able to cope with the pain better, and actually report experiencing less pain. Conversely, if a person experiences negative sensations from sources other than the painful experience in combination with the painful experience, the subject cannot endure as much pain and reports experiencing more pain than other subjects (2).

CHAPTER 4 SUMMARY

SENSATION AND PERCEPTION

<u>Sensation</u> is the process by which the body gathers information about the environment.
<u>Perception</u> is the process by which the brain organizes and interprets sensory information.
* Sensation and perception are really two sides of the same coin.
* Perception is an active process, rather than a passive process.
* Ambiguous figures give rise to different perceptions (see Figure 4.1)
* Other examples include:
* Face-vase figure
* Necker cube
* Old Woman-Young Woman

Other ambiguous figures can be found at: **http://dragon.uml.edu/psych/index.html**

BASIC PRINCIPLES OF SENSATION-PERCEPTION

Three principles emerge with regard to sensation and perception:
* There is not a one-one correspondence between physical and psychological reality.
* Sensation and perception are active processes.
* Sensation and perception are adaptive.

COMMON FEATURES OF SENSORY SYSTEMS

Sensory receptors translate physical stimulation into neural signals (the "transduction" process)
* Receptors detect physical energy.
    - Light, sound waves, heat, vibration
* Law of specific nerve energies: The nature of a sensation depends on the brain pathways activated by the stimulus.

Each system has a minimum amount of energy required to activate the system (termed the threshold).
* Sensation involves decision making ("is that stimulus relevant?")
* Sensory systems are sensitive to change in stimulation. e.g. A frog has receptors in its eyes that only respond to a small moving black dot.
* Receptors show adaptation to constant sensory input.
* Adaptation is important lest we be constantly reminded of our clothes, our watch, and our shoes.
* Constant stimuli provide no new information about the environment.

THRESHOLDS

Sensory receptors are tuned to a particular form of energy.

- Auditory receptors in the ear code for sound pressure changes, but not for light

Sensory systems require a minimum amount of energy for activation.

- The <u>absolute threshold</u> is the level a person can detect 50% of the time.

Vision: A candle 30 miles away on a dark clear night.

Hearing: a watch ticking 20 feet away in a quiet place.

- <u>Just-noticeable difference</u> (JND): The minimum difference in stimulation that is just noticeable.
- Weber noted that the JND is a fraction of the original stimulus intensity.
- The Weber fraction is different for different senses.

VISION

The function of the eye is to detect electromagnetic radiation (light).

- Vision is functional in that it allows for detection of
- Movement ("Is that moving object a predator or a friend?")
- Color ("Is that fruit ripe or is it spoiled?")

Light detection is particularly useful because:

- Light travels rapidly (in contrast to sound waves in hearing) allowing for rapid detection of events in the environment.
- Light travels in straight lines (no distortion); the geometry of objects is preserved in visual perception.
- Light interacts with the surfaces of objects in the environment (is reflected or absorbed).

Note however, that vision requires light; limits the utility of vision at night.

ELECTROMAGNETIC SPECTRUM

<u>Electromagnetic</u> (EM) energy travels in waves or oscillations

- The waves vary in frequency with gamma waves at the low end (10^{-5} nM) and radio waves at the upper end (10^{-13} nM).
- Humans are sensitive to only a small range of the EM scale (400-700 nM)

DETAILS OF THE HUMAN EYE AND RETINA

Figures 4.5 and 4.6 illustrate the organization of the

- Eye: Key elements are the pupil, the lens and the retina.
- Retina: Composed of 3 layers of cells; the photoreceptors are found at the back of the retina. The photoreceptors, in turn connect to bipolar cells, which connect to ganglion cells. The ganglion cells axons leave the eye (blind spot) and form the optic nerve.

TRANSDUCTION OF LIGHT

Light travels through the retina and impinges on photoreceptors at the back of the eye.

- Light bleaches a pigment contained within the photoreceptors:

- Bleaching leads to a graded receptor potential that eventually produces an action potential in the ganglion cell.
- Two types of photoreceptors
  - <u>Cones</u>: found in center of retina (fovea) and are sensitive to fine detail and color.
  - <u>Rods</u>: found in periphery of retina and are sensitive to movement but not fine detail.

RECEPTIVE FIELDS

<u>Receptive field</u>: That aspect of the external world that produces a change in firing rate of a given sensory cell.

- Insert a microelectrode into a retinal ganglion cell: Then record electrical potentials as various stimuli are shown onto the cell.
- Key concept: Sensory neurons show a baseline rate of firing; rate of firing can increase or decrease in response to external stimuli.
- Center-surround shape: A spot of light placed on the center of the field produces an <u>on</u> response (increase in firing rate), the same spot of light placed on the outside of the field <u>reduces</u> the firing rate.

VISUAL PATHWAYS IN BRAIN

From the retina, the visual pathways project through the optic chiasm to the lateral geniculate (thalamus) and then on to the primary visual cortex (occipital lobe).

Visual processing does not stop at the primary visual cortex:

- Two pathways: the "Where" versus "What" pathways process where an object is in the environment versus judging the form of an object.

PERCEPTION OF COLOR

Color is a psychological perception.

- Three dimensions of color:
- <u>Hue</u> is the apparent color of an object (e.g. "blue").
- <u>Brightness</u> is the intensity of a color.
- <u>Saturation</u> is the purity of the color.
- Three different types of cones are found in the eye.
- Cones are sensitive to different wavelengths of light:
  - S-cones: code for blue light.
  - M-cones: code for green light.
  - L-cones: code for red light.

COLOR VISION THEORIES

Young-Helmholtz Trichromatic Theory

- Color is explained by differential activation of 3 color elements in eye.

- Each element is maximally sensitive to either red, green, or blue.
    - This theory could not account for negative color afterimages.

Hering: Opponent-Process Theory

- Colors are derived from activity of 3 antagonistic systems.
    - Black-white
    - Red-green
    - Blue-yellow

DEPTH PERCEPTION CUES

- Binocular Cues
- Monocular Cues
- Interposition: One object blocks another.
- Linear perspective: Parallel lines converge in the distance.
- Texture gradient: Texture of distant objects appears finer rather than coarser.
- Shading: 3D objects cast shadows.
- Aerial Perspective: Far objects appear fuzzy.
- Familiar size: Familiar objects that appear small are inferred to be distant.
- Relative size: When looking at 2 objects of known similar size, the smaller object is seen as further away.

MOTION PERCEPTION

The visual system is wired to detect motion

- Rods in retina are sensitive to motion.
- Visual neurons in cortex respond to motion.
- Two systems exist for the processing of movement.

PERCEPTUAL CONSTANCY

Color: Tendency to perceive object color as stable even under conditions of changing illumination

Shape: We recognize an object as having the same shape although we may view it in a different angle, at a different distance.

Size: Objects do not differ in size when viewed from different distances.

LECTURE TOPIC EXTENSIONS

Pain and Culture

Women from a society in which childbirth was honored suffer more intense pain than do women from a society in which childbirth was considered polluting. This is a good place to review problems of reporting and self-reporting. It also provides an opportunity to discuss an assumption that many people carry along with them, assuming that if a perception is based on culture or "attitudes" it is somehow less real or valid than perceptions that can be traced to purely physiological causes. At the same time, students often assume that "cultural" perceptions are more malleable than other sorts.

Primary versus Secondary Cortex

Sensory signals travel along distinct pathways to reach distinct regions of the cortex. Once a signal arrives at a primary sensory region (e.g. area 17 of striate cortex), the signal is then transmitted to other regions of cortex for further analysis. These analyses modify the perception perhaps relating it to its location in the environment (e.g. "where") or to its form ("what"). Other connections may link the stimulus to memory, allowing us to recognize the stimulus and to link it with other sensory inputs (voice=audition; perfume=olfaction).

Sensation and Perception

Although students are generally able to grasp this distinction, in some instances they may find themselves wondering whether they are investigating a sensation or a perception. Two points will help clarify this issue. (1) Organization is one of the hallmarks of perception. Perception generally involves putting sensations in a context or relating them to one another in a meaningful way. (2) It is better to think of a sensation and perception as running along a continuum rather than being mutually exclusive categories. After all, even the simplest sensation, the firing of a single neuron, is already organized and interpreted to a certain degree, this neuron fired rather than another one.

LEARNING: THE PROCESS OF KNOWLEDGE

5

> patterns of responding
> resistance to extinction
> - Explain the role of context in operant conditioning.
> - Explain how shaping is used to mold new behaviors in an organism.
> - Discuss the role of preparedness in operant conditioning.
> - Discuss the role of drive reduction for learning.
> - Sum up the distinction between primary and secondary reinforcers.
> - Explain the role of expectancies in conditioning in animals and in complex human behavior.
> - Discuss how learned helpless develops and how it affects an individual's ability to adapt to situations.
> - Describe how observational learning and modeling are studied in children.

INTRODUCTION

What if we all could learn how we learn? Then if some kinds of learning were harder than others, we could find the source of that difficulty rather than rejecting what is being taught or feeling bad about ourselves for not learning. In the final analysis of life, we are all born to learn. Learning is how we grow and develop and eventually impact the world in which we live. It is how we adjust and adapt to an ever-changing and demanding world. There are three factors that should be examined when considering the construct of learning: What? How? Who? When?

1. What—the content or skill to be learned
2. How—the learning context
3. Who—the learning style of the learner
4. When—the period of time to learn the skill set

When all of these factors are congruent, the learner will be successful in the learning process. When they are not congruent, at best the leaner will experience some gains, but inconsistent with the overall goals of the learning task. To take charge of the learning process, it is important to learn lessons from the past and apply the lessons learned to the future.

To learn is to acquire knowledge or skill that is enduring and can be used over time to accomplish a task or reach a goal. Learning also may involve a change in attitude or behavior. Children learn to identify objects at an early age; teenagers may learn to improve study habits; and adults can learn to solve complex problems. This chapter addresses that branch of psychology directly concerned with how people learn.

LEARNING DEFINED

The ability to learn is one of the most outstanding abilities of human kind. Learning is a continuous process that occurs across a person's lifespan. To define learning, it is necessary to analyze what happens to the individual. For example, an individual's way of perceiving, thinking, feeling, and doing may change as a result of a learning experience. Thus, **learning** can be defined any enduring change in behavior based on experience. Thus learning includes enduring change in behavior and mental processes. If a behavior does not change, then learning did not take place. Next, learning is based on experience that is actualized or observed. We encounter learning and we learn through observation, which results in experience. The nature of learning will be different for each person depending on their prior experience, resources, cognitive sets, and readiness. In 1979 Säljö (1979) carried out a simple test and asked a number of adult students to define and describe the construct of learning. Their responses fell into five main categories:

1. ***Learning is Quantitative*** increase in knowledge. Learning is acquiring information or 'knowing a lot'.
2. Learning as memorizing. Learning is storing information that can be reproduced.
3. ***Learning as Acquiring*** facts, skills, and methods that can be retained and used as necessary.
4. ***Learning as making sense or abstracting*** meaning. Learning involves relating parts of the subject matter to each other and to the real world.
5. ***Learning as interpreting*** and understanding reality in a different way. Learning involves comprehending the world by reinterpreting knowledge. (quoted in Ramsden 1992: 26)

Overall, learning can be physical and overt, or it may involve complex intellectual or attitudinal changes which affect behavior in more subtle ways. In spite of numerous theories and contrasting views, psychologists generally agree on many common characteristics of learning.

CHARACTERISTICS OF LEARNING

Learning is Purposeful

Each student sees a learning situation from a different perspective. That perspective is unique to the individual whose past experiences affect readiness to learn and understanding of the requirements in the learning process. For example, an instructor may give two students the same assignment of learning certain research procedures. One student may learn quickly and be able to competently present the assigned material. The combination of an educational background and future goals may enable that student to realize

the need and value of learning the process. A second student's educational goals and experiences may only be to comply with the instructor's assignment, and may result in only minimum preparation. The responses differ because each student will respond to the instructor based on what he or she sees in the situation and knows cognitively based on their individual experiences and levels of motivation.

Each student will enter into a learning experience with specific intentions and goals. Their individual needs and attitudes may determine what they learn as much as what the instructor is trying to get them to learn. In the process of learning, the student's goals are of paramount significance. To be effective, instructors need to find ways to relate new learning to the student's goals.

Learning is a Result of Experience

Since learning is an individual process, the student can learn only from personal experiences; therefore, learning and knowledge cannot exist apart from a person. A person's knowledge is a result of experience, and no two people have had identical experiences. Even when observing the same event, two people react differently; they learn different things from it, according to the manner in which the situation affects their individual needs. Previous experience conditions a person to respond to some things and to ignore others.

All learning is by experience, but learning takes place in different forms and in varying degrees of richness and depth. For instance, some experiences involve the whole person while others may be based only on hearing and memory. If an experience challenges the students, requires involvement with feelings, thoughts, memory of past experiences, and physical activity, it is more effective than a learning experience in which all the students have to do is commit something to memory.

It seems clear enough that the learning of a physical skill requires actual experience in performing that skill. Mental habits are also learned through practice. If students are to use sound judgment and develop decision-making skills, they need learning experiences that involve knowledge of general principles and require the use of judgment in salving realistic problems.

Learning Is Multifaceted

Psychologists sometimes classify learning by types, such as verbal, conceptual, perceptual, motor, problem solving, and emotional. Other classifications refer to intellectual skills, cognitive strategies, and attitudinal changes, along with descriptive terms like surface or deep learning. However useful these divisions may be, they are somewhat artificial. For example, a class learning to apply the scientific method of problem solving may learn the method by trying to solve real problems. But in doing so, the class also engages in verbal learning and sensory perception at the same time. Each student approaches the task with preconceived ideas and feelings, and for many students, these ideas change as a result of experience. Therefore, the learning process may include verbal elements, conceptual elements, perceptual elements, emotional elements, and problem solving elements all taking place at once.

Learning is multifaceted in still another way. While learning the subject at hand, students may be learning other things as well. They may be developing attitudes about aviation-good or bad-depending on what they experience. Under a skillful instructor, they may learn self-reliance. The list is seemingly endless. This type of learning is sometimes referred to as incidental, but it may have a great impact on the total development of the student.

What will impact learning most, is the individual's learning style. That is the manner in which they learn information the best. Learning styles are directly related to use of neurological sense modalities which include visual, auditory, kinesthetic, intuitive, and incremental learning processes. After the neurological transfer of raw sensory data to the brain, all learning will form from perceptions which are directed to the brain by one or more of the five senses: sight, hearing, touch, smell, and taste. Perceiving involves more than the reception of stimuli from the five senses.

Perceptions result when a person gives meaning to sensations. People base their actions on the way they believe things to be. Real meaning comes only from within a person, even though the perceptions which evoke these meanings result from external stimuli. The meanings which are derived from perceptions are influenced not only by the individual's experience, but also by many other factors such as **physical health**, which provides individuals with the perceptual apparatus for sensing the world around them; A person's **basic need** is to maintain and enhance the organized self. The self is a person's past, present, and future combined; it is both physical and psychological.

Psychologists have also found that learning occurs most rapidly when information is received through more than one sensory modality. What is predicted is that when learning is occurring, 75% of the time, SIGHT is used in learning, 13% of the time, HEARING is used in learning, 6% of the time TOUCH, 3% of time SMELL, and 3% of the time, TASTE. Overall, learning differences certainly depend on how much information is retained through our senses. Once information is received through the senses, perception and processing of information is different for every person. Some people rely heavily on visual references while others depend more on auditory presentations. For example, visual students learn readily through reading and graphic displays, and auditory students have more success if they hear the subject matter described. Another difference is that some learn more easily when an idea is presented in a mathematical equation, while others may prefer a verbal explanation of the same idea. In addition, where hands-on activities are involved, students also learn by touch and physical manipulation of an object, which is sometimes called kinesthetic learning.

Although characteristics of learning and learning styles are related, there are distinctions between the two. **Learning style** is a concept that can play an important role in improving instruction and student success. It is concerned with student preferences and orientation at several levels

LEARNING STYLES

The key point is that all people learn differently based on the strength of their sensory modality. That is which sense organ dominates in the learning process. Some individuals process information quickly while others are slow and deliberate in processing information. Learning and rate of learning will be impacted by motivation, experience, and previous training affect learning style. There are many concepts that are used to describe learning styles. Some common examples include:

- **Right/left brain**
- **Holistic vs. Serialist**
- **Dependent vs. Independent**
- **Reflective vs. impulsive**
- **Collaborative vs. Individual**

Right and Left Brain

Theories abound concerning right- or left-brain dominance. In general, those with right-brain dominance are characterized as being spatially oriented, creative, intuitive, and emotional. As discussed in Chapter 3, those with left-brain dominance are more verbal, analytical, and objective. However, the separate hemispheres of the brain do not function independently. For example, the right hemisphere may recognize a face, while the left associates a name to go with the face.

Holistic Serialist Theory

Information processing theories contain several other useful classifications. As an example, in the holistic/serialist theory, the holist strategy is a top-down concept where individuals have a big picture, global perspective. These individuals seek overall comprehension, especially through the use of analogies. In contrast, the serialist student focuses more narrowly and needs well-defined, sequential steps where the overall picture is developed slowly, thoroughly, and logically. This is a bottom-up strategy.

Dependent and Independent

As indicated, personality also affects how individuals learn. Dependent individuals require a lot of guidance, direction, and external stimulation. These individuals tend to focus on the instructor. The more independent individuals require only a minimum amount of guidance and external stimulation. They are not overly concerned with how the lesson is presented.

Reflective and Impulsive

Individuals with a reflective-type personality may be described as tentative. They tend to be uncertain in problem-solving exercises. The opposite applies to impulsive individuals. Typically, they dive right in with enthusiasm and are prone to make quick, and sometimes faulty, decisions.

Collaborative and Individual

The social interaction concept contains further classifications of student learning styles. Like most of the other information on learning styles, these classifications are derived from research on tendencies that collaborative, sharing individuals who enjoy working with others, and competitive individuals who are grade conscious and feel they must do better than their peers. Participant individuals normally have a desire to learn and enjoy attending class, and avoidant individuals do not take part in class activities and have little interest in learning.

All five cognitive processes play a role in learning. We all enter a learning situation with some perceptions already formed and some judgments already made. We are more open to certain kinds of information and more inclined to organize that information in certain ways.

Learning is a relatively permanent change in behavior that is the result of experience. During the first half of the twentieth century, the school of thought known as behaviorism rose to dominate psychology and sought to explain the learning process. The three major types of learning described by behavioral psychology are classical conditioning, operant conditioning and observational learning. In addition humanism and behavioral perspectives of learning will be discussed in the next phase of this chapter.

LEARNING THEORY

A **learning theory** is an attempt to describe how people and animals learn; thereby helping us understands the inherently complex process of learning. **Learning theories** have two major goals. One goal is to provide the vocabulary and a conceptual framework for interpreting the phenomenon that is being observed, such as learning. The other goal is to provide research and practical strategies for explaining and interpreting the construct or phenomenon. Theories do not give solutions, but they direct the process of investigation toward variables that are crucial in finding solutions. Learning theory may be described as a body of principles advocated by psychologists, educators, and other research scientists to explain how people acquire skills, knowledge, and attitudes. Various branches of learning theory are used in formal training programs to improve and accelerate the learning process.

Over the years, many theories have attempted to explain how people learn. Even though psychologists and educators are not in complete agreement, most do agree that there are three main categories or philosophical frameworks under which learning theories fall: *Behaviorism*, *Cognitivism*, and *Constructivism*. However, other theoretical frameworks will be presented. Behaviorism focuses only on the objectively observable aspects of learning. Cognitive theories look beyond behavior to explain brain-based learning. And Constructivism views learning as a process in which the learner actively constructs or builds new ideas or concepts. Each of these theoretical perspectives will be discussed below.

BEHAVIORISM

Behaviorism is a worldview maintained by a community of psychologists that assumes a learner is essentially passive, responding to environmental stimuli that occur randomly or deliberately within an environment. Upon birth, a child starts off as a clean slate (i.e. *tabula rasa*) and behavior is shaped through positive reinforcement or negative reinforcement as predicted in the "12 Healthy Infant" postulation by J.B. Watson. Both positive reinforcement and negative reinforcement increase the probability that the antecedent behavior will happen again. In contrast, *punishment* (both positive and negative) decreases the likelihood that the antecedent behavior will happen again. Positive indicates the application of a stimulus; Negative indicates the withholding of a stimulus. Learning is therefore defined as a change in behavior in the learner. Early behavioral scientist performed their work with animals (e.g. Pavlov's dogs) and generalized to humans.

While other formidable originators and important contributors of behaviorism are noted: John B. Watson, Ivan Pavlov, B.F. Skinner, E. L. Thorndike (connectionism), Bandura, Tolman (moving toward cognitivism) are the most well known and quoted.

John B. Watson is generally given credit for creating and popularizing the term *behaviorism* with the publication of his seminal 1913 article "Psychology as the Behaviorist Views It." In the article, Watson argued that psychology had failed in its quest to become a natural science, largely due to a focus on consciousness and other unseen phenomena. Watson urged the careful scientific study of observable behavior. He and other early behaviorists believed that controlled laboratory studies were the most effective way to study learning. With this approach, manipulation of the learner's environment was the key to fostering development. This approach stands in contrast to techniques that placed the emphasis for learning in the mind of the learner. The 1913 article is often given credit for the founding of behaviorism, but it had a minor impact after its publication. His popular 1919 psychology text is probably more responsible for introducing behaviorist principles to a generation of future scholars of learning. In this way, Watson prepared psychologists and educators for the highly influential work of Skinner and other radical behaviorists in subsequent decades. In addition, his experiments were effective in the demonstration of behavioral principles discussed in his publications, for example, "Little Albert" and the "Twelve Health Kids."

The Little Albert Study

In 1920 Watson and an assistant, Rosalie Rayner, published one of the most famous research studies of the past century. Watson attempted to condition a severe emotional response in Little Albert, a nine-month-old child. Watson determined that white, furry objects, such as a rat, a rabbit, and cotton, did not produce any negative reaction in the baby. But by pairing together a neutral stimulus (white, furry animals and objects) with an unconditioned stimulus (a very loud noise) that elicited an unconditioned response (fear), Watson was able to create a new stimulus-response link: When Albert saw white, furry objects, this conditioned stimulus produced a conditioned response of fear. This study is generally presented as a seminal work that provided evidence that even complex behaviors, such as emotions, could be learned through manipulation of one's environment. As such, it became a standard bearer for behaviorist approaches to learning and is still widely cited in the early twenty-first century.

The "Dozen Healthy Infants"

To a behaviorist, manipulation of the environment is the critical mechanism for learning (e.g., the Little Albert study). To illustrate this point, Watson wrote in 1930, "Give me a dozen healthy infants, well-formed, and my own specified world to bring them up in and I'll guarantee to take any one at random and train him to become any type of specialist I might select–doctor, lawyer, artist–regardless of his talents, penchants, tendencies, abilities, vocations and race of

his ancestors" (p. 104). This quote routinely appears in introductory texts in education and psychology and is used to express the views of behaviorists that proposed that the environment influenced the development of behavioral patterns. This quote was also in response to other psychologists and educators who believed that heredity was solely responsible for human development and learning. In contrast to early behaviorists who held different views regarding behavior and learning.

Key Assumptions for Behaviorism

- Observable behavior rather than internal thought processes are the focus of study. In particular, learning is manifested by a change in behavior.
- The environment shapes one's behavior; what one learns is determined by the elements in the environment, not by the individual learner.
- The principles of contiguity (how close in time two events must be for a bond to be formed) and reinforcement (any means of increasing the likelihood that an event will be repeated) are central to explaining the learning process. (Merriam and Caffarella 1991)

Researchers like Edward L. Thorndike build upon these foundations and, in particular, developed a S-R (stimulus-response) theory of learning. He noted that that responses (or behaviors) were strengthened or weakened by the consequences of behavior. This notion was refined by Skinner and is perhaps better known as operant conditioning—reinforcing what you want people to do again; ignoring or punishing what you want people to stop doing.

EDWARD THRONDIKE'S LAW OF STIMULUS AND RESPONSE

Edward Thorndike proposed a theory that suggests that all learning consists primarily of the strengthening of the relationship between the stimulus and the response. In developing this theory, Thorndike proposed three laws: the Law of Effect, the Law of Exercise, and the Law of Readiness.

A law effect states that rewarding a behavior increases the probability that the behavior will be repeated, while punishing a behavior decreases the probability that the behavior will be repeated. Thus, the law suggests that the effect of a particular behavior, whether it is pleasing or displeasing, influences the chances of its recurrence: behaviors resulting in pleasant sensations tend to be repeated, while those associated with unpleasant sensations tend to be avoided

The Law of Exercise states that, in learning, the more frequently a stimulus and response are associated with each other, the more likely the particular response will follow the stimulus. The law implies that one learns by doing and one cannot learn a skill, for instance, by watching others. It is necessary to practice the skill, because by doing so the bond between stimulus and response is strengthened. In applying this to motor learning, the more often a given movement is repeated, the more firmly established it becomes. The performance of drills attempts to utilize this law.

The Law of Readiness states that learning is dependent upon the learner's readiness to act, which facilitates the strengthening of the bond or relationship between stimulus and response. Thus, a student musician who is highly motivated and eager to learn is more likely to be receptive to learning than one who is poorly motivated

Edward Thorndike's Puzzle Box Experiments

One of Thorndike's major contributions to the study of Psychology was his work with animals. Through long, extensive research with these animals, he constructed devices called "puzzle boxes," (see Figure X).

This work on animal intelligence used equipment that became both famous and controversial. Thorndike's setup of the puzzle boxes is an example of instrumental conditioning: An animal makes some response, and if the response is right, it is rewarded. If repeated, the response is learned. If the response

is not rewarded, it gradually disappears. The entire experiment was based on animals being placed into the puzzle boxes with the intent to escape by making contrived responses. Hence, the cat could only escape by making some specific response. Such escape procedures would be pulling a sting or pushing a button. The way his experiment worked was by placing a hungry cat into the box, then observing its behavior as it tried to escape and obtain some food. Consistently, Thorndike noticed that the cats obtained the food only by "trial-and-error." On repeated attempts, the mere trial-and-error behavior decreased and the cat would escape at a quicker rate. Thorndike studied several cats, and plotted the time it took for them to escape from the puzzle box on successive trials. These learning curves did not suddenly improve, but rather the amount of time the animal spent in the box gradually shortened. From this, the animal did not merely realize what it had to do to escape, but the connection between the animal's situation and the response that gradually freed him was stamped in. With these observations, Thorndike suggested that certain stimuli and responses become connected or dissociated from each other according to his law of effect. He stated, "When particular stimulus-response sequences are followed by reward, those responses tend to be repeated leading to learned behavior. Responses followed by pain tend to be "stamped out." or not repeated and eventually eliminated.

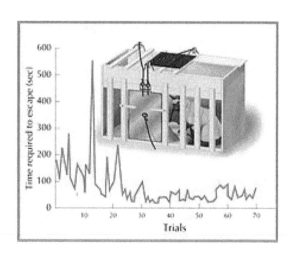

This evaluation led Thorndike to conclude that animals learn, solely, by trial and error, or reward and punishment. Thorndike used the cat's behavior in a puzzle box to describe what happens when all beings learn anything. All learning involves the formation of connections, and connections were strengthened according to the law of effect. Intelligence is the ability to form connections and humans are the most evolved animal because they form more connections than any other animal being. He continued his study with learning by writing his famous *Animal Intelligence*. In this he argued that we study animal behavior, not animal consciousness, for the ultimate purpose of controlling behavior. Edward Thorndike is mostly known for his development of the Law of Effect.

The Law of Effect

The Law of Effect was published by Edward Thorndike in 1905 and states that when the stimulus and response are associated, the response is likely to occur without the stimulus being present. It holds that responses that produce a satisfying or pleasant state of affairs in a particular situation are more likely to occur again in a similar situation. Conversely, responses that produce a discomforting, annoying or unpleasant effect are less likely to occur again in the situation. Thorndike emphasized the importance of the situation in eliciting a response; the cat would not go about making the lever-pressing movement if it was not in the puzzle box but was merely in a place where the response had never been reinforced. The situation involves not just the cat's location but also the stimuli it is exposed to, for example, the hunger and the desire for freedom. The cat recognized the inside of the box, the bars, and the lever and remembers what it needs to do to produce the correct response. This shows that learning and the law of effect are context-specific.

Thorndike's Law of Effect can be compared to *Darwin's theory of* natural selection in which successful organisms are more likely to prosper and survive to pass on their genes to the next generation, while the weaker, unsuccessful organisms are gradually replaced and "stamped out". It can be said that the environment selects the "fittest" behavior for a situation, stamping out any unsuccessful behaviors, in the same way it selects the "fittest" individuals of a species. In Thorndike's experiment, the cats that chose the appropriate (i.e. fittest) behavior and successfully escaped the puzzle box were more likely to chose this behavior and be successful again the next time they were placed in that situation.

Influence of Law of Effect

The law of effect provided a framework for psychologist B.F. Skinner almost half a century later on the principles of operant conditioning. Skinner would later use an updated version of Thorndike's puzzle box and contribute greater to our perception and understanding of the law of effect today and how it relates to operant conditioning, a learning process that is influenced by positive and or negative consequence, and ultimately will influences the rate at which a behavior is repeated in the presence of a stimulus.

Operant Conditioning

Under this view, it is believed that any type of *Classical* conditioning will form an association between two stimuli, thus forming a stimulus response relationship. *Operant* conditioning forms an association between a behavior and a consequence. It is called *response-stimulus* or RS conditioning because it forms an association between the animal's response [behavior] and the stimulus that follows [consequence])

There are four possible consequences to any behavior, which are:

1. Something Good can start or be presented;
2. Something Good can end or be taken away;
3. Something Bad can start or be presented;
4. Something Bad can end or be taken away.

In operant conditioning, in order for behavior change to occur, consequences have to be immediate, or clearly linked to the behavior. With verbal humans, we can explain the connection between the consequence and the behavior, even if they are separated in time. For example, you might tell a friend that you'll buy dinner for them since they helped you move, or a parent might explain that the child can't go to summer camp because of her bad grades. With very young children, humans who don't have verbal skills, and animals, you can't explain the connection between the consequence and the behavior; you must show them how consequences are related to behavioral responses. For the nonverbal persons, children learning language and behavior management, persons who are impulsive and animal, the consequence have to be immediate to assist with forming a cognitive link between consequences and behaviors. The next section of this chapter will discuss operant conditioning and famous experiments conducted to further enhance research knowledge about learning principles and processes.

Burrhus Frederic (B.F.) Skinner's Behavioral Operant Conditioning

B.F. Skinner is regarded as the father of *Operant Conditioning*. His work was based on Thorndike's law of effect. BF Skinner coined the term *operant conditioning*; which is defined as the process of changing of behavior by the use of reinforcement which is given immediately after the desired response. Skinner introduced a new term into the Law of Effect, namely Reinforcement. Reinforcement is responses from the environment that increases the probability of a behavior being repeated. Reinforcers can be either positive or negative. Behaviors that are reinforced tend to be strengthened and thus repeated; a behavior which is not reinforced tends to become weak and eventually cease to exist and can be weakened and eventually extinguished.

Skinner studied operant conditioning by conducting experiments using animals which he placed in a "*Skinner Box*" which was similar to Thorndike's puzzle box.

Based on this experiment, Skinner identified three types of responses or operants that can follow a desired or undesired behavior.

1. **Neutral operants**: responses from the environment that neither increase nor decrease the probability of a behavior being repeated.
2. **Reinforcers**: Responses from the environment that increase the probability of a behavior being repeated. Reinforcers can be either positive or negative.
3. **Punishers**: Response from the environment that decrease the likelihood of a behavior being repeated. Punishment weakens behavior.

Research Outcomes Learned from the Skinner Box

There are four primary lessons that were learned from Skinner's experiment with the hungry rat.

First and most importantly, he demonstrated that reinforcement strengthens behavior. Skinner demonstrated how positive reinforcement worked by placing a hungry rat in his Skinner box. The box contained a lever in the side and as the rat moved about the box it would accidentally knock the lever. Immediately a food pellet would drop into a container next to the lever. The rats quickly learned to go straight to the lever after a few times of being put in the box. The consequence of receiving food if they pressed the lever ensured that they would repeat the action again and again. The Second lesson learned was that Positive reinforcement strengthens a behavior by providing a consequence an individual finds rewarding. For example, if your teacher gives you $5 each time you complete your homework (i.e. a reward) you are more likely to repeat this behavior in the future, thus strengthening the behavior of completing your homework. Third, the removal of an unpleasant reinforcer can also strengthen behavior. This is known as Negative Reinforcement because it is the removal of an adverse stimulus which is 'rewarding' to the animal. Negative reinforcement strengthens behaviors because it stops or removes an unpleasant experience. For example, if you do not complete your homework you give your teacher $5. You will complete your homework to avoid paying $5, thus strengthening the behavior of completing your homework. Finally, Skinner showed how negative reinforcement worked by placing a rat in his Skinner box and then subjecting it to an unpleasant electric current which caused it some discomfort. As the rat moved about the box it would accidentally knock the lever. Immediately, the electric current would be switched off. The rats quickly learned to go straight to the lever after a few times of being put in the box. The consequence of escaping the electric current ensured that they would repeat the action again and again. It is also believed that Skinner taught the rats to avoid the electric current by turning on a light just before the electric current came on. The rats soon learned to press the lever when the light came on to avoid being shocked by an electric current. These two learned responses are known as Escape Learning and Avoidance Learning.

Unlike Reinforcement, which strengthens behaviors, Punishment is designed to weakens undesired behaviors. Punishment is defined as the opposite of reinforcement since it is designed to weaken or eliminate a response rather than increase it. Like reinforcement, punishment can work either by directly applying an unpleasant stimulus like a shock after a response or by removing a potentially rewarding stimulus, for instance, deducting someone's pocket money to punish undesirable behavior.

Note: It is not always easy to distinguish between punishment and negative reinforcement but the Table XX below provides a visual example of consequences and behaviors.

Table 10. Reinforcement and Punishment Table

	Reinforcement (behavior increases)	Punishment (behavior decreases)
Positive (something added)	Positive Reinforcement Something added increases behavior	Positive Punishment Something added decreases behavior
Negative (something removed)	Negative Reinforcement Something removed increases behavior	Negative Punishment Something removed decreases behavior

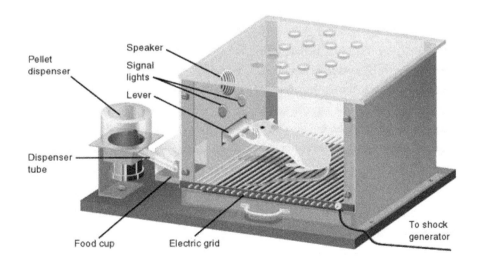

SKINNER BOX EXPERIMENT

Burhus Frederick Skinner's work was influenced by Pavlov's experiments and the ideas of John Watson, father of behaviorism. He especially was interested in stimulus-response reactions of humans to various situations, and experimented with pigeons and rats to develop his theories. He took the notion of conditioned reflexes developed by Ivan Pavlov and applied it to the study of behavior.

One of his best known inventions is the Skinner box (operant conditioning chamber). It contains one or more levers which an animal can press, one or more stimulus lights and one or more places in which reinforcers like food can be delivered.

In one of Skinners' experiments a starved rat was introduced into the box. When the lever was pressed by the rat a small pellet of food was dropped onto a tray. The rat soon learned that when he pressed the lever he would receive some food. In this experiment the lever pressing behavior is reinforced by food.

If pressing the lever is reinforced (the rat gets food) when a light is on but not when it is off, responses (pressing the lever) continue to be made in the light but seldom, if at all, in the dark. The rat has formed discrimination between light and dark. When one turns on the light, a response occurs, but that is not a Pavlovian conditioned reflex response.

In this experiment Skinner demonstrated the ideas of "operant conditioning" and "shaping behavior." Unlike Pavlov's "classical conditioning," where an existing behavior (salivating for food) is shaped by associating it with a new stimulus (ringing of a bell or a metronome), operant conditioning is the rewarding of an act that approaches a new desired behavior.

Skinner applied his findings about animals to human behavior and even developed teaching machines so students could learn bit by bit, uncovering answers for an immediate "reward." Computer-based self-instruction uses many of the principles of Skinner's technique.

Operant Conditioning Summary

Looking at **Skinner's** classic studies on rat, pigeons,' and other animal behavior we can identify some of the **major assumptions of behaviorists approach**. First, Psychology should be seen as a **science**, to be studied in a scientific manner. Skinner's study of behavior in rats was conducted under carefully controlled laboratory conditions. Second, Behaviorism is primarily concerned with **observable behavior**, as opposed to internal events like thinking and emotion. Note that Skinner did not say that the rats learned to press a lever because they wanted food. He instead concentrated on describing the easily observed behavior that the rats acquired. Third, the major influence on human behavior is **learning from our environment**. In the Skinner study, because food followed a particular behavior the rats learned to repeat that behavior, e.g. classical and operant conditioning and.

Fourth, there is **little difference between the learning that takes place in humans and that in other animals**. Therefore research (e.g. classical conditioning) can be carried out on animals (Pavlov's dogs) as well as on humans (Little Albert). Skinner proposed that the way humans learn behavior is much the same as the way the rats learned to press a lever.

CLASSICAL CONDITIONING (IVAN PAVLOV)

Several types of learning exist. The most basic form is *associative learning*, i.e., making a new association between events in the environment. There are two forms of associative learning: classical conditioning (made famous by Ivan Pavlov's experiments with dogs) and operant conditioning. The next section will discuss Ivan Pavlov's experiment with dogs.

Pavlov's Dogs

In the early twentieth century, Russian physiologist Ivan Pavlov did Nobel prize-winning work on digestion. While studying the role of saliva in dogs' digestive processes, he stumbled upon a phenomenon he labeled "psychic reflexes." While an accidental discovery, he had the foresight to see the importance of it. Pavlov's dogs, restrained in an experimental chamber, were presented with meat powder and they had their saliva collected via a surgically implanted tube in their saliva glands. Over time, he noticed that his dogs who begin salivation before the meat powder was even presented, whether it was by the presence of the handler or merely by a clicking noise produced by the device that distributed the meat powder.

Fascinated by this finding, Pavlov paired the meat powder with various stimuli such as the ringing of a bell. After the meat powder and bell (auditory stimulus) were presented together several times, the bell was used alone. Subsequently, Pavlov's dogs, began to salivate as predicted. They responded by salivating to the sound of the bell (without the food). The bell began as a neutral stimulus (i.e. the bell itself did not produce the dogs' salivation). However, by pairing the bell with the stimulus that did produce the salivation response, the bell was able to acquire the ability to trigger the salivation response. Pavlov therefore demonstrated how stimulus-response bonds (which some consider as the basic building blocks of learning) are formed. He dedicated much of the rest of his career further exploring this finding.

In technical terms, the meat powder is considered an unconditioned stimulus (UCS) and the dog's salivation is the unconditioned response (UCR). The bell is a neutral stimulus until the dog learns to associate the bell with food. Then the bell becomes a conditioned stimulus (CS) which produces the conditioned response (CR) of salivation after repeated pairings between the bell and food. Table XX presents a visual representation of this experiment.

Description of Classical Conditioning

Classical (or Respondent or Reflex) Conditioning (Pavlov and Watson)

- Naturally occurring stimulus and the reflex response are unconditioned—they occur together without training.
- Naturally occurring stimulus is known as the unconditioned stimulus (UCS) and the naturally occurring response is known as the unconditioned response (UCR.)
- After training (paring the UCS with the new stimulus), the new stimulus elicits the reflex response.
- The new stimulus is known as the conditioned stimulus (CS) and the resulting response is known as the conditioned response (CR)
- Instrumental Conditioning (Thorndike)
- Conditioning of known voluntary behaviors to new stimuli
- Discovery learning

In summary, Operant conditioning is reinforcement of the behavior by a reward or a punishment. The theory of operant conditioning was developed by Skinner and is known as Radical Behaviorism. The word 'operant' refers to the way in which behavior 'operates on the environment'. Briefly, a behavior may result either in reinforcement, which increases the likelihood of the behavior recurring, or punishment, which decreases the likelihood of the behavior recurring. It is important to note that, a punishment is not considered to be applicable if it does not result in the reduction of the behavior, and so the terms punishment and reinforcement are determined as a result of the actions. Within this framework, behaviorists are particularly interested in measurable changes in behavior.

CONSTRUCTIVIST LEARNING THEORY

The learning theories of Jean Piaget, Jerome Bruner, Lev Vygotsky and John Dewey serve as the foundation of constructivist learning theory. Constructivism is a theory based on observation and scientific study about how people learn. Constructivism views learning as a process in which the learner actively constructs or builds new ideas or concepts based upon current and past knowledge or experience. "Learning involves constructing one's own knowledge from one's own experiences." It says that people construct their own understanding and knowledge of the world, through experiencing things and reflecting on those experiences. When we encounter something new, we have to reconcile it with our previous ideas and experience, maybe changing what we believe, or maybe discarding the new information as irrelevant. To do this, we must ask questions, explore, and assess what we know. There are, however, two major forms of the constructivist perspective. These two types of constructivism are *cognitive constructivism* and *social constructivism.* These two constructivist views share many common perspectives about teaching and learning, however there are differences as well.

Cognitive Constructivism

Cognitive constructivism is based on the work of Jean Piaget. His theory has two major parts: an ages and stages component that predicts what children can and cannot understand at different ages, and a theory of development that describes how learners develop cognitive abilities. Piaget's theory of cognitive development proposes that humans cannot be **given** information, in which they immediately understand and use. Instead, learners must **construct** their own knowledge. They build their knowledge through experience. Experiences enable them to create *schemas* or mental models of the world. These schemas are changed, enlarged, and made more sophisticated through two complimentary processes: assimilation and accommodation.

Cognitive constructivism is based on two different senses of construction. First, on the idea that people learn by actively constructing new knowledge, not by having information poured into their heads. Moreover, constructivism asserts that people learn with particular effectiveness when they are engaged

Table 11. Pairing of CS and UCS in Pavlov's Dog Experiment

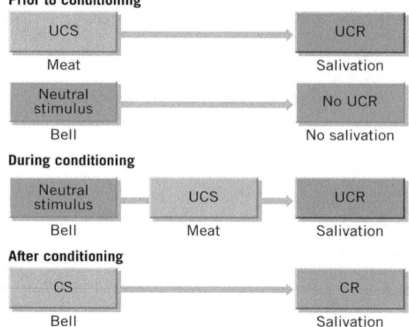

in constructing personally meaningful artifacts (e.g. computer programs, animations). There are several branches of cognitive theory. Two of the major theories may broadly be classified as the *Information Processing Model* and the *Social Interaction Model*.

Information Processing Model

The Information Processing Model purports that the student's brain has internal structures which select and process incoming material, store and retrieve it, use it to produce behavior, and receive and process feedback on the results. These abilities involves a number of cognitive processes, including executive functions of recognizing expectancies, planning and monitoring performance, encoding and chunking information, and producing internal and external responses. This involves a number of cognitive processes, including executive functions of recognizing expectancies, planning and monitoring performance, encoding and chunking information, and producing internal and external responses

Social Constructivism

Lev Vygotsky, a Russian psychologist and philosopher in the 1930's, is most often associated with the social constructivist theory. He emphasizes the influences of cultural and social contexts in learning and supports a discovery model of learning. This type of model places the teacher in an active role while the students' mental abilities develop naturally through various paths of discovery. Social constructivists posit that knowledge is constructed when individuals engage socially in talk and activity about shared problems or tasks. Learning is seen as the process by which individuals are introduced to a culture by more skilled members". Social constructivism emphasizes the importance of culture and context in understanding what occurs in society and constructing knowledge based on this understanding (Derry, 1999; McMahon, 1997). This perspective is closely associated with many contemporary theories, most notably the developmental theories of Vygotsky and

Bruner, and Bandura's social cognitive theory (Shunk, 2000).

Assumptions of Social Constructivism

Social constructivism is based on specific assumptions about reality, knowledge, and learning. To understand and apply models of instruction that are rooted in the perspectives of social constructivists, it is important to know the premises that underlie them.

Reality: Social constructivists believe that reality is constructed through human activity. Members of a society together invent the properties of the world (Kukla, 2000). For the social constructivist, reality cannot be discovered: it does not exist prior to its social invention.

Knowledge: To social constructivists, knowledge is also a human product, and is socially and culturally constructed (Ernest, 1999; Gredler, 1997; Prat & Floden, 1994). Individuals create meaning through their interactions with each other and with the environment they live in.

Learning: Social constructivists view learning as a social process. It does not take place only within an individual, nor is it a passive development of behaviors that are shaped by external forces (McMahon, 1997). Meaningful learning occurs when individuals are engaged in social activities.

Social Interaction Model

The social interaction theories gained prominence in the 1980s. They stress that learning and subsequent changes in behavior take place as a result of interaction between the student and the environment. Behavior is modeled either by people or symbolically. Cultural influences, peer pressure, group dynamics, and film and television are some of the significant factors. Thus, the social environment to which the student is exposed demonstrates or models behaviors, and the student cognitively processes the observed behaviors and consequences. The cognitive processes include attention, retention, motor responses, and motivation. Techniques for learning include direct modeling and verbal instruction. Behavior, personal factors, and environmental events all work together to produce learning.

Both models of the cognitive theory have common principles. For example, they both acknowledge the importance of reinforcing behavior and measuring changes. Positive reinforcement is important, particularly with cognitive concepts such as knowledge and understanding. The need to evaluate and measure behavior remains because it is the only way to get a clue about what the student understands. Evaluation is often limited to the kinds of knowledge or behavior that can be measured by a paper-and-pencil exam or a performance test. Psychologists agree that measuring student knowledge, performance, and behavior is necessary.

Social Learning Theory

The social learning theory proposed by Albert Bandura has become perhaps the most influential theory of learning and development. While rooted in many of the basic concepts of traditional learning theory, Bandura believed that direct reinforcement could not account for all types of learning. His theory added a social element, arguing that people can learn new information and behaviors by watching other people. Known as observational learning (or modeling), this type of learning can be used to explain a wide variety of behaviors.

There are three core concepts at the heart of social learning theory. First is the idea that people can learn through observation. Next is the idea that internal mental states are an essential part of this process. Finally, this theory recognizes that just because something has been learned, it does not mean that it will result in a change in behavior.

Behaviors that can be learned through modeling

Many behaviors can be **learned**, at least **partly**, **through** modeling. Examples that can be cited are, individuals can watch parents **read**, individuals can watch the demonstrations of **mathematics** problems,

or seen someone acting bravely and a fearful situation. **Aggression** can be learned through models. Much research indicates that children become more aggressive when they observed aggressive or violent models. Moral thinking and **moral behavior** are influenced by observation and modeling. This includes **moral judgments** regarding right and wrong which can in part, develop through modeling.

Effects of modeling on behavior:

- Modeling teaches **new** behaviors.
- Modeling influences the **frequency** of previously learned behaviors.
- Modeling may **encourage** previously **forbidden** behaviors.
- Modeling increases the **frequency** of **similar** behaviors. For example a student might see a friend excel in basketball and he tries to excel in football because he is not tall enough for basketball.

Self Efficacy and Learning

People are **more likely** to engage in certain behaviors when they believe they are **capable** of executing those behaviors **successfully**. This means that they will have high self-efficacy. Self-efficacy is the one's confidence towards learning. Perceived self-efficacy is defined as people's beliefs about their capabilities to produce designated levels of performance that exercise influence over events that affect their lives. Self-efficacy beliefs determine how people feel, think, motivate themselves and behave. Such beliefs produce these diverse effects through four major processes. They include cognitive, motivational, affective and selection processes.

Persons with a *high self-efficacy* will complete tasks with a greater motivations and belief in skill. Their focus and approach to difficult tasks is to master rather than avoid through procrastination. They set themselves challenging goals and maintain strong commitment to them. They heighten and sustain their efforts in the face of failure. They quickly recover their sense of efficacy after failures or setbacks. They attribute failure to insufficient effort or deficient knowledge and skills which are acquirable. They approach threatening situations with assurance that they can exercise control over them. Such an efficacious outlook produces personal accomplishments, reduces stress and lowers vulnerability to depression.

In contrast, people with *low self-efficacy* will doubt their capabilities and avoid tasks which they view as difficult. They have low aspirations and weak commitment to the goals they choose to pursue. When faced with difficult tasks, they dwell on their personal deficiencies, on the obstacles they will encounter, and all kinds of adverse outcomes rather than concentrate on how to perform successfully. They are slow to recover their sense of efficacy following failure or setbacks. Because they view insufficient performance as deficient aptitude it does not require much failure for them to lose faith in their capabilities. They fall easy victim to stress and depression.

Sources of Self-Efficacy

People's beliefs about their efficacy can be developed by four main sources of influence. The most effective way of creating a strong sense of efficacy is through mastery experiences. Successes build a robust belief in one's personal efficacy and self-esteem. Failures undermine and devalue efficacy and self-esteem, especially if failures occur before a sense of efficacy is firmly established. This is seen today in people struggling to survive a 21st century recession that is characterized by high rates of job loss, high rates of foreclosures, and high rates in decline of income. Person's who maintained hopes based on external rewards may show higher levels of low efficacy and esteem due to these losses. Persons, who maintain self-efficacy and esteem independent of the type of job, house, and income acquired will experience resilient efficacy. There are strategies to build a positive self-efficacy.

First, learning to overcome obstacles as described above builds self efficacy. If people experience only easy successes they come to expect quick results and are easily discouraged by failure. A resilient sense of efficacy requires experience in overcoming obstacles through perseverant effort. Some setbacks and difficulties in human pursuits serve a useful purpose in teaching that success usually requires sustained effort. After people become convinced they have what it takes to succeed, they persevere in the face of adversity and quickly rebound from setbacks. By having a persevering focus during the most difficult times, people will see themselves emerging as a strong self.

Second, observing vicariously those deemed as social models succeed is another way to build self-efficacy and esteem. The model will need to similar to the observer for an impact to be made. The greater the assumed similarity the more persuasive is the models' successes and failures. If people see the models as very different from themselves their perceived self-efficacy is not influenced much by the models' behavior and the results its produces.

People learn through observing others' behavior, attitudes, and outcomes of those behaviors. *Observational learning* is also known as imitation or modeling. In this process, learning occurs when individuals observes and imitate others' behavior. There are four component processes influenced by the observer's behavior following exposure to models. These components include: *attention; retention; motor reproduction; and motivation* (Bandura, 1977: pp.24-28). Social learning theory explains human behavior in terms of continuous reciprocal interaction between cognitive, behavioral, and environmental influences. The theory has often been called a bridge between behaviorist and cognitive learning theories because it encompasses attention, memory, and motivation.

Necessary conditions for effective modeling:

1. Attention — various factors increase or decrease the amount of attention paid. Includes distinctiveness, affective valence, prevalence, complexity, functional value. One's characteristics (e.g. sensory capacities, arousal level, perceptual set, past reinforcement) affect attention. Attention is the first component of observational learning. Individuals cannot learn much by observation

unless they perceive and attend to the significant features of the modeled behavior. For example, children must attend to what the aggressor is doing and saying in order to reproduce the model's behavior (Allen & Santrock,1993: p.139) In the Bobo doll experiment, the children witnessed the Bobo doll being verbally and/or physically abused by live models and filmed models.

2. Retention — remembering what you paid attention to. Includes symbolic coding, mental images, cognitive organization, symbolic rehearsal, motor rehearsal Retention is the next component. In order to reproduce the modeled behavior, the individuals must code the information into long-term memory. Therefore, the information will be retrieval. For example, a simple verbal description of what the model performed would be a known as retention (Allen & Santrock, 1993: p139). Memory is an important cognitive process that helps the observer code and retrieve information. In the Bobo doll experiment, the children imitated the aggression they witnessed in the video. They aggressively hit the Bobo doll because it was coded and store in their memory.

3. Reproduction — reproducing the image. Including physical capabilities, and self-observation of reproduction. Motor reproduction is another process in observational learning. The observer must be able to reproduce the model's behavior. The observer must learn and posses the physical capabilities of the modeled behavior. An example of motor reproduction would to be able to learn how to ski or ride a bike. Once a behavior is learned through attention and retention, the observer must possess the physically capabilities to produce the aggressive act. The children had the physically capabilities of hitting and pummeling the doll to the ground.

4. Motivation — having a good reason to imitate. Includes motives such as past (i.e. traditional behaviorism), promised (imagined incentives) and vicarious (seeing and recalling the reinforced model). The final process in observational learning is motivation or reinforcements. In this

process, the observer expects to receive positive reinforcements for the modeled behavior. In the Bobo doll experiment, the children witnessed the adults being rewarded for their aggression. Therefore, they performed the same act to achieve the rewards. For example, most children witnessed violence on television being rewarded by the media. Historically, bank robbers were heroes. Many people were highly upset about the death of Bonnie and Clyde. When individuals, especially children witness this type of media, they attend, code, retrieve, posses the motor capabilities and perform the modeled behavior because of the positive reinforcement determined by the media (Bootzin, Bowers, Crocker, 1991: 201-202). The Bobo doll experiment helped Bandura to theorized that "As children continue to age, the experience still effected their personality, turning them into violent adults http://www.mhcollegeco/socscienc/comm/bandur-s.mhtml

Observational Learning

In his famous "Bobo doll" studies, Bandura demonstrated that children learn and imitate behaviors they have observed in other people. The children in Bandura's studies observed an adult acting violently toward a Bobo doll. When the children were later allowed to play in a room with the Bobo doll, they began to imitate the aggressive actions they had previously observed.

Environmental experiences is a second influence of the social learning of violence in children. Albert Bandura reported that individuals that live in high crime rates areas are more likely to act violently than those who dwell in low-crime areas (Bandura, 1976: p.207). This assumption is similar to Shaw and McKay's theory of social disorganization. They believed that a neighborhood surrounded by culture conflict, decay and insufficient social organizations was a major cause of criminality (Bartollas, 1990: pp.145).

Albert Bandura believed *television* was a source of behavior modeling. Today, films and television shows illustrate violence graphically. Violence is often expressed as an acceptable behavior, especially for heroes who have never be punished. Since aggression is a prominent feature of many shows, children who have a high degree of exposure to the media may exhibit a relatively high incidence of hostility themselves in imitation of the aggression they have witnessed (Berkowitz, 1962: pp. 247). For example, David Phillips reported homicide rates increase tremendously after a heavy weight championship fight (Cloward & Ohlin, 1960). There have been a number of deaths linked to violence on television. For example, John Hinckley attempted to assassinate President Ronald Reagan after he watched the movie "Taxi Driver" fifteen times. In the movie "Born Innocent," a girl was raped with a bottle by four other girls. In 1974, a similar incident happened to a California's girl. The girls who raped her testified in court that they had witness the same scene in "Born Innocent." In addition, Ronald Zamora brutally killed an elderly woman and pleaded the insanity defense. His attorney argued that Zamora's was addicted to the violence on television. As a result, he could not differentiate between reality and fantasy. However, Zamora was founded guilty because the jury did not believe his defense (Siegel, 1992: p.172).

Contemporary Views

Today, many social learning theorists have indicated that crime is a product of learning the values and aggressive behaviors linked with criminality. Sutherland developed the differential association theory that suggests that individuals learn criminal behavior while in their adolescence from family members and peers (Sutherland, 1939, pp25). In "Deviant Behavior: A Social Learning Approach," Akers believed individuals learned aggressive acts through operant condition (Akers, 1977). In this process, the aggression was acquired after through direct conditioning and modeling others' actions. He believed that positive rewards and the avoidance of punishment reinforced aggression (Akers, 1977). William Benson found that adolescents that watched

excessive amounts of television during their childhood became adult criminals. They committed crimes, such as rape and assault, "at a rate 49% higher than teenage boys who had watched below average quantities of television violence (Centerwall, 1993: pp.70-71) Also, Bandura's theory has made the public and political affairs realize that violence does cause aggression in children. He has spoken at a number of political conferences concerning the Bobo doll experiment and the effects television has on children. Several political candidates have indicated that violence on television does cause aggression. President Clinton has implemented policies that would deter violence on television.

Criticisms

The social learning theory advocates that individuals, especially children, imitate or copy modeled behavior from personally observing others, the environment, and the mass media. Biological theorists argue that the social learning theory completely ignores individual's biological state. Also, they state that the social learning theory rejects the differences of individuals due to genetic, brain, and learning differences (Jeffery, 1985: p.238). For example, if a person witnessed a hanging or a violent murder, he or she might respond in many different ways. "Biological theorists believed that the responses would be normal and come from the autonomic nervous system. In the autonomic nervous system, the heart rate, increase blood pressure, nausea, and fainting would be normal symptoms of the responses that individuals might expressed in this particular situation. Therefore, the symptoms and behavior are not learned, but partially inherited. In addition, the social learning theory rejects the classical and operant conditioning processes. The biological preparedness of the individual to learn as well as the role of the brain in processing information from the social environment, are critical to learning theory, but they are ignored by the social learning theory. Social reinforcement is conditioned reinforcement based on the relationship of the conditioned stimulus to an unconditioned stimulus" (Jeffery, 1985: p.239).

BOBO DOLL EXPERIMENT

Albert Bandura is most famous for the Bobo doll experiment. Albert Bandura believed that aggression must explain three aspects: First, how aggressive patterns of behavior are developed; second, what provokes people to behave aggressively, and third, what determines whether they are going to continue to resort to an aggressive behavior pattern on future occasions (Evans, 1989: p.22). In this experiment, he had children witness a model aggressively attacking a plastic clown called the Bobo doll. There, children would watch a video where a model would aggressively hit a doll and " '...the model pummels it on the head with a mallet, hurls it down, sits on it and punches it on the nose repeatedly, kick it across the room, flings it in the air, and bombards it with balls...'(Bandura, 1973: p.72). After the video, the children were placed in a room with attractive toys, but they could not touch them. The process of retention had occurred. Therefore, the children became angry and frustrated. Then the children were led to another room where there were identical toys used in the Bobo video. The motivation phase was in occurrence. Bandura and many other researchers founded that 88% of the children imitated the aggressive behavior. Eight months later, 40% of the same children reproduce the violent behavior observed in the Bobo doll experiment.

In the Bobo doll experiment, critics have argued that the children were manipulated into responded to the aggressive movie. The children were teased and became frustrated because they could not touch the toys. Many critics believed the experiment conducted was unethical and morally wrong because the children were trained to be aggressive. "How many more of the experiments finding a link between violence on television and aggressive behavior have ethical problems? It is not surprising that the children had long-term implications because of the methods imposed in this experiment"(Worthman and Loftus, p.45)

There have been many debates over whether or not violence on television causes aggressive behavior in children. Many studies have indicated that television does not lead to aggressive behavior. For instances, psychologists have found that some cartoons are very violent and cause children to illustrate aggressive behavior. However, the general public believes that children view cartoons such as Elmer Fudd shooting the rabbit as funny and humorous. It is the parents' responsibility to inform their children that the cartoons are not real.

Cooke believed that individuals tend to support the theory that television violence causes aggression because the public needs to justify the aggression they see in others. He also believed television was a form of education and positive role models. "If violence in television causes people to be more aggressive, than shouldn't the good-hearted qualities in television cause its audience to be kinder to others (Cooke,1993, p.L19)?" Therefore, television can serve as deterrence if individuals focus on the positive qualities. Despite these criticisms, Albert Bandura's Social Learning Theory has maintained an important place in the study of aggression and criminal behavior. In order to control aggression, he believed family members and the mass media should provide positive role models for their children and the general public (Bandura, 1976).

Julian Rotter on Social Learning Theory

Julian B. Rotter has been cited as one of the 100 most eminent psychologists of the 20th century. Haggbloom et al. (2002) found that Rotter was 18th in frequency of citations in journal articles and 64th in overall eminence. The main idea in Julian Rotter's social learning theory is that personality represents an interaction of the individual with his or her environment. One cannot speak of a personality, internal to the individual, that is independent of the environment. Neither can one focus on behavior as being an automatic response to an objective set of environmental stimuli. Rather, to understand behavior, one must take both the individual (i.e., his or her life history of learning and experiences) and the environment (i.e., those stimuli that the person is aware of and responding to) into account. Rotter has four main components to his social learning theory model predicting behavior. These are behavior potential, expectancy, reinforcement value, and the psychological situation.

Behavior Potential. Behavior potential is the likelihood of engaging in a particular behavior in a specific situation. In other words, what is the probability that the person will exhibit a particular behavior in a situation? In any given situation, there are multiple behaviors one can engage in. For each possible behavior, there is a behavior potential. The individual will exhibit whichever behavior has the highest potential.

Expectancy. Expectancy is the subjective probability that a given behavior will lead to a particular outcome, or reinforcer. How likely is it that the behavior will lead to the outcome? Having "high" or "strong" expectancies means the individual is confident the behavior will result in the outcome. Having low expectancies means the individual believes it is unlikely that his or her behavior will result in reinforcement. If the outcomes are equally desirable, we will engage in the behavior that has the greatest likelihood of paying off (i.e., has the highest expectancy). Expectancies are formed based on past experience. The more often a behavior has led to reinforcement in the past, the stronger the person's expectancy that the behavior will achieve that outcome now.

It is important to note that expectancy is a **subjective** probability, because one common source of pathology is irrational expectancies. There may be no relationship whatsoever between the person's subjective assessment of how likely a reinforcement will be and the actual, objective probability of the reinforcer's occurring. People can either over- or underestimate this likelihood, and both distortions can potentially be problematic.

Reinforcement Value. Reinforcement is another name for the outcomes of our behavior. Reinforcement value refers to the desirability of these outcomes. Things we want to happen, that we are attracted to, have a high reinforcement value. Things we don't want to happen, that we wish to avoid, have a low reinforcement value. If the likelihood of achieving reinforcement is the same, we will exhibit the behavior with the greatest reinforcement value (i.e., the one directed toward the outcome we prefer most).

Psychological Situation. Although the psychological situation does not figure directly into Rotter's formula for predicting behavior, Rotter believes it is always important to keep in mind that different people interpret the same situation differently. Again, it is people's subjective interpretation of the environment, rather than an objective array of stimuli, that is meaningful to them and that determines how they behave.

A strength of Rotter's social learning theory is that it explicitly blends specific and general constructs, offering the benefits of each. In social learning theory, all general constructs have a specific counterpart. For every situationally specific expectancy there is a cross-situational **generalized expectancy**. Social learning theory blends generality and specificity to enable psychologists to measure variables and to make a large number of accurate predictions from these variables.

"Locus of Control." For many people, their only exposure to the ideas of Julian B. Rotter is his concept of generalized expectancies for control of reinforcement, more commonly known as locus of control. Locus of control refers to people's very general, cross-situational beliefs about what determines whether or not they get reinforced in life. People can be classified along a continuum from very internal to very external.

People with a strong internal locus of control believe that the responsibility for whether or not they get reinforced ultimately lies with themselves. Internals believe that success or failure is due to their own efforts. In contrast, externals believe that the reinforcers in life are controlled by luck, chance, or powerful others. Therefore, they see little impact of their own efforts on the amount of reinforcement they receive.

Rotter has written extensively on problems with people's interpretations of the locus of control concept. First, he has warned people that locus of control is not a typology. It is not an either/or proposition. Second, because locus of control is a generalized expectancy it will predict people's behavior across situations. However, there may be some specific situations where people, for example, who are generally external behave like internals. That is because their learning history has shown them that they have control over the reinforcement they receive in certain situations, although overall they perceive little control over what happens to them. Again, one can see the importance of conceiving of personality as the **interaction** of the person and the environment.

Locus of Control of Reinforcement

Julian Rotter gave the construct the name Locus of Control of Reinforcement. In giving it this name, Rotter was bridging behavioral and cognitive psychology. Rotter's view was that behavior was largely guided by "reinforcements" (rewards and punishments) and that through contingencies such as rewards and punishments, individuals come to hold beliefs about what causes their actions. These beliefs, in turn, guide what kinds of attitudes and behaviors people maintain as a part of their personality expression. This understanding of Locus of Control is consistent, for example, with Philip Zimbardo (a famous psychologist): A locus of control orientation is a belief about whether the outcomes of our actions are contingent on what we do (internal control orientation) or on events outside our personal control (external control orientation)." (Zimbardo, 1985, p. 275).

Thus, locus of control is conceptualized as referring to a unidimensional continuum, ranging from *external* to *internal*:

External Locus of Control	Internal Locus of Control
Individual believes that his/her behavior is guided by fate, luck, or other external circumstances	Individual believes that his/her behavior is guided by his/her personal decisions and efforts.

Humanistic Perspective to learning

In this orientation the basic concern is for human growth. The work of Abraham Maslow and Carl Rogers as expressions of this approach. A great deal of the theoretical writing about adult education in the 1970s and 1980s drew on humanistic psychology. In this orientation the basic concern is for the human potential for growth. Perhaps the most persuasive exploration of a humanistic orientation to learning came from **Carl Rogers**. His passion for education that engaged with the whole person and with their experiences; for learning that combines the logical and intuitive, the intellect and feelings; found a ready audience. 'When we learn in that way', he said, 'we are *whole*, utilizing all our masculine and feminine capacities' (1983 20).

Benjamin Bloom (1956) identified three domains of educational activities and purported that there is more than one type of learning. These domains are known as *Bloom's Taxonomy of Learning Domains*. In this taxonomy, he explains that learning involves Cognition, Affective, and Psychomotor Abilities. The cognitive domain involves knowledge and the development of intellectual skills. This includes the recall or recognition of specific facts, procedural patterns, and concepts that serve in the development of intellectual abilities and skills. The Affective Domain defines the manner in which we deal with things emotionally, such as feelings, values, appreciation, enthusiasms, motivations, and attitudes. The psychomotor domain (Simpson, 1972) includes physical movement, coordination, and use of the motor-skill areas. Development of these skills requires practice and is measured in terms of speed, precision, distance, procedures, or techniques in execution. These domains or categories are employed by Trainers that refer to these three categories as KSA (Knowledge, Skills, and Attitude). This taxonomy of learning behaviors can be thought of as "the goals of the learning process." That is, after a learning episode, the learner should have acquired new skills, knowledge, and/or attitudes.

Bloom's taxonomy is easily understood and is probably the most widely applied one in use today.

Perhaps the best known example of learning principles is Abraham Maslow's hierarchy of motivation. Unlike others researchers in the earlier days of psychology, Abraham Maslow's based his theory of *human needs* on creative people who used all their talents, potential, and capabilities (Bootzin, Loftus, Zajonc, Hall, 1983). His methodology differed from most other psychological researchers at the time in that these researchers mainly observed mentally unhealthy people. However, Maslow based his theoretical premise on normal healthy individuals. He addressed the humanity in its purist state. Maslow (1970) felt that *human needs* were arranged in a hierarchical order that could be divided into two major groups: basic needs and metaneeds (higher order needs):

- **Basic Needs** are physiological, such as food, water, and sleep; and psychological, such as affection, security, and self-esteem. These basic needs are also called "deficiency needs" because

if they are not met by an individual, then that person will strive to make up the deficiency.
- **Metaneeds** or *being needs* (growth needs). These include justice, goodness, beauty, order, unity, etc. Basic needs normally take priority over these meta needs. For example, a person who lacks food or water will not normally attend to justice or beauty needs.

These needs are normally listed in a hierarchical order in the form of a pyramid to show that the basic needs (bottom ones) must be met before the higher order needs, see Figure 6 below.

Figure 6

At the lowest level are physiological needs, at the highest self actualization. Only when the lower needs are met is it possible to fully move on to the next level. A motive at the lower level is always stronger than those at higher levels. Tennant (1997) summarizes these as follows:

- **Level one:** *Physiological needs* such as hunger, thirst, sex, sleep, relaxation and bodily integrity must be satisfied before the next level comes into play.

- **Level two**: *Safety needs* call for a predictable and orderly world. If these are not satisfied people will look to organize their worlds to provide for the greatest degree of safety and security. If satisfied, people will come under the force of level three.

- **Level three**: *Love and belonginess needs* cause people to seek warm and friendly relationships.

- **Level four**: *Self-esteem needs* involve the desire for strength, achievement, adequacy, mastery and competence. They also involve confidence, independence, reputation and prestige.

- **Level five:** *Self-actualization* is the full use and expression of talents, capacities and potentialities.

Self actualizers are able to submit to social regulation without losing their own integrity or personal independence; that is they may follow a social norm without their horizons being bounded in the sense that they fail to see or consider other possibilities. They may on occasion transcend the socially prescribed ways of acting. Achieving this level may mean developing to the full stature of which they are capable, (Tennant 1997: 13). It is also a point in development that the individual seeks to reproduce themselves through their own abilities. So they seek to give back to their communities in acts of altruism.

Learning can, thus, be seen as a form of self-actualization, it contributes to psychological health (Sahakian 1984 in Merriam and Caffarella 1991: 133). Yet while self actualization may be seen as the primary goal, other goals (linked to the other stages) are also around. These include a sense of accomplishment and the controlling of impulses (Maslow 1970: 439).

Characteristics of Self-Actualized People

- Have better perceptions of reality and are comfortable with it.
- Accept themselves and their own natures.
- Lack of artificiality.
- They focus on problems outside themselves and are concerned with basic issues and eternal questions.
- They like privacy and tend to be detached.
- Rely on and their own development and continued growth.
- Appreciate the basic pleasures of life (e.g. do not take blessings for granted).
- Have a deep feeling of kinship with others.
- Are deeply democratic and are not really aware of differences.
- Have strong ethical and moral standards.
- Are original, inventive, less constricted and fresher than others

BIOLOGICAL THEORIES OF LEARNING

Brain Based Learning–Brain-based learning is based on the structure and function of the brain ("Brain-based learning," 2008). Learning will occur as long as the brain is not prohibited from fulfilling its normal processes.

Physicians began observing patients with severe head injuries and noticed deficits in language, memory, personality, and behavior. Mark Dax in 1836 presented a paper suggesting that lesions on the left side of the brain were associated with *"aphasia," a language disorder.* Paul Broca (1824 – 1880) discovered that person with brain injuries in the front section of the left hemisphere were often unable to speak fluently but could comprehend language, (i.e., expressive and receptive language).

Later, Carl Wernicke (1848—1904): showed that damage to an area a few centimeters behind the Broca could lead to another form of aphasia that is difficulty with receptive language. Receptive difficulty deals with a person's ability to understand or comprehend spoken language. Today neuroscientist believe that psychological functions are no longer localized to certain areas of the brain, but are intertwined throughout the brain by neurological circuitry that creates emotions or thoughts of which contribute to ones total experience. This is further described when discussing right and left brain lateralization.

Left Brain vs. Right Brain Function in Learning

The notion that some people are left-brained (analytical and critical thinkers) versus right brain (intuitive and creative) is a continuous viewpoint in psychology today. Dr. Paul Broca in the 1860's and Dr. Carl Wernicke discovered areas in the left hemisphere of the brain that were used for language. Robert Louis Stevenson's in 1886 discussed the uncanny Case of Dr. Jekyll and Mr. Hyde. This article explores left brain vs. right brain function in learning theories.

CHAPTER 5 SUMMARY

LEARNING

Learning is any process that results in a change in how the organism responds to the environment.

CLASSICAL CONDITIONING

- Unconditioned stimuli: Produces a response automatically when an organism is exposed to this stimulus.
- Unconditioned response: The response of the organism to the unconditioned stimulus (UCS)
- Conditioned stimuli: A stimulus that, when associated with the UCS, produces the UCR.
- Conditioned response: A response that is the same as the UCR, but now occurs as a result of the CS.

SPECIAL CLASSICALLY CONDITIONED RESPONSES

- Taste Aversions
- Evolutionary significance for learning due to nausea
- Irrational taste aversions
- Conditioned emotional responses
- Formerly neutral stimuli produce emotional responses when associated with emotional stimuli (or, emotional UCSs). Classic examples include Watson & Raynor's illustration with 'Little Albert.'
- Phobias have been proposed as clear illustration of classical conditioning in humans. Further, knowledge of irrationality illustrates that classically conditioned responses are beyond ability to exercise reason.
- Conditioned immune responses
- With increased exposure to stimuli that weaken immune response, these stimuli serve to regulate later immune response (even without exposure to material that weakened immune system initially; the UCSs).
- Generalization: Stimuli that resemble the CS produce similar a CR. As the stimulus becomes less similar to the original CS, the CR either reduces, or eventually does not occur at all.

ELEMENTS OF CLASSICAL CONDITIONING

- Discrimination: For some discrete situations, classical conditioning is restricted to that situation only. Pavlov demonstrated this by conditioning salivation in dogs to a 60MHz bell tone, and extinguished salivation for 50 and 70MHz tones.

- Extinction: When exposure to the CS occurs repeatedly without the UCS, eventually the CS fails to produce the CR. However, there remain residual elements of the conditioning experience, as noted in spontaneous recovery.
- Inter-stimulus Interval: Presumably, as time passes between the association of CS and UCS, the likelihood of conditioning should decrease. When the CS and UCS occur closely together, the bond between CS and CR is strengthened. There are notable exceptions to when this happens, and the novelty of the CS should also be considered in discussing this relationship. That is, conditioning happens rapidly for CS-UCS associations where the CS is unique to the individual. As the CS is an increasingly familiar object, conditioning occurs more slowly.
- Types of classical conditioning:

Forward conditioning: CS precedes the UCS; most effective means of conditioning
Simultaneous conditioning: CS and UCS occur at the same temporal moment; produces learned responses, but less effective
Backward conditioning: CS occurs after the UCS; produces limited learned responses.

- Preparedness: Since the presentation of CSs with UCSs occurs frequently and at random, then there should be a random distribution of CSs for most organisms. This, however, is not the case. In the case of phobias, individuals are commonly afraid of certain things (such as spiders, snakes, heights, enclosed places) but rarely fearful of other things (such as flowers, electrical outlets). This is an illustration of 'prepared learning.' That is, individuals are biologically 'hard-wired' to develop fears more readily for certain CSs over others.

OPERANT CONDITIONING

Operant conditioning begins with Thorndike's Law of Effect-Behaviors. Operant conditioning is dependent on the consequence on the organism. Operants (behaviors emitted) are of interest here, in contrast to behaviors elicited by the environment (as in classical conditioning). In this learning paradigm, reinforcers and punishers are the key aspects to altering behavior. Reinforcement increases the future probability that a response will occur, whereas punishers prevent behavior from occurring. Terms to be covered include:

- Positive reinforcement: The presentation of a reward follows a behavior.
- Negative reinforcement: The cessation of an aversive stimulus following a behavior.
- Escape: Here, the aversive stimulus occurs and it is quickly terminated (i.e., turning off an alarm clock)
- Avoidance: The source of the aversive stimulus is prevented from emitting the noxious stimuli (i.e., waking before the alarm clock and turning it off).
- Positive punishment: The presentation of an aversive stimulus following a behavior.
- Negative punishment: The removal of a positive stimulus following a behavior (for example, grounding).

Extinction: This happens when rewards no longer follow behavior. Typically, when extinction first occurs, the organism responds more (response burst) followed by an emotional reaction. For example, a soda machine failing to dispense soda after money has been deposited results in more button pressing, followed by an emotional reaction (such as frustration). After these two reactions, then extinction follows.

SCHEDULES OF REINFORCEMENT

Skinner found that arranging reinforcers according to schedules where responses were occurring, but not necessarily rewarded every time, produced orderly patterns in behavior. Further, some schedules were more difficult to extinguish responses.

- Fixed ratio: A reward is given for a set number of responses (i.e., every tenth response).
- Variable ratio: A reward is given for an average number of responses (a good example of this is the one-armed bandit in casinos).
- Fixed interval: A reward is given for the first response following a set time period (for example, being paid weekly one is reinforced for coming to work on pay-day but not on other days).
- Variable interval: A reward is given for the first response following an average elapsed time (i.e., unannounced quizzes in a class).

DISCRIMINATIVE STIMULI

Important in the maintenance of behavior is the notion that other environmental stimuli signal the presence of reinforcement, extinction, or punishment. For example, approaching a soda machine that is lit, humming, and visually observing that it is plugged in, all constitute discriminant stimuli for reinforcement. However, if the lights were not on it would be discriminant stimuli for extinction. Finally, if a sign were posted on the machine stating that the soda machine delivers electric shock, this is a discriminant stimulus for punishment.

SHAPING AND CHAINING

In order to develop more complex behavior, reinforcement is delivered such that there are 'successive approximations.' That is, smaller units of the complex behavior are reinforced. Once sequences of desired behaviors have been established, then they may be 'chained' to form a novel complex behavior sequence, with reinforcement of course accompanying the successive chaining of responses.

ENDURING CHARACTERISTICS OF THE LEARNER

Operant conditioning acknowledges individual differences among organisms, within as well as between species. Accordingly, there are characteristics that appear to predict differential learning ability. For example, it has been well studied that persons with antisocial personality fail to learn from punishment (or do so at a greatly reduced rate). Similar effects have been noted with some populations of drug and alcohol abusers.

SPECIES-SPECIFIC BEHAVIOR AND PREPAREDNESS

In many instances, learning set up by the experimenter is overridden by instinctual behaviors associated with the reward. The text clearly illustrates how this effect occurred in research conducted by the Brelands with pigs, porpoises, cats, and raccoons. This has been considered conceptually similar to preparedness in classical conditioning.

SIMILARITIES BETWEEN CLASSICAL AND OPERANT CONDITIONING

It appears that both classical and operant conditioning share common features despite different emphases on how behaviors are acquired and maintained. For example, both place importance on
- Extinction
- Discrimination
- Preparedness
- Generalization
- Irrational association

Therefore, a meaningful discussion of both types of learning may be completed with a capstone discussion of similar and distinctive aspects.

COGNITIVE-SOCIAL THEORY

Some of the history of cognition and its link to learning theory may be traced back to Tolman's work showing that organisms form 'cognitive maps' of their surroundings. Tolman demonstrated this in classical conditioning research with rats by varying stimulus elements of the maze, suggesting that the rat formed a more complex understanding of the environment than a mere reflex account could support.

Since the time of Tolman, a great deal of attention has been paid to cognitive accounts of behavior. Among those that have received attention are:
- Expectancies
- Generalized expectancies
- Locus of control (internal or external) or reinforcement
- Learned helplessness

SOCIAL LEARNING THEORY

As an extension, it appears that much learning may be accounted for by merely observing someone experience the contingencies directly. For example, modeling occurs when one observes someone engaging in a behavior and receiving reinforcement for that behavior (the famous studies on aggressive behavior in children by Bandura demonstrate this well). This is also referred to as 'vicarious conditioning.'

The Role of Memory in Practical Life

- Defend the notion that different neural subsystems are involved in explicit versus implicit memory.
- Explain the functional importance of the various forms of everyday memory.
- Explain the functional significance of prospective memory.
- Describe the impact of spacing of rehearsal sessions on memory formation.
- Contrast the method of Loci and the SQ3R mnemonic methods.
- Outline and critique the evidence for the use of schemas in encoding and retrieval.
- Discuss the various factors that affect the formation of long-term memory.
- Describe the "seven sins of memory" articulated by Daniel Schacter.
- Explain the significance of flashbulb memories.
- Outline the factors that could explain forgetting or failure to retrieve information from long-term memory.
- Explain how the concept of false memory may be used to explain repressed memories of sexual abuse.

INTRODUCTION

Memory is one of the most fundamental abilities that humans have to connect with the world over time. It is a picture of life happening in real time that helps us create history and futuristic events. Without memory, the existence of life and our connection with others appears obsolete and meaningless. The ability to create new memories, store them for periods of time, and recall them when they are needed allows us to learn, connect, network, and interact within our environment. The study of human memory has been a subject of science and philosophy for thousands of years and has become one of the major topics of interest within cognitive psychology. Memory is one of the most fundamental mental processes.

The brain is the organ that is responsible for what we call the mind. It is the basis for thinking, feeling, wanting, perceiving, learning and memory, curiosity, and behavior. Memory is a fundamental mental process, and without memory we are capable of nothing but simple reflexes and stereotyped behaviors. Our 5 Senses (vision, hearing, touch, taste, and smell) help us to receive and record information. This recorded information becomes our "memory". Thus, learning and memory is one of the most intensively studied subjects in the field of neuroscience. Various approaches have been used to understand the mechanisms underlying this process.

MEMORY DEFINED

Memory is defined as an internal record of some prior event or experience; a set of mental processes that receives, encodes stores, organizes, alters, and retrieves information overtime that results in behavioral and mental process change caused by an experience. Hence, memory engages processes that are used to acquire, store, retain and later retrieve information. The first process of memory is attention. There is so much information in the environment that happens at once, that decision will need to be made to as to what you should attend. Thus, you must make choices (conscious and unconscious) regarding the stimuli to which you will attend. This is called *Attention* and *Selection*. Three other major processes are involved in memory: encoding, storage and retrieval. In order to form new memories, information must be changed into a usable form this starts with the process of encoding.

ENCODING

Once something is attended to, it must be encoded to be remembered. Encoding refers to translating incoming information into a mental representation that can be stored in memory. Information can be encoded in a many different ways. For example, you can encode information according to its sound (acoustic code), what it looks like (visual code), or what it means (semantic code). Suppose, for example, that you are trying to remember these three types of encoding from your notes. You might say each of the terms aloud and encode the sounds of the words (acoustic), you might see the three types of encoding on your page and visualize the way the words look (visual), or you might think about the meanings of each of the terms (semantic).

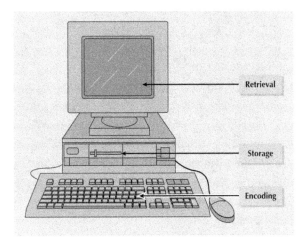

You may be able to remember information best if you use techniques (while retrieving the information)

that are related to the way you encoded it. For example, if you encoded something visually, you will be able to recall it most easily by drawing on visual cues. You will find that many of the memory techniques discussed in this section are designed to help you encode the information in different ways. Encoding prepares the perceived information for storage in LTM. It is usually achieved by "making new information meaningful and integrating it with known information" (Schunk, 2004). If this does not occur between STM and LTM, transfer will not happen and information is forgotten.

Storage

Storage is the process of holding information in your memory. A distinction is often made between short-term and long-term memory. Short-term memory is just that, brief and transient. Think about looking up a new phone number in the phone book and making a call. You may remember it long enough to make the call, but do not recall it later. This is your short-term memory, which can hold a small amount of information for a short period of time. In order to remember the number for a longer period of time (and after attending to other things), you would need to store it in your long-term memory.

Retrieval

Retrieval is the process of actually remembering something when you want to. If you think about tip-of-the-tongue experiences, when you know a word or name but just can't seem to recall it, you will understand how retrieval is different from storage. In terms of memory improvement, it can help to understand how the retrieval process relates to encoding and storage. Consider the relationship between retrieval and encoding. If you encoded something visually, but are trying to retrieve it acoustically, you will have difficulty remembering. Like encoding, information can be retrieved through visualizing it, thinking about the meaning, or imagining the sound, etc. The more ways information has been encoded, the more ways there are for retrieving it. Imagine that you are taking a test in which you are given a definition and asked to recall the word it describes. You may recall the page of your notes that the word was on and visualize the word, or you might say the definition to yourself and remember yourself repeating the word. Thus, memory is aided by encoding and retrieving information in multiple ways.

Retrieval relates to storage as well. Obviously the memory has to be stored in order for you to retrieve it, but knowing *how* it was stored can help. This is where elaboration and processing come in. When attempting to retrieve information, it helps to think about related ideas. For example, you are trying to remember a chemistry formula during an exam. Although you are able to visualize the page of your chemistry notes, you cannot recall the exact formula. You do remember, however, that this same formula was used in the biology class you took last semester. As you think about that class, you are able to recall the formula. This is one reason why intentionally organizing information

in your memory when you are learning it helps you recall it later.

SUMMARY

In summary, memorization is a process that occurs in a deliberate and stepwise manner. If first requires attention, encoding, storage, and retrieval.

Attention ----> Encoding ----> Storage ----> Retrieval

Here are the steps of memory discussed thus far. First, you select the information to which you will attend. You then code the information for storage (where it can be practiced and processed more deeply). Later, when needed, information is retrieved by using a search strategy that parallels how the information was coded and stored.

INFORMATION PROCESSING

When we take in information, we do so in steps. It is a like a process of acquiring, retaining, and using information as an activity called information processing, which is diagrammed in Figure X. Information comes from the outside world into the sensory registers in the human brain using our five senses. The best understood of the five sensory registers (SRs) are hearing (echoic) and seeing (iconic). Very little is known about tactile (touch), olfactory (smell), and gustatory (taste) SRs. *Iconic Storage* describes momentary memory for visual information. *Echoic Storage* describes momentary memory for auditory information. The process take by SRs is 1. to detect that something is there; 2. to hold information for a fraction of a second; and 3. to create a mental representation that it passes onto short term memory.

No human brain can encode the amount of input available to it at any given time. It is necessary to narrow the range of available information to the most useful. The brain does this by through the process of focusing more specific attention and selection on information and moving it into *working memory*. We focus our attention on information when it somehow arouses our curiosity (as when there is a physical novelty in what we see or when information presents us with an optimal discrepancy, as described in Chapter 9), or when we consciously focus our attention for some other relevant reason. We then will choose to focus our attention to these stimuli and place them in our *working memory*.

MODELS OF INFORMATION PROCESSING

It is difficult to conceive of any model of information processing that does not first deal with the issue of 'memory' and how the brain deals with information that is newly gathered, newly processed, or existing knowledge. Thus how memory is dealt with becomes a key feature in the models of Cognitive Information Processing Theory. The Stage Theory also addresses the construct of memory.

Stage Theory

Based on the work of Atkinson and Shiffrin, it is postulated that information is processed and memorized in three distinct stages: Sensory Memory Stage, Short-Term Memory Stage, and Long Term Memory Stage. The dual store model elaborates on the requirements for human learning: *attention, perception, encoding, storage and retrieval.*

1. Sensory Memory Stage—The biological sensors of our body are triggered and then the information is relayed through our nerves to the brain where it must either be processed immediately or ignored. Approximate sensory memory is about 1/2 a second, shorter for vision, longer for hearing.

2. Short Term Memory Stage—(Also known as Short Term Memory) We exist primarily in this state, dealing with the immediate and near-term moments. With its operation we can pay attention to our thoughts, the world around us or both simultaneously. Nonetheless, it is a short-term memory stage of variable length and thus we can only store a very finite amount of information in it before the information is stored in the third stage, long term memory, or discarded. If an experience or stimulus can be organized into something that relates to a previous experience, it is more likely to be recalled in the future.

For example, you are reading the words on this screen, you know the individual letters, but they are quickly processed into *chunks* of information as *words* and then as *sentences* and finally into a set of ideas. All of this takes advantage of pre-existing organization and also serves to emphasize the importance of organization in the learning and comprehension process. Note the difference if you try and remember something by rote immediately after the fact (i.e. the numerical sequence 3.141519 or the letters b-l-e-s-s---d) compared to recognizing a number pattern or word pattern (in this case 'pi=3.141519' and 'blessed without the finale'

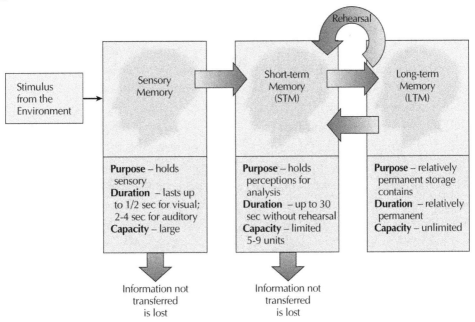

Figure 7. Information Processing Model

Limitations to this storage ‹medium› are its very shallow capacity for events to be stored. For some individuals, recalling more than 3 events that took place in the past few moments may be a challenge while others can recall up to 7 events. [link to the NASA human factors web site with the audio recording]

3.   Long Term Memory—Long Term Memory involves the storage and recall of past experiences. Some types of recall will be immediate (the name of your best friend) and others will require a bit more time until the information ‹arrives› – i.e. the name of your first ‹Best Friend Forever› in elementary school or the best way to get from A-B in a town you've last been in 10 years ago, see Figure X.

TYPES OF MEMORY

Memory actually takes many different forms. We know that when we store a memory, we are storing information. But, what that information is and how long we retain it determines what type of memory it is. The biggest categories of memory are short-term memory (or working memory) and long-term memory, based on the amount of time the memory is stored. Both can weaken due to age, or a variety of other reasons such as health and mental disabilities. In this section, I will discuss types of memory: Short Term Memory (Working Memory) and Long-Term Memory and the defining features that distinguish these types of memory forms.

Short Term Memory

Short Term Memory is remembering something that you recently saw or heard. An example of short term memory is remembering the color of the car that just passed by you. Short term memory is very brief. It only lasts about 5 seconds. In order to remember the same information at a later time, your brain transfers this information from your Short Term Memory to Long Term Memory, if relevance is applied. Short Term Memory can be transferred to Long Term Memory by repeating the information, or visualizing it. Short-term memories can become long-term memory through the process of consolidation, involving rehearsal and meaningful association. Unlike short-term memory (which relies mostly on an acoustic, and to a lesser extent a visual, code for storing information), long-term memory encodes information for storage semantically (i.e. based on meaning and association). However, there is also some evidence that long-term memory does also encode to some extent by sound. For example, when we cannot quite remember a word but it is "on the tip of the tongue", this is usually based on the sound of a word, not its meaning.

Long Term Memory

Long term memory has no limit on capacity and can store vast amounts of information. Long-term memory is intended for storage of information over a long period of time. Despite our everyday impressions and claims of "forgetting," it seems likely that the storage has more to do with access and recall of information from long-term memory. If information is stored, it is accessible at any time, unless the decaying process is occurring. LTM has the capacity to store an unlimited amount of information and almost indefinitely. While there is some debate as to whether we actually ever "forget" anything at all, or whether it just becomes increasingly difficult to access or retrieve certain items from memory.

Over the years, several different types of long-term memory have been distinguished, including explicit and implicit, declarative and procedural, episodic

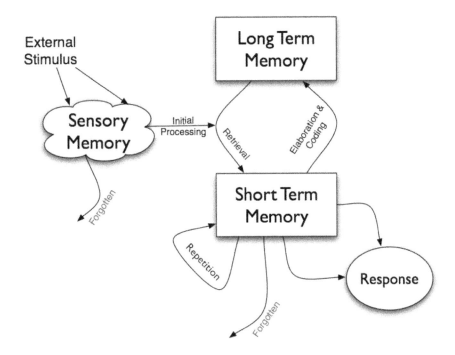

Figure 8. Stage Theory

and semantic, as well as retrospective and prospective memory.

Types of Long Term Memory

Semantic memory stores facts and generalized information. It contains verbal information, concepts, rules, principles, and problem-solving skills. While *episodic memory* stores information as images, *semantic memory* stores information in networks or schemata. Information is most easily stored in semantic memory when it is meaningful and relates to existing and well-established schemata. When we retrieve information from schematic memory, we mentally follow cognitive paths taken during the process of storage. By using information on numerous occasions after it has been initially learned, we solidify the connections among elements of information, make it easier to retrieve when we need to use it, and make it more likely that this information will be available to help us accept and store additional information in the future.

Procedural memory refers to the ability to remember how to perform a task or to employ a strategy. The steps in various procedures are apparently stored in a series of steps, or stimulus-response pairings. When we retrieve information from procedural memory, we retrieve one step, which triggers the next, which triggers the next, etc.

1. **Declarative memory** includes semantic and episodic from which information can be intentionally recalled
   • Vocabulary, concepts, language rules, and facts are stored in **SEMANTIC memory**.
   • In **episodic memory**, life events and personal experiences are stored (time-related experiences are stored in chronological order).

2. **Nondeclarative or procedural memory** involves the acquisition of, retention and retrieval of, performance skills, like a tennis stroke or a golf swing

Explicit vs. Implicit memory is the conscious recollection, recall of information. For example, completing an essay examination, or a multiple choice examination. Implicit memory involves behavior not requiring conscious recollection, like riding a bike, getting a glass of water, or putting on a pair of gloves. Figure 8 described the types of long term memory.

These various parts of long-term memory do not operate in isolation from one another. When transferring information to long-term memory, there are two major considerations that must be observed: (1) to transfer the information accurately to long-term memory and (2) to retrieve the information accurately. The primary strategy for transferring information from working memory into long-term memory is referred to as *encoding* or *elaboration*. These terms refer to the process of relating information to other information that is already stored in long-term memory. Piaget and other constructivists have developed detailed theories regarding how information is stored in long-term memory, and some aspects of these schemata theories are described in Chapter 4 of this book. That information should be considered directly compatible with the information presented in this chapter.

Memory Recall and Retrieval

There are two main methods used to access memory: recognition and recall. **Recognition** is the association of an event or physical object with one previously experienced or encountered, and involves a process of comparison of information with memory, e.g. recognizing a known face, true/false or multiple choice questions, etc. **Recall** is the process of remembering a fact, event or object that is not currently physically present (in the sense of retrieving a representation, mental image or concept), and requires the direct uncovering of information from memory, e.g. remembering the name of a recognized person, fill-in the blank questions, etc.

There are three **Types of Recall**: *Free Recall, Cued Recall, and Serial Recall.*

1. **Free recall** is the process in which a person is given a list of items to remember and then is asked to recall them in any order (hence the name "free"). This type of recall often displays evidence of either the **primacy effect** (when the person recalls items presented at the beginning of the list earlier and more often) or the **recency effect** (when the person recalls items presented at the end of the list earlier and more often), and also of the **contiguity effect** (the marked tendency for items from neighboring positions in the list to be recalled successively).

2. **Cued recall** is the process in which a person is given a list of items to remember and is then tested with the use of cues or guides. When cues are provided to a person, they tend to remember items on the list that they did not originally recall without a cue, and which were thought to be lost to memory. This can also take the form of **stimulus-response recall**, as when words, pictures and numbers are presented together in a pair, and the resulting associations between the two items cues the recall of the second item in the pair.

3. **Serial recall** refers to our ability to recall items or events in the order in which they occurred, whether chronological events in our autobiographical memories, or the order of the different parts of a sentence (or phonemes in a word) in order to make sense of them. Serial recall in long-term memory appears to differ from serial recall in short-term memory, in that a sequence in long-term memory is represented in memory as a whole, rather than as a series of discrete items.

The efficiency of memory recall can be increased to some extent by making **inferences** from our personal stockpile of world knowledge, and by our use of **schemata**. A **schema** (plural: schemata) is an organized mental structure or framework of pre-conceived ideas about the world and how it works, which we can use to make realistic inferences and assumptions about how to interpret and process information. Thus, our everyday communication consists not just of words

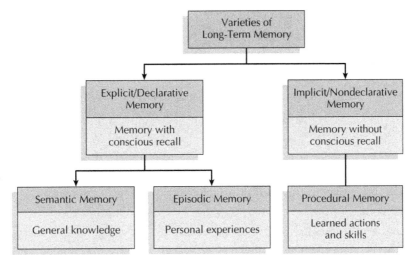

Figure 9. Types of Long Term Memory

and their meanings, but also of what is left out and mutually understood (e.g. if someone says "it is 3 o'clock", our knowledge of the world usually allows us to know automatically whether it is 3am or 3pm). Such schemata are also applied to recalled memories, so that we can often flesh out details of a memory from just a skeleton memory of a central event or object.

Biological Pathways to Memory

Since the early neurological work of Karl Lashley and Wilder Penfield in the 1950s and 1960s, it has become clear that long-term memories are not stored in just one part of the brain, but are widely distributed throughout the cortex. It seems that sometimes memories may be encoded redundantly, that is several times across different parts of the cortex. Therefore, contrary to the popular notion, memories are stored in our brains like books on library shelves, must be revisited. Memory storage is therefore an ongoing process of reclassification resulting from continuous changes in our neural pathways, and parallel processing of information in our brains.

Scientists believe that long-term memories are stored in groups of brain cells or "neurons" that

are activated in response to particular experiences. The thought is that the initial experience triggers biochemical or structural changes in networks of neurons. These neurons are then more likely than other neurons to be activated during recall, which create memories that are believed to leave traces.

Brain Regions Involved in Memory

It's been difficult to study memory. Humans have about 100 billion neurons and each neuron can interact with thousands of others. And the cells involved in memory are distributed in different parts of the brain. For example, regions of the brain associated with memory include the cerebral cortex, cerebellum, striatum, hippocampus and amygdala.

Each of these regions is associated with a different type of memory. Amygdala: emotional memory and memory consolidation; Basal ganglia & cerebellum: memory for skills, habits and CC responses; Hippocampus: memory recognition, spatial, episodic memory, laying down new declarative long-term memories; Thalamus, formation of new memories and working memories; Cortical Areas: encoding of factual memories, storage of episodic and semantic memories, skill learning, priming. The hippocampus plays an important role in spatial learning, while the amygdala plays a role in learning during arousal (e.g., during a fear response). The different regions of the brain also work together to create memories. There's no single region of the brain that functions as a "memory bank."

The Limbic System

The limbic system is a complex set of structures that lies on both sides of the thalamus, just under the cerebrum. It includes the hypothalamus, the hippocampus, the amygdala, and several other nearby areas. It appears to be primarily responsible for our emotional life, and has a lot to do with the formation of memories. In this drawing, you are looking at the brain cut in half, but with the brain stem intact. The part of the limbic system shown is that which is along the left side of the thalamus (hippocampus and amygdala) and just under the front of the thalamus (hypothalamus).

Forgetting

Forgetting is the inability to recall previously learned information. Although information can be stored in long-term memory for extended periods of time, "memory decay" does take place under certain conditions, such as stress, health related problems, and trauma. While forgetting sometimes occur, it is important to distinguish between normal forgetting and abnormal memory loss. It's normal to forget things from time to time. Healthy people can experience memory loss or memory distortion at any age. Some of these memory flaws become more pronounced with age, but unless they are extreme and persistent they are not considered indicators of Alzheimer's or other memory-impairing illnesses.

There are three (3) possible reasons why people sometimes forget. 1. Fading (trace decay) over time; 2. Interference or overlaying new information over the old; and 3. There is a lack of retrieval cues.

Seven Normal Memory Problems

1. **Transience**—This is the tendency to forget facts or events over time. You are most likely to forget information soon after you learn it. However, memory has a use-it-or-lose-it quality: memories that are called up and used frequently are least likely to be forgotten. Although transience might seem like a sign of memory weakness, brain scientists regard it as beneficial because it clears the brain of unused memories, making way for newer, more useful ones.

2. **Absentmindedness**—This type of forgetting occurs when you don't pay close enough attention. You forget where you just put your pen because you didn't focus on where you put it in the first place. You were thinking of something else (or, perhaps, nothing in particular), so your brain didn't encode the information securely. Absentmindedness also involves forgetting to do something at a prescribed time, like taking your medicine or keeping an appointment.

3. **Blocking**—Someone asks you a question and the answer is right on the tip of your tongue — you know that you know it, but you just can't think of it. This is perhaps the most familiar example of blocking, the temporary inability to retrieve a memory. In many cases, the barrier is a memory similar to the one you're looking for, and you retrieve the wrong one. This competing memory is so intrusive that you can't think of the memory you want. A common example is calling your older son by your younger son's name, or vice versa.

Scientists think that memory blocks become more common with age and that they account for the trouble older people have remembering other people's names. Research shows that people are able to retrieve about half of the blocked memories within just a minute.

4. **Misattribution**—Misattribution occurs when you remember something accurately in part, but misattribute some detail, like the time, place, or person involved. Another kind of misattribution occurs when you believe a thought you had was totally original when, in fact, it came from something you had previously read or heard but had forgotten about. This sort of misattribution explains cases of

unintentional plagiarism, in which a writer passes off some information as original when he or she actually read it somewhere before.

As with several other kinds of memory lapses, misattribution becomes more common with age. Age matters in at least two ways. First, as you age, you absorb fewer details when acquiring information because you have somewhat more trouble concentrating and processing information rapidly. Second, as you grow older, your memories grow older as well. And old memories are especially prone to misattribution.

5. **Suggestibility**—Suggestibility is the vulnerability of your memory to the power of suggestion — information that you learn about an occurrence after the fact becomes incorporated into your memory of the incident, even though you did not experience these details. Although little is known about exactly how suggestibility works in the brain, the suggestion fools your mind into thinking it's a real memory.

6. **Bias**—Even the sharpest memory isn't a flawless snapshot of reality. In your memory, your perceptions are filtered by your personal biases — experiences, beliefs, prior knowledge, and even your mood at the moment. Your biases affect your perceptions and experiences when they're being encoded in your brain. And when you retrieve a memory, your mood and other biases at that moment can influence what information you actually recall.

Although everyone's attitudes and preconceived notions bias their memories, there's been virtually no research on the brain mechanisms behind memory bias or whether it becomes more common with age.

7. *Persistence*—Most people worry about forgetting things. But in some cases people are tormented by memories they wish they could forget, but can't. The persistence of memories of traumatic events, negative feelings, and ongoing fears is another form of memory problem. Some of these memories accurately reflect horrifying events, while others may be negative distortions of reality. People suffering from depression are particularly prone to having persistent, disturbing memories. So are people with post-traumatic stress disorder (PTSD). PTSD can result from many different forms of traumatic exposure — for example, sexual abuse or wartime experiences. Flashbacks, which are persistent, intrusive memories of the traumatic event, are a core feature of PTSD.

In summary, forgetting is a condition that is common to most people for different reasons. Forgetting only becomes a problem when it is persistent and begins to interfere with everyday functioning. If this begins to happen, then other neurological problems may be inherent. The next section of this chapter will discuss conditions associated with pervasive memory loss.

By 2050, there will be many older adults in wealthy, developed countries. It is predicted that there will be twenty-six percent (26%) more than children under age 15 and approximately sixteen percent (16%) of the total population according to J. E. Cohen, 2003. The aging of the population represents both an opportunity and threat for society. The opportunity comes from the tremendous reserve of human capital and experience represented by older citizens; the threat emerges from the disconcerting fact that at this time, adults aged 85 and older have a dementia rate (typically in the form of Alzheimer's disease) of nearly 50% (Herbert et al. 2003), with a very high cost to affected individuals and families, as well as to limited medical resources. At present, it is fair to say that neurocognitive frailty is the biggest threat to successful aging in our society.

Fortunately, as our aging population has grown, so has our knowledge about the aging mind. For the past 25 years, our understanding of the behavioral changes that occur in cognition with age has increased tremendously, and in the past 10 years, the advent of neuroimaging tools has presented a truly stunning increase in what we know about the aging mind. Neuroimaging techniques such as structural and functional magnetic resonance imaging (fMRI) and positron emission tomography (PET) allow medical scientists to see how both brain structure and function change with age. In the present review, scientist integrates the vast body of behavioral research in cognitive aging with recent data revealed by imaging techniques. It is argued that the unprecedented opportunity to look into the operation of the mind afforded by neuroimaging indicates the brain and cognitive system to be more dynamic and adaptive then was ever previously suspected. We propose that the extant behavioral and brain data can best be understood within a new model: the scaffolding theory of aging and cognition (STAC).

After reviewing the range of data examining brain and behavioral function with age, it is believed that the corpus of these data suggests that the brain is a dynamic organism seeking to maintain homeostatic cognitive function. With age, the number of dopaminergic receptors declines; many brain structures show volumetric shrinkage; white matter becomes less dense; and brains of even very highly functioning individuals are frequently characterized by destructive neurofibrillary plaques and tangles. We argue that the brain responds to these neural insults by engaging in continuous functional reorganization and functional repairs that result in self-generated support of cognitive function. We term this *homeostatic, adaptive model* of aging *the scaffolding theory of aging and cognition.* Encarta defines scaffolding as "a supporting framework." In this context, scaffolding is defined

as a process that results in changes in brain function through strengthening of existing connections, formation of new connections, and disuse of connections that have become weak or faulty.

A second important approach to understanding cognitive aging comes from evidence that working memory function decreases with age and, along with speed, mediates age-related variance on a broad array of cognitive behaviors (Park et al. 1996, 2002; Wingfield et al. 1988). Indeed, working memory, which encompasses both the short-term maintenance and active manipulative processing of information, figures prominently in a third view of cognitive aging that emphasize declines in executive control processes, namely inhibitory function (Hasher & Zacks, 1988, Hasher et al. 2007). According to this view, age-related deficits in cognition stem from the inefficiency of inhibitory processes that normally control the contents of consciousness (i.e., working memory). Older adults show working memory deficiencies and slowing due to selection of irrelevant information into the contents of working memory, along with inefficient deletion of working memory contents that are no longer relevant to task performance. Inhibitory dysfunction with age is a source of general attentional dysregulation and accounts for age-related deficits in other cognitive domains such as task switching, response competition, and response suppression.

In summary, age-related cognitive declines may be best understood in terms of a range of mechanisms including speed, working memory, inhibition, and cognitive control (Moscovitch & Winocur, 1992, West 1996) that show varying degrees of vulnerability in different individuals. Although these mechanisms can all be categorized as executive processes, other sources of decline, such as dedifferentiation of cognitive function, must also be considered. Given the broad spectrum of cognitive changes with age, it is unlikely that any single process or unitary mechanism can fully explain age-related deficits across all individuals. Some memory loss is due to neurological dysfunctions that result in some disorder developing. The next section will discuss type of memory related disorders.

MEMORY DISORDERS

If you suffer from regular mental blocks or memory slips, you are not alone. Our mental speed seems to decline from our late-teens and early-20s—and especially when we are under stress.

There are many different types of memory loss that affect us. Here, we look at the main memory disorders.

KORSAKOFF'S SYNDROME

Korsakoff's syndrome, or **Wernicke-Korsakoff syndrome**, is a brain disorder caused by extensive **thiamine deficiency**, a form of malnutrition which can be precipitated by over-consumption of alcohol and **alcoholic beverages** compared to other foods. Its main symptoms are anterograde amnesia (inability to form new memories and to learn new information or tasks) and retrograde amnesia (severe loss of existing memories), **confabulation** (invented memories, which are then taken as true due to gaps in memory), meager content in conversation, lack of insight and apathy.

Korsakoff's syndrome is caused by a deficiency of **thiamine** (**vitamin B1**), which is thought to cause damage to the **thalamus** and to the **mammillary bodies** of the **hypothalamus** (which receives many neural connections from the **hippocampus**), as well as generalized cerebral atrophy, neuronal loss and damage to neurons.

Typically, the retrograde amnesia of Korsakoff's syndrome follows a distinct **temporal curve**: the more remote the event in the past, the better it is preserved and the sharper the recollection of it. This suggests that the more recent memories are not fully consolidated and therefore more vulnerable to loss, indicating that the process of consolidation may continue for much longer than initially thought, perhaps for many years.

RETROGRADE AMNESIA

Retrograde amnesia is a form of amnesia where someone is unable to recall events that occurred **before** the development of the amnesia, even though they may be able to encode and memorize new things that occur after the onset.

Retrograde amnesia usually follows damage to areas of the brain other than the **hippocampus** (the part of the brain involved in encoding new memories), because already existing long-term memories are stored in the neuron and synapses of various different brain regions. For example, damage to Broca's or Wernicke's areas of the brain, which are specifically linked to speech production and language information, would probably cause language-related memory loss. It usually results from damage to the brain regions most closely associated with declarative memory, such as the temporal lobe and prefrontal cortex. The damage may result from a cranial trauma (a blow to the head), a cerebrovascular accident or stroke (a burst artery in the brain), a tumor (if it presses against part of the brain), hypoxia (lack of oxygen in the brain), certain kinds of encephalitis, and chronic alcoholism.

Typically, episodic memory is more severely affected than semantic memory, so that the patient may remember words and general knowledge (such as who their country's leader is, how everyday objects work, colors, etc) but not specific events in their lives. Procedural memories (memory of skills, habits and how to perform everyday functions) are typically not affected at all.

MEMORY SLIP

How many times have you searched the house for lost car keys—or tried to introduce someone at a party and forgotten their name? If this sounds familiar, you could be suffering from a 'memory slip'.

According to Ian Robinson, professor of psychology at Trinity College, Dublin, this common trait is actually a disorder of attention—rather than memory loss.

'As we get older, we find it harder to split our attention between several tasks,' says Professor Robinson. 'This is because too many thoughts in our head clutter up our memory centre found deep in our brain. When our brain can't cope it turns off the electricity that fires up our neurotransmitters—substances that send messages to our brain and switches on our memory.'

Studies show that the frontal lobes in the brains of older people are much more vulnerable to ageing than other parts of the body—and more prone to temporary memory loss than younger people. 'It is thought that as we get older, we get out of the habit of learning new experiences leaving our brain unexercised,' says Professor Robinson.

But the good news is there is plenty we can to do to improve our memory. *Click on the link below to discover six ways to boost your brain power.*

Alcohol-Related Dementia

Dementia can be caused by the effect of toxins on the brain. General alcohol dementia is characterized by damage throughout the brain caused by the abuse of alcohol.

This brain disorder is associated with heavy drinking over a long period of time. While not strictly speaking a dementia, those with the condition experience loss of short-term memory. According to the Alzheimer's Society, 10 per cent of younger people are affected by alcohol-related dementia.

It has been estimated that about a quarter of those affected from alcohol-related dementia will make a very good recovery. About half will make a partial recovery and need support to manage their lives. Another quarter will make no recovery and may need long-term care.

Mental blocks

People often complain of their mind going blank, especially as they get older. This common experience happens when the frontal lobes of our brain temporarily lose track of what our brain plans to do.

As we get older our memory appears to have a more limited capacity, holding a smaller number of thoughts than when we were younger. Typically this happens when one thought is easily erased by another thought.

The good news is that a regular workout of the brain can help to overcome mental blanks. Regular meditation, mind games and physical exercise is said to have instant improvements on memory loss.

Apart from common memory lapses that many of us experience, there are also some serious medical conditions that involve long-term memory loss.

Dementia

The term 'dementia' describes a group of symptoms caused by the impact of disease on the brain. Symptoms typically include problems with memory, speech and perception.

Short-term memory is usually affected. This may mean that the person with dementia forgets the names of family or friends—or how to perform simple everyday tasks. They may, however, retain their long-term memory, clearly remembering events from the past.

The person with dementia might have problems finding the right words, or may seem to have difficulties understanding what is being said to them.

Alzheimer's

Alzheimer's disease is the most common cause of dementia, affecting around 500,000 people in the UK. Dementia affects one in 20 people over the age of 65—and one in five over the age of 80.

During the course of the disease, the chemistry of the brain changes and cells, nerves and transmitters are attacked. Eventually the brain shrinks as gaps develop.

Early Onset Alzheimer's Disease

Dementia in people under the age of 65 is relatively rare, but around 17,000 people aged between 30 and 64 suffer from early onset Alzheimer's in the UK.

Researchers have found that there are a small number of families where early onset Alzheimer's appears to be caused by the particular type of genes they inherit. However, it is also thought that 10 per cent of those suffering from the disease is alcohol-related and 18 per cent is due to vascular dementia.

Vascular Dementia

Vascular dementia describes all those forms of dementia caused by damage to the blood vessels leading to the brain. The brain relies on a network of vessels to bring it oxygen-bearing blood. If the oxygen supply to the brain fails, brain cells are likely to die.

Symptoms of vascular dementia can either happen suddenly following a stroke, or over time through a series of small strokes in the brain, known as multi-infarct dementia. In vascular dementia some mental abilities may be unchanged, but symptoms may include depression or mood swings.

Post-Traumatic Memory Loss

When stress is severe it can cause physical changes to the brain cells leading to long-term memory loss. This can happen after a bad accident and can be experienced by soldiers fighting at war.

Studies show that Vietnam War soldiers experienced shrinkage of the memory centre. This happens when the brain is flooded with a brain chemical called glutamate which reduces the brain cells.

For more information on Alzheimer's contact the Alzheimer's society at www.alzheimers.org.uk

Parkinson's Disease

Parkinson's Disease (PD) can be a fairly common disorder with increased age, tending to occur more often in men. It affects movement, resulting in tremors and shakiness, stiffness, difficulty with walking, lack of facial expression and impaired speech. Many individuals with Parkinson's develop dementia in later stages of the disease, which does not affect memory like in Alzheimer's disease, but rather affects concentration, visual spatial skills, and speed of thinking.

Head Injury

The purpose of the head, including the skull and face, is to protect the brain against injury. In addition to the bony protection, the brain is covered in tough fibrous layers called meninges and bathed in fluid that may provide a little shock absorption.

When an injury occurs, loss of brain function can occur even without visible damage to the head. Force applied to the head may cause the brain to be directly injured or shaken, bouncing against the inner wall of the skull. The trauma can potentially cause bleeding in the spaces surrounding the brain, bruise the brain tissue, or damage the nerve connections within the brain.

Traumatic head injury affects more than 1.7million people in the United States each year including almost a half million children; 52,000 people die. As well, 80-90,000 people sustain long-term or lifelong disabilities because of a brain injury each year.

Adults suffer head injuries most frequently due to falls, motor vehicle crashes, colliding or being struck by an object, and assaults. Falls and being struck are the most common causes of head injury in children.

Symptoms of Head Injury

The symptoms of a head injury can occur immediately or develop slowly over several hours or days. Even if the skull is not fractured, the brain can bang against the inside of the skull and be bruised. The head may look fine, but complications could result from bleeding or swelling inside the skull.

In any serious head trauma, always assume the spinal cord is also injured.

Some head injuries result in prolonged or nonreversible brain damage. This can occur as a result of bleeding inside the brain or forces that damage the brain directly. More serious head injuries may cause the following symptoms:

- Changes in, or unequal size of pupils
- Chronic or severe headaches
- Coma
- Fluid draining from nose, mouth, or ears (may be clear or bloody)
- Fracture in the skull or face, bruising of the face, swelling at the site of the injury, or scalp wound
- Irritability (especially in children)
- Loss of consciousness, confusion, or drowsiness
- Loss of or change in sensation, hearing, vision, taste, or smell
- Low breathing rate or drop in blood pressure
- Memory loss
- Mood, personality, or behavioral changes
- Paralysis
- Restlessness, clumsiness, or lack of coordination
- Seizures
- Speech and language problems
- Slurred speech or blurred vision
- Stiff neck or vomiting
- Symptoms improve, and then suddenly get worse (change in consciousness)

Types of Head Injuries

The location of a head injury is important because some skull bones are thinner and more fragile than others. For example, the temporal bone above the ear is relatively thin and can be more easily broken than the occipital bone at the back of the skull. The middle meningeal artery is located in a groove within the temporal bone. It is susceptible to damage and bleeding if the fracture crosses that groove. Types of injuries are discussed below.

- **Basilar skull fractures** occur because of blunt trauma and describe a break in the bones at the base of the skull. These are often associated with bleeding around the eyes (raccoon eyes) or behind the ears (Battle's sign). The fracture line may extend into the sinuses of the face and allow bacteria from the nose and mouth to come into contact with the brain, causing a potential infection.
- In infants and young children, whose skull bones have not yet fused together, a skull fracture may cause a **diastasis fracture**, in which the bone junctions (called suture lines) widen.
- **Penetrating skull fractures** describe injuries caused by an object entering the brain. This includes gunshot and stab wounds, and impaled objects to the head.
- A **depressed skull fracture** occurs when a piece of skull is pushed toward the inside of the skull (think of pressing in on a ping pong ball). Depending upon circumstances, surgery may be required to elevate the depressed fragment.
- It is important to know whether the fracture is open or closed (this describes the condition of the skin overlying the broken bone). An **open fracture** occurs when the skin is torn or lacerated over the fracture site. This increases the risk of infection, especially with a depressed skull fracture in which brain tissue is exposed. In a **closed fracture**, the skin is not damaged and continues to protect the underlying fracture from contamination from the outside world.
- **Intracranial Bleeding**—Intracranial (intra=within + cranium=skull) describes any bleeding within the skull. Intracerebral bleeding describes bleeding within the brain itself. More specific descriptions are used based upon where the blood is located. Bleeding in the skull may or may not be associated with a skull fracture. An intact skull is no guarantee that there is not

underlying bleeding, or hemorrhage, in the brain or its surrounding spaces. For that reason, plain X-rays of the skull are not routinely performed.

- Epidural, subdural, and subarachnoid bleeding are terms that describe bleeding in the spaces between the meninges, the fibrous layered coverings of the brain. Sometimes, the terms hemorrhage (bleeding) and hematoma (blood clot) are interchanged. Because the skull is a solid box, any blood that accumulates within the skull can increase the pressure within it and compress the brain. Moreover, blood is irritating and can cause edema or swelling as excess fluid leaks from the surrounding blood vessels. This is no different than the swelling that can occur surrounding a bruise on an arm or leg. The only difference is that there is no room within the skull to accommodate that swelling.

- **Subdural Hematoma**—When force is applied to the head, bridging veins that cross through the subdural space (sub=beneath +dura= one of the meninges that line the brain) can tear and bleed. The resultant blood clot increases pressure on the brain tissue. Subdural hematomas can occur at the site of trauma, or may occur on the opposite side of the injury (contracoup: contra=opposite + coup=hit) when the brain accelerates toward the opposite side of the skull and crushes or bounces against the opposite side. Chronic subdural hematoma may occur in patients who have had atrophy (shrinkage) of their brain tissue. These include the elderly and chronic alcoholics. The subdural space increases and the bridging veins get stretched as they cross a much wider distance. Minor or

unnoticed injuries can lead to some bleeding, but because there is enough space in the skull to accommodate the blood, there may be minimal initial symptoms. Asymptomatic (producing no symptoms) chronic subdural hematomas may be left to resolve on their own; however, it may require attention if the individual's mental status changes or further bleeding occurs. Depending upon the neurologic status of the affected individual, surgery may be required.

- **Epidural Hematoma**—Thee dura is one of the meninges or lining membranes that covers the brain. It attaches at the suture lines where the bones come together. If the head trauma is epidural (epi=outside +dura) the blood is trapped in a small area and cause a hematoma or blood clot to form. Pressure can increase quickly within the epidural space, pushing the clot up against the brain and causing significant damage. While individuals who sustain small epidural hematomas may be observed, most require surgery. Patients have improved survival and brain function recovery if the operation to remove the hematoma and relieve pressure on the brain occurs before they have lost consciousness and become comatose. An epidural hematoma may often occur with trauma to the temporal bone located on the side of the head above the ear. Aside from the fact that the temporal bone is thinner than the other skull bones (frontal, parietal, occipital), it is also the location of the middle meningeal artery that runs just beneath the bone. Fracture of the temporal bone is associated with tearing of this artery and may lead to an epidural hematoma.

NEUROLOGICAL EVALUATION

Evaluation Topics Covering:	
Cognitive Problems	**Psychological Problems**
Alzheimer's Dementia versus Age-Related Memory Impairment or....... • Vascular Dementia • Fronto/Temporal Dementia • Differential Cognitive Diagnosis • Word Finding Problems • Competency • Language Lateralization • Learning Disability Evaluation • Attention/Concentration Deficits • Forensic Evaluation of Cognition	• Depression • Anxiety • Learning Disorders • Sleep Disorders • Headaches and Chronic Pain • Impulsivity • Autistic Spectrum Disorders • Social/Emotional Skill Deficits • Counseling and Therapy may be provided or referrals can be initiated for these problems • Forensic Evaluation of Psychological Status
Problems may be due to medical, neurological, psychological, or genetic causes.	
• Comprehensive Neuropsychological and Psychological Exams. Review of records and cases for defense of plaintiff counsel.	

MEMORY LOSS AND MEDICAL TREATMENT

Drugs currently available for the treatment of memory loss

Various drugs and classes of drugs are currently available for the treatment of memory loss related to several types of illnesses. The following is a list of some of the drugs that are currently approved or under investigation for the treatment of memory loss.

Drugs in this section are used to treat several types of memory disorders including Alzheimer's disease, dementia due to Lewy bodies, vascular dementia and other types of memory loss. The choice of drug depends on the condition and the physician's preference. Some physicians use one or more medications in combination.

Tacrine (Cognex) Donepezil (Aricept) Rivastigmine (Exelon) Memantine (Akatinol) Galantamine (Reminyl) Neotropin Nootropics Alpha-tocopherol Selegeline (Eldepryl)	Non-steroidal Anti-inflammatory Agents Intravenous Immunoglobulin (IVIg) Gingko Biloba Estrogen B-secretase inhibitors B vitamins Calcium channel blockers Cholesterol lowering agents Clioquinol, an earlier generation antibiotic

Tacrine, or Cognex, was the first drug approved by the Food and Drug Administration (FDA) for the treatment of Alzheimer's. It slows progression of Alzheimer's by increasing levels of the neurotransmitter acetylcholine. It needs to be taken four times a day and blood tests for liver function need to be monitored. Up to six out of ten people are unable to reach the maximum dosage due to side effects.

Donepezil, or Aricept, was the second drug approved by the FDA to treat Alzheimer's. It works by raising the level of the chemical acetylcholine in the brain, slowing progression of some types of dementias. The dosing is once a day. Side effects include gastrointestinal discomfort.

Rivastigmine, or Exelon, was approved by the FDA to treat Alzheimer's. It also, like Cognex and Aricept, increases levels of acetylcholine in the brain. It is given twice a day and side effects include gastrointestinal discomfort.

Galantamine, or Razadyne, is last in the class of drugs that raise brain levels of acetylcholine. It has been approved by the FDA for treating Alzheimer's disease. It is given twice a day. Side effects include gastrointestinal discomfort.

Memantine, or Akatinol, is an NMDA receptor agent, which prevents the harm to brain cells from excessive activity of the chemical glutamate. It was approved by the FDA for treating moderate to severe

Alzheimer's dementia. Although approved for twice a day use, it may be given once a day.

Intravenous Immunoglobulin (IVIg) is derived from the pooled blood of thousands of donors. It is used for treating various autoimmune conditions and may have utility in treating Alzheimer's disease.

Neotropin, as the name suggests, is drug that possibly promotes the growth of nerve cell processes and maintains nerve cell viability. It is currently in clinical trials

Nootropics, the first class of agents used for treatment of memory loss have not been shown to be consistently effective and are not used routinely in the US.

Alpha-tocopherol, or vitamin E, in doses of 2000 international units has been shown to slow progression of Alzheimer's disease. The drug works as a free radical scavenger and promotes nerve cell viability.

Selegeline, or Eldepryl, is an agent that both raises the levels of certain neurochemicals and promotes nerve cell viability, has been used in the US for the treatment of Parkinson's disease. It has been shown to be effective for the treatment of Alzheimer's.

Non-steroidal anti-inflammatory agents, or NSAIDS, include drugs such as ibuprofen (Motrin, Advil, etc) may have some utility in *preventing* Alzheimer's disease. However, NSAIDs were not effective in *treating* Alzheimer's.

Gingko biloba, a free radical scavenger and possible brain activator, is said to be the third most commonly prescribed drug for the treatment of dementia in Germany. Preparations of the drug in the US vary and the right dose of the right preparations may slow progression of some types of memory loss.

Estrogen may increase or reduce risk for Alzheimer's disease in women, although data on this topic is exceptionally confusing and controversial. Please see the section on menopause and memory for more on this topic.

B-secretase inhibitors are the newest and most exciting class of drugs being developed for treating memory loss. These drugs stop formation of amyloid plaque and may halt progression of illnesses like Alzheimer's.

Vaccines that dissolve plaques in the brain are also in development. A clinical trial using a vaccine developed by Elan was recently stopped because of possible side effects in some patients.

Certain classes of the B vitamins are felt to be neuroprotective and are being used in clinical trials for treating memory loss.

Calcium channel blockers, a class of drugs used to treat illnesses like hypertension and migraine, have been used to treat memory loss.

Statins, a class of drugs used to lower cholesterol levels, may reduce amyloid plaque formation and thus may be helpful in some types of memory loss.

Clioquinol, an antibiotic withdrawn from the US market in the 1970s because of adverse effects may reduce plaque formation by binding to zinc and copper. A recent Swedish study found some benefit in patients with Alzheimer's disease.

> Please note that all material contained herein is provided for informational purposes only and should not be considered as medical advice or instruction for treatment. Consult your health care professional for advice relating to a medical problem or condition. Information is for class use only.

COGNITIVE BEHAVIOR STRATEGIES FOR IMPROVING MEMORY

Improving your memory is easier than it sounds. Most people of think of memory as something static and unchanging. But it is not. You can improve your memory just as you can improve your math or foreign language skills, simply by practicing a few tried and true memory building exercises.

Your Memory is in Your Brain

Although it may seem obvious, memory is formed within your brain. So anything that generally improves your brain health may also have a positive impact on your memory. Physical exercise and engaging in novel brain-stimulating activities — such as the crossword puzzle or Sudoku — are two proven methods for helping keep your brain healthy.

Remember, a healthy body is a healthy brain. Eating right and keeping stress at bay helps not only your mind focus on new information, but also is good for your body too. Getting a good night's <u>sleep</u> every night is important as well. Vitamin supplements and herbal extracts aren't the same thing as getting vitamins and omega-3 fatty acids naturally, through the food you eat.

Strategies to Improve Your Memory

So you want to improve your memory? You need to focus on what you're doing and the information you're looking to encode more strongly in your brain. These tips will help you do just that:

1. **Focus on it.** So many people get caught up in multi-tasking, that we often fail to do the one thing that will almost always improve your memory — paying attention to the task at hand. This is important, because your brain needs time to encode the information properly. If it never makes it into your memory, you won't be able to recall it later. If you need to memorize something, quit multitasking.

2. **Smell, touch, taste, hear and see it.** The more senses you involve when you need to encode memory, usually the more strong a memory it becomes. That's why the smell of mom's home-baked cookies can still be recalled as fresh as though she were downstairs making them just now. Need to remember someone's name you met for the first time? It may help to look them in the eye when you repeat their name, and offer a handshake. By doing so, you've engaged 4 out of your 5 senses.

3. **Repeat it.** One reason people who want to memorize something repeat it over and over again is because repetition (what psychologists sometimes refer to as "over learning") seems to work for most people. It helps not to cram, though. Instead,

repeat the information spaced out over a longer period of time.

4. **Chunk it.** Americans remember their long 10-digit telephone numbers despite being able to hold only 7 pieces of information in their brain at one time. They do because we've taught ourselves to chunk the information. Instead of seeing 10 separate pieces of information, we see 3 pieces of information — a 3 digit area code, a 3 digit prefix, and a 4 digit number. Because we've been taught since birth to "chunk" the telephone number in this way, most people don't have a problem remembering a telephone number. This technique works for virtually any piece of information. Divide the large amount of information into smaller chunks, and then focus on memorizing those chunks as individual pieces.

5. **Organize it.** Our brains like organization of information. That's why books have chapters, and outlines are recommended as a studying method in school. By carefully organizing what it is you have to memorize, you're helping your brain better encode the information in the first place.

6. **Learn it the way that works for you.** People often get caught up in thinking there's a "one size fits all" learning style for memorizing new material. That's simply not the case — different people prefer different methods for taking in new information. Use the style that works for you, even if it's not the way most people study or try and learn new information. For instance, some people like to write things down when they're learning something new. Others may benefit more from recording what they're hearing, and going back to take more detailed notes later on at their own leisure.

7. **Connect the dots.** When we learn, we often forget to try and make associations until later on. However, research has shown that memory can be stronger when you try and make the associations when you first take in the information. For instance, think about how two things are related, and the memory for both will be enhanced.

Connect new information to existing information or experiences in your mind.

Mneumonics

Mnemonic devices are techniques a person can use to help them improve their ability to remember something. In other words, it's a <u>memory</u> technique to help your brain better encode and recall important information. It's a simple shortcut that helps us associate the information we want to remember with an image, a sentence, or a word.

Mnemonic devices are very old, with some dating back to ancient Greek times. Virtually everybody uses them, even if they don't know their name. It's simply a way of memorizing information so that it "sticks" within our brain longer and can be recalled more easily in the future.

Popular mnemonic devices include:

The Method of Loci

The Method of Loci is a mnemonic device that dates back to Ancient Greek times, making it one of the oldest ways of memorizing we know of. Using the Method of Loci is easy. First, imagine a place with which you are familiar. For instance, if you use your house, the rooms in your house become the objects of information you need to memorize. Another example is to use the route to your work or school, with landmarks along the way becoming the information you need to memorize.

You go through a list of words or concepts needing memorization, and associate each word with one of your locations. You should go in order so that you will be able to retrieve all of the information in the future.

Acronyms

An acronym is a word formed from the first letters or groups of letters in a name or phrase. An acrostic is a series of lines from which particular letters (such as the first letters of all lines) from a word or phrase. These can be used as mnemonic devices by taking the

first letters of words or names that need to be remembered and developing an acronym or acrostic.

For instance, in music, students must remember the order of notes so that they can identify and play the correct note while reading music. The notes of the treble staff are EGBDF. The common acrostic used for this are *Every Good Boy Does Fine* or *Every Good Boy Deserves Fudge*. The notes on the bass staff are ACEG, which commonly translates into the acrostic *All Cows Eat Grass.*

Rhymes

A rhyme is a saying that has similar terminal sounds at the end of each line. Rhymes are easier to remember because they can be stored by acoustic encoding in our brains. For example:

- In fourteen hundred and ninety-two Columbus sailed the Ocean Blue.
- *Thirty days hath September, April, June, and November; All the rest have thirty-one, Save February, with twenty-eight days clear, And twenty-nine each leap year.*

Chunking & Organization

Chunking is simply a way of breaking down larger pieces of information into smaller, organized "chunks" of more easily-managed information. Telephone numbers in the United States are a perfect example of this — 10 digits broken into 3 chunks, allowing almost everyone to remember an entire phone number with ease. Since short-term human memory is limited to approximately 7 items of information, placing larger quantities of information into smaller containers helps our brains remember more, and more easily.

Organizing information into either objective or subjective categories also helps. Objective organization is placing information into well-recognized, logical categories. Trees and grass are plants; a cricket is an insect. Subjective organization is categorizing seemingly unrelated items in a way that helps you recall the items later. This can also be useful because it breaks down the amount of information to learn. If you can divide a list of items into a fewer number of categories, then all you have to remember is the categories (fewer items), which will serve as memory cues in the future.

Imagery

Visual imagery is a great way to help memorize items for some people. For instance, it's often used to memorize pairs of words (green grass, yellow sun, blue water, etc.). The Method of Loci, mentioned above, is a form of using imagery for memorization. By recalling specific imagery, it can help us recall information we associated with that imagery.

Imagery usually works best with smaller pieces of information. For instance, when trying to remember someone's name you've just been introduced to. You can imagine a pirate with a wooden leg for "Peggy," or a big grizzly bear for "Harry."

STRATEGIES FOR STUDYING FOR AN EXAM

Before you study for your next exam, you might want to use a few strategies to boost your memory of important information. There are a number of tried and tested techniques for improving memory. These strategies have been established within cognitive psychology literature and offer a number of great ways to improve memory, enhance recall and increase retention of information.

1. *Focus your attention on the materials you are studying*.

Attention is one of the major components of memory. In order for information to move from short-term memory into long-term memory, you need to actively attend to this information. Try to study in a place free of distractions such as television, music and other diversions.

2. *Avoid cramming by establishing regular study sessions*.

According to Bjork (2001), studying materials over a number of session's gives you the time you need to adequately process the information. Research has shown that students who study regularly remember the material far better than those who did all of their studying in one marathon session.

3. *Structure and organize the information you are studying*.

Researchers have found that information is organized in memory in related clusters. You can take advantage of this by structuring and organizing the materials you are studying. Try grouping similar concepts and terms together, or make an outline of your notes and textbook readings to help group related concepts.

4. *Utilize mnemonic devices to remember information*.

Mnemonic devices are a technique often used by students to aid in recall. A mnemonic is simply a way to remember information. For example, you might associate a term you need to remember with a common item that you are very familiar with. The best mnemonics are those that utilize positive imagery, humor or novelty. You might come up with a rhyme, song or joke to help remember a specific segment of information.

5. *Elaborate and rehearse the information you are studying*.

In order to recall information, you need to encode what you are studying into long-term memory. One of the most effective encoding techniques is known as elaborative rehearsal. An example of this technique would be to read the definition of a key term, study the definition of that term and then read a more detailed description of what that term means. After repeating this process a few times, your recall of the information will be far better.

6. *Relate new information to things you already know*.

When you are studying unfamiliar material, take the time to think about how this information relates to things that you already know. By establishing relationships between new ideas and previously existing memories, you can dramatically increase the likelihood of recalling the recently learned information.

7. ***Visualize concepts to improve memory and recall.***

Many people benefit greatly from visualizing the information they study. Pay attention to the photographs, charts and other graphics in your textbooks. If you do not have visual cues to help, try creating your own. Draw charts or figures in the margins of your notes or use highlighters or pens in different colors to group related ideas in your written study materials.

8. ***Teach new concepts to another person.***

Research suggests that reading materials out loud significantly improves memory of the material. Educators and psychologists have also discovered that having students actually *teach* new concepts to others enhances understanding and recall. You can use this approach in your own studies by teaching new concepts and information to a friend or study partner.

CHAPTER 6 SUMMARY

MEMORY
This is a process of storing and retrieving previously presented material.

INFORMATION PROCESSING
An apt metaphor to describe this is the brain as computer processing unit. This may help someone understand how that information is presented, stored, manipulated, and output is generated based upon this information. From a definition standpoint, it is frequently referred to as a process involving memory of all types, as well as attention and learning.

TYPES OF MEMORY
The standard model of memory includes:
- Sensory memory: Discuss iconic and echoic memory as visual and auditory memory respectively.
- Short-term memory: Here, it is useful to consider methods of enhancing memory. Practicing these approaches using different methods with the class can be most informative. For example, by showing how the method of loci works with a list of ideas that is all unrelated might profitably illustrate how these processes work.
- Long-term memory: This is also best illustrated by example, with particular effects easily noted here as well. Three important ideas in long-term memory involve serial position effects, primacy, and recency effects. Each of these can be illustrated using word lists and relative recall over the session. Interference effects can also be illustrated by presenting competing lists. Students can be quizzed for personal examples of long-term memory effects.

WORKING MEMORY
Brain areas involved in specific memory processes can be presented here in lecture format. Most of the material may focus upon the prefrontal cortex and the directing of material from the hippocampus to relevant brain areas for storage. Also important at this point is the difference between working memory and long-term memory. Here, a discussion of the difference between styles of encoding and chunking of material into memory can be pursued.

LONG-TERM MEMORY
Long-term memory (LTM) is divided into a number of categories. Declarative memory is material that is being learned in an ongoing manner. It has not become automatic in process yet. An example that illustrates this well, and is usually fresh in students' minds involves learning to drive. When this task is first initiated, all the steps involved are declarative. One has to think carefully about each step in beginning and ending the

task. This example can lead to a discussion of how declarative memory is transferred to procedural memory. For many students, driving is now procedural. That is, they can get in a car and drive away, with little thought required regarding the steps involved in driving a vehicle.

RECALL AND RECOGNITION

These are important topics to consider, and can also be illustrated on the basis of example. If the class is structured with multiple-choice exams, then the primary memory function relied upon is recognition; if they are short-answer, then recall in a more pure form is utilized for performance. Memories of these sorts can be primed. This is accomplished when information related to the memory is presented, activating the relevant memory. This can be illustrated by the common example by the reaction of some students who upon receiving their exam back (with an answer key) note that they knew the information (there is also frequently a disappointed noise that follows as well).

ENCODING/ORGANIZATION OF LONG-TERM MEMORY

Here, it is important to detail the varieties of processing, such as deep (elaborate details in memory) versus shallow (bare minimum of details in memory) processing describes how memory is encoded. Context effects can be illustrated by how certain environments can aid in memory retrieval.

In order to discuss spaced and distributed practice, studying provides the perfect example (and may spark a change in student behavior with regard to exam preparation).

Many students 'pull all-nighters.' The value of this method of study can be discussed from the perspective of stress, ability to continue encoding, and efficiency of recall and performance. Contrast this with distributive practice, which distributes not only the activity, but also the stress level associated with studying. In this context, the varying mnemonic devices may be covered as well.

While furthering the class understanding of memory and encoding, a more elaborate theory may be covered, that of association networks, and schemas. Although separate, these items may be treated in the same context in order to develop the idea. Schemas, as well as association networks provide frameworks for organizing memory. This can be shown from the perspective of efficiency when describing the notion that different, unrelated stimuli and information is encoded, but it all has to be arranged meaningfully or it will be difficult to utilize. One can rely on the computer processing unit metaphor to show that each item is in a file, which is in a database, with key terms in each file associated with other key terms.

FORGETTING

Any discussion of forgetting should also focus on relative accuracy of memories, and the decay of memory over time. Here, discussion may center on flashbulb memories, eyewitness memory and two different effects upon forgetting. These are proactive interference and retroactive interference. Finally, there are times when one might attempt to forget information, and this can be highlighted as well (motivated forgetting).

KEY TERMS

Amnesia	The loss of memory.
anterograde amnesia	memory disorder that affects the retention of new information and events.
decay theory	Theory stating that when something new is learned, a neurochemical memory trace is formed, but over time this trace tends to disintegrate.
Elaboration	Extensiveness of processing at any given level of memory.
Encoding	The process by which information gets into memory storage.
episodic memory	The retention of information about the where, when, and what of life's happenings.
explicit memory (declarative memory)	The conscious recollection of information, such as specific facts or events and, at least in humans, information that can be verbally communicated.
flashbulb memory	The memory of emotionally significant events that people often recall more accurately and vividly than everyday events.
implicit memory (nondeclarative memory)	Memory in which behavior is affected by prior experience without that experience being consciously recollected.

6

interference theory	Theory stating that people forget not because memories are lost from storage but because other information gets in the way of what they want to remember.
levels of processing	The idea that coding occurs on a continuum from shallow to deep, with deeper processing producing better memory.
long-term memory	A relatively permanent type of memory that stores huge amounts of information for a long time.
Memory	The retention of information over time the processes of encoding, storage, and retrieval.
Mnemonics	Specific visual and/or verbal memory aids.
motivated forgetting	An act of forgetting something because it is so painful or anxiety-laden that remembering it is intolerable.
Priming	A type of implicit memory process involving the activation of information that people already have in storage to help them remember new information better and faster.
proactive interference	Situation in which material that was learned earlier disrupts the recall of material learned later.
procedural memory	Memory for skills.
prospective memory	Remembering information about doing something in the future.
Retrieval	The memory process of taking information out of storage.
retroactive interference	Situation in which material learned later disrupts the retrieval of information learned earlier.
retrograde amnesia	A memory disorder that involves memory loss for a segment of the past but not for new events.
retrospective memory	Remembering the past.

Schema	A concept or framework that already exists at a given moment in a person's mind and that organizes information and provides a structure for interpreting it.
Script	A schema for an event.
semantic memory	A person's knowledge about the world.
sensory memory	Information from the world that is held in its original form only for an instant, not much longer than the brief time it is exposed to the visual, auditory, and other senses.
serial position effect	The tendency for items at the beginning and at the end of a list to be recalled more readily than those in the middle of the list.
short-term memory	A limited-capacity memory system in which information is retained for only as long as 30 seconds unless strategies are used to retain it longer.
storage	Retention of information over time and the representation of information in memory.
tip-of-the-tongue phenomenon (TOT state)	The "effortful retrieval" that occurs when people are confident that they know something but cannot pull it out of memory.

LANGUAGE AND THOUGHT: THE BRIDGE BETWEEN COMMUNICATION AND SOCIALIZATION

LEARNING OBJECTIVES

After completing Chapter 7, students should be able to:

- Discuss the role of mental representations in forming concepts and categories.
- Classify different sorts of concepts.
- Describe how people categorize objects.
- Outline the goal-directed aspects of reasoning, problem solving, and decision-making.
- Discuss the interplay between explicit and implicit reasoning in our everyday thinking.
- Discuss ways in which specific languages shape thought, along with the ways that concrete social situations shape languages.
- Outline the connectionist models of thinking.
- Describe the areas of the brain associated with various kinds of thinking.
- Outline the building blocks of language.
- Define what psychologists mean by the "pragmatics" of language.
- Outline Chomsky's major claims about universal grammar.
- Outline the stages of language acquisition in children.
- Discuss the interplay between nature and nurture in language acquisition

LANGUAGE AS A HUMAN PHENOMENON

INTRODUCTION

Even the most formal and abstract work on linguistic structure is colored by the awareness that language is uniquely a human phenomenon. It is innately implanted in the human brain; it is passed on across generations; it is intimately bound up with the forms of human thought. Unlike other specialized system such as science and mathematics, language meets a wide range of social needs that are met through verbal and nonverbal needs, for example, getting your neighbor control their children, CNN reporting national and international news, telling jokes, expressing emotions of love and satisfaction, or praying to a higher power. Furthermore, language serves as a marker and or identifier of a social class, ethnic group, or nation.

Psychologists are interested in how language shapes the way persons perceive the world and then respond to its influence. Linguists document the remarkable diversity of means of expression employed in the languages of the world. At the same time, though, researchers have come to understand that many of the features of language are universal, both because there are universal aspects to human experience and because language has a built-in biological basis.

The American linguist Benjamin Lee Whorf (1897-1941) proposed that a relationship exists between language and thought, which is known as the Whorfian hypothesis (or the Sapir-Whorf hypothesis).

The Language of Thought Hypothesis (LOTH) postulates that thought and thinking take place in a mental language. This language consists of a system of representations that is physically realized in the brain of thinkers. Most of the arguments for LOTH derive their strength from their ability to explain certain empirical phenomena like productivity and systematicity of thought and thinking.

The ability to use language is a very important part of human cognition. In fact, some would argue that it is this ability which distinguishes us from other animals. Regardless of one's view of the capability of animals to use language or language-like symbols, the fact that humans have language abilities far superior to those of other animals is not disputed. The focus of this chapter is to explore how language helps us and how we use language to develop and maintain existence and socialization within the world. First, it is clear that language is used to communicate one's thoughts to other people. In the expression and exchange of thought through language, relationships are formed or broken, strengthened or weakened, ideas are developed, improved, or dissolved, the expression of emotions are projected, and business networks are formed. Language is the link to socialization and human connections with each other and the world. The expression of thought through language is heard and sometimes silenced. People use language in many different forms. How one communicates is based on the strength of their language, whether verbal or nonverbal, letters, electronic emails, or avoidance. It is all a form of language used to express thinking. What is key in the expression of language is that the message intended is conveyed correctly. Therefore, the means of transferring a message via language must be clear to avoid the error of miscommunication of thoughts and facts.

Howard Gardner and Andy Clark have identified other reasons for the use of language as discussed in his book *Frames of Mind: The Theory of Multiple Intelligences.*

1. Language is used to create an action and or reaction in other people, for example, the cry of a baby depending on the pitch will indicate the need of food, sleep, or to help relieve pain. The higher the pitch, the greater the need.

2. Language is used to provide cues or guides that can help an individual remember a skill or steps to complete a tasks. Mnuemonics are often used to complete mathematics problems.

3. language is used to provide knowledge in a didactic or cooperative fashion. For example, a teacher in a classroom teaching a lesson on photosynthesis or students completing a group project requires language and the exchange of knowledge between individuals.

4. Language is used as means to reflect and critically analyze points of interests. A child asking his or her parents, "where do babies come from?" is a means of critical thought that extends beyond the cognitive abilities of a 5 year old.

As you can see, language is used for many reasons to create an exchange between one person and another. The need for communication is common across all races, cultures, and age groups. Language is a skill that is uniquely committed to humans and is acquired throughout a life span.

LANGUAGE DEFINED

Language is the predominant means by which human beings communicate with each other. In broad terms, language is an ability to understand and systematically use symbols. Humans especially make use of verbal symbols (i.e. the spoken word) for communicating. The symbol-words are combined according to specific rules in order to create and convey meanings. These words are selected through cognitive reflection and used to express a thought regarding the current situation.

We can use language to describe novel events, situations which have happened in the past and situations that will happen in the future. Moreover, we can communicate concrete ideas about the here-and-now as well as abstract concepts such as feelings, attitudes and perceptions. There is seemingly a near infinite flexibility to what human beings are capable of communicating. The way we communicate is a reflection of learned speech, language, and personality traits.

SPEECH

Human beings use speech as the most effective and flexible means of communicating ideas and sharing experiences and knowledge. This is true of all human social groups. In fact, throughout history there have been societies that have existed without being able to read or write but it is not known to have societies that exist without the use of speech.

Speech is the transmission system of language. It is highly complex and, arguably, it has to be learned. It involves rapid, coordinated movements of the lips, tongue, palate of the mouth, vocal folds (popularly, although inaccurately, also known as vocal cords) and breathing to articulate sounds which are then used to add a form meaning to words, such as intonation.

As with language, speech also has its own set of rules that govern which particular sound combinations may or may not be produced. For example, in English, the sound 'ng' is allowable at the ends of words, such as in *wing*, *sing* and *ring*. However, this sound never occurs at the beginning of words, i.e. there are no words in English which begin with 'ng'.

THE THEORETICAL DEBATE OF LANGUAGE

The Issues

Howard Gardner, along with Noam Chomsky and many others, believes that parts of the brain have evolved over time specifically for the purpose of producing and understanding language. Thinkers such as Andy Clark and Jean Piaget, on the other hand, believe that public language utilizes brain structures and psychological functions that were already present before the development of this important tool. In the first ("nature") school of thought, linguistic abilities have developed over time as a result of Darwinian evolution. In the conflicting ideology (a "nurture" position), there is no innate linguistic ability; and linguistic evolution occurs as a result of learning and cultural evolution, which will be explained in greater detail below, rather than through natural selection. The beliefs do overlap; and oftentimes the proponents of one side argue against what they suppose the other side would believe, when in fact the other side subscribes to no such ideology. For example, the nature proponents argue that human brains are biologically different from the brains of other animals; and that at least part of this difference is due to innate, inherited differences in genes.

Similarly, both sides agree that language draws from and influences other thought processes. However, there is a controversy centered on the extent of this interaction. It appears that the two schools of thought agree on almost all basic tenets of language use, and disagree only on the exact recipe for combining these tenets.

Chomsky, Gardner, and others of similar ideologies believe that infants are born with a significant prewired knowledge of how languages work and how they do not work. Views within this group vary slightly, but they all hold to this basic tenet that proponents of the innateness of linguistic ability has a genetic basis for language development. This view stems from Darwinian evolution and by an extension of the "survival of the fittest" argument. Again, individual views vary slightly, but all supporters of this school of thought see language as a product of Darwinian evolution.

On the other hand, Piaget, Clark, and others see the newborn as possessing only a few basic cognitive abilities. The more specific abilities we see in the developing child, they argue, are due to interactions with the environment and are independent of any inheritable code found in the genes. They place language skills in this category, and so they disagree completely with Chomsky's assertion that humans inherit certain linguistic knowledge (Gardner 80). In addition, proponents of the Nurture ideology view public language as a tool constructed by people for use by people, and they believe its development is due to cultural evolution, a completely different mechanism for change (Clark 200-213).

Cultural evolution, like Darwinian evolution, brings about changes within the human species. However, these changes occur at a much faster rate and by different mechanisms. Whereas traits in "Darwinian" evolution are passed from one generation to the next through genes only, without regard to what progress one generation has made or what it has learned during its lifetime, traits in cultural evolution are passed on through language from one generation to the next. This means that progress made by one generation can be selectively passed on to the next, which does not occur with random genetic mutations. The focus and ease of transfer characteristic of cultural evolution lead to changes that takes place at such a fast rate that the effects of Darwinian evolution, in comparison, are practically negligible. As scientist Stephen Jay Gould remarks, "While the gene for sickle-cell anemia declines in frequency among black Americans, we have invented the railroad, the automobile, radio and television, the atom bomb, the computer, the airplane and spaceship." Clearly, cultural evolution is a distinct process from Darwinian evolution and accounts for many changes in human behavior (324).

"Nurture" advocates in the language debate believe that humans invented language as they did computers through the process of cultural evolution. Again, subscribers to this school of thought have gathered much evidence in support of their theories. Indeed, determining which of these two theories better describes human linguistic ability will require careful examination of the arguments and evidence and even after such examination will nonetheless prove to be a difficult task.

PSYCHOLOGY OF LANGUAGE

Psycholinguistics studies explain how human beings develop and use language. This provides deeper knowledge into how the human brain functions and how the use of language and emotion is closely tied together. Determining what words were used, and in what context, hundreds of years ago and comparing those words to the one's used today can provide psychologists of a greater idea of where humans have been and what direction they may be taking.

Language as a Social Phenomenon

The social life of language begins with the smallest and most informal interactions. Every conversation is a social transaction, governed by rules that determine how sentences are put together into larger discourses—stories, jokes, or whatever—and how participants take turns speaking and let each other know that they are attending to what is being said. The organization of these interactions is the subject of the subfield called discourse analysis.

At a larger level, the field of sociolinguistics is also concerned with the way the divisions of societies into social classes and ethnic, religious, and racial groups are often mirrored by linguistic differences. Of particular interest here, too, is the way language is used differently by men and women.

In most parts of the world, communities use more than one language, and the phenomenon of bilingualism or multilingualism has a special interest for linguists. Multilingualism raises particular psychological questions: How do two or more languages coexist within an individual mind? How do bilingual individuals decide when to switch from one language to another? It also raises questions at the level of the community, where the question of which language to use is determined by tacit understandings, and sometimes by official rules and regulations that may invoke difficult questions about the relation of language to nationality. In many nations, including the US, there are currently important debates about establishing an official language.

Multilingual communities are interesting to linguists for another reason: Languages that come into contact can influence each other in various ways, sometimes converging in grammar or other features. Under certain social conditions, a mix of languages can give rise to 'new' languages called pidgins and creoles, which have a particular interest for linguists because of the way they shed light on language structure and function. Often, though, the result when languages come into contact is that one becomes dominant at the expense of the other, especially when the contact pits a widely used language of a powerful community against a local or minority language. Modern communications have accelerated this process, to the point where the majority of the languages currently used in the world are endangered, and may disappear within a few generations—a situation that causes linguists concerns that go beyond the purely academic.

Psychological Body Language

Body language is any type of non-verbal communication. Unlike linguistics, a mostly conscious act, humans display and interpret body language at a subconscious level. Psychologists study body posture, gestures and expressions to determine the moods and thoughts of humans. The study of body language also provides a look into the subconscious mind, allowing psychologists to better understand how human's communicate, and how their words differ from their actual meaning.

Psychology of Eye Contact

The study of eye contact, also known as oculesics, is used in psychology and unconsciously by society to determine to mood and personality of a person. There are several nuances in the psychology of eye contact, most easily understood by an initial meeting between strangers. Making eye contact when being introduced to someone sends an unconscious signal to the other person that you hold him or her in high regard and are confident. However, when taken to the extreme of staring, which is prolonged eye contact, this can make others feel threatened or held in contempt, sending the opposite message. Psychologists have also determined a pattern to tell when a person is lying, which is fairly accurate. This study of eye contact is based on the eye movements a person makes before they make a statement, and where their eyes are when speaking.

THE BASIC COMPONENTS OF HUMAN LANGUAGE

Human language involves both receptive and productive use. Receptive language use occurs during the comprehension or understanding of words and sentences. Productive language use involves idea generation and the articulation of words in speech. Both reception and production utilize the fiver basic structural components of language:

1. *Phonology*: The system of the sound segments that humans use to build up words. The study of the sounds of language is called phonology. The sounds of human language are special because they are produced by a set of organs, the speech organs, that belong only to the human species. The actual sounds that come out of our mouths are called phones, and they vary continuously in acoustic properties. However, we hear all the phones within a particular range of variation as functionally equivalent allophones of the same phoneme, or characteristic speech sound, in the language. Each language has a different set of these segments or phonemes, and children quickly come to recognize and then produce the speech segments that are characteristic of their native language.

2. *Semantics*: The system of meanings that are expressed by words and phrases. In order to serve as a means of communication between people, words must have a shared or conventional meaning. In the 1960s, formal semantics took off when Chomsky argued that grammars needed to represent all of the linguistic knowledge in a speaker's head, and word meanings were part of that knowledge. Formal semanticists focused attention on how words are linked to each other within a language, exploring such relations as synonymy, or "same meaning" (old and aged);

homophony, or "same sound, different meaning" (would and wood); and antonymy, or "opposite meaning" (tall and short). They also defined words in terms of denotation, or what they referred to in the "real world." Picking out the correct meaning for each new word is a major learning task for children.

3. *Syntax*: **Sentence Structure** A third component of language is syntax, or sentence structure. Linguists began to study syntax when they discovered that morphological rules alone could not account for certain patterns of morpheme use. In languages like English, for example, rules governing word order cannot explain what is puzzling about the following English sentence:

    1. Grammar: The system of rules by which words and phrases are arranged to make meaningful statements. Children need to learn how to use the ordering of words to mark grammatical functions such as subject or direct object.

    2. Pragmatics: The system of patterns that determine how humans can use language in particular social settings for particular conversational purposes. Children learn that conversations customarily begin with a greeting, require turn taking, and concern a shared topic. They come to adjust the content of their communications to match their listener's interests, knowledge, and language ability.

These five basic systems can be extended and elaborated when humans use language for special purposes, such as for poetry, song, legal documents, or scientific discourse. The literate control of language constructs additional complex social, cognitive, and linguistic structures that are built on top of the four basic structural components.

SUMMARY OF LANGUAGE

Almost every human child succeeds in learning language. As a result, people often tend to take the process of language learning for granted. To many, language seems like a basic instinct, as simple as breathing or blinking. But language is not simple at all; in fact it is the most complex skill that a human being will ever master. That nearly all people succeed in learning this complex skill demonstrates how well language has adapted to human nature. In a very real sense, language is the complete expression of what it means to be human. All humans use language in one form or another, and psychologists and linguists has noted many similarities in how children acquire language and their use of the language to convey a message. Therefore, in the case with most humans, the acquisition of language occurs as a combined act of nature and nurture.

Psychologists and those linguists who reject the Chomskyan approach often view language learning from a very different perspective. To the psychologist, language acquisition is a window on the operation of the human mind. The patterns of language emerge not from a unique instinct but from the operation of general processes of evolution and cognition. For researchers who accept this emergentist approach, the goal of language acquisition studies is to understand how regularities in linguistic form emerge from the operation of low-level physical, neural, and social processes. Before considering the current state of the dialog between the view of language as a hard-wired instinct and the view of language as an emergent process, it will be useful to review a few basic facts about the shape of language acquisition and some of the methods that are used to study it.

ANATOMY OF LANGUAGE

THE STRUCTURE OF THE BRAIN

A basic understanding of the structure and form of the essential body parts that allow humans to communicate by language through the transmission system of speech is enlightening. It helps us appreciate the relationship between the brain and language. There are two major areas of the human brain that are responsible for language: **Broca's area**, which is thought to be partially responsible for language production (putting together sentences, using proper syntax, etc.) and **Wernicke's area**, which is thought to be partially responsible for language processing (untangling others' sentences and analyzing them for syntax, inflection, etc.). Other areas involved in language are those surrounding the **Sylvian fissure**, a cleavage line separating the portions of the brain that are exclusively human from those we share with other animals, (Catherwood, D., 2000).

The brain is divided into three parts: cerebrum, cerebellum and brain stem. The cerebrum is responsible for reasoning, emotion, memory, motor movements, and speech and language skills. The cerebellum

co-ordinates motor movements and the brain stem controls automatic functions such as breathing.

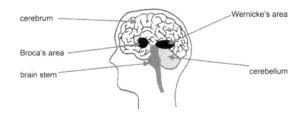

Figure X. Anatomy of the Brain

Cerebrum

The cerebrum is divided along the **longitudinal fissure** into two almost identical halves: the left and the right **cerebral hemispheres**. The outer layer of each hemisphere is known as the **cerebral cortex** and it is highly convoluted, with many intricate folds. These serve to increase the surface area of the brain. The left hemisphere controls the movements of the right-hand side of the body and the right hemisphere controls the left side. In most people one of the hemispheres is dominant over the other and, for most people, it is the left hemisphere that is dominant. Therefore, most people are right-handed, as it is the left hemisphere that dominates.

For many years, people had wondered which hemisphere controlled speech. In 1836, the Frenchman Marc Dax noticed that people who suffered a paralysis of the right-hand side of their body, as a result of a stroke, frequently lost their speech as well. A paralysis of the right side of the body must be due to damage to the left hemisphere, as the left hemisphere controls the right side of the body. As the loss of speech was also due to brain damage and as it was the left hemisphere that was damaged then, Dax deduced, it must be the left hemisphere that controls speech. Speech, then, is said to be localized in one half of the brain, usually the left hemisphere. As stated above, the production of speech is localized in **Broca's area** and the ability to comprehend spoken language is localized in **Wernicke's area**.

In summary, the cerebrum is responsible for such things as reasoning ability, emotion, memory, motor movements, and speech and language skills.

Phases in Language Development

William James (1890) described the world of the newborn as a "blooming, buzzing confusion." It is now known, however, that, on the auditory level at least, the newborn's world is remarkably well structured. The cochlea (in the inner ear) and the auditory nerve (which connects the inner ear with the brain) provide extensive preprocessing of signals for pitch and intensity. In the 1970s and 1980s, researchers discovered that human infants were specifically adapted at birth to perceive contrasts in sounds such as that between /p/ and /b/, as in the words *pit* and *bit*. Subsequent research showed that even chinchillas are capable of making this distinction. This suggests that much of the basic structure of the infant's auditory world can be attributed to fundamental processes in the mammalian ear. Moreover, there is evidence that some of these early perceptual abilities are lost as the infant begins to acquire the distinctions actually used by the

native language. Beyond this basic level of auditory processing, it appears that infants have a remarkable capacity to record and store sequences of auditory events. It is as if the infant has a tape recorder in the brain's auditory cortex that records input sounds, replays them, and accustoms the ear to their patterns.

Children tend to produce their first words sometime between nine and twelve months. One-year-olds have about 5 words in their vocabulary on average, although individual children may have none or as many as thirty; by two years of age, average vocabulary size is more than 150 words, with a range among individual children from as few as 10 to as many as 450 words. Children possess a vocabulary of about 14,000 words by six years of age; adults have an estimated average of 40,000 words in their working vocabulary at age forty. In order to achieve such a vocabulary, a child must learn to say at least a few new words each day from birth.

One of the best predictors of a child's vocabulary development is the amount and diversity of input the child receives. Researchers have found that verbal input can be as great as three times more available in educated families as in less educated families. These facts have led educators to suspect that basic and pervasive differences in the level of social support for language learning lie at the root of many learning problems in the later school years. Social interaction (quality of attachment; parent responsiveness, involvement, sensitivity, and control style) and general intellectual climate (providing enriching toys, reading books, encouraging attention to surroundings) predict developing language competence in children as well. Relatively uneducated and economically disadvantaged mothers talk less frequently to their children compared with more educated and affluent mothers, and correspondingly, children of less educated and less affluent mothers produce less speech. Socioeconomic status relates to both child vocabulary and to maternal vocabulary. Middle-class mothers expose their children to a richer vocabulary, with longer sentences and a greater number of word roots.

Whereas vocabulary development is marked by spectacular individual variation, the development of grammatical and syntactic skills is highly stable across children. Children's early one-word utterances do not yet trigger the need for syntactic patterns, because they are still only one-word long. By the middle of the second year, when children's vocabularies grow to between 50 and 100 words, they begin to combine words in what has been termed "telegraphic speech." Utterances typical of this period include forms such as "where Mommy," "my shoe," "dolly chair," and "allgone banana."

At this same time, children are busy learning to adjust their language to suit their audience and the situation. Learning the pragmatic social skills related to language is an ongoing process. Parents go to great efforts to teach their children to say "please" and "thank you" when needed, to be deferential in speaking to adults, to remember to issue an appropriate greeting when they meet someone, and not to interrupt when others are speaking. Children fine-tune their language skills to maintain conversations, tell stories, ask or argue for favors, or tattle on their classmates. Early on, they also begin to acquire the metalinguistic skills involved in thinking and making judgments about language.

As children move on to higher stages of language development and the acquisition of literacy, they depend increasingly on broader social institutions. They depend on Sunday school teachers for knowledge about Biblical language, prophets, and the geography of the Holy Land. They attend to science teachers to gain vocabulary and understandings about friction, molecular structures, the circulatory system, and DNA. They rely on peers to understand the language of the streets, verbal dueling, and the use of language for courtship. They rely on the media for role models, fantasies, and stereotypes. When they enter the workplace, they will rely on their coworkers to develop a literate understanding of work procedures, union rules, and methods for furthering their status. By reading to their children, telling stories, and engaging in supportive dialogs, parents set the stage for their children's entry into the world of literature and

schooling. Here, again, the parent and teacher must teach by displaying examples of the execution and generation of a wide variety of detailed literate practices, ranging from learning to write through outlines to taking notes in lectures.

The overarching goal of language is to engage in some form of mutual communication with others. Communication is a process that engages encoding, reception, and some form of response. However, the recipients and responders of language must do so with an intended purpose.

COMMUNICATION PROCESS

One model that defines the process of communication is the **transmission model**, which includes three basic elements of communication:

PRODUCTION → TRANSMISSION → RECEPTION

1. Production refers to the process by which a human agent expresses himself or herself through first deciding what message he or she wishes to communicate, then planning and encoding the appropriate linguistic utterance and, finally, producing this utterance through the suitable co-ordination of the vocal apparatus. Production is sometimes simply referred to as **expression**.

2. Transmission refers to the sending of the linguistic utterance through some medium to the recipient. As we are only concerned with oral verbal communication in this book, there is only one medium of consequence and that is air, i.e. the spoken utterance travels through the medium of air to the recipient's ear.

3. Reception refers to the process by which the recipient of a verbal utterance detects the utterance through the sense of hearing and then decodes the linguistic expression. Reception is often referred to as **comprehension**.

CONVERSATION PROCESSES

The **transmission model** is helpful in explaining the processes of communication; it does not fully emphasize the two-way nature of human communication. Indeed, the transmission model focuses on a single act of communication from one person to another without regard to reciprocation.

Communication is a **reciprocal social activity**. There is a constant interplay between the participants, with each taking turns at either initiate or respond to a transmission of some verbalized thought. The model below clarifies that conversational processes involve the act of encoding, interpreting, and decoding messages from a responder.

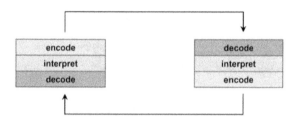

This reciprocal, interactive discourse is known as conversation. Indeed, conversation is the archetypal language used through which people participate in social interactions. An ability to converse easily is a major feature of <u>good communication skills.</u> <u>Communication involves all of the skills discussed above, which sometimes makes effective communication difficult if it is not practiced perfectly. Some individuals may experience language problems that make communication even more challenging. These are sometimes expressed in the form of language disabilities.</u>

LANGUAGE DISABILITIES

As discussed earlier, language is the expression of human communication through which knowledge, belief, and behavior can be experienced, explained, and shared. This sharing is based on systematic, conventionally used signs, sounds, gestures, or marks that convey understood meanings within a group or community. Recent research identifies "*windows of opportunity*" for acquiring language in the forms of written, spoken, or signed language. Signs of these will normally occur within the first few years of life.

However, between 6 and 8 million individuals in the United States have some form of language impairment. Disorders of language affect children and adults differently. For children who do not use language normally from birth, or who acquire impairments during childhood, language may not be fully developed or acquired. These children often will not perform at grade level. They may struggle with reading, have difficulty understanding and expressing language, misunderstand social cues, avoid attending school, show poor judgment, and have difficulty with tests.

Difficulty in learning to listen, speak, read, or write can result from problems in language development. Problems can occur in the production, comprehension, and awareness of language sounds, syllables, words, sentences, and conversation. Individuals with reading and writing problems also may have trouble using language to communicate, think, and learn.

Many children who are deaf in the United States use a natural sign language known as American Sign Language (ASL). ASL shares an underlying organization with spoken language and has its own syntax and grammar. Many adults acquire disorders of language because of stroke, head injury, dementia, or brain tumors. Language disorders also are found in adults who have failed to develop normal language skills because of mental disabilities, autism, hearing impairment, or other congenital or acquired disorders of brain development. Types of language disabilities are discussed below.

Expressive Language Disorder

A person with an *expressive language disorder* (as opposed to a mixed receptive/expressive language disorder) understands language better than he/she is able to communicate. In speech-language therapy terms, the person's *receptive language* (understanding of language) is better than his/her *expressive language* (use of language). This type of language disorder is often a component in *developmental language delay* (see section on this disorder). Expressive language disorders can also be *acquired* (occurring as a result of brain damage/injury), as in *aphasia*. The developmental type is more common in children, whereas the acquired type is more common in the elderly. An expressive language disorder could occur in a child of normal intelligence, or it could be a component of a condition affecting mental functioning more broadly (i.e. mental retardation, autism).

Children with expressive language delays often do not talk much. In school-aged children, expressive language difficulties may be evident in writing as well. These children may have difficulties with spelling, using words correctly, composing sentences, and performing written composition. These children may act out in school, or in later school years and reject learning completely without help. They may express frustration because they recognize that they cannot express the idea they wish to communicate. These children may become withdrawn socially because they cannot use language to relate to peers.

Receptive Language Disorder

Receptive language involves the comprehension of spoken language. Children with a receptive language disorder have difficulty understanding and processing what is said to them. They may have difficulty following directions, may often ask the speaker to repeat themselves, or may appear not to be listening. For a child with this diagnosis, spoken words may sound like a foreign language; the child can hear the words being said, but does not understand what they mean.

Receptive Language Disorders are a broad category and often overlap with other diagnoses. These diagnoses are often used by many people in different ways. Other names for a receptive language disorder may include:

- Auditory processing disorder;
- Auditory-linguistic processing disorder;
- Central auditory processing disorders (CAPD);

- Aphasia;
- Comprehension deficit;
- Word deafness;
- "Delayed language"

Developmental language disorders and expressive language disorders do not disappear with time. A speech-language pathologist can best diagnose an expressive language disorder. Parents and classroom teachers are in key positions to help in the evaluation as well as in the planning and implementation of treatment. Other professionals involved in assessment and treatment, especially as related to academics, include educational therapists, resource specialists, and tutors.

Voice

Voice (or vocalization) is the sound produced by humans and other vertebrates using the lungs and the vocal folds in the larynx, or voice box. Voice is not always produced as speech, however. Infants babble and coo; animals bark, moo, whinny, growl, and meow; and adult humans laugh, sing, and cry. Voice is generated by airflow from the lungs as the vocal folds are brought close together. When air is pushed past the vocal folds with sufficient pressure, the vocal folds vibrate. If the vocal folds in the larynx did not vibrate normally, speech could only be produced as a whisper. Your voice is as unique as your fingerprint. It helps define your personality, mood, and health.

Approximately 7.5 million people in the United States have trouble using their voices. Disorders of the voice involve problems with pitch, loudness, and quality. Pitch is the highness or lowness of a sound based on the frequency of the sound waves. Loudness is the perceived volume (or amplitude) of the sound, while quality refers to the character or distinctive attributes of a sound. Many people who have normal speaking skills have great difficulty communicating when their vocal apparatus fails. This can occur if the nerves controlling the larynx are impaired because of an accident, a surgical procedure, a viral infection, or cancer.

Speech

Humans express thoughts, feelings, and ideas *orally* to one another through a series of complex movements that alter and mold the basic tone created by voice into specific, decodable sounds. Speech is produced by precisely coordinated muscle actions in the head, neck, chest, and abdomen. Speech development is a gradual process that requires years of practice. During this process, a child learns how to regulate these muscles to produce understandable speech.

However, by the first grade, roughly 5 percent of children have noticeable speech disorders; the majority of these speech disorders have no known cause. One category of speech disorder is fluency disorder, or stuttering, which is characterized by a disruption in the flow of speech. It includes repetitions of speech sounds, hesitations before and during speaking, and the prolonged emphasis of speech sounds. More than 15 million individuals in the world stutter, most of who began stuttering at a very early age. The majority of speech sound disorders in the preschool years occur in children who are developing normally in all other areas. Speech disorders also may occur in children who have developmental disabilities.

The Onset of Stuttering

Stammering was recognized as long ago as the 4th Century BCE, when the philosopher Aristotle regarded it as being caused by 'too thick a hard tongue' leading to malfunction. Today we would reject his conclusion regarding the cause but we must acknowledge that stammering is not a condition to which only modern people have been prone. For any one individual, the onset of stuttering may be gradual or sudden. For most preschool children the onset is gradual. If the onset is sudden, however, it is important to investigate if there were any situations or events that may have induced the stutter.

It is relatively common for dysfluent people to have periods of fluency. The duration of these periods, however, can vary widely – ranging from a few minutes to weeks or months. But what causes stuttering?

Unfortunately, there still remain no clear cut answers. Several suggestions have been put forward but no one proposal appears to provide a complete explanation. A few of these proposals are outlined below.

The causes of stuttering are unknown but neurological development, parental reaction, trauma and a predisposition to stuttering have all been suggested.

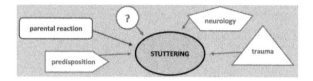

Stuttering Causes

Neurological development—Parents of young children may remark that 'the brain is racing ahead of the mouth' or something similar. In part, this may apply to children between 2-4 years of age. The infant's ability to co-ordinate the movements of their lips, mouth and tongue in a flowing, smooth and easy manner is much less well developed than their mental ability to think of what they want to say. This rationale may go some way to explaining why more males then females stutter, as we know that the neurological development of males is slower than that of females. However, as children mature neurologically, and develop greater control over their oral musculature, the suggestion that mental ability outstrips motor skills no longer provides a satisfactory answer as to the cause of a persistent stutter after the age of about 6;00 years.

Adult reaction—The essential difference between a primary stutter and a secondary stutter is the speaker's awareness of the negative impact of his or her involuntary repetitions, prolongations and hesitations on communication. Children who exhibit a primary stutter have no such awareness. However, some adults (e.g. parents, teachers, careers) will be more alert to the disruptive features of a primary stammer and may react negatively to the child's speech. They may focus attention on the disruptions by asking the child to, "Say it again," "Slow down and think!" and so on. Thus, believing that a child is developing a stutter may cause adults to respond negatively to a child's speech. This may then creates anxiety in the child and aggravate any dysfluency.

A speech therapist's job is to help parents better understand stuttering so that they can respond to their child's dysfluency in ways that will help their child speak more fluently. A speech therapist's job is to help parents better understand stammering so that they can respond differently to their child's dysfluency. It is not about judging people.

Typically a speech therapist will work with parents, and other adults who care for the child, to demonstrate new ways of interacting when their child is dysfluent and, thereby, minimize any potential negative effects.

Trauma—Many people who stammer find that the stammer becomes more severe under conditions of stress. Some traumatic experiences may create the psychological conditions that lead to the onset of stammering. In some instances, the stammer may persist even when the effects of the initial trauma have been minimized.

Predisposition—We know that stuttering may run in families and it appears that some people are predisposed to stutter whereas others are not. Under certain conditions of stress such people may begin to stutter because they are predisposed to do so.

In summary, some researchers consider the cause of stuttering to be **psychological** whereas others ascribe an **organic basis**. However, at present, the true cause (if indeed there is only one cause) remains unknown.

Strategies for Improving Language Disabilities

Fluency shaping is a stuttering treatment that aims to replace stuttered speech with fluent speech. Prolonged Speech is a fluency therapy which is particularly useful when overt stuttering features are more significant than any covert stuttering features. A new speech pattern is taught that focuses on slowed speech, easy phrase initiation, soft contacts, breath-stream management, deliberate flow between words and pitch control. Some research suggests that prolonged speech

techniques reduce stuttering and that the benefits are maintained over time. Other studies claim that fluency shaping therapies are relapse prone and produce speech that sounds unnatural to the listener and feels unnatural to the speaker.

Prolonged Speech

Typically, speech therapists use variations of Goldiamond's (1965) original **prolonged speech** technique. Stuttering is, therefore, modified by deliberately prolonging speech. This is typically achieved through the following modifications.

Slowed speech

To begin with, prolonged speech will sound unnatural, as the individual is encouraged to begin speaking extremely slowly, at around only 40-60 syllables per minute (spm). This is gradually quickened over the following weeks, aiming for a speed of about 120-150 spm. This is the typical rate of speech of most adult speakers who are considered to be fluent.

Soft contacts

The individual is encouraged to ensure that all speech sounds are produced gently and without excess muscle tension. However, plosive consonants (such as /b/, /d/ and /g/) are more likely to have a hard, 'punchy' quality if produced with too much effort. Rather like easy phrase initiation (see above) the individual can be encouraged to "blow the sounds away gently," accompanying them with a slight puff of air if needs be. For example, the /b/ in the word bin would be softened so that the word sounds more like the word pin, and the /d/ indin would be softened so that the word sounds quite similar to the word tin. Using soft contacts makes all so-called hard consonants sound gentler and more relaxed.

Breath-stream management

The individual is encouraged to divide their speech up into manageable sizes that they can speak on one breath. There should be sufficient breath to speak each short phrase. There should be no straining or gasping for breath. The individual should be reminded about the importance of monitoring their breath support for speaking. In addition, they should monitor their chest and upper shoulder tension, and keep the neck and jaw as relaxed as possible.

Deliberate flow between words

The individual should be encouraged to run each word of a short phrase into the next one. This will create a continuous stream of <u>words</u>. This promotes the concept of an easy, flowing, smooth production of continuous speech. It reduces the possibility of hesitating or halting between words.

Stuttering Cure

Does prolonged speech cure stuttering or indeed stop stuttering completely? Well, the evidence is mixed. There are studies that suggest that prolonged speech techniques do contribute to reducing stuttering (e.g. Packman, Onslow and van Doorn (1994); Onslow, Costa, Andrews, Harrison and Packman (1996)) and that the gains can be maintained over time (Howie, Tanner, and Andrews (1981)).

However, there are investigations suggesting that fluency shaping therapies are "relapse prone, and they produce speech that sounds unnatural to the listener and feels unnatural to the speaker" (Onslow, Menzies and Packman, 2001:116).

Many individuals remain vulnerable to dysfluency throughout their life. Arguably, their stuttering is never cured but, rather, they learn to manage their dysfluent speech at different times in their life. Consequently, it is likely that they will require several treatment episodes – and a number of treatment approaches may be necessary.

LANGUAGE AND CULTURE

Language as Determined by Culture and Part of Culture

Early anthropologists, followed the theory that words determine thought. They also believed that language and its structure were entirely dependent on the cultural context in which they existed. This was a logical extension of what is termed the **Standard Social Science Model**, which views the human mind as an indefinitely malleable structure capable of absorbing any sort of culture without constraints from genetic or neurological factors.

For many people, language is not just the medium of culture but also is a part of culture. It is quite common for immigrants to a new country to retain their old customs and to speak their first language amid fellow immigrants, even if all present are comfortable in their new language. This occurs because the immigrants are eager to preserve their own heritage, which includes not only customs and traditions but also language. Linguistic differences are also often seen as the mark of another culture, and they very commonly create divisiveness among neighboring peoples or even among different groups of the same nation. A good example of this is in Canada, where French-speaking natives of Quebec clash with the English-speaking majority. This sort of conflict is also common in areas with a great deal of tribal warfare. It is even becoming an issue in America as speakers of standard American English—mainly whites and educated minorities—observe the growing number of speakers of black English vernacular. Debates are common over whether it is proper to use "Ebonics" in schools, while its speakers continue to assert that the dialect is a fundamental part of the "black culture".

However language is expressed, it is a mirrored view of one's innermost thoughts. Express thoughts and ways of thinking, whether culturally defined, gender related, or age governed, language is defined.

PSYCHOLOGY OF THOUGHT

INTRODUCTION

Thinking is the highest mental activity present in man. All human achievements and progress are simply the products of thought. The evolution of culture, art, literature, science and technology are all the results of thinking. Thought and action are inseparable—they are actually the two sides of the same coin. All our deliberate action starts from our deliberate thinking. For a man to do something he should first see it in his *mind's eye* -- he should imagine it, think about it first, before he can do it. All creations-- whether artistic, literal or scientific --first occur in the creator's mind before it is actually given life in the real world.

The concept of thought content is integral to the expressive theory of linguistic communication inasmuch as it is the content of the speaker's thought that the speaker intends the hearer to grasp on the basis of the speaker's choice of words. Apart from the conception of content as something shareable between speaker and hearer, the expressive theory of communication would amount to little more than the thesis that *something* happens in the speaker, which causes the speaker to speak, and as a result of the speaker's speaking *something* happens in the hearer. The expressive theory is distinguished from this completely vacuous theory primarily by the idea that in successful communication there must be a certain relation between what happens in the mind of the speaker and what happens in the mind of the hearer, and that relation is a relation of common content (although the hearer's attitude toward that common content may be different from the speaker's attitude toward it).

Psychologists have concentrated on thinking as an intellectual exertion aimed at finding an answer to a question or the solution of a practical problem. Cognitive psychology is a branch of psychology that investigates internal mental processes such as problem solving, memory, and language. The school of thought arising from this approach is known as cognitivism which is interested in how people mentally represent information processing. Cognitive psychologists use psychophysical and experimental approaches to understand, diagnose, and solve problems, concerning themselves with the mental processes which mediate between stimulus and response. They study various aspects of thinking, including the psychology, and how people make decisions and choices, solve problems, as well as engage in creative discovery and imaginative thought. Language is the median that is used to communicate thought. Cognitive theory contends that solutions to problems take the form of algorithms— rules that are not necessarily understood but promise a solution, or heuristics—rules that are understood but that do not always guarantee solutions.

In developmental psychology, Jean Piager was a pioneer in the study of the development of thought from birth to maturity. In his theory of cognitive development, thought is based on actions on the environment. Hence thought evolves from perceptions and actions at the sensorimotor level and interpreted cognitively. In recent years, the Piagetian conception of thought was integrated with information processing conceptions. Thus, thought is considered as the result of information processing mechanisms that are responsible for the representation and processing of information. In this conception, speed of processing, congnitive control, and working memory are the main functions underlying thought.

Human thought often does not take the form of language. People think without words and the mind works with concepts instead of words. Language, on the other hand, is a means of expressing these thoughts. When we hear the word "dog" we think of the four-legged, furry thing that makes the sound we call "bark." But what do we think when we hear a word like "love," or any other word representing an abstract concept? Here the use of language as a medium for expression of thought begins to break down. This is the problem faced by a writer like Willam Faulkner, who uses a stream-of-consciousness technique, which attempts to simulate pure thought patterns directly in language. How can a book, whose only possible means of expressing an idea is through the use of language, express "pure thought," where language is usually absent? In *As I Lay Dying*, Faulkner disembodies the language from his characters in order to create the thoughts and ideas of the characters in the readers mind.

THE PURPOSE OF THINKING

The purpose of thinking, paradoxically, is to arrive at a state where thinking is no more necessary at all. In other words, thinking starts with a problem and ends in a solution. Thus, thinking is a tool for adapting ourselves to the physical and social environment in which we are in. It is reasoning and processing of information to attain maximized adaptation and success.

Factors Influencing Types of Thinking

Your thinking pattern is mostly influenced by many factors other than your lifestyle and current surroundings. The following play a crucial role in shaping your types of thinking:

- Your financial background
- Your educational background
- Your peer group with whom you spend most of your time
- The attitude of your family members and relatives
- Upbringing and values
- Your memes (Memetics is the study of inherited mannerisms from our elders via mimicking)
- The society you live in
- Your religion

So you see, a huge number of factors collectively determine your types of thinking. In spite of the sheer cumulative influence of all these significant factors, you are always the master of your thought processes. You are the sole captain who steers the ship through choppy waters, and you alone have it in you to shape your thinking patterns and optimize your mental capacity to its fullest.

Though all this may sound alien to you, the fact is that many are blatantly unaware of their competence and their intrinsic power to achieve something by way of positive and constructive thoughts paving a surefire way to success.

"Different Types of Thinking"

1. Critical thinking—This is convergent thinking. It assesses the worth and validity of something existent. It involves precise, persistent, objective analysis. When teachers try to get several learners to think convergently, they try to help them develop common understanding.

2. Creative thinking—This is divergent thinking. It generates something new or different. It involves having a different idea that works as well or better than previous ideas.

3. Convergent thinking—This type of thinking is cognitive processing of information around a common point, an attempt to bring thoughts from different directions into a union or common conclusion.

4. Divergent thinking—This type of thinking starts from a common point and moves outward into a variety of perspectives.

5. Inductive thinking—This is the process of reasoning from parts to the whole, from examples to generalizations.

Types of Reasoning

Reasoning relies on forms of logic, a system of rules for making correct inferences. The two best recognized types of reasoning are inductive and deductive reasoning.

1. Inductive Reasoning

Inductive reasoning begins with specific facts or experiences and concludes with general principles. For example, one day you observe a particular bird, a bluejay, building a nest. You might then inductively reason that all local birds have begun to build nests today. Since inductive reasoning makes inferences about an entire class based on only a few members of that class, it is an expedient but risky form of reasoning.

2. Deductive Reasoning

Deductive reasoning begins with general principles and applies these to particular cases. For example, you know that in spring birds begin to build nests, and that today is the first day of spring. You might then deductively reason that a particular bird you see in your neighborhood is commencing to build a nest somewhere. Deductive reasoning is more conservative than inductive reasoning and generally more reliable.

3. Analogical Reasoning

An analogue is a likeness in form or proportion; for example, an analogue wristwatch is equipped with a dial like a clock or sundial, while a digital watch displays digits but not a dial.

An analogy is an inference that two things or ideas that are similar in some ways share other qualities as well. Analogical reasoning involves forming a concept about something new based on its similarity to something familiar.

For example, in the analogy, "tines are to fork as teeth are to comb," one must first understand the relation between teeth and comb—that "teeth" are the serrations in a comb—in order to conclude that "tines" must be the word for the prongs of a fork.

Analogical reasoning takes commonplace forms as well. For example, if you turn down a friend's request to borrow your car because "the last time you borrowed something of mine you ruined it'" you are drawing an analogy between the old behavior and the new request, and making your decision by carrying the inference forward.

Problem-solving is one of the most obvious functions of thinking. Several processes have been proposed to account for effective problem-solving.

The Information Processing Approach to Thinking

More and more people are employed in the information segment of the economy, and it is the fastest growing segment. In the information age, we earn our living by generating, analyzing, categorizing, evaluating, and communicating information. An information processing approach to thinking skills aligns well with preparation of students for 21st century life. This approach divides thinking skills into three types: understanding information, manipulating information, and generating information. In each of the three categories are specific skills. For example, recall is related to understanding information; deduction is related to manipulating information; and brainstorming is related to generating information. This division of skills into three sets of five is not perfect (for example, questioning is related to understanding, manipulating, and generating); nevertheless, it is quite useful.

Summary

In summary, language is a verbal and nonverbal behavior that is used to express the feeling, emotions, and knowledge concering humanbeings.

When thoughts are expressed sometimes or not in the purest since, language will provide the median. Therefore, language is expressed thought, although all langue is not expressed. Language, due to its specific properties, is one aspect that makes human beings unique in comparison to other animals and species. The properties include: communication, arbitrary symbolism, regular structure, structure at multiple levels, generation and production, and dynamism (Sternberg, 1999). However, language seems to vary across different cultures and with different people. Different languages use distinctive phonemes, which are the smallest units of sound, as well as describe and name ideas and concepts differently. Consequently, some cognitive psychologists believe that language may influence thought processes. Thus, thinking is a tool for adapting ourselves to the physical and social environment in which we are in. It is reasoning and processing of information to attain maximized adaptation and success.

The issue of whether or not language influences thought is tricky since more than one factor affects thought patterns. Many researchers have used differing languages to study the relationship between language and thought, and they have come up with many different hypotheses. Although specific languages would affect the part of the brain that one uses, it is not language alone that produces "linguistically" differentiated thought patterns. Rather it is one's culture.

Though different linguistic cultures have specific language for certain ideas and concepts, the culture they are raised in most likely produce their differentiated ways of thinking. In the United States of America, where English is the predominate language, school systems have a specific method of teaching their curriculum to students. Though not all students are able to grasp this teaching process, most are; this method, taught to them by their teachers, becomes a large part of their thought processes. If one takes into account the idea of society and its impact on thought processes, then both the linguistic universalism and linguistic relativity theories are applicable. Humans are biologically capable of learning any language, but once an individual has passed a certain age, he/she is less likely to develop new language skills. At that point, culture will use the knowledge of words from education to teach a specific way of analyzing the world. It is the culture, not purely language, which facilitates a different way of thinking.

Chapter 7 Summary

Development: A Definition
Development, the orderly, durable changes that occur over a lifetime, results from the interaction of the environment and heredity. Although development proceeds in a relatively orderly fashion, individuals can vary considerably in the ways and rates at which they develop. Brain research attempts to forge links between descriptions of how the brain physically grows and operates and cognitive development.

Piaget's Theory of Intellectual Development
Piaget suggested that development is an orderly process that occurs in stages. The quality of experiences in the physical and social world, together with the drive for equilibrium, combine to influence development. Intellectually, developing children organize their experiences into schemes that help them understand the world. Compatible experiences are assimilated into existing schemes; incongruent experiences require an accommodation of these schemes to reestablish equilibrium.

As children develop, they progress through stages characterized by unique ways of understanding the world. During the sensorimotor stage, young children develop eye–hand coordination schemes and object permanence. The preoperational stage includes the growth of symbolic thought, as evidenced by increased use of language. During the concrete operational stage, children can perform basic operations such as classification and serial ordering on concrete objects. In the final stage, formal operations, students develop the ability to think abstractly, reason hypothetically, and think about thinking. Computer-based simulations can provide learners with valuable experiences in controlling variables and systematically analyzing data.

Piaget's work has influenced curriculum and instruction, as evidenced by the emphasis on manipulatives, language experience, hands-on activities, and discovery-oriented instruction.

A Sociocultural View of Development: The Work of Lev Vygotsky
Lev Vygotsky offered an alternate view of development. His theory focuses heavily on language and social interaction, and the role they play in helping learners acquire an understanding of the culture in which they live. Language is a tool people use for cultural transmission, communication, and reflection on their own thinking.

Vygotsky's work has begun to exert influence in classrooms. Teachers are encouraged to engage students in meaningful learning tasks that involve language and social interaction. Learners who can benefit from assistance are in what Vygotsky calls the zone of proximal development. Learners within this zone can profit from instructional scaffolding in the form of modeling, questions, prompts, and cues.

Piaget and Vygotsky both agree that active learners and social interaction are important for development, but they differ in their reasons why. Piaget focuses on manipulation of objects and ideas, together with the validation of schemes; Vygotsky emphasizes participation in verbal cultural exchange.

Language Development

All views of cognitive development are closely linked to language and its development. Behaviorism, social cognitive theory, and nativist theory explain language development differently; each contributes unique perspectives on this process. Children progress from one- and two-word utterances to elaborate language that involves complex sentence structures by the time they reach school.

Language diversity poses new challenges for teachers. Schools respond to this challenge with bilingual and ESL programs that use differing strategies to teach English.

CHAPTER SUMMARY

In this chapter, we distinguish among theory, science, and practice, and demonstrate how the three complement one another in the field of language development. A theory of language development is a claim or hypothesis that provides explanations for how and why children develop their capacity for language. Science in the field of language development describes the process of generating and testing theories of language, and practice in the field of language development includes the areas of people's lives that are influenced by language development theories and science, including second language teaching methods and methods for the prevention of language difficulties, for language intervention and remediation, and for language enrichment.

Scientists from many disciplines (including psychology, linguistics, psycholinguistics, anthropology, speech–language pathology, education, and sociology, among others) study language development. Some scientists conduct basic research in language development, with the goal of generating and refining the existing knowledge base. Other scientists conduct applied research, with the goal of testing approaches and practices that pertain to real-world settings.

Scientists use various approaches to study language development. For example, to study infants' speech perception abilities, scientists can measure the infants' heart rate, kicking rates, and visual responses to auditory stimuli. To measure young children's language production abilities, scientists might use observational studies, in which children's language is examined in naturalistic or semi-structured contexts, or experimental studies, in which variables of interest to the researcher are manipulated. To study children's language comprehension abilities, scientists might measure looking time or pointing toward a stimulus.

Several nurture-inspired and nature-inspired language development theories can be examined in the context of three questions: (a) What do infants bring to the task of language learning? (b) What mechanisms drive language acquisition? (c) What types of input support the language learning system?

Nurture-inspired or empiricist theories of language development include behaviorist theory, social-interactionist theory, cognitive theory, the intentionality model, the competition model, and usage-based theory.

Nature-inspired or nativist theories of language development include modularity theory, universal grammar, syntactic bootstrapping, semantic bootstrapping, and connectionist theories.

Language development theories influence practices in several areas. These areas include instruction in English as a second language, prevention of language difficulties, intervention and remediation, and enrichment.

Intelligence

8

Introduction

Intelligence is the mental capacity to reason, plan, solve problems, think abstractly, comprehend ideas and language and learn. Although many generally regard the concept of intelligence as having a much broader scope, in some schools of psychology, the study of intelligence generally regards this trait as distinct from creativity, personality, character or wisdom.

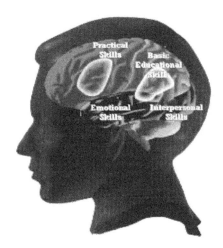

The study and measurement of intelligence is a complex concept primarily because of how it is defined, measured, and utilized as a measure of intellectual aptitude. While there are different theoretical views

and methods of what constitutes IQ, each researcher, psychologist, and educator will need to decide independently what community of theorist best represents their frame of reference concerning the construct of intelligence. There is an extensive and continually growing collection of research papers on the topic. Howard Gardner (1983, 1993), Robert Sternberg (1988, 1997), and David Perkins (1995) have written widely sold books that summarize the literature and present their own specific points of view.

Intelligence Defined

The following definition is a composite from various authors. Intelligence is a combination of the ability to:

1. Learn. This includes all kinds of informal and formal learning via any combination of experience, education, and training.
2. Pose problems. This includes recognizing problem situations and transforming them into more clearly defined problems.
3. Solve problems. This includes solving problems, accomplishing tasks, fashioning products, and doing complex projects.

ISSUES SURROUNDING THE USE OF IQ TESTS

Intelligence tests have encountered criticism from some. For example, minority and economically disadvantaged students tend to score lower than other students and, consequently, are often underrepresented in gifted and talented programs.

Further, some critics charge that the current, widely used, IQ tests are not guided by a plausible theory of how the brain actually operates and do not accurately measure more contemporary ideas of what "intelligence" actually is. Indeed, some feel that an expanded view of intelligence should guide the testing process (e.g. Plucker, 1998). An example of such an expanded view would be Gardner's theory of Multiple Intelligences (Gardner, 1983). Gardner's theory has gained a lot of momentum in the last twenty years. It proposes the existence of at least eight distinct areas in which a student may be particularly adept. Proponents of this theory like the way that it widens the net in terms of identifying more areas in which a student may be talented and, so, in how many different children might be identified. This has particular implications for the identification of some minority groups who traditionally have been under-identified with more conventional approaches. Critics of Gardner's theory contend that it has not been thoroughly validated through statistical measures.

Another major issue is the inconsistent use of these tests. Some school districts rely heavily, or even exclusively, on standardized IQ test scores to identify giftedness, yet other districts may use a multidimensional procedure that views test scores as only one piece of a much larger picture of a child's talents. Indeed, opponents of "IQ-only" identification point out that these tests may assess only a narrow range of ability, neglecting a child's strengths in other areas, such as spatial reasoning or nonacademic talents.

Still, such tests have their merits. Individually administered tests, such as the Wechsler Intelligence Scale for Children, Fourth Edition (WISC-IV) and the Stanford-Binet, Fourth Edition (SB-IV). While they do not lend themselves perfectly to some views of intelligence, they have historically been fairly good predictors of school achievement (expected "ability"). These tests are highly reliable—they provide similar results if taken, say, several months apart—and they have been studied and refined over many years or decades with thousands of children. So, intelligence tests can, and do, provide valuable information regarding a child's abilities and, despite some criticism, they are still widely used to make placement decisions for gifted, as well as learning disabled and intellectually challenged students. Because they have been standardized and researched to a great deal, they are often seen as adding a degree of accountability to the identification process.

This definition of intelligence is a very optimistic one. It says that each of us can become more intelligent. We can become more intelligent through study and practice, through access to appropriate tools, and through learning to make effective use of these tools (Perkins, 1995).

This is discussed further in the chapter. Historical perspectives of intelligence will be discussed to provide background concerning the existence of intelligence.

HISTORY OF INTELLIGENCE

As long ago as 2200 B.C., Chinese emperors used large-scale "aptitude" testing for the selection of civil servants, and stories such as that of the *Wild Boy of Averyon* (see story below) in the 18th century, have captured the imagination regarding the relative difference between "normal" and "abnormal" intelligence. By the end of the 19th century, the foundation was laid for how intelligence is assessed today. I will start

THE WILD BOY OF AVERYON

In 1799 three French sportsmen were exploring a wood in southern France when they came upon a young boy. They guessed that he was eleven or twelve years old, and he was filthy, naked, and covered with scars. The boy ran from them, but he was caught when he stopped to climb a tree. The sportsmen brought him to a nearby village and gave him over into the care of a widow. As the story of his capture spread, local residents began reporting that a young naked boy had been seen in the woods five years earlier. It was presumed that he had lived alone for many years, and that he had survived by eating whatever he could find or catch (Itard, 1801/1962).

The boy escaped from the widow, and spent the next winter roaming the woods alone. He was eventually recaptured and placed in safe custodial care. An official in the French government heard about him, and suggested that he be taken to Paris where he could be studied as an example of the human mind in its primitive state (Itard, 1801/1962). However, the prominent Parisian physicians who examined him declared that he was not "wild" at all; their collective opinion was that the boy was mentally deficient, and that he had been recently abandoned by his parents. The famous psychiatrist Philippe Pinel put it succinctly when he said that the boy was in fact "an incurable idiot" (Gaynor, 1973).

Itard disagreed. He believed that the boy had survived alone in the woods for at least seven years, citing as evidence his "profound aversion to society, its customs, and its artifacts" (Itard, 1801/1962). He asserted that his apparent mental deficiency was entirely due to a lack of human interaction. Moreover, he believed that this could be overcome. He brought the boy-whom he eventually named "Victor"--to The National Institution for Deaf-Mutes, and devoted the next five years to an intensive, individualized educational program (Humphrey, 1962; French, 2000). This was the first example of an IEP, and the beginning of modern special education (Gaynor, 1973; Humphrey, 1963; Pinchot, 1948).

Itard identified five primary goals for his pupil:

1. To interest him in social life
2. To improve his awareness of environmental stimuli
3. To extend the range of his ideas (e.g. introduce him to games, culture, etc.)
4. To teach him to speak
5. To teach him to communicate by using symbol systems, such as pictures and written words

Itard had been influenced by the empiricist philosophers John Locke and Etienne Condillac, both of whom advanced the idea that all knowledge comes through the senses. Victor's eyesight and hearing were normal, but his responses to sensory input were often sluggish or nonexistent. For example, he would perk up at the slightest sound of a nutshell cracking, but would not startle at the sound of a gunshot. Itard reasoned that Victor could not learn effectively until he became more attuned to his environment. Therefore, his educational approach relied heavily on sensory-training and stimulation. (Humphrey, 1962; Itard, 1801/1962).

Victor improved, but he never approached normalcy. After five years he could read and speak a few words, demonstrated affection for his caretakers, and could carry out simple commands. Itard was disappointed in this lack of progress, but he maintained his environmentalist position, stating that would have been successful if Victor had been a few years younger. (Pinchot, 1948). As it turns out, Philippe Pinel and the other physicians were probably right; modern readers of Itard's personal account usually come to the conclusion that Victor was indeed mentally retarded or autistic (French, 2000; Humphrey, 1962; Pinchot, 1948).

The fact that Itard failed to make Victor "normal" is relatively unimportant to this story. The important thing is that he *tried*. He was the first physician to declare that an enriched environment could compensate for developmental delays caused by heredity or previous deprivation (French, 2000). Up to this time, it had been assumed that mentally retarded people were uneducable (Humphrey, 1962). As one writer put it, Itard's work with Victor "did away with the paralyzing sense of hopelessness and inertia that had kept the medical profession and everybody else from trying to do anything constructive for mental defectives" (Kanner, 1967).

this historical account of intelligence by discussing the work of Sir Francis Glton, who sought to predict individuals' intellectual capacity through tests of sensory discrimination and motor coordination. Although his belief that such capacities were necessarily correlated with intelligence was eventually determined to be unfounded, he ushered in an age of individual psychology and the pursuit of measuring intelligence by quantifying traits assumed to be correlated.

In addition to measuring intelligence, Galton is most highly recognized for his heredity studies and his proliferation of the eugenics ideology. Galton is recognized as the "father of behavioral genetics" for his ground laying twin studies where he looked at the differences between monozygotic and dizygotic twins. His observations and testing approaches led to findings examining the nature versus nurture elements of mental abilities. While he may have led claim to this still widely studied dichotomy, his beliefs weighed heavily on the genetic predisposition to abilities in general.

Galton is also hailed as having made lasting contributions to the fields of psychology and statistics. In his passionate drive to quantify the passing down of characteristics, qualities, traits, and abilities from generation to generation, he formulated the statistical notion of correlation which led to his understanding of how generations were related to each other (Bynum, 2002). He also established that "numerous heritable traits, including height and intelligence, exhibited regression to the mean—meaning that extreme inherited results tended to move toward average results in the next generation" (Seligman, 2002).

Galton was the first to demonstrate that the Laplace-Gauss distribution or the "normal distribution" could be applied to human psychological attributes, including intelligence (Simonton, 2003). From this finding, he coined the use of percentile scores for measuring relative standing on various measurements in relation to the normal distribution (Jensen, 2002). He even established the world's first mental testing center, in which a person could take a battery of tests and receive a written report of the results (Irvine, 1986).

ALFRED BINET AND THE FIRST IQ TEST

"It seems to us that in intelligence there is a fundamental faculty, the alteration or the lack of which, is of the utmost importance for practical life. This faculty is judgment, otherwise called good sense, practical sense, initiative, the faculty of adapting one's self to circumstances. A person may be a moron or an imbecile if he is lacking in judgment; but with good judgment he can never be either. Indeed the rest of the intellectual faculties seem of little importance in comparison with judgment" (Binet & Simon, 1916, 1973, pp.42-43).

In 1905, the French psychologist Alfred Binet published the first modern intelligence test, the Binet-Simon intelligence scale. His principal goal was to identify students who needed special help in coping with the school curriculum. Along with his collaborator Theodore Simon, Binet published revisions of his intelligence scale in 1908 and 1911, the last appearing just before his untimely death. In 1912, the abbreviation of "intelligence quotient" or I.Q., a translation of the German Intelligenz-Quotient, was coined by the German psychologist William Stern.

Binet and Simon, in creating what historically is known as the Binet-Simon Scale, comprised a variety of tasks they thought were representative of typical children's abilities at various ages. This task-selection process was based on their many years of observing children in natural settings. They then tested their measurement on a sample of fifty children, ten children per five age groups. The children selected for their study were identified by their school teachers as being average for their age. The purpose of this scale of normal functioning, which would later be revised twice using more stringent standards, was to compare children's mental abilities relative to those of their normal peers (Siegler, 1992).

The first intelligence test. Binet took a pragmatic approach, choosing a series of 30 short tasks related to everyday problems of life (e.g. attend to simple instructions).

- name parts of the body
- compare lengths and weights
- counting coins,
- assessing which of several faces is 'prettier',
- naming objects in a picture,
- digit span (the number of digits a person can recall after being shown a long list),
- word definition
- filling in the missing words in sentences, etc.

Supposedly all these tasks involved basic processes of reasoning. The tests were arranged so as to be of increasing difficulty. Each level of tests matched a specific developmental level—i.e. all tests at a given level were capable of being solved by any normal child in that specific age-group.

A further refinement of the Binet-Simon scale was published in 1916 by Lewis M. Terman, from Stanford University, who incorporated Stern's proposal that an individual's intelligence level be measured as an intelligence quotient (IQ). Terman's test, which he named the Stanford-Binet Intelligence Scale formed the basis for one of the modern intelligence tests still commonly used today.

In 1916, Terman adopted William Stern's suggestion that the ratio between mental and chronological age be taken as a unitary measure of intelligence.

William Sterns Intelligence Quotient (IQ)

The term 'intelligence quotient' was first coined in 1912 by German psychologist, William Stern in reference to the intelligence tests developed by psychologists Alfred Binet and Theodore Simon, who wanted to identify students that needed special help with the school curriculum. The original formula for calculating IQ was:

Mental Age (MA) divided by Chronological Age (CA) x 100 = IQ

IQ is a number meant to measure people cognitive abilities (intelligence) in relation to their age group.

Terman is also well known for his studies with intelligence in children. Terman's "Termites" as they are known were chosen to test the early ripe-early rot myth." In other words, Terman wanted to know if high IQ children had intellectual success or failure as adults. According to Terman, unusually precocious children were more likely to turn out well than poorly in their later lives. Terman found, among other things, that the gifted were taller, healthier, physically better developed, superior in leadership and social adaptability, dispelling the often held contrary opinion. Terman's points of view regarding gifted youth include:

- They are the top 1 percent in intelligence,
- They should be identified as early as possible in childhood,
- They should be accelerated through school
- They should have a differentiated curriculum and instruction,
- They should have specially trained teachers,
- They should be viewed as a national resource for the betterment of society, and
- They should be allowed to develop in whatever directions their talents and interests dictate.

Charles Spearman—General Intelligence

British psychologist Charles Spearman (1863-1945) described a concept he referred to as general intelligence, or the *g factor*. After using a technique known as factor analysis to examine a number of mental aptitude tests, Spearman concluded that scores on these tests were remarkably similar. People who performed well on one cognitive test tended to perform well on other tests, while those who scored badly on one test tended to score badly on other. He concluded that intelligence is general cognitive ability that could be measured and numerically expressed (Spearman, 1904).

But the main thrust of Spearman's analysis was this idea of a general intellectual capacity. This formed a major theoretical platform for many subsequent approaches to intelligence.

It might be also noted, however, that Spearman was perhaps excessively enthusiastic about g. For example, he advocated restricting voting rights to people whose g exceeded a certain level, and he was a eugenicist (eugenics comes from the Greek "eugenes" meaning well-born)—arguing that only people with a certain level of g should be allowed to have offspring. "g" was controversial then as now.

Historically, General intelligence is considered a good predictor of a child's current learning ability and performance in school. While many people claim that their intelligence seems to decline as they age, research suggests that while fluid intelligence begins to decrease after adolescence, crystallized intelligence continues to increase throughout adulthood. Other tests were developed to assess abilities, such as the Army Alpha-Beta Test.

Intelligence Testing During World War I

At the outset of World War I, U.S. Army officials were faced with the monumental task of screening an enormous number of army recruits. In 1917, as president of the APA and chair of the Committee on the Psychological Examination of Recruits, psychologist Robert Yerkes developed two tests known as the Army Alpha and Beta tests. The Army Alpha was designed as a written test, while the Army Beta was administered orally in cases where recruits were unable to read. The tests were administered to over two million soldiers in an effort to help the army determine which men were well suited to specific positions and leadership roles (McGuire, 1994).

At the end of WWI, the tests remained in use in a wide variety of situations outside of the military with individuals of all ages, backgrounds and nationalities. For example, IQ tests were used to screen new immigrants as they entered the United States at Ellis Island. The results of these mental tests were inappropriately used to make sweeping and inaccurate generalizations about entire populations, which led some intelligence "experts" to exhort Congress to enact immigration restrictions (Kamin, 1995).

Wechsler Intelligence Scales—David Wechsler

The next development in the history of intelligence testing was the creation of a new measurement instrument by American psychologist David Wechsler. Much like Binet, Wechsler believed that intelligence involved a number of different mental abilities, describing intelligence as, "the global capacity of a person to act purposefully, to think rationally, and to deal effectively with his environment" (1939). In 1939 David Wechsler published the first intelligence test explicitly designed for an adult population, the

Wechsler Adult Intelligence Scale, or WAIS. The Wechsler scales contained separate subscores for verbal and performance IQ, thus being less dependent on overall verbal ability than early versions of the Stanford-Binet scale, and was the first intelligence scale to base scores on a standardized normal distribution rather than an age-based quotient.

Wechsler also developed two different tests specifically for use with children: the Wechsler Intelligence Scale for Children (WISC) and the Wechsler Preschool and Primary Scale of Intelligence (WPPSI). The adult version of the test has been revised since its original publication and is now known as the WAIS-III.

The WAIS-III contains 14 subtests on two scales and provides three scores: a composite IQ score, a verbal IQ score and a performance IQ score. Subtest scores on the WAIS-III can be useful in identifying learning disabilities, such as cases where a low score on some areas combined with a high score in other areas may indicate that the individual has a specific learning difficulty (Kaufman, 1990).

At this juncture, the approaches to intelligence had been very pragmatic—i.e. tests were developed for particular needs. However, another approach to understanding intelligence, involved analyzing data that was already collected. Charles Spearman led the charge in further defining intelligence.

Fluid and Crystallized Intelligence

Raymond Cattell (1971) and John Horn (1985), further expanded the concept of general intelligence and included other dimensions, namely, fluid intelligence (Gf) and crystallized intelligence (Gc). and visual-spatial reasoning (Gv). Cattell and Horn describe them as follows:

Fluid intelligence is the ability to develop techniques for solving problems that are new and unusual, from the perspective of the problem solver. Cattell defined fluid intelligence as "…the ability to perceive relationships independent of previous specific practice or instruction concerning those relationships." Fluid intelligence is the ability to think and reason abstractly

and solve problems. This ability is considered independent of learning, experience, and education. Examples of the use of fluid intelligence include solving puzzles and coming up with problem-solving strategies.

Crystallized intelligence is the ability to bring previously acquired, often culturally defined, problem-solving methods to bear on the current problem. Note that this implies both that the problem solver knows the methods and recognizes that they are relevant in the current situation. Crystallized intelligence is learning from past experiences and learning. Situations that require crystallized intelligence include reading comprehension and vocabulary exams. This type of intelligence is based upon facts and rooted in experiences. This type of intelligence becomes stronger as we age and accumulate new knowledge and understanding.

Visual-spatial reasoning is a somewhat specialized ability to use visual images and visual relationships in problem solving--for instance, to construct in your mind a picture of the sort of mental space that I described above in discussing factor-analytic studies. Interestingly, visual-spatial reasoning appears to be an important part of understanding mathematics.

Measuring Intelligence

Intelligence testing is used to assess the all around effectiveness of an individual's mental processes, especially understanding, reasoning, and the ability to recall information. Tests exist that are appropriate for both children and adults. The use of standardized tests to produce a numerical value for these abilities is a very popular tool among educators. Correctly administered, some intelligence tests can also detect learning impairments.

Men and women seem to score approximately the same on IQ testing, though men exhibit a greater variance in testing, and have more very high and very low scores than do women. The American Psychological Association conducted studies on IQs and came up with the following conclusions:

- IQ score was a fairly good predictor for school performance.

- IQ score may also predict fairly well the degree to which a person may be successful in occupations.
- IQ scores tend to exhibit some racial bias.
- Test scores may be influenced by personal genetic history.

There is much contentious debate in evaluating the IQ test, as to whether nature or nurture most influences IQ scores. As well, debate exists as to how much IQ scores should be used as a predictor of behavior. Some are concerned that IQ scores might negatively affect the perception of colleges, private schools or employers if used to determine employability or acceptance into schools.

CHARACTERISTICS OF A GOOD TEST

There are three basic elements to look for when judging the quality of a psychological test -- reliability, validity, and standardization.

RELIABILITY is a measure of the test's consistency. A useful test is consistent over time. As an analogy, think of a bathroom scale. If it gives you one weight the first time you step on it, and a different weight when you step on it a moment later, it is not reliable. Similarly, if an IQ test yields a score of 95 for an individual today and 130 next week, it is not reliable. Reliability also can be a measure of a test's internal consistency. All of the items (questions) on a test should be measuring the same thing -- from a statistical standpoint, the items should correlate with each other. Good tests have reliability coefficients which range from a low of .65 to above .90 (the theoretical maximum is 1.00).

VALIDITY is a measure of a test's usefulness. Scores on the test should be related to some other behavior, reflective of personality, ability, or interest. For instance, a person who scores high on an IQ test would be expected to do well in school or on jobs requiring intelligence. A person who scores high on a scale of depression should be diagnosed as depressed by mental health professionals who assess him. A validity coefficient reflects the degree to which such relationships exist. Most tests have validity coefficients (correlations) of up to .30 with "real world" behavior. This is not a high correlation, and emphasizes the need to use tests in conjunction with other information. Relatively low correlations mean that some people may score high on a scale of schizophrenia without being schizophrenic and some people may score high on an IQ test and yet not do well in school. Correlations are high as .50 are seen between IQ and academic performance.

STANDARDIZATION is the process of trying out the test on a group of people to see the scores which are typically obtained. In this way, any test taker can make sense of his or her score by comparing it to typical scores. This standardization provides a mean (average) and standard deviation (spread) relative to a certain group. When an individual takes the test, she can determine how far above or below the average her score is, relative to the normative group. When evaluating a test, it is very important to determine how the normative group was selected. For instance, if everyone in the normative group took the test by logging into a website, you are probably being compared to a group which is very different from the general population.

Standardized Tests

Psychological assessment is a process of testing that uses a combination of techniques to help arrive at some hypotheses about a person and their behavior, personality and capabilities. Psychological assessment is also referred to as psychological testing, or performing a psychological battery on a person. Psychological testing is nearly always performed by a licensed psychologist, or a psychology trainee (such as an intern). Psychologists are the only profession that is expertly trained to perform and interpret psychological tests.

Psychological assessment should never be performed in a vacuum. A part of a thorough assessment of an individual is that they also undergo a full medical examination, to rule out the possibilities of a medical, disease or organic cause for the individual's symptoms. It's often helpful to have this done first, before psychological testing (as it may make psychological testing moot).

Components of Psychological Assessment

Norm-references psychological tests are standardized on a clearly defined group, termed the *norm group*, and scaled so that each individual score reflects a rank within the norm group. Norm-referenced tests have been developed to assess many areas, including intelligence; reading, arithmetic, and spelling abilities; visual-motor skills; gross and fine motor skills; and adaptive behavior. Psychologists have a choice of many well-standardized and psychometrically sound tests with which to evaluate an individual.

Norm-referenced tests have several benefits over non-norm-referenced tests. They provide valuable information about a person's level of functioning in the areas covered by the tests. They relatively little time to administer, permitting a sampling of behavior within a few hours. Each appraisal can provide a wealth of information that would be unavailable to even the most skilled observer who did not use testing.

Finally, norm-referenced tests also provide an index for evaluating change in many different aspects of the child's physical and social world.

Good test use requires:

- Comprehensive assessment using history and test scores
- Acceptance of the responsibility for proper test use
- Consideration of the Standard Error of Measurement and other psychometric knowledge
- Maintaining integrity of test results (such as the correct use of cut-off scores)
- Accurate scoring
- Appropriate use of norms
- Willingness to provide interpretive feedback and guidance to test takers

A good test is both reliable and valid, and has good norms.

- Reliability, briefly, refers to the consistency of the test results. For example, IQ is not presumed to vary much from week to week, and as such, test results from an IQ test should be highly reliable. On the other hand, transient mood states do not last long, and a measurement of such moods should not be very reliable over long periods of time. A measurement of transient mood state may still be shown reliable if it correlates well with other tests or behavior observations indicative of transient mood states.
- Validity, briefly, refers to how well a test measures what it says it does. In a simple way, validity tells you if the hammer is the right tool to fix a chair, and reliability tells you how good a hammer you have. A test of intelligence based on eye color (blue eyed people are more intelligent than brown eyed people) would certainly be reliable, because eye color doesn't change, but it would not be very valid, because IQ and eye color have little to do with each other.
- Norms are designed to tell you what the result of measurement (a number) means in relation to other results (numbers). The "normative sample" should be very representative of the sample of people who will be given the test. Thus, if a test is to be used on the general population, the normative sample should be large, include people from ethnically and culturally diverse backgrounds, and include people from all levels of income and educational status.

Test Taker Rights

The test taker has the right:

- To have the directions of testing as well as the results of an evaluation explained in language that they can understand.
- To have the confidentiality of that information maintained within the limits promised during informed consent.
- To have the results of the testing explained to them in a meaningful way, and in most cases

to know to whom and how these results were shared.

Sources of Invalidity

- Unreliability
- Response sets = psychological orientation or bias towards answering in a particular way:
- Acquiescence: tendency to agree, i.e. say "Yes☐. Hence use of half -vely and half +vely worded items (but there can be semantic difficulties with -vely wording)
- Social desirability: tendency to portray self in a positive light. Try to design questions which so that social desirability isn't salient.
- Faking bad: Purposely saying ‹no' or looking bad if there's a ‹reward' (e.g. attention, compensation, social welfare, etc.).
- Bias
- Cultural bias: does the psychological construct have the same meaning from one culture to another; how are the different items interpreted by people from different cultures; actual content (face) validity may be different for different cultures.
- Gender bias may also be possible.
- Test Bias
- Bias in <u>measurement</u> occurs when the test makes systematic errors in measuring a particular characteristic or attribute e.g. many say that most IQ tests may well be valid for middle-class whites but not for blacks or other minorities. In interviews, which are a type of test, research shows that there is a bias in favor of good-looking applicants.
- Bias in <u>prediction</u> occurs when the test makes systematic errors in predicting some outcome (or criterion). It is often suggested that tests used in academic admissions and in personnel selection under-predict the performance of minority applicants Also a test may be useful for predicting the performance of one group e.g. males but be less accurate in predicting the performance of females.

External validity is dependent on the adequacy of the sample. If the sample is representative of the desired population then our results will generalize. This is called generalizability. Thus, if we study patients in a free clinic can we generalize to patients of a private physician? The answer is no, to be able to generalize to both groups we must include subjects from both care sources.

To have a generalizable sample, first define your population, then randomly select a large sample. With a random sample of sufficient size research findings can generalize to the larger population. As a rule of thumb random sample sizes of twenty subjects per group are minimally sufficient.

Internal validity refers to the adequacy of our study design and the degree of control we have exercised in our data gathering. Good internal validity is insured by application of the concept of control. This concept is very important in research. By control we mean that all variables except the dependent variable are controlled by the experimenter. In this way if the dependent variable changes during the study then that change is due to the changes the experimenter made in the independent variable(s). The concept of control has six major parts:

1. Groups have equal scores on the dependent variable at the start of the study and are of large size. Random assignment will insure they are equal without testing if sample size is large
2. Extraneous variables are controlled so no group is affected by them during the study.
3. Each group receives identical treatment during the study except for the manipulations of the independent variable
4. Large numbers of subjects are not lost from the study and any losses are distributed evenly across the groups
5. The treatment (manipulation of the independent variable) was of sufficient magnitude and duration to expect it to change the dependent variable(s).
6. The dependent variable(s) are accurately measured.

In evaluating the internal validity of a study we ask this question: Was the experimental manipulation the only possible cause of a change in the dependent variable? In general, if a study adequately responds to the six factors above, then it will have controlled for many extraneous influences, will allow the researcher a good chance of detecting any change in the dependent variable, and will have internal validity. Note that a study can have good internal validity and <u>NOT</u> find any changes in the dependent variable due to the independent variable. Also, a study can have good internal validity, but without a generalizable sample, it may have no external validity. Finally, remember that a study with no external validity still found true relationships for the sample that was studied. If I study Mongolian fishermen in Cleveland, I cannot generalize to Vietnamese shrimpers in the Gulf, but I still know more about Mongolian fishermen.

Do not confuse internal validity with the validity of the method by which the dependent variable is measured, called <u>test validity</u>. Internal validity refers to the overall degree of control exercised. Test validity refers to the suitability of the measuring instrument used.

Over the years a number of terms have been introduced that describe various factors that can adversely influence the internal validity. We have already discussed most of these factors, but we have not necessarily used these common terms before. The list below will familiarize you with these names and their definitions.

1. History: Specific events unrelated to the study, occurring between the first and second measurements in addition to the experimental treatment.
2. Maturation: General events/experiences occurring to participants over an extended period of time, e.g., growing older, fatiguing, etc.
3. Pre-Test Influence (Test Practice): The effects (e.g., cueing and practice) of taking one test upon the results of taking a second test. Sometimes the subjects can learn about the dependent variable by just taking the pre-test. This additional learning

can confound the effect of the independent variable on the dependent variable.

4. Statistical Regression: Changes in scores over time due to unreliability of measuring devices; especially troublesome when using subjects selected on the basis of extreme scores.
5. Experimental Mortality: Loss of more subjects from one group than from the other. This may make groups unequal.
6. Instrumentation Error: Error of measurement due to:
   a. Changes in the assessment instrument (e.g., shortening a test, adding different items, changing the scoring procedure),
   b. Changes in the observers (e.g., different observers at O1 and O2, some observers using different standards than others, or training of observers changes from one treatment to the next), and
   c. Changes in the equipment (e.g., a fault in the equipment, non-standardization of equipment prior to study, loss of calibration).
7. Bias in Group Composition (Differential Selection): Biases or conveniences in creating comparison groups that cannot be assumed to be equivalent (e.g., the groups are not equal because they were not randomly chosen. For example, if one hospital uses one treatment method and a second hospital uses a second method, then the groups are biased because it is unrealistic to assume the hospital populations are the same).
8. Selection-Maturation Interaction: Biases in the selection of groups to be included in the study may differentially be affected by the time between assessments. For example, if the subjects are children and the average age of one group is older than the others, then the maturation process will affect the older group differently than the younger groups. If changes due to maturation can be confounded with changes due to the independent variable then the internal validity of the study is reduced.
9. Hawthorne Effect: Being in an experiment sometimes changes the response of the subjects.

New treatment methods may be exciting, and people improve due to the thrill of it all and the increased attention.

PSYCHOMETRIC APPROACH TO INTELLIGENCE

The **Wechsler Adult Intelligence Scale (WAIS)** tests are the primary clinical instruments used to measure adult and adolescent intelligence, (Kaufamn, A. 2006). The original WAIS (Form I) was published in February 1955 by David Wechsler, as a revision of the Wechsler-Bellevue Intelligence Scale, (Kaufman, A. 2006). The fourth edition of the test (WAIS-IV) was released in 2008 by Person Publishing.

The Wechsler-Bellevue tests were innovative in the 1930s because they gathered tasks created for non-clinical purposes for administration as a "clinical test battery", (Kaufman, A. 2006). The Wechsler tests included non-verbal items (known as *performance scales*) as well as verbal items for all test-takers. Wechsler defined intelligence as "... the global capacity of a person to act purposefully, to think rationally, and to deal effectively with his environment, "(Wechsler, D.,1939)

CLASSIFICATIONS OF INTELLIGENCE

While people often talk about test scores, many people are confused about exactly what these test scores mean. In order to adequately assess and interpret test scores, psychometritians use a process known as standardization. The standardization process involves administering the test to a representative sample of the entire population that will eventually take the test. Each test taker completes the test under the same conditions as all other participants in the sample group. This process allows psychometricians to establish norms, or standards, by which individual scores can be compared.

Intelligence test scores typically follow what is known as a normal distribution, a bell-shaped curve in which the majority of scores lie near or around the average score. For example, the majority of scores (about 68%) on the WAIS-III tend to lie between plus 15 or minus 15 points from the average score of 100. As you look further toward the extreme ends of the distribution, scores tend to become less common. Very few individuals (approximately 0.2%) receive a score of more than 145 (indicating a very high IQ) or less than 55 (indicating a very low IQ) on the test.

Range of Scores	% of Population	Description
130 +	2%	Very superior
120—129	7%	Superior
110 -119	16%	High average
90—109	50%	Average
80—89	16%	Low average
70—79	7%	Borderline
70 & below	2%	Deficient

COGNITIVE APPROACH TO INTELLIGENCE

Howard Gardner

Some researchers in the field of intelligence have long argued that people have a variety of different intelligences. A person may be good at learning languages and terrible at learning music--or vice versa. A single number (a score on an IQ test) cannot adequately represent the complex and diverse capabilities of a human being.

Howard Gardner proposed a theory of multiple intelligences. He originally identified seven components of intelligence (Gardner, 1983). He argues that these intelligences are relatively distinct from each other and that each person has some level of each of these seven intelligences. More recently, he has added an eighth intelligence to his list (Educational Leadership, 1997).

The following table lists the eight intelligences identified by Howard Gardner. It provides some examples of the types of professionals who exhibit a high level of intelligence. The eight intelligences are listed in alphabetical order, See Table 12.

1. Naturalist Intelligence ("Nature Smart")

Designates the human ability to discriminate among living things (plants, animals) as well as sensitivity to other features of the natural world (clouds, rock configurations). This ability was clearly of value in our evolutionary past as hunters, gatherers, and farmers; it continues to be central in such roles as botanist or chef. It is also speculated that much of our consumer society exploits the naturalist intelligences, which can be mobilized in the discrimination among cars, sneakers, kinds of makeup, and the like.

2. Musical Intelligence ("Musical Smart")

Musical intelligence is the capacity to discern pitch, rhythm, timbre, and tone. This intelligence enables us to recognize, create, reproduce, and reflect on music, as demonstrated by composers, conductors, musicians, vocalist, and sensitive listeners. Interestingly, there is often an affective connection between music and the emotions; and mathematical and musical intelligences may share common thinking processes. Young adults with this kind of intelligence are usually singing or drumming to themselves. They are usually quite aware of sounds others may miss.

3. Logical-Mathematical Intelligence (Number/ Reasoning Smart)

Logical-mathematical intelligence is the ability to calculate, quantify, consider propositions and hypotheses, and carry out complete mathematical operations. It enables us to perceive relationships and connections and to use abstract, symbolic thought; sequential reasoning skills; and inductive and deductive thinking patterns. Logical intelligence is usually well developed in mathematicians, scientists, and detectives. Young adults with lots of logical intelligence are interested in patterns, categories, and relationships. They are drawn to arithmetic problems, strategy games and experiments.

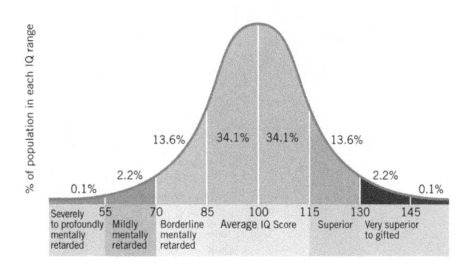

4. Existential Intelligence

Sensitivity and capacity to tackle deep questions about human existence, such as the meaning of life, why do we die, and how did we get here.

5. Interpersonal Intelligence (People Smart")

Interpersonal intelligence is the ability to understand and interact effectively with others. It involves effective verbal and nonverbal communication, the ability to note distinctions among others, sensitivity to the moods and temperaments of others, and the ability to entertain multiple perspectives. Teachers, social workers, actors, and politicians all exhibit interpersonal intelligence. Young adults with this kind of intelligence are leaders among their peers, are good at communicating, and seem to understand others' feelings and motives.

6. Bodily-Kinesthetic Intelligence ("Body Smart")

Bodily kinesthetic intelligence is the capacity to manipulate objects and use a variety of physical skills. This intelligence also involves a sense of timing and the perfection of skills through mind–body union. Athletes, dancers, surgeons, and craftspeople exhibit well-developed bodily kinesthetic intelligence.

7. Linguistic Intelligence (Word Smart)

Linguistic intelligence is the ability to think in words and to use language to express and appreciate complex meanings. Linguistic intelligence allows us to understand the order and meaning of words and to apply meta-linguistic skills to reflect on our use of language. Linguistic intelligence is the most widely shared human competence and is evident in poets, novelists, journalists, and effective public speakers. Young adults with this kind of intelligence enjoy writing, reading, telling stories or doing crossword puzzles.

Table 12. Multiple Intelligence Traits

Intelligence	Examples	Discussion
Bodily-kinesthetic	Dancers, athletes, surgeons, crafts people	The ability to use one's physical body well.
Interpersonal	Sales people, teachers, clinicians, politicians, religious leaders	The ability to sense other's feelings and be in tune with others.
Intrapersonal	People who have good insight into themselves and make effective use of their other intelligences	Self-awareness. The ability to know your own body and mind.
Linguistic	Poets, writers, orators, communicators	The ability to communicate well, perhaps both orally and in writing, perhaps in several languages.
Logical-mathematical	Mathematicians, logicians	The ability to learn higher mathematics. The ability to handle complex logical arguments.
Musical	Musicians, composers	The ability to learn, perform, and compose music.
Naturalistic	Biologists, naturalists	The ability to understand different species, recognize patterns in nature, classify natural objects.
Spatial	Sailors navigating without modern navigational aids, surgeons, sculptors, painters	The ability to know where you are relative to fixed locations. The ability to accomplish tasks requiring three-dimensional visualization and placement of your hands or other parts of your body.

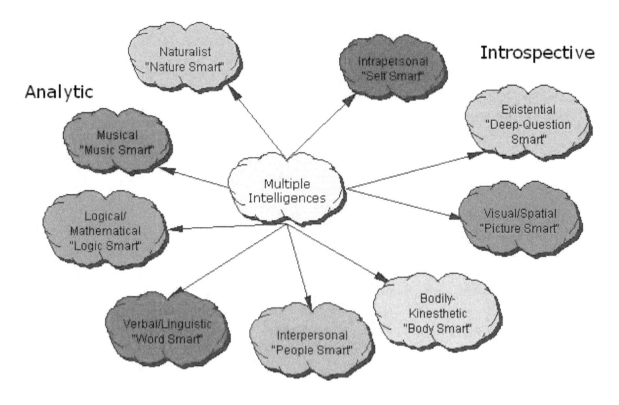

Analytic

Naturalist "Nature Smart"

Intrapersonal "Self Smart"

Introspective

Musical "Music Smart"

Existential "Deep-Question Smart"

Multiple Intelligences

Logical/ Mathematical "Logic Smart"

Visual/Spatial "Picture Smart"

Verbal/Linguistic "Word Smart"

Interpersonal "People Smart"

Bodily- Kinesthetic "Body Smart"

Interactive

8. Intra-personal Intelligence (Self Smart")

Intra-personal intelligence is the capacity to understand oneself and one's thoughts and feelings, and to use such knowledge in planning and directioning one's life. Intra-personal intelligence involves not only an appreciation of the self, but also of the human condition. It is evident in psychologist, spiritual leaders, and philosophers. These young adults may be shy. They are very aware of their own feelings and are self-motivated.

9. Spatial Intelligence ("Picture Smart")

Spatial intelligence is the ability to think in three dimensions. Core capacities include mental imagery, spatial reasoning, image manipulation, graphic and artistic skills, and an active imagination. Sailors, pilots, sculptors, painters, and architects all exhibit spatial intelligence. Young adults with this kind of intelligence may be fascinated with mazes or jigsaw puzzles, or spend free time drawing or daydreaming.

Robert Sternberg

Many teachers have provided testimonial evidence that PBL encourages participation on the part of their students who do not have a high level of "school smarts." They report that some of their students who were not doing well in school have become actively engaged and experienced a high level of success in working on projects. These observations are consistent with and supportive of the research of Robert Sternberg.

As noted earlier in this chapter, different researchers have identified different components of intelligence. Sternberg (1988, 1997) focuses on just three main components:

1. Practical intelligence--the ability to do well in informal and formal educational settings; adapting to and shaping one's environment; street smarts.
2. Experiential intelligence--the ability to deal with novel situations; the ability to effectively automate ways of dealing with novel situations so

they are easily handled in the future; the ability to think in novel ways.

3. Componential intelligence--the ability to process information effectively. This includes metacognitive, executive, performance, and knowledge-acquisition components that help to steer cognitive processes.

Sternberg provides examples of people who are quite talented in one of these areas but not so talented in the other two. In that sense, his approach to the field of intelligence is somewhat like Howard Gardner's. However, you can see that Sternberg does not focus on specific components of intelligence that are aligned with various academic disciplines. He is far more concerned with helping people develop components of intelligence that will help them to perform well in whatever they chose to do.

Sternberg strongly believes that intelligence can be increased by study and practice. Quite a bit of his research focuses on such endeavors. Some of Sternberg's work focuses specifically on "street smarts" versus "school smarts." He notes that some people are particularly talented in one of these two areas, and not in the other. This observation is consistent with the work of Lev Vygotsky (Fosnot, 1996) who argues that the type of learning that goes on outside of school is distinctly different than the type of learning that goes on in school. While some students are talented in both informal and formal education, others are much more successful in one rather than the other. A teacher who is skillful in developing PBL can help students to design projects that are consistent with their learning abilities and interests.

Sternberg's Triarchic Theory of Human Intelligence (1977, 1985, 1995) subsumes both Spearman's *g* and underlying information processing components. His triarchic theory includes three facets or subtheories:

- Analytical (componential)
- Creative (experiential)
- Practical (contextual)

Overview of Sternberg's Triarchic Theory of Intelligence

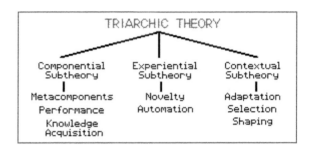

Sternberg's theory builds on his earlier componential approach to reasoning. His theory is mostly based on observing Yale graduate students. Sternberg believes that if intelligence is properly defined & measured it will translate to real-life success.

Sternberg's Triarchic Theory is an important effort to synthesize the various theories of intelligence.

Analytical (componential) Facet (or Subtheory)

Analytical Intelligence similar to the standard psychometric definition of intelligence e.g. as measured by Academic problem solving: analogies and puzzles, and corresponds to his earlier componential intelligence. Sternberg considers this reflects how an individual relates to his internal world.

Sternberg believes that Analytical Intelligence (Academic problem-solving skills) is based on the joint operations of metacomponents and performance components and knowledge acquisition components of intelligence

Metacomponents: control, monitor and evaluate cognitive processing. These are the *executive* functions to order and organize performance and knowledge acquisition components. They are the higher-order processes that order and organize the performance components. Used to analyze problems and pick a strategy for solving them. They decide what to do and the performance components actually do it.

Performance Components: execute strategies assembled by the metacomponents. They are the basic operations involved in any cognitive act. They are the cognitive processes that enable us to encode stimuli, hold information in short-term memory, make calculations, perform mental calculations, mentally compare different stimuli, retrieve information from long-term memory.

Knowledge acquisition components: are the processes used in gaining and storing new knowledge—i.e. capacity for learning. The strategies you use to help memorize things exemplify the processes that fall into this category.

WHAT IS EMOTIONAL INTELLIGENCE

Emotional intelligence (EI) refers to the ability to perceive, control and evaluate emotions. Some researchers suggest that emotional intelligence can be learned and strengthened, while others claim it is an inborn characteristic.

Since 1990, Peter Salovey and John D. Mayer have been the leading researchers on emotional intelligence. In their influential article "Emotional Intelligence," they defined emotional intelligence as, "the subset of social intelligence that involves the ability to monitor one's own and others' feelings and emotions, to discriminate among them and to use this information to guide one's thinking and actions" (1990).

The Four Branches of Emotional Intelligence

Salovey and Mayer proposed a model that identified four different factors of emotional intelligence: the perception of emotion, the ability reason using emotions, the ability to understand emotion and the ability to manage emotions.

1. **Perceiving Emotions:** The first step in understanding emotions is to accurately perceive them. In many cases, this might involve understanding nonverbal signals such as body language and facial expressions.
2. **Reasoning With Emotions:** The next step involves using emotions to promote thinking and cognitive activity. Emotions help prioritize what we pay attention and react to; we respond emotionally to things that garner our attention.

3. **Understanding Emotions:** The emotions that we perceive can carry a wide variety of meanings. If someone is expressing angry emotions, the observer must interpret the cause of their anger and what it might mean. For example, if your boss is acting angry, it might mean that he is dissatisfied with your work; or it could be because he got a speeding ticket on his way to work that morning or that he's been fighting with his wife.
4. **Managing Emotions:** The ability to manage emotions effectively is a key part of emotional intelligence. Regulating emotions, responding appropriately and responding to the emotions of others are all important aspect of emotional management.

According to Salovey and Mayer, the four branches of their model are, "arranged from more basic psychological processes to higher, more psychologically integrated processes. For example, the lowest level branch concerns the (relatively) simple abilities of perceiving and expressing emotion. In contrast, the highest level branch concerns the conscious, reflective regulation of emotion" (1997).

A Brief History of Emotional Intelligence

Interest in intelligence dates back thousands of years, but it wasn't until psychologist Alfred Binet was commissioned to identify students who needed educational assistance that the first IQ test was born.

INTELLIGENCE AND GENETICS

Influences of genetics and environment

The role of genes and environment (nature and nurture) in determining IQ has been debated for decades and the degree to which nature versus nurture influences the development of human traits (especially intelligence) is one of the most intractable scholarly controversies of modern times.

Traditional View of Intelligence vs. MI Theory

Traditional View of Intelligence	Multiple Intelligences Theory
Intelligence can be measured by short-answer tests: • Stanford-Binet Intelligence Quotient • Wechsler Intelligence Scale for Children (WISCIV) • Woodcock Johnson test of Cognitive Ability • Scholastic Aptitude Test	Assessment of an individual's multiple intelligences can foster learning and problem-solving styles. Short answer tests are not used because they do not measure disciplinary mastery or deep understanding. They only measure rote memorization skills and one's ability to do well on short answer tests. Some states have developed tests that value process over the final answer, such as PAM (Performance Assessment in Math) and PAL (Performance Assessment in Language)
People are born with a fixed amount of intelligence.	Human beings have all of the intelligences, but each person has a unique combination, or profile.
Intelligence level does not change over a lifetime.	We can all improve each of the intelligences, though some people will improve more readily in one intelligence area than in others.
Intelligence consists of ability in logic and language.	There are many more types of intelligence which reflect different ways of interacting with the world
In traditional practice, teachers teach the same material to everyone.	M.I. pedagogy implies that teachers teach and assess differently based on individual intellectual strengths and weaknesses.
Teachers teach a topic or "subject."	Teachers structure learning activities around an issue or question and connect subjects. Teachers develop strategies that allow for students to demonstrate multiple ways of understanding and value their uniqueness.

As it relates to intelligence, overall, except in unusual cases, the role of genes and heredity is far greater than the role of environment. However, environmental factors can, and do, play a role in determining IQ in extreme situations. Proper childhood nutrition appears critical for cognitive development; malnutrition can lower IQ. Other research indicates environmental factors such as prenatal exposure to toxins, duration of breastfeeding, and micronutrient deficiency can affect IQ. In the developed world, there are some family effects on the IQ of children, accounting for up to a quarter of the variance. However, by adulthood, this correlation disappears, so that the IQ of adults living in the prevailing conditions of the developed world may be more heritable.

It is reasonable to expect that genetic influences on traits like IQ should become less important as one gains experience with age. Surprisingly, the opposite occurs. Heritability measures in infancy are as low as

20%, around 40% in middle childhood, and as high as 80% in adulthood.

The heritability of IQ measures the extent to which the IQ of children appears to be influenced by the IQ of parents. Because the heritability of IQ is less than 100%, the IQ of children tends to "regress" towards the mean IQ of the population. That is, high IQ parents tend to have children who are less bright than their parents, whereas low IQ parents tend to have children who are brighter than their parents.

Intelligence and Heredity

Our genes determine the quality of our intelligence, our ability to integrate and process information. The level of our intelligence determines how well we cope with changes in our environment. We express the processing capacity of our intelligence by a unit of

measurement called the Intelligence Quotient, IQ for short. Our IQ represents the ratio of the measured level of intelligence to the physiological age of the subject, multiplied by 100.

Some people are very smart; some people are not very smart. If we compile a large number of individual intelligence measurements, it is statistically inevitable that the graphic display of such results appears in the shape of a bell curve. The bell-curve represents a cross-section of the intellectual capacity of a population group.

Caucasians of predominantly European ancestry were the first subjects of standardized intelligence tests. The mean achievement level of these tests was set at 100 and this arbitrary level represents the norm against which the intelligence of individuals and groups is measured.

In the past, considerable conflict existed regarding the proportional importance of hereditary factors versus environmental factors, in determining the level of intelligence displayed by individuals or population groups. From the 1960s to the 1990s, a trend prevailed among sociologists in the United States to attribute 80% or even 100% of measured intelligence to environmental determinants, with negligible ascription to heredity.

This anomaly was the result of political concessions, demanded by some members of the non-scientific academic community. These persons insisted on a strict interpretation of the Jeffersonian pronouncement that "all men are created equal".

However, only politically motivated sociologists in purportedly egalitarian societies, such as the United States and the Soviet Union, adopted this unrealistic view. Scientists in all other countries of the world accept the irrefutable fact that men are not created equal.

Parallel to the unrealistic attitude of American politicians, a political trend persisted in the Soviet Union in the form of the state-approved teachings of the Russian biologist Lysenko. Similar to the Jeffersonian position, the Soviets invested all people with equal human attributes, including equal rational thought processes.

Jefferson pronounced the equality of all men but, simultaneously, he subjugated many of the same human beings he referred to as equal, in a state of severe slavery for his own gain. Russia, as the successor to the Soviet Union, abandoned the politically motivated position that all men are born with equal attributes. Eventually, rationality prevailed in the United States, where such untenable positions disappeared towards the end of the 20th century.

Intelligence and Race

The reality and validity of IQ measurements lies in the fact that different people have different IQs. Different population groups, races or ethnic groups exhibit different statistical levels of intelligence as measured by standard IQ tests.

Blacks consistently score 15% lower than Whites on standard IQ tests, even after adjusting for environmental exposures. This deviation occurs without regard to the geographical area of the world or the society where we administer such IQ tests.

The Japanese population has a mean IQ level of 110, Mexican mestizos score in the low 90's. Indeed, it would be truly astounding if all people of the world had the same level of intelligence, because it might indicate that all people where produced in the same mold and had identical genes.

The graphical display of normal population statistics invariably produces bell-curved graphs with regard to human characteristics. The bell curve merely reflects the fact that all humans are different. It is difficult to conceive of a reason why this well-established attribute should not apply to human intelligence. Indeed, human intelligence displays results in the shape of a bell curve.

Intelligence levels of groups of people conform to the law of evolution and do not change rapidly. Significant change might occur over time spans measured in thousand or tens of thousands of years.

However, evolution can accelerate dramatically in the face of violent societal upheavals. Such tumultuous and dangerous periods encourage the survival and subsequent propagation of only those members of a population group who are best equipped to survive. Intelligence is a crucial survival factor.

It is illuminating to consider the two opposites of American societal IQ levels: African American Negroes, as opposed to American Jews. These population groups have sorted themselves out into different occupational structures based on their respective IQs.

Black Americans prevail in occupations that require limited intellectual acuity but a high level of physical prowess, such as manual labor or sports activities. The opposite holds true of Jews who predominate in intellectual and artistic pursuits that require a higher level of intelligence than physical activities.

It is therefore not surprising that IQ levels for both groups diverge drastically. The peak of the bell curve charting IQ level of American urban Blacks falls in the 80-85 range. Jews consistently score in the 115-120 range.

Since IQs do not exist in a vacuum but are broad predictors of financial success in life, the income levels of Blacks and Jews are similarly representative of their different intellectual capacity. Earnings of Jews are almost twice as high as the earnings of Blacks and are slightly ahead of the Japanese.

These facts confirm the old expression: The dull people of this world do not run the world, the smart people run this world. The highest standard of living does not accrue to the unintelligent people of this world; it is the smart people, the people with the higher IQ, who are affluent. This fact is self-evident.

The explanation for this discrepancy in IQ levels becomes obvious when we refer to the source of all innate human faculties. The evolution of man over a millions of years resulted in a variety of innate traits that reflected survival characteristics demanded by differing environments.

Negroes developed in a benign tropical environment where nature readily provided sustenance without substantial competitive pressures for natural resources. The lack of a need for higher intellectual accomplishments did not encourage the elimination of the intellectually disadvantaged from their society.

After the transfer of Negroes to the Americas, slave owners further discouraged intellectual activities by slaves and placed higher value on the physical prowess of slaves. Manual field labor provided no evolutionary impetus for high levels of intelligence.

The reverse situation applied to Jews. Their religious beliefs and their shrewdness set them apart from most other population groups with whom they interacted. This separateness frequently placed them into the position of scapegoats and consequentially subjected them to pogroms. In order to survive they had to live by their wits, not by their brawns. The harsh atmosphere of such persecutions favored and honed their intellectual ability to survive constant onslaughts of malevolence and violence.

After thousands of years of pogroms, the weaker and less adroit elements of Jewish societies gradually diminished in numbers. The surviving Jewish population groups attained a higher standard of living due to the constant rise in IQ levels required by their survival needs. This evolutionary process resulted in the survival of the more intelligent Jews.

The evolution of the Jews gained momentum during the extermination of Jews in World War II. During those calamitous times, Jews of innately higher intelligence had a better chance of survival than intellectually less endowed Jews. Einstein survived because he had the intelligence to foresee the looming catastrophe; a Jewish street vendor in Berlin lacked this acuity and perished.

This perspective on the formation of intelligence levels is statistical in nature. It does not imply that only bright Jews survived and that only dull Jews perished. When faced with a disaster that is largely beyond one's personal control or anticipation, even the best and the brightest can perish where a less intellectually capable person may survive.

In any analysis of evolutionary characteristics, statistical results determine the outcome, rather than individual abilities. In this statistical arena, results speak for themselves: Jews have become a super-race.

Evolution has no moral connotations. It does not concern itself with the sufferings of individuals or even vast numbers of people. Evolution is not a selective factor with a preordained purpose.

The process of evolution is the prerequisite of all life on earth. It follows only one principle: The survival and the perpetuation of those persons who are most fit to adjust to changing environmental conditions. Evolution has no moral or political agenda; it is merely a manifestation of the fact that some persons have superior survival mechanisms than others. Evolution has endowed human beings with intelligence because intelligence is the most potent survival mechanism.

Bright black professionals, who were capable of achieving success without the crutch of affirmative action, are strongly opposed to Affirmative Action laws, because these laws provide for preferential treatment of Blacks. Affirmative Action makes it impossible for other persons to judge whether the accreditation of Blacks is due to merit or to preferential treatment based on their color.

The high esteem attributed to many Jewish professionals may in part be due to the quota system that elite colleges maintained in order to reduce access by Jews. The public has learned that, if a Jew graduated from a prestigious medical school, he had to have superior qualifications than even the average white applicant.

Instead of fighting rampant discrimination against them in the employment market, and instead of clamoring for preferential treatment, Jews simply proved their superior abilities. They overcame racial prejudice in employment by becoming very successful professionals and artists.

CHAPTER 8 SUMMARY

INTELLIGENCE

In order to place intelligence in its proper context, it is important to demonstrate that intelligence has been difficult to define and to operationalize. This will allow for students to clearly see that intelligence is multifaceted. Once this has been accomplished, then discussion of testing and other likely preconceived notions of intelligence may be covered effectively.

INTELLIGENCE TESTING

Beginning with the Binet scales, intelligence testing has focused on skills that are acquired and compared against some predetermined value. Trace the history of the Binet scales first in covering testing, then move on to group tests, and then to the Wechsler scales. Discuss the validity and limitations of intelligence tests by a) cultural bias inherent in tests, and b) the multidimensionality of intelligence does not allow for a test to satisfactorily measure all aspects of intelligence.

APPROACHES TO INTELLIGENCE

The psychometric approach to measuring intelligence relies upon a statistical method for delineating broader categories from a group of measured skills. This method has been cast into two different theories. One, Spearman's Two Factor theory, posits that intelligence is divided into a g-factor (general abilities) and an s-factor (specific abilities). Typical measures of g are tests of comprehension, spatial skills, and verbal abilities. Typical measures of s are speed and accuracy tests, and rote memory skills. The general message conveyed by this theory is that there are overarching abilities that can be assessed in all persons, with other specific skills that some have while others do not. Another psychometric-based theory is the Gf-Gc theory. Gf refers to fluid intelligence, which is a set of innate skills that are not dependent upon environment. Gc refers to crystallized intelligence, which is based upon academic learning.

INFORMATION PROCESSING AND INTELLIGENCE

A richer theoretical tradition is based upon the manner of information processing and its relation to intelligence. Accordingly, it has been suggested that intelligence has been predicated upon personal attributes such as speed of processing, knowledge base, and the ability to acquire and apply new cognitive approaches to problem solving. Taken together, these represent a predictive approach to intelligence based on skills acquisition and ability to use these skills effectively.

MULTIPLE INTELLIGENCES

Howard Gardner proposed a theory of intelligence that suggests individuals have a conglomeration of skills that all fall on different normal curves (that is, each area is distinct from the others), referred to as multiple intelligences. He has proposed seven different intelligences: musical, bodily/kinesthetic, spatial, linguistic, logical/mathematical, intra-personal, and interpersonal. The data that he has relied upon to marshal support for this theory is primarily based on idiosyncratic situations where persons display one of these areas in deference to the other intelligences. For example, savants (persons determined to have mental retardation) may appear totally lacking in most of these areas, yet display exceptional musical ability, or mathematics skill (such as the main character in the movie Rain Man). Other illustrations have been based upon examining persons with head injuries, where a portion of the brain has been damaged, thus isolating a circumscribed area defining one of these intelligences. The MI theory is the focus of the following site:

HEREDITY AND INTELLIGENCE

This area has been controversial, most notably with regard to racial differences in intel-ligence. However, the most salient feature of this material (twin, adoption, and family studies) leads to a demonstration of a research methodology that has been developed to answer questions such as these. It has been shown that there appears to be a strong genetic effect when examining twin studies and adoption data, although environmental factors can also play a significant role in one's performance on intelligence tests.

Regarding race differences, this issue has been a source of controversy for some time, with a recent increase in interest based upon the text by Murray and Hernstein, The Bell Curve. Since the publication of this book, there has been considerable debate about the findings suggesting group differences in performance. Notably, scholars have pointed out that nutrition and relative education differences are also significant between these groups, and that the effects of these differences likely account for more of the differences in IQ than heredity.

The work of Sir Cyril Burt focused on twin studies of intelligence. After his death, serious questions were raised as to the validity of his methods and conclusions. This topic can lead to a discussion of ethics in research. For a discussion of these issues, visit the following site:

MENTAL DISABILITIES

Mental disability is associated with IQ scores below 70, as well as poor performance in adaptive functioning. There are a number of reasons one may develop mental re-tardation. Two notable genetic disorders are Down Syndrome, characterized by an additional chromosome, and Phenylketonuria (PKU), where an inability to produce an enzyme is present. There are other notable environmental causes of mental retardation, such as ingestion of lead-based paints during childhood, brain damage before birth, or alcohol and cocaine abuse by the mother during pregnancy.

Treatments for mental retardation focus primarily upon attempts at normalizing the affected individual so that the deficits in functioning are not persistently brought to attention. It has been shown that the more one can 'mainstream' mentally retarded individuals, the more they can function outside of classroom situations.

GIFTEDNESS AND HIGH INTELLIGENCE

At the other end of the spectrum, many people exhibit high levels of intellectual functioning. This can be expressed in a number of ways. One way that this may be demonstrated is by divergent thinking. Frequently, persons with high intelligence will view problem solutions in novel ways or in non-normative ways. Creativity is an interesting element associated with high intelligence that shows a unidirectional relationship. That is, for one to be creative they must be intelligence. However, the presence of intelligence in no way guarantees creativity.

STATES OF CONSCIOUSNESS

9

After completing Chapter 9, students should be able to:

- Describe the functions of consciousness.
- Discuss the role of attention as a part of consciousness.
- Define what is meant by the term mindlessness.
- Outline Freud's views of conscious, preconscious, and unconscious states.
- Compare and contrast the concepts of the psychodynamic and the cognitive unconscious.
- Explain the significance of the split-brain procedure for our understanding of consciousness.
- Discuss the brain structures that regulate wakefulness and arousal.
- Define the term circadian rhythm.
- Discuss the impact of sleep deprivation on human function.
- Discuss the most common forms of sleep disorders.
- Describe four suggestions for avoiding or reducing insomnia.
- Outline the various phases of sleep and dreaming.
- Contrast the biological, cognitive and psychodynamic views on dreaming.
- Describe how meditation differs from normal consciousness.
- Discuss the effects of hypnosis on pain perception, memory, and cognitive function.
- Outline how various psychoactive substances operate on the nervous system to alter patterns of perception, thought, feeling, and behavior.

Consciousness refers to your individual awareness of your unique thoughts, memories, feelings, sensations and environment. Your conscious experiences are constantly shifting and changing. For example, in one moment you may be totally focused on reading this chapter. Then later, your consciousness may shift to the memory of a conversation you had earlier with a friend.. Next, you might notice how uncomfortable your chair is or maybe you may begin to budget your money mentally while planning for dinner at the same time. This ever-shifting stream of thoughts can change dramatically from one moment to the next, but your experience of it seems smooth and effortless.

INTRODUCTION

The conscious experience was one of the first topics studied by early psychologists. Structuralists used a process known as *introspection* to analyze and report conscious sensations, thoughts, and experiences. American psychologist William James compared consciousness to a stream; unbroken and continuous despite constant shifts and changes. While the focus of much of the research in psychology shifted to purely observable behaviors during the first half of the twentieth century, research on human consciousness has grown tremendously since the 1950s. William James (1842–1910), the great pioneer of the study of consciousness, wrote in the *Varieties of Religious Experience* what is called "normal waking consciousness." This is a type of consciousness that is separated by the slightest of barriers, "there lie potential forms of consciousness entirely different." While many individuals may go through life without suspecting the existence of these states of consciousness, "...apply the requisite stimulus, and at a touch they are there in all their completeness…No account of the universe in its totality can be final which leaves these forms of consciousness disregarded."

Researchers who study aspects of human consciousness have suggested that within the course of a single day an individual may flicker in and out of several states of consciousness. Some theorize that there are six states of "nonreflective consciousness," characterized by the absence of self-consciousness. These states include:

1. Bodily feelings, which are induced by normal bodily functioning and are characterized by nonreflective awareness in the organs and tissues of the digestive, glandular, respiratory, and other bodily systems. This awareness does not become self-conscious unless such stimuli as pain or hunger intensify a bodily feeling.

2. Stored memories, which do not become self-conscious until the individual reactivates them.

3. Coma, which is induced by illness, epileptic seizures, or physical injuries to the brain, and is characterized by prolonged nonreflective consciousness of the entire organism.

4. Stupor, which is induced by psychosis, narcotics, or over-indulgence in alcohol, and is characterized by greatly reduced ability to perceive incoming sensations.

5. Non-rapid-eye-movement sleep, which is caused by a normal part of the sleep cycle at night or during daytime naps, and is characterized by a minimal amount of mental activity, which may sometimes be recalled upon awakening.

6. Rapid-eye-movement sleep, which is a normal part of the nighttime sleep cycle, and is characterized by the mental activity known as dreams.

The reflective, or self-conscious, states of consciousness are:

1. Pragmatic consciousness, the everyday, waking conscious state, characterized by alertness, logic, and rationality, cause-and-effect thinking, goal-directedness. In this level of consciousness, one has the feeling that he or she is in control and has the ability to move at will from perceptual activity to conceptual thinking to idea formation to motor activity.

2. Lethargic consciousness, characterized by sluggish mental activity that has been induced by

fatigue, sleep deprivation, feelings of depression, or certain drugs.

3. Hyperalert consciousness, brought about by a period of heightened vigilance, such as sentry duty, watching over a sick child, or by certain drugs, such as amphetamines.

Levels or types of consciousness with varying degrees of what could be considered an altered state might include:

1. Rapturous consciousness, characterized by intense feelings and overpowering emotions and induced by sexual stimulation, the fervor of religious conversion, or the ingestion of certain drugs.

2. Hysterical consciousness, induced by rage, jealousy, fear, neurotic anxiety, violent mob activity, or certain drugs. As opposed to rapturous consciousness, which is generally evaluated as pleasant and positive in nature, hysterical consciousness is considered negative and destructive.

3. Fragmented consciousness, defined as a lack of integration among important segments of the total personality, often results in psychosis, severe neurosis, amnesia, multiple personality, or dissociation. Such a state of consciousness is induced by severe psychological stress over a period of time. It may also be brought about temporarily by accidents or psychedelic drugs.

4. Relaxed consciousness, characterized by a state of minimal mental activity, passivity, and an absence of motor activity. This state of consciousness may be brought about by lack of external stimulation, such as sunbathing, floating in water, or certain drugs.

5. Daydreaming, induced by boredom, social isolation, or sensory deprivation.

6. Trance consciousness, induced by rapt attentiveness to a single stimulus, such as the voice of a hypnotist, one's own heartbeat, a chant, certain drugs, or trance-inducing rituals and primitive dances. The trance state is characterized by hypersuggestibility and concentrated attention on one stimulus to the exclusion of all others.

7. Expanded consciousness, comprising four levels: A) the sensory level, characterized by subjective reports of space, time, body image, or sense impressions having been altered; B) the recollective-analytic level, which summons up memories of one's past and provides insights concerning self, work, or personal relationships; C) the symbolic level, which is often characterized by vivid visual imagery of mythical, religious, and historical symbols; D) the integrative level, in which the individual undergoes an intense religious illumination, experiences a dissolution of self, and is confronted by God or some divine being. Each of these four levels might be induced by psychedelic drugs, hypnosis, meditation, prayer, or free association during psychoanalysis. Through the ages, many of humankind's major material and spiritual breakthroughs may have come from these virtually unmapped, uncharted regions of the mind.

CONSCIOUSNESS AND BRAIN WAVES

Consciousness is the awareness we have of ourselves and our environment. Different states of consciousness are associated with different patterns of brain waves. Brain waves are tracings of electrical activity that is going on in the brain. Scientists record brain waves using an electroencephalograph (EEG), which monitors electrical activity through electrodes placed on the scalp. There are four main types of brain waves: alpha, beta, theta, and delta each with a corresponding mental state:

Type of Brain Wave—Corresponding Mental State

1. Alpha—Very relaxed or meditating
2. Beta—Awake and alert
3. Theta—Lightly asleep
4. Delta—Deeply asleep
5. Gamma

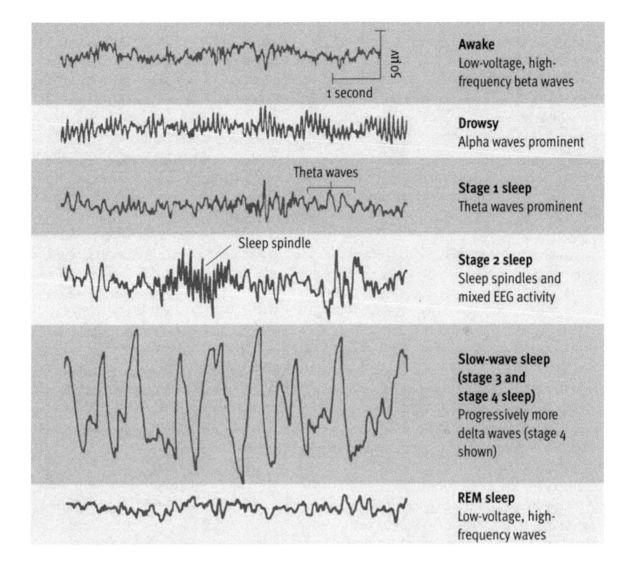

The table below tells the patterns of brain wave activity across different ages and states of awareness with the number of repetitions required to learn new behavior patterns.

Every part of your body vibrates to its own rhythm. Your brain has a unique set of brain waves. In neuroscience, there are five distinct brain wave frequencies, namely Beta, Alpha, Theta, Delta and the lesser known Gamma. Learning mind control at the deeper states of consciousness opens you up to the world of your subconscious mind where you can create your reality at will and with exact precision.

Each frequency, measured in cycles per second (Hz), has its own set of characteristics representing a specific level of brain activity and hence a unique state of consciousness.

Beta (12-30Hz): Beta brain waves are associated with normal waking consciousness and a heightened state of alertness, logic and critical reasoning. As you go about your daily activities you are at Beta. Although important for effectively functioning in everyday life, higher Beta levels translate into stress, anxiety and restlessness. With the majority of adults primarily operating at Beta during their waking hours it is little wonder that stress is today's most common health problem. The voice of Beta is the little nagging chatterbox of your inner critic, which becomes louder and more relentless the higher you go in the range.

Alpha (7.5-12Hz): Alpha brain waves are present in deep relaxation with the eyes usually closed and while day-dreaming. The relaxed detached awareness achieved during light meditation is characteristic of

Alpha and is optimal for programming your mind for success. Alpha heightens your imagination, visualization, memory, learning and concentration. It lies at the base of your conscious awareness and is the gateway to your subconscious mind. The renowned Silva Method by Jose Silva is premised on the power of Alpha. The voice of Alpha is your intuition, which becomes clearer and more profound the closer you get to 7.5Hz.

Theta (4-7.5Hz): Theta brain waves are present during deep meditation and light sleep, including the REM dream state. Theta is the realm of your subconscious mind. It is also known as the twilight state as it is normally only momentarily experienced as you drift off to sleep (from Alpha) and arise from deep sleep (from Delta). A sense of deep spiritual connection and oneness with the Universe can be experienced at Theta. Vivid visualizations, great inspiration, profound creativity, exceptional insight as well as your mind's most deep-seated programs are all at Theta. The voice of Theta is silence.

Delta (0.5-4Hz): The Delta frequency is the slowest and is present in deep, dreamless sleep and in very deep, transcendental meditation where awareness is completely detached. Delta is the realm of your unconscious mind. It is the gateway to the Universal mind and the collective unconscious whereby information received is otherwise unavailable at the conscious level. Delta is associated with deep healing and regeneration, underlining the importance of deep sleep to the healing process.

The Alpha-Theta border, from 7 to 8Hz, is the optimal range for visualization, mind programming and using the creative power of your mind. It is the mental state at which you consciously create your reality. At this frequency of mind control you are conscious of your surroundings but your body is in deep relaxation.

Gamma (30-100Hz): The most recently discovered range is Gamma which is the fastest in frequency at above 40Hz (some researchers do not distinguish Beta from Gamma waves). Although little is known about this state of mind, initial research shows

EEG Brain Frequency Chart

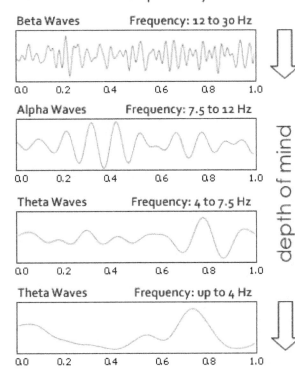

Beta Waves   Frequency: 12 to 30 Hz

0.0   0.2   0.4   0.6   0.8   1.0

Conscious Mind

Normal waking state of consciousness. Alertness, concentration, focus, cognition and the five physical senses.

Alpha Waves   Frequency: 7.5 to 12 Hz

0.0   0.2   0.4   0.6   0.8   1.0

Gateway to the Subconscious Mind

Deep relaxation and light meditation usually with eyes closed. Relaxation, visualization, creativity and super learning.

Theta Waves   Frequency: 4 to 7.5 Hz

0.0   0.2   0.4   0.6   0.8   1.0

Subconscious Mind

Usually light sleep, including REM dream state. Deep meditation, intuition, memory and vivid visual imagery.

Theta Waves   Frequency: up to 4 Hz

0.0   0.2   0.4   0.6   0.8   1.0

Unconscious or Supra-Conscious Mind

Usually deep sleep, dreamless state. Transcendental meditation. Automatic self-healing, immune system function.

depth of mind

image source of graphs: wikipedia

Gamma waves are associated with bursts of insight and high-level information processing.

The following chart shows the EEG (Electroencephalography) graphs of the four major levels of brain activity.

In a nutshell, there are five major brain wave ranges: Beta (14-40Hz) is present in normal waking consciousness and stress; the Alpha brain wave (7.5-14Hz) in deep relaxation; Theta (4-7.5Hz) in meditation and light sleep; and the slowest, Delta (0.5-4Hz) in deep dreamless sleep and transcendental meditation. The less recognized Gamma is fastest (above 40Hz) and associated with sudden insight. The optimal level for visualization is the Alpha-Theta Border at 7-8Hz. It is the gateway to your subconscious mind.

BRAIN IMAGING: ALTERED STATES OF CONSCIOUSNESS

An altered state of consciousness is a brain state wherein one loses the sense of identity with one's body or with one's normal sense perceptions. A person may enter an altered state of consciousness through such things as sensory deprivation or overload, neuro-chemical imbalance, fever, trauma, or sleep. One may also achieve an altered state by chanting, meditating, entering a trance state, or ingesting psychedelic drugs.

Perspectives on Consciousness

In this section of the chapter, a variety of different perspectives on the nature of consciousness will be critically examined. Different approaches to therapeutic intervention that result from the respective views on consciousness. Five broad streams of thought that relate to the question of consciousness have been identified and will be discussed. These are: the *psychodynamic* school of thought that originated with the ideas of Sigmund Freud; the *phenomenological existentialist* approach, that originated with the ideas of Edmund Husserl and Jean-Paul Sartre; the *humanist* approach that is best exemplified by Karl Rogers; the *behaviorist* approach, that originated with the ideas of J.B. Watson and B.F. Skinner; the *cognitive-behaviorist* approach, a pioneer of which was Stanley Beck. Lastly, some of the more recent theoretical developments will be discussed, including *postmodern* and/or *poststructuralist* theorists like Michel Foucault, Gille Deleuze and Felix Guattari.

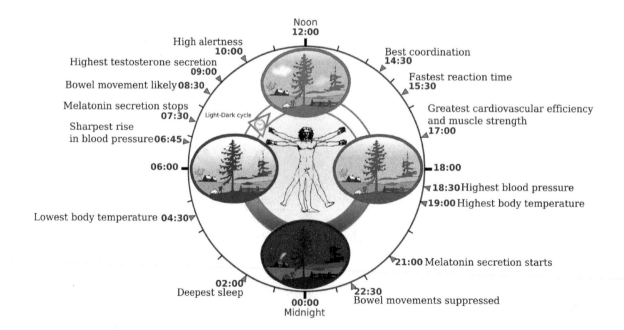

The Biological Perspective

It is necessary to repeat that all aspects of human life is impacted by levels of consciousness. Particularly important are the nervous system, comprising brain and spinal cord, and the endocrine system, comprising a number of ductless glands that secrete hormones into the bloodstream. Many biological scientists today implicitly believe that these structures not only shape consciousness, but are actually the source of conscious awareness. This view is known as the *Biological Identity Theory*.

Psychodynamic Perspective

Sigmund Freud held the view that the mind was divided into three functional structures, consciousness, preconsciousness, and unconsciousness. He suggested that the existence of an "unconscious," resulting particularly in irrational impulses, unconscious desire and sexual drives. Freud argued (in his first topography) that there were different psychical systems within the mind -the unconscious, pre-conscious and conscious. The unconscious was separated from the other two by a censor, or deliberate attempts to avoid painful emotions associated with an experience or memory of that experience. Freud later modified his position and introduced the second topography in <u>On Narcissism</u> (Freud, 1914) by referring to three structures in the mind: the id, which was the source of all biological drives and demands for immediate gratification; the super-ego, which was the internalization of the parental representations of the values and morality of the society in which individuals found themselves; and the ego, which was the mediator between the two structures, having to satisfy the individual's demands for gratification, while keeping them out of danger from the environment (Freud, 1923: 439-483). However, there was still a division between consciousness and unconsciousness (Wollheim, 1985: 153).

Freud's therapeutic technique was to look at the dreams produced by his patients as their neurotic symptoms and interpret these. He also encouraged his patients to "free associate, " by which he intended that they should speak about everything that came to

mind and omit nothing. This was done in order to reveal their chains of associations to him. He argued that patients would be cured through the transference, which rearticulated the Oedipal bonds and enabled the patient to work through unresolved conflicts. This would enable them to overcome any "fixations" that may have taken place as a result of trauma in their life that they were unable to deal with effectively at the time of their occurrence (Freud, 1926: 7-23). Using this technique, Freud was able to provide effective and convincing accounts of clinical phenomena, such as somatization and other hysterical sympapplelogy (which are arguably not done at a conscious level).

Humanistic Perspective

An approach that is closely related to the existentialist one is the Humanist approach, as exemplified by the ideas of Carl Rogers. He founded the "individual centered" approach to psychotherapy. Rogers argued that all individuals have the "germ" within them that, if allowed to grow and develop, would result in their self-actualization. For Rogers, psychopathology arose when individuals' own unique personalities are made to conform to the demands of their environment. Rogers argues that this state comes about when individuals receive conditional positive regard from their care-givers in childhood. That is, they are not encouraged and supported to develop their own unique potential, but are made to feel that they will only be loved if they behave in a certain manner. A state of incongruence results between the demands of the environment (i.e., the family, the workplace) and the demands of the self (Thorne, 1993: 312).

His view of consciousness is that individuals are not victims of unknown (environmental or unconscious) forces that decide their destinies on their behalf. They are able to know their desires and are able to change their lives consciously and rationally for the better (Thorne, 1993: 312).

The Rogerian therapeutic approach is therefore aimed at providing unconditional positive regard to the individual, who is thus encouraged to live his/her life in accordance with his/her own true self (Thorne, 1993: 312).

Cognitive Information Consolidation Theory of Sleep

The information consolidation theory of sleep is based on cognitive research and suggests that people sleep in order to process information that has been acquired during the day. In addition to processing information from the day prior, this theory also argues that sleep allows the brain to prepare for the day to come. Some research also suggests that sleep helps cement the things we have learned during the day into long-term memory. Support for this idea stems from a number of sleep deprivation studied demonstrating that a lack of sleep has a serious impact on the ability to recall and remember information.

While there is research and evidence to support each of these theories of sleep, there is still no clear-cut support for any one theory. It is also possible that each of these theories can be used to explain why we sleep. Sleeping impacts many physiological processes, so it is very possible that sleep occurs for many reasons and purposes.

The invention of the electroencephalograph allowed scientists to study sleep in ways that were not previously possible. During the 1950s, a graduate student named Eugene Aserinsky used this tool to discover what is known today as REM sleep. Further studies of human sleep have demonstrated that sleep progresses through a series of stages in which different brain wave patterns are displayed.

Behaviorism

Another approach that gained widespread currency in the earlier part of the last century was the behaviorist approach of J.B. Watson and B.F. Skinner. Watson argued that the science of psychology should only be interested in phenomena that were observable and measurable. He built on the experiments of Ivan Pavlov (on dogs) and developed the concepts of behavioral conditioning. Skinner introduced the notion of reinforcement as an aid for learning and behavior modification. The behaviorists were not interested in "mind" at all as they argued that this notion was a relic of a superstitious interpretation of human behavior (Watson, 1930; Skinner, 1953).

The behaviorists maintained that it was far more important to consider the environmental stimuli—the conditioners and the reinforcers of behavior. Mind was viewed as an epiphenomenon, and as such was seen to be unable to exert any causal transformations of (or in) the environment. One could diagrammatize their view of the relationship between (environmental) stimulus and (behavioral) response thus:

STIMULUS → RESPONSE

The focus was on the nature of that which takes place between the stimulus and the response.

The therapeutic approach that emerged from these ideas was one that sought to ignore the mental and "psychological" material that had been of central importance until then. It was argued that pathological behavior should be modified by means of a schedule of conditioners and reinforcers that would have the effect of rewarding good behavior and punishing the bad. Many of these techniques proved to be remarkably effective, particularly with obsessive-compulsive disorders, anxiety disorders and phobias (Watson, 1930; Skinner, 1953).

Although behaviorism was an important step forward, it was widely criticized by philosophers as being inadequate. The major criticism was failure to account for the (cognitive) processes that are involved in the production of any particular response.

Cognitive Behavior Approach

These and other criticisms of the behavioral approach fostered the emergence and development of the Cognitive-Behaviorist approach. One of its pioneers was Stanley Beck, who argued that it was necessary to view mental events as being causally related to behavior. An analogy was also drawn between a computer and the human mind. Thus, between stimulus and response was the "black box," and it was the task of psychologists to explain the mechanisms and functionings of the contents of the black box.

STIMULUS → MENTAL PROCESSES → RESPONSE

The therapeutic approach that followed from Beck's cognitive model was to include various mental conditioners and reinforcers in the behavior schedule that was administered. Thus, an individual that was suffering from poor self-esteem could not only be placed on a fitness, health and beauty training course, but could also be instructed to monitor themselves for "automatic negative self appraisals." That is, they would be made to monitor their own mental activities and record these in a schedule. The occurrences of the negative thoughts would be progressively diminished, while the positive ones strengthened and reinforced. This approach has proved to be remarkably effective in a number of areas. For example, depression, anxiety, obsessive-compulsive disorders, phobias and other behavioral problems.

Social Perspective

Social Psychology is a branch of psychology that studies the behavior and consciousness of individuals. While it is true that social psychology focuses especially on social situations (as individual's react to and serve as stimuli for others), this subdiscipline of psychology grounds itself on the assumption that all social behavior can be explained in terms of the principles of individual psychological functioning. The notion promulgated by some that there are phenomena of collective behavior or group consciousness beyond the simple reactions of individualism and self-identity.

Fundamental, then, to the nature of social behavior is its quality as a social stimulus and its potential to control the behavior of others, a potential that varies phylogenetically, culminating in the human ability to exert social influence through direct forms of expression (gesture, language, facial movement), custom, tradition, and social institutions.

Discussion of elementary social response is restricted to sympathy, imitation, suggestion, and laughter; and Allport's primary point, in each instance, is that these are not instinctive processes, but depend on the responder's own system of habits, formed in past experience. Thus, for example, the effects of suggestion (in which one person "*controls the behavior and consciousness of the recipient in an immediate manner, relatively uninfluenced by thoughs that a*re attributed to the power of a social stimulus to establish or release habitual response tendencies or augment such responses as they are being carried out.

More complex forms of response to social stimulation are those that take place in groups and crowds. For Allport, groups are distinguished from crowds by the fact that groups are assembled for deliberate activities, whereas crowds are driven by motives "of the more primitive and prepotent level." In groups, the individual's behavior is influenced by perception of others engaged in the same activity. This influence may take the form of social facilitation, (the activity is guided), social rivalry (created competition with external and internal reward).

In conclusion it can be stated that, while a number of widely diverging theoretical perspectives have been discussed in this chapter, there is no one dominant paradigm in evidence. Each theoretical approach can be put to productive use, depending upon the specific context within which an individual finds him/herself.

ALTERED STATES OF CONSCIOUSNESS

An altered state of consciousness (ASC) is a state of mind that is significantly different from any normal state of mind, which is consciousness. An ASC is almost always a temporary state of mind where one enters into an altered state of mind. When a person is in an ASC, they often have a morphed sense of identity with their own body, along with their own sense of perception. Their ability to encode sensations from the environment, perceive and interpret stimuli is significantly decreased. ASC does not allow persons to function at a honestatic level due to the imbalances that are occurring with consciousness. There are two major reasons that ASC will occur, *accidents* and *intentional enforcement*. **Accidental ASC** will may occur due to a car crash, lack of sleep, deep lucid dreams, high fever, lack of oxygen to the brain, hallucinogenic states. **Intentional Enforcement** of ASC can occur on purpose for religious and or during socialized recreation. Examples of intentional enforcement include sensory deprivation, mind-control (prayer, hypnosis, meditation), use of psychoactive drugs (opiates, alcohol), and the use of entheogenic drugs (marijuana, psychedelic mushrooms, LSD, DMT, Peyote, etc.). Sleep is another form of ASC. The behavior of sleep is intentional and required for human sustainability.

Types of Altered States of Consciousness

Any various states of awareness such as dreaming sleep, a drug-induced hallucinogenic state, or a trance that deviates from and are usually clearly demarcated from ordinary waking consciousness or state of awareness.

Sleep: A Dynamic Activity

Sleep is sometimes called "*the forgotten third of existence.*" It is an altered state of consciousness. For the first half of the 20th Century, sleep was recognized minimally by psychological researchers. A typical psychology textbook of the 1920s through 1940s devoted only a few paragraphs to the subject of sleep. However, information about sleep and dreaming accumulated at a rapid pace during the 1950s and 1960s, an era known as the Golden Age of Sleep Research.

Until the 1950s, most people thought of sleep as a passive, dormant part of life. It is now known that the brain is very active during sleep as it affects the physical and mental health in many ways promoting the daily functions of humans.

N*eurotransmitters* control whether we are asleep or awake by acting on different groups of nerve cells, or neurons, in the brain. Neurons in the brainstem, which connects the brain with the spinal cord, produce neurotransmitters such as serotonin and norepinephrine that keep some parts of the brain active while we are awake. Other neurons at the base of the brain begin signaling when we fall asleep. These neurons appear to "switch off" the signals that keep us awake. Research also suggests that a chemical called adenosine builds up in our blood while we are awake and causes drowsiness. This chemical gradually breaks down while we sleep.

THEORY OF SLEEP

Evolutionary psychology theories of dreams

Evolutionary theory, also known as the adaptive theory of sleep, suggests that periods of activity and inactivity evolved as a means of conserving energy. According to this theory, all species have adapted to sleep during periods of time when wakefulness would be the most hazardous.

Support for this theory comes from comparative research of different animal species. Animals that have few natural predators, such as bears and lions, often sleep between 12 to 15 hours each day. On the other hand, animals that have many natural predators have only short periods of sleep, usually getting no more than 4 or 5 hours of sleep each day. Evolutionary psychologists believe dreams serve some adaptive function for survival, (Deirdre Barrett).

Psychosomatic theory

Dreams are a product of dissociated imagination that occurs in a state of altered consciousness. By simulating the sensory signals to drive the autonomous nerves, dreams can affect mind-body interaction. In the brain and spine, the autonomous "repair nerves," this can expand the blood vessels; connect with compression and pain nerves. Repair nerves are grouped into many chains called meridians in Chinese medicine. When a repair nerve is prodded by compression or pain to send out its repair signal, a chain reaction spreads out to set other repair nerves in the same meridian into action. While dreaming, the body also employs the meridians to repair the body and help it grow and develop by simulating very intensive movement-compression signals to expand the blood vessels when the level of growth enzymes increase.

While we can now investigate sleep and related phenomena, not all researchers agree on exactly *why* we sleep. A number of different theories have been proposed to explain the necessity of sleep as well as the functions and purposes of sleep.

Sleep and Circadian Rhythms

Circadian rhythms are regular changes in mental and physical characteristics that occur in the course of a day (*circadian* is Latin for "around a day"). Most circadian rhythms are controlled by the body's biological "clock." This clock, called the *suprachiasmatic nucleus* or *SCN* , is actually a pair of pinhead-sized brain structures that together contain about 20,000 neurons. The SCN rests in a part of the brain called the *hypothalamus,* just above the point where the optic nerves cross. Light that reaches photoreceptors in the *retina* (a tissue at the back of the eye) creates signals that travel along the optic nerve to the SCN.

Signals from the SCN travel to several brain regions, including the *pineal gland,* which responds to light-induced signals by switching off production of the hormone melatonin. The body's level of melatonin normally increases after darkness falls, making people feel drowsy. The SCN also governs functions that are synchronized with the sleep/wake cycle, including body temperature, hormone secretion, urine production, and changes in blood pressure.

By depriving people of light and other external time cues, scientists have learned that most people's biological clocks work on a 25-hour cycle rather than a 24-hour one. But because sunlight or other bright lights can reset the SCN, our biological cycles normally follow the 24-hour cycle of the sun, rather than our innate cycle. Circadian rhythms can be affected to some degree by almost any kind of external time cue, such as the beeping of your alarm clock, the clatter of a garbage truck, or the timing of your meals.

To reduce the effects of jet lag, some doctors try to manipulate the biological clock with a technique called light therapy. They expose people to special lights, many times brighter than ordinary household light, for several hours near the time the subjects want to wake up. This helps them reset their biological clocks and adjust to a new time zone.

Symptoms much like jet lag are ·common in people who work nights or who perform shift work. Because these people's work schedules are at odds with powerful sleep-regulating cues like sunlight, they often become uncontrollably drowsy during work, and they may suffer insomnia or other problems when they try to sleep. Shift workers have an increased risk of heart problems, digestive disturbances, and emotional and mental problems, all of which may be related to their sleeping problems. Daily supplements of melatonin may improve night-time sleep for such patients. However, since the high doses of melatonin found in most supplements can build up in the body, long-term use of this substance may create new problems. Because the potential side effects of melatonin supplements are still largely unknown, most experts discourage melatonin use by the general public.

SLEEP CYCLE

One complete sleep cycle takes about 90 to 100 minutes, thus for an average sleep time of 8 hours there will be a 4 to 5 complete sleep cycles. The sleep cycle begins with four stages of sleep called by Slow Wave Sleep (SWS) or non rapid eye movement (NREM or Non-REM) sleep. After the completion of the first 4th stages, instead of proceed to 5th REM sleep the first 4 stages quickly reversed and then followed by REM sleep. The first REM sleep will occur approximately after 90 minutes of falling asleep and it will last only about 10 minutes, gives the starting length of sleep cycle being approximately 100 minutes. The length of the stages of sleep is not fixed and it varies, in particular the length of sleep stage 3 and 4 (also called delta or deep sleep) slowly wane, and the length of stage 5 (REM sleep) increases, up to about one hour in length after certain sleep cycles. Therefore, as the night proceeds, dream may be of longer periods of time.

The Beginnings of Sleep

During the earliest phases of sleep, you are still relatively awake and alert. The brain produces what are known as beta waves, which are small and fast. As the brain begins to relax and slow down, slower waves known as alpha waves are produced. During this time when you are not quite asleep, you may experience strange and extremely vivid sensations known as hypnagogic hallucinations. Common examples of this phenomenon include feeling like you are falling or hearing someone call your name.

Another very common event during this period is known as a ***myoclonic jerk***. If you've ever startled suddenly for seemingly no reason at all, then you have experienced this odd phenomenon. While it may seem unusual, these myoclonic jerks are actually quite common.

Stages of Sleep

Sleep researchers distinguish between several different phases of sleep. They follow each other in a cycle that is repeated three or four times per night. Each complete cycle takes about an hour and a half. A group of researchers proposed in 1937 that the cycle be divided into 5 stages identifiable in the EEG record, labeled A through E. Now these stages are labeled 1 to 4, with the fifth being REM sleep. Some researchers refer to the wakefulness before sleep as stage 0.

What is stage zero?

During Stage 0, while a person is still awake but sleepy, the EEG shows mostly *alpha* waves: waves in the 8-12 per second frequency range. Alpha waves are normally blocked by eye movements or focused attention, so the appearance of alpha waves indicates that a person is resting the eyes and letting go of the day's concerns. If alpha waves are present, the individual is still awake and resting quietly.

Stage 1 sleep (the earliest stage) marks the onset of sleep. It is characterized by the disappearance of alpha waves and a simultaneous *cut-off of attention to the environment*. **Sleep stage 1** is the light sleep where there is a drift in and out of sleep and one can be awakened easily during this stage. This stage is characterized by slow eyes movement and slow muscle activity. During this stage, many people experience sudden muscle contractions preceded by a sensation of falling.

Common characteristics of stage 1

- transition between sleep and wakefulness
- eyes rolls slightly
- mostly contains of theta waves (high amplitude & low frequency – slow wave)
- briefly contains of alpha waves, similar to those present while awake

Stage 1 lasts only for a few minutes

Researchers can observe when a person has fallen asleep. The switch of attention from outside to inside is often accompanied by odd thoughts or imagery that are distinctly dream-like (hypnagogic mentation). At the same time, the alpha waves in the EEG disappear. Independent observers can agree when sleep onset occurs to within 2 minutes of each other 80% of the time using only EEG records.

Stage 2 non-REM is identified by two distinctive EEG patterns called *sleep spindles* and *K-complexes*. Except for the first one or two cycles of sleep stages, when REM sleep follows stage 4 sleep, REM sleep usually follows stage 2 sleep. **Sleep stage 2** with eye movement stopped and the brain waves become slower with only an occasional burst of rapid brain waves.

Common characteristics of stage 2

- Amplitude of brain wave peaks become higher and higher (sleep spindles)
- k-complexes (peaks suddenly descends and then rises) follow spindles
- Stage 2 lasts for a few minutes

Sleep stage 3 with extremely slow brain waves called delta waves are interspersed with smaller, faster waves. This stage is considered as deep sleep and so it is difficult to waken someone from this stage.

Common characteristics of stage 3

- Called as delta sleep or deep sleep
- very slow brain waves, called delta waves (lower frequency than theta waves)
- 20—50% of brain waves are delta waves; the balance are theta waves

Stages 3 and 4 of non-REM sleep are identified by increasingly prominent brain waves on the EEG called *delta waves*. Delta waves are large, slow waves caused by the synchronized firing of many neurons. The neurons are in a resting pattern, pulsing together. This phase of non-REM sleep is called *slow wave sleep* or *delta sleep*. It is the deepest stage of sleep for humans, if deepness is defined by how hard it is to awaken a creature. In cats and other animals, the REM state is the deepest state.

Stage 4 non-REM sleep is deepest. **Sleep stage 4** with the brain produces delta waves almost exclusively. This stage is also considered as a deep or "sound" sleep and so it is difficult to wake someone from this stage. In deep sleep, there is no eye movement or muscle activity. This is when some children experience bedwetting, sleepwalking or night terrors.

People describe a good sleep as *sound*, which means "solid and unmoving." As the expression suggests, the type of sleep that feels deepest to humans is a sleep with little body movement. Usually this indicates lots of stage 3 or stage 4 sleep. Tossing and turning accompanies lighter sleeps with more time in stages 1 and 2. People often get all the delta sleep they need during the first two sleep cycles, so they remain in lighter stages of sleep after that, often alternating between stage 2 and REM sleep for the remainder of the night.

Common characteristics of stage 4

- Called as delta sleep or deep sleep
- more than 50% of brain waves are delta waves; the balance are theta waves

- last sleep stages before REM sleep; sleep stages reverses and then REM sleep begins

Sleep stage 5. REM stage with breathing becomes more rapid and shallow, eyes jerk rapidly and limb muscles are temporarily paralyzed. The waveform during REM has low amplitudes and high frequencies, just like the waking state. Early researchers actually called it "paradoxical sleep". REM stage has increased heart rate, raised blood pressure, males have erections and the body does not regulate its temperature. Most of the vivid dreams occur during REM sleep, once awaken at this stage a person can remember the dreams. Most people experience three to five times of REM sleep each night.

Common characteristics of stage 5

- Beta waves—have a high frequency and it happens when the brain is quite active, that is during REM sleep and while awake
- frequent bursts of rapid eye movement, along with infrequent muscular twitches
- heart beat faster with shallow and rapid breathing
- most vivid dreaming occurs during REM

Infants spent almost 50% of their sleep time in REM stage. Adults spend nearly half of sleep time in stage 2, about 20% in REM and the other 30% is divided between the other three stages. Older adults spend progressively less time in REM sleep.

TYPES OF SLEEP

Sleep follows a certain regular sleep cycle every night. There are two main types of sleep, Non-Rapid Eye Movement (NREM) Sleep (also known as *quiet sleep)* and Rapid Eye Movement (REM) Sleep (also known as *active sleep* or *paradoxical sleep)*. Infants have about half of their sleep time in REM sleep. Adults have approximately 20% of their sleep time in REM and balance NREM sleep. Elderly people have less than

15% of their sleep time in REM sleep balance NREM sleep.

How does non-REM sleep contrast with REM sleep?

The phrase *REM sleep* refers to more than just eye movements. REM sleep is a distinctive stage of sleep identified by many criteria. The eyes do not move constantly; sometimes there are 5 minutes between bursts of REMs while a person remains in REM sleep by other criteria. During REM sleep there is an aroused EEG pattern, muscle relaxation below the neck, fluctuating heart rate and rapid changes in breathing rate. Human males have an erection and women have increased vaginal blood flow during REM sleep. This generally has nothing to do with sexual content of dreams; it is part of the overall REM sleep pattern.

During the other type of sleep, called *non-REM sleep*, the EEG shows large, regular waves. Breathing and heart rate are slower and more regular than during REM sleep. During non-REM sleep large, slow eye movements occur.

Sleep is just one of many types of consciousness we experience, and sleep itself comprises several states of consciousness. Even when we're sleeping, our brains and bodies continue to work.

How Much Sleep Do We Need?

The amount of sleep each person needs depends on many factors, including age. Infants generally require about 16 hours a day, while teenagers need about 9 hours on average. For most adults, 7 to 8 hours a night appears to be the best amount of sleep, although some people may need as few as 5 hours or as many as 10 hours of sleep each day. People tend to sleep more lightly and for shorter time spans as they get older, although they generally need about the same amount of sleep as they needed in early adulthood. About half of all people over 65 have frequent sleeping problems, such as insomnia, and deep sleep stages in many elderly people often become very short or stop completely. This change may be a normal part of

aging, or it may result from medical problems that are common in elderly people and from the medications and other treatments for those problems.

Experts say that if you feel drowsy during the day, even during boring activities, you haven't had enough sleep. If you routinely fall asleep within 5 minutes of lying down, you probably have severe sleep deprivation, possibly even a sleep disorder. *Microsleeps,* or very brief episodes of sleep in an otherwise awake person, are another mark of sleep deprivation. In many cases, people are not aware that they are experiencing microsleeps. The widespread practice of "burning the candle at both ends" in western industrialized societies has created so much sleep deprivation that what is really abnormal sleepiness is now almost the norm.

Sleep Deprivation Risks

Many studies make it clear that sleep deprivation is dangerous. Sleep-deprived people who are tested by using a driving simulator or by performing a hand-eye coordination task perform as badly as or worse than those who are intoxicated. Sleep deprivation also magnifies alcohol's effects on the body, so a fatigued person who drinks will become much more impaired than someone who is well-rested. Driver fatigue is responsible for an estimated 100,000 motor vehicle accidents and 1500 deaths each year, according to the National Highway Traffic Safety Administration. Since drowsiness is the brain's last step before falling asleep, driving while drowsy can – and often does – lead to disaster. Caffeine and other stimulants cannot overcome the effects of severe sleep deprivation. The National Sleep Foundation says that if you have trouble keeping your eyes focused, if you can't stop yawning, or if you can't remember driving the last few miles, you are probably too drowsy to drive safely.

The Benefits of Sleep

Sleep appears necessary for our nervous systems to work properly. Too little sleep leaves us drowsy and unable to concentrate the next day. It also leads to impaired memory and physical performance and reduced ability to carry out math calculations. If sleep deprivation continues, hallucinations and mood swings may develop. Some experts believe sleep gives neurons used while we are awake a chance to shut down and repair themselves. Without sleep, neurons may become so depleted in energy or so polluted with byproducts of normal cellular activities that they begin to malfunction. Sleep also may give the brain a chance to exercise important neuronal connections that might otherwise deteriorate from lack of activity.

Deep sleep coincides with the release of growth hormone in children and young adults. Many of the body's cells also show increased production and reduced breakdown of proteins during deep sleep. Since proteins are the building blocks needed for cell growth and for repair of damage from factors like stress and ultraviolet rays, deep sleep may truly be "beauty sleep." Activity in parts of the brain that control emotions, decision-making processes, and social interactions is drastically reduced during deep sleep, suggesting that this type of sleep may help people maintain optimal emotional and social functioning while they are awake. A study in rats also showed that certain nerve-signaling patterns which the rats generated during the day were repeated during deep sleep. This pattern repetition may help encode memories and improve learning.

Sleep and Disease

Neurons that control sleep interact closely with the immune system. As anyone who has had the flu knows, infectious diseases tend to make us feel sleepy. This probably happens because *cytokines,* chemicals our immune systems produce while fighting an infection, are powerful sleep-inducing chemicals. Sleep may help the body conserve energy and other resources that the immune system needs to mount an attack.

Sleep and sleep-related problems play a role in a large number of human disorders and affect almost every field of medicine. For example, problems like stroke and asthma attacks tend to occur more

frequently during the night and early morning, perhaps due to changes in hormones, heart rate, and other characteristics associated with sleep.

Sleeping problems occur in almost all people with mental disorders, including those with depression and schizophrenia. People with depression, for example, often awaken in the early hours of the morning and find themselves unable to get back to sleep. The amount of sleep a person gets also strongly influences the symptoms of mental disorders. Sleep deprivation is an effective therapy for people with certain types of depression, while it can actually cause depression in other people. Extreme sleep deprivation can lead to a seemingly psychotic state of paranoia and hallucinations in otherwise healthy people, and disrupted sleep can trigger episodes of mania (agitation and hyperactivity) in people with manic depression.

Sleeping problems are common in many other disorders as well, including Alzheimer's disease, stroke, cancer, and head injury. These sleeping problems may arise from changes in the brain regions and neurotransmitters that control sleep, or from the drugs used to control symptoms of other disorders. Once sleeping problems develop, they can add to a person's impairment and cause confusion, frustration, or depression. Patients who are unable to sleep also notice pain more and may increase their requests for pain medication. Better management of sleeping problems in people who have other disorders could improve these patients' health and quality of life.

Sleep Disorders

At least 40 million Americans each year suffer from chronic, long-term sleep disorders each year, and an additional 20 million experience occasional sleeping problems. These disorders and the resulting sleep deprivation interfere with work, driving, and social activities. They also account for an estimated $16 billion in medical costs each year, while the indirect costs due to lost productivity and other factors are probably much greater. Doctors have described more than 70 sleep disorders, most of which can be managed effectively once they are correctly diagnosed. The most common sleep disorders include insomnia, sleep apnea, restless legs syndrome, and narcolepsy.

Insomnia

Almost everyone occasionally suffers from short-term insomnia. This problem can result from stress, jet lag, diet, or many other factors. Insomnia almost always affects job performance and well-being the next day. About 60 million Americans a year have insomnia frequently or for extended periods of time, which leads to even more serious sleep deficits. Insomnia tends to increase with age and affects about 40 percent of women and 30 percent of men. It is often the major disabling symptom of an underlying medical disorder.

For short-term insomnia, doctors may prescribe sleeping pills. Most sleeping pills stop working after several weeks of nightly use, however, and long-term use can actually interfere with good sleep. Mild insomnia often can be prevented or cured by practicing good sleep habits. For more serious cases of insomnia, researchers are experimenting with light therapy and other ways to alter circadian cycles.

Sleep Apnea

Sleep apnea is a disorder of interrupted breathing during sleep. It usually occurs in association with fat buildup or loss of muscle tone with aging. These changes allow the windpipe to collapse during breathing when muscles relax during sleep. This problem, called *obstructive sleep apnea,* is usually associated with loud snoring (though not everyone who snores has this disorder). Sleep apnea also can occur if the neurons that control breathing malfunction during sleep.

During an episode of obstructive apnea, the person's effort to inhale air creates suction that collapses the windpipe. This blocks the air flow for 10 seconds to a minute while the sleeping person struggles to breathe. When the person's blood oxygen level falls, the brain responds by awakening the person enough to tighten the upper airway muscles and open the windpipe. The person may snort or gasp, then resume snoring. This cycle may be repeated hundreds of times a night. The frequent awakenings that sleep apnea patients experience leave them continually sleepy and may lead to personality changes such as irritability or depression. Sleep apnea also deprives the person of oxygen, which can lead to morning headaches, a loss of interest in sex, or a decline in mental functioning. It also is linked to high blood pressure, irregular heartbeats, and an increased risk of heart attacks and stroke. Patients with severe, untreated sleep apnea are two to three times more likely to have automobile accidents than the general population. In some high-risk individuals, sleep apnea may even lead to sudden death from respiratory arrest during sleep.

An estimated 18 million Americans have sleep apnea. However, few of them have had the problem diagnosed. Patients with the typical features of sleep apnea, such as loud snoring, obesity, and excessive daytime sleepiness, should be referred to a specialized sleep center that can perform a test called *polysom-nography.* This test records the patient's brain waves, heartbeat, and breathing during an entire night. If sleep apnea is diagnosed, several treatments are available. Mild sleep apnea frequently can be overcome through weight loss or by preventing the person from sleeping on his or her back. Other people may need special devices or surgery to correct the obstruction. People with sleep apnea should never take sedatives or sleeping pills, which can prevent them from awakening enough to breathe.

Restless Legs Syndrome

Restless legs syndrome (RLS), a familial disorder causing unpleasant crawling, prickling, or tingling sensations in the legs and feet and an urge to move them for relief, is emerging as one of the most common sleep disorders, especially among older people. This disorder, which affects as many as 12 million Americans, leads to constant leg movement during the day and insomnia at night. Severe RLS is most common in elderly people, though symptoms may develop at any age. In some cases, it may be linked to other conditions such as anemia, pregnancy, or diabetes.

RLS and PLMD often can be relieved by drugs that affect the neurotransmitter dopamine, suggesting that dopamine abnormalities underlie these disorders' symptoms. Learning how these disorders occur may lead to better therapies in the future.

Narcolepsy

Narcolepsy affects an estimated 250,000 Americans. People with narcolepsy have frequent "sleep attacks" at various times of the day, even if they have had a normal amount of night-time sleep. These attacks last from several seconds to more than 30 minutes. People with narcolepsy also may experience cataplexy (loss of muscle control during emotional situations), hallucinations, and temporary paralysis when they awaken, and disrupted night-time sleep. These symptoms seem to be features of REM sleep that appears during waking, which suggests that narcolepsy is a disorder of sleep regulation. The symptoms of narcolepsy typically appear during adolescence, though it often takes years to obtain a correct diagnosis. The disorder (or at least a predisposition to it) is usually hereditary, but it occasionally is linked to brain damage from a head injury or neurological disease.

Once narcolepsy is diagnosed, stimulants, antidepressants, or other drugs can help control the symptoms and prevent the embarrassing and dangerous effects of falling asleep at improper times. Naps at certain times of the day also may reduce the excessive daytime sleepiness.

SCIENTIFIC FUTURE OF SLEEP

Sleep research is expanding and attracting more and more attention from scientists. Researchers now know that sleep is an active and dynamic state that greatly influences our waking hours, and they realize that we must understand sleep to fully understand the brain. Innovative techniques, such as brain imaging, can now help researchers understand how different brain regions function during sleep and how different activities and disorders affect sleep. Understanding the factors that affect sleep in health and disease also may lead to revolutionary new therapies for sleep disorders and to ways of overcoming jet lag and the problems associated with shift work. We can expect these and many other benefits from research that will allow us to truly understand sleep's impact on our lives.

TIPS FOR A GOOD NIGHT'S SLEEP:

Adapted from "When You Can't Sleep: The ABCs of ZZZs," by the National Sleep Foundation

Set a schedule:

Go to bed at a set time each night and get up at the same time each morning. Disrupting this schedule may lead to insomnia. "Sleeping in" on weekends also makes it harder to wake up early on Monday morning because it re-sets your sleep cycles for a later awakening.

Exercise:

Try to exercise 20 to 30 minutes a day. Daily exercise often helps people sleep, although a workout soon before bedtime may interfere with sleep. For maximum benefit, try to get your exercise about 5 to 6 hours before going to bed.

Avoid caffeine, nicotine, and alcohol:

Avoid drinks that contain caffeine, which acts as a stimulant and keeps people awake. Sources of caffeine include coffee, chocolate, soft drinks, non-herbal teas, diet drugs, and some pain relievers. Smokers tend to sleep very lightly and often wake up in the early morning due to nicotine withdrawal. Alcohol robs people of deep sleep and REM sleep and keeps them in the lighter stages of sleep.

Relax before bed:

A warm bath, reading, or another relaxing routine can make it easier to fall sleep. You can train yourself to associate certain restful activities with sleep and make them part of your bedtime ritual.

Sleep until sunlight:

If possible, wake up with the sun, or use very bright lights in the morning. Sunlight helps the body's internal biological clock reset itself each day. Sleep experts recommend exposure to an hour of morning sunlight for people having problems falling asleep.

Don't lie in bed awake:

If you can't get to sleep, don't just lie in bed. Do something else, like reading, watching television, or listening to music, until you feel tired. The anxiety of being unable to fall asleep can actually contribute to insomnia.

Control your room temperature:

Maintain a comfortable temperature in the bedroom. Extreme temperatures may disrupt sleep or prevent you from falling asleep.

See a doctor if your sleeping problem continues:

If you have trouble falling asleep night after night, or if you always feel tired the next day, then you may have a sleep disorder and should see a physician. Your primary care physician may be able to help you; if not, you can probably find a sleep specialist at a major hospital near you. Most sleep disorders can be treated effectively, so you can finally get that good night's sleep you need.

DREAMING

Dreams are cinematic images and imagery, thoughts, sounds and voices, and subjective sensations experienced when we sleep. This can include people you know, people you've never met, places you've been, and places you've never visited. Sometimes they're as mundane as recalling events that happened earlier in the day. They can also be your deepest and darkest fears and secrets, and most private fantasies. There's no limit to what the mind can experience during a dream and really no identifiable reason why certain dreams occur. Stresses in waking life can manifest in dreams plainly or be cleverly disguised with imagery. For instance, a dream about a grizzly bear chasing you through your house could be the stress you feel about the relationship with a friend. A dream about being stuck inside of a room with no door might echo your feelings about a dead-end job.

Dreams are most abundant and best remembered during the R.E.M. stage of sleep. This is the deepest stage of the sleep cycle, when your eyes are moving rapidly, your heart rate and breathing become inconsistent, and paralysis of your skeletal muscles occurs. This last part may sound pretty frightening, but it's actually a safeguard that keeps us from acting out our dreams physically. R.E.M. sleep makes up about 20 to 25 percent of the sleep cycle in adults in short increments, first for only a few minutes at a time, but growing increasingly longer as the sleep cycle progresses. Some stages of R.E.M. sleep can last for as long as 30 minutes at a time. Since long, detailed dreams can sometimes only last a couple of minutes, these long R.E.M. stages can be rich with dream activity.

It's believed that we all dream, even though not everyone remembers their dreams with the same frequency, or at all, in some cases. Consider that we may dream as much as six to eight hours per night and you have a clue as to how many dreams are left behind. Waking up during a R.E.M. cycle will make it more likely that you'll remember your dreams, but there's no hard and fast rule regarding dream memory. Scientists know waking experiences have an impact on our dreams, but they aren't sure how much or if it's consistent among humans. In one study, participants wore red goggles before going to sleep and reported seeing more red images in their dreams than those who didn't wear them. Another theory posits that dreams are our brain's attempt to make sense of what would otherwise be meaningless stimuli, random messages created from the arousal of the posterior segment of the brain. Others think dreams are merely the brain firing signals as it organizes the previous day's thoughts and experiences that may end up as memory. The problem with any theory about dreams is that we can't really prove or disprove any of them, and they aren't necessarily mutually exclusive. If dreams are psychologically significant, they can still be the result of random brain stimuli. Dreams are most likely a combination of theories.

There's still so much we don't know about the brain and how it operates, waking or sleeping, that we may never be able to pinpoint exactly what dreams are, and how they're meaningful or necessary for humans. But that doesn't stop science from trying. Dream studies are always among the most popular in universities and research facilities, which probably has something to do with their ubiquitous nature.

Whether we'd like to admit it or not, whether we are able to remember them or not, we all dream. People awakened from REM periods in sleep experiments report they've been dreaming 80%- 100% of the time. REM dreams are considered to be more perceptual and emotional as opposed to NREM (non-rapid eye-movement) dreams. Content of NREM dreams is often a recreation of some psychologically important event. According to Freud REM dreams are like primary-process thinking which is often unrealistic and emotional, and NREM dreams are like secondary-process thinking which is more realistic (Franken, 1988).

Meaningful Dreams

DREAM THEORIES

Freudian Theory—believes that dreams reveal information in the unconscious mind

Manifest content- literal content

Latent content—deeper meaning

Activation-synthesis Theory—dreams are nothing more than the brains interpretation of what is happening physiologically during REM sleep

Information-processing Theory—dreams may be a way to integrate the information processed during the day into our memories

Psychoanalytic Theory of Dreams:

Consistent with the psychoanalytic perspective, Sigmund Freud's theory of dreams suggested that dreams were a representation of unconscious desires, thoughts and motivations. According to Freud's psychoanalytic view of personality, people are driven by aggressive and sexual instincts that are repressed from conscious awareness. While these thoughts are not consciously expressed, Freud suggested that they find their way into our awareness via dreams.

In his famous book *The Interpretation of Dreams*, Freud wrote that dreams are "...disguised fulfillments of repressed wishes."[1] He also described two different components of dreams: manifest content and latent content. Manifest content is made up of the actual images, thoughts and content contained within the dream, while the latent content represents the hidden psychological meaning of the dream.

Freud's theory contributed to the popularity of dream interpretation, which remains popular today. However, research has failed to demonstrate that the manifest content disguises the real psychological significance of a dream.[2]

Activation- Synthesis Model of Dreaming:

The activation-synthesis model of dreaming was first proposed by J. Allan Hobson and Robert McClarley in 1977. According to this theory, circuits in the brain become activated during REM sleep, which causes areas of the system involved in emotions, sensations and memories, including the amygdala and hippocampus, to become active. The brain synthesizes and interprets this internal activity and attempts to find meaning in these signals, which results in dreaming. This model suggests that dreams are a subjective interpretation of signals generated by the brain during sleep.[3]

While this theory suggests that dreams are the result of internally generated signals, Hobson does not believe that dreams are meaningless. Instead, he suggests that dreaming is "…our most creative conscious state, one in which the chaotic, spontaneous recombination of cognitive elements produces novel configurations of information: new ideas. While many or even most of these ideas may be nonsensical, if even a few of its fanciful products are truly useful, our dream time will not have been wasted."[4]

Other Theories of Dreams:

Many other theories have been suggested to account for the occurrence and meaning of dreams. The following are just of few of the proposed ideas:

- One theory suggests that dreams are the result of our brains trying to interpret external stimuli during sleep. For example, the sound of the radio may be incorporated into the content of a dream.
- Another theory uses a computer metaphor to account for dreams. According to this theory, dreams serve to 'clean up' clutter from the mind, much like clean-up operations in a computer, refreshing the mind to prepare for the next day.
- Yet another model proposes that dreams function as a form of psychotherapy. In this theory, the dreamer is able to make connections between different thoughts and emotions in a safe environment.
- A contemporary model of dreaming combines some elements of various theories. The activation of the brain creates loose connections between thoughts and ideas, which are then guided by the emotions of the dreamer.

Hall: Dreams as a Cognitive Process:

Calvin S. Hall proposed that dreams are part of a cognitive process in which dreams serve as 'conceptions' of elements of our personal lives. Hall looked for themes and patterns by analyzing thousands of dream diaries from participants, eventually creating a quantitative coding system that divided the content of dreams into a number of different categories.

According to Hall's theory, interpreting dreams requires knowing:

- The actions of the dreamer within the dream
- The objects and figures in the dream
- The interactions between the dreamer and the characters in the dream
- The dream's setting, transitions and outcome

The ultimate goal of this dream interpretation is not to understand the dream, however, but to understand the dreamer.

Lucid Dreams

One of the most intriguing types of dream is the *lucid dream*. This is a dream in which *you suddenly realize you are dreaming*; yet you remain asleep and the dream continues, so you can experiment with the dream or intervene in the activity of the dream. For most people lucid dreams are rare; for other people they are commonplace.

Students report that lucid dreams often end with a surge of self-consciousness. The dreamer becomes increasingly self-conscious and wakes up. This can be frustrating if the dreamer wants the lucid dream to continue.

Lucid dreams can be cultivated, according to Stephen LaBerge (1980). He developed an intensive, 5-step method for inducing lucid dreams:

HYPNOSIS

Early Investigations of Hypnosis

A Viennese physician, Franz Anton Mesmer (1734-1815), is often credited with discovering hypnosis. For many years *mesmerization* was a synonym for hypnosis. But Mesmer's procedures were a far cry from those of modern-day hypnosis. Mesmer had patients sit in a wooden tub that contained metal bottles of water. Beneath the patients was a layer of iron filings and ground glass. Mesmer covered the tub and inserted metal rods through openings to touch a patient's body. Although he did not know it, Mesmer had created a crude battery. The resulting electric charges sometimes knocked his patients unconscious or gave them seizures. Some of the patients reported miraculous cures of their aches and pains from this treatment.

Summary: Hypnosis

During hypnosis, a person is *hypersuggestible* or easily influenced. The hypnotized person is focused on the instructions given by another person. Hypnotism is sometimes described as *imagined involvement*.

During the induction of hypnosis, a person is asked to concentrate on small changes in the body or the environment. When the hypnotist notices changes which indicate acceptance of these suggestions (such as fluttering eyes, or swaying) the hypnotist makes new, slightly more demanding suggestions, and the subject is led into deep levels of imagined involvement.

Under deep hypnosis suggestions can be issued for later execution (post-hypnotic suggestion) or a person can be told to forget the events of hypnosis. Hypnosis can sometimes enhance memory for long-forgotten events. However, hypnotized people are notorious for fabricating false memories that they later believe to be true.

CONSCIOUSNESS AND MIND-ALTERING DRUGS

PSYCHOACTIVE DRUGS

Drugs that affect states of consciousness are called *psychoactive* drugs. This part of the chapter will review the physical and psychological effects of many different substances. All psychoactive drugs seem to have certain things in common.

1. *They are able to cross the blood/brain barrier.* In order to affect consciousness, a drug must penetrate the biological filter that prevents many other substances from reaching the brain.

2. *They alter brain chemistry at the level of individual brain cells.* Most drugs act at the level of *neurotransmitters*, for example, by blocking their re-uptake, interfering with their synthesis, or mimicking their effects. Some drugs alter the permeability characteristics of cell membranes or interfere with metabolic processes in neurons.

3. *Their effects depend on dosage.* Researchers are able to vary the amount of the drug and observe resulting changes in behavior, from no change at all (at very low dosages) to toxicity or poisoning (at high levels). A *dose/response curve* is a graph relating dosage to some measure of behavior.

4. *Their effects are altered by prior experience with the drug.* Drugs can *sensitize* individuals to future exposures, leading to a larger reaction. Constant exposure to a drug leads eventually to the opposite phenomenon, *tolerance*, as the body re-establishes a new equilibrium in which presence of the drug is felt as normal. Few drugs produce the same effects in experienced users as they do in beginners.

5. *Their effects depend on expectancy.* In all psychoactive drugs yet studied, the response to the drug depends partly on what people expect to happen. Individuals who think they are receiving alcohol will act drunk, even if they receive drinks without alcohol. Similar things happen with marijuana and other drugs.

6. *They can be addictive.* If a psychoactive drug produces pleasurable effects, some people will chose to repeat the experience. As they repeat the experience, their bodies adapt to the presence of the drug, sometimes producing uncomfortable or dangerous *withdrawal*

Domhoff: Dreams as a Reflection of Waking Life

G. William Domhoff is a prominent dream researcher who studied with Calvin Hall at the University of Miami. In large-scale studies on the content of dreams, Domhoff has found that dreams reflect the thoughts and concerns of a dreamer's waking life.[6] Domhoff suggests a neurocognitive model of dreams in which the process of dreaming results from neurological processes and a system of schemas. Dream content, he suggests, results from these cognitive processes.[5]

A small number of dreams contain important insights about emotional or psychological problems. Here are some common categories of meaningful dreams, each with two examples provided by students.

1. *Warning* dreams point to dangerous situations in the future.
(A student dreams about his drunk-driving friends dying in a wreck. Another student dreams about the ill consequences of dropping out of school.)
2. *Guilt* and *worry* dreams express concern about past or present events.
(A student is "haunted" by dreams of her grandfather, whose last wishes concerning burial were not carried out. A young man dreams that another man fathered his wife's new baby.)
3. *Inspirational* dreams set goals or ideals to attain.
(A tennis-playing student, ranked at the state level, has a recurring dream of beating a famous star in a tournament match. A student having trouble in school dreams of rising to the occasion at the end of the term, doing well on his exams. Inspired by the dream, he makes it come true.)
4. *Post-traumatic* dreams contain flashbacks to stressful events.
(One girl relives a serious traffic accident in recurrent dreams. Another dreams of her near drowning in Hawaii.)
5. *Problem-solving* dreams present solutions to difficulties.
(A boy dreams of sticking little numbered labels to wires, which allows him to figure out how to wire his car stereo. A girl loses her bracelet then remembers, in a dream, where she put it.)
6. *Death-reconciliation* dreams help people deal with death of loved ones.
(A boy dreams that his father comes back to life to catch up on the news of his life. A girl dreams her recently killed boyfriend returns and gives her the chance to say she loves him.)

reactions when they try to quit. Psychologists studying *addictive behavior* point out the failure rate for overcoming all addictions is about the same, whether the addiction is alcohol, cigarettes, or heroin.

One way to operationally define the danger of a drug is to calculate a dose/toxicity ratio. This is a ratio formed by dividing a typical dose of a drug by the amount that will kill a person.

Categories of Psychoactive Drugs

Depressants are drugs that *lower the overall level of activity in the nervous system*. Among the chemically distinct families of depressant drugs are *sedatives, hypnotics*, and *alcohol*. All are capable of producing relaxation or sluggish and lethargic behavior. In large doses all can produce coma or death. Sedatives include drugs like

> ### A classic report of a lucid dream comes from van Eeden (1913, in Tart, 1973):
>
> On September 9, 1904, I dreamed that I stood at a table before a window. On the table were different objects. I was perfectly well aware that I was dreaming and I considered what sorts of experiments I could make. I began by trying to break glass, by beating it with a stone. I put a small tablet of glass on two stones and struck it with another stone. Yet it would not break. Then I took a fine claret-glass from the table and struck it with my fist, with all my might, at the same time reflecting on how dangerous it would be to do this in waking life; yet the glass remained whole. But lo! When I looked at it again after some time, it was broken.
>
> It broke all right, but a little too late, like an actor who misses his cue. This gave me a very curious impression of being in a fake-world, cleverly imitated, but with small failures. I took the broken glass and threw it out of the window, in order to observe whether I could hear the tinkling. I heard the noise all right and I even saw two dogs run away from it quite naturally. I thought what a good imitation this comedy-world was. Then I saw a decanter with claret and tasted it, and noted with perfect clearness of mind: "Well, we can also have voluntary impressions of taste in this dream-world; this has quite the taste of wine." (p.47)

PCP (phencyclidine), a drug commonly abused in the 1970s and 1980s, and *barbiturates*, used in sleeping potions and pills from the 1800s through the first half of the 20th Century. Depressants are often *potentiated* (made much more powerful) by combination with alcohol.

Stimulants are drugs that *increase* overall activity and excitability in the nervous system. Commonly known stimulants are caffeine, amphetamines ("speed"), and cocaine. Stimulants increase alertness and activity. In large amounts, they cause nervousness, shaking movements or jitters, insomnia, and irregular heartbeats. Sometimes they cause anxiety or panic states accompanied by hyperventilation and lightheadedness.

Opiates are drugs derived from the opium poppy or synthetic drugs similar to natural opiates in chemical structure and action. Opiates include heroin, morphine, and codeine, as well as the endorphins-natural pain-killing substances secreted by the body. To pharmacologists, opiates are the only drugs properly termed *narcotics*. Cocaine, marijuana, sedatives, and LSD are *not* narcotics, unless the term is used loosely to refer to all illegal drugs.

Marijuana (cannabis) is in a category by itself, because it does not resemble other drugs either in chemical structure or effect. The active ingredient in marijuana is delta-4-tetrahydrocannabinol or THC. Marijuana achieves its effect by altering levels of a particular type of transmitter-anandamide-that is not affected by other drugs. Anandamide receptors are very common in the human nervous system, so the transmitter must be involved in important brain processes, but its normal function is not yet clear. *Hashish* is a form of concentrated cannabis resin.

Hallucinogens or *psychedelic* drugs include LSD (lysergic acid diethylamide or "acid"), mescaline (the active ingredient in peyote buttons), and psilocybin (the active ingredient in psychoactive mushrooms). They cause a dreamlike state ("trip") with dramatic alterations of thought and emotion. The major psychedelics are all chemically related. Their hallucinogenic effects are thought to be caused by reduction in a variety of the neurotransmitter serotonin.

The internet provides many web sites about drugs and their effects, ranging from sites focusing on prevention of substance abuse (such as <http://www.drugnet.net/> to sites where users share experiences and cautions about drugs ranging from caffeine to hallucinogens <http://www.erowid.org>.

Alcohol is the most familiar drug in our society. Although alcohol makes some people more active by reducing their inhibitions or shyness, it is a depressant in its chemical action. A person who drinks a fifth of whiskey in one gulp can die, because that amount of alcohol can depress the centers controlling respiration in the brain, causing breathing to stop.

Stimulants

Stimulants raise the general level of activity in the nervous system. The heart rate increases, nerve cells fire more easily, and a person reacts more quickly or intensely to challenging situations. Just as heroin mimics the actions of the body's natural painkillers, stimulants mimic the function of the adrenal cortex in the brain that secretes adrenaline (epinephrine) into the bloodstream.

Types of Stimulants

Amphetamines

In the 1960s dextroamphetamine (brand name Dexedrine) was the most commonly prescribed amphetamine. For many, the drug was synonymous with the term "diet pills." After dextroamphetamine because a controlled substance in the U.S., diet pills containing other ingredients would mimic the old brand name, using trademarked names such as Dexatrim, although the new products contained no amphetamines.

Another type of amphetamine, methamphetamine or "meth," has more potent effects than dextroamphetamine. It was used frequently by Hitler and may account for some of his erratic behavior during World War II.

During the mid to late 1960s a drug called "crystal" (crystallized methamphetamine) became popular in motorcycle clubs such as the Hell's Angels. Crystal meth was sometimes snorted (inhaled up the nose), but people who used it often ended up injecting it to get the maximum effect. Because tolerance to amphetamines built quickly, users soon had to inject massive doses to maintain the effects. The effects of injection were dramatic: people would stay awake up to 12 days at a time, eating little if at all, engaged in nervous activity. After that they would "crash," sometimes sleeping for days.

So-called *speed freaks* could be identified on the streets of major United States cities in the 1960s by their extremely thin arms and legs. Activated by the methamphetamine for days at a time, but lacking appetite, they were digesting their own muscles.

Methamphetamine returned in the 1990s as "ice." Ice is typically smoked rather than injected. It shares with cocaine the tendency to raise blood pressure and heart rate at the same time, increasing the likelihood of heart attack. In 1990, Cho described the manufacture of methamphetamine as "a $3-billion industry with indications of expansion." By the late 1990s, Cho's prediction came true: there was an epidemic of methamphetamine production and addiction, particularly in the Southwestern United States. Methamphetamine abuse also spread well beyond the borders of the U.S. By 2000, methamphetamine production was a major problem in Myanmar, the country formerly called Burma, and by 2007 it was reportedly a common drug of abuse throughout southeast Asia, where it was often used by workers to stay awake and work faster, just as in the U.S.

The key ingredient of methamphetamine is the adrenaline-like chemical *pseudoephedrine*. For years, pseudoephedrine was found in most cold remedies, where it functioned as a decongestant. Trying to imitate their success with PCP and methaqualone, U.S. government agencies attempted as early as the 1990s to eliminate methamphetamine abuse by limiting the production of pseudoephedrine. This time, however, major pharmaceutical companies fought representatives of law enforcement. Drug companies claimed millions of people would be inconvenienced by changes in top-selling cold remedies such as Sudafed that contained pseudoephedrine. U.S. administrations sympathetic to business interests decided not to limit this $3 Billion industry, and valuable time was lost. By the time ephedrine-containing products were moved behind the counters at drug stores, in 2005 and 2006, a full-scale meth epidemic was underway.

A PBS Frontline documentary called this "the unnecessary epidemic" because of how it developed. The story, along with lots of information about methamphetamine and its effects, can be found online at this URL: http://www.pbs.org/wgbh/pages/frontline/meth/

How did one student die on his 23rd birthday?

One student belonged to a fraternity in which the birthday tradition (supposedly) was to drink the same number of shots of whiskey as one's age. The student was found dead the day after his birthday with the words "23 shots" written on his forehead. His friends assumed he simply passed out after so much drinking. The anguished parents brought these details to the attention of news media in an attempt to prevent such episodes from occurring in the future.

Amphetamines are interesting to psychologists not only as a public health problem but also because they imitate the natural effects of stress. In fact, Antelman, Eichler, Black, and Kocan (1980) showed that a dose of amphetamine was biochemically interchangeable with the effects of environmental stress. In non-human primates, amphetamines were observed to cause a "staggering increase in aggression." In humans, long-term administration of amphetamines produces a syndrome indistinguishable from <u>paranoid schizophrenia</u> complete with delusions of persecution and extreme suspicion.

Cocaine

Cocaine is said to be the most reinforcing drug known, as defined by repetitive use. Methamphetamine may be equally or more reinforcing as defined by <u>capture ratio</u>. The effects of cocaine fade sooner than methamphetamine, so cocaine induces more repetitive behavior. Rats will press a bar more times for a dose of cocaine than for any other drug. Rhesus monkeys forced to choose between food and cocaine will choose cocaine almost exclusively, losing weight and continuing their "binge" until either they die or the experiment is discontinued (Aigner & Balster, 1978).

Why does cocaine have this effect? Like methamphetamine, cocaine acts directly on the dopaminergic (dopamine-using) areas of the midbrain that are normally activated by biologically significant events such as victories in combat, pride over creative accomplishments, love and sex. Because such events are followed by great pleasure, an individual will try to repeat them. Cocaine short-circuits the process and brings pleasure without accomplishment. Instead

of trying to repeat a biologically adaptive response, individuals try to repeat the intake of cocaine.

Cocaine is most pleasurable to people who are depressed or in pain. In this respect, it is like direct stimulation of the so-called <u>pleasure centers</u> of the limbic system. Pleasure and pain normally act as an accelerator and a brake in the so-called hedonic control system of the body (in other words, the pleasure/pain control system). Like all control systems, the hedonic control system seeks equilibrium or an ideal state (homeostasis) by counteracting disturbances. (See the discussion of biological motives at the beginning of Chapter 9: Motivation.)

Heavy use of cocaine, like heavy use of heroin or methamphetamine, leads the body to form a new equilibrium. With cocaine hitting the accelerator all the time, the body starts to compensate by riding the brakes, so to speak. Anti-cocaine substances are secreted into the bloodstream and the areas around neurons to counteract or take up the extra transmitters released by cocaine. If a long-time user stops taking the drug, the result is a rebound effect or "crash" in the body's hedonic control system. This explains why long-term cocaine users say the drug is needed just to feel normal or un-depressed, and life seems unexciting and colorless without it.

Smoking and injecting are the most dangerous forms of cocaine administration, because they carry massive amounts of the drug directly to the bloodstream, producing a quick rush or euphoric sensation that soon wears off. The crash which ensues leaves a person feeling tired and depressed, or just bored. Cocaine users universally report, "You want more." Methamphetamine users report the same sorts of reactions. Ironically, the ability of the drug to produce joy (the so-called honeymoon phase) diminishes just as tolerance begins, because tolerance—the ability to withstand more of the drug, with less reaction—indicates that the body has adjusted to the drug's presence and is compensating or fighting it. At this point pleasure decreases and a user may claim to need the drug just to feel normal.

Cocaine or methamphetamine use may produce delayed health problems. By the 2000s, health professionals noticed an increase in the number of *aneurysms* (strokes caused by bulging blood vessels in the brain) among middle-aged people who had binged on cocaine in the 1970s and 1980s. Apparently the high blood pressure spikes of a cocaine binge weakened artery walls in the brain, resulting in an increased tendency to have strokes in later life. Methamphetamine has been observed to produce similar damage, such as tears in artery walls, even in younger people (McIntosh, Hungs, Kostanian, and Yu, 2006).

Caffeine

The most widely used stimulant drug is caffeine. Adults in the United States consume, on the average, over 10 pounds of coffee a year. Coffee can be dangerous for a person with epilepsy or a heart condition, but researchers have found no dangers for normal healthy people. Heavy coffee drinking (more than 4 or 5 cups a day, less if a person is not used to the drug) can lead to irregular heartbeats, insomnia, and nervousness-the same effects produced by other stimulants and by adrenaline.

Oddly enough, *grapefruit juice* potentiates caffeine. Grapefruit juice inhibits an enzyme that normally removes caffeine from the blood; so combining grapefruit juice with coffee may give even a veteran coffee drinker the jitters. Sudden withdrawal from caffeine may produce headaches, so a coffee drinker who wishes to stop usually must taper off gradually.

The response of individuals to caffeine varies. For example, people who are prone to anxiety disorders often show an exaggerated response to caffeine. Charney, Heninger, and Jatlow (1985) found that people meeting the criteria for panic attacks and phobias (see p.551) responded to caffeine with more

"anxiety, nervousness, fear, nausea, palpitations, restlessness, and tremors" compared to healthy subjects. Every year, caffeine pills send numerous college students to hospital Emergency Rooms with panic attacks. Pills contain a concentrated form of the drug that may have a powerful effect in people who are not used to it.

In most people, caffeine produces a state of wakefulness and alertness. This may be related to basic regulation of the waking/sleeping cycle in the nervous system. Caffeine has a molecular shape similar to adenosine and occupies the receptor sites on neurons where adenosine would normally have its effect, so coffee cuts the effect of adenosine and restores alertness.

Like other psychoactive drugs, caffeine produces the phenomena of sensitization and tolerance (Meliska, Landrum, & Landrum, 1990). *Sensitization* occurs when caffeine is taken occasionally. Then a person becomes more reactive to it. *Tolerance* occurs when caffeine is taken in regular, high doses. Then the effect of caffeine is reduced. As with other drugs, caffeine has its largest effect if it is used only occasionally or moderately. In a heavy user, it produces less effect. That is why a person who seldom drinks coffee may experience insomnia (sleeplessness) after having a cup of coffee at dinner hours before bedtime, while a person who drinks a lot of coffee may be able to have a cup before bedtime with little effect.

Opiates

Heroin and morphine

Heroin and morphine are opiates, substances that resemble the body's natural pain-fighting substances: endorphins. Endorphins are secreted into the bloodstream naturally during times of stress. They reduce physical and psychological pain and may produce a diffuse feeling that all is well. However, the first time a person takes heroin, it may not even be pleasurable. Beecher (1959) gave non-addicted subjects injections of heroin or a harmless placebo. The subjects preferred the placebo.

Sandoz (1922) made these comments about morphine, a derivative of heroin:

The widely spread belief that morphine brings about an uncanny mental condition, accompanied by fantastic ideas, dreams, and whatnot, is wrong... The most striking thing about morphine, taken in ordinary doses by one who is not an addict, is that it dulls general sensibility, allays or suppresses pain or discomfort, physical or mental, whatever its origin, and that disagreeable sensations of any kind, including unpleasurable states of mind are done away with.

Why does the addict require progressively higher doses? The body adapts to constant presence of the drug and learns to combat it with natural *opiate antagonists*. If opiates are constantly added to the body, the body starts producing antagonists in large amounts, neutralizing the effect of the drug. However, this also means the addict will feel great pain if he or she stops taking the drug. The body's own pain-relief system, involving relatively low levels of endorphins, has little effect in the presence of high concentrations of opiate antagonists. This explains why *dependence* is greatest just when *enjoyment* starts to fade: both are the result of high levels of antagonists. At that point, if a person tries to quit, the result is great pain.

Nitrous Oxide and Inhalants

Some dentists use nitrous oxide or "laughing gas" as an anesthetic. (It is not the same as "nitric oxide," the gas which functions as a transmitter) Mixed with oxygen, nitrous oxide induces a state of altered awareness in which pain is diminished or ignored. Its drug action is related to that of opiates. Naloxone, an opiate antagonist (drug which blocks opiates) also eliminates the anesthetic effects of nitrous oxide. Chronic exposure to morphine, which builds up tolerance to opiates, also builds up tolerance to nitrous oxide. This effect is called *cross-tolerance* : exposure to one drug produces tolerance for another drug. It is evidence for an underlying chemical relationship between drugs.

Overdoses of nitrous oxide can be fatal. One news report told of how containers of nitrous oxide were stolen from a hospital. They turned up at a party where three people died by breathing the concentrated nitrous oxide without oxygen. A container diverted from legitimate medical use contains pure nitrous oxide, intended for mixing with oxygen. Breathing nitrous oxide directly from a tank will smother the user. In addition, it will produce a numb, faraway, fainting sensation similar to the feeling of standing up too quickly after being at rest. Amyl nitrate and other *inhalants* such as glue and paint remover produce an altered state of consciousness primarily by depriving the brain of oxygen.

Many inhalants produce harmful effects over the long term, including permanent brain damage. They are inexpensive and easy to obtain, however, so they are sometimes abused by young teenagers or by very poor people who have no access to more expensive consciousness-altering drugs. In the mid-1990s, for example, Brazil experienced an epidemic of inhalant abuse among impoverished city children who sniffed an inexpensive glue to get high.

Marijuana

Marijuana is derived from the *cannabis sativa* or *cannabis indicus* plant. Historically it has been smoked, put into teas, or eaten. Since the late 1990s vaporization or volatilization (extracting the active ingredients with hot air) has become increasingly common. Marijuana smoking reached a peak of popularity in the United States during the late 1960s and early 1970s, when soldiers, blue-collar workers, and college students used it most widely. Overall levels of marijuana use in the United States declined in the 1980s, went up again in the early 1990s, declined again in the mid 1990s, and went up again in 2000s.

Marijuana resembles a brain chemical called anandamide, discovered in 1988. The researchers who discovered anandamide concluded that it was responsible for the reinforcing effects of marijuana. They put the word ananda (the Sanskrit word for bliss) in the chemical's name. Scientists use the term *cannabinoids* to describe anadamide and similar psychoactive compounds found in marijuana. Cannabinoids appear in brain areas such as the frontal lobes and hippocampus, a pattern unlike other psychoactive drugs. Receptors for these chemicals are found in both the brain and the spleen of many species, from sea urchins to rats to humans, suggesting an "ancient-and widespread-signaling system for organisms." (Pennisis, 1993)

Effects of Marijuana

First-time users of marijuana often feel nothing unless they take a very potent form of the drug. Second- or third-time users may experience profound changes in consciousness. Colors may seem brighter, music more vivid, humor more hilarious. Many experience a desire to eat. This well-known association of cannabis consumption with eating has inspired scientists to look for compounds that curb appetite by blocking cannabinoid receptors in the brain. A team of 10 researchers from the Psychology Department at the University of Connecticut found that cannabinoid receptor *antagonists* (substances that block or oppose the action of cannabanoid receptors) did indeed reduce food consumption by laboratory rats (McLaughlin, Winston, Swezey, Wisniecki, Aberman, Tardif, Betz, Ishiwari, Makriyannis and Salamone, 2003).

In 1969 researchers at the National Institutes of Mental Health felt it was necessary to seek a "long-term, multi-disciplinary study of chronic marijuana smokers who weren't taking a lot of other drugs." The result was a two-year study involving more than 2,000 regular marijuana users in Jamaica. Marijuana has been used for 100 years in Jamaica, and nearly 60% of the rural, working-class males smoke it, usually mixed with tobacco. Jamaican ganja (marijuana) is a powerful variety. Women and children also use the drug, but typically they take it in the form of teas and tonics.

Studies by Robert Block and colleagues in the early 1990s suggested that chronic marijuana use could have damaging effects on cognitive abilities (Block & Ghoneim, 1993) Similar findings were reported by Pope and Yurgelun-Todd (1996). Block said these findings justified serious concern, but he noted, "There is far more extensive, consistent evidence of cognitive deficits associated with heavy use of alcohol relative to marijuana" (Block, 1996, p.560).

A discussion of the issue by Block, written as an editorial for the *Journal of the American Medical Association* (JAMA) is at this location: <http://www.druglibrary.org/schaffer/hemp/medical/block.htm>.

Hallucinogens

Hallucinogens are drugs like LSD (lysergic acid diethylamide), mescaline (the active ingredient of the peyote cactus), and psilocybin (the active ingredient of psychoactive mushrooms). They cause profound changes in thought processes similar to a waking dream or temporary psychosis. Hallucinogens do not always cause hallucinations, so some specialists prefer the term *psychedelic* (mind-altering) for these drugs.

LSD, lysergic acid diethylamide, is the most powerful psychoactive substance known to science. Tiny amounts of it, measured in micrograms-thousandths of a gram-produce powerful effects. LSD is notorious for producing traumatic "bad trips" in some people. However, these experiences are rare when the drug is given in pure form under controlled circumstances. The United States Army and CIA tested LSD on hundreds of subjects. When the research suddenly became public in 1975, due to a lawsuit by a man who claimed lasting ill effects from his participation as a subject, Army drug experts hastened to reassure the public that the research was safe and most of the subjects experienced no harm. However, in a subsequent report, LSD was re-classified at that time as a Schedule 3 drug, a classification reserved for the most dangerous substances. This made it difficult for researchers to obtain permission to do research on LSD.

SUMMARY: PSYCHOACTIVE DRUGS

Psychoactive drugs are those that affect states of consciousness. They come in several varieties: stimulants,

Findings of the "Jamaica study"

In the Jamaica study, 30 male ganja users were matched with 30 non-users of the same age. Men in the ganja-using group averaged seven pounds lighter and tended to have bloodshot eyes. Other than that, few differences turned up in biological or intellectual tests. Testosterone levels in the two groups were identical. The only medical difference was a tendency to hyposia (reduced oxygen delivery to tissues) in the ganja-using group, probably due to the carbon monoxide present in smoke. Research with long-term marijuana users in Costa Rica produced similar conclusions.

which increase activity, depressants, which reduce activity, opiates, which reduce pain and produce a numb feeling; hallucinogens, which produce a state resembling a waking dream; and hypnotics, which produce a feeling of altered perception and thought without the dramatic changes of hallucinogens.

The most commonly used drug is alcohol. Researchers describe the characteristic mental state produced by alcohol as "alcohol myopia." Attention to long-term plans and problems is reduced, while attention to immediate events and stimulation is increased.

Stimulant drugs include amphetamines, cocaine, and caffeine. Cocaine can cause sudden heart attacks because it reduces activity in the vagus nerve, which normally lowers the heart rate as blood pressure rises. Behaviorally, both cocaine and methamphetamine mimic the natural effects of stress.

Opiates are drugs such as heroin and morphine, similar to the endorphins, natural pain-killing drugs in the body. Nitrous oxide, a gas used as an anesthetic by some dentists, produces cross-tolerance to opiates and therefore must involve similar neural mechanisms.

Marijuana does not fit easily into other drug classifications. Its chemical action is unique, affecting mostly the cerebral cortex and hippocampus of the brain. Chemicals that block cannabanoid receptors may prove useful as anti-obesity drugs.

Psychedelics such as LSD produce dramatic, dream-like experiences while awake. MDMA (ecstasy) has become a popular recreational drug. Users often report that it makes them feel like they "love everybody." MDMA has a dose/toxicity ratio less dangerous than that of alcohol, when toxicity is defined as death. However, animal experiments suggest that MDMA may be neurotoxic (neuron-killing) at three times the minimal psychoactive dose.

Chapter 9 Summary

Consciousness is the state or condition of being conscious. A sense of one\'s personal or collective identity, especially the complex of attitudes, beliefs, and sensitivities held by or considered characteristic of an individual or a group. There are several different stages of consciousness. Waking consciousness, altered states of consciousness and sleep.

Waking consciousness is the mental state that includes moving and thinking, along with anything else done while we are awake and alert. Behavior during this period is as normal as it can be. Although behavior can differ from person to person, although most people go through the relatively same behavioral patterns. While awake, people go through feelings of happiness, depression, anger, and boredom, to name a few. These feelings can cause people to do different things and act differently than normal. For instance, happiness, caused by having something give them pleasure in some way, can cause people to smile more or be more kind to other people, like doing other things for people just to be nice, or giving presents and gifts to people. Depression is caused by bad, non-pleasurable things happening to you. While depressed, people may become distanced from their family and friends, not want to interact with other people, and even, in severe cases, hurt themselves and/or others, and even commit suicide. Many things cause anger and aggression also. They can be caused by the interaction with other people like family and peers, but also frustration, hot weather, physical pain, and even noise. While angry people may act overly aggressive, lash out at others, even loved ones, and also commit violent acts. Being bored can also cause people to act differently. While bored people may do things like act and think hastily and also commit crimes in hopes of satisfying their urge for fun and pleasure. All these feelings have different causes but most include interaction with people, television and different chemical balances and imbalances within the a person's body.

Another type of consciousness is altered consciousness. There are many different types of altered consciousness. Daydreaming is one form of this type of consciousness. Daydreaming is when, due to boredom or mental fatigue, a person enters a dream-like state while awake. While not necessarily bad, daydreaming can be a problem, especially at a time in which it is important to be on full alert, like a security guard, or even a school student . It can cause a school student to miss something important or not react to a be-ing called upon by a teacher. Another type of altered consciousness is a drug induced one. Each different type of drug can have a different effect on behavior, depending on the drugs potency and side effects. Alcohol is one of the most widely used drugs there are. It's effects on behavior and personalities are known by most, whether they abuse it, use it, or neither. Since alcohol is a depressant while being intoxicated, people's response time, and decision making are effected strongly as the amount of alcohol taken in rises. At a blood-alcohol level of .05%, a person feels good and is a little less alert than normal. At .1%, a person is slow to react and much less cautious. At .15%, a person's reaction time is much slower. At .2%, the sensory motor skills are largely suppressed. At .25%, a person will most likely be staggering and have very bad perception. At .3%, the person is at a semi-stupor. At .35%, a person is at a level for anesthesia and, depending on tolerance and body weight, could possibly die; And finally at .4% death is likely. People like drinking alcoholic beverages because of the feeling of courage, being care-free and spontaneous. While drinking, the user may exuberate all of these feelings and act more sexual and aggressive than they normally would. After abusing alcohol for a long period of time a person may become an alcoholic. The behavioral changes can be visible when a person is an alcoholic. The person may become easily irritable, disenfranchised, overly aggressive, and suicidal. The causes of these problems are not only caused by alcohol, but also from alcohol-related health problems including memory loss, decrease in sexual desire, impotence, menstrual problems, liver and kidney damage, cancer, insomnia, and brain damage. There are many other drugs that can cause changes in behavior. With stimulants such as caffeine, cocaine, nicotine, and amphetamines, the user can be more excited, and have insomnia which may cause irritability, paranoia, and dependency. With hallucinogens such as marijuana, LSD, and PCP, behavioral changes include loss of contact with reality, disorientation, and fatigue. Long term effects include physical and mental dependence, insanity for LSD users, and possible death for PCP users.

The last stage of consciousness is sleep. Sleep can be defined as a natural state of rest with reduced body movement and awareness of surroundings. Lack of sleep is very influential in a person's behavior. A person who is tired can be less alert , appear uninterested in what people are discussing, and seem to distance themselves from other people. People who suffer from the most common sleep disorder, insomnia, have difficulty falling or staying asleep. This can affect their behavior by causing reduced concentration, and slow reaction time while in the waking state of consciousness. Behavioral changes from lack of sleep include, of course, fatigue. When a person is fatigued and tired it may cause them to be drawl, and uninterested irritable, and lash out in fits of psychotic rages. All these behavioral changes can cause a person to lose their job due to lack of motivation towards completing a task, can cause a person to become distanced from their friends, break up with their companions or spouses and act odd in everyday life. Another type of sleeping disorder is narcolepsy. Narcolepsy affects REM sleep and it's mechanisms. People who are narcoleptic are persistently tired and fatigued and experience loss of muscle tone. This loss of muscle tone can cause brief paralysis of functions and even for a standing person to fall to the ground. This disorder can effect a person's behavior negatively because of the difficulty in conducting everyday activities with the fear of possibly losing consciousness or falling and getting severely injured. It is also harder to lead a normal sex life because the sudden sleep and loss of muscle tone can cause a person to become embarrassed to be close to someone or a person to be frustrated with their partner's disorder.

In conclusion, the three states of consciousness can effect behavior in many different ways, whether it be positive or negative. Behavior is an important part of life although getting enough sleep and avoiding drug abuse can help, there are different things that can also affect people's behavior in waking consciousness. Relationships with other people like friends and family can make a person have a lot of feelings like anger and happiness, and even television can also effect a person's behavior by violent show's making people more aggressive.

10

MOTIVATION AND EMOTION

- Describe the four phases of the human sexual response cycle.
- Define and contrast the organizational versus the activational effects of hormones.
- Discuss the prevalence of homosexuality as a function of species.
- Discuss the potential biological causes of homosexuality.
- Outline the most common sexual dysfunctions.
- Outline the most common psychosocial motivations.
- Compare and contrast needs for relatedness and needs for agency.
- Compare and contrast the major theories relating bodily experience and emotional response.
- Describe the benefits that accrue to expressing one's emotions.
- Explain the relationship between culture and happiness.
- Discuss the respects in which emotional expression is innate or cross-culturally variable.
- Make a tentative list (taxonomy) of the basic emotions of all humans.
- Outline the neural pathways that control approach and avoidance reactions.
- Explain the view that there exist two circuits that control emotional responses such as fear.
- Contrast the psychodynamic, cognitive, and evolutionary perspectives on emotion.
- Discuss the role of attributions in emotions

INTRODUCTION

At its highest level, motivation achieves flow. Flow is a state of mind, where people become totally immersed in their tasks and lose all sense of time. It is a state, where people work for the pure enjoyment of completing the task and not for any external reward. The neuro-modulator dopamine is released when you successfully cope with challenging tasks, by uncovering novel solutions. Dopamine increases alertness and provides clarity to immediate objectives and makes a person feel more energetic and elated.

Research has shown that people achieve flow, when they feel that they are in control of tasks, which are goal directed, provide feedback and give them a sense of meaning. Studies indicate that flow does not require engagement in creative or artistic tasks. Flow has been shown to be experienced even in tasks such as analyzing data, or filling out income tax returns.

Flow occurs, because the system finds swift answers to the challenges of a job. When this happens motivation increases to assist with the task at hand.

MOTIVATION DEFINED

Motivation refers to the driving force behind behavior that leads us to pursue some things and avoid others. It is the process that arouses, directs, and maintains behavior. There is a general consensus that motivation is an internal state or condition (sometimes described as a need, desire, or want) that serves to activate or energize behavior and give it direction (see Kleinginna and Kleinginna, 1981a). Motivation involves the following:

- internal state or condition that activates behavior and gives it direction;

- desire or want that energizes and directs goal-oriented behavior;
- influence of needs and desires on the intensity and direction of behavior.
- the arousal, direction, and persistence of behavior, (Franken (2006).

While still not widespread in terms of introductory psychology textbooks, many researchers are now beginning to acknowledge that the factors that energize behavior are likely different from the factors that provide for its persistence.

A person's mental energy is a consequence of both the motivational and emotional systems. Motives serve to develop an individual's psychic energy and to guide the person toward important tasks and goals. Emotions serve to amplify or diminish specific motives, and help integrate motivated behavior in a person's social interactions.

For example, the need to achieve will motivate a person to attain excellence in a given field. Emotions of pride and happiness may sustain such achievement; emotions of regret and guilt (for example, over harming others) can help ensure that the individual achieves while respecting the rights of others.

Overall, motivation is what causes us to act, whether it is getting a glass of water to reduce thirst or reading a book to gain knowledge.

It involves the biological, emotional, social and cognitive forces that activate behavior. In everyday usage, the term *motivation* is frequently used to describe *why* a person does something. For example, you might say that a student is so motivated to get into a school psychology program that she spends every night studying.

Historically, psychologists have proposed a number of different reasons for motivation which include, instincts, drives, excitement (arousal), goals (incentives), achievement, power, friendship (affiliation), self-fulfillment

Today, human needs are now viewed as dispositions toward action (i.e., they create a condition that is predisposed towards taking action or making a change and moving in a certain direction). Action or overt behavior may be initiated by either positive or negative incentives or a combination of both. The following chart provides a brief overview of the different sources of motivation (internal state) that have been studied. While initiation of action can be traced to each of these domains, it appears likely that initiation of behavior may be more related to emotions and/or the affective area (optimism vs. pessimism; self-esteem; etc.) while persistence may be more related to conation (volition) or goal-orientation.

Sources of Motivational Needs

Behavioral	• elicited by stimulus associated/connected to innately connected stimulus • obtain desired, pleasant consequences (rewards) or escape/avoid undesired, unpleasant consequences
Social	• imitate positive models • be a part of a group or a valued member
Biological	• increase/decrease stimulation (arousal) • activate senses (taste, touch, smell, etc. • decrease hunger, thirst, discomfort, etc. • maintain homeostasis, balance
Cognitive	• maintain attention to something interesting or threatening • develop meaning or understanding • increase/decrease cognitive disequilibrium; uncertainty • solve a problem or make a decision • figure something out • eliminate threat or risk
Affective	• increase/decrease affective dissonance • increase feeling good • decrease feeling bad • increase security of or decrease threats to self-esteem • maintain levels of optimism and enthusiasm
Cognitive	• meet individually developed/selected goal • obtain personal dream • develop or maintain self-efficacy • take control of one's life • eliminate threats to meeting goal, obtaining dream • reduce others' control of one's life
Spiritual	• understand purpose of one's life • connect self to ultimate unknowns

Components of Motivation

There are three major components to motivation: activation, persistence and intensity. Activation involves the decision to initiate a behavior, such as enrolling in a psychology class. Persistence is the continued effort toward a goal even though obstacles may exist, such as taking more psychology courses in order to earn a degree although it requires a significant investment of time, energy and resources. Finally, intensity can be seen in the concentration and vigor that goes into pursuing a goal. For example, one student might coast by without much effort, while another student will study regularly, participate in discussions and take advantage of research opportunities outside of class.

Extrinsic Vs. Intrinsic Motivation

Different types of motivation are frequently described as being either extrinsic (external) or intrinsic (internal). External motivations are those that arise from outside of the individual and often involve rewards such as trophies, money, social recognition or praise. Internal motivations are those that arise from within the individual.

THEORIES OF MOTIVATION

Instinct Theory of Motivation

Instinct is an unlearned, complex pattern of behavior that occurs in the presence of certain stimuli

According to instinct theories, people are motivated to behave in certain ways because they are evolutionarily programmed to do so. An example of this in the animal world is seasonal migration. These animals do not learn to do this; it is instead an inborn pattern of behavior. Instinct Theory Instinct theory was the earliest theory of motivation. Instincts are inherited, unlearned forces that help all species survive. Animals like salmon, bears, and turtles are preprogrammed at birth to engage in specific instinctive reproductive and feeding patterns.

For example, salmon instinctively return to the same stream in which they were spawned to lay their eggs. Humans are also born with instincts. The extent to which these instincts are under conscious control has been a subject of vigorous debate. Psychologists like William McDougall (1908) saw instincts as volitional and purposive: The human mind has certain innate or inherited tendencies which are the essential springs or motive powers of all thought and action.

Drive Reduction Theory

Clark Hull is the psychologist principally identified with drive theory (Hull, 1943). Drives, according to Hull, are of two types: primary and acquired (secondary). Primary drives are forces within the individual that are triggered by biological needs such as hunger and thirst. These drives produce random activity (recall Skinner's animal experiments, described in Chapter 4). This activity is essentially directionless until the need is satisfied. Whatever behavior satisfies the need eventually becomes learned as a habit through the processes of drive reduction and reinforcement.

Acquired or secondary drives include desires for money, for love, to play sports, to write, or to create music. They do not spring from a biological need. Rather, they areBORICP07.d acquired through a process of association with a primary drive. Drive theory assumes that almost all psychological motives are acquired drives. Hull believed that all activity is directed toward reducing the tension triggered by needs and drives. Drive reduction, therefore, is the psychological mechanism underlying both activity and learning. Whatever behavior results in lessening the tension (and consequently the drive) will be repeated until it becomes habitual.

The drive theory of motivation provides the foundation for behavioral learning theory and, unlike instinct theory, still has its proponents. Extrinsic reinforces (i.e., money or good grades) are viewed as incentives that activate acquired drives. The behavior that is instrumental in getting each incentive is learned through a combination of both drive reduction and reinforcement processes. Table 13. provide

Hierarchy of the Four Sources of Motivation

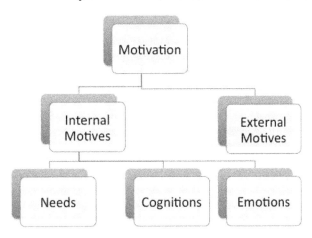

Adapted from Reeve (2009) p9.

a lists of behaviors that represent primary (biological) and secondary (social) motives.

William James created a list of human instincts that included such things as attachment, play, shame, anger, fear, shyness, modesty and love. The main problem with this theory is that it did not really explain behavior, it just described it. By the 1920s, instinct theories were pushed aside in favor of other motivational theories, but contemporary evolutionary psychologists still study the influence of genetics and heredity on human behavior.

Abraham Maslow

Maslow's work lead to additional attempts to develop a theory of motivation, a theory that would put all of the factors influencing motivation into one model (discussed below). An example is provided by Leonard Beauvais Scholl (1995). These authors propose 5 factors as the sources of motivation: 1) Instrumental Motivation (rewards and punishers), 2) Intrinsic Process Motivation (enjoyment, fun), 3) Goal Internalization (self-determined values and goals), 4) Internal Self Concept-based Motivation (matching behavior with internally-developed ideal self), 5) External Self Concept-based Motivation (matching behavior

with externally-developed ideal self). Individuals are influenced by all five factors, though in varying degrees that can change in specific situations.

Factors one and five are both externally-oriented. The main difference is that individuals who are instrumentally motivated are influenced more by immediate actions in the environment (e.g. operant conditioning) whereas individuals who are self-concept motivated are influenced more by their constructions of external demands and ideals (e.g., social cognition).

Factors two, three, and four are more internally-oriented. In the case of intrinsic process, the specific task is interesting and provides immediate internal reinforcement (e.g., cognitive or humanistic theory). The individual with a goal-internalization orientation is more task-oriented (e.g., humanistic or social cognition theory) whereas the person with an internal self-concept orientation is more influenced by individual constructions of the ideal self (humanistic or psychoanalytic theory).

Social Learning Theory

Social learning theory suggests that modeling of behavior (imitating others) and vicarious learning

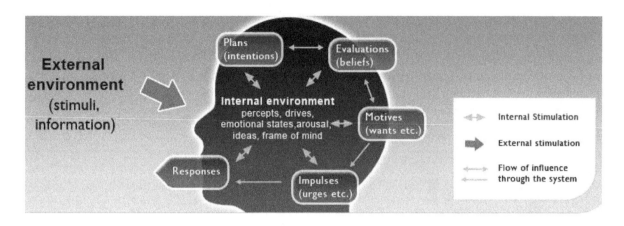

Table 13. Primary and Secondary Drives

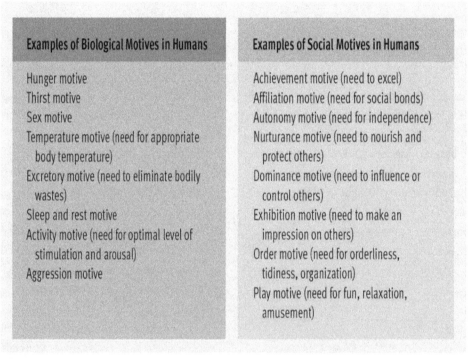

Examples of Biological Motives in Humans	Examples of Social Motives in Humans
Hunger motive	Achievement motive (need to excel)
Thirst motive	Affiliation motive (need for social bonds)
Sex motive	Autonomy motive (need for independence)
Temperature motive (need for appropriate body temperature)	Nurturance motive (need to nourish and protect others)
Excretory motive (need to eliminate bodily wastes)	Dominance motive (need to influence or control others)
Sleep and rest motive	Exhibition motive (need to make an impression on others)
Activity motive (need for optimal level of stimulation and arousal)	Order motive (need for orderliness, tidiness, organization)
Aggression motive	Play motive (need for fun, relaxation, amusement)

(watching others have consequences applied to their behavior) are important motivators of behavior.

Social cognition theory proposes reciprocal determination as a primary factor in both learning and motivation. In this view, the environment, an individual's behavior, and the individual's characteristics (e.g., knowledge, emotions, and cognitive development) both influence and are influenced by each other two components. Bandura (1986, 1997) highlights self-efficacy (the belief that a particular action is possible and that the individual can accomplish it) and self-regulation (the establishment of goals, the development of a plan to attain those goals, the commitment to implement that plan, the actual implementation of the plan, and subsequent actions of reflection and modification or redirection.

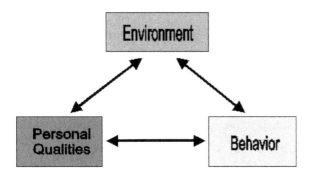

Transpersonal or Spiritual Theories

Most of the transpersonal or spiritual theories deal with the meaningfulness of our lives or ultimate meanings. Abraham Maslow (1954) has also been influential in this approach to motivation. Other influential scholars included Gordon Allport (1955), Victor Frankl (1998), William James (1997), Carl Jung (1953, 1997), Ken Wilber (1998).

THERE ARE MANY TYPES OF MOTIVATION

Motivational techniques have been experienced by every person from birth. We learn behavior through motivation. We live our whole lives because of motivation. The question that remains however is this: What motivation should a person have? This is important because our motivation decides our behavior. Some types of motivation are more effective than others. However, the perfect motivation for you can only be decided by one person, and that person is YOU.

Motivation is the force that draws you to move toward something. It can come from a desire or a curiosity within you or can be from an external force urging you on. In either case, you make the decision to seize or to skip a chance to learn. Motivation styles vary for different situations and topics but nonetheless, you draw on them all the time, especially when you try to learn something challenging. If you can recognize your predominant motivational style you can identify the situations that best satisfy your needs. Likewise, you can't motivate anyone else. All you can do is invite them to learn.

Six Types of Motivation

1. **Achievement:** This is an intrinsic thing. A burning desire to achieve certain goal can be one of the most power motivations. When you set a goal worthy of you and keep thinking about it day in and day out, it soon becomes an all consuming desire and this alone can drive you to achieve any goal you set for yourself.

2. **Change:** It is the drive to bring about a change in your environment. This is usually a result of frustration with the way things are and you want to change it for the better. This causes you to think of a better place you want to be rather than where you are currently. Intensity is determined by the level of frustration and commitment to make a change.

3. **Power:** This is the drive to influence others to get what you want. This is mostly observed in Politics and intensely competitive work place. You have heard the phrase 'Power Hungry'. This is a strong motivational force which could affect the people immensely (positive or negative if not directed properly).

4. **Incentive:** It is the drive to perform a task in anticipation of a reward. This is the 'carrot' piece of 'carrot and stick approach' used by some managers. This is very temporary and may not get the best and sincere efforts. If you are one of those managers in a dire need to keep the team motivated to complete a project, you are best served by enrolling your team on the true purpose of the project and get them emotionally involved rather than short term incentives.

5. **Fear:** In some situations, you may be driven to do certain task out of fear (of losing job or losing friendship or trust). In the work environment, some managers use this tactic. This is the 'stick' part of the carrot and stick approach. If you are currently performing certain task out of fear, it is a clear indication that it is something you don't want to do. You should take a step back and think. Is it really worth it? Just remember that doing anything out of fear is not in harmony with your style of being motivated.

What's Your Motivation Style?

Take a few minutes to complete the following questionnaire assessing your preferred motivation style. These questions have no right or wrong answers. Your response offers insight about how you're motivated to learn. Begin by reading the words in the left-hand column. Of the three responses to the right, circle the one that best characterizes you, answering as honestly as possible with the description that applies to you now. Count the number of circled items and write your total at the bottom of each column.

1. I am proud when I …	Get things done.	Help other people.	Solve problems by thinking things through.
2. I mostly think about …	What's next.	People.	Different ideas.
3. To relax, I tend to …	Rely on a consistently relaxing activity.	Talk with friends.	Learn something new.
4. I like to do things …	Right away or on a schedule.	When everyone else can do it with me.	When it feels right to me.
5. When online, I like to …	Search for specific information.	Write emails, text message, or chat.	Follow links in many directions.
6. Projects should be …	Finished on time.	Done in groups.	Meaningful to my life.
7. In school, I liked to …	Ask questions.	Make friends.	Explore many topics.
8. I believe schedules …	Keep me organized.	Help me coordinate plans with other people.	Are useful tools to keep me on track.
9. I like to be recognized for …	Being organized, neat, and on time.	Being kind, thoughtful, and considerate to others.	Being clever, curious, and a good problem solver.
10. In terms of completing things …	I finish what I start.	I like to enlist the help of other people.	I want to be learning from start to finish.
Totals	Goal:	Social:	Learning:

The column with the highest total represents your primary motivation style. The column with the second-highest total is your secondary motivation style.

Your primary motivation style: _____
Your secondary motivation style: _____

If you are **goal-oriented**, you probably reach for your goals through a direct and obvious route. This might lead you to a reference book, your computer, or to call an expert—whatever means is available. You usually prefer meeting in-person when it's the most effective method and don't find learning, itself, much fun.

If you are **relationship-oriented**, you take part in learning mainly for social contact. When you meet and interact with people, you learn things along the way. You may not like working independently or focusing on topics (separately from the people) because that doesn't give you the interactivity you crave.

If you are **learning-oriented**, the practice of learning, itself, drives you. You search for knowledge because learning delights you and you may become frustrated by anything that requires you to spend more time following procedures than on actual learning.

There is also a fourth motivation style I haven't yet addressed, primarily because it's far less common than the other three styles and because you might not think of it as a motivation style at all. That style is **thrill-oriented**, drawn not to any particular thing but, rather, away from anything that people perceive as tying them down, bounding them, or pulling them in any predictable direction. This isn't to say that thrill-oriented learners can't acquire goals, relationships, or curiosity, but if any of these feel too time-consuming, invasive, or binding, the learner becomes restless and perhaps experiences a compulsion to go in another direction—any other direction—to feel free. If you're thrill-oriented, you're likely to be impulsive and you want to remain impulsive; you seek thrills and flee anything that doesn't offer you that sensation. All of us at one time or another feel impulsive or have an urge to do something else, but we usually moderate these urges when they come, instead of always following where they lead.

6. **Social:** This is an external driver. Intense desire to be recognized by others (either as an equal or part of a group). If you constantly worry about being accepted or appreciated by others, it is likely that actions you take are geared towards pleasing others. This is a social or affiliate motivation. While there may be circumstances that require you to act this way, you need to watch out for this behavior as this may be distracting you from what you truly want to accomplish in your life.

In summary, there are various types of motivation and in order to truly live a productive life, you need to constantly evaluate what motivates you. If you uncover any fear based motivation, reassess your purspose and skill set to complete the task..

CLASSICAL THEORIES OF MOTIVATION

Many of the theories of motivation address issues introduced previously in these materials. The following provides a brief overview to any terms or concepts that have not been previously discussed.

Behavioral

Each of the major theoretical approaches in behavioral learning theory posits a primary factor in motivation. Classical Conditioning states that biological responses to associated stimuli energize and direct behavior. Operant learning states the primary factor is consequences: the application of reinforcers provides incentives to increase behavior; the application of punishers provides disincentives that result in a decrease in behavior.

Cognitive

There are several motivational theories that trace their roots to the *information processing* approach to learning. These approaches focus on the categories and labels people use help to identify thoughts, emotions, dispositions, and behaviors.

A first cognitive approach is *Attribution Theory* (Heider, 1958; Weiner, 1974 and 1985). This theory proposes that every individual tries to explain success or failure of self and others by offering certain "attributions." These attributions are either internal or external and are either under control or not under control. The following chart shows the four attributions that result from a combination of internal or

Diagrammatic summary of Weiner's (1985) Locus of Control

	Internally Perceived Locus	Externally Perceived Locus
Attributions of No Control	Ability	Chance/Luck
Attributions of Control	Effort	Task Difficulty

external locus of control and whether or not control is possible.

In a teaching/learning environment, it is important to assist the learner to develop a self-attribution explanation of effort (internal, control). If the person has an attribution of ability (internal, no control) as soon as the individual experiences some difficulties in the learning process, he or she will decrease appropriate learning behavior (e.g., I'm not good at this). If the person has an external attribution, then nothing the person can do will help that individual in a learning situation (i.e., responsibility for demonstrating what has been learned is completely outside the person). In this case, there is nothing to be done by the individual when learning problems occur.

A second cognitive approach is *Expectancy Theory* (Vroom, 1964) which proposes the following equation:

Motivation = Perceived Probability of Success (Expectancy)*
Connection of Success and Reward (Instrumentality)*
Value of Obtaining Goal (Valance, Value)

Since this formula states that the three factors of Expectancy, Instrumentality, and Valance or Value are to be multiplied by each other, a low value in one will result in a low value of motivation. Therefore, all three must be present in order for motivation to occur. That is, if an individual doesn't believe he or

she can be successful at a task **OR** the individual does not see a connection between his or her activity and success **OR** the individual does not value the results of success, then the probability is lowered that the individual will engage in the required learning activity. From the perspective of this theory, all three variables must be high in order for motivation and the resulting behavior to be high.

Summary

To summarize the cognitive approaches, notice the relationship between William James' formula for self-esteem (**Self-esteem = Success / Pretensions**) and the attribution and expectancy theories of motivation. If a person has an external attribution of success, self-concept is not likely to change as a result of success or failure because the person will attribute it to external factors. Likewise, if the person has an Internal/Ability explanation, his or her self-concept will be tied to learning to do a new activity quickly and easily (I do well because I'm naturally good at it). If failure or difficulty occurs, the person must quickly lower expectations in order to maintain self-esteem. However, if the person has a Internal/Effort explanation and high expectations for success, the person will persevere (i.e., stay motivated) in spite of temporary setbacks because one's self-esteem is not tied to immediate success.

Cognitive dissonance theory suggests that we will seek balance or homeostasis in our lives and will

The third cognitive approach is cognitive dissonance theory which is in some respects similar to disequilibrium in Piaget's theory of cognitive development. This theory was developed by Leon Festinger (1957), as social psychologist, and states that when there is a discrepancy between two beliefs, two actions, or between a belief and an action, we will act to resolve conflict and discrepancies. The implication is that if we can create the appropriate amount of disequilibrium, this will in turn lead to the individual changing his or her behavior which in turn will lead to a change in thought patterns which in turn leads to more change in behavior.

resist influences or expectations to change. How, then, does change or growth occur. One source, according to Piaget, is biological development. As we mature cognitively we will rework our thinking and organizations of knowledge (e.g., schemas, paradigms, explanations) to more accurately reflect our understanding of the world. One of those organizations involves our explanations or attributions of success or failure. After puberty, when biological change slows down considerably, it is very difficult to change these attributions. It requires a long-term program where constant feedback is given about how one's behavior is responsible for one's success.

PSYCHOANALYTIC THEORIES

The psychoanalytic theories of motivation propose a variety of fundamental influences. Freud (1990) suggested that all action or behavior is a result of internal, biological instincts that are classified into two categories: life (sexual) and death (aggression). Many of Freud's students broke with him over this concept. For example, Erikson (1993) and Sullivan (1968) proposed that interpersonal and social relationships are fundamental, Adler (1989) proposed power, while Jung (1953, 1997) proposed temperament and search for soul or personal meaningfulness.

BIOLOGICAL THEORY

All creatures are born with specific innate knowledge about how to survive. Animals are born with the capacity and often times knowledge of how to survive by spinning webs, building nests, avoiding danger, and reproducing. These innate tendencies are preprogrammed at birth, they are in our genes, and even if the spider never saw a web before, never witnessed its creation, it would still know how to create one.

Humans have the same types of innate tendencies. Babies are born with a unique ability that allows them to survive; they are born with the ability to cry. Without this, how would others know when to feed the baby, know when he needed changing, or when she wanted attention and affection? Crying allows a human infant to survive. We are also born with particular reflexes which promote survival. The most important of these include sucking, swallowing, coughing, blinking. Newborns can perform physical movements to avoid pain; they will turn their head if touched on their cheek and search for a nipple (rooting reflex); and they will grasp an object that touches the palm of their hands.

DRIVE REDUCTION THEORY

According to Clark Hull (1943, 1952), humans have internal biological needs which motivate us to perform a certain way. These needs, or drives, are defined by Hull as internal states of arousal or tension which must be reduced. A prime example would be the internal feelings of hunger or thirst, which motivates us to eat. According to this theory, we are driven to reduce these drives so that we may maintain a sense of internal calmness. The table below provides examples of other internal drives.

HUMANISTIC THEORY

One of the most influential writers in the area of motivation is Abraham Maslow (1954).

Maslow (1954) attempted to synthesize a large body of research related to human motivation. Prior to Maslow, researchers generally focused separately on such factors as biology, achievement, or power to explain what energizes, directs, and sustains human behavior. Maslow posited a hierarchy of human needs based on two groupings: deficiency needs and growth needs. Within the deficiency needs, each lower need must be met before moving to the next higher level. Once each of these needs has been satisfied, if at some future time a deficiency is detected, the individual will act to remove the deficiency. The first four levels are:

1) Physiological: hunger, thirst, bodily comforts, etc.;

2) Safety/security: out of danger;

3) Belonginess and Love: affiliate with others, be accepted; and

4) Esteem: to achieve, be competent, gain approval and recognition.

According to Maslow, an individual is ready to act upon the growth needs if and only if the deficiency needs are met. Maslow's initial conceptualization included only one growth need--self-actualization. Self-actualized people are characterized by: 1) being problem-focused; 2) incorporating an ongoing freshness of appreciation of life; 3) a concern about personal growth; and 4) the ability to have peak experiences. Maslow later noted the difference between growth need and self-actualization specifically naming two lower-level growth needs prior to general level of self-actualization (Maslow & Lowery, 1998) and one beyond that level (Maslow, 1971). They are:

5) Cognitive: to know, to understand, and explore;

6) Aesthetic: symmetry, order, and beauty;

7) Self-actualization: to find self-fulfillment and realize one's potential; and

8) Self-trancendenc: to connect to something beyond the ego or to help others find self-fulfillment and realize their potential.

Maslow's basic position is that as one becomes more self-actualized and self-transcendent, one becomes more wise (develops wisdom) and automatically knows what to do in a wide variety of situations.

The few major studies that have been completed on the hierarchy seem to support the proposals of William James (1892/1962) and Mathes (1981) that there are three levels of human needs. James hypothesized the levels of material (physiological, safety), social (belongingness, esteem), and spiritual. Mathes proposed the three levels were physiological, belonginess, and self-actualization; he considered security and self-esteem as unwarranted. Alderfer

Table 14. Examples of Drives

acquisitiveness	escape	mating	rivalry	submission
cleanliness	fear	modesty	secretiveness	sympathy
combativeness	food-seeking	parental love	self-assertion	
constructiveness	hunting	play	shyness	
curiosity	jealousy	repulsion	sociability	

In an article in the May 4, 2006, Neuron, Alison Adcock and colleagues report brain-scanning studies in humans that reveal how specific reward-related brain regions "alert" the brain's learning and memory regions to promote memory formation.

In their studies, the researchers asked volunteers to participate in two types of reward-related tasks as they scanned the subjects' brains using functional magnetic resonance imaging. In this technique, harmless magnetic fields and radio waves are used to detect regions of higher blood flow in the brain, which reflects higher activity.

In the first task, the researchers aimed at identifying the region involved in anticipating rewards. This task involved presenting the subjects with such symbols as circles or squares that indicated an amount of money the subjects could gain or lose--from no money to $5--by rapidly responding to a subsequently presented target by pressing a button. The subjects were notified immediately whether they had received the reward. The researchers found that reward anticipation activated specific brain structures in the "mesolimbic" region involved in the processing of emotions.

In the second task, the researchers sought to measure how this reward center promoted memory formation. They first showed subjects a "value" symbol that signified whether the image of a scene that followed would yield $5 or ten cents if they remembered it the next day. Then they showed the subjects the scene, and the next day tested their ability to pick the scene out of a group.

The researchers found that the subjects were far more likely to remember high-value scenes than low-value scenes. Importantly, they found that the cues to the high-reward scenes that were later remembered--but not those scenes later forgotten--activated the reward areas of the mesolimbic region as well as the learning-related hippocampus in the medial temporal lobe (MTL) of the brain. Activation prior to scene visualization suggests that the brain actually prepares in advance to filter incoming information rather than simply reacting to the world. Activation of the MTL is associated with higher brain functions, including learning and memory, and subjects who showed greater activation in these regions also showed better memory performance, found Adcock and colleagues.

The researchers concluded that the learning mechanism they identified "may let an organism's expectations and motivation interact with events in the physical world to influence learning. Thus, anticipatory activation of this mesolimbic circuit may help translate motivation into memory."

(1972) developed a comparable hierarchy with his ERG (existence, relatedness, and growth) theory. His approach modified Maslow's theory based on the work of Gordon Allport (1960, 1961) who incorporated concepts from systems theory into his work on personality.

Maslow recognized that not all personalities followed his proposed hierarchy. While a variety of personality dimensions might be considered as related to motivational needs, one of the most often cited is that of introversion and extroversion. Reorganizing Maslow's hierarchy based on the work of Alderfer and considering the introversion/extraversion dimension of personality results in three levels, each with an introverted and extroverted component. This organization suggests there may be two aspects of each level that differentiate how people relate to each set of needs. Different personalities might relate more to one dimension than the other. For example, an introvert at the level of Other/Relatedness might be more concerned with his or her own perceptions of being included in a group, whereas an extrovert at that same level would pay more attention to how others value that membership.

At this point there is little agreement about the identification of human basic needs and how they are ordered. For example, Ryan & Deci (2000) also suggest three needs, although they are not necessarily

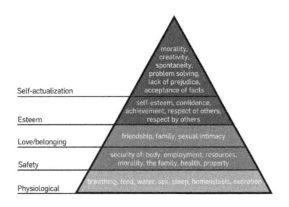

Maslow's Hierarchy of Needs Pyramid

arranged hierarchically: the need for autonomy, the need for competence, and the need for relatedness. Thompson, Grace and Cohen (2001) state the most important needs for children are connection, recognition, and power. Nohria, Lawrence, and Wilson (2001) provide evidence from a sociobiology theory of motivation that humans have four basic needs: (1) acquire objects and experiences; (2) bond with others in long-term relationships of mutual care and commitment; (3) learn and make sense of the world and of ourselves; and (4) to defend ourselves, our loved ones, beliefs and resources from harm. The Institute for Management Excellence (2001) suggests there are nine basic human needs: (1) security, (2) adventure, (3) freedom, (4) exchange, (5) power, (6) expansion, (7) acceptance, (8) community, and (9) expression.

Notice that bonding and relatedness are a component of every theory. However, there do not seem to be any others that are mentioned by all theorists. Franken (2001) suggests this lack of accord may be a result of different philosophies of researchers rather than differences among human beings. There is much work still to be done in this area before we can rely on a theory to be more informative than simply collecting and analyzing data. However, this body of research can be very important to parents, and educators.

Other Psychosocial Motivation

Hunger Motivation

Most people love food. Some people live to eat, while others eat to live. In fact, it is belied that most people think about food probably more than other points of motivations in their lives. At different points in time people are constantly thinking about what they will eat for their next meal (or snack). If a person is in a Vegan or Vegetarian phase, they will about nuts, pasta and fruits. If a person is carnivourous, they will think about big juicy cheeseburgers, steaks, fried chicken, fresh warm Krispy Crème donuts and a thick chemical enhanced Micky D's chocolate shake.

Whatever your diet, it is true that our bodies need food for survival and health. However, we sometimes eat even when we do not need food. Thus, the motivation for hunger goes beyond simple nourishment and nutrition. There are both biological and psychological factors around the motivation of hunger.

Biological Basis of Hunger

When your stomach feels stuffed you probably do not feel hungry and when your stomach is empty you probably get that take me to Taco Bell feeling. Researchers used to believe that the feeling of hunger comes from our stomach. To test the theory out, they made some dude swallow a balloon and inflated the balloon inside his stomach.

The dude felt full for awhile. But after a few hours he began to feel hungry again (even with the full stomach). The dude showed us that hunger does not come just from our stomach. In fact, most of the biological feeling of hunger comes from the brain in a structure that you should already know called the **hypothalamus**. There are two areas on the hypothalamus that control hunger. First, there is the *lateral hypothalamus* that, if stimulated, causes you to feel hunger. So every time you feel hungry, you know your lateral hypothalamus is working. If I took a knife and lesioned your lateral hypothalamus, you would

Alderfer's Hierarchy of Motivational Needs

Level of Need	Definition	Properties
Growth	Impel a person to make creative or productive effects on himself and his environment	Satisfied through using capabilities in engaging problems; creates a greater sense of wholeness and fullness as a human being
Relatedness	Involve relationships with significant others	Satisfied by mutually sharing thoughts and feelings; acceptance, confirmation, understanding, and influence are elements
Existence	Includes all of the various forms of material and psychological desires	When divided among people one person's gain is another's loss if resources are limited

A Reorganization of Maslow's and Alderfer's Hierarchies

Level	Introversion	Extroversion
Growth	Self-Actualization (development of competencies [knowledge, attitudes, and skills] and character)	Trancendence (assisting in the development of others' competencies and character; unknown relationships)
Other (Relatedness)	Personal identification with group, significant others (Belongingness)	Value of person by group (Esteem)
Self (Existence)	Physiological, biological (including basic emotional needs)	Connectedness, security

NEVER again feel hungry from a physical perspective. You would probably lose a lot of weight.

Next there is the ***ventromedial hypothalamus***, which when stimulated, makes you feel full. Whenever you eat a big meal and don't even want to think about eating another bite, the ventromedial hypothalamus is doing its job. If I lesioned out your ventromedial hypothalamus, you would never feel full again, and given the right amount of food, would gain a whole lotta weight.

If the hypothalamus is functioning normally, these two areas oppose each other and signal impulses to eat and stop eating at appropriate times. **Set-point theory** describes how the hypothalamus might decide what impulse to send. This theory states that the hypothalamus wants to maintain a certain optimum body weight. When we drop below that weight, the hypothalamus tells us we should eat and lowers our *metabolic rate-* how quickly our body uses energy. The

hypothalamus tells us to stop eating when that set point is reached and raises our metabolic rate to burn any excess food.

Psychological Factors in Hunger Motivation

Some of us eat even though our hypothalamus is not sending us any cues. If you are motivated to eat by external cues, such as stress, smell, or just the fact that food is in front of you, then you are en ***external***. If you are more motivated to eat by internal cues, empty stomach, feelings of hunger, then you are an ***internal***. Most of us are a combination of both, although I believe that most Americans lean toward the external side of the fence.

Culture and background also affect our food preferences. For example, when I was growing up my mother would make me a peanut butter and jelly omelet. It was really good!!! But when I made one for my wife, she almost upchucked. But she can eat fried pig skin and ask for more where that makes me gag. Think about what various cultures might eat around the world. Here are some examples- camel eyes, dog, beer-jelly, monkey brains, fish flavored ice cream etc.... Just realize that hunger goes way beyond the body and nurture plays a large part in the foods we choose.

Eating Disorders

Eating disorders remain problematic today. There three major types of eating disorders, obesity, Bulimia, and Anorexia Nervosa. It is important to be aware that although there is a biological component to eating disorders, these conditions are also influenced by society and culture.

- **Bulimia**- Bulimics eat large amounts of food in a short period of time (binging) and then get rid of the food (purging) by vomiting, excessive exercise or the use of laxatives. Bulimics are obsessed with food and their body weight. The majority of bulimics are women.
- **Anorexia Nervosa**- Anorexics starve themselves to below 85% of their normal body weight and refuse to eat due to their obsession with weight. The vast majority of anorexics are women.
- **Obesity**- People with diagnosed obesity are severely overweight, often over 100 pounds, and the excess weight threatens their health. Obese people typically have unhealthy eating habits rather than the food obsessions of the other two disorders. Some people may also be genetically predisposed to obesity.

Sexual Motivation

Next to procreation, sexual motivation is a pursuit of erotic pleasure and is a primary reason to engage in sexual behavior, (Abramson et al., 1995; Hatfield et al., 1993). Kinsey and colleagues (1948; 1953) found that children between the ages of 2 and 5 years of age spontaneously touch their genitals. At this age, one could not argue that this sexual behavior is learned or designed to contribute to reproduction. Abramson and Pinkerton (1995) point out that the pleasure of sexual behavior is physiologically and psychologically-based and that the sex organs do not exist merely to guarantee reproductive behavior. As an example, they cite the female orgasm, uncommon during vaginal penetration, but very common by more direct means

of clitoral stimulation. Sexual pleasure does not occur merely to ensure procreation. We engage in sexual behavior because it is enjoyable. However, as discussed below, what is considered pleasurable, may well be influenced by one's interpretation of the stimuli.

Physical pleasure has both a physiological component (the physical sensations associated with touch) and a subjective psychological component. Pleasure is an emotion (Cofer, 1972), which, according to the Schacter-Singer theory, is a subjective feeling based upon physiological arousal and interpretations of the stimuli that are linked to the arousal (Cornelius, 1996). Thus emotions are both physiologically- and cognitively-based. Pleasure is influenced by both our cognitions and our physiological functioning. As a factor involved in sexual motivation, it is not unusual to be associated with motivation and to simultaneously be associated with other variables that are themselves identified as related to sexual motivation and which may or may not belong to the same category.

Physiological Correlates – As discussed in Chapter 3, the influence of hormones in sexual behavior is well-supported by research. Both men and women produce estrogens, progestins and androgens,

though women produce far more estrogens and progestin and men more androgens (Hokanson, 1969; Leger, 1992). In lower species, hormone levels are almost directly correlated with sexual behavior, however, as one moves up the phylogenetic scale, other elements become involved (Fisher, 1993; Hokanson, 1969). In humans, hormones are also related to sexual desire, but are not the entire story.

In males, a minimum level of testosterone is necessary to maintain normal sexual motivation in males (Leger, 1992). If males' testosterone levels fall below the threshold, sexual motivation is greatly reduced. However, once the threshold level is reached, it no longer predicts sexual behavior. Women's studies also show correlations between hormones and sexual desire (Leger, 1992; Sherwin & Gelfan, 1987; Sherwin, Gelfan, & Brender, 1985), however, the results are inconsistent (Leger, 1992). Since neither increases nor decreases in hormones in either males or females are perfectly correlated with sexual desire, it stands to reason that there must be other factors involved. As Hokanson (1969) concludes, hormones serve the primary purpose of readying the individual for action, but other factors determine whether the individual actually engages in sexual activity.

Another physiological factor in sexual motivation may well be *odor and sense of smell*. Of all the elements researched, odor and sense of smell have received the least attention, probably because, as Kohl and Francoeur (1995) state, their influence on sexual behavior is difficult to ascertain. However, body odor (i.e., airborne hormones) definitely influences our behaviors. In their review of numerous studies such as synchronization of menstrual cycles of women who live together, and the influence of hormone-scented masks on individuals' ratings of others, Kohl and Francoeur (1995) state that odor must be involved in our sexual behaviors also. Helen Fisher (1993) also agrees that odors may influence sexual behavior and cites that some men in Greece swear by body-odor scented handkerchiefs which they use to lure women into relationships.

Attraction—Numerous elements have been identified as playing a role in attraction. For example, attraction is a function of proximity (how frequently you cross paths with someone), familiarity and similarity (e.g. in looks, or attitudes) (Kalat, 1996). This has been supported both with studies of attraction to friends and to romantic partners.

Playing hard-to-get also contributes to human's attraction to one another (Hatfield, Walster, Piliavin & Schmidt, 1988). Apparently individuals make attributions about potential significant others based upon how quickly that person returns a show of interest. Those who are easily attained are less attractive than those who are more difficult to attain due to the traits the relationship-seeker attributes to her. For example, relationship seekers fear that easy-to-get women might display inappropriate behaviors in public. However, a hard-to-get woman who indicates interest in the relationship-seeker has positive traits attributed to her such as warmth and friendliness.

Another overwhelmingly important element in attraction is *physical attractiveness*. As stated previously, research between attitudes and behaviors are not always consistent. Research on what individuals find attractive in potential dates provides further evidence

for this inconsistency in human sexual behavior. Although subjects stated that physical attractiveness was one of the least important elements in their attraction to someone else, in actual experiments using blind dates, the only factor which predicted whether subjects desired a second date with the same person was the attractiveness of the blind date (Walster, Aronson, Abrahams, & Rottman, 1966). This was true for both male and female participants of the study. Attraction to others is yet another element of sexual motivation that has its roots in both nature and nurture -- it is obviously innate to seek out attractive others, yet we still lean towards mates who are more similar to us, an apparent influence of culture and learning in addition to an inherited predisposition.

Learning—Learning is, of course, highly influential in sexual motivation. We copy the behaviors of those we respect and admire. We learn to repeat behaviors that are rewarded (and sexual behavior is rewarding for most) and we learn to discontinue behaviors that have negative outcomes. Conditioning is believed to influence sexual motivation. Certain stimuli may increase sexual arousal. For example, one might become sexually aroused by candlelight due to the learned association with sexual pre-encounters such as a romantic, candlelight dinner. These modeled behaviors will continue to teach learned behaviors associated with romance.

Attitudes and Culture—Attitudes are defined as relatively stable evaluations of a person, object, situation or issue (Wood et al., 1996). Studies have shown that behaviors normally considered proper in one culture, may be improper or unarousing in another. In other words, attitudes towards sexual behaviors are culturally learned. For example, some cultures find kissing repulsive (Tiefer, 1995) while other cultures insist on same-gender sex as a rite of passage into adulthood (Herdt, 1984).

It is still noted, even in newer surveys in the United States (e.g., Laumann et al., 1994), that men and women have different attitudes toward sexual behaviors. For example, men are more interested in a variety of sexual behaviors, such as group sex, than are women. These divergences are undoubtedly, as mentioned earlier, a function of the gender roles each society impresses upon its members. A comparison of Swedish and American college students sought to examine if indeed the difference in men's and women's attitudes could be definitively tied to culture, rather than inherent gender differences (Weinberg, Lottes, Shaver, 1995). Specifically, it was believed that men and women in Sweden would have more convergent and relaxed attitudes toward sexual behaviors than the American participants. Sweden is generally known to have more relaxed sexual standards. It is believed that this is due, in part, to several years of mandatory sex education and the relatively equal power that women have in society. The study indeed showed that Swedish men and women had very similar attitudes towards sexual behaviors. Americans, as expected, had very different attitudes about what constituted appropriate sexual behaviors. While the current author cautioned earlier against drawing causal conclusions from a descriptive study such as this, the information further indicates that culture is associated with differences in sexual attitudes.

The influence of learning on sexual motivation is quite profound. Attraction, cognitions, and sexual orientation, variables mentioned previously, are also influenced by learning. Thus a key component which determines the level of our sexual motivation is learning.

In conclusion, sexual motivation is influenced by complex relationships among numerous factors including hormones, cognitions, learning and culture. Because these variables are also associated with one another, in addition to sexual motivation, it is difficult to place them in discrete categories. Finally, the inability to clearly isolate the many variables involved in human sexual motivation ensures that this topic will continue to fascinate researchers for a very long time.

Scientists say that sexual motivation is one of the most important aspects of humanity. If we were not motivated to have sex, then we probably would not procreate (have babies) and the human species would end. So according to that logic, feeling like you want to have sex (being horny) are just you doing your job

as part of the human species (way to take one for the team).

Although we have been having sex since the dawn of humans, we have only began serious scientific study of sex in the United States 60 years ago. The first major scientist to analyze human sexual behavior in the U.S. was **Alfred Kinsey**.

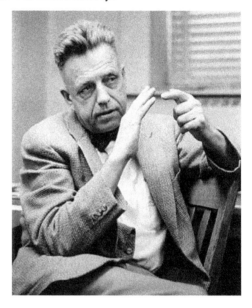

Kinsey, who studied the genealogy of flies by trade, set out and surveyed thousands of people of their sexual behaviors. He discovered some pretty interesting things about human sexual being (like the % of people masturbating and having pre-marital sex). But what made Kinsey so important was 1. he attempted to use the scientific method to study sex and 2. he showed us that our perceptions about what others are doing are a whole lot different than our reality. Before Kinsey, many people believed that they were part of the dirty few who masturbated, but after Kinsey's reports they realized that everyone and their mom did it (hopefully not literally).

Sexual Response Cycle

In the late 1950s and early 1960s a husband wife team of William Masters and Virginia Johnson brought sex into their lab.

They brought hundreds of volunteers into their lab and observed them having various types of sex. They used tools to measure penile length and blood flow and vaginal expansion and lubrication. They perform thousands of trials and their results over a twenty year period were extensive. They even tried to "cure" homosexuality and claimed a 30% failure rate. The highlight of their research was the physiological breakdown of the sexual act called the ***sexual response cycle***, which is broken down into four stages (and there will be no pictures- use your imagination):

1. **Initial excitement**: Genital areas become engorged with blood, penis becomes erect, clitoris swells, respiration and heart rate increases.
2. **Plateau phase**: Respiration and heart rate continue at an elevated level, genitals secrete fluids in preparation for orgasm.
3. **Orgasm**: Rhythmic genital contractions that may help conception. Respiration and heart rate increase further, males ejaculate (there is evidence of female ejaculation as well), often accompanied by a pleasurable euphoria.
4. **Resolution phase**: Respiration and heart rate return to normal resting states. Men experience a refractory period- a time period that must elapse before another orgasm. Women do not have a similar ***refractory period*** and can repeat the cycle immediately.

Psychological factors in Sexual Motivation

Unlike many animals, our sexual desire is not motivated strictly by hormones. Many studies demonstrate that sexual motivation is controlled to a great extent by psychological rather than biological sources. Sexual desire can be present even when the capacity to have sex is lost. Accident victims who lose the ability to have sex still have sexual desires. Erotic material can inspire sexual feelings and physiological responses in men and women, including elevated levels of hormones (remind me to tell you about the research on this in class). The interaction between our physiology and psychology creates the myriad of sexual desires we see in society and ourselves.

Sexual Orientation

Our desire to engage in sexual behavior with someone is also influenced by sexual orientation. Sexual orientation refers to the direction of an individual's sexual attraction (Wood, et al., 1996). Most individuals are heterosexual (Laumann, 1994; Wellings, et al., 1994) which means they are primarily attracted to the opposite sex. Homosexuals are individuals who are attracted to the same sex and bisexuals are attracted to both sexes.

Why are individuals attracted to one sex rather than another? LeVay (1995) believes that most researchers of the topic agree it is a combination of multiple factors including genetic makeup, hormones and social experiences. He further believes that newer studies (e.g., Bailey & Pillard, 1991; Bailey, Pillard, Neale, & Agyei, 1993) indicate that genes are perhaps more influential than the other factors. Studies indicate that the percentage of individuals who call themselves homosexual is quite small, ranging from about .5% to 2.8% (Laumann, 1994; Wellings, et al., 1994) . This estimate is significantly lower than the rates given in the problematic Kinsey Reports (1948; 1953).

In his review of several studies on the prevalence of homosexuality, LeVay (1995) states that it is best to keep an open mind towards reviewing new evidence since changing attitudes and beliefs appear to be linked to self-stated homosexuality. What he was referring to was the indication that individuals are more likely to express their gay behavior within their own culture as that culture becomes more accepting of homosexuality. Thus it is apparent that culture influences the expression of one's sexual orientation which in turn influences sexual motivation.

Ok- let's just get the myths out of the way. Studies have shown again and again that homosexuality is NOT related to traumatic childhood experiences, parenting styles, the quality of relationships with parents, masculinity or femininity, or whether we are raised by heterosexual or homosexual parents. Although researchers believe that environmental strongly influence probably affect sexual orientation, research is still being performed.

Researchers HAVE identified possible biological influences. Scientist Simon LeVay discovered that certain brain structures are different in homosexual and heterosexual males. But that does not mean than genetics caused the brain differences (one can argue that environmental influences change neural structures.). But twin studies indicate a genetic influence on sexual orientation since a twin is much more likely to be gay if his or her identical twin is gay.

The most current research points to the prenatal environment (the womb) that may alter brain structures and influence sexual orientation. Since 3-10% of the population is homosexual, it is suspected that research in this area will continue and the differences become more clear.

Achievement Motivation

One classification of motivation differentiates among achievement, power, and social factors (see McClelland, 1985; Murray, 1938, 1943). In the area of achievement motivation, the work on Goal Theory has differentiated three separate types of goals: **mastery goals** (also called learning goals) which focus on gaining competence or mastering a new set of knowledge or skills; **performance goals** (also called ego-involvement goals) which focus on achieving normative-based standards, doing better than others, or doing well without a lot of effort; and **social goals**

which focus on relationships among people (see Ames, 1992; Dweck, 1986; Urdan & Maehr, 1995). In the context of school learning, which involves operating in a relatively structured environment, students with mastery goals outperform students with either performance or social goals. However, in life success, it seems critical that individuals have all three types of goals in order to be very successful.

One aspect of this theory is that individuals are motivated to either avoid failure (more often associated with performance goals) or achieve success (more often associated with mastery goals). In the former situation, the individual is more likely to select easy or difficult tasks, thereby either achieving success or having a good excuse for why failure occurred. In the latter situation, the individual is more likely to select moderately difficult tasks which will provide an interesting challenge, but still keep the high expectations for success.

Achievement motivation seems to vary from person to person. Some people have high achievement motivations in school, maintaining healthy lifestyles, job success, while others in nothing at all. Motivation is the basic drive for all of our actions. Motivation refers to the dynamics of our behavior, which involves our needs, desires, and ambitions in life. Achievement motivation is based on reaching success and achieving all of our aspirations in life. Achievement goals can affect the way a person performs a task and represent a desire to show competence (Harackiewicz, Barron, Carter, Lehto, & Elliot, 1997). These basic physiological motivational drives affect our natural behavior in different environments. Most of our goals are incentive-based and can vary from basic hunger to the need for love and the establishment of mature sexual relationships. Our motives for achievement can range from biological needs to satisfying creative desires or realizing success in competitive ventures. Motivation is important because it affects our lives every day. All of our behaviors, actions, thoughts, and beliefs are influenced by our inner drive to succeed.

Implicit and Self-Attributed Motives

Motivational researchers share the view that achievement behavior is an interaction between situational variables and the individual subject's motivation to achieve. Two motives are directly involved in the prediction of behavior, implicit and explicit. Implicit motives are spontaneous impulses to act, also known as task performances, and are aroused through incentives inherent to the task. Explicit motives are expressed through deliberate choices and more often stimulated for extrinsic reasons. Also, individuals with strong implicit needs to achieve goals set higher internal standards, whereas others tend to adhere to the societal norms. These two motives often work together to determine the behavior of the individual in direction and passion (Brunstein & Maier, 2005).

Explicit and implicit motivations have a compelling impact on behavior. Task behaviors are accelerated in the face of a challenge through implicit motivation, making performing a task in the most effective manner the primary goal. A person with a strong implicit drive will feel pleasure from achieving a goal in the most efficient way. The increase in effort and overcoming the challenge by mastering the task satisfies the individual. However, the explicit motives are built around a person's self-image. This type of motivation shapes a person's behavior based on their own self-view and can influence their choices and responses from outside cues. The primary agent for this type of motivation is perception or perceived ability. Many theorists still cannot agree whether achievement is based on mastering one's skills or striving to promote a better self-image (Brunstein & Maier, 2005). Most research is still unable to determine whether these different types of motivation would result in different behaviors in the same environment.

Achievement Goals and Information Seeking

Theorists have proposed that people's achievement goals affect their achievement-related attitudes and behaviors. Two different types of achievement-related attitudes include task-involvement and ego-involvement. Task-involvement is a motivational state in which a person's main goal is to acquire skills and understanding whereas the main goal in ego-involvement is to demonstrate superior abilities (Butler, 1999). One example of an activity where someone strives to attain mastery and demonstrate superior ability is schoolwork. However situational cues, such as the person's environment or surroundings, can affect the success of achieving a goal at any time.

Studies confirm that a task-involvement activity more often results in challenging attributions and increasing effort (typically in activities providing an opportunity to learn and develop competence) than in an ego-involvement activity. Intrinsic motivation, which is defined as striving to engage in activity because of self-satisfaction, is more prevalent when a person is engaged in task-involved activities. When people are more ego-involved, they tend to take on a different conception of their ability, where differences in ability limit the effectiveness of effort. Ego-involved individuals are driven to succeed by outperforming others, and their feelings of success depend on maintaining self-worth and avoiding failure. On the other hand, task-involved individuals tend to adopt their conception of ability as learning through applied effort (Butler, 1999). Therefore less able individuals will feel more successful as long as they can satisfy an effort to learn and improve. Ego-invoking conditions tend to produce less favorable responses to failure and difficulty.

Competence moderated attitudes and behaviors are more prevalent in ego-involved activities than task-involved. Achievement does not moderate intrinsic motivation in task-involving conditions, in which people of all levels of ability could learn to improve. In ego-involving conditions, intrinsic motivation was higher among higher achievers who demonstrated superior ability than in low achievers who could not demonstrate such ability (Butler, 1999). These different attitudes toward achievement can also be compared in information seeking.

Task- and ego-involving settings bring about different goals, conceptions of ability, and responses to difficulty. They also promote different patterns of information seeking. People of all levels of ability will seek information relevant to attaining their goal of improving mastery in task-involving conditions. However they need to seek information regarding self-appraisal to gain a better understanding of their self-capacity (Butler, 1999). On the other hand people in ego-involving settings are more interested in information about social comparisons, assessing their ability relative to others.

Approach and Avoidance Goals

Achievement motivation theorists focus their research attention on behaviors involving competence. The desire for success and the desire to avoid failure were identified as critical determinants of aspiration and behavior by a theorist named Lewin. In his achievement motivation theory, McClelland proposed that there are two kinds of achievement motivation, one oriented around avoiding failure and the other around the more positive goal of attaining success.

Presently, achievement goal theory is the predominant approach to the analysis of achievement motivation. Most contemporary theorists use the frameworks of Dweck's and Nicholls' revised models in two important ways. First, most theorists institute primary orientations toward competence, by either differentiating between mastery and ability goals or contrasting task and ego involvement. A contention was raised toward the achievement goal frameworks on whether or not they are conceptually similar enough to justify a convergence of the mastery goal form (learning, task involvement and mastery) with the performance goal form (ability and performance, ego involvement, competition). Secondly, most modern theorists characterized both mastery and performance goals as approach forms of motivation, or they failed to consider approach and avoidance as independent motivational tendencies within the performance goal orientation (Elliot & Harackiewicz, 1996).

Three motivational goal theories have recently been proposed based on the tri-variant framework by achievement goal theorists: mastery, performance-approach, and performance-avoidance. Performance-approach and mastery goals both represent approach orientations according to potential positive outcomes, such as the attainment of competence and task mastery. These forms of behavior and self-regulation commonly produce a variety of affective and perceptual-cognitive processes that facilitate optimal task engagement. They challenge sensitivity to information relevant to success and effective concentration in the activity, leading to the mastery set of motivational responses described by achievement goal theorists. The performance-avoidance goal is conceptualized as an avoidance orientation according to potential negative outcomes. This form of regulation evokes self-protective mental processes that interfere with optimal task engagement. It creates sensitivity to failure-relevant information and invokes an anxiety-based preoccupation with the appearance of oneself rather than the concerns of the task, which can lead to the helpless set of motivational responses. The three goal theories presented are very process oriented in nature. Approach and avoidance goals are viewed as exerting their different effects on achievement behavior by activating opposing sets of motivational processes (Elliot & Harackiewicz, 1996).

Intrinsic Motivation and Achievement Goals

Intrinsic motivation is defined as the enjoyment of and interest in an activity for its own sake. Fundamentally viewed as an approach form of motivation, intrinsic motivation is identified as an important component of achievement goal theory. Most achievement goal and intrinsic motivational theorists argue that mastery goals are facilitative of intrinsic motivation and related mental processes and performance goals create negative effects. Mastery goals are said to promote intrinsic motivation by fostering perceptions of challenge, encouraging task involvement, generating excitement, and supporting self-determination while performance goals are the opposite. Performance goals are portrayed as undermining intrinsic motivation by instilling perceptions of threat, disrupting task involvement, and creating anxiety and pressure (Elliot & Harackiewicz, 1996).

An alternative set of predictions may be derived from the approach-avoidance framework. Both performance-approach and mastery goals are focused on attaining competence and foster intrinsic motivation. More specifically, in performance-approach or mastery orientations, individuals perceive the achievement setting as a challenge, and this likely will create excitement, encourage cognitive functioning, increase concentration and task absorption, and direct the person toward success and mastery of information which facilitates intrinsic motivation. The performance-avoidance goal is focused on avoiding incompetence, where individuals see the achievement setting as a threat and seek to escape it (Elliot & Harackiewicz, 1996). This orientation is likely to elicit anxiety and withdrawal of effort and cognitive resources while disrupting concentration and motivation.

Management Theory

Organizational psychologists are the psychologists of the business world and spend the most time studying motivations and how we can use these ideas to increase employee performance in the workplace. Organizational psychologists spend a lot of time looking at managers (bosses) in the workplace and how they treat the people under them. They divide managers into two different styles. If you want to make this more applicable to your lives change the word manager to teacher, and the word employee to student- it will make more sense to you.

- **Theory X:** Managers believe that employees will work only if rewarded with benefits or threatened with punishment. In other words, they believe that employees are only *extrinsically motivated.*
- **Theory Y:** Mangers believe that employees are internally motivated to do good work and policies should encourage this internal motive. Thus these managers believe that employees can be *intrinsically motivated.*

Which environment would you rather work under? Organizations are starting to move to the Theory Y style of leadership and are hiring organizational psychologists to help promote intrinsic motivation in the workplace.

When Motives Conflict

Sometimes what you want to do in a situation is clear to you, but at other times you no doubt find yourself conflicted about what choice to make. Psychologists discuss four types of motivational conflicts.

- **Approach-approach conflict**: occurs when you must choose between two desirable outcomes. On Friday night, should you go to the movies with your best friend or dinner with that really cute guy/girl from history class. Assuming both choices appeal to you, you have a conflict because you can only chose one.
- **Avoidance-avoidance conflict**: occurs when you must choose between two unattractive outcomes. If your parents tell you to clean your room or rake leaves and you desire neither one you are experiencing an avoidance-avoidance conflict.
- **Approach-avoidance**: exists when ONE event or goal has both attractive and unattractive features. Let's say you love cotton candy but the sugar gives you gas. Cotton candy has both attractive (tastes good) and unattractive (farting) features.
- **Multiple approach-avoidance conflicts**: here you must choose between two or more things, each of which has both desirable and undesirable features. The best example is choosing a college that you want to go to. Obviously you are deciding between Duke and Harvard. Well Duke has better weather (attractive), but their lacrosse team is not the most upstanding (unattractive). Harvard has a great legacy (attractive) but crimson is such a horrid color (unattractive).

THE PSYCHOLOGY OF EMOTION

The relationship of motivation and emotion

Emotion (an indefinite subjective sensation experienced as a state of arousal) is different from motivation in that there is not a goal orientation affiliated with it. Emotions occur as a result of an interaction between perception of environmental stimuli, neural/hormonal responses to these perceptions (often labeled feelings), and subjective cognitive labeling of these feelings (Kleinginna and Kleinginna, 1981b). Evidence suggests there is a small core of core emotions (perhaps 6 or 8) that are uniquely associated with a specific facial expression (Izard, 1990). This implies that there are a small number of unique biological responses that are genetically hard-wired to specific facial expressions. A further implication is that the process works in reverse: if you are motivated to change how you feel and your feeling is associated with a specific facial expression, you can change that feeling by purposively changing your facial expression. As most people would rather feel happy than experience some other negative emotion, the most desired facial expression by most people today is a *smile*.

EMOTION DEFINED

In psychology, emotion is often defined as a complex state of feeling that results in physical and psychological changes that influence thought and behavior. Emotionality is associated with a range of psychological phenomena including temperament, personality, mood and motivation. According to author David G. Meyers, human emotion involves "...physiological arousal, expressive behaviors, and conscious experience." This section will present the various theories related to the acquisition of emotion.

The definition of emotion refers to feeling state involving thoughts, physiological changes, and an outward expression or behavior.

Theories of Emotion

The major theories of emotion can be grouped into three main categories: physiological, neurological and cognitive. Physiological theories suggest that responses within the body are responsible for emotions. Neurological theories propose that activity within the brain leads to emotional responses. Finally, cognitive theories argue that thoughts and other mental activity play an essential role in the formation of emotions. Each of these categories are supported in the theories noted below.

The James-Lange Theory of Emotion

The James Lange Theory is one of the best-known examples of a physiological theory of emotion. Independently proposed by psychologist William James and physiologist Carl Lange, the James-Lange theory of emotion suggests that emotions occur as a result of physiological reactions to events.

It is an event that will cause a physiological arousal first and then we interpret this arousal. Only after our interpretation of the arousal can we experience emotion. If the arousal is not noticed or is not given any thought, then we will not experience any emotion based on this event.

EVENT ····➔ AROUSAL ····➔ INTERPRETATION ····➔ EMOTION

According to this theory, you see an external stimulus that leads to a physiological reaction. Your emotional reaction is dependent upon how you interpret those physical reactions. For example, suppose you are walking in the woods and you see a grizzly bear. You begin to tremble and your heart begins to race. The James-Lange theory proposes that you will interpret your physical reactions and conclude that you are frightened ("I am trembling, therefore I am afraid").

The Cannon-Bard Theory of Emotion

Another well-know physiological theory is the Cannon-Bard theory of emotion. The Cannon-Bard theory argues that we experience physiological arousal and emotion at the same time, but gives no attention to the role of thoughts or outward behavior. This theory differs from the James Lange Theory, which states that we feel emotions and experience physiological reactions such as sweating, trembling and muscle tension simultaneously. More specifically, it is suggested that emotions result when the thalamus sends a message to the brain in response to a stimulus, resulting in a physiological reaction.

The Schachter-Singer Theory

Also known as the two-factor theory of emotion, the Schachter-Singer Theory is an example of a cognitive theory of emotion. This theory suggests that the physiological arousal occurs first, and then the individual must identify the reason behind this arousal in order to experience and label it as an emotion.

EVENT ···→ AROUSAL ···→ REASONING ···→ EMOTION

EMOTIONAL EXPRESSION

EVENT ···→ AROUSAL
···→ EMOTION

There is a great deal of evidence to support the idea that people can reliably identify facial expressions of emotion. This ranges from identifying major classes of emotional states (such as anger, anxiety, and happiness) to more subtle distinctions (such as irritation, fear, and amusement). Further, people seem capable of identifying whether the facial display is genuine, or faked, based upon the extent to which the whole face is involved (fake expressions are typically limited to the mouth). There are some features that are culture-bound, and other features of facial recognition that are cross-culturally consistent. These effects are also different between genders. In general, research indicates that women are better at identifying emotions, experience emotions with greater intensity, and express emotions with greater directness.

Facial Feedback Theory

According to the facial feedback theory, emotion is the experience of changes in our facial muscles, for example when we smile, we then experience pleasure, or happiness. When we frown, we then experience sadness, frustration, and anger. It is the changes in facial muscles that cue our brains and provide the basis of our emotions. Just as there are an unlimited number of muscle configurations in our face, so too are there a seemingly unlimited number of emotions.

BIOLOGICAL BASIS OF EMOTIONS

The limbic system regulates many emotions. Some emotional reactions are triggered automatically by the amygdala and others involve the cerebral cortex. No single region of the cortex that regulates all feelings has been discovered.

When an event prompts an emotional reaction, the sympathetic nervous system mobilizes the body

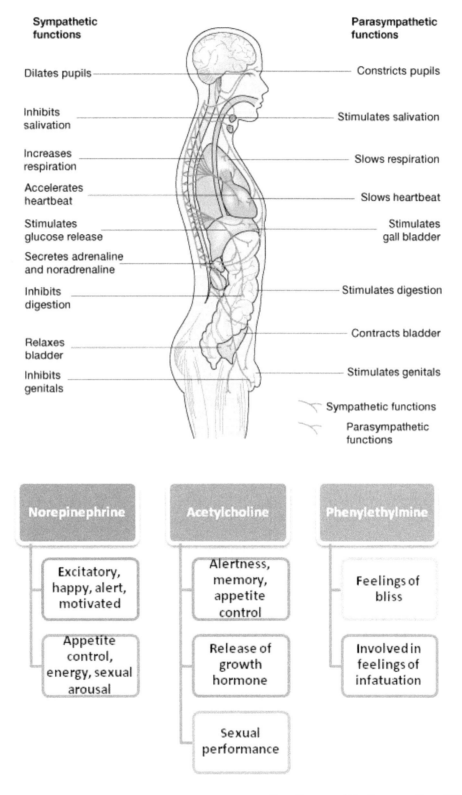

Sympathetic functions

Dilates pupils

Inhibits salivation

Increases respiration

Accelerates heartbeat

Stimulates glucose release

Secretes adrenaline and noradrenaline

Inhibits digestion

Relaxes bladder

Inhibits genitals

Parasympathetic functions

Constricts pupils

Stimulates salivation

Slows respiration

Slows heartbeat

Stimulates gall bladder

Stimulates digestion

Contracts bladder

Stimulates genitals

Sympathetic functions

Parasympathetic functions

Norepinephrine
- Excitatory, happy, alert, motivated
- Appetite control, energy, sexual arousal

Acetylcholine
- Alertness, memory, appetite control
- Release of growth hormone
- Sexual performance

Phenylethylmine
- Feelings of bliss
- Involved in feelings of infatuation

for an adaptive fight-or-flight response. Afterward, the parasympathetic nervous system restores the body to its pre-aroused, calm state. Research supports the notion that each emotion has unique symptoms.

Emotions and Feelings are Broad Thoughts

Any emotion or feeling can be broken down into the sensations and real events that caused it. And you can think about any of those things with thoughts.

As discussed in Chapter X, a thought is thinking about something in specific. You can have a thought about your entire day, but it is going to be just a thought, it is going to be about one thing, and that one thing might be a summary of the paragraph—but it is still a thought. So what we think of as thought is really just a short period of thinking—one unit of thinking that lasts for a short period of time. An essay is composed of many thoughts, but just one thought would be "I went to the movie today".

Thoughts are in general talked about as being verbal, people rarely think of emotions and feelings as thoughts. But emotions and feelings are thoughts if you think about that emotion and feeling. The short period of time in which you think about the emotion or feeling is a thought. So thoughts can be about emotions and feelings. They are just harder to identify because they aren't verbal.

The reason that verbal things are easier to identify is because they are distinct sounds (that we have definitions for). Distinct sounds, different sounds, are easy to separate. It is easy to identify one sound from another sound, and that is all words are, different sounds. So it could be that someone is talking and you don't have any thoughts about them talking, or you are not thinking about them talking. In that case you just aren't listening to them, or you are not paying attention to the sounds they are making.

So thought then is really just any short period of high attention. And thinking is long or short periods of high attention. So if you are thinking for more than a few seconds, then you are probably going to be thinking about several thoughts. Since you can think about emotions and feelings too, however, you can think about your emotions or feelings for long periods of time.

Just as thinking is made up of individual components of thought, feeling, or emotion, each of those components is made up of their own further components. In fact, when you think about an emotion or feeling you intensify that feeling or emotion a lot. Each emotion, however, is made up of experiences in the real world. The real world can include thoughts and feelings in your head as well.

Since emotions are made up of many parts which are real, then intelligence is ultimately just your ability to manipulate real things, and therefore your emotions are going to determine what it is in your mind, and give a larger pool of things for your intellect to explore.

Summary

Some things in life cause people to feel, these are called emotional reactions. Some things in life cause people to think, these are sometimes called logical or intellectual reactions. Thus life is divided between things that make you feel and things that make you think. The question is, if someone is feeling, does that mean that they are thinking less? It probably does. If part of your brain is being occupied by feeling, then it makes sense that you have less capacity for thought. That is obvious if you take emotional extremes, such as crying, where people can barely think at all. This does not mean that emotional people are not intelligent; it just means that they might be dumber during the times in which they are emotional. Emotion goes on and off for everyone, sometimes people cry, and sometimes they are completely serious.

Some things in life can identifiably cause more emotion than other things.

1. Color causes more emotion than black and white. So anything with more color in it is going to be more emotional to look at, whether it is the difference between a gold or silver sword, or a gold or silver computer. In both cases the gold is going to be more emotional.

2. Things that are personal are emotional, personal things that people like and that they feel are "close" to them. Things like home or anything someone likes actually. That is a definition of emotion after all, something that causes feeling. So if you like it, it is probably going to cause more feeling. Other things aside from liking something could cause emotions from it, such as curiosity, but usually like is one of the stronger emotions. You could say that the two are

directly proportional, the more you like something, the more it is going to cause feeling.

The difference between emotions, feelings and thoughts is that you know what thoughts are about, but you don't have as good an idea of what emotions and feelings are, as they are more obscure and harder to identify. Thus once you find out what is causing the emotion, it is no longer an emotion, but it is a thought (that is, you now call the emotion a thought, so the thought is still probably generating emotion. When you identify an emotion, it is a thought because thoughts can generate emotions, so if the emotion is still there after you identified it you would say it falls under the category "thought", because the thought is making it. Therefore, emotional things are really any feelings that cause unconscious or conscious thought. Feeling is also another word for unconscious thought. That then leads to the conclusion that thought can be emotional (because thoughts are going to be about things that can cause emotion).

Since emotion is all your feelings being affected at once, emotions are stronger than feelings. Feelings however are a more directed focus. When you feel something you can always identify what that one thing is. When you have an emotion, the emotion is more distant, but stronger. All your feelings must feel a certain way about whatever is causing the emotion. So that one thing is affecting your entire system. Feelings can then be defined as immediate unconscious thought and emotions as unconscious thought.

CHAPTER 10 SUMMARY

Motivation and emotion go hand in hand. Motivation is what motivates us and makes us strive towards our set goals and emotion is how we react when we have succeeded in meeting our goals, or when we are not quite able to reach the goal we had originally set for ourselves.

THE EVOLUTIONARY APPROACH:

The evolutionary approach emphasizes the role of instincts in motivation. An **instinct** is an innate (unlearned) biological pattern of behavior that is assumed to be universal throughout a species. According to evolutionary psychologists, if we can understand the roots of the people that went before us it paints a pretty good picture of the pattern that takes place down generations. However human behavior is far too complex to map a pattern from people in the past to determine actions were done my instinct.

DRIVE REDUCTION THEORY:

The drive reduction theory states that motivation and emotion can be explained by these two present things: A **drive** is an aroused state that occurs because of a physiological need. A **need** is a deprivation that energizes the drive to eliminate or reduce the deprivation. Drive reduction theory explains that as a drive becomes stronger, we are motivated to reduce it. The goal of drive reduction is **homeostasis,** the body's tendency to maintain equilibrium, or a steady state.

OPTIMUM AROUSAL THEORY:

Psychologists are generally referring to a person's feelings of being alert and engaged when they refer to this theory. When we are very excited, our arousal levels are high. When we are bored, they are low. Thus, when we are motivated to do something we do it and try to do it well and when we are not motivated to do something we do not do it. **Yerkes-Dodson law:** performance is best under conditions of moderate arousal rather than either low or high arousal.

THE BIOLOGY OF HUNGER:

GASTRIC SIGNALS: A growling stomach needs food. The stomach tells the brain not only how full it is but also how much nutrient is present, which is why rich food stops hunger faster than the same amount of water.

BLOOD CHEMISTRY: Glucose (blood sugar) is an important factor in hunger, probably because the brain critically depends on sugar for energy. So do other factors such as insulin and leptin.

BRAIN PROCESSES: The lateral hypothalamus is involved in stimulating eating. When this area is electrically stimulated in a well-fed animal, the animal begins to eat.

OBESITY

There are two main factors to obesity the biological and the psychological. Te biological states that obesity has a genetic component and the psychological:Psychologists used to think that obesity stemmed from factors such as unhappiness and external food cues

EMOTIONS

Biological Factors in Emotion-The body is a crucial part of our emotional experience. There are many different factors that control one's emotional factors. For instance, if your mom or dad tells you "we need to talk," you could automatically assume you did something wrong or are in trouble, when they really may just want to ask you what you did at school that day. Depending on the body language or verbal cues the person speaking to you uses, you may or may not know if what they want to talk to you about will have a positive or negative outcome. If you are nervous that your parents want to talk to you and you think you might be in trouble, your body may move through a vast array of emotions, such as fear, anticipation, worry, and disappointment. However, if you realize you weren't getting into trouble after all, your body may go through an array of more positive emotions, such as relief, happiness, and joy.

The sympathetic nervous system is responsible for rapid reactions to different stressors. During the "fight or flight" response, the sympathetic nervous system increases your blood pressure, makes your heart rate speed up, makes you breathe more rapidly, and causes you to have more efficient blood flow to the brain and all major muscles. These changes help prepare our body for action.

The parasympathetic nervous system is responsible for calming the body. When the parasympathetic nervous system is activated, your heart rate and blood pressure drop, your stomach activity and food digestion increases, and your breathing slows down. These changes help promote relaxation and healing.

Behavioral Factors in Emotion-The behavioral component in emotions can be verbal or nonverbal. Verbal components could include telling someone you love them, telling someone you dislike them, or telling your best friend how much they mean to you. Nonverbal components include showing someone you care about them by giving them a hug, smiling when someone does something nice for you, or frowning when someone does something you don't like. Different facial expressions we use can influence and reflect emotions. Our facial muscles send signals to the brain that help us recognize different emotions we are experiencing. For example, when we smile, we feel happier and when we frown, we feel sadder. Thanks to James-Lange's theory of emotion, we know that emotional experiences can be generated by changes in the awareness of our bodily states.

Cognitive Factors in Emotion-Cognitive theories of emotion center around the premise that emotion always has a cognitive component. Thinking is responsible for feelings of love, hate, joy, and sadness.

The two-factor theory of emotion was developed by Stanley Schachter and Jerome Singer. The two-factor theory of emotion states that emotion is determined by two factors: physiological arousal and cognitive labeling. We interpret external cues and label the emotion. For instance, if you feel good after someone has given you a compliment, you can label the emotion as «happy.»

Sociocultural Factors in Emotion-Charles Darwin stated that "Facial expressions of human beings are innate, not learned; are the same in all cultures of the world; and have evolved from the emotions of animals." Today, psychologists still believe emotions, especially facial expressions of emotion, have strong biological ties. Paul Ekman's observations observed that the many faces we use to show emotion do not differ significantly from culture to culture. People from all different cultures have been observed to accurately label emotions that lie behind facial expressions. Even though facial expressions for basic emotions are universal for all cultures, display rules for emotion vary between cultures. Display rules are sociocultural standards that determine when, where, and how emotions should be expressed. For example, happiness may be a universally expressed emotion, but when, where, and how it should be displayed varies between different cultures.

The Adaptive Functions of Emotions-Everyone show emotions such as happiness, sadness, fear, and anger. Emotions are a huge part of daily life between human beings. Negative emotions indicate that something is wrong and that a person must take action to combat the problem. Positive emotions, however, do not signal that there is anything wrong, thus there is no problem to fix. Because of Barbara Fredrickson's "broaden-and-build model" of positive emotion, we know that the function of positive emotions lies in their effects on an individual's attention and ability to build resources. For instance, positive moods, such as humor, enjoyment, and contentment, have been shown to broaden a human's attentional focus, thus allowing us to see things for how they really are, instead of just making broad assumptions.

HEALTH, STRESS, AND COPING MANAGEMENT OF PSYCHOLOGICAL AND HEALTH PROBLEMS

LEARNING OBJECTIVES

After completing Chapter 11, students should be able to:

- Briefly summarize the history of health psychology.
- Defend the proposition that lifestyle choices and health-compromising behaviors are major determinants of early mortality.
- Describe four approaches for why people engage in positive and/or negative health habits.
- Outline the key issues regarding obesity as a health disorder.
- Describe the underlying factors that are thought to contribute to cigarette smoking.
- Explain why alcoholism represents a health issue and explain how this issue is treated.
- Describe the health consequences of alcoholism.
- Describe the factors that act as barriers to health promotion.
- Define stress and describe its principal causes.
- List at least three forms of stressors.
- Sketch the relationship between response to stress and overall physical health.
- Contrast problem-focused coping with emotion-focused coping mechanisms in dealing with stress.
- Describe the interaction of social support and stress.

INTRODUCTION

In today's fast paced world, everyone is exposed to innumerable pressures to cope with some problem that causes stress. Sometimes, you may feel that the pressures are just too much to deal with. You feel stressed. Stress is your physical and emotional reaction to pressures inside and outside your home. Therefore, stress is very personal, depending on your level of tolerance to the stressful scenarios that you have to cope with. Your stress level and tolerance also depend on how you react to situations and things around you. In fact, each individual probably has his or her own personal stress gauge. This is the reason why the signs and symptoms of stress vary from one person to another. What is important to know, however, is what you can do about stress.

Stress: A Motivation or Emotion?

In the everyday usage of the word, motivation is defined as "a sense of need, desire, fear etc., that prompts an individual to act", and emotion is defined as "a strong feeling often accompanied by a physical reaction" (Webster's Dictionary, 1988). But in the field of psychology, both motivation and emotion are hypothetical constructs, processes which cannot be directly observed or studied. Motivation is thought of as a process that both energizes and directs goal-oriented behavior, as where emotions are subjective experiences, feelings that accompany motivational states (Weber, 1991). I believe that stress is primarily a process of motivation since it requires some sort of adaptation (coping) to the demand or set of demands. On the other hand, the emotions that we experience due to stress can also be studied. This does relate stress to emotions, but stress in itself is not considered a particular emotion. For example, one could experience different kinds of emotions due to stress, such as that of anger, anticipation, and fear.

STRESS DEFINED

At one time or another, everyone will experience some form of stress, positive or negative. The term stress has been used to describe a variety of negative feelings and reactions that accompany threatening or challenging situations. However, not all stress reactions are negative. A certain amount of stress is actually necessary for survival. For example, birth is one of the most stressful experiences of life. The high level of hormones released during birth, which are also involved in the stress response, are believed to prepare the newborn infant for adaptation to the challenges of life outside the womb. These biological responses to stress make the newborn more alert promoting the bonding process and, by extension, the child's physical survival. The stress reaction maximizes the expenditure of energy which helps prepare the body to meet a threatening or challenging situation and the individual tends to mobilize a great deal of effort in order to deal with the event. Both the sympathetic/adrenal and pituitary/adrenal systems become activated in response to stress. The sympathetic system is a fast-acting system that allows us to respond to the immediate demands of the situation by activating and increasing arousal. The pituitary/adrenal system is slower-acting and prolongs the aroused state. However, while a certain amount of stress is necessary for survival, prolonged stress can affect health adversely (Bernard & Krupat, 1994).

Stress has generally been viewed as a set of neurological and physiological reactions that serves an adaptive function (Franken, 1994). Traditionally, stress research has been oriented toward studies involving the body's reaction to stress and the cognitive processes that influence the perception of stress. However, social perspectives of the stress response have noted that different people experiencing similar life conditions are not necessarily affected in the same manner (Pearlin, 1982). Research into the societal and cultural influences of stress may make it necessary to re-examine how stress is defined and studied.

There are a number of definitions of stress as well as number of events that can lead to the experience of stress. People say they are stressed when they take an examination, when having to deal with a frustrating work situation, or when experiencing relationship difficulties. Stressful situations can be viewed as harmful, as threatening, or as challenging. With so many factors that can contribute to stress it can be difficult to define the concept of "stress". Hans Selye (1982) points out that few people define the concept of stress in the same way or even bother to attempt a clear-cut definition. According to Selye, an important aspect of stress is that a wide variety of dissimilar situations are capable of producing the stress response such as fatigue, effort, pain, fear, and even success. This has led to several definitions of stress, each of which highlights different aspects of stress. One of the most comprehensive models of stress is the Biopsychosocial Model of Stress (Bernard & Krupat, 1994). According to the Biopsychosocial Model of Stress, stress involves three components: an external component, an internal component, and the interaction between the external and internal components.

Events that involve very strong demands and are imminent tend to be seen as stressful (Kelly and Lazarus, 1983).

Life transitions tend to be stressful (Moos and Schaefer, 1986). Changing from one phase to another in life is called a transition; examples include:

- Starting school
- Moving home
- Reaching puberty
- Starting college, especially away from home
- Starting a career
- Getting married
- Becoming a parent
- Losing a spouse through divorce or death
- Retiring.
- Economic Depression
- Economic Recession
- Unemployment
- Loss of a Home

Becoming a parent can be stressful before and after the birth (Miller and Sollie, 1986). Before birth there is the physiological burden of pregnancy on the mother's body and concern about the babies and mothers health. After birth, stress can result from the parents feeling tied down, having a less orderly and predictable lifestyle, and having their sleep interrupted often, among other things.

The timing of a life transition can affect the stress it produces. If a life events occur as at a time when it is not expected then this is stressful. One reason could be that having an event too early or too late could mean that one is deprived of the support of peers. An example of this would be having a baby at the age of 38 or later. Achieving life events late in life could be seen as failing. Some people who graduated late or were promoted late in life feel as though they have failed.

Ambiguity can cause stress. Two types of ambiguity are:

1. Role ambiguity
2. Harm ambiguity.

Role ambiguity can occur in the workplace, for instance when there are no clear guidelines, standards for performance and no clear consequences. Role ambiguity is stressful because people are uncertain about what actions and decisions to make.

Harm ambiguity occurs when people are not sure what to do to avoid harm. Stress will depend upon the person's personality, beliefs and general experience (Lazarus and Folkman, 1984). A person who is seriously ill and has no clear information might draw hope from this ambiguity, believing that they will get well. Another person in the same situation may believe that people are deliberately giving ambiguous information because the prognosis is poor.

The desirability of the situation is also another important factor. An event like losing your home is undesirable and therefore stressful. Buying and selling a house could be because one is moving to a more desirable house but still there will be many demands that tax or exceed the individuals resources. Many of life's events, whether desirable or undesirable, can produce stress (for example getting a parking ticket or preparing to throw party). Generally, undesirable events are more likely to be appraised as stressful (McFarlane et al., 1980)

Controllability is another factor that will affect the perception of stress. People tend to appraise uncontrollable events as being more stressful than controllable events (Miller, 1979). There are two types of control:

1. Behavioral
2. Cognitive.

Behavioral control means performing some action. For example, being unable to take a tablet for a headache will make experiencing a headache less stressful. In the case of **cognitive** control, we can affect the impact of the events by using some mental strategy, such as distraction or by developing a plan to overcome the problem.

TYPES OF STRESS

Distress

For example, you may experience a high level of stress (distress) if you awaken in the middle of the night, hear a noise and think that someone is breaking into your home. You might have goose bumps, your heart might pound fast and you might find yourself sweating profusely. You believe that there is danger, so you experience distress (fear, anxiety, physical symptoms, etc.) This can happen, even if the noise was your neighbor's cat knocking over a garbage can. The *definition of stress* changes when you talk about **distress**. When you experience a lot of stress and you don't cope well with it, you experience **distress**, the kind of stress that most of us already know about. Distress can lead to anxiety, withdrawal, depression, and even to physical problems—if it isn't handled well and it continues for a long time.

Eustress

Eustress enhances function. It helps you emotionally, mentally or physically. You can experience positive stress when you go through strength training or when you take on a challenging assignment at work. Let's see how the same situation could produce eustress. You awaken in the middle of the night, hear a noise and remember that your husband, who was away on a business trip, would be coming in late. You are anxious to see him and tell him some good news that you learned today. You quickly put on your robe and slippers and go to meet him. Eustress enhances function. It helps you emotionally, mentally or physically. You can experience positive stress when you go through strength training or when you take on a challenging assignment at work. Eustress enhances function. It helps you emotionally, mentally or physically. You can experience positive stress when you go through strength training or when you take on a challenging assignment at work.

CAUSES OF STRESS

The causes of stress are known as ***stressors*** and there are literally hundreds of different types of stressors. Any event in life that a person finds threatening, difficult to cope with or causes excess pressure can be a potential cause of stress. It is important to bear in mind that stress is an individualistic, subjective experience and therefore what one person finds stressful another may not. Stressors can be broken down roughly into either external or internal (or a mixture of both.)

Here are some examples of events that you and someone else might interpret or handle in different ways. Your experience will determine whether each event will be positive or negative for you:

- Falling in love
- Marriage
- Childbirth
- Riding a roller coaster
- Winning a race
- Speaking in front of a group

- Getting a promotion and a raise
- Watching a suspenseful movie
- Moving to a new home and a new city
- Holidays and getting together with family
- Starting a new business
- Going to a job interview
- A challenging project at work

Work and Stress

In a study of 46,000 workers, health care costs were 147% higher in workers who were stressed or depressed than in others who were not. Furthermore, according to one survey, 40% of American workers describe their jobs as very stressful, making job-related stress an important and preventable health hazard.

Several studies are now suggesting that job-related stress is as great a threat to health as smoking or not exercising. Stress impairs concentration, causes sleeplessness, and increases the risk for illness, back problems, accidents, and lost time from work. Work stress can lead to harassment or even violence while on the job. At its most extreme, chronic stress places a burden on the heart and circulation that in some cases may be fatal. The Japanese even have a word for sudden death due to overwork, *karoushi*.

Not all work stress is harmful. However, studies suggest the following job-related stressors may increase people's -- particularly men's -- health risks:

- Having no say in decisions that affect one's responsibilities
- Unrelenting and unreasonable performance demands
- Lack of effective communication and conflict-resolution methods among workers and employers
- Lack of job security
- Night-shift work, long hours, or both
- Too much time spent away from home and family
- Wages not matching levels of responsibility

Reducing Stress on the Job. Many institutions within the current culture, while paying lip service to stress reduction, put intense pressure on individuals to behave in ways that increase tension. Yet, there are numerous effective management tools and techniques available to reduce stress. Furthermore, treatment for work-related stress has proven benefits for both the employee and employer. In one study, at the end of 2 years, a company that instituted a stress management program saved nearly $150,000 in workers compensations costs (the cost of the program was only $6,000). Other studies have reported specific health benefits resulting from workplace stress-management programs. In one of the studies, workers with hypertension experienced reduced blood pressure after even a brief (16-hour) program that helped them manage stress behaviorally.

In general, however, few workplaces offer stress management programs, and it is usually up to the employee to find their own ways to reduce stress. Here are some suggestions:

- Seek out someone in the Human Resources department or a sympathetic manager and communicate concerns about job stress. Work with them in a non-confrontational way to improve working conditions, letting them know that productivity can be improved if some of the pressure is off.
- Establish or reinforce a network of friends at work and at home.
- Restructure priorities and eliminate unnecessary tasks.
- Learn to focus on positive outcomes.
- If the job is unendurable, plan and execute a career change. Send out resumes or work on transfers within the company.
- If this isn't possible, be sure to schedule daily pleasant activities and physical exercise during free time. It may be helpful to keep in mind that bosses are also victimized by the same stressful conditions they are imposing. For example, in one study of male managers in three Swedish companies, those who worked in a bureaucracy

had greater stress-related heart risks than those who worked in companies with social supports.

Problems at work are more strongly associated with health complaints than are any other life stressor-more so than even financial problems or family problems.[5] Many studies suggest that psychologically demanding jobs that allow employees little control over the work process increase the risk of cardiovascular disease, hypertension, and muscular disorders. High levels of stress are associated with substantial increases in health service utilization.

There are four Main physiological reactions to stress:

- Blood is shunted to the brain and large muscle groups, and away from extremities, skin, and organs that are not currently serving the body.
- An area near the brain stem, known as the reticular activating system, goes to work, causing a state of keen alertness as well as sharpening of hearing and vision.
- Energy-providing compounds of glucose and fatty acids are released into the bloodstream.
- The immune and digestive systems are temporarily shut down.

Job stress results from the interaction of the worker and the conditions of work. Views differ on the importance of worker characteristics versus working conditions as the primary cause of job stress. The differing viewpoints suggest different ways to prevent stress at work. According to one school of thought, differences in individual characteristics such as personality and coping skills are very important in predicting whether certain job conditions will result in stress. This viewpoint underlies prevention strategies that focus on workers and ways to help them cope with demanding job conditions.

A person's status in the workplace can also affect levels of stress. While workplace stress has the potential to affect employees of all categories; those who have very little influence to those who make major decisions for the company. However, less powerful employees (that is, those who have less control over their jobs) are more likely to suffer stress than powerful workers. Managers as well as other kinds of workers are vulnerable to work overload (Primm, 2005).

Economic factors that employees are facing in the 21st century have been linked to increased stress levels. Researchers and social commentators have pointed out that the computer and communications revolutions have made companies more efficient and productive than ever before. This boon in productivity however, has caused higher expectations and greater competition, putting more stress on the employee (Primm, 2005).

The following economic factors may lead to workplace stress:

- Pressure from investors, who can quickly withdraw their money from company stocks.
- The lack of trade and professional unions in the workplace.
- Inter-company rivalries caused by the efforts of companies to compete globally
- The willingness of companies to swiftly lay off workers to cope with changing business environments.
- Bullying in the workplace can also contribute to stress

Parental Stress

Parental stress, especially in mothers, is a particularly powerful source of stress in children, even more important than poverty or overcrowding. Young children of mothers who are highly stressed (particularly if they were depressed) tend to be at high risk for developing stress-related problems. This may be especially true if the mothers were stressed during both the child's infancy and early years. Some evidence even supports the old idea that stress during pregnancy can have adverse effects on the infant's mood and behavior. Older children with stressed mothers may become aggressive and anti-social. Another study suggested that stress-reduction techniques in parents may improve their children's behavior.

Gender Differences in Adolescent Stress

Adolescent boys and girls experience equal amounts of stress, but the source and effects may differ. Girls tend to become stressed from interpersonal situations, and stress is more likely to lead to depression in girls than in boys. For boys, however, specific events, such as changing schools or getting poor grades, appear to be the major sources of stress.

Caregiving

Caregivers of Family Members. Studies show that caregivers of physically or mentally disabled family members are at risk for chronic stress. One study reported that overall mortality rates were over 60% higher in caregivers who were under constant stress. Spouses caring for a disabled partner are particularly vulnerable to a range of stress-related health threats, including influenza, depression, heart disease, and even poorer survival rates. Caring for a spouse with even minor disabilities can induce severe stress.

Specific risk factors that put caregivers at higher risk for severe stress, or stress-related illnesses, include:

- Caregiving wives: Some studies suggest that wives experience significantly greater stress from caregiving than husbands do.
- Having a low income.
- Being African-American: African-Americans tend to be in poorer physical health, and have

lower incomes, than Caucasians. They therefore face greater stress as caregivers to their spouses than their white counterparts.
- Living alone with the patient.
- Helping a highly dependent patient.
- Having a difficult relationship with the patient.

Intervention programs that are aimed at helping the caregiver approach the situation positively can reduce stress, and help the caregiver maintain a positive attitude. A 2002 program also demonstrated that moderate-intensity exercise was very helpful in reducing stress and improving sleep in caregivers.

MODELS OF STRESS

Biological Models of Stress

Stress has both physiological and psychological components. We respond to external events or even imagined events with a generalized set of responses called **General Adaptation Syndrome** or the **stress response**, but our responses are to some degree tailored to the nature of the event. The fight or flight response is designed for response to acute (or short-term) stressors, however many of the stressors that affect modern man may be chronic in nature. Hans Selye developed the General Adaptation Syndrome model to describe the effect of chronic stressors on the body. The first stage of the model is the alarm phase. This is where the fight or flight response is activated causing the organism's ability to resist the stressor to increase. In the resistance phase, the body starts to adapt to the existence of a chronic stressor. In the exhaustion phase the body's resources become depleted, and body systems start to deteriorate.

Selye was an endocrinologist who spent much of his life studying the stress response. He noticed that both good news and bad news stimulated this general response calling negative stress distress and positive stress eustress. Selye saw stress as a generic response which occurred in reaction to any stressor (1974).

Cannon originally found this response in animals, but it was later found to also present in humans. The fight or flight response describes the way mammals respond to a threat. When our ancestors were walking through the jungle, and they came across a threat they needed to decide very quickly if they should fight or run away. The fight or flight response prepares the body almost instantly for these actions.

The Fight or Flight Response

The first stage of the fight or flight response is activation of the sympathetic nervous system. This causes a system-wide response. Adrenaline and nor-adrenaline are released leading to increased alertness. Blood is diverted from the internal organs and the skin to skeletal muscles. The heart-rate, force of heart contractions, and respiratory rate are increased. The body begins to convert stored glycogen into glucose. All of these changes allow the body to exert a large amount of energy over a short period of time so that the individual may either fight effectively, or run away effectively.

One well-known phenomena which has its roots in the fight or flight response is the reporting of people lifting cars off their loved ones after a car accident. The amount of energy that such a task demands seems inconceivable to most people, and indeed it would be without the fight or flight response.

The Relaxation Response

In 1976 a medical researcher called Herbert Benson in his studies of transcendental meditation practitioners discovered what he called the relaxation response (Payne, 2005). This is the direct opposite of the fight or flight response. The relaxation response is mediated by the parasympathetic nervous system, which is also called the resting and digesting system. It works in opposition to the fight or flight response by decreasing heart rate, force of contraction, rate of respiration, and diverting blood away from skeletal muscles to the internal organs, therefore stimulating digestion.

The Autonomic Nervous System

Both the fight or flight response and the relaxation response are mediated by the autonomic nervous system which is composed of the sympathetic nervous system and the parasympathetic nervous system. These branches of the nervous system are like the yin and the yang of our being. Their relative levels of stimulation dictate whether we are alert or lethargic, and an appropriate balance between the two systems is essential for our good health and functioning.

A Psychological Model

Twenty years after Selye developed his General Adaptation Syndrome model of stress, Cox and MacKay redefined stress as a psychological phenomena. Stress is "a perceptual phenomenon arising from a comparison between the demand on the person and his ability to cope. An imbalance…gives rise to the experience of stress and to the stress response" (Cox & MacKay, 1976)

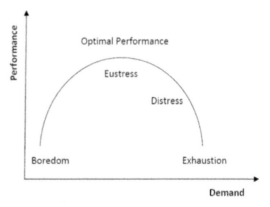

According to this model, demands placed on an individual result in an increase in performance. There is a point however where optimal performance is reached, and further demands will act to decrease an individual's performance. This relationship is sometimes illustrated by the human performance curve (shown to the right). The most interesting implication of this model is that it's not so much the actual demands that are significant, it's how we perceive these demands and our ability to cope with them. A person who perceives their ability to cope as weak will experience more stress & vice-versa.

Another interesting implication is that mental wellbeing comes from having an ideal level of stimulation. When we say we are stressed, we really mean that we are under more stress than we can handle. The only time that we are completely free from stress is at death (Payne, 2005). Psychological stressors are the most common stressors in modern life. Stress caused by worrying about things that may never happen such as losing a job, or our loved ones being hurt is much more common than actually being in a situation where we are physically threatened.

Effects of Stress on the Body

The human body is designed to experience stress and react to it. Stress can be positive, keeping us alert and ready to avoid danger. Stress becomes negative when a person faces continuous challenges without relief or relaxation between challenges. As a result, the person becomes overworked and stress-related tension builds.

Stress that continues without relief can lead to a condition called distress -- a negative stress reaction. Distress can lead to physical symptoms including headaches, upset stomach, elevated blood pressure, chest pain, and problems sleeping. Research suggests that stress also can bring on or worsen certain symptoms or diseases.

Stress also becomes harmful when people use alcohol, tobacco, or drugs to try and relieve their stress. Unfortunately, instead of relieving the stress and returning the body to a relaxed state, these substances tend to keep the body in a stressed state and cause more problems. Consider the following:

- Forty-three percent of all adults suffer adverse health effects from stress.
- Seventy-five percent to 90% of all doctor's office visits are for stress-related ailments and complaints.
- Stress can play a part in problems such as headaches, high blood pressure, heart problems, diabetes, skin conditions, asthma, arthritis, depression, and anxiety.

- The Occupational Safety and Health Administration (OSHA) declared stress a hazard of the workplace. Stress costs American industry more than $300 billion annually.
- The lifetime prevalence of an emotional disorder is more than 50%, often due to chronic, untreated stress reactions.

When we experience stress we can develop a wide variety of physical, psychological and behavioral symptoms. These symptoms are not a sign of disease because stress is not a disease; they are brought about by the body's Fight-Flight Response, which is designed to give us extra energy and speed to cope with the threat.

When under stress we may experience a pounding, speeding heart. This is not a sign of heart disease, but is in fact, caused by stress hormones stimulating the heart to pump harder and beat faster to get extra oxygen to vital muscles and organs so we can fight or run away. Once the stressful event has passed, the levels of stress hormones in our blood stream will fall again and our heart will return to its normal rhythm.

The heart and the rest of our body's organs and systems can cope with this speeding up and working harder; they are designed to be able to do this, just as a car can speed up or slow down with extra pressure on the accelerator and less pressure on the brake. Our sympathetic and parasympathetic nervous systems, which deal with the fight/flight response, work in a similar manner. Stress stimulates the sympathetic nervous system (the accelerator) and increases the levels of stress hormones in the blood stream, whereas relaxation stimulates the parasympathetic nervous system (the brake), which reduces the levels of stress hormones in the blood stream.

There are numerous signs and symptoms of stress that many are unaware of. Not everybody develops exactly the same symptoms and research has indicated that, although there are common symptoms of stress, individuals vary in the symptoms they present some of us may have mainly physical symptoms such as muscle pain/tension, others may present with symptoms such as crying or anger. Learning the signs and symptoms

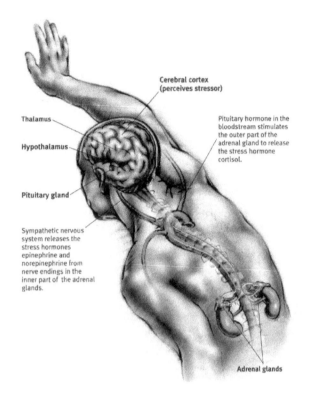

Cerebral cortex
(perceives stressor)

Thalamus

Hypothalamus

Pituitary hormone in the
bloodstream stimulates
the outer part of the
adrenal gland to release
the stress hormone
cortisol.

Pituitary gland

Sympathetic nervous
system releases the
stress hormones
epinephrine and
norepinephrine from
nerve endings in the
inner part of the adrenal
glands.

Adrenal glands

of stress can help person become more aware of the problems stress can cause stress in our lives.

Stress is difficult for scientists to define because it is a highly subjective phenomenon that differs for each of us. Things that are distressful for some individuals can be pleasurable for others. We also respond to stress differently. Some people blush, some eat more while others grow pale or eat less. There are numerous physical as well as emotional responses as illustrated by the following list of some **50 common signs and symptoms of stress**.

THEORIES OF STRESS

There are several theoretical positions devised for examining and understanding stress and stress-related disorders. Brantley and Thomason (1995) categorized them into three groups: response theories, stimulus theories, and interaction (or transaction) theories. Given the distinction made earlier between stress as a stimulus and as a response, this system serves as a

useful way to present the various theories and associated research.

Response Theories and Research

Because chronic stress responses involve actual physiological changes to body systems and organs, a good bit of attention has been paid to acute physiological stress responses and how they might possibly lead to subsequent chronic stress responses (McEwen and Stellar, 1993).

Historically, both Walter Cannon (1929) and Hans Selye (1956) provided the foundation for the current interest in this physiological process.

The Work of Walter Cannon

Cannon was a physiologist at Harvard University who was the first to use the term 'homeostasis.' According to Cannon (1929), the body possesses an internal mechanism to maintain stable bodily functioning or equilibrium. As the environment presents the organism with various challenges, the body must respond to each new situation by adjusting various physiological systems to compensate for the resources being taxed. A classic example of this type of compensation involves fluid regulation.

When an organism ingests a large amount of water, the kidney releases more waste fluid into the bladder for eventual disposal in an effort to maintain bodily equilibrium. Many of the feedback mechanisms that regulate blood pressure presented in Chapter 1 share similar characteristics with bodily systems that maintain homeostasis. According to Cannon (1935), failure of the body to respond to environmental challenges by maintaining bodily homeostasis results in damage to target organs and eventually death.

Translating his work with physical challenges associated with eating, drinking, and physical activity into those of a psychological nature, Cannon hypothesized that common homeostatic mechanisms were involved. Accordingly, if an organism's response to threat involves significant sympathetic nervous system arousal so that respiration and heart rate increase

Table 15. Fifty Common Signs and Symptoms of Stress

1. Frequent headaches, jaw clenching or pain	26. Insomnia, nightmares, disturbing dreams
2. Gritting, grinding teeth	27. Difficulty concentrating, racing thoughts
3. Stuttering or stammering	28. Trouble learning new information
4. Tremors, trembling of lips, hands	29. Forgetfulness, disorganization, confusion
5. Neck ache, back pain, muscle spasms	30. Difficulty in making decisions.
6. Light headedness, faintness, dizziness	31. Feeling overloaded or overwhelmed.
7. Ringing, buzzing or "popping sounds	32. Frequent crying spells or suicidal thoughts
8. Frequent blushing, sweating	33. Feelings of loneliness or worthlessness
9. Cold or sweaty hands, feet	34. Little interest in appearance, punctuality
10. Dry mouth, problems swallowing	35. Nervous habits, fidgeting, feet tapping
11. Frequent colds, infections, herpes sores	36. Increased frustration, irritability, edginess
12. Rashes, itching, hives, "goose bumps"	37. Overreaction to petty annoyances
13. Unexplained or frequent "allergy" attacks	38. Increased number of minor accidents
14. Heartburn, stomach pain, nausea	39. Obsessive or compulsive behavior
15. Excess belching, flatulence	40. Reduced work efficiency or productivity
16. Constipation, diarrhea	41. Lies or excuses to cover up poor work
17. Difficulty breathing, sighing	42. Rapid or mumbled speech
18. Sudden attacks of panic	43. Excessive defensiveness or suspiciousness
19. Chest pain, palpitations	44. Problems in communication, sharing
20. Frequent urination	45. Social withdrawal and isolation
21. Poor sexual desire or performance	46. Constant tiredness, weakness, fatigue
22. Excess anxiety, worry, guilt, nervousness	47. Frequent use of over-the-counter drugs
23. Increased anger, frustration, hostility	48. Weight gain or loss without diet
24. Depression, frequent or wild mood swings	49. Increased smoking, alcohol or drug use
25. Increased or decreased appetite	50. Excessive gambling or impulse buying

significantly, the body's compensatory response should involve either reducing sympathetic nervous system activity or increasing parasympathetic nervous system counter-activity.

If the compensatory response is inadequate, tissue damage can result, placing the organism at a greater risk for subsequent medical problems associated with the damaged tissue.

In brief, the concept of homeostasis introduced by Cannon has proved to be very valuable in explaining how acute physiological stress responses to threats of survival lead toward chronic stress responses.

The Work of Hans Selye

Selye (1956) was the first investigator to use the term 'stress' to describe the problems associated with homeostasis identified by Cannon decades earlier. Although he borrowed the term from physics, he used it to describe the effects on the organism rather than the environmental stressors he examined in his empirical work.

According to Selye, the 'stress' response of the organism represented a common set of generalized physiological responses that were experienced by all organisms exposed to a variety of environmental challenges like temperature change or exposure to noise. From his perspective, the stress response was nonspecific; that is, the type of stressor experienced did not affect the pattern of response. In other words, a wide variety of stressors elicited an identical or general stress response. He termed this nonspecific response the General Adaptation Syndrome, which consisted of three stages: Alarm Reaction, Resistance, and Exhaustion.

Selye reasoned that the first stage, Alarm Reaction, involved the classic 'fight-flight' response described above. As a result, the body's physiological system dropped below optimal functioning. As the body attempted to compensate for the physiological reactions observed in the Alarm Reaction stage, the organism entered the Resistance stage. Physiological compensatory systems began working at peak capacity to resist the challenges the entire system was confronting, and according to Selye, actually raised the body's resistance to stress above homeostatic levels.

However, because this response consumed so much energy, a body could not sustain it forever. Once energy had been depleted, the organism entered the stage of Exhaustion. In this stage, resistance to environmental stressors broke down and the body became susceptible to tissue damage and perhaps even death. In Selye's terminology, the Alarm Reaction Stage was comparable to the acute stress response described above and the Exhaustion Stage was comparable to a chronic stress response.

The Work of Bruce McEwen

More recently, the historic works of Cannon and Selye that have attempted to explain how acute physiological stress responses evolved into chronic stress responses have been revisited by Bruce McEwen and colleagues (McEwen and Stellar, 1993; McEwen, 1998) at Rockefeller University. In contrast to the state of physiological equilibrium of homeostasis essential for survival that Cannon discussed, McEwen used the term 'allostasis,' referring to the body's ability to adapt to a changing environment in situations that did not challenge survival.

From his perspective, an organism that maintained a perfectly stable physiological equilibrium during a stressful encounter (a nonresponse) might be just as problematic as an organism that exhibited an exaggerated physiological response. Allostasis referred to the body's ability to adjust to a 'new steady state' in response to the environmental challenge (McEwen and Stellar, 1993).

To clarify the distinction between homeostasis and allostasis, consider two physiological parameters: body temperature and heart rate. For an organism to survive in a changing environment there exist a very narrow window of acceptable body temperatures. Even though the temperature of the environment can change 50 degrees over the course of a single day, body temperature remains constant.

Deviations from a normal temperature are met with a range of symptoms (sweating, chills) that occur as part of our body's attempt to regain homeostasis. For body temperature, homeostasis is a very important mechanism of survival. In contrast to body temperature, our body can tolerate a wide range of heart rates. When we are asleep, our heart rate drops to basal levels. When we are awake, heart rates increase substantially, and when we are engaged in aerobic exercise, heart rates climb even higher.

Rather than maintaining stability in the face of a changing environment, as body temperature does, heart rate adjusts to a changing environment to optimize functioning. In this case, the ability of the body to adjust to aerobic exercise by resetting heart rate at a higher level is called allostasis, not homeostasis. McEwen argues that most acute stress responses represent challenges to the body's allostasis, not challenges to its homeostasis.

According to the work of McEwen and colleagues, 'allostatic load' is a term that refers to the price the body pays for being challenged repeatedly by a variety of environmental stressors. Increased allostatic load, or what McEwen and Wingfield (2003) called 'allostatic overload,' occurs with increased frequency of exposure to stressors, increased intensities of these stressors, or decreased efficiency in coordinating the onset and termination of the physiological response.

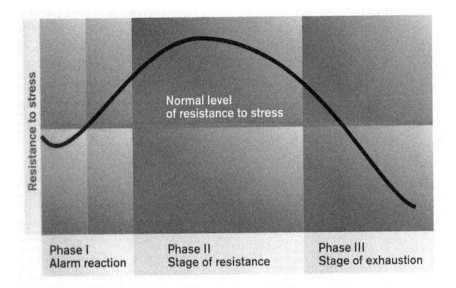

Hans Selye's General Adaptation Syndrome   T-123

McEwen (1998) outlined four distinct types of allostatic overload. In the first type, the organism is exposed to multiple environmental stressors during a short period of time. In this type of allostatic overload, the problem is associated with the frequency of the stressors encountered.

In the second form of allostatic overload, repeated stressors elicit responses that fail to habituate. Consider an example in which you are dealing with five consecutive irate customers who are demanding their money back for a defective product that you sold them. Normally, one's physiological response to this series of encounters would decrease, or habituate, with each subsequent encounter. When the body fails to exhibit the normal habituation response, this type of allostatic overload occurs.

A third form of allostatic overload involves delayed physiological recovery from a given environmental stressor. In this case, the frequency or magnitude of the physiological response may be entirely normal; however, it is the length of time that the response is sustained that leads to allostatic overload. For example, imagine having an argument with a spouse and experiencing some physiological arousal associated with the argument. Rather than the arousal gradually declining after the argument, in this type of allostatic overload the physiological recovery is delayed and the

arousal is still apparent hours or days later. What will determine the delayed overload is the content of the argument or stressor.

The final form of allostatic overload involves an inadequate physiological response. In this case, the organism encounters a stressful circumstance or environmental change, but the physiological response is either very weak or entirely absent.

According to McEwen and Stellar (1993), allostatic overload, whatever its source, is the mechanism through which acute physiological responses result in permanent tissue damage. Research using animals documents not only changes in peripheral tissues associated with increased allostatic load, but also altered functioning in the cerebral cortex (McEwen, 1998).

This altered brain functioning has included atrophy of dendrites on neurons, suppression of neurogenesis (creation and proliferation of new neurons), and permanent loss of pyramidal neurons. Obviously, McEwen and other contemporary stress researchers have extended the theories and empirical work of Cannon and Selye to further our understanding of how stress results in actual tissue damage in the brain and peripheral body systems.

Selye's (1956) General Adaptation Syndrome described below is a classic representation of a theoretical perspective that focuses upon stress as a response. In fact, Selye went so far as to state that the nature of the stimulus was irrelevant to the stress response. To support his view, he subjected animals to a wide variety of experimental conditions that elicited very similar physiologic stress responses including temperature change, pain stimulation, and exposure to infection.

Likewise, although acknowledging the importance of the stress stimulus in their theoretical models, McEwen and colleagues have also focused on the physiological stress response, paying less attention to the type or nature of the eliciting stimulus (McEwen and Stellar, 1993; McEwen, 1998).

Although response theories have contributed greatly to our understanding of the physiological response systems that mediate the relation between environmental stressors and chronic stress responses, they have typically neglected a detailed exploration of types of environmental stressors and how they might influence the disease process.

Component Analysis of Coping

The effects of stress are directly linked to coping. The study of coping has evolved to encompass large variety of disciplines beginning with all areas of psychology such as health psychology, environmental psychology, neuro psychology and developmental psychology to areas of medicine spreading into the area of anthropology and sociology. Dissecting coping strategies into three broad components, (biological/physiological, cognitive, and learned) will provide a better understanding of what the seemingly immense area is about.

Biological/physiological component—The body has its own way of coping with stress. Any threat or challenge that an individual perceives in the environment triggers a chain of neuroendocrine events. These events can be conceptualized as two separate responses, that being of sympathetic/adrenal response, with the secretion of catecholamines (epinephrine, norepinephrine) and the pituitary/adrenal response, with the secretion of corticosteroids (Frankanhauser, 1986). The sympathetic/adrenal response takes the message from the brain to the adrenal medulla via the

sympathetic nervous system, which secretes epinephrine and norepinephrine. This is the basic "fight or flight" response (Cannon, 1929), where the heart rate quickens and the blood pressure rises. In the pituitary/adrenal response, the hypothalamus is stimulated and produces the corticotrophin releasing factor (CRF) to the pituitary gland through the blood veins, then the adrenal corticotropic hormone (ACTH) is released from the pituitary gland to the adrenal cortex. The adrenal cortex in turn secretes cortisol, a hormone that will report back to the original brain centers together with other body organs to tell it to stop the whole cycle. But since cortisol is a potent hormone, the prolonged secretion of it will lead to health problems such as the breakdown of cardiovascular system, digestive system, musculoskeletal system, and the recently established immune system. Also when the organism does not have a chance for recovery, it will lead to both catecholamine and corisol depletion and result in the third stage of the General Adaptation Syndrome of exhaustion (Seyle, 1956).

Social support has also been established by studies to be linked to stress (Bolger & Eckenrole, 1991; House, et. al, 1988). This can be seen as a dimension of the biological component since it is closely linked to the biological environment of that individual. There are many aspects to social support, the major categories would be of emotional, tangible, and informational.

Personality types as so called Type A Personality have been defined to have such characteristics as competitive, impatient and hostile. Hostility has been linked to coronary heart disease which is thought be caused by stress (Rosenman, 1978). Eysenck (1988) has coined the term Type C Personality for those who are known to be repressors and are prone to cancer. Hardiness also is a personality that seems to have much to do with how an individual handles stress. Hardiness is defined as having a sense of control, commitment, and challenge towards life in general. Kobasa (1979) has studied subjects who were laid off in large numbers by AT&T when the federal deregulation took place, and found that the people who were categorized as having hardy personalities were

11

Selye's Concept of a General Adaptation Syndrome

Hans Selye (1907-1982) started the modern era of research into something called *stress*. In 1950, Selye addressed the American Psychological Association convention. He described a theory of stress-induced responses that become the standard model of stress, the one people usually refer to (or criticize) in academic journal articles about stress.

Selye's discovery of the stress response was an accident. He was doing research on the effect of hormone injections in rats. Initially he thought he detected a harmful effect from the hormones, because many of the rats became sick after receiving the injections. But when Selye used a control group of rats, injected only with a neutral solution containing no hormones, he observed that they became sick, too.

As it turned out, the rats responded more profoundly to the trauma of being injected than they did to the hormones. The experience of being handled and injected led to high levels of sympathetic nervous system arousal and eventually to health problems such as ulcers. Selye coined the term "stressor" to label a stimulus that had this effect.

The immediate response to stress is the release of adrenaline into the blood plasma (the liquid part of the bloodstream). "Mild stressors such as opening a cage door or handling a rat produces an eightfold increase in plasma epinephrine [adrenaline] concentrations" (Axelrod and Reisine, 1984). The sentence is ambiguous; does the rat or the human experience the eightfold increase in adrenaline? In this case, it is the rat which is having its adrenaline (plasma epinephrine) measured. However, many lab assistants probably experience a burst of adrenaline, too, when handling a rat for the first time.

Selye proposed a three-stage pattern of response to stress that he called the *General Adaptation Syndrome (GAS)*. He proposed that when the organism first encountered stress, in the form of novelty or threat, it responded with an *alarm reaction*. This is followed by a *recovery* or *resistance* stage during which the organism repairs itself and stores energy. If the stress-causing events continue, *exhaustion* sets in. This third stage is what became known popularly as burn-out. Classic symptoms of burn-out include loss of drive, emotional flatness, and (in humans) dulling of responsiveness to the needs of others.

mentally and emotionally better off than the others. Although it may be possible to modifying ones personality, research has shown it to be heritable (Rahe, Herrig, & Rosenman, 1978; Parker, & Barret, 1992).

Cognitive component—The cognitive approach to coping is based on a mental process of how the individual appraises the situation. Where the level of appraisal determines the level of stress and the unique coping strategies that the individual partakes. (Lazarus & Folkman, 1984). There are two types of appraisals, the primary and the secondary. A primary appraisal is made when the individual makes a conscious evaluation of the matter at hand of whether it is either a harm or a loss, a threat or a challenge. Then secondary

appraisal takes place when the individual asks him/herself "What can I do?" by evaluating the coping resources around him/her. These resources include, physical resources, such as how healthy one is, or how much energy one has, social resources, such as the family or friends one has to depend on for support in his/her immediate surroundings, psychological resources, such as self-esteem and self-efficacy, and also material resources such as how much money you have or what kind of equipment you might be able to use.

Learned component—The learned component of coping includes everything from various social learning theories, which assume that much of human motivation and behavior is the result of what is learned through experiential reinforcement, learned helplessness phenomena which is believed to have a relationship to depression, and even implications of the particular culture or society that the stress at hand is affected by can also be included in this component. Some of the examples for the social learning theories would be the wide range of stress management techniques that have been found to help ease stress. Changing how you cognitively process a particular situation, so called cognitive restructuring, changing how you behave in a particular situation, so called behavior modification, biofeedback which uses operant conditioning to alter involuntary responses mediated by the autonomic nervous system, and the numerous relaxation techniques such as meditation, breathing, and exercise are all part of what is learned through experiential reinforcement. The learned helplessness phenomena has been linked to depression by such researchers as Coyne, Aldwin, and Lazarus (1981) when they studied subjects who tried to exert control when it was not possible to do so.

Cultures and societies have their own set of rule of what they perceive to be stressful or not (Colby, 1987). For example, educational systems differ greatly from culture to culture. In Asian cultures such as Japan and Korea, there is a great deal of importance attributed to how they do in schools. Access to higher education, leading to better jobs is determined solely through academic performance. The amount of stress that the students experience due to this is very high. High enough to report a number of suicides each year for not passing an important exam. People will have different responses in a monogamous culture to that of a polygamous culture. In Africa, where polygamy is the norm, when they find out that the significant other has another partner, it means more workforce to take care of the children and the household chores. If the husband does not take on many wives, it can become a strain on the rest of the wives. An interesting study was done by using Holmes and Rahe's (1967) stressful life event measure in South Africa, and found that it correlated very little with standard distress measures (Swartz, Elk, & Teggin, 1983). This suggests the existence of such cultural/societal differences.

BIOLOGICAL PATHWAYS OF STRESS

Effects of Stress on the Brain

So you know that stress has negative effects on your body, right? But did you also know that the effects of stress on the brain can be equally as damaging Yes, stress can kill the brain. Researchers found that at high levels, the hormones released during stress response, cortisol, and in particular glucocorticoids, kill brain cells in experimental animals. Researchers believe that the same happens in humans.

Prolonged exposure to glucocorticoids also seems to reduce the brain's ability to create new connections to new brain cells and re-route connections to other brain cells. This problem is mostly seen in the area of hippocampus—part of brain that controls memory.

Brain scans of people who have suffered long term stress—children who have been abused, and Vietnam veterans with post traumatic stress disorder—show that their hippocampus has shrunk.

Their ability to plan, concentrate, learn quickly, think ahead and act decisively has been compromised as a result of long term flood of stress hormones into the body and brain.

These **brain chemicals, elicited by the fight-fight response, in turn, cause the following** to occur:

1. Acceleration of heart rate
2. Dilation of coronary arteries
3. Dilation of bronchial tubes
4. Increase in force of heart contractions
5. Increase in rate of metabolism
6. Increase in anxiety
7. Increase in gastrointestinal motility
8. Increase in rate and depth of respiration
9. Decrease in feeling of tiredness
10. Decrease in Salvation (dry mouth)
11. Dilation of pupils

Walter Cannon (1929) describes the **fight or flight** response of the body after perceiving danger or stress. This response mobilizes the organism to respond quickly to danger but the state of higher arousal can be harmful to health if it is prolonged.

General Adaptation Syndrome

Selye (1956) observed in laboratory animals and in human patients the body's reaction to stress. He found that the fight or flight response was only the first in a series of reactions, which he called the general adaptation syndrome (GAS). The GAS consists of three stages:

1. Alarm reaction
2. Stage of resistance
3. Stage of exhaustion.

The **alarm** reaction is like the fight or flight response to an emergency. The body is mobilized. At the beginning of the arousal blood pressure drops below normal for a moment, but then quickly rises to above normal. This arousal is produced by the release of hormones by the endocrine system: the pituitary glands secrete ACTH, which causes a heightened release of adrenaline, noradrenaline, and cortisol by the adrenal glands into the bloodstream. The body cannot stay in this state for long without serious consequences. Some organisms in a continuous state of alarm have died within hours or days

Stage of resistance. If the reaction continues and is not strong enough to cause death the physiological reaction enters the stage of resistance. The body tries to adapt to the stressor. Physiological arousal declines but remains higher than normal and the body replenishes the hormones released by the adrenal glands. The organism may show few outward signs of stress. However, the body may not be able to resist new stresses. The body becomes increasingly vulnerable to health problems. These health problems include ulcers, high blood pressure, asthma, and illnesses that result from impaired immune function.

Stage of exhaustion. Severe long-term or repeated stress will cause the organism to enter the third stage, the stage of exhaustion. The immune system and the body's energy reserves are weakened until resistance is very limited. If the stress continues, disease and physiological damage become increasingly likely and death may result.

Impact of Stress on Health

Stress is thought to be an important factor in many health problems. Early stress researchers found that regardless of the environmental stressor, a generalized physiological response was activated in the organism **called the "fight or flight," or stress response** and termed the General Adaptation Syndrome by Hans Selye. When an individual encounters a stressor, the body part that first notes the stimulus passes the signal to the brain. The message passes through the reticular activating system to the hypothalamus and thalamus. When the hypothalamus experiences the stressor signal, it simultaneously activates the two major stress pathways: the autonomic nervous system and the endocrine system. When the sympathetic part of the autonomic nervous system is activated by the hypothalamus, involuntary functions such as heart rate, blood pressure, respiration, and body fluid regulation are affected. At the same time, the pituitary gland is stimulated, which in turn orders the release of several chemical hormones. The chemical cortisol provides fuel for the "fight or flight" response by increasing blood sugar so that there is energy for action. Aldosterone increases the blood pressure. Epinephrine (adrenaline) and norepinephrine are also produced, along with thyroxine.

The physical problems related to chronic stress include the lowering of the immune response, chronic muscle tension, and increased blood pressure. These problems can eventually lead to serious life-threatening illnesses such as heart attacks, kidney disease, and cancer. Holmes and Rahe and others have found that individuals who have undergone several stressful life events over a year's time have a much higher probability of developing these types of serious illness, within a few years of the events, than non-stressed individuals. During the middle 1970s, research by Mason et al. And Lazarus demonstrated that vast individual differences exist in how individuals respond to stress-producing stimuli.

Some health problems that may be caused by stress

• diarrhea	• colds	• high blood
• nausea	and sinus	pressure
• indigestion	infections	• heart
• sphincter	• vaginal yeast	disease
of Oddi	infection	• hyperventi-
spasms	• bladder	lation
• spastic colon	infections	• asthma
• irri-	• fiber myalgia	• headaches
table bowel	• arthritis	• migraines
syndrome		
• constipation		

Some individuals react with the "fight or flight" response, whereas other individuals either suppress the response or do not react to it at all. To accommodate the individual differences in the activation of the stress response, the concept of cognition was proposed. In other words, the **thought process of the individual in response to the stressor is considered important. What might be perceived as a stressor by one person might not be seen as a stressor by another.** As an example, if a professor announces a surprise quiz, student "A" might then experience extreme anxiety and the fight-flight response. Student "B" may experience no activation. This could occur because student "A" had never reviewed the notes from the class while student "B" had.

This concept of selectively responding to a stress stimulus was coined by Lazarus, Stensrud and Stensrud, and others as the coping theory of stress. **An individual being stimulated by a stressor appraises the stimulus to determine if it is a source of a) threat, b) loss or harm, c) challenge, or d) irrelevanc**y. If upon appraisal it is determined that the stimulus is irrelevant or harmless, no stress response is activated. However, if the stressor is seen as harmful and the stress response is activated, a coping response occurs. If the coping response, such as taking three deep breaths before beginning the speech before the large group of people, is successful, normal physiological functioning will soon resume. According to Stensrud and Stensrud, if the coping response is not successful and/or the person experiences chronic stressful arousal from a variety of stimuli, unhealthy results, including physical and psychological health problems, can occur.

According to various authors in the book The Addictive Behaviors, **individuals with compulsive disorders, including alcoholism, gambling, overeating, or smoking, often increase negative behavior, or undergo a relapse, after they have been through a stressful time period.** Herman and Polivy feel that emotional stress leads to increases in binge eating. Hooker and Convisser believe that **anger resulting from stressful situations also plays a part in some addictive disorders.** As an example, individuals who do not express anger outwardly often turn it inward. When this occurs, it may lead to depression. To relieve the discomfort they feel because they have not expressed their anger, these individuals begin to overeat or engage in other addictive behaviors. Some researchers in feel that stress contributes to addictive behaviors. Individuals begin to use the drugs as a way of relieving the anxiety and tension associated with the stress response and to feel good. **However, getting involved with substances, or any other addictive behavior, only increases the anxiety and stress, thus perpetuating a vicious circle.** Why some individuals engage in an addictive behavior or develop an illness while others do not is not known at this time. Perhaps an individual inherits a "trait" to develop a health or an addictive behavior problem. Depending upon early family and environmental influences, including ways of coping with everyday stressors, the person either learns to cope with stress in a positive manner or develops physical, emotional or addictive behavior problems.

Have you ever heard of illnesses caused by stress? You may think that health problems are the result of bacteria or viruses. What many people do not realize is that stress can also disable the body's immune system to make you more susceptible to germs in the environment. Many kinds of infirmities result from your immune system's inability to function properly. Stress, especially the unrelenting kind for which there is no relief, can play havoc with your body's ability to fight off microscopic invaders or to operate the way it is supposed to. There are many kinds of illnesses caused by stress involving both the body and the mind. Here are some of the health problems and diseases that may be related to your body's battle with stress.

1. Insomnia. Stress keeps people awake at night due to worry, anxiety, or uncertainty about the future. Some people worry about their jobs, while others are concerned over family issues or health problems. Many things in life can be stressful and stress, if left unmanaged, can interrupt or delay sleep. To combat sleeplessness caused by stress, try drinking a glass of milk before bedtime, avoid caffeine, do not exercise at least four hours before going to bed and keep your bedroom cool, dimly lit and comfortable. Do not think about stress-related problems when you get ready for bed. Instead, fill your mind with peaceful or happy thoughts to prepare for a good night's rest. Keep the television in the family room, since many violent or dramatic programs can increase stress.

- **Eating disorders.** Have you ever reached for something sweet and tasty when you felt overwhelmed by stress? You are not alone. Thousands of people react to stress by feeding an eating pattern that typically reaches for sweets or carbohydrate-laden foods for a quick sugar rush. While your blood sugar may skyrocket briefly, it is sure to plummet afterward, often leaving you feeling worse than before. If you must nibble when stress has you in its clasp, stick to crisp veggies or light butter popcorn. Fiber will make you feel full and keep you healthy, too. Don't let stress drive you to the cookie jar or candy counter. Eat a balanced diet to calm your nerves and stay on top of stressful situations.

3. Depression. Unresolved stress can make a person feel angry or hopeless, both of which can lead to depression. If you feel chronically sad, have trouble thinking clearly, feel alone or unloved, struggle with guilt or shame, chances are you are battling a serious case of depression related to stress. Illnesses caused by stress may appear unrelated, but when doctors, counselors, or the patients themselves take a closer look, often there is a cause-and-effect relationship between stress and conditions like depression. A doctor should be able to diagnose the source of the stress-related depression and prescribe appropriate treatment.

4. Anxiety and panic attacks. Like depression, anxiety disorders and panic attacks frequently have a stress-related connection. People who struggle with ongoing situations that make them feel uneasy may experience high levels of stress that can manifest in nervousness and fear, seemingly for an unknown cause. Through careful analysis, it can be discerned whether a stressful situation may be the cause for one of these disorders. If the disorders continue to occur or increase in frequency, it is a good idea to meet with a counselor or psychologist to deal with root issues.

5. Colds and viruses. Physical illnesses caused by stress may be as common as the garden variety cold or a seasonal virus. People who are stressed often have immune systems that are not functioning properly. Consequently, they can get sick faster and easier than they otherwise might. To alleviate stress that may be contributing to a prolonged cold or sickness, be sure to get plenty of rest, eat healthily and avoid worrying. Take care of your physical needs to keep your body resistant to germs, especially during the winter months.

6. Circulatory problems. Stress can make your body's arteries and veins tighten up in response to the fight-or-flight complex. This compression can reduce blood flow throughout the body and create problems like blood clots, poor circulation, or even strokes. In addition to dealing with the causes of stress with your doctor or a counselor, temporary relief may be found in a warm bath or shower, hot tea consumption, or mental relaxation therapy, such as daydreaming or positive imaging. Do not let this advice substitute for a thorough medical examination and professional diagnosis, however.

7. Systemic or local infections. Ironically, mental or emotional stress can even delay physical healing of local infections, like a bug bite, or systemic infections, like food poisoning. Stress drains the body of positive energy as it strives to cope with the demanding worry of the stress-related issues. This leaves inadequate energy to sustain bodily immune functions that heal infectious illnesses and injuries. It is important to get plenty of rest when you have an infection and try to put stress out of your mind until you are well again. Learn how to delegate tasks at work and at home so that you do not have to worry about them while trying to get well.

8. Diabetes. One of the common illnesses caused by stress is out-of-control blood sugar for diabetes patients. People with diabetes have to follow a lifestyle that keeps their blood sugar within acceptable limits. Stress can throw off the body, sending sugar levels skyrocketing or plummeting. Those with diabetes who are experiencing significant stress need to check their blood sugar routinely and take their medication consistently.

9. Heart problems. Stress can make anyone's heart palpitate wildly and increase pulse rate as well as blood pressure. Over time, serious stress can damage the heart with increased wear and tear for the reasons just mentioned. Elevated stress levels can even raise your blood cholesterol. That is why it is important to check blood pressure regularly If your blood pressure is elevated, see your doctor to find out why. If it is due to stress, take steps to deal with the underlying causes.

10. Cancer. More and more studies are showing links between stress and various types of cancer. Since stress is known to depress the body's immune system, someone who is struggling with ongoing stress may be ill equipped to battle a major illness such as cancer. Newer treatments for cancer patients include with medical treatments such innovations as relaxation therapy, musical therapy and even pet therapy, all of which can help to deflect stress associated with the disease as well as external factors.

Stress can be harder on the body than harsh physical labor. If you are concerned about contracting one of these illnesses caused by stress, take time to evaluate the factors that may be contributing anxiety to your life. If you experience symptoms for these or other illnesses, make an appointment with your doctor to get a complete examination and medical assessment. Do not let stressful situations continue to cause problems with your immune system and perhaps lead to one of the common illnesses caused by stress. Learn how to take steps now to manage stressful factors in your life before stress takes control of you.

Psychological Effects of Stress

Psychological effects of stress today are more complex than ever. We live in an increasingly complex and fast paced world. Modern civilization has created many stressors that our ancestors did not have to deal with. Daily stressors, microstressors, and major life events are often common triggers for symptoms of stress to manifest.

These symptoms manifest on both physiological and psychological levels. Physiological reactions to stress are common to all animals with a developed nervous system. But in humans, there is an added dimension of complexity—the human mind. It is our mind that leads to certain psychological effects of stress.

Some common psychological effects of stress are:

- Mood swings
- Irritability
- Resentment
- Feeling of powerlessness
- Low self esteem
- Low self worth
- Lack of interest in activities
- Cognitive effects of stress
- Effects of stress on memory

- Anxiety
- Depression
- Panic attacks
- Feeling of guilt
- Angry outbursts
- Increased cynicism
- Isolation/few close friends
- Feeling overwhelmed
- Unable to feel happy
- Feeling of hopelessness

PSYCHOSOCIAL ASPECTS OF STRESS

Cognition and Stress

A high level of stress impairs people's memory and attention during cognitive activities such as when taking examinations (Cohen et al 1986).

Noise can be a stressor, for example when people live next to a busy railway or motorway. People cope by tuning out the noise. Cohen (1980) has proposed that children who tried to tune out chronic noise may develop generalized cognitive deficits because they have difficulty knowing which sounds to attend to and which to tune out

One study tested primary school children who lived in a block of flats that was built on bridges spanning a busy highway. The children in the noisy flats had more difficulty discriminating between pairs of words (for example, house and mouse) (Cohen et al., 1973).

People living near the three mile island nuclear power plant in Pennsylvania who had difficulty in coping with the stress that was produced by the fear that the nuclear emissions would affect their health, found it difficult to keep their minds from thinking about the accident. Thoughts can perpetuate stress and make it chronic.

Social behavior and stress

In some stressful situations, such as train crashes, earthquakes, etc. people may work together to help each other survive. This could be because they have a common goal that requires co-operative efforts (Sherif & Sherif, 1953).

When stress is accompanied by anger, negative social behaviors tend to increase. **Stress-produced anger** increases aggressive behavior, and these negative effects continue after the stressful event is over. Child abuse is often related to parental stress (Kempe, 1976). Prior to a parent battering their child the parent usually has experienced a stressful crisis, such as the loss of a job. At high levels of stress the parent is at risk of losing control. If a child is running around

making a lot of noise in the house the parent could become very angry and lose control.

Stress affects **helping behavior**. An experiment was conducted in a shopping centre (Cohen & Spacapan, 1978). The subjects either had a difficult shopping task or uneasy one and the shopping centre was either crowded or uncrowded. The difficult shopping task as well as the crowded shopping centre therefore produced stress. After completing the shopping task, each subject walked through a deserted hallway to meet with the researcher. In the hallway the subjects encountered a woman who pretended to have dropped a contact lens. Subjects who had experienced a lot of stress did not help as much as those that had completed an easy shopping task in uncrowded conditions.

Personality Type and Stress Response

What's stressful to one person may be all in a day's work for another. The difference appears to lie in our perceptions of various events. Mental health professionals believe personality plays a significant role in how we perceive stress.

People with "Type A" personalities, for example, are rushed, ambitious, time-conscious and driven. Studies suggest these traits, if not properly managed, can create stress-related illnesses. In contrast, the "Type B" personality is a much more relaxed, less time-conscious and driven person. Type B personalities are able to view things more adaptively. They are better able to put things into perspective, and think through how they are going to deal with situations. Consequently they tend to be less stress-prone.

A variety of social, biological, psychological and behavioral factors influence the development of our character. Scientists agree that a largely genetic personal chemistry, or in-born temperament, influences an infant to react to its environment in ways that can be assertive or shy. Such tendencies are further influenced by experiences. The combination of inheritance and experience form an individual's characteristic way of behaving, feeling and thinking, which is personality.

Studies also show that men and women handle stress differently, a difference that some scientists attribute, in part, to estrogen. This hormonal difference may also account for the fact that women are three times more likely to develop depression in response to the stress in their lives than are men. Women, unlike men, also tend to have stronger social support networks to which they turn during times of stress. These social supports may help explain why women, in general, seem to be better able to cope with stress than men.

We all have certain features to our personality that make us unique as people; however there are many aspects of our personality that are similar to other people. These similar personality factors are called Personality Traits. Research has indicated that certain personality traits can make us more vulnerable to stress. People with such traits are known as Type A personalities. Type A's tend to be more competitive, more impatient, have time urgency when compared to the more relaxed and laid back Type B personalities. It's important to realize that we are all a mixture of type A and B personality traits but if we are excessively type A this can make us more vulnerable to stress. Examples of Type A and Type B Personality Traits are listed below:

Type A Personality Traits	Type B Personality Traits
· Must get things finished	· Do not mind leaving things unfinished for a while
· Never late for appointments	· Calm and unhurried about appointments
· Excessively competitive	· Not excessively competitive
· Can't listen to conversations, interrupt, finish other's sentences	· Can listen and let the other person finish speaking
· Always in a hurry	· Never in a hurry even when busy
· Do not like to wait	· Can wait calmly
· Very busy at full speed	· Easy going
· Trying to do more than one thing at a time	· Can take one thing at a time
· Want everything to be perfect	· Do not mind things not quite perfect
· Pressurized speech	· Slow and deliberate speech
· Do everything fast	· Do things slowly
· Hold feelings in	· Can express feelings

· Not satisfied with work/life	· Quite satisfied with work/life
· Few social activities/interests	· Many social activities/interests
· If in employment, will often take work home	· If in employment, will limit working to work hours

Personality Disorders and Stress

The difference between common stress and abnormal stress is that the symptoms of stress from a common view are temporary, while the symptoms of mental illness are ongoing. Even the so-called normal person might require medications to treat stress, but most of time when a mental illness is involved; the person will need long-term medicines.

Stress affects both the body and mind and can lead to a series of problems. Stress is a force that compels one part of the mind against another part of the mind, pulling and pushing against the positive forces or compressing emotions and thoughts. When this occurs, a person feels as though they're losing control of their life. This will often lead them to lean on their emotions to try to solve their problems.

When a person leans on the emotions within them that create anger or sadness, often leads to negative thought patterns. Now it's up to that person to decide when they've had enough and take charge by doing something to resolve their problems.

If a person fails to initiate this decision-making process in their mind and instead dwells constantly on negative emotions, then that person is subject to mental illness, providing it lingers for longer than a few weeks or even months. **What happens is stress changes the equilibrium in the brain and this applies pressure to the mind.** When the equilibrium is not reinstated, then the mind is subject to chemical imbalances, tumors, and diseases.

If the mind has a faulty area, it makes it difficult for a person to cope with their stress. This creates additional thinking patterns, including suicidal tendencies or thoughts, and consistent negative thinking. When a person feels negative or suffering and is unaware of the cause, it often creates a higher level of stress for the individual, decreasing the persons coping mechanism. However, a person may not have a disease, chemical imbalance or tumor and still suffer beyond normal stress.

Posttraumatic Stress Disorder (PTSD)

PTSD is a psychological reaction that reoccurs consistently after a person has witnessed or experienced a high level of trauma. This person will suffer anxiety attacks, depression, reoccurring nightmares, night sweats, flashbacks and they'll do everything in their power to avoid social gatherings and triggers that link their minds back to the tragedy. This person will also suffer abnormal stress on a daily basis and do everything in their power to avoid stress at the same time.

Posttraumatic Stress Disorder is a mental health issue, because this person has endured extreme trauma. This marks the person as a candidate for heart attacks, strokes, high-blood pressure and other medical related illnesses.

As you can see, there's a fine line between common stress and mental illness and stress. The levels of stress for the common society are often tolerable, while the mentally ill have to fight a million times harder to avoid stress and/or cope with stress.

If you or someone you love is suffering stress, you may want to consider stress management techniques that can benefit everyone.

The symptoms of PTSD

For many people, symptoms begin almost right away after the trauma happens. For others, the symptoms may not begin or may not become a problem until years later. Symptoms of PTSD may include:

- **Repeatedly thinking about the trauma.** You may find that thoughts about the trauma come to mind even when you don't want them to. You might also have nightmares or flashbacks about the trauma or may become upset when something reminds you of the event.
- **Being constantly alert or on guard.** You may be easily startled or angered, irritable or anxious and preoccupied with staying safe. You may also

find it hard to concentrate or sleep or have physical problems, like constipation, diarrhea, rapid breathing, muscle tension or rapid heart rate.
- **Avoiding reminders of the trauma.** You may not want to talk about the event or be around people or places that remind you of the event. You also may feel emotionally numb, detached from friends and family, and lose interest in activities.

These are other symptoms of PTSD

- **Panic attacks**: a feeling of intense fear, with shortness of breath, dizziness, sweating, nausea and racing heart.
- **Physical symptoms**: chronic pain, headaches, stomach pain, diarrhea, tightness or burning in the chest, muscle cramps or low back pain.
- **Feelings of mistrust**: losing trust in others and thinking the world is a dangerous place.
- **Problems in daily living**: having problems functioning in your job, at school, or in social situations.
- **Substance abuse**: using drugs or alcohol to cope with the emotional pain.
- **Relationship problems**: having problems with intimacy, or feeling detached from your family and friends.
- **Depression**: persistent sad, anxious or empty mood; loss of interest in once-enjoyed activities; feelings of guilt and shame; or hopelessness about the future. Other symptoms of depression may also develop.
- **Suicidal thoughts**: thoughts about taking one's own life.

Stress and Health Disease

Traditionally, stress research has been oriented toward studies involving the body's reaction to stressors (a physiological perspective) and the cognitive processes that appraise the event or situation as a stressor (a cognitive perspective). However, current social perspectives of the stress response have noted that different people experiencing similar life conditions are not necessarily affected in the same manner. There is a growing interest in the epidemiology of diseases thought to result from stress. It has been noted that the incidence of hypertension, cardiovascular ailments, and depression varies with such factors as race, sex, marital status, and income. This kind of socioeconomic variation of disease indicates that the stressors that presumably dispose people toward these illnesses are somehow linked to the conditions that people confront as they occupy their various positions and status's in the society. Pearlin (1982) observes that individuals' coping strategies are primarily social in nature. The manner in which people attempt to avoid or resolve stressful situations, the cognitive strategies that they use to reduce threat, and the techniques for managing tensions are largely learned from the groups to which they belong. Although the coping strategies used by individuals are often distinct, coping dispositions are to a large extent acquired from the social environment.

Physical Diseases

Stress-related physical illnesses are commonly referred to as psycho-physiological disorders or psychosomatic illnesses. Even though the general perception is that stress causes psychological problems, the reality is that psycho-physiological disorders and illnesses are nearly as common. Stress produces a response from the central nervous system that initiates certain actions within the body. We do not have conscious control over these actions. Continuous stress results in constant alertness, something that can adversely affect certain organs. For example, the stress response can cause the heart to beat faster, something that the blood vessels may not be able to tolerate if the pressure is maintained at high levels for a long time.

The link between stress and cardiovascular disease is fairly well known. As age advances, the fatty deposits often cause constriction in blood vessels. Prolonged stress causes high blood pressure, and a simultaneous constriction of blood vessels leads to cardiovascular problems like heart attack, stroke and even heart failure.

Other physical illnesses related to stress can differ in magnitude and seriousness. It can range to extremes; from simple fatigue after a bad night of sleep resulting from the mewing over of a stressful situation past, present or future, to the life changing event such as a heart attack or stroke. Of course, in the worst case scenario the more extreme end of the physical illnesses related to stress can be deadly. It is therefore vitally important that you take note of changes in your body and consult professional medical advice if any of these symptoms concern you.

Below is discussed three of the 3 most common physical illnesses related to stress which come at the extreme end of the spectrum and serves to encourage you to lead a less stressful life due to the potential severity of these conditions.

1. Heart Disease

Individuals are known to deal with stress through alcohol, smoking of cigarettes, eating to excess and use of drugs. All of these activities are known to put undue stress on vital organs leading to an increased risk of heart disease developing in later life. If left unchecked this heart disease could lead to heart attacks which could be deadly or irreparably change the lifestyle of the individual in question.

- If you know that you are responsible for indulging in these guilty pleasures then it's never too late to change your behavior.
- Try and indulge instead in some alternative methods of stress relief such as power napping or going for a walk and you could reduce the risk you are under of developing heart related physical illnesses related to stress.

2. Strokes

People who feel stressed on a day today basis as a result of their career or other demands on their life are almost ninety percent more likely to experience a stroke in their life than those who lead less stressful existences. Similarly to the factors associated with the development of heart disease the link is associate with the correlation between the highly stressed and those who indulge in drinking, smoking, drug use and indulgence in food.

- Again, the advice given is that individuals who are aware of their leading of unhealthy lifestyles and who feel highly stressed need to develop more healthy coping mechanisms to avoid the possibility of experiencing a stroke in later life.

3. Irritable Bowel Syndrome (IBS)

The third from the 3 most common physical illnesses related to stress is the Irritable bowel syndrome. This is caused by the spasm of the nerves controlling the digestive tract; this condition results in abdominal pain and changes in bowel habits. Stress is a major contributory factor to the establishment and causing of further abdominal pain and changes in bowel habits.

This is a hereditary illness meaning that to an extent an individual is predetermined to be more susceptible to experience irritable bowel syndrome. If a family member has irritable bowel syndrome you must endeavor all you can to adopt effective stress coping mechanisms to avoid episodes of pain and changes in bowel habits caused by one of many physical illnesses related to stress.

Stress and Culture

The orientation toward stress research is changing as awareness of the social and cultural contexts involved in stress and coping are examined. The biopsychosocial model of stress incorporates a variety of social factors into its model that influence stress reaction and perception. However, research into the cultural differences that may exist in stress reactions are also needed to examine how various social and cultural structures influence the individual's experience of stress. Culture and society may shape what events are perceived as stressful, what coping strategies are acceptable to use in a particular society, and what institutional mechanisms we may turn to for assistance (Fumiko Naughton, personal communication). Pearlin (1982) suggests that society, its value systems, the stratified ordering of its populations, the organization of its institutions, and the rapidity and extent of changes in these elements can be sources of stress. For example, Merton (1957) suggests that society can elicit stress by promoting values that conflict with the structures in which they are acted upon. Merton argues that the system of values in the United States promotes attainment of monetary and

honorable success among more people than could be accommodated by the opportunity structures available. As a consequence, many of those individuals who internalize these culturally prized goals are doomed to failure.

As researchers incorporate a social-cultural perspective to stress research, the definitions of stress, which currently incorporate the physiological and cognitive components of stress, need to be re-examined and re-defined to reflect both social and cultural differences. These social and cultural differences may increase our knowledge about stress and how stress can be effectively managed given the constraints imposed upon the individual by the existing values in a particular culture. A re-definition of stress, that would reflect cultural mediation in the experience of stress, might be that "stress is a set of neurological and physiological reactions that serve an adaptive function in the environmental, social, and cultural values and structures within which the individual acts upon."

Behavioral Medicine

Behavioral medicine is a multidisciplinary field of medicine concerned with the development and integration of knowledge in the biological, behavioral, psychological, and social sciences relevant to health and illness. The term is often used interchangeably, and incorrectly, with health psychology, whereas the practice of behavioral medicine also includes applied psychophysiological therapies such as biofeedback, hypnosis, and biobehavioral therapy of physical disorders.

Medical psychology is a very broad field and has been defined in various ways. The Academy of Medical Psychology's definition applies to both the practices of consultation and prescribing in Medical Psychology, when allowed by statutes. These professionals are trained in a specialty of psychology concerned with the application of psychological principles to the practice of medicine and both physical, as well as, mental disorders. They apply psychological theories, scientific psychological findings, and techniques of psychotherapy, behavior modification, cognitive, interpersonal, family, and lifestyle therapy to improve the psychological and physical health of the patient. Clinical psychologists with post doctoral specialty training as medical psychologists are the practitioners with refined skills in clinical observation in of the field of psychology, learning, central nervous system adaptation and change, and adaptation and lifestyle change applying a number of different methods in several different mediums of treatment.

Medical psychology, as defined by most medical dictionaries is defined as "the branch of psychology concerned with the application of psychological principles to the practice of medicine". Other similar definitions include: "the application of clinical psychology or clinical health psychology, usually in hospital, medical, or health care settings" and "the study and application of psychological factors related to any and all aspects of physical health, illness, and its treatment at the individual, groups, and systems level"

Medical psychology, as defined by Division 55 of the American Psychological Association (APA), "is that branch of psychology that integrates somatic and psychotherapeutic modalities into the management of mental illness and emotional, cognitive, behavioral and substance use disorders." Division 55 is the organization within APA that represents medical psychologist who have prescriptive authority and is a leader in defining this new practice area for clinical psychological practitioners with prescriptive authority.

The Academy of Medical Psychology defines medical psychology as a specialty trained at the post doctoral level and designed to deliver advanced diagnostic and clinical interventions in Medical and Healthcare Facilities utilizing the knowledge and skills of clinical psychology, health psychology, behavioral medicine, psychopharmacology and basic medical science.

Health Psychology—distinct from behavioral medicine in that is specifically involved with the role of psychology in health and illness. **Health psychology** is concerned with understanding how biological, psychological, environmental, and cultural factors are involved in physical health and the prevention of illness. Health psychologists work alongside other medical professionals in clinical settings, work on behavior change in public health promotion, teach at universities, and conduct research. Health psychologists conduct research to identify behaviors and experiences that promote health, give rise to illness, and influence the effectiveness of health care. They also recommend ways to improve health care and health-care policy.

Health psychology is also concerned with contextual factors, including economic, cultural, community, social, and lifestyle factors that influence health. Health psychologists also aim to change health behaviors for the dual purpose of helping people stay healthy and helping patients adhere to disease treatment regimens. Health psychologists employ cognitive behavior therapy, and applied behavior analysis.

Health Prevention and Stress

Health Psychologists work towards promoting health through behavioral change, as mentioned above; however, they attempt to prevent illness in other ways as well. Campaigns informed by health psychology have targeted health disparity issues, such as diabetes, breast cancer, and hypertension. In addition, practitioners emphasize education and effective communication as a part of illness prevention because many people do not recognize, or minimize, the risk of illness present in their lives.

Coping with Stress and Management Techniques

Stress management gives you a range of tools to reset your alarm system. Without stress management, all too often your body is always on high alert. Over time, high levels of stress lead to serious health problems. Don't wait until stress has a negative impact on your health, relationships or quality of life. Start practicing a range of stress management techniques today.

Stress Management Introduction

People use coping and defense mechanisms in more or less spontaneous ways. There is no shortage of popular self-help guides concerning how to deal with stress. Some are based firmly on research findings about stress itself and coping mechanisms, while others are more anecdotal.

One influential way to classify the wide variety of is in terms of Lazarus & Folkman (1984) suggestion that there are two coping strategies that people use to deal with stress:

- **Problem-focused coping:** An attempt is made to control stress by trying to change the event or situation that produces the stress.
- **Emotion focused coping:** Focuses on changing the person's response to stress. This may be the only realistic option when the source of stress is outside the person's control.

Psychologists and medical researchers have examined a range of ways of stress management. For convenience these can be divided into physical approaches (e.g. drugs, biofeedback) and psychological approaches.

Physical approaches to managing the effects of stress. In some cases, chronic stress reactions are treated by the use of anti-anxiety (anxiolytic) drugs. This might occur, for example, in post-traumatic stress disorder. The most commonly prescribed drugs are the benzodiazapines: Valium (diazapam) and Librium (chlorodiazepoxide). They act by facilitating the activity of GABA, an important chemical transmitter in the brain. They do this in a complex way, binding with receptor sites in a way that enhances the effectiveness of GABA. Barbiturates and alcohol have a similar effect. Because GABA is an inhibitory neurotransmitter, the effect of benzodiazapines, barbiturates and alcohol is neural inhibition. It is suggested that anti-anxiety drugs mimic the effect of the brain's own anti-anxiety compounds that are released in times of stress, though no-one has yet been able to find these compounds.

Disadvantages of anti-anxiety drugs

Anti-anxiety drugs have a number of disadvantages. They can have serious side effects and can be very addictive. Although helpful in the short term, their disadvantages may sometimes outweigh their advantages.

For example, benzodiazapines may be used to treat insomnia (frequently a consequence of stress) but the sleep they induce is not as refreshing as natural sleep. In fact, it has been claimed that the most common cause of insomnia is dependency on sleep medication.

The problem with all physical methods is that they treat the *symptoms* of stress and not its *causes* (i.e. coping with stress rather than managing stress). Someone suffering from stress at work would be better advised to examine his or her work patterns and relationships than to take tablets for stress symptoms.

Biofeedback

Another physical approach to stress management is biofeedback. This is based on the idea that giving a person information about the state of their body (for example blood pressure readings) provides them with the potential means to control it. Biofeedback has been shown to be successful in treating some stress related conditions, such as migraine and high blood pressure, but the results are no better than those of conventional relaxation training. Since it requires complex and expensive equipment, critics argue that there are simpler and more cost effective remedies for stress.

Psychological methods of stress management include various types of cognitive therapy. The aim of these predominantly emotion-focused techniques is to replace irrational and negative thoughts with more positive ways of thinking about a problem. The assumption is that in many cases there is little that a person can do about the objective situation, as stress is an inevitable consequence of modern life (a single-women trying to cope with young children can't just abandon the children and go off to live in Ibiza). What can be changed is the way that she thinks about the situation (e.g. seeing child-rearing as a time of opportunity and taking satisfaction from the children's progress). Restructuring beliefs about a problem can make that problem disappear, or at least become more manageable.

Stress inoculation training (Meichenbaum)

Unlike many cognitive therapies, stress inoculation training (SIT) is a more problem-focused coping strategy. It was developed by Donald Meichenbaum and the basic idea is to prepare individuals to cope with potential stressors. According to Meichenbaum (1985), the best way to cope with stressors is to go on the offensive and try to pre-empt them. People should try to anticipate sources of stress and have effective coping strategies ready to put in place.

SIT usually involves a therapist working with a individual. The training takes place in three phases, each of which has the aim of achieving specific goals. The phases are:

- Conceptualization phase
- Skills acquisition and rehearsal phase
- Application and follow through phase

Although there were initially few studies that have evaluated SIT, recent research has shown it to be effective in a range of settings, including helping people deal with stressful jobs such as teaching, nursing and the police, as well as with professional athletes (e.g. Cox, 1991). However, SIT takes time and effort and as individuals have to go through a rigorous program of training over a long period, it can only work with people who have a sufficiently high level of motivation and commitment. It also may not suit certain individuals, for example those whose basic personality makes them resistant to changing cognitions (see locus of control, below).

Relaxation Training

A variety of different relaxation techniques can help you bring your nervous system back into balance by producing the relaxation response. The relaxation response is not lying on the couch or sleeping but a mentally active process that leaves the body relaxed, calm, and focused.

Learning the basics of these relaxation techniques isn't difficult, but it does take practice. Most stress experts recommend setting aside at least 10 to 20 minutes a day for your relaxation practice. If you'd like to get even more stress relief, aim for 30 minutes to an hour. You can practiced at your desk over lunch or on the bus during your morning commute.

Finding the relaxation technique that's best for you

There is no single relaxation technique that is best for everyone. When choosing a relaxation technique, consider your specific needs, preferences, fitness level, and the way you tend to react to stress. The right relaxation technique is the one that resonates with you, fits your lifestyle, and is able to focus your mind and interrupt your everyday thoughts in order to elicit the relaxation response. In many cases, you may find that alternating or combining different techniques will keep you motivated and provide you with the best results.

How you react to stress may influence the relaxation technique that works best for you:

Stress Response	Symptoms	Relaxation Technique
Overexcited	You tend to become angry, agitated, or keyed up under stress	You may respond best to relaxation techniques that quiet you down, such as meditation, deep breathing, or guided imagery
Under excited	You tend to become depressed, withdrawn, or spaced out under stress	You may respond best to relaxation techniques that are stimulating and that energize your nervous system, such as rhythmic exercise
Frozen (both overexcited and under excited at the same time – like pressing on the brakes and gas simultaneously)	You tend to freeze: speeding up in some ways while slowing down in others	Your challenge is to identify relaxation techniques that provide both safety and stimulation to help you "reboot" your system. Techniques such as mindfulness walking or power yoga might work well for you

CHAPTER 11 SUMMARY

Overall, stress is a normal condition that impacts every human being at some point in their lives. Stress will influence both the psychological and physiological state of an individual. With medical and mental health intervention, stress conditions can be managed when confronted.

Focus is on identifying factors that impair physical and emotional health
>   Stress
>   Drug use
>   Other factors

STRESS

Stress has been described as a process with both psychological and biological aspects, with three distinct phases in a general adaptation syndrome. These are
>   Alarm
>   Resistance
>   Exhaustion

One can readily describe this process by illustrating the life of a student during finals week. Here, one becomes alarmed at how much needs to be studied (typically during reading days), followed by physical resistance (noted by higher levels of ailments during the last week of a semester), followed by physical exhaustion (at the end of the last final exam).

During any stressful situation, there are two important processes at play. The first, primary appraisal, involves a determination of the importance of the situation (should it be considered neutral or stressful). The second is secondary appraisal. This involves determining a plan of action. There have been three types of stress described, as follows:
>   harm or loss
>   threat
>   challenge (opportunities for positive experience or growth)

As part of this listing, there have been categorizations of stressors, mostly based upon life events. Some of these are referred to as major stressors, which involve significant life events such as marriage, birth of a child, death of a loved one, to name a few. Other major stressors are out of the ordinary human experience, such as catastrophes (natural or man-made). In some significant circumstances, people can develop psychological symptoms in response to major stressors such as Posttraumatic Stress Disorder (PTSD).

Other problems that are stress inducing can be insidious. For example, daily hassles have been shown to be stressful, but no one event alone would be considered very stressful. Some daily hassles include traffic, difficulties at work, and minor arguments.

Stress and Health

Under prolonged stress, people experience declines in physical health with great regularity. One of the first areas that decline is the immune system. Here it is worth describing some of the biological features of the immune system (such as B and T cells, as well as natural killer cells). It appears from research that on the one hand, avoiding stress is worthwhile for better physical health. However, there are personality variables that interact with stress in that some people seek stress, and find it more stressful to avoid stressful situations. This paradoxical situation is sometimes aptly described by considering people who go on vacation only to bring some occupational material with them, as well as a cell-phone and laptop computer. On the one hand, the vacation is design to be a stress reliever, but if asked how much they would enjoy the vacation without the reminders of the job, they would suggest that it would be difficult. This has also been described as Type A personality (people with this style are sometimes referred to as workaholics). People with this personality style also tend to be at greater risk for coronary heart disease and other illnesses associated with stress.

Coping

At this point, the lectures would seem to suggest that stress only leads to negative physical health. However, there are other insulating factors that can reduce the stress response cycle. Most of these are problem-focused strategies or emotion-focused strategies. So one might engage in activities designed to minimize associated stress. If this cannot be achieved, then one may focus on altering the negative emotions associated with stress. An additional insulating effect on stress is social support. Social support has been extensively studied, and most research suggests that increased social networks are associated with better stress response. However, there is a bi-directional relationship between social support and stress. That is, as stress increases one's social network can erode depending on how the person responds to stress. Therefore, one can regulate their social network if they are effective at regulating stress.

Lecture Topic Extensions

Obesity

Obesity refers to the excessive accumulation of fat in the body. The government had a goal of eliminating obesity by the year 2000 (Healthy People 2000 Initiative). In spite of research and educational programs, the prevalence of obesity has increased such that most Americans are now overweight. Moreover, we are eating more calories now than we did on 1971 (men: up by 8%; women up by 22%), and mostly in the form of

carbohydrates. This section would be a place to explore a number of issues relating to obesity
stigmatization of the obese person
development of drug treatments to replace the failed treatment
e.g. fenfluramine-phentermine; ephedra-containing products

Stress and Coping
Stress and coping are frequently the source of questions by students, such as what are the long-term health effects if a stressful career is pursued. This is a weighty matter, and one should have a sense of how to best adjust to stress in order to avoid the negative physical symptoms commonly associated with stress.

12

PERSONALITY TRAITS AND TYPES

LEARNING OBJECTIVES

After completing Chapter 12, students should be able to:

- Define "individual differences in personality" and "structure of personality."
- Outline the basic features of Freud's psychodynamic theories.
- Discuss the notion of psychodynamic conflict.
- Outline Freud's drive model of personality.
- Discuss Freud's developmental model of personality.
- Outline Freud's structural model of personality.
- Explain the general features of a defense mechanism.
- Discuss how object relations theory grew out of Freud's personality theories.
- Contrast the life history approach with the projective test approach of personality assessment.
- Outline the basic features of the behaviorist account of personality.
- Discuss the role that encoding, expectancies, and self-regulation play in various cognitive-social theories of personality.
- Define the concept of emotional intelligence.
- Discuss the general features of the trait approach to personality.
- Outline Eysenck's personality model and discuss the interactions between the various model factors.
- Outline the general features of the Five Factor Model of personality.
- Discuss what Mischel means by "person-by-situation interactions."

- Outline Rogers's person-centered approach and discuss how compatible or incompatible his work is with respect to other theories of personality.
- Outline the key features of existential personality theories.
- Discuss the methods used to probe the interaction of genetics with personality.
- Discuss at least two examples of the interaction between culture and individual personality (concentrating on how various cultures value and shape certain kinds of personalities).

Introduction

We are known by our reputation or the typical manner in how we respond within our environment. Our habitual patterns of response based on our temperament makes up personality. According to the *Diagnostic and Statistical Manual of the* American Psychiatric Association, personality traits are "enduring patterns of perceiving, relating to, and thinking about the environment and oneself that are exhibited in a wide range of social and personal contexts." Theorists generally assume a) traits are relatively stable over time, b) traits differ among individuals (e.g. some people are outgoing while others are reserved), and c) traits influence behavior.

Almost every day we describe and assess the personalities of the people around us. Whether we realize it or not, these daily musings on how and why people behave as they do are similar to what personality psychologists do. While our informal assessments of personality tend to focus more on individuals, personality psychologists instead use conceptions of personality that can apply to everyone. Personality research has led to the development of a number of theories that help explain how and why certain personality traits develop. The most common models of traits incorporate three to five broad dimensions or factors. The least controversial dimension, observed as far back as the ancient Greeks, is simply *extraversion* and *introversion* (outgoing and physical-stimulation-oriented vs. quiet and physical-stimulation-averse).

Temperament and Personality

Personality is determined by the interaction of temperament traits with the environment. Each person comes with a predetermined genetics. How genes express themselves in our lives can determine whether they will be easy or difficult. How well their temperament fits with the environment and how well they are received by the people in the environment will determine how a person sees self and others. Temperament is biologically based: Heredity, neural, and hormonal factors affect response to the environment. Temperament can be modulated by environmental factors, such as parental response. Babies with easy temperaments adjust easily to new situations, quickly establish routines, are generally cheerful and easy to calm. Babies with Difficult temperaments are slow to adjust to new experiences, are likely to react negatively and intensely to stimuli and events. Babies with Slow-to-warm-up temperaments are somewhat difficult at first but become easier over time. The role of temperament is observed in social skills and adjustment differences will manifest as anger/irritability, positive emotion, and ability to regulate emotions are associated with social competence and adjustment. Children who are negative, impulsive, and unregulated tend to have poor peer relations and get in trouble with the law. They will develop into adults who are difficult with their spouse, friends, and roommates. Behaviorally inhibited children are more likely to experience anxiety, depression, and phobias. The "Goodness of fit "model is used to examine temperament. It is the degree to which an individual's temperament is compatible with the demands and expectations of his or her social environment.

Temperament Defined

Temperament is a set of in-born traits that organize the child's approach to the world. They are instrumental in the development of the child's distinct personality. These traits also determine how the child interacts in the world.

These traits appear to be relatively stable from birth. They are enduring characteristics that are actually never "good" or "bad." How they are expressed through personality and how they are received determines whether they are perceived as appropriate or challenging.

When the demands and expectations of people and the environment are compatible with the child's temperament there is said to be a "goodness-of-fit." When incompatibility exists, you have what is known as a "personality conflict." The sooner personality traits are conditioned to the environment through adaptation, the better the effects of fit will occur.

Four Temperament Types

The Four Temperaments, also known as the Four Humours, is arguably the oldest of all personality profiling systems, and it is fascinating that there are so many echoes of these ancient ideas found in modern psychology.

The Four Temperaments ideas can be traced back to the traditions of the Egyptian and Mesopotamian civilizations over 5,000 years ago, in which the health of the body was connected with the elements, fire, water, earth and air, which in turn were related to body organs, fluids, and treatments. Some of this thinking survives today in traditional Eastern ideas and medicine.

The ancient Greeks however first formalized and popularized the Four Temperaments methodologies around 2,500 years ago, and these ideas came to dominate Western thinking about human behavior and medical treatment for over two-thousand years.

Most of these concepts for understanding personality, behavior, illness and treatment of illness amazingly persisted in the Western world until the mid-1800s.

The Four Temperaments or Four Humours can be traced back reliably to Ancient Greek medicine and philosophy, notably in the work of Hippocrates (c.460-377/359BC—the 'Father of Medicine') and in Plato's (428-348BC) ideas about character and personality.

In Greek medicine around 2,500 years ago it was believed that in order to maintain health, people needed an even balance of the four body fluids: blood, phlegm, yellow bile, and black bile. These four body fluids were linked (in daft ways by modern standards) to certain organs and illnesses and also represented the Four Temperaments or Four Humours (of personality) as they later became known. As regards significant body fluids no doubt natural body waste products were discounted, since perfectly healthy people evacuate a good volume of them every day.

Each of the four types of humours or temperaments that corresponded to a different personality type.

Sanguine

The Sanguine temperament personality is fairly extroverted. People of a sanguine temperament tend to enjoy social gatherings, making new friends and tend to be boisterous. They are usually quite creative and often daydream. However, some alone time is crucial for those of this temperament. Sanguine can also mean very sensitive, compassionate and thoughtful. Sanguine personalities generally struggle with following tasks all the way through, are chronically late, and tend to be forgetful and sometimes a little sarcastic. Often, when pursuing a new hobby, interest is lost quickly when it ceases to be engaging or fun. They are very much people persons. They are talkative and not shy. People of sanguine temperament can often be emotional.

Choleric

A person who is choleric is task oriented. They are highly motivated with ambition and passion toward their goals. They can dominate people of other temperaments, especially phlegmatic types. Many great charismatic military and political figures were choleric. They is a strong desire to be leaders and in charge of many activities. They can be very manipulative.

Melancholic

A person who is a thoughtful and reflective has a *melancholic* disposition. Often are very considerate and worry when late attending scheduled events. They are very creative in activities such as poetry and art. A *melancholic* is also often a perfectionist. They are often self-reliant and independent; one negative part of being a melancholic is sometimes they can get so involved in what they are doing they forget to think of others.

Phlegmatic

Phlegmatics tend to be self-content and kind. They can be very accepting and affectionate. They may be very receptive and shy and often prefer stability to uncertainty and change. They are very consistent, relaxed, calm, rational, curious, and observant, making them good administrators. They can also be very passive-aggressive.

The Four Temperaments also provided much inspiration and historical reference for Carl Young's work, which in turn provided the underpinning structures and theory for the development of Myers Briggs and David Keirsey's modern-day personality assessment systems, which correlate with the Four Temperaments thus:

Isabel Myers 1950s	Galen c.190AD	David Keirsey 1998
SP sensing-perceiving	sangine	artisan
SJ sensing-judging	melancholic	guardian
NF intuitive-feeling	choleric	idealist
NT intuitive-thinking	phlegmatic	rationalist

Nine Temperament Characteristics of Thomas and Chess

Research by Thomas and Chess used the following nine temperament traits in children based on a classification scheme developed by Dr. Herbert Birch:

Activity

Activity refers to the child's physical energy. Is the child constantly moving, or does the child have a relaxing approach? A high-energy child may have difficulty sitting still in class, whereas a child with low energy can tolerate a very structured environment. The former may use gross motor skills like running and jumping more frequently. Conversely, a child with a lower activity level may rely more on fine motor skills, such as drawing and putting puzzles together. This trait can also refer to mental activity, such as deep thinking or reading.

Regularity

Regularity, also known as **Rhythmicity**, refers to the level of predictability in a child's biological functions, such as waking, becoming tired, hunger, and bowel movements. It depicts a child's routine in eating and sleeping habits, or are these events more random.

Initial reaction

Initial reaction is also known as **Approach or Withdrawal**. This refers to how the child responds (whether positively or negatively) to new people or environments. Does the child approach people or things in the environment without hesitation, or does the child shy away? A bold child tends to approach things quickly, as if without thinking, whereas a cautious child typically prefers to watch for a while before engaging in new experiences.

Adaptability

Adaptability refers to how long it takes the child to adjust to change over time (as opposed to an initial reaction). Does the child adjust to the changes in their environment easily, or is the child resistant? A child who adjusts easily may be quick to settle into a new routine, whereas a resistant child may take a long time to adjust to the situation.

Intensity

Intensity refers to the energy level of a positive or negative response. Does the child react intensely to a situation, or does the child respond in a calm and quiet manner? A more intense child may jump up and down screaming with excitement, whereas a mild-mannered child may smile or show no emotion.

Mood

Mood refers to the child's general tendency towards a happy or unhappy demeanor. All children have a variety of emotions and reactions, such as cheerful and stormy, happy and unhappy. Yet each child biologically tends to have a generally positive or negative outlook.

Distractibility

Distractibility refers to the child's tendency to be sidetracked by other things going on around them. An easily distracted child is engaged by external events and has difficulty returning to the task at hand, whereas a rarely distracted child stays focused and completes the task at hand.

Persistence and attention span

Persistence and attention span refer to the child's length of time on a task and ability to stay with the task through frustrations

Sensitivity

Sensitivity refers to how easily a child is disturbed by changes in the environment. This is also called sensory threshold or threshold of responsiveness.

A sensitive child may lose focus when a door slams, whereas a child less sensitive to external noises will be able to maintain focus.

"Easy", "difficult", and "slow-to-warm-up"

Thomas, Chess, Birch, Hertzig and Korn found that many babies could be categorized into one of three groups: *easy*, *difficult*, and *slow-to-warm-up* (Thomas & Chess 1977). Not all children can be placed in one of these groups. Approximately 65% of children fit one of the patterns. Of the 65%, 40% fit the easy pattern, 10% fell into the difficult pattern, and 15% were slow to warm up. Each category has its own strength and weakness and one is not superior to another.

Thomas, Chess, Birch, Hertzig and Korn showed that *Easy* babies readily adapt to new experiences, generally display positive moods and emotions and also have normal eating and sleeping patterns. *Difficult* babies tend to be very emotional, irritable and fussy, and cry a lot. They also tend to have irregular eating and sleeping patterns. *Slow-to-warm-up* babies have a low activity level, and tend to withdraw from new situations and people. They are slow to adapt to new experiences, but accept them after repeated exposure.

Thomas, Chess, Birch, Hertzig and Korn found that these broad patterns of temperamental qualities are remarkably stable through childhood. These traits are also found in children across all cultures.

Traits and Personality Expression

According to the DSM, personality traits are "enduring patterns of perceiving, relating to, and thinking about the environment and oneself that are exhibited in a wide range of social and personal contexts." Theorists generally assume a) traits are relatively stable over time, b) traits differ among individuals (e.g. some people are outgoing while others are reserved), and c) traits influence behavior.

The most common models of traits incorporate three to five broad dimensions or factors. The least controversial dimension, observed as far back as the ancient Greeks, is simply extraversion and introversion (outgoing and physical-stimulation-oriented vs. quiet and physical-stimulation-averse).

The trait approach to personality is one of the major theoretical areas in the study of personality. The trait theory suggests that individual personalities are composed broad dispositions. Consider how you would describe the personality of a close friend. Chances are that you would list a number of traits, such as *outgoing*, *kind* and *even-tempered*. A trait can be thought of as a relatively stable characteristic that causes individuals to behave in certain ways. Trait theory is focused on identifying and measuring these individual personality characteristics. Different theories are discussed below.

Hans Eysenck's Three Dimensions of Personality

British psychologist Hans Eysenck developed a model of personality based upon just three universal trails:

1. **Introversion/Extraversion:** Introversion involves directing attention on inner experiences, while extraversion relates to focusing attention outward on other people and the environment. So, a person high in introversion might be quiet and reserved, while an individual high in extraversion might be sociable and outgoing.
2. **Neuroticism/Emotional Stability:** This dimension of Eysenck's trait theory is related to moodiness versus even-temperedness. Neuroticism refers to an individual's tendency to become upset or emotional, while stability refers to the tendency to remain emotionally constant.
3. **Psychoticism:** Later, after studying individuals suffering from mental illness, Eysenck added a personality dimension he called psychoticism to his trait theory. Individuals who are high on this trait tend to have difficulty dealing with reality and may be antisocial, hostile, non-empathetic and manipulative.[4]

The Five-Factor Theory of Personality

Both Cattell's and Eysenck's theory have been the subject of considerable research, which has led some theorists to believe that Cattell focused on too many traits, while Eysenck focused on too few. As a result, a new trait theory often referred to as the "Big Five" theory emerged.

Lewis Goldberg proposed a five-dimension personality model, nicknamed the "Big Five.":

1. **Openness to Experience**: the tendency to be imaginative, independent, and interested in variety vs. practical, conforming, and interested in routine.
2. **Conscientiousness**: the tendency to be organized, careful, and disciplined vs. disorganized, careless, and impulsive.
3. **Extraversion**: the tendency to be sociable, fun-loving, and affectionate vs. retiring, somber, and reserved.
4. **Agreeableness**: the tendency to be softhearted, trusting, and helpful vs. ruthless, suspicious, and uncooperative.
5. **Neuroticism**: the tendency to be calm, secure, and self-satisfied vs. anxious, insecure, and self-pitying

The Big Five contain important dimensions of personality. However, some personality researchers argue that this list of major traits is not exhaustive. See the table X. Five Fasctor Model.

Personalities are distinctive. Each individual behaves according to certain distinctive patterns throughout a variety of situations. Humans are finely tuned to observe these behavior patterns of acquaintances and to notice behavior differences among people. You might use words such as talkative, cheerful, cold, disorganized, compulsive, intellectual, shrewd, shortsighted, flirtatious, or ruthless to describe various people you know. Also, you have probably observed that these various behaviors stay with the person consistently over time and throughout a variety of circumstances. These persistent behavior patterns, called *personality traits,* are stable over time, consistent in a variety of situations, and differ from one individual to the next.

Table 16a. Five Factor Model of Personality

TABLE 12.2
THE FIVE-FACTOR MODEL AND ITS FACETS

Neuroticism	Extraversion	Agreeableness	Conscientiousness	Openness
Anxiety	Warmth	Trust	Competence	Fantasy (active fantasy life)
Angry hostility	Gregariousness	Straightforwardness	Order	Aesthetics (artistic interests)
Depression	Assertiveness	Altruism	Dutifulness	Feelings (emotionally open)
Self-consciousness	Activity	Compliance	Achievement striving	Actions (flexible)
Impulsivity	Excitement seeking	Modesty	Self-discipline	Ideas (intellectual)
Vulnerability	Positive emotion	Tenderness	Deliberation	Values (unconventional)

Note: These are the higher-order and lower-order traits (facets) that constitute the Five-Factor-Model. Within each factor, traits are highly correlated; across factors, they are not.
Source: Adapted from McCrae & Costa, 1997, p. 513.

Table 16b. The American-English form of the structure identifies these five personality factors:

Factor	Trait Characteristics	Inverse Trait Characteristics
I Extraversion/Surgency	Talkative, extroverted Aggressive, verbal Sociable, bold Assertive, social Unrestrained, confident	Shy, quiet Introverted, silent Untalkative, bashful Reserved, withdrawn Timid, unaggressive
II Agreeableness	Sympathetic, kind Warm, understanding Soft-hearted, helpful Considerate, cooperative Trustful, affectionate	Cold, unsympathetic Unkind, rude Harsh, inconsiderate Insensitive, insincere Hard, uncharitable
III Conscientiousness	Organized, neat Orderly, systematic Efficient, responsible Precise, thorough Practical, dependable	Disorganized, disorderly Careless, unsystematic Inefficient, sloppy Haphazard, inconsistent Impractical, negligent
IV Emotional Stability	Unenvious, relaxed Unexcitable, patient Undemanding, imperturbable Unselfconscious, uncritical Masculine, optimistic	Moody, temperamental Jealous, touchy Envious, irritable Fretful, emotional Self-pitying, nervous
V Intellect	Creative, intellectual Imaginative, philosophical Artistic, complex Inventive, intelligent Innovative, deep	Uncreative, unimaginative Unintellectual, unintelligent Simple, unreflective Shallow, imperceptive Unsophisticated, uniquisitive.

PHILOSOPHICAL ASSUMPTIONS OF PERSONALITY

Many of the ideas developed by historical and modern personality theorists stem from the basic philosophical assumptions they hold. The study of personality is not a purely empirical discipline, as it brings in elements of philosophy to draw general conclusions. The following five categories are some of the most fundamental philosophical assumptions on which theorists disagree:

Freedom versus Determinism

This assumption is based on whether we have control over our own behavior and understand the motives behind it (*Freedom*), or if our behavior is causally determined by forces beyond our control, that is our behaviors are predetermined based on influences out of our control (Determinism). Determinism has been considered unconscious, environmental, or biological by various theories.

Heredity versus Environment (Nature vs. Nurture)

Personality is thought to be determined largely by genetics and biology, by environment and experiences, or by some combination resulting thereof. There is evidence for all possibilities. Contemporary research suggests that most personality traits are based on the joint influence of genetics and environment.

Uniqueness versus Universality

The argument over whether we are all truly unique individuals (Unique) or if humans are basically similar in their nature (Universal Traits). Gordon Allport, Abraham Maslow, and Carl Roges were all advocates of the uniqueness of individuals. Behaviorists and cognitive theorists, in contrast, emphasized the importance of universal principles such as reinforcement and self-efficacy.

Active versus Reactive

Do we primarily act through our own initiative (Individualistic Actions), or react to outside stimuli (Rective Nature)? Behavioral theorists typically believe that humans are passively shaped by their environments, whereas humanistic and cognitive theorists believe that humans are more active.

Optimistic versus Pessimistic

Personality theories differ on whether people can change their personalities (Optimistic), or if they are doomed to remain the same throughout their lives (Pessimistic). Theories that place a great deal of emphasis on learning are often, but not always, more optimistic than theories that do not emphasize learning.

THEORY OF PERSONALITY

The study of personality has a broad and varied history in psychology, with an abundance of theoretical traditions. The major theories include dispositional (trait) perspective, psychodynamic, humanistic, biological, behaviorist and social learning perspective. There is no consensus on the definition of "personality" in psychology. Most researchers and psychologists do not explicitly identify themselves with a certain perspective and often take an eclectic approach. Some research is empirically driven such as the "Big 5" personality model whereas other research emphasizes theory development such as psychodynamics. There is also a substantial emphasis on the applied field of personality testing. In psychological education and training, the study of the nature of personality and its psychological development is usually reviewed as a prerequisite to courses in abnormal or clinical psychology.

PERSONALITY THEORIES

Critics of personality theory claim personality is "plastic" across time, places, moods, and situations. Changes in personality may indeed result from diet (or lack thereof), medical effects, significant events, or learning. However, most personality theories emphasize stability over fluctuation. Several theories are discussed below.

Psychoanalytic Theory

Psychoanalytic theories explain human behavior in terms of the interaction of various components of personality. Freud was the founder of this school. Freud drew on the physics of his day (thermodynamics) to coin the term psychodynamics. Based on the idea of converting heat into mechanical energy, he proposed psychic energy could be converted into behavior. Freud's theory places central importance on dynamic, unconscious psychological conflicts.

Structure of Personality

Freud divides human personality into three significant components: the id, ego, and super-ego. The **id** acts according to the *pleasure principle*, demanding immediate gratification of its needs regardless of external environment; the **ego** then must emerge in order to realistically meet the wishes and demands of the id in accordance with the outside world, adhering to the *reality principle*. Finally, the **superego**(conscience) inculcates moral judgment and societal rules upon the ego, thus forcing the demands of the id to be met not only realistically but morally. The superego is the last function of the personality to develop, and is the embodiment of parental/social ideals established during childhood. According to Freud, personality is based on the dynamic interactions of these three components.[8]

Psychosexual Stages of Development

The channeling and release of sexual (libidal) and aggressive energies, which ensues from the "Eros" (sex; instinctual self-preservation) and "Thanatos" (death; instinctual self-annihilation) drives respectively, are major components of his theory. It is important to note that Freud's broad understanding of sexuality included all kinds of pleasurable feelings experienced by the human body.

Freud proposed five psychosexual stages of personality development. He believed adult personality is dependent upon early childhood experiences and largely determined by age five.[8] Fixations that develop during the Infantile stage contribute to adult personality and behavior.

One of Sigmund Freud's earlier associates, Alfred Adler, did agree with Freud early childhood experiences are important to development, and believed birth order may influence personality development. Adler believed the oldest was the one that set high goals to achieve to get the attention they lost back when the younger siblings were born. He believed the middle children were competitive and ambitious possibly so they are able to surpass the first-born's achievements, but were not as much concerned about the glory. He also believed the last born would be more dependent and sociable but be the baby. He also believed that the only child loves being the center of attention and matures quickly, but in the end fails to become independent.

Heinz Kohut thought similarly to Freud's idea of transference. He used narcissism as a model of how we develop our sense of self. Narcissism is the exaggerated sense of oneself in which is believed to exist in order to protect one's low self esteem and sense of worthlessness. Kohut had a significant impact on the field by extending Freud's theory of narcissism and introducing what he called the 'self-object transferences' of mirroring and idealization. In other words, children need to idealize and emotionally "sink into" and identify with the idealized competence of admired figures such as parents or older siblings. They also need to have their self-worth mirrored by these people. These experiences allow them to thereby learn the self-soothing and other skills that are necessary for the development of a healthy sense of self.

Another important figure in the world of personality theory was Karen Horney. She is credited with the development of the "real self" and the "ideal self". She believes all people have these two views of their own self. The "real self" is how you really are with regards to personality, values, and morals; but the "ideal self" is a construct you apply to yourself to conform to social and personal norms and goals. Ideal self would be "I can be successful, I am CEO material"; and real self would be "I just work in the mail room, with not much chance of high promotion".

helped promote analysis of behavior based on the "Stimulus—Response—Consequence Model" in which the critical question is: "Under which circumstances or antecedent 'stimuli' does the organism engage in a particular behavior or 'response', which in turn produces a particular 'consequence'.

Behaviorist theories

Behaviorists explain personality in terms of the effects external stimuli have on behavior. It was a radical shift away from Freudian philosophy. This school of thought was developed by B. F. Skinner who put forth a model which emphasized the mutual interaction of the person or "the organism" with its environment. Skinner believed children do bad things because the behavior obtains attention that serves as a reinforcer. According to this theory, people's behavior is formed by processes such as operant conditioning. Skinner put forward a "three term contingency model" which

Social cognitive theories

In cognitive theory, behavior is explained as guided by cognitions (e.g. expectations) about the world, especially those about other people. Cognitive theories are theories of personality that emphasize cognitive processes such as thinking and judging.

Albert Bandura, a social learning theorist suggested the forces of memory and emotions worked in conjunction with environmental influences. Bandura was known mostly for his "Bobo Doll experiment". During these experiments, Bandura videotaped a college student kicking and verbally abusing a bobo doll.

Oral Fixation: (0-18 mos.) Fixations at the oral stage may be extremely clingy and dependent, with an exaggerated need for approval, nurturance, and love. Soothing sensations from sucking may lead to fixated behavior such as thumb sucking and nail biting.

Anal Fixation: (2-3 years). Fixations at the anal stage may exhibit a variety of behaviors: May be very orderly, neat, punctual, or may be the opposite, extremely messy, stubborn, or constantly late. May have conflict with compliance vs. noncompliance, giving and receiving. Can experience regression at this stage and revert back to the oral stage.

Phallic Fixation: (4-6 years). Children enjoy the pleasure they can obtain from touching their genitals and even from masturbating. Children become aware of female and male differences. Identification-process by which the child identifies with a significant other of the same sex. Making the person apart of them by internalizing motives, behaviors, beliefs, and ideals.

Oedipus Complex: Freud hypothesizes that boys want an exclusive relationship with their mother and little girls want an exclusive relationship with their father (Electra).

Castration Complex: For boys there is a conscious effort to renounce or rid sexual feelings toward their mother, as they unconsciously fear that their fathers will castrate them for these feelings.

Penis Envy: Refers to the envy girls develop in society n which men's activities seem more interesting and valued.

Latency Fixation: (7 – 11yrs). May be preoccupied with attracting mares or take on stereotypical characteristics of their own or the opposite gender, individuals fixated at the latency stage may seem asexual.

Genital Fixation: (12yrs and older). Goal is the development of mature sexuality and a capacity for emotional intimacy.

He then showed this video to a class of kindergarten children who were getting ready to go out to play. When they entered the play room, they saw bobo dolls, and some hammers. The people observing these children at play saw a group of children beating the doll. He called this study and his findings observational learning, or modeling.

Early examples of approaches to cognitive style are listed by Baron (1982). These include Witkin's (1965) work on field dependency, Gardner's (1953) discovering people had consistent preference for the number of categories they used to categories heterogeneous objects, and Block and Petersen's (1955) work on confidence in line discrimination judgments. Baron relates early development of cognitive approaches of personality to ego psychology. More central to this field have been:

- Self-efficacy work, dealing with confidence people have in abilities to do tasks;[9]
- Locus of control theory dealing with different beliefs people have about whether their worlds are controlled by themselves or external factors;
- Attributional style theory dealing with different ways in which people explain events in their lives. This approach builds upon locus of control, but extends it by stating we also need to consider whether people attribute to stable causes or variable causes, and to global causes or specific causes.

Humanistic theories

In humanistic psychology it is emphasized people have free will and they play an active role in determining how they behave. Accordingly, humanistic psychology focuses on subjective experiences of persons as opposed to forced, definitive factors that determine behavior. Abraham Maslow and Carl Rogers were proponents of this view, which is based on the "phenomenal field" theory of Combs and Snygg (1949).[18]

Maslow spent much of his time studying what he called "self-actualizing persons", those who are "fulfilling themselves and doing the best they are capable

of doing". Maslow believes all who are interested in growth move towards self-actualizing (growth, happiness, satisfaction) views. Many of these people demonstrate a trend in dimensions of their personalities. Characteristics of self-actualizers according to Maslow include the four key dimensions:

1. **Awareness**—maintaining constant enjoyment and awe of life. These individuals often experienced a "peak experience". He defined a peak experience as an "intensification of any experience to the degree there is a loss or transcendence of self". A peak experience is one in which an individual perceives an expansion of his or herself, and detects a unity and meaningfulness in life. Intense concentration on an activity one is involved in, such as running a marathon, may invoke a peak experience.
2. **Reality and problem centered**—they have tendency to be concerned with "problems" in their surroundings.
3. **Acceptance/Spontaneity**—they accept their surroundings and what cannot be changed.
4. **Unhostile sense of humor/democratic**—they do not like joking about others, which can be viewed as offensive. They have friends of all backgrounds and religions and hold very close friendships.

Maslow and Rogers emphasized a view of the person as an active, creative, experiencing human being who lives in the present and subjectively responds to current perceptions, relationships, and encounters. They disagree with the dark, pessimistic outlook of those in the Freudian psychoanalysis ranks, but rather view humanistic theories as positive and optimistic proposals which stress the tendency of the human personality toward growth and self-actualization. This progressing self will remain the center of its constantly changing world; a world that will help mold the self but not necessarily confine it. Rather, the self has opportunity for maturation based on its encounters with this world. This understanding attempts to reduce the acceptance of hopeless redundancy.

Biopsychological theories

Some of the earliest thinking about possible biological bases of personality grew out of the case of Phineas Gage. In an 1848 accident, a large iron rod was driven through Gage's head, and his personality apparently changed. Graphic by Damasio *et al.* showing how the tamping iron may have damaged both frontal lobes. (A 2004 study by Ratiu and colleagues suggests the damage was more limited.)

In general, patients with brain damage have been difficult to find and study. In the 1990s, researchers began to use Electroencephalography (EEG), Positron Emission Tomography (PET) and more recently functional Magnetic Resonance Imaging (fMRI), which is now the most widely used imaging technique to help localize personality traits in the brain. One of the founders of this area of brain research is Richard Davidson of the University of Wisconsin–Madison. Davidson's research lab has focused on the role of the prefrontal cortex (PFC) and amygdala in manifesting human personality.

Trait models have been criticized as being purely descriptive and offering little explanation of the underlying causes of personality. Finally, trait models often underestimate the effect of specific situations on people's behavior. It is important to remember that traits are statistical generalizations that do not always correspond to an individual's behavior.

Biological Pathways to Personality

Underlying the question of whether brain equals behavior is the possibility that one's personality may be understood on a neurobiological level. Personality affects how a person will behave in certain situations. Peoples' attitudes towards their environments, their dispositions, personal preferences and dislikes all help determine their everyday actions. If behavior is controlled by the nervous system, these factors which make up a person's personality must also fall under its direction. This does not refer to whether one's personality is a result of environment or genomic make-up. It has already been proposed that personality is 50%-70% hereditary and that home environment has other levels of impact on the development of personality. The higher ordered personality trait which has been most studied for its neurobiological link is extraversion. On a hierarchical level extraversion often describes a person who is sociable, active, assertive and impulsive. It seems likely that these traits fall under neuronal influence.

Further supporting Depue's theory, a direct relationship has been found between dopamine response and extraversion levels. Extraverted subjects were found (indirectly) to have significantly higher levels of dopamine than non-extraverted subjects. The enzyme monoamine oxidase, a dopamine inhibitor, is inversely related to extraversion. Other research has described this dopamine model of personality as a behavioral on and off switch. The BFS (behavioral activation or facilitation system) regulates exploratory and goal-directed behavior through the release of dopamine. The off switch (behavioral inhibition system) is believed to be controlled by serotonin levels. Low levels cause impulsiveness and oversensitivity (characteristics of extraversion) while high levels can cause anxiety (characteristic of intraversion). Extreme levels of either dopamine or serotonin play a role in personality disorders.

Sick Nos. 949, 5106.

Of course a complex personality trait such as extraversion is not controlled solely by two or three neurotransmitters. It is most likely an elaborate interaction between many different chemicals and neurons in the brain. However, dopamine is a good place to begin investigation. Dopamine has far reaching influences in the nervous system. A single dopamine releasing neuron can form 500,000- 1,000,000 synapses with neighboring neurons. The amine neurotransmitters (dopamine, serotonin, norepinephrine) have been shown to be active in brain structures associated with emotion, motivation and cognition, all processes involved in personality formation.

Personality research has a long history in the field of psychology. Only in the last forty years, however, have scientists begun to look for biological explanations. Is it possible that eventually neurobiology will be able to explain personality on the same level as motor responses or our sense of hearing? It is unlikely in the near future that biology will confirm or refute Freud's theories on personality development. Still, the chemical basis of personality gives us great insight into how and why we behave as we do. It can help explain why different people react differently to similar situations. Perhaps most importantly, it offers the potential to alter such behavior, from treating mild cases of anxiety to severe personality disorders.

Assessing the Trait Approach to Personality

While most agree that people can be described based upon their personality traits, theorists continue to debate the number of basic traits that make up human personality. While trait theory has objectivity that some personality theories lack (such as Freud's psychoanalytic theory), it also has weaknesses. Some of the most common criticisms of trait theory center on the fact that traits are often poor predictors of behavior. While an individual may score high on assessments of a specific trait, he or she may not always behave that way in every situation. Another problem is that trait theories do not address how or why individual differences in personality develop or emerge.

Assessing Personality

Personality tests

There are two major types of personality tests. **Projective** tests assume personality is primarily unconscious and assess an individual by how he or she responds to an ambiguous stimulus, like an ink blot. The idea is unconscious needs will come out in the person's response, e.g. an aggressive person may see images of destruction. **Objective** tests assume personality is consciously accessible and measure it by self-report questionnaires. Research on psychological assessment has generally found objective tests are more valid and reliable than projective tests

A personality test is a standardized diagnostic instrument (test) that records non-cognitive traits (e. g. achievement motivation, conscientiousness or interests) as clearly defined dimensions or factors. Personality tests are used in different domains, from psychological assessments to job interviews or even when joining military institutions. The main purpose of personality tests is to identify different characteristics of the subject and compare them against common and objective normative samples for the purpose of placement or therapeutic treatment.

Types of Personality Tests

Beck Depression Inventory—Pencil/paper test used in conjunction with professional where subjects rate themselves on a variety of symptoms/experiences. Used to assess depression / level of depression.

Burns Depression / Anxiety checklists—Pencil/paper tests where subject is asked to rate themselves on different symptoms, thoughts, and feelings. Ratings then yield scores which are used to determine a subject's level of depression or anxiety. These are two different checklists that are used in conjunction with a trained professional.

Eysenck Personality Questionnaire—Pencil/paper test where subject is asked to complete a brief questionnaire in a yes/no format, depending on how questions apply to them. Test yields four scores,

(Extraversion, Psychoticism, Neuroticism, and Lie—Note, the meaning of these scales does not refer to the use of these four words as we commonly know them. I.E., Psychoticism does not measure one's psychotic potential, etc.) which then correspond to levels of four different personality traits.

House—Person—Tree Test—This is a projective test where a subject is usually asked to draw separate pictures of a house, a person, and a tree. They may be asked to draw in pencil, or in colored crayon. They may also be asked to draw additional pictures, and are often asked to create stories regarding these pictures. Professional generally interprets these pictures/answers based on themes evident in the drawing, and also based on other methods and theories. Scoring method for this type of test often varies greatly.

MMPI2 (Minnesota Multiphasic Personality Inventory 2)—This is a pencil and paper test, or can also be completed on a computer, where subjects answer yes/no to various questions depending on how they pertain to them. Can take upwards of one hour to complete. Is statistically well-normed and validated, but must be interpreted by an experienced professional. Measures various personality characteristics, including depression, anxiety, obsessiveness, social introversion. Can also provide some measure of thought disorder.

Myers—Briggs Type Indicator—Traditionally a simple pencil/paper self-report test, subjects are asked to answer questions based on their likes/dislikes and experiences. Test yields a four digit code that sorts subjects into 16 personality types. Is often used to help individuals make career-related decisions, or to understand their own way of looking at and/or perceiving the world around them.

Rorschach Inkblot Test—Projective test where subject is shown a series of inkblots and is asked what they see in these inkblots. Test can be scored in a variety of different ways, and is used primarily to uncover personality traits.. However, other uses of this test have also been to investigate thought disorders, perception, and emotional issues. There are several scoring systems for this test, many of which do not have adequate reliability and/or scientific validity.

Test should only be used by a licensed mental health professional skilled in the use and scoring of this test.

Sentence Completion Blank—There are numerous types of sentence-completion tests available, depending on population to be tested. Generally, subject is given a 1-2 page form of incomplete sentences. Sentences are started, and subject is asked to complete them. Professional scores the test, usually on themes that are evident in the completed sentences. Test is considered projective, and scoring methods vary greatly. Can yield information on personality, stress, depression, etc.

Suicide Probability Scale—Pencil/paper test administered by a trained professional where subjects rate themselves on various thoughts, feelings, and ideas. Ratings are then turned into scores, which are interpreted as a Suicide Risk profile. Suicide risk is determined by scores, but also by various risk categories that a subject may fall into.

Thematic Apperception Test (TAT)—Administered by a highly trained professional, subject is shown a series of several cards depicting people in various situations. Subject is asked to tell a detailed story about each card. Story is then interpreted by professional. Scoring methods for this test vary greatly, as does the experience of examiner. Is often used to assess personality, depression, world outlook, etc.

PERSONALITY AND CULTURE

Ruth Benedict

'Culture and personality' is the name given to the earliest school of thought in what came to be the sub-disciplinary field of psychological anthropology.

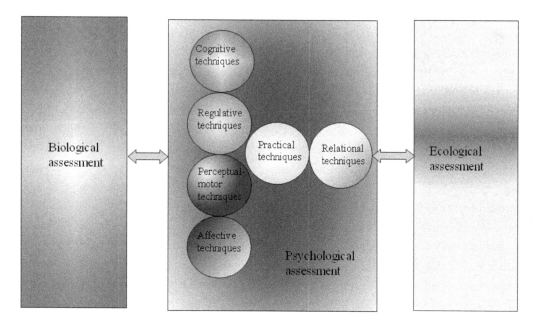

Culture and personality movement was a core of anthropology in the first half of the 20th century. It attempts to find general traits repeating in a specific culture to lead to a discovery of a national character, model personality types and configurations of personality by seeking the individual characteristics and personalities. The field of personality and culture gives special attention to socialization of children and enculturation. Theorists of culture and personality school argue that socialization creates personality patterns. It helps shape people's emotions, thoughts, behaviors, cultural values and norms to fit into and function as productive members in the surrounding human society. The study of culture and personality demonstrates that different socialization practices such as childrearing in different societies (cultures) result in different personality types. This conception is demonstrated in the work of anthropologists, such as Margaret Mead and Ruth Benedict, Barbara Rogoff and Shirley Brice Heath.

Culture influences socialization patterns, which in turn shapes some of the variance of personality (Maccoby 2000). Because of distinctive socialization practices in different societies, each society has unique culture and history. Based on this perspective, one should not assume universal laws govern how cultures run. As Boas (2001) states: "We rather see that each cultural group has its own unique history, dependent partly upon the peculiar inner development of the social group, and partly upon the foreign influences to which it has been subjected.

Leading Figures in discussing culture and personality:

Sigmund Freud (1856-1939) Theorists of culture and personality school in the early twentieth century borrowed the insights of Sigmund Freud, the father of psychoanalysis to explain the phenomena of mind as revealed in different cultures. Freud claims dreams are royal roads to the unconscious. That is, dream interpretation can be an access to understand aspects of personality. His work *The Interpretation of Dreams* reveals that nothing happens by chance and human action and thoughts are driven by the unconscious at the extent level. He coined the Oedipus complex in psychoanalytical theory. It is a universal phenomenon in which a group of unconscious feelings and ideas desiring to possess the parent of the opposite sex and harbor hostility towards the parent of the same sex. The Oedipus complex is Freud's self-analysis.

Erik Erikson (1902 – 1994) He is known for his socio-cultural theory and its impact on human development. Erikson theorizes eight stages of human socialization. He elaborates Freud's genital stage into adolescence plus three stages of adulthood. He coins the phrase *identity crisis,* an adolescent period of intensive role confusion and exploration of different ways to see oneself. Erikson also emphasizes mutuality in generation influence. Unlike Freud's emphasis to dramatic parental influence on children, Erikson believes that children impact on their parents' development as well. He integrates information from cultural anthropology about the role of culture in human development.

Edward Sapir (1884-1939) Edward Sapir was recognized as one of the first to explore the relationship between language and anthropology. He perceives language as a tool in shaping human mind. He describes language is a verbal symbol of human relations. His key work concerns ethnography and linguistics of native American groups. He is noted for exploring the connection among language, personality and social behavior. His illuminating exploration in language, culture and personality has been collected in the book entitled *Language, Culture, and Personality* published in 1949 by the University of California Press.

Benjamin Lee Whorf (1897 – 1941) He is an American linguist. Whorf was interested in the American Indians and the Hopi language. He was Edward Sapir's student. Whorf believes in linguistic determinism, that is, language shapes thought and language structure affects cognition and behaviors of language users. He has been seen as the primary proponent of linguistic relativity. Linguistic relativity means the differences in various languages reflect the different views of language speakers. Linguistic relativity often refers to «Sapir-Whorf hypothesis." He uses observation techniques to perceive linguistic differences and their consequences in human thoughts and behaviors.

Ruth Benedict (1887-1948) Ruth Benedict believed the cultural whole determines personality of individuals of the culture. She argues "the crystallization of a culture pattern is not a necessary result of circumstances, but rather is a creative formulation of the human imagination." Her interpretation guides people toward further understanding of the concept of culture and cultural relativism. Cultural relativism suggests that each society be interpreted in its own

norms. People from other cultures should not use their standards to disparage the norms, values and customs of a culture different from their own. She further points out that morality is evaluated by the values of the culture. Benedict's conceptualization of culture best reflects her ideas on cultural particularism that emphasizes the importance of exploring each culture itself. She explains: "A culture, like an individual, is a more or less consistent pattern of thought and action. Within each culture there came into being characteristic purposes not necessarily shared by other types of society. In obedience to these purposes, each people further and further consolidates its experience, and in proportion to the urgency of these drives the heterogeneous items of behavior take more and more congruous shape" (1934:46). Benedict, Sapir and Mead are the major figures in progressing culture and personality movement.

Margaret Mead (1901-1978) Margaret Mead works explore human development in a cross-cultural perspective and cover the topics on gender roles and childrearing in primitive cultures and American own. Her first work, *Coming of Age in Samoa,* is a best seller and built up Mead as a Leading Figure in Cultural Anthropology. The book tells that individual development is determined by cultural expectations. Human development experiences differently in each culture. As she points out "...man made for himself a fabric of culture with which each human life was dignified by form and meaning...Each people makes this fabric differently, selects some clues and ignores others, emphasizes a different sector of the whole arc of potentialities."(1935: 1)

Abram Kardiner (1891-1981) Kardiner contribution concerns the interplay of individual personality development and the situated cultures. He develops a psycho-cultural model for the relationship between child-rearing, housing and decent types in the different cultures. He distinguishes primary institutions (e.g. child training, toilet behavior and family structure form individual basic personality) and secondary institutions. He explains that basic personality structures in a society further influences the product of secondary institutions as religion and arts.

Cora Dubois (1903- 1991) In this social-psychological study, she advanced the concept of modal personality structure. Cora Dubois states that individual variation within a culture exists and each culture shares the development of a particular type which might not exist in its individuals. She is also the author Social Forces in Southeast Asia (1949). Cora Dubois, Abram Kardiner and Ralph Linton coauthored the book, *the Psychological Frontiers of Society*, published by Columbia University Press in 1945. The book consists of careful descriptions and interpretations of three cultures, namely, the Comanche culture, the Alorese culture, and the culture of an American rural community. It explains the basic personality formed by the diversity of subject matter in each culture.

Clyde Kluckhohn (1905 – 1960) Clyde Kluckhohn is noted for his long-term ethnographic work about the Navajo located in part of northern Arizona. Based on his experiences in Navajo country, he finished the books entitled *To the Foot of the Rainbow* (1927) and *Beyond the Rainbow* (1933). Kluckhohn initially held the view of the biological equality of races. Later he reversed his position to the belief that humans are the product of a mix of biology and culture. His ideas are collected into *Personality in Nature, Society, and Culture* (1953) edited by Kluckhohn and a psychologist Henry Murray.

CHAPTER 12 SUMMARY

It is worth beginning a discussion of personality by offering a concise definition, with a discussion of the multifaceted lay conceptions of what is meant by personality. This usually allows for a discussion of traits as well, which then dovetails into more detailed theoretical lecture material.

FREUD'S MODEL OF PERSONALITY

Freud described two different models that describe personality, one being a stage theory of the development of the unconscious. The more basic topographic model organizes the mind into three distinct functional aspects:

- conscious
- preconscious
- unconscious

Each of these are processes that organize our experience of the world. An important feature of this model involves how conflict and ambivalence are handled by the organism, which Freud suggested are everyday aspects of life. That is, resolving conflicts and ambivalence is a necessary aspect of the human condition.

The psychosexual stages describe a developmental process for the basic structures of the unconscious, and how one shows different personality styles later in life. The psychosexual stages are divided into the following sequence:

- oral (0-18 months)
- anal (2-3 years)
- phallic (4-6 years)
- latency (7-11 years)
- genital (12 years and above)

It is worthwhile to emphasize and clarify Freud's original intent in describing each of these stages, and dispel any misconceptions about each developmental stage. For example, students may have heard about Freud's notions of the phallic stage, but be grossly misinformed about the basic theoretical idea behind it.

Each stage is characterized by conflict that must be resolved, usually by a defense mechanism housed within the unconscious. Specifically, in lectures it is worthwhile to describe the conflict, method of adaptive resolution, and the co-occurring development of unconscious structures. These structures are the id, ego, and superego. By doing this, one can also begin to describe the defense mechanisms utilized by the ego in resolving conflicts.

Fixations refer to developmental difficulties encountered at each stage, usually involving an inability to resolve one of the stage related conflicts. Overlaid on the whole model is the drive model, which suggests that all behaviors can be reduced to two basic instinctual drives:

- sex
- aggression

In the structural model (that is, the organization of the unconscious into id, ego, super-ego), there are characteristic processes associated with each structure. Each one can be depicted as follows:

- id → primary process
- ego → secondary process
- superego → ideals

DEFENSE MECHANISMS

Primary process refers to wishful and illogical thinking that typically cannot be manifested in the everyday world. At the other extreme, the superego offers ideals and standards that also may be unreasonably high. In order to counterbalance these forces, the ego works from secondary process, which is goal directed and rational.

Because the ego is under such strain from acting as an intermediary between id and superego, there are a number of defense mechanisms that the ego constructs to alleviate tension. Some of these are

- identification
- repression
- denial
- projection
- reaction formation
- sublimation
- rationalization

Following the theorizing of Freud, several of his followers developed different ideas about how personality is organized, and how it develops.

OBJECT RELATIONS THEORIES

These theoreticians developed from following Freud and his basic ideas about the unconscious and the motivating factors involved in driving behavior, but took different notions and changed them according to differing views, and in order to accommodate shortcomings in the original theory. Each of these theorists developed a special language that served as an outgrowth of the original Freudian model (such as Jung with collective and personal unconscious).

Most contemporary psychodynamic thinking centers upon object relations theory. Unlike previous theories of unconscious behavior, this line of thinking has been empirically examined, with some positive results. At its basis, object relations suggests that there are unconscious representations of relationships that drive our behavior when in the presence of those people, or others that are similar. Representations center on the self, significant others, and relationships in particular.

ASSESSMENT OF UNCONSCIOUS PATTERNS

Typically, students have encountered notions about personality measurement such as projective tests. This is an opportunity to bring to life the ideas that are conveyed by the projective hypothesis—the idea that unconscious responses are borne out by examining ambiguous stimuli. In describing this method of measurement, one can cover popular projective tests such as the Rorschach, TAT, and sentence completion tests.

Throughout the discussion of psychodynamic theories of personality, it is important to highlight the strengths (such as the rich description of personality) and weaknesses (such as the limited empirical support for different parts of these theories) in order to set the tone for examining other theories of personality.

COGNITIVE-SOCIAL THEORIES

A major aspect of cognitive-social theories involves traits, and differential methods of encoding information. These theories suggest that depending on personality styles, one encodes and understands the environment different. Part of the original notion of encoding and traits comes from the theory forwarded by George Kelly, where one has a set of personal constructs that determine how one interprets the world.

Since the early theorizing of traits and encoding, there have been gains in examining more general trends across people that predict behavior. Specifically, expectancies and competencies predict how people behave in later situations. Two particular expectancies deserve special mention: behavior-outcome expectancies and self-efficacy expectancies. The first involves the belief that a behavior will lead to a particular outcome, while the second refers to the sense that one is capable of performing the behavior necessary to attain the desired outcome.

Self-regulation involves the ability to set goals and adjust these goals according to competencies. This ability interacts with both behavior-outcome expectancies and self-efficacy expectancies in predicting behavior. It may be fruitful to consider the strengths and limits of this model as well, now that students have been exposed to two different theoretical frameworks for personality.

TRAIT THEORIES

As noted earlier, at this point students should have been exposed to a psychological definition of traits when discussing the meaning of personality per se. Here is an opportunity to expand upon that definition by couching the terms within a theoretical framework that is not inconsistent with either of the previous theoretical models. That is, trait theories may serve to contribute greatly within each of the other theories, without being contradictory to the basic tenets of each.

Eysenck's theory of traits helped set the foundation for scientific trait research, and specifically, an examination of psychophysiological processes that accompany different traits. There are essentially three major factors associated with Eysenck's model:

- Extroversion
- Neuroticism
- Psychoticism

It is important to emphasize that each of these are on continua, and therefore all students in the class have some levels on each dimension. This sets the occasion to discuss the basic meaning of each construct more fully without individuals in the class remaining stuck on a more stereotyped meaning of particular terms (such as psychoticism).

Another popular, and some have argued more inclusive, trait theory is the Five-Factor Model. This theory posits five basic dimensions that organize personality:

- Openness to experience
- Conscientiousness
- Extroversion
- Agreeableness
- Neuroticism

Although there have been some minor differences depending on the sample used to determine these factors, there has been fairly consistent findings across cultures.

GENETIC FACTORS IN PERSONALITY

It appears that some personality traits are genetically transmitted, although some have greater heritable salience than others. Rather than expect students to commit all of this information to memory, it is instead worthwhile to consider how genetic factors work (such as dominant and recessive genes) and place that discussion in the context of a heritability lecture. Trait theory, and the associated labels, is largely consistent with the language used in genetics.

CONSISTENCY OF PERSONALITY

If traits are to be called traits, then these behaviors should be consistent across situations and time. However, it appears that the picture is more complex than that would suggest. There are situational variables that can produce different behaviors—even contrary to the measured traits in an individual. Interestingly, it also appears that personality patterns can change over time—either in intensity or degree. This is worth pointing out by illustrating how people may 'mellow' with age, or under new situations people may adopt different styles of responding to environmental events.

HUMANISTIC THEORIES

This framework is based largely upon the writings of Carl Rogers. The basic element to convey to students involves a two-pronged idea regarding personality suggested by Rogers—true self and false self. In a related vein, existential approaches involve the idea that one creates their self, often as a means of avoiding anxiety. Anxiety in this case is often existential in nature, typically involving death or a broader life issue. I sometimes describe to students the 'pre-life crises that one goes through as part of the college experience of determining life goals and aspirations.

13

PSYCHOLOGICAL DISORDERS

- Outline Rogers's person-centered approach and discuss how compatible or incompatible his work is with respect to other theories of personality.
- Outline the key features of existential personality theories.
- Discuss the methods used to probe the interaction of genetics with personality.
- Discuss at least two examples of the interaction between culture and individual personality (concentrating on how various cultures value and shape certain kinds of personalities).

Szasz and the "Myth of Mental Illness

At least one prominent theorist argued since the 1960s that the concept of mental illness was a myth and that society should abandon the effort to judge people as sane or insane. Thomas Szasz (1961) claimed that there was no real evidence for biological causes of mental illness, so a person who was labeled mentally ill was essentially the victim of a political act. Such a person was perceived as threatening to society, and that (according to Szasz) was the real reason the person was likely to be locked away in a mental hospital, with no rights and few freedoms. Szasz argued strongly that it was dishonest to label such a person mentally ill and wrong to use illness as an excuse to deprive people of their rights.

Szasz believed that so-called mentally ill people should have the same rights and responsibilities as everybody else. His position was not simply lenient and forgiving, however, because he also felt that in exchange for having the same freedom as every other citizen, an "insane" person should also have the same responsibilities as every other citizen and should not be exempted from moral or legal blame for deviant behavior. Therefore Szasz was against the insanity defense in our legal system, with its implication that people who fall into a special category (insane) should be exempted from punishment for illegal behavior. Instead (Szasz argued) such an individual should be treated just like everybody else. If the person's behavior endangered other people, the person should be arrested and sent to jail. If the person did not endanger other people, the person should be left alone.

Szasz's position was very radical when he first put it forward, but a lot of people agreed with the essence of his argument about freedom and responsibility. Eventually, the laws in the United States changed to resemble Szasz's recommendations. Many states passed legislation making it illegal to put people in mental hospitals against their will, unless they presented a danger to others. In modern day America, people are no longer locked up just for acting crazy. They are allowed to remain free unless they endanger the property or personal safety of other people. If they do pose a danger, they are more likely to be put in a prison than in a mental hospital. That has caused problems for the prison system and mentally ill people who end up there. (See the next page, on deinstitutionalization.)

13

Introduction

Psychological Disorders are widespread all over the world. In the United States, they affect adults, children & adolescents. Over 50% of adult population will experience some type of Psychological Disorder at some point in their life. These disorders will range from depression, anxiety, Post Traumatic Stress Disorder, Globally, Psychological Disorders rank second only to cardiovascular disease.

Psychological Disorders have been known to human kind at least for as long as human history had been recorded. Misunderstanding, stigma & discrimination have always followed alongside, and all of these are still present even in developed & educated societies. Information and education are the main means to reduce these. Even today, with all the research done by scientists, psychologists & psychiatrists in order to understand causes & improve treatments for psychological disorders, misunderstanding, stigma & mystery are still around the subject.

The definition and classification of psychological disorders are a key issue for effective treatment by providers of mental health services. Most international clinical documents use the term "mental disorder". The Surgeon General states that psychological disorders are health conditions characterized by alterations in thinking, mood, or behavior or some combination thereof, associated with distress and/or impaired functioning.

Psychological disorder is not a sign of weakness in individual's character or lack of intelligence. It affects people of diverse groups that belong to all ages, genders, religions, occupational, economic & social circles. Psychological disorders may last a short period or many years or even a lifetime. Symptoms may occur from early childhood or develop later in life, with varying intensity, duration & consistency. The causes are often explained in terms of a diathesis-stress model or biopsychosocial model. In biological psychiatry, psychological disorders are conceptualized as disorders of brain circuits likely caused by developmental processes shaped by a complex interplay of genetics and life experiences, thus there are inborn, inherited & environmental factors.

A large percentage of people with psychological disorders remain untreated for various reasons. Some of the reasons are stigma, cost, unawareness & misunderstanding. Stigma can lead to mistreatment or discrimination towards mentally ill, which can affect person's ability to have a functional social life or even ability to find a decent employment. The cost of treatment is generally expensive, in many cases the mentally ill have no means of affording these expenses, so many remain untreated because of this. For this reason mental health advocates are trying to push the treatment of the mentally ill to be more accessible through better insurance coverage & governmental health services, stating the financial, physical & psychological burden to the mentally ill, their families & society caused by psychological disorders. Unawareness by those who suffer & those around them can last for years causing a significant distress to their lives & relationships. Misunderstanding by families of the sufferers may also leave many untreated, which is more affecting children, teens & younger adults. Torrcy (1983, 1988) underlined the importance of families' understanding the "inner world of mental madness", the sympathy of family, friends & relatives is what makes the disorder bearable, where sympathy is the ability to put oneself in other person's shoes, which is not as simple is it may sound.

Recently, there has been paid more attention to the influence of culture in person's psychological distress. More psychologists & psychiatrists, practitioners as well as theorists, factor in culture for diagnosis & treatment. Cultural norms dictate whether a set of symptoms are considered "normal" or not. Culture can also make help for mental treatment more accessible or the other way around. Cultural concepts, values & beliefs can shape the way psychological disorders develop or are being treated, in many cases these values & beliefs can be the cause of the psychological disorder. Depending on culture symptoms may be expressed differently, public response to these expressions can greatly vary too, in many ways they are interconnected. Effective mental care can't exist without taking the culture into the context. This can greatly affect diagnosis & coping strategies for the patient.

PERSONALITY DEFINED

In psychological idioms "personality" refers to a person's *unique and enduring pattern of thinking, feeling, and behaving.* When viewed in this manner it becomes evident that "personality" encompasses nearly every aspect of human experience. Subsequently, our personalities have the potential to greatly impact our well-being. In particular, the quality of our relationships with others is significantly affected by our personalities.

Psychologists use the term "environment" to refer to these external events going on around us. As we receive this information from our environment, it undergoes a subjective, internal process of evaluation and interpretation. This process of interpretation (our thoughts) and assigning meaning and importance (our feelings about those thoughts) will then determine our behavioral response to these external events in our environment; i.e., what I think and feel determines how I will behave.

Not only does the environment impact our behavior but our behavior will subsequently impact the environment. Therefore, there is a dynamic, interactive exchange between the environment and our personalities (what we think and feel, and how we behave). These habitual patterns form the foundation of "personality." Therefore, the environment influences the development of our personalities, and our personalities' influence how we respond to the environment.

THE GENETICS OF BEHAVIOR AND MENTAL ILLNESS

The influence of genes on behavior, normal and abnormal, has long been established (Plomin et al., 1997). Sorting out which genes are involved and determining how they influence behavior present the greatest challenge. Research suggests that many mental disorders arise in part from defects not in single genes, but in *multiple* genes.

First, genes are the blueprints of cells. The products of genes, proteins, work together in pathways or in building cellular structures, so that finding variants within genes will suggest pathways that can be targets of opportunity for the development of new therapeutic interventions. Genes will also be important clues to what goes wrong in the brain when a disease occurs. For example, once we know that a certain gene is involved in risk of a particular mental illness such as schizophrenia or autism, we can ask at what time during the development of the brain that particular gene is active and in which cells and circuits the gene is expressed. Finally, genes will provide tools for those scientists who are searching for environmental risk factors. Information from genetics will tell us at what age environmental cofactors in risk must be active, and genes will help us identify homogeneous populations for studies of treatment and of prevention.

Heritability refers to how much genetics contributes to the variation of a disease or trait in a population at a given point in time (Plomin et al., 1997). Once a disorder is established as running in families, the next step is to determine its heritability (see below), then its mode of transmission, and, lastly, its location through genetic mapping (Lombroso et al., 1994).

One powerful method for estimating heritability is through twin studies. Twin studies often compare the frequency with which identical versus fraternal twins display a disorder. Since identical twins are from the same fertilized egg, they share the exact genetic inheritance. Fraternal twins are from separate eggs and thereby share only 50 percent of their genetic inheritance. If a disorder is heritable, identical twins should have a higher rate of concordance. Such studies, however, do not furnish information about *which* or *how many* genes are involved. They can only be used to estimate heritability. For example, the heritability of bipolar disorder, according to the most rigorous twin study, is about 59 percent, although other estimates vary (NIMH, 1998). The heritability of schizophrenia is estimated, on the basis of twin studies, at a somewhat higher level (NIMH, 1998).

Even with a high level of heritability, however, it is essential to point out that environmental factors (e.g., psychosocial environment, nutrition, health care access) can play a significant role in the severity and course of a disorder.

OTHER CAUSES OF MENTAL ILLNESS

Biological Factors Involved in Mental Illness

Some mental illnesses have been linked to an abnormal balance of special chemicals in the brain called neurotransmitters. Neurotransmitters help nerve cells in the brain communicate with each other. If these chemicals are out of balance or are not working properly, messages may not make it through the brain correctly, leading to symptoms of mental illness. In addition, defects in or injury to certain areas of the brain have also been linked to some mental conditions.

Other biological factors that may be involved in the development of mental illness include:

Genetics (heredity): Many mental illnesses run in families, suggesting that people who have a family member with a mental illness are more likely to develop a mental illness. Susceptibility is passed on in families through genes. Experts believe many mental illnesses are linked to abnormalities in many genes -- not just one. That is why a person inherits a susceptibility to a mental illness and doesn't necessarily develop the illness. Mental illness itself occurs from the interaction of multiple genes and other factors --such as stress, abuse, or a traumatic event -- which can influence, or trigger, an illness in a person who has an inherited susceptibility to it.

Infections: Certain infections have been linked to brain damage and the development of mental illness or the worsening of its symptoms. For example, a condition known as pediatric autoimmune neuropsychiatric disorder (PANDA) associated with the Streptococcus bacteria has been linked to the development of obsessive-compulsive disorder and other mental illnesses in children.

Brain defects or injury: Defects in or injury to certain areas of the brain have also been linked to some mental illnesses.

Prenatal damage: Some evidence suggests that a disruption of early fetal brain development or trauma that occurs at the time of birth -- for example, loss of oxygen to the brain -- may be a factor in the development of certain conditions, such as autism.

Substance abuse: Long-term substance abuse, in particular, has been linked to anxiety, depression, and paranoia.

Other factors: Poor nutrition and exposure to toxins, such as lead, may play a role in the development of mental illnesses.

Psychological Factors Contribute to Mental Illness

Psychological factors that may contribute to mental illness include: Severe psychological trauma suffered as a child, such as emotional, physical, or sexual abuse An important early loss, such as the loss of a parent, Neglect and Poor ability to relate to others

Environmental Factors Contribute to Mental Illness

Certain stressors can trigger an illness in a person who is susceptible to mental illness. These stressors include:

- Death or divorce
- A dysfunctional family life
- Living in poverty
- Feelings of inadequacy, low self-esteem, anxiety, anger, or loneliness
- Changing jobs or schools
- Social or cultural expectations (For example, a society that associates beauty with thinness can be a factor in the development of eating disorders.)
- Substance abuse by the person or the person's parents

Psychosocial Influences on Mental Health and Mental Illness

Stressful life events, affect (mood and level of arousal), personality, and gender are prominent psychological influences. Social influences include parents, socioeconomic status, racial, cultural, and religious background, and interpersonal relationships. These psychosocial influences, taken individually or together, are integrated into many chapters of this report in discussions of epidemiology, etiology, risk factors, barriers to treatment, and facilitators to recovery.

Psychodynamic Theories

Psychodynamic theories of personality assert that behavior is the product of underlying conflicts over which people often have scant awareness. Sigmund Freud (1856–1939) was the towering proponent of psychoanalytic theory, the first of the 20th-century psychodynamic theories. Many of Freud's followers pioneered their own psychodynamic theories, but this section covers only psychoanalytic theory. A brief discussion of Freud's work contributes to a historical perspective of mental health theory and treatment approaches.

Freud's theory of psychoanalysis holds two major assumptions: (1) that much of mental life is unconscious (i.e., outside awareness), and (2) that past experiences, especially in early childhood, shape how a person feels and behaves throughout life (Brenner, 1978).

Freud's structural model of personality divides the personality into three parts—the id, the ego, and the superego. The id is the unconscious part that is the cauldron of raw drives, such as for sex or aggression. The ego, which has conscious and unconscious elements, is the rational and reasonable part of personality. Its role is to maintain contact with the outside world in order to help keep the individual in touch with society. As such, the ego mediates between the conflicting tendencies of the id and the superego. The latter is a person's conscience that develops early in life and is learned from parents, teachers, and others. Like the ego, the superego has conscious and unconscious elements (Brenner, 1978).

When all three parts of the personality are in dynamic equilibrium, the individual is thought to be mentally healthy. However, according to psychoanalytic theory, if the ego is unable to mediate between the id and the superego, an imbalance would occur in the form of psychological distress and symptoms of mental disorders. Psychoanalytic theory views symptoms as important only in terms of expression of underlying conflicts between the parts of personality. The theory holds that the conflicts must be understood by the individual with the aid of the psychoanalyst who would help the person unearth the secrets of the unconscious. This was the basis for psychoanalysis as a form of treatment, as explained later in this chapter.

Cognitive Theory

The way in which we interpret an event is critically linked to another type of cognition: our core beliefs. A complex blend of factors derived from both «nature» and «nurture» are thought to drive the formation of people's core beliefs. Cognitive theory assumes there are certain inherited dispositions such as temperament (nature), which interact with children's environments (nurture), to influence the ultimate shape of their personality, and their characteristic interpersonal strategies. Moreover, cognitive theory emphasizes the importance of social learning with respect to personality development. Childhood experiences, including childhood trauma and abuse, are seen as important factors that establish these core beliefs about the world. These core beliefs will later color, and potentially distort, people's perceptions and interpretations of subsequent experiences.

Behaviorism and Social Learning Theory

Behaviorism (also called learning theory) posits that personality is the sum of an individual's observable responses to the outside world (Feldman, 1997). As charted by J. B. Watson and B. F. Skinner in the early part of the 20th century, behaviorism stands

Classical Theoretical Perspectives: Models of Abnormal Behavior

Biological Model: is the concept that behavior is caused by biological factors. Thus when behavior is abnormal it is caused by biochemical imbalance. Medical means are used to correct this problem such as medication or surgery. This can also be referred to as the Medical Model.

Psychoanalytic Model: approaches abnormal behavior from the psychodynamic theoretical base that there are issues with anxiety and conflicts which are too immense for the defense mechanisms. Abnormal behavior is the symptom of internal issues. Treatment is focused on the curing of the sources of anxiety and conflicts.

Cognitive Model: approaches abnormal behavior as non- effective thinking and problem solving. The treatment approach is to help the person understand his/her problems and learn effective ways of problem solving.

Behavioral Model: Consider abnormal behavior the result of learned social maladjustment. This results in learned inappropriate role expectations and behaviors. Treatment is focused on learning new behavior and unlearning behaviors that are maladaptive.

Sociocultural Model: cultural and social variables influence and define behavior and what is considered abnormal. Also, one must look at what forces in the society and culture cause or creates deviance.

Legal Model: Society sets up laws, regulations and standards of conduct. Violation of these is not acceptable therefore 'deviance or abnormal'.

Statistical Model: Abnormal behavior is considered deviation from the statistical norm.

at loggerheads with psychodynamic theories, which strive to understand underlying conflicts. Behaviorism rejects the existence of underlying conflicts and an unconscious. Rather, it focuses on observable, overt behaviors that are learned from the environment (Kazdin, 1996, 1997). Its application to treatment of mental problems, which is discussed later, is known as behavior modification.

Learning is seen as behavior change molded by experience. Learning is accomplished largely through either classical or operant conditioning. Classical conditioning is grounded in the research of Ivan Pavlov, a Russian physiologist. It explains why some people react to formerly *neutral* stimuli in their environment, stimuli that previously would not have elicited a reaction. Pavlov's dogs, for example, learned to salivate merely at the sound of the bell, without any food in sight. Originally, the sound of the bell would not have elicited salvation. But by repeatedly pairing the

sight of the food (which elicits salvation on its own) with the sound of the bell, Pavlov taught the dogs to salivate just to the sound of the bell by itself.

The movement beyond behaviorism was spearheaded by Albert Bandura (1969, 1977), the originator of social learning theory (also known as social cognitive theory). Social learning theory has its roots in behaviorism, but it departs in a significant way. While acknowledging classical and operant conditioning, social learning theory places far greater emphasis on a different type of learning, particularly observational learning. Observational learning occurs through selectively observing the behavior of another person, a model. When the behavior of the model is rewarded, children are more likely to imitate the behavior. For example, a child who observes another child receiving candy for a particular behavior is more likely to carry out similar behaviors. Social learning theory asserts that people's cognitions—their views, perceptions, and expectations toward their environment—affect what they learn. Rather than being passively conditioned by the environment, as behaviorism proposed, humans take a more active role in deciding what to learn as a result of cognitive processing. Social learning theory gave rise to cognitive-behavioral therapy, a mode of treatment described later in this chapter and throughout this report.

Cognitive-Behavior Theory

Originally based on the works of Aaron Beck, M.D.. and Albert Ellis, Ph.D., CBT emerged from the observation that people react emotionally and behaviorally to events according to their *interpretation* of those events. In other words, our thoughts (cognitions) lead to our emotions and subsequent behavior. By way of illustration, suppose someone stepped on your foot. You might interpret this action by concluding that this person was intentionally trying to hurt you. In response to this "assault," you might become angry and maybe even retaliate against the foot-stepper. Alternatively, you could interpret the same event as an indication of the other person's clumsiness, in which case you might laugh, and feel compassionate and forgiving. Notice, the identical environmental event (someone stepping on your foot) resulted in two entirely different sets of emotions and behaviors, simply by the way your mind interpreted the event.

Humanistic Theory

The humanistic theory centers around four basic principles: (1) the primary interest on the person, (2) the preference on human choice and self-actualization, (3) the emphasis on meaningfulness, and (4) the ultimate value on human dignity. Two of the most influential persons in the humanistic bandwagon are Carl Rogers and Abraham Maslow.

Carl Rogers introduced client-centered therapy and published a book entitled "On Becoming A Person" in 1961. Rogers emphasized that all living organisms possess an innate actualizing tendency, a drive to survive, grow and develop. He also stressed

out the importance of positive regard. He also defined unconditional positive regard as "a situation in which the acceptance and love a person receives from significant others is unqualified" and contrasted it with conditional positive regard as "a situation in which the acceptance and love one receives is contingent upon one's behavior". When the need for self-actualization does not parallel with the need for self-discrepancies, positive regard, frustration, anxiety and incongruence may result. Rogers also pointed out the importance of a person's self-concept and this is usually formed from social interactions.

The second important name is Abraham Maslow, who shifted from behaviorism to humanism, after the birth of his first child. Maslow described this life event as his eye-opener, describing that he felt "not being in control" and further explained that "anyone who has a baby could not be a behaviorist". In humanism, he focused on motivation. According to Maslow, each person strives to achieve a certain level of living, development and stability. The achievement or fulfillment of this desire further pushes a person to strive for self-actualization, where a person strives to become the best person he/she can become. Simply put, self-actualization is the desire to fulfill a person's potential. He also further explained that in order for self-actualization to be attained, the lower needs (survival needs, stability, acceptance and affection, self-esteem) should be gratified first. Most self-actualized persons also enjoy a peak experience, which Maslow described as "a fleeting but intense moment of self-actualization in which a person feels happy, absorbed, and extraordinarily capable".

Biological Theory

The Biosocial Theory of Creativity is that there is a definitive link between madness, also known as irrationality, and creativity. Many of the greatest creative thinkers, Van Gogh as an example, went mad later in their lifetime. Also, mad people who are held in psychotic wards have been found to create masterpieces of art, especially in the avant-garde style. It has been proposed that the suffering of mentally ill people is compensated when they perform great works of art, as an opposite end of their mental spectrum.

The second part is that creativity is just an outlet to deal with the madness within the patients. There is also the opposite of this being put forth, in that, madness is just a form of creativity that is misunderstood by the general populace. Both of these forms are extremely controversial and are being debated. A conclusion for this may not be available for many years to come.

The third part is that madness is ultimately just a result of some imbalance or defect within the brain. Some examples of these defects are brains that have unusual EEG (Electroencephalography) readings, an unbalanced neurochemistry, abnormal brain structures, or unusual hemisphere lateralization.

The fourth and last part is that the creativity associated with madness is inherited, but where the inheritance comes from is not so clear. Genes and DNA is a possibility, but parental trauma that caused a defect within the womb is also possible. Then, there are environmental that could create such a madness. Drugs could affect the brain, which then would become an inherited defect. All of these things are possible within the bounds of modern science.

Social Learning Theories

The most prominent name under the social learning bandwagon is Albert Bandura. He suggested that people acquire a certain set of behaviors through observation and imitation. He used the term modeling to refer to people's tendency to observe and imitate behaviors of other people. He emphasized that learning and acquiring behaviors operate in a social context. Bandura also popularized the concept on self-efficacy defined as "the belief that one is capable of performing the behaviors required to producing a desired outcome". A person's self-efficacy corresponds to his or her competencies. A person may also have a different self-efficacy in some situations and a different self-efficacy in others. Bandura also further explained that self-efficacy is gained through a person's past experiences either at success or failures,

a person's observation of other persons, encouraging words received from significant persons, feelings of calmness and relaxation.

Julian Rotter, another disciple of the social learning approach, also suggested that human behavior is influenced by two factors: the expectancy that a certain action will be reinforced and the value of that reinforcement to the person. Rotter also coined the term "locus of control", referring to the "expectancy that one's reinforcements are generally controlled by internal or external factors". Those who have internal locus of control attribute their reinforcements to personal will, determination, characteristics or abilities. They believe they control everything that will happen to them. On the other hand, persons who have external locus of control attribute their reinforcements to luck, destiny, karma, or to other powerful persons. Rotter also emphasized the possibility of practicing internal locus of control in some situations and external in others. Another possibility that he also stressed out is the difference in persons' perceptions of control.

Based on that proposition by Rotter, another branch of theory was introduced by Walter Mischel, the cognitive social-learning theory. Mischel suggested that there are five "person variables" necessary to understand the interaction between individuals and social environment. These variables are as follows: competencies, encoding strategies, expectancies, subjective values, and self-regulatory systems. Mischel also further emphasized the importance of self-regulation.

Developmental Theories

The earliest stage is characterized with the basic trust vs. mistrust dilemma. During this stage, the virtue of hope remains significant. This stage is also the stage of numinous ritualization, or the baby's longing for the presence of the mother. Lack of affection from the mother may result to estrangement, sense of separation and abandonment. Too much numinous ritualization causes idolism, or hero worship in adult life. During the second stage of life, the child tries to learn the necessary basic skills. This striving for activities and experiences produce the necessity of autonomy vs. shame and doubt. The virtue of will becomes dominant and is characterized by the judicious ritualization, when a child begins to learn to judge itself and its actions. Perversion of the ritualization is legalism or too much emphasis on the law.

The third psychosocial stage is described through initiative vs. guilt forces. The virtue cited is purpose that results from playing, exploring, attempting and failing to discover new things and experimenting. The ritualization is dramatic as a child begins to participate in playacting, imitating adults and pretending. The ritualization's negative pole is impersonation, or playing of roles not representing the true personality. The fourth dilemma is industry vs. inferiority. This stage, the school stage, is described with the formal ritualization, as the child learns to strive for quality and perfection. The distorted sense of formal ritualization is formalism, or "the repetition of meaningless formalities and empty rituals".

The fifth stage, adolescence, is marked with the struggle for identity vs. confusion. A person now begins to acquire a sense of uniqueness, a sense of self. However, a person may also begin to suffer from confusion or overlapping of roles. During this stage, the phenomenon "identity crisis" is also highlighted. The virtue of fidelity and the ritualization of ideology also develop. But if distorted, ideology may turn into totalism. Young adults also deal with intimacy vs. isolation dilemma. They seek intimate relationships and social interactions. The virtue of love becomes dominant as they develop in mutuality with a loved partner. The ritualization is affiliative or sharing, but may be perverted into elitism or exclusivity.

The seventh stage is characterized by generativity vs. stagnation, when adults are concerned with helping the later generations. The virtue of care develops and expressed by concern for others. The ritualization at this stage is generational, and distortion of this ritualization is authoritism. The last stage is labeled with integrity vs. despair. It is partnered with wisdom. The ritualization is termed integral but also corresponds to a ritualism called sapientism.

PERSONALITY TRAITS AND DISORDERS

Personality traits are thought to confer either beneficial or detrimental effects on mental health during adulthood. Here too, however, there may be insufficient attention to gender and culture. The culture-bound nature of much of behavior has limited widespread predictive validity of personality research. (Mischel & Shoda, 1968). With this caveat in mind, a brief summary of healthy and maladaptive characteristics follows.

Self-Esteem

Self-esteem refers to an abiding set of beliefs about one's own worth, competence, and abilities to relate to others (Vaughan & Oldham, 1997). Self-esteem also has been conceptualized as buffering the individual from adverse life events. Emotional well-being is often associated with a slightly positive, yet realistic, outlook (Alloy & Abramson, 1988). The opposite outlook is characterized by pessimism, demoralization, or minor symptoms of anxiety and depression. One seminal aspect of self-esteem has garnered much research attention: self-efficacy (Bandura, 1977). Self-efficacy is defined as confidence in one's own abilities to cope with adversity, either independently or by obtaining appropriate assistance from others. Self-efficacy is a major component of the construct known as resilience (i.e., the ability to withstand and overcome adversity). Other components of resilience include intelligence and problem solving, although resilience is also facilitated by having adequate social support (Beardslee & Vaillant, 1997).

Neuroticism

Neuroticism is a construct that refers to a broad pattern of psychological, emotional, and psychophysiologic reactivity (Eysenck & Eysenck, 1975). The opposite of neuroticism is stability or equanimity, which are major components of mental health. A high level of neuroticism is associated with a predisposition toward recognizing the dangerous, harmful, or defeating aspects of a situation and the tendency to respond with worry, anticipatory anxiety, emotionality, pessimism, and dissatisfaction. Neuroticism is associated with a greater risk of early-onset depressive and anxiety disorders (Clark et al., 1994). Neuroticism also may be linked to a particular cognitive attributional style in which life events are perceived to be large in impact and more difficult to change (Alloy et al., 1984). For example, this attributional style is embodied by pessimists who see every setback or failure as lasting forever, undermining everything, and being their fault (Seligman, 1991). Neuroticism also is associated with more rigid or distorted attitudes and beliefs about one's competence (Beck, 1976).

Psychosis

Though distinctively different, psychosis may appear as a symptom of a number of mental disorders, including mood and personality disorders, schizophrenia, delusional disorder, and substance abuse. It is also the defining feature of the psychotic disorder (i.e., brief psychotic disorder, shared psychotic disorder, psychotic disorder due to a general medical condition, and substance-induced psychotic disorder). Patients suffering from psychosis are unable to distinguish the real from the unreal. They experience hallucinations and/or delusions that they believe are real, and they typically behave in an inappropriate and confused manner. Psychosis may be caused by a number of biological and social factors, depending on the disorder underlying the symptom. Trauma and stress can induce a short-term psychosis known as *brief psychotic disorder*. This psychotic episode, which lasts a month or less, can be brought on by the stress of major life-changing events (e.g., death of a close friend or family member, natural disaster, traumatic event), and can occur in patients with no prior history of mental illness.

Psychosis can also occur as a result of an organic medical condition (known as *psychotic disorder due to a general medical condition*). Neurological conditions (e.g., epilepsy, migraines, Parkinson's Disease, cerebrovascular disease, dementia), metabolic imbalances

(hypoglycemia), endocrine disorders (hyper- and hypothyroidism), renal disease, electrolyte imbalance, and autoimmune disorders may all trigger psychotic episodes.

Avoidance

Avoidance describes an exaggerated predisposition to withdraw from novel situations and to avoid personal challenges as threats. This is the behavioral state that often accompanies the distress of someone who has a high level of neuroticism and low self-efficacy (Vaughan & Oldham, 1997). Closely related to the characteristics of behavioral inhibition or introversion, the trait of avoidance appears to be partly inherited and is associated with shyness, anxiety, and depressive disorders in both childhood and adult life, as well as the subsequent development of substance abuse disorders (Vaughan & Oldham, 1997; Kagan et al., 1988). The people with low levels of harm avoidance are described as "healthy extroverts" and are characterized by confident, carefree, or outgoing behaviors.

Impulsivity

Impulsivity is a trait that is associated with poor modulation of emotions, especially anger, difficulty delaying gratification, and novelty seeking. There is some developmental continuity between high levels of impulsivity in childhood and several adult mental disorders, including attention deficit hyperactivity disorder, bipolar disorder, and substance abuse disorders (Svrakic et al., 1993; Rothbart & Ahadi, 1994). Impulsivity also is associated with physical abuse (both as victim and, subsequently, as perpetrator) and antisocial personality traits (Vaughan & Oldham, 1997).

Sociopathy

This set of traits and behaviors refers to the predisposition to engage in dishonest, hurtful, unfaithful, and at times dangerous conduct to benefit one's own ends. The opposite of sociopathy may be referred to as character or integrity. In its full form, sociopathy is referred to as antisocial personality disorder (DSM-IV). Sociopathy is characterized by a tendency and ability to disregard laws and rules, difficulties reciprocating within empathic and intimate relationships, less internalization of moral standards (i.e., a weaker conscience or superego), and an insensitivity to the needs and rights of others. People scoring high in sociopathy often have problems with aggressivity and are overrepresented among criminal populations. Although not invariably associated with criminality, sociopathy is associated with problematic, unethical, and morally questionable conduct in the workplace and within social systems. Marked sociopathy is much more common among men than women, although several other disorders (borderline and histrionic personality disorders and somatization disorder) are overrepresented among women within the same families (Widiger & Costa, 1994).

In summary, the various traits and behavioral patterns that epitomize strong mental health do not, of course, exist in a vacuum: they develop in a social context, and they underpin people's ability to handle psychological and social adversity and the exposure to stressful life events. Furthermore, as reviewed in Chapter 3, severe or repeated trauma during youth may have enduring effects on both neurobiological and psychological development, altering stress responsivity and adult behavior patterns. Perhaps the best documented evidence of such enduring effects has been shown in young adults who experienced severe sexual or physical abuse in childhood. These individuals experience a greatly increased risk of mood, anxiety, and personality disorders throughout adult life.

CLASSIFICATION OF THE PSYCHOLOGICAL DISORDERS

In medicine, classification of the various medical disorders typically is based on the particular combinations of symptoms that patients present to the physician; the physician then renders a diagnosis based on those

symptoms. Thus, if a patient comes into the doctor's office complaining about chills and fever, muscular aches and pains, nausea, and so, the physician might conclude from these symptoms that the patient has the flu. The idea here is that patients who present the same symptoms are probably suffering from the same underlying disorder, a common cause for which there will be a specific treatment. Psychiatrists, clinical psychologists, school psychologists, and other mental health workers confronted with a variety of behavioral, cognitive, and emotional "symptoms" of their individuals likewise began to identify combinations of these symptoms that seemed to hang together, for the purpose of diagnosing. Historically, category labels were developed for the different syndromes and it was hoped that those falling into the same category might turn out to be suffering from the same set of underlying causes and syptomology of the condition. Thus was born labels such as "schizophrenia," "hysteria," and "manic-depressive psychosis.

Such labels can be very helpful to practitioners. They make it relatively easy to communicate the major features of a person's disorder to other practitioners and layperson, to explain the type of abnormalities a person is diagnosed, for example, as "bipolar" is likely to display extreme mood swings, ranging from exteme elatedness to depression. And once a person has been identified as having a particular disorder, this immediately suggests which treatments are likely to be the most beneficial to the individual.

The initial system of categories developed slowly over decades and in some ways proved unsatisfactory in practice. Eventually the American Psychiatric Association convened a committee to develop a new classification system that would reorganize some of the major categories and provide additional ones based on the latest information. The result of the committee's deliberations was a publication called the **Diagnostic and Statistical Manual** or DSM. Over the years this has been revised several times, the current revision is the DSM IV.

A main approach to psychiatric classification is the "medical model." This holds that psychiatric classification is capable of being both scientific and objective.

The best-known defender of such an approach is Christopher Boorse, in a series of influential papers (1975, 1976, 1977, 1997). A middle range of views, sometimes called "mixed" (e.g., Wakefield 1992), hold that diagnostic categories do match real mental illnesses but that their determination is grounded both in facts about the world and an irreducible element of value or normativity. Two classification models are discussed further, the Diagnostic Statistical manual of Mental Disorders (DSM) and the International Classification of Diseases and Related Health Problems (ICD).

Classification of Abnormal Behavior

The American Psychiatric Association in 1952 developed a standard that is used to determine and diagnose abnormal behavior. This is called the Diagnostic Statistical manual of Mental Disorders or DSM. Currently, the latest addition is called the DSM-IV [4th revision] . The World Health Organization standard is called the International Statistical Classification of Diseases and Related Health Problems or ICD-10 [10th revision] Both the DSM and ICD are coordinated with each other.

The DSM-4 classifies the individual on five axis or dimensions.

> Axis I—Primary Clinical diagnosis which concerns the major problem and symptoms
> Axis II --long-term personality characteristics or developmental problems
> Axis III—any medical problems that might be relevant to the disorder
> Axis IV—environmental and psychosocial problems
> Axis V—global assessment is made on how the person is functioning

The DSM uses a number code that is associated with agreed upon disorders. An example would be 300.14 -Associative Identity Disorder.

Although there is disagreement on how DSM describes disorders, or includes or not includes certain disorders, it does provide an objective established system and standard to operate from. The DSM and ICD are continually being reviewed and when there is significant change then a revised addition comes out.

The DSM covers or identifies over 200 classifications of abnormal conduct these classifications are further categorized into major categories.

International Classification of Diseases (ICD)

The International Classification of Diseases (ICD) is an international standard diagnostic classification for a wide variety of health conditions and consists of 10 main groups. Within each group there are more specific subcategories. The ICD includes personality disorders on the same domain as other mental disorders, unlike the DSM. The ICD-10 states that mental disorder is "not an exact term", although is generally used "to imply the existence of a clinically recognizable set of symptoms or behaviors associated in most cases with distress and with interference with personal functions." (WHO, 1992).

ICD Categories

- F0: Organic, including symptomatic, mental disorders
- F1: Mental and behavioral disorders due to use of psychoactive substances
- F2: Schizophrenia, schizotypal and delusional disorders
- F3: Mood [affective] disorders
- F4: Neurotic, stress-related and somatoform disorders
- F5: Behavioral syndromes associated with physiological disturbances and physical factors
- F6: Disorders of personality and behavior in adult persons
- F7: Mental retardation
- F8: Disorders of psychological development
- F9: Behavioral and emotional disorders with onset usually occurring in childhood and adolescence

- In addition, a group of "unspecified mental disorders".

The World Health Organization (WHO) is revising their classifications in this section as part of the development of the ICD-11 (scheduled for 2014). The WHO (organization) develops and promotes the use of evidence-based tools, norms and standards to support Member States to inform health policy options. It regularly publishes a World Health Report including an expert assessment of a specific global health topic. The organization has published tools for monitoring the capacity of national health systems and health workforces to meet population health needs, for example the WHO endorsed the world's first official HIV/AIDS Toolkit for Zimbabwe (from 3 October 2006), making it an international standard.

PREVALENCE AND AGE-OF-ONSET OF MENTAL DISORDERS

Unlike most disabling physical diseases, mental illness begins very early in life. Half of all lifetime cases begin by age 14; three quarters have begun by age 24. Thus, mental disorders are really the chronic

MENTAL ILLNESS AND AGE OF ONSET RESEARCH NATIONAL COMORBIDITY SURVEY REPLICATION (NCS-R) STUDY

Researchers supported by the National Institute of Mental Health (NIMH) have found that half of all lifetime cases of mental illness begin by age 14, and that despite effective treatments, there are long delays and sometimes decades between first onset of symptoms and when people seek and receive treatment. The study also reveals that an untreated mental disorder can lead to a more severe, more difficult to treat illness, and to the development of comorbid mental illnesses.

The landmark study is described in four papers that document the prevalence and severity of specific mental disorders. The papers provide significant new data on the impairment — such as days lost from work — caused by specific disorders, including mood, anxiety, and substance abuse disorders. These measures will allow researchers to determine the degree of disability and the economic burden caused by mental illness, as well as trends over time.

The papers are reported in the June 6 issue of the *Archives of General Psychiatry* by Ronald Kessler, Ph.D., and colleagues. The study was a collaborative project between Harvard University, the University of Michigan, and the NIMH Intramural Research Program.

This study, called the National Comorbidity Survey Replication (NCS-R), is a household survey of 9,282 English-speaking respondents, age 18 and older. It is an expanded replication of the 1990 National Comorbidity Survey, which was the first to estimate the prevalence of mental disorders (using modern psychiatric standards) in a nationally representative sample. The expansion includes detailed measures that will significantly improve estimates of the severity and persistence of mental disorders, and the degree to which they impair individuals and families, and burden employers and the U.S. economy.

"These studies confirm a growing understanding about the nature of mental illness across the lifespan," says Thomas Insel, M.D., Director of the National Institute of Mental Health. "There are many important messages from this study, but perhaps none as important as the recognition that mental disorders are the chronic disorders of young people in the U.S."

diseases of the young. For example, anxiety disorders often begin in late childhood, mood disorders in late adolescence, and substance abuse in the early 20's. Unlike heart disease or most cancers, young people with mental disorders suffer disability when they are in the prime of life, when they would normally be the most productive.

The risk of mental disorders is substantially lower among people who have matured out of the high-risk age range. Prevalence increases from the youngest group (age 18-29) to the next-oldest age group (age 30-44) and then declines, sometimes substantially, in the oldest group (age 60 +). Females have higher rates of mood and anxiety disorders. Males have higher rates of substance use disorders and impulse disorders.

The survey found that in the U.S., mental disorders are quite common; 26 percent of the general population reported that they had symptoms sufficient for diagnosing a mental disorder during the past 12 months. However, many of these cases are mild or will resolve without formal interventions.

It is likely, however, that the prevalence rates in this paper are underestimated, because the sample was drawn from listings of households and did not include homeless and institutionalized (nursing homes, group homes) populations. In addition, the study did not assess some rare and clinically complex psychiatric disorders, such as schizophrenia and autism, because a household survey is not the most efficient study design to identify and evaluate those disorders.

TYPES OF PSYCHOLOGICAL DISORDERS

Depression

Depression is a psychological condition that changes how you think and feel, and also affects your social behavior and sense of physical well-being. We have all felt sad at one time or another, but that is not depression. Sometimes we feel tired from working hard, or discouraged when faced with serious problems. This too, is not depression. These feelings usually pass within a few days or weeks, once we adjust to the stress. But, if these feelings linger, intensify, and begin to interfere with work, school or family responsibilities, it may be depression.

Depression is one of the most common psychological problems, affecting nearly everyone through either personal experience or through depression in a family member. Each year over 17 million American adults experience a period of clinical depression. The cost in human suffering cannot be estimated. Depression can interfere with normal functioning, and frequently causes problems with work, social and family adjustment. It causes pain and suffering not only to those who have a disorder, but also to those who care about them. Serious depression can destroy family life as well as the life of the depressed person.

Impact of Depression:

- Causes tremendous emotional pain
- Disrupts the lives of millions of people
- Adversely affects the lives of families and friends
- Reduces work productivity and absenteeism
- Has a significant negative impact on the economy, costing an estimated $44 billion a year

Depression causes changes in thinking, feeling, behavior, and physical well-being.

Changes in Thinking—Many people experience difficulty with concentration and decision making. Some people report problems with short term memory, forgetting things all the time. Negative thoughts and thinking are characteristic of depression. Pessimism, poor self-esteem, excessive guilt, and self-criticism are all common. Some people have self-destructive thoughts during more serious depression.

Changes in Feelings—Many people report feeling sad for no reason. Others report that they no longer enjoy activities that they once found pleasurable. You might lack motivation, becoming more apathetic. You might feel "slowed down" and tired all the time. Sometimes irritability is a problem, and more difficulty controlling your temper. Often, Dysthymic disorder leads to feelings of helplessness and hopelessness.

Changes in Behavior—You might act more apathetic, because that's how you feel. Some people do not feel comfortable with other people, so social withdrawal is common. Some people experience a change in appetite, either eating more or less. Because of the chronic sadness, excessive crying is common. Some people complain about everything, and act out their anger with temper outbursts. Sexual desire may disappear, resulting in lack of sexual activity. In the extreme, people may neglect their personal appearance, even neglecting basic hygiene.

Changes in Physical Well-being—We already talked about the negative emotional feelings experienced during depression, but these are coupled with negative physical emotions as well. Chronic fatigue, despite spending more time sleeping is common. Some people can't sleep, or don't sleep soundly.

Types of Depression
1. Unspecified Depression

This category includes people with serious depression, but not quite severe enough for a diagnosis of a major depression, so moderate depression would be included here. This would include people with mild to moderate depression, who have not been depressed long enough to be diagnosed with *Dysthymic disorder*, which requires depressive symptoms for two years. It also includes those individuals who continue to be depressed, in response to some traumatic event, but the depression has lasted longer than expected for an *adjustment disorder with depression*. In an adjustment disorder, the expectation is that the depression will last no more than about six months after the stressor has ended.

2. Adjustment Disoder with Depression

This category describes depression that occurs in response to a major life stressor or crisis. It is also called a "reactive depression." The diagnosis of an adjustment disorder implies that specific psychological symptoms have developed in response to a specific and identifiable psychosocial stressor. Also, the depressive

symptoms related to an adjustment disorder should be treated and dissipate within six months following the end of the stress that produced the reaction. If the symptoms last longer, then the above diagnosis of Depression, not otherwise specified, is probably more appropriate. There is an exception to this rule, as some stressors continue over a long period of time, rather than occurring as a single event. For example, if a person is harassed on the job, that can continue for months. In such a case, the depression may not be severe enough for a diagnosis of major depression, but it would continue for more than six months. But, since the stress is continuing, then the adjustment disorder diagnosis could still be used.

3. Bipolar Depression

This type includes both high and low mood swings, as well as a variety of other significant symptoms not present in other depressions. The distinguishing characteristic of Bipolar Disorder, as compared to other mood disorders, is the presence of at least one manic episode. Every individual with bipolar disorder has a unique pattern of mood cycles, combining depression and manic episodes, that is specific to that individual, but predictable once the pattern is identified. Research studies suggest a strong genetic influence in bipolar disorder.

Bipolar disorder typically begins in adolescence or early adulthood and continues throughout life. It is often not recognized as a psychological problem, because it is episodic.

Effective treatment is available for bipolar disorder. Without treatment, marital breakups, job loss, alcohol and drug abuse, and suicide may result from the chronic, episodic mood swings. The most significant treatment issue is noncompliance with treatment. Most individuals with bipolar disorder do not perceive their manic episodes as needing treatment, and they resist entering treatment. In fact, most people report feeling very good during the beginning of a manic episode. As the manic episode progresses, concentration becomes difficult, thinking becomes more grandiose, and problems develop. Many individuals with bipolar disorder abuse drugs or alcohol during manic episodes, and some of these develop secondary substance abuse problems.

Features of a Depressive Episode
• Persistent sad, anxious, or empty mood
• Feeling helpless, guilty, or worthless
• Hopeless or pessimistic feelings
• Loss of pleasure in usual activities
• Decreased energy
• Loss of memory or concentration
• Irritability or restlessness
• Sleep disturbances
• Loss of or increase in appetite
• Persistent thoughts of death

Features of a Manic Episode
• Extreme irritability & distractibility
• Excessive "high" or euphoric feelings
• Sustained periods of unusual, even bizarre, behavior with significant risk-taking
• Increased energy, activity, rapid talking & thinking, agitation
• Decreased sleep
• Unrealistic belief in one's own abilities
• Poor judgment
• Increased sex drive
• Substance abuse
• Provocative or obnoxious behavior
• Denial of a problem

Anxiety Disorders

Different anxiety problems are reviewed including panic disorder, post traumatic stress, social anxiety, agoraphobia, generalized anxiety, obsessive compulsive disorder and specific phobias. Everyone has experienced significant anxiety at one time or another, although perhaps not severe enough to warrant a diagnosis by a professional. Anxiety is a danger or an alert signal. The physiological arousal experienced as anxiety is directly related to fear of harm. When faced with a threat to one's physical well-being that can result in either serious physical harm or death. Individuals will respond psychologically and physically. This response has been called the "fight or flight" response because it activates us to either defend ourselves, or to run away and escape injury. In a life threatening crisis, this fight or flight response can save our lives.

Anxiety problems are very common. The prevalence of anxiety disorders varies by type, ranging from 1% of the population for some disorders, to as high as 58% of combat veterans experiencing post traumatic stress to some degree. The use of medications for anxiety management is very common, but not effective without psychotherapy. In fact, many anti-anxiety medications produce dependency, and the withdrawal symptoms are often similar to anxiety symptoms. These medications control the symptoms without eliminating the cause for the problem. Psychological treatment focuses on reducing the inappropriate anxiety response, so medication is not necessary. Types of anxiety disorders will be discussed below.

Panic Disorder

A panic attack is an episode of extreme anxiety that includes a specific pattern of symptoms associated with extreme physiological arousal. There may be heart palpitations, trembling or shaking. Often, there are chest pains which cause the person to believe he/she is experiencing a heart attack. The person may feel dizzy, may sweat profusely, have hot flashes, or experience numbness in the extremities. The person may also experience shortness of breath. Nausea is often present, and sometimes the person has difficulty swallowing or feels like he/she is choking. There may be a feeling of unreality, or being detached from oneself. A panic attack often results in a fear of dying, losing control or going crazy. This attack comes on suddenly, and often occurs without a trigger.

Treatment for panic disorder, and the associated anxiety and avoidance behavior, involves psychotherapy, desensitization and other cognitive and behavioral techniques. The goal is to be able to regain control and interrupt a panic attack if one occurs. Frequently, other anxiety issues have to be treated as part of controlling panic disorder.

Post Traumatic Stress Disorder (PTSD)

The essential element of PTSD, is that a person either experienced or observed an event which involved actual or threatened death or serious injury to self or someone else. This disorder was first described in Vietnam War veterans, but has also been called "battle fatigue" and "war neurosis" in past wars. More than 50 percent of combat veterans may experience some form of PTSD, although the milder forms may not be diagnosed or treated. Combat veterans tend to experience more severe forms of PTSD because the duration and severity of trauma during war is greater, but the disorder is frequently diagnosed in civilians who have experienced and survived serious trauma. For example, the victims of serious accidents, rape survivors, and people burned out of their homes, survivors of other natural disasters such as tornadoes, hurricanes and earthquakes, and violent crime victims all may develop PTSD. In each of these events, the threat of death or serious injury is present, and those who develop PTSD realized, or believed, that their lives were on the line.

Another characteristic of PTSD is the remembering of the trauma, and sometimes actually reliving the events in your mind. Survivors have recurrent recollections of the event, distressing dreams about what happened, or some other form of psychological rehashing of the event. (For example, the survivor of a head-on car crash may sometimes "see" another car coming toward him/her, even though there is no other car.) These violent recollections can have a serious impact on a person's life. As a result, the person avoids all situations that might be a reminder of the trauma, and tends to react with significant anxiety whenever there is a reminder of the event.

People with PTSD may experience a variety of somatic and psychological complaints, including sleep disturbance, outbursts of anger, or an exaggerated startle response. (They jump at sudden noises or movements). Social relationships often suffer, as the person becomes more withdrawn and detached. If you have experienced a serious trauma, and have some of these symptoms, you may want to consult with a psychologist about your condition to determine if you have PTSD, and to learn what can be done to help you.

Treatment is available for PTSD, including the more severe forms seen in combat veterans. A combination of cognitive therapy to alter the recollections of the trauma, supportive counseling while expressing the feelings associated with the events, and behavioral interventions to control the stress responses appears to be most effective. In more severe cases of PTSD, your physician may prescribe medication to be used in addition to the psychological treatment, but medication alone will not resolve these problems.

Generalized Anxiety Disorder

This disorder exemplifies the definition of chronic anxiety, with excessive worrying about a lot of different life events over a period of at least six months. You might feel restless, tense and tired, have difficulty sleeping, find it hard to concentrate, and be more irritable than usual. Many people with generalized anxiety disorder (GAD) describe themselves as chronic worriers, who often become more upset by problems than the average person. The key component of this disorder is not worry, but excessive worry.

Many people with generalized anxiety experience panic attacks at some point in their lives, in response to more severe stress. Eventually, you might begin to worry about worrying. That is, because you see yourself as an anxious person who can't handle stress very well, you develop additional anticipatory anxiety when you must face a stressful situation. (eg. going for a job interview, entering the hospital for a medical procedure, etc.)

Many primary care physicians treat generalized anxiety disorder exclusively by prescribing anti-anxiety medications, especially the benzodiazepines, rather than referring the person for psychotherapy. However, these drugs are not without risk. They cause impairment of cognitive functioning, including reaction time. Many individuals experience rebound anxiety if they abruptly stop taking the medications. Research has also suggested that the benzodiazepines may produce functional changes in the central nervous system that make it difficult for people to withdraw from these drugs.

Generalized anxiety disorder is not a biological problem, it is a psychological problem with pronounced physical symptoms. It requires psychological treatment, most often a combination of behavioral and cognitive therapy. Psychologists have used behavioral treatment effectively to teach individuals how to reduce their anxiety through relaxation exercises. Cognitive therapy techniques help identify and change the expectations you might have that triggers anxiety. A combination of cognitive and behavioral interventions has shown very positive results, without the drawbacks of medication. The development of cognitive coping strategies for managing anxiety is a particularly effective treatment for individuals with generalized anxiety disorder.

Agoraphobia

Agoraphobia produces intense anxiety when you are in a place where escape is difficult or embarrassing. Those people who have had panic attacks often worry about being in a place where help may not be available, if they have another attack. This fear causes the person to withdraw into safer surroundings, and many agoraphobics will only frequent a few secure locations, such as their home, a specific route to work, or sometimes the homes of friends or relatives. They typically avoid bridges, tunnels, elevators, highways without shoulders, limited access roads with infrequent exits, or being in crowded places. In the extreme, they will not leave their home.

Agoraphobia almost always occurs with panic disorder, but can sometimes occur on its own. It is more appropriate to look at agoraphobia as the best explanation for a problem, rather than specific phobias, when there are many phobias, and when the theme common to all of the fears is a difficult escape. The most difficult part of treatment for agoraphobia is maintaining regular treatment appointments. People suffering with agoraphobia often have difficulty getting to the office of a psychologist, and frequently

cancel appointments because of their fears. This must be addressed as part of treatment.

Phobia

Phobias are also called Specific Phobias. These disorders are the phobias with which we are all familiar. A person has an anxiety response when exposed to a specific event or object, such as fear of snakes, or fear of flying. Phobias are divided into types, including animal type (fear of animals or insects), natural environment type (storms, heights, etc), blood-injection-injury type (seeing blood, getting a shot, etc.), and situational type (flying, tunnels, bridges, etc.).

Psychologists provide treatment for specific phobias using behavioral and cognitive therapy procedures. Desensitization is very effective, as well as the development of cognitive coping strategies. However, many people never seek treatment, unless the specific phobia interferes with life functioning in a significant way. For example, if a person has a fear of flying, they cannot accept a promotion that requires frequent travel without learning how to cope with their fear, or overcome it.

Obsessive Compulsive Disorder

Obsessive compulsive disorder (OCD) is an anxiety disorder in which the person experiences either obsessions or compulsions that interfere with normal life functioning. Obsessions are persistent ideas or thoughts or impulses that intrude on your thoughts, and cause significant distress in your life. Compulsions are repetitive behaviors that are performed in an effort to reduce anxiety. (Typically the anxiety is caused by obsessions). Approximately 2 percent of the population develops an obsessive compulsive disorder during their lifetime.

It is important to note that obsessions are not just excessive worrying about real problems, as that would be a generalized anxiety disorder. Also, the person with OCD typically tries to ignore these thoughts and ideas. An individual with a psychotic disorder may ruminate on a single idea, but would not try to avoid thinking about it, as obsessive ideas do not generate the same kind of personal distress when they occur as part of a psychotic process.

This disorder results in significant distress. Most people with OCD spend a lot of time during the day dealing with either obsessions, compulsions, or both. These obsessions and compulsions significantly interfere with their normal life functioning. OCD can develop in childhood, but most often it develops in adolescence or young adults.

Intrusive thoughts are very common in the general population. Most of the time, stress leads to intrusive thoughts, and individuals who are depressed are also more likely to develop intrusive thoughts. It appears that those people who develop an OCD response to these intrusive thoughts may have a severe biologically based emotional response to stress. It should be noted that OCD is very resistant to treatment, and an individual with OCD will need treatment over an extended period of time.

Schizophrenia

Schizophrenia is a chronic, severe, and disabling brain disease. Schizophrenia is found all over the world. The severity of the symptoms and the long-lasting, chronic pattern of schizophrenia often results in disability, and many individuals need ongoing assistance to manage the most basic functions of independent living. People with schizophrenia may have perceptions of reality that are strikingly different from the reality seen and shared by others around them. Their behavior may seem odd, unusual or even bizarre at times. They sometimes hear voices, talk to themselves, or respond to imaginary fears. At times, normal individuals may feel, think, or act in ways that resemble schizophrenia. Normal people may sometimes be unable to "think straight." They may become extremely anxious, for example, when speaking in front of groups and may feel confused, be unable to pull their thoughts together, and forget what they had intended to say. This is not schizophrenia. At the same time, people with schizophrenia do not always act abnormally. Indeed, some people with the

illness can appear completely normal and be perfectly responsible, even while they experience hallucinations or delusions. An individual's behavior may change over time, becoming bizarre if medication is stopped and returning closer to normal when receiving appropriate treatment.

Symptoms of Schizophrenia

People with schizophrenia may have perceptions of reality that are strikingly different from the reality seen and shared by others around them. Living in a world distorted by hallucinations and delusions, individuals with schizophrenia may feel frightened, anxious, and confused.

In part because of the unusual realities they experience, people with schizophrenia may behave very differently at various times. Sometimes they may seem distant, detached, or preoccupied and may even sit as rigidly as a stone, not moving for hours or uttering a sound. Other times they may move about constantly – always occupied, appearing wide-awake, vigilant, and alert.

1. Hallucinations

Hallucinations are disturbances of perception that are common in people suffering from schizophrenia. Hallucinations are perceptions that occur without connection to an appropriate source. Although hallucinations can occur in any sensory form – auditory (sound), visual (sight), tactile (touch), gustatory (taste), and olfactory (smell) – hearing voices that other people do not hear is the most common type of hallucination in schizophrenia. Voices may describe the patient's activities, carry on a conversation, warn of impending dangers, or even issue orders to the individual. Illusions, on the other hand, occur when a sensory stimulus is present but is incorrectly interpreted by the individual.

2. Delusions

Delusions are false personal beliefs that are not subject to reason or contradictory evidence and are not explained by a person's usual cultural concepts. Delusions may take on different themes. For example, patients suffering from paranoid-type symptoms – roughly one-third of people with schizophrenia – often have delusions of persecution, or false and irrational beliefs that they are being cheated, harassed, poisoned, or conspired against. These patients may believe that they, or a member of the family or someone close to them, are the focus of this persecution. In addition, delusions of grandeur, in which a person may believe he or she is a famous or important figure, may occur in schizophrenia. Sometimes the delusions experienced by people with schizophrenia are quite bizarre; for instance, believing that a neighbor is controlling their behavior with magnetic waves; that people on television are directing special messages to them; or that their thoughts are being broadcast aloud to others.

3. Disordered Thinking

Schizophrenia often affects a person's ability to "think straight." Thoughts may come and go rapidly; the person may not be able to concentrate on one thought for very long and may be easily distracted, unable to focus attention. People with schizophrenia may not be able to sort out what is relevant and what is not relevant to a situation. The person may be unable to connect thoughts into logical sequences, with thoughts becoming disorganized and fragmented. This lack of logical continuity of thought, termed "thought disorder," can make conversation very difficult and may contribute to social isolation. If people cannot make sense of what an individual is saying, they are likely to become uncomfortable and tend to leave that person alone.

4. Emotional Expression

People with schizophrenia often show "blunted" or "flat" affect. This refers to a severe reduction in emotional expressiveness. A person with schizophrenia may not show the signs of normal emotion, perhaps may speak in a monotonous voice, have diminished facial expressions, and appear extremely apathetic. The person may withdraw socially, avoiding contact with others; and when forced to interact, he or she may have nothing to say, reflecting "impoverished thought." Motivation can be greatly decreased, as can interest in or enjoyment of life. In some severe cases, a person can spend entire days doing nothing at all, even neglecting basic hygiene. These problems with emotional expression and motivation, which may be extremely troubling to family members and friends, are symptoms of schizophrenia – not character flaws or personal weaknesses.

Causes of Schizophrenia

There is no known single cause of schizophrenia. Many diseases, such as heart disease, result from interplay of genetic, behavioral, and other factors; and this may be the case for schizophrenia as well. Scientists do not yet understand all of the factors necessary to produce schizophrenia, but all the tools of modern biomedical research are being used to search for genes, critical moments in brain development, and other factors that may lead to the illness.

Genetics and Schizophrenia

It has long been known that schizophrenia runs in families. People who have a close relative with schizophrenia are more likely to develop the disorder than are people who have no relatives with the illness. For example, a monozygotic (identical) twin of a person with schizophrenia has the highest risk – 40 to 50 percent – of developing the illness. A child whose parent has schizophrenia has about a 10 percent chance. By comparison, the risk of schizophrenia in the general population is about 1 percent.

Scientists are studying genetic factors in schizophrenia. It appears likely that multiple genes are involved in creating a predisposition to develop the disorder. In addition, factors such as prenatal difficulties like intrauterine starvation or viral infections, perinatal complications, and various nonspecific stressors, seem to influence the development of schizophrenia. However, it is not yet understood how the genetic predisposition is transmitted, and it cannot yet be accurately predicted whether a given person will or will not develop the disorder.

Several regions of the human genome are being investigated to identify genes that may confer susceptibility for schizophrenia. The strongest evidence to date leads to chromosomes 13 and 6 but remains unconfirmed. Identification of specific genes involved in the development of schizophrenia will provide important clues into what goes wrong in the brain to produce and sustain the illness and will guide the development of new and better treatments. To learn more about the genetic basis for schizophrenia, the NIMH has established a Schizophrenia Genetics Initiative (see website at http://www-grb.nimh.nih.gov/gi.html) that is gathering data from a large number of families of people with the illness.

Schizophrenia and Chemical Defects

Basic knowledge about brain chemistry and its link to schizophrenia is expanding rapidly. Neurotransmitters, substances that allow communication between nerve cells, have long been thought to be involved in the development of schizophrenia. It is likely, although not yet certain, that the disorder is associated with some imbalance of the complex, interrelated chemical systems of the brain, perhaps involving the neurotransmitters dopamine and glutamate.

Schizophrenia and Brain Abnormality

There have been dramatic advances in neuro-imaging technology that permit scientists to study brain structure and function in living individuals. Many studies of people with schizophrenia have found abnormalities in brain structure (for example, enlargement of the fluid-filled cavities, called the ventricles, in the interior of the brain, and decreased size of certain brain regions) or function (for example,

decreased metabolic activity in certain brain regions). It should be emphasized that these abnormalities are quite subtle and are not characteristic of all people with schizophrenia, nor do they occur only in individuals with this illness. Microscopic studies of brain tissue after death have also shown small changes in distribution or number of brain cells in people with schizophrenia. It appears that many (but probably not all) of these changes are present before an individual becomes ill, and schizophrenia may be, in part, a disorder in development of the brain.

Developmental neurobiologists funded by the National Institute of Mental Health (NIMH) have found that schizophrenia may be a developmental disorder resulting when neurons form inappropriate connections during fetal development. These errors may lie dormant until puberty, when changes in the brain that occur normally during this critical stage of maturation interact adversely with the faulty connections. This research has spurred efforts to identify prenatal factors that may have some bearing on the apparent developmental abnormality.

In other studies, investigators using brain-imaging techniques have found evidence of early biochemical changes that may precede the onset of disease symptoms, prompting examination of the neural circuits that are most likely to be involved in producing those symptoms. Scientists working at the molecular level, meanwhile, are exploring the genetic basis for abnormalities in brain development and in the neurotransmitter systems regulating brain function.

Personality Disorders

Personality disorders are a group of mental disturbances defined by the fourth edition, text revision (2000) of the *Diagnostic and Statistical Manual of Mental Disorders (DSM-IV)* as "enduring pattern[s] of inner experience and behavior" that are sufficiently rigid and deep-seated to bring a person into repeated conflicts with his or her social and occupational environment. *DSM-IV* specifies that these dysfunctional patterns must be regarded as nonconforming or deviant by the person's culture, and cause significant emotional <u>pain</u> and/or difficulties in relationships and occupational performance. In addition, the patient usually sees the disorder as being consistent with his or her self-image (ego-syntonic) and may blame others for his or her social, educational, or work-related problems.

Description

To meet the diagnosis of personality disorder, which is sometimes called character disorder, the patient's problematic behaviors must appear in two or more of the following areas:

- perception and interpretation of the self and other people
- intensity and duration of feelings and their appropriateness to situations
- relationships with others
- ability to control impulses

Personality disorders have their onset in late adolescence or early adulthood. Doctors rarely give a diagnosis of personality disorder to children on the grounds that children's personalities are still in the process of formation and may change considerably by the time they are in their late teens. In retrospect, however, many individuals with personality disorders could be judged to have shown evidence of the problems in childhood.

It is difficult to give close estimates of the percentage of the population that has personality disorders. Patients with certain personality disorders, including antisocial and borderline disorders, are more likely to get into trouble with the law or otherwise attract attention than are patients whose disorders chiefly affect their capacity for intimacy. On the other hand, some patients, such as those with narcissistic or obsessive-compulsive personality disorders, may be outwardly successful because their symptoms are useful within their particular occupations. It has, however, been estimated that about 15% of the general population of the United States has a personality disorder, with higher rates in poor or troubled neighborhoods.

The rate of personality disorders among patients in psychiatric treatment is between 30% and 50%. It is possible for patients to have a so-called dual diagnosis; for example, they may have more than one personality disorder, or a personality disorder together with a substance-abuse problem.

By contrast, *DSM-IV* classifies personality disorders into three clusters based on symptom similarities:

- Cluster A (paranoid, schizoid, schizotypal): Patients appear odd or eccentric to others.
- Cluster B (antisocial, borderline, histrionic, narcissistic): Patients appear overly emotional, unstable, or self-dramatizing to others.
- Cluster C (avoidant, dependent, obsessive-compulsive): Patients appear tense and anxiety-ridden to others.

Cluster A: Odd or Eccentric Behavior

Paranoid Personality: People with a paranoid personality are distrustful and suspicious of others. Based on little or no evidence, they suspect that others are out to harm them and usually find hostile or malicious motives behind other people's actions. Thus, people with a paranoid personality may take actions that they feel are justifiable retaliation but that others find baffling. This behavior often leads to rejection by others, which seems to justify their original feelings. They are generally cold and distant in their relationships. (<u>more detailed info on Paranoid Personality Disorder</u>)No Iframes

People with a paranoid personality often take legal action against others, especially if they feel righteously indignant. They are unable to see their own role in a conflict. They usually work in relative isolation and may be highly efficient and conscientious.

Sometimes people who already feel alienated because of a defect or handicap (such as deafness) are more likely to suspect that other people have negative ideas or attitudes toward them. Such heightened suspicion, however, is not evidence of a paranoid personality unless it involves wrongly attributing malice to others.

Schizoid Personality: People with a schizoid personality are introverted, withdrawn, and solitary. They are emotionally cold and socially distant. They are most often absorbed with their own thoughts and feelings and are fearful of closeness and intimacy with others. They talk little, are given to daydreaming, and prefer theoretical speculation to practical action. Fantasizing is a common coping (defense) mechanism. (more detailed info on Schizoid Personality Disorder)

Schizotypal Personality: People with a schizotypal personality, like those with a schizoid personality, are socially and emotionally detached. In addition, they display oddities of thinking, perceiving, and communicating similar to those of people with schizophrenia (see Schizophrenia and Delusional Disorder: Schizophrenia). Although schizotypal personality is *Here are the different types of personality disorders along with the characteristics of each type of personality disorder.*

As mentioned previously, personality disorders are grouped into three clusters. Cluster A personality disorders involve odd or eccentric behavior; cluster B, dramatic or erratic behavior; and cluster C, anxious or inhibited behavior.

sometimes present in people with schizophrenia before they become ill, most adults with a more detailed info on Schizotypal Personality Disorder)

Some people with a schizotypal personality show signs of magical thinking that is, they believe that their thoughts or actions can control something or someone. For example, people may believe that they can harm others by thinking angry thoughts. People with a schizotypal personality may also have paranoid ideas.

Cluster B: Dramatic or Erratic Behavior

Histrionic (Hysterical) Personality: People with a histrionic personality conspicuously seek attention, are dramatic and excessively emotional, and are overly concerned with appearance. Their lively, expressive manner results in easily established but often superficial and transient relationships. Their expression of emotions often seems exaggerated, childish, and contrived to evoke sympathy or attention (often erotic or sexual) from others. People with a histrionic personality are prone to sexually provocative behavior or to sexualizing nonsexual relationships. However, they may not really want a sexual relationship; rather, their seductive behavior often masks their wish to be dependent and protected. Some people with a histrionic personality also are hypochondriacal and exaggerate their physical problems to get the attention they need. (more detailed info on Histrionic Personality Disorder)

Narcissistic Personality: People with a narcissistic personality have a sense of superiority, a need for admiration, and a lack of empathy. They have an exaggerated belief in their own value or importance, which is what therapists call grandiosity. They may be extremely sensitive to failure, defeat, or criticism. When confronted by a failure to fulfill their high opinion of themselves, they can easily become enraged or severely depressed. Because they believe themselves to be superior in their relationships with other people, they expect to be admired and often suspect that others envy them. They believe they are entitled to having their needs met without waiting, so they exploit others, whose needs or beliefs they deem to be less important. Their behavior is usually offensive to others, who view them as being self-centered, arrogant, or selfish. This personality disorder typically occurs in high achievers, although it may also occur in people with few achievements. (more detailed info on Narcissistic Personality Disorder)

Antisocial Personality: People with an antisocial personality (previously called psychopathic or sociopathic personality), most of whom are male, show callous disregard for the rights and feelings of others. Dishonesty and deceit permeate their relationships. They exploit others for material gain or personal gratification (unlike narcissistic people, who exploit others because they think their superiority justifies it).

Characteristically, people with an antisocial personality act out their conflicts, impulsively and irresponsibly. They tolerate frustration poorly, and sometimes they are hostile or violent. Often they do not anticipate the negative consequences of their antisocial behaviors and, despite the problems or harm they cause others, do not feel remorse or guilt. Rather, they glibly rationalize their behavior or blame it on others. Frustration and punishment do not motivate them to modify their behaviors or improve their judgment and foresight but, rather, schizotypal personality does not develop schizophrenia. (usually confirm their harshly unsentimental view of the world.

People with an antisocial personality are prone to alcoholism, drug addiction, sexual deviation, promiscuity, and imprisonment. They are likely to fail at their jobs and move from one area to another. They often have a family history of antisocial behavior, substance abuse, divorce, and physical abuse. As children, many were emotionally neglected and physically abused. People with an antisocial personality have a shorter life expectancy than the general population. The disorder tends to diminish or stabilize with age. (more detailed info on Antisocial Personality Disorder)

Consequences of Personality Disorders

- People with a personality disorder are at high risk of behaviors that can lead to physical illness (such as alcohol or drug addiction); self-destructive behavior, reckless sexual behavior, hypochondriasis, and clashes with society's values.
- They may have inconsistent, detached, over-emotional, abusive, or irresponsible styles of parenting, leading to medical and psychiatric problems in their children.
- They are vulnerable to mental breakdowns (a period of crisis when a person has difficulty performing even routine mental tasks) as a result of stress.
- They may develop a mental health disorder; the type (for example, anxiety, depression, or psychosis) depends in part on the type of personality disorder.
- They are less likely to follow a prescribed treatment regimen; even when they follow the regimen, they are usually less responsive to drugs than most people are.

They often have a poor relationship with their doctor because they refuse to take responsibility for their behavior or they feel overly distrustful, deserving, or needy. The doctor may then start to blame, distrust, and ultimately reject the person.

Borderline Personality: People with a borderline personality, most of whom are women, are unstable in their self-image, moods, behavior, and interpersonal relationships. Their thought processes are more disturbed than those of people with an antisocial personality, and their aggression is more often turned against the self. They are angrier, more impulsive, and more confused about their identity than are people with a histrionic personality. Borderline personality becomes evident in early adulthood but becomes less common in older age groups.

People with a borderline personality often report being neglected or abused as children. Consequently, they feel empty, angry, and deserving of nurturing. They have far more dramatic and intense interpersonal relationships than people with cluster A personality disorders. When they fear being abandoned by a caring person, they tend to express inappropriate and intense anger. People with a borderline personality tend to see events and relationships as black or white, good or evil, but never neutral.

When people with a borderline personality feel abandoned and alone, they may wonder whether they actually exist (that is, they do not feel real). They can become desperately impulsive, engaging in reckless promiscuity , substance abuse, or self-mutilation. At times they are so out of touch with reality that they have brief episodes of psychotic thinking, paranoia, and hallucinations.

People with a borderline personality commonly visit primary care doctors. Borderline personality is also the most common personality disorder treated by therapists, because people with the disorder relentlessly seek someone to care for them. However, after repeated crises, vague unfounded complaints, and failures to comply with therapeutic recommendations, caretakers including doctors often become very frustrated with them and view them erroneously as people who prefer complaining to helping themselves. (more detailed info on Borderline Personality Disorder)

Cluster C: Anxious or Inhibited Behavior

Avoidant Personality: People with an avoidant personality are overly sensitive to rejection, and they fear starting relationships or anything new. They have a strong desire for affection and acceptance but avoid intimate relationships and social situations for fear of disappointment and criticism. Unlike those with a schizoid personality, they are openly distressed by their isolation and inability to relate comfortably to others. Unlike those with a borderline personality, they do not respond to rejection with anger; instead, they withdraw and appear shy and timid. Avoidant personality is similar to generalized social phobia (see Anxiety Disorders: Social Phobia). (more detailed info on Avoidant Personality Disorder)

Dependent Personality: People with a dependent personality routinely surrender major decisions and responsibilities to others and permit the needs of those they depend on to supersede their own. They lack self-confidence and feel intensely insecure about their ability to take care of themselves. They often protest that they cannot make decisions and do not know what to do or how to do it. This behavior is due partly to a reluctance to express their views for fear of offending the people they need and partly to a belief that others are more capable. People with other personality disorders often have traits of a dependent personality, but the dependent traits are usually hidden by the more dominant traits of the other disorder. Sometimes adults with a prolonged illness or physical handicap develop a dependent personality. (more detailed info on Dependent Personality Disorder)

Obsessive-Compulsive Personality: People with an obsessive-compulsive personality are preoccupied with orderliness, perfectionism, and control. They are reliable, dependable, orderly, and methodical, but their inflexibility makes them unable to adapt to change. Because they are cautious and weigh all aspects of a problem, they have difficulty making decisions. They take their responsibilities seriously, but because they

cannot tolerate mistakes or imperfection, they often have trouble completing tasks. Unlike the mental health disorder called obsessive-compulsive disorder (see Anxiety Disorders: Obsessive-Compulsive Disorder (OCD)), obsessive-compulsive personality does not involve repeated, unwanted obsessions and ritualistic behavior.

People with an obsessive-compulsive personality are often high achievers, especially in the sciences and other intellectually demanding fields that require order and attention to detail. However, their responsibilities make them so anxious that they can rarely enjoy their successes. They are uncomfortable with their feelings, with relationships, and with situations in which they lack control or must rely on others or in which events are unpredictable. (more detailed info on Obsessive-Compulsive Personality Disorder)

Other Personality Types

Some personality types are not classified as disorders. These are briefly discussed.

Passive-Aggressive (Negativistic) Personality: People with a passive-aggressive personality behave in ways that appear inept or passive. However, these behaviors are actually ways to avoid responsibility or to control or punish others. People with a passive-aggressive personality often procrastinate, perform tasks inefficiently, or claim an implausible disability. Frequently, they agree to perform tasks they do not want to perform and then subtly undermine completion of the tasks. Such behavior usually enables them to deny or conceal hostility or disagreements.

Cyclothymic Personality: People with cyclothymic personality alternate between high-spirited buoyancy and gloomy pessimism. Each mood lasts weeks or longer. Mood changes occur regularly and without any identifiable external cause. Many gifted and creative people have this personality type (Depression and Mania: Symptoms and Diagnosis).

Depressive Personality: This personality type is characterized by chronic moroseness, worry, and self-consciousness. People have a pessimistic outlook, which impairs their initiative and disheartens others.

To them, satisfaction seems undeserved and sinful. They may unconsciously believe their suffering is a badge of merit needed to earn the love or admiration of others.

Common Characteristics

Personality Disorders are mental illnesses that share several unique qualities. They contain symptoms that are enduring and play a major role in most, if not all, aspects of the person's life. While many disorders vacillate in terms of symptom presence and intensity, personality disorders typically remain relatively constant.

To be diagnosed with a disorder in this category, a psychologist will look for the following criteria:

1. Symptoms have been present for an extended period of time, are inflexible and pervasive, and are not a result of alcohol or drugs or another psychiatric disorder. The history of symptoms can be traced back to adolescence or at least early adulthood.
2. The symptoms have caused and continue to cause significant distress or negative consequences in different aspects of the person's life.
3. Symptoms are seen in at least two of the following areas:
   * *Thoughts* (ways of looking at the world, thinking about self or others, and interacting)
   * *Emotions* (appropriateness, intensity, and range of emotional functioning)
   * *Interpersonal Functioning* (relationships and interpersonal skills)
   * *Impulse Control*

Symptomology of Personality Disorders

Personality disorder symptoms include:
* Frequent mood swings
* Stormy relationships
* Social isolation
* Angry outbursts
* Suspicion and mistrust of others
* Difficulty making friends
* A need for instant gratification
* Poor impulse control
* Alcohol or substance abuse

Etiology of Personality Disorders

Causes and symptoms

Personality disorders are thought to result from a bad interface, so to speak, between a child's temperament and character on one hand and his or her family environment on the other. Temperament can be defined as a person's innate or biologically shaped basic disposition. Human infants vary in their sensitivity to light or noise, their level of physical activity, their adaptability to schedules, and similar traits. Even such traits as shyness or novelty-seeking may be at least in part determined by the biology of the brain and the genes one inherits.

Other factors that have been cited as affecting children's personality development are the mass media and social or group hysteria, particularly after the events of September 11, 2001. Cases of so-called mass sociogenic illness have been identified, in which a group of children began to vomit or have other physical symptoms brought on in response to an imaginary threat. In two such cases, the children were reacting to the suggestion that toxic fumes were spreading through their school. Some authors believe that overly frequent or age-inappropriate discussions of terrorist attacks or bioterrorism may make children more susceptible to sociogenic illness as well as other distortions of personality.

Personality is the combination of thoughts, emotions and behaviors that makes you unique. It's the way you view, understand and relate to the outside world, as well as how you see yourself. Personality forms during childhood, shaped through an interaction of two factors:
* **Inherited tendencies, or your genes.** These are aspects of your personality passed on to you by your parents, such as shyness or having a

happy outlook. This is sometimes called your temperament. It's the "nature" part of the nature vs. nurture debate.

- **Environment, or your life situations.** This is the surroundings you grew up in, events that occurred, and relationships with family members and others. It includes such things as the type of parenting you had, whether loving or abusive. This is the "nurture" part of the nature vs. nurture debate.
- Personality disorders are thought to be caused by a combination of these genetic and environmental influences. You may have a genetic vulnerability to developing a personality disorder and your life situation may trigger the actual development of a personality disorder.

Risk Factors

Although the precise cause of personality disorders isn't known, certain factors seem to increase the risk of developing or triggering personality disorders, including:

- A family history of personality disorders or other mental illness
- Low socioeconomic status
- Verbal, physical or sexual abuse during childhood
- Neglect during childhood
- An unstable or chaotic family life during childhood
- Being diagnosed with childhood conduct disorder
- Loss of parents through death or traumatic divorce during childhood

Personality disorders often begin in childhood and last through adulthood. There's reluctance to diagnose personality disorders in a child, though, because the patterns of behavior and thinking could simply reflect adolescent experimentation or temporary developmental phases.

CHILDHOOD DISORDERS

Childhood psychological problems related to behavioral control problems, including ADHD, conduct disturbance, and oppositional behavior are discussed. Separation anxiety, a common problem in young children, is also reviewed in this section.

Many psychological disorders first diagnosed in children involve physiological and/or genetic components. However, there are many other psychological disorders found in children without any physical causes. Disorders caused by physiological or biological problems are more likely to be identified early in life, but some of these problems are not identified until adulthood.

Oppositional Defiant Disorder

Children and adolescents with this problem usually exhibit a pattern of defiant and disobedient behavior, including resistance to authority figures. However, this behavior pattern is not as severe as conduct disorder. The behavior pattern may include recurrent temper problems, frequent arguments, especially with adults, and evidence of anger and resentment. Additionally, the defiant child or adolescent will often try to annoy others, and will become easily annoyed by others. When mistakes are made, he/she will almost always blame others, avoiding taking responsibility for mistakes. Active defiance of adult authority is common, and the child or adolescent may also display vindictive behavior.

The child may be stubborn and unwilling to compromise, but you will usually not see the more severe acts of aggression that are common with a conduct disturbance. This problem is fairly common, occurring in between 2 percent and 16 percent of children and adolescents. In younger children, it is more common in boys, but during adolescence, it occurs as often in boys and girls. The onset is usually gradual, and the severity of behavior problems increases over time. Some children will eventually develop a conduct disturbance, if the oppositional disorder is left untreated.

Generally, treatment for oppositional disorder requires a combination of counseling for the child, and parental training in behavior management techniques. Often, parents become too severe in reacting to the child, out of frustration. This causes their efforts to become ineffective, as the child ignores the punishment. If a child believes s/he cannot "be good" the child will stop trying.

Conduct Disorder

Conduct Disorder is a serious behavioral problem involving repeated violations of the rights of others, or violation of basic age-appropriate social rules expected of a child. Conduct disorder involves a pattern of aggressive behavior toward people or animals, destruction of property, a pattern of deceitfulness, and/or serious violations of social rules at home or at school.

Aggressive behavior toward people or animals—These children may bully other children, or repeatedly get into fights. Some children and adolescents have even used weapons in fights, or used weapons to intimidate others. In the extreme, there is a history of crimes involving violence, including mugging, extortion or forced sexual activity, and harm to animals. Little to no remorse is observed.

Destruction of property—Some children have intentionally set fires, with the intention of destroying property, while others have vandalized property. In conduct disorder, the child destroys the property of others, rather than destroying his/her own property.

Deceitfulness—This involves a pattern of breaking rules by lying or stealing from others. Shoplifting is common, often of minor objects, or taking objects from the home of a friend. In more serious cases, the child/adolescent may be a con artist, fooling others or lying to obtain something for nothing. In the extreme, the child or adolescent may have a history of breaking and entering, either of houses, cars, or stores.

Serious violations of social rules—Beginning at a young age, the child stays out late, without parental permission, or skips school, even before age 13. In the extreme, the child or adolescent has run away from home multiple times, staying away at least one overnight.

Most children with these problems are referred to a psychologist by the juvenile justice system, usually as a condition of probation, after committing a serious crime. This is a relatively common problem in children, which may occur in approximately 10 percent of males and 5 percent of females. Most of these children show evidence of problems in later childhood or early adolescence. It rarely begins after age 16. Fortunately, most cases are treated successfully, and result in normal behavior during adulthood. However, a large percentage continue to show evidence of antisocial behavior into adulthood, with some developing into antisocial personality disorders. Such individuals usually have lifelong social adjustment problems, with frequent arrests and periods of incarceration.

Attention Deficit Hyperactivity Disorder

Attention Deficit Hyperactive Disorder, commonly referred to by its initials, either ADHD or ADD, recently has been diagnosed with such frequency that some professionals are questioning whether it is over-diagnosed. The diagnostic criteria for this disorder have changed over the years, and new research is continuing to refine our understanding of ADHD. In many respects, this diagnosis represents two distinctly different problems, although they appear to be linked together. Children may have ADHD, primarily with inattention, or ADHD primarily with impulsive and hyperactive behavior. There is a third option, which is called ADHD, mixed type, which incorporates attributes of both of these problems.

Inattention is usually identified by problems in school work. The child may fail to finish most work, often making careless mistakes, and often forgetting many things. Almost anything will distract the child. Disorganization is common, and the child may lose personal items regularly. Even when spoken to directly, the child may not pay attention to what is said, and be unable to provide feedback when asked. The child will regularly fail to complete assignments in school, and chores at home, but because of forgetfulness and disorganization rather than defiance or resistance to authority.

Of course, the age of the child is important when assessing these factors, as younger children are more likely to exhibit these behaviors normally. This is one reason that ADHD is often not identified until a child is in school.

Hyperactive and impulsive behavior is easier to identify, because the ADHD child is all over the place, and rarely sits still for very long. Even when sitting, the child fidgets and bounces in his/her seat. (More boys than girls are diagnosed with ADHD). In school, the child has trouble remaining seated, and frequently blurts out answers or questions, out of turn and without waiting to be called. The child may be very talkative and will demonstrate difficulty listening and following directions. As a result, these children will frequently get into minor difficulties in school because of their activity level and poor conduct in school.

Separation Anxiety Disorder

Separation Anxiety Disorder is self-descriptive. It involves excessive anxiety that occurs when a child is separated from home or a family caregiver. These children tend to come from very close-knit families. The most significant social development problem is school refusal. Some children with separation anxiety will refuse to go to school, to the point of having tantrums at the bus stop or at the school door. This may lead to academic adjustment problems, and social problems with their peer group. This problem sometimes develops after a traumatic life event, such as the death of a relative or a pet, or prolonged illness in the child or a family member. At times, it occurs after relocating to a new environment, or following the divorce or separation of his/her parents.

Children with this psychological behavior problem display inappropriate, excessive anxiety when separating from home or a caregiver. The child may worry about something bad happening to a parent, or may worry that they will experience a disaster if separated from the parent (being kidnapped, etc.).

The child may be reluctant to go to school, or may be very fearful of being alone, without a parent. They may be fearful of sleeping away from home, or away from their parent. They may experience recurrent nightmares with separation themes, and sometimes will complain of a variety of physical symptoms to avoid separation (headache, vomiting, etc.).

Assessing Psychological Disorders

Interviews

The doctor may schedule two or three interviews with the patient, spaced over several weeks or months, in order to rule out an adjustment disorder caused by job loss, bereavement, or a similar problem. An office interview allows the doctor to form an impression of the patient's overall personality as well as obtain information about his or her occupation and family. During the interview, the doctor will note the patient's appearance, tone of voice, body language, eye contact, and other important non-verbal signals, as well as the content of the conversation. In some cases, the doctor may contact other people (family members, employers, close friends) who know the patient well in order to assess the accuracy of the patient's perception of his or her difficulties. It is quite common for people with personality disorders to have distorted views of their situations or to be unaware of the impact of their behavior on others.

Psychologic Testing

Doctors use psychologic testing to help in the diagnosis of a personality disorder. Most of these tests require interpretation by a professional with specialized training. Doctors usually refer patients to a clinical psychologist for this type of test.

Personality Inventories. Personality inventories are tests with true/false or yes/no answer that can be used to compare the patient's scores with those of people with known personality distortions. The single most commonly used test of this type is the Minnesota

Multiphasic Personality Inventory, or MMPI. Another test that is often used is the Millon Clinical Multiaxial Inventory, or MCMI.

Projective Tests. Projective tests are unstructured. Unstructured means that instead of giving one-word answers to questions, the patient is asked to talk at some length about a picture that the psychologist has shown him or her, or to supply an ending for the beginning of a story. Projective tests allow the clinician to assess the patient's patterns of thinking, fantasies, worries or anxieties, moral concerns, values, and habits. Common projective tests include the Rorschach, in which the patient responds to a set of ten inkblots; and the Thematic Apperception Test (TAT), in which the patient is shown drawings of people in different situations and then tells a story about the picture.

Psychological Assessment

In the early times, psychological tests were used to measure intelligence and detect personality disorders. As defined by Robert Gregory in his 1996 book, "Psychological Testing: History, Principles and Applications", a psychological test is "a standardized procedure for sampling behavior and describing it with categories or scores". To aid the interpretation of such categories or scores, norms or standards have been set as basis for comparison. Standardization of a test is valid provided that the procedures for administration of the test are uniform and consistent.

Before a test will be considered standardized, a test should establish norms or standards. Norms are "summaries of test results for a large and representative group of subjects" called the "sample". Aside from indicating the required average performance, the norms also indicate the degree to which a score compares with the expectations. The selection of the standardization sample is also highly significant. The sample should be "representative of the population for whom it is intended". The validity and reliability of the test is also highly emphasized. A test is considered valid if it measures what it intends to measure. Reliability of a test refers to the consistency of the scores a test-taker gets, regardless of the examiner, the setting, the time or the date.

Psychological tests can be either norm-referenced or criterion-referenced. For norm-referenced tests, examinee's performance is interpreted through a comparison against the standardization sample. For criterion-referenced tests, an examinee is judged as to where he stands in pre-set categories. Tests can also be grouped into individual tests that should be administered one-to-one or group tests that are suitable to administering to groups of examiners at the same time. These tests can also be classified under intelligence tests, aptitude tests, achievement tests, creativity tests, personality tests, interest inventories, behavioral assessments, and neurophysiological tests. Psychological tests are now widely used in placement, screening, certification, selection and diagnosis and treatment.

Minnesota Multiphasic Personality Inventories

Minnesota Multiphasic Personality Inventory (MMPI) was originally devised for psychiatric diagnosis. To identify the clinical scales, the psychologists contrasted item responses of psychiatric patients with item responses of control subjects. The initial version consisted of 566 items and was later revised restandardized with 567 items. The general themes of MMPI-2 include health concerns, family difficulties, marital relationships, neurological illnesses, antisocial practices, among many others. The requirement to take the test is a sixth-grade reading level. It can be completed by a test-taker in a maximum of 1.5 hours.

The clinical scales of MMPI-2 are hypochondriasis, depression, hysteria, psychopathic deviation, masculinity-femininity orientation, paranoia, psychasthenia, schizophrenia, hypomania and social introversion. The first scale, hypochondriasis, measures the test-takers excessive concern over one's own physical condition while scale 2 indicates sad feelings and hopelessness. Hysteria measures immaturity and rampant use of defense mechanisms while psychopathic deviation signifies conflicts with authority and impulsive behavior. The scale on masculinity-femininity

DIAGNOSTIC AND STATISTICAL MANUAL OF MENTAL DISORDERS, FOURTH EDITION (DSM-IV)

Psychiatric Diagnoses are categorized by the <u>Diagnostic and Statistical Manual of Mental Disorders, 4th.</u> <u>Edition</u>. Better known as the DSM-IV, the manual is published by the American Psychiatric Association and covers all mental health disorders for both children and adults. It also lists known causes of these disorders, statistics in terms of gender, age at onset, and prognosis as well as some research concerning the optimal treatment approaches.

Mental Health Professionals use this manual when working with patients in order to better understand their illness and potential treatment and to help 3rd party payers (e.g., insurance) understand the needs of the patient. The book is typically considered the 'bible' for any professional who makes psychiatric diagnoses in the United States and many other countries. Much of the diagnostic information on these pages is gathered from the DSM IV.

The DSM IV is published by the American Psychiatric Association. Much of the information from the Psychiatric Disorders pages is summarized from the pages of this text. Should any questions arise concerning incongruencies or inaccurate information, you should always default to the DSM as the ultimate guide to mental disorders.

The DSM uses a multiaxial or multidimensional approach to diagnosing because rarely do other factors in a person's life not impact their mental health. It assesses five dimensions as described below:

<u>Axis I: Clinical Syndromes</u>
This is what we typically think of as the diagnosis (e.g., depression, schizophrenia, social phobia)

Axis II: Developmental Disorders and Personality Disorders

Developmental disorders include autism and mental retardation, disorders which are typically first evident in childhood

Personality disorders are clinical syndromes which have a more long lasting symptoms and encompass the individual's way of interacting with the world. They include Paranoid, Antisocial, and Borderline Personality Disorders.

Axis III: Physical Conditions which play a role in the development, continuance, or exacerbation of Axis I and II Disorders

Physical conditions such as brain injury or HIV/AIDS that can result in symptoms of mental illness are included here.

Axis IV: Severity of Psychosocial Stressors

Events in a person's life, such as death of a loved one, starting a new job, college, unemployment, and even marriage can impact the disorders listed in Axis I and II. These events are both listed and rated for this axis.

Axis V: Highest Level of Functioning

On the final axis, the clinician rates the person's level of functioning both at the present time and the highest level within the previous year. This helps the clinician understand how the above four axes are affecting the person and what type of changes could be expected.

orientation uncovers gender interests while paranoia indicates suspicious and hostile demeanor. Psychasthenia signifies anxiety and obsessive thinking while schizophrenia suggests preference for alienation. Hypomania scale indicates extremely high energy while the last scale refers to shyness and preference for social isolation.

Aside from the ten clinical scales, the assessment also contains four validity scales referred to as Cannot Say (or ?), L scale, F scale, and K scale. The first scale refers to the total numbers unanswered or double-answered. High scores on this scale signify a reading problem, conflicts with authority, defensiveness, or indecisiveness. The second scale, L, consists of 15 statements scored in the false direction. High scores in the L scale also indicate a defensive test-taking attitude. The F scale consists of 60 items that were answered no more than 10 percent of the time, thus high scores on this scale characterize serious maladjustment. The last validity scale, K, is used to spot a subtle form of defensiveness. High scores serve as signals for defensiveness while normal scores suggest normal functioning and ego strength in the face of internal conflict.

Rorschach Inkblot Test

The Rorschach Inkblot Test was designed in the 1900s by Herman Rorschach. The assessment consists of 10 inkblots formed by putting ink on sheets of paper and folding the sheets of paper in half. Half of the set of inkblots are in black or gray while the other half is in color. Though it can be used by persons of age five years old and above, majority of the users are usually adults. This assessment necessitates close administering. The examiner should sit beside the examinee to reduce nonverbal messages. The assessment also uses free association process, where the examinee identifies to what object can he or she associate the inkblot.

It is a given standard that the examiner responds to the questions or inquiries of the examinee in a non-directive manner. The examinee may also choose to give more than one answer to a specific card. However, the

card may also be rejected or ignored by the examinee. All of the ten cards should also be presented to the test-taker in a uniform or consistent manner.

To interpret the responses to the assessment, the examiner uses a scoring guide. The scoring guide provides key points for interpretation. The scoring criteria interpret according to the perception of the test-taker. Important details including the location of the percept on the blot, the feature of the blot that is closest to the percept, the percept itself, and the originality of the test-taker's response, compared to others who have taken the test are also taken into consideration during interpretation.

Despite the interesting appeal of the Rorschach Inkblot Test, critics have argued that the reliability, validity and clinical application of the assessment are questionable. The assessment was initially devised for psychiatric diagnosis, psychotherapy, detection of suicidal tendencies, and formulation of personality profiles. Some psychologists also disagreed that the assessment should even be classified as a test. It should only be regarded as a method to extract personality information.

Thematic Apperception Test

Similar to the Rorschach Inkblot Test, the Thematic Apperception Test (TAT) is a highly visual projective technique. With 30 pictures portraying different subject matters and themes and 1 blank card, the assessment requires the test-takers to make up a story for each picture. The story may revolve around what events caused the event shown in the picture, what is the actual event portrayed in the picture or what the characteristics are doing. The examiner should take note of the test-taker's response in the exact manner it was described by the examinee.

The Thematic Apperception Test was devised by Henry Murray, with the assistance of his colleagues at the Harvard Psychological Clinic. The test was rooted and founded on Murray's personality theory, focusing on needs and press. The TAT measured 36 different needs and various aspects of press.

Murray stressed out that the test is highly imaginative. The test-taker is encouraged to speak everything that comes to his or her mind. Again, it uses the free association process. However, it becomes a disadvantage as examiners forget to emphasize imagination in the instructions given to the test-taker. The interpretation starts with the analysis of the main character or the protagonist. According to Murray, the protagonist or the main character is a personality with whom the test-taker identifies himself or herself. The main character reflects the dreams, aspirations, attitudes, needs and feelings of the examinee.

But, the danger comes with the great possibility of the examinee denying negative past experiences. The examiner should then be quick to explore these issues of denial. Researchers have likewise insisted that reliability of this assessment is questionable. The interpretation of this test is also based on concepts with fairly established reliability and validity. In response to this criticism, psychologists have also designed contemporary scoring and interpreting techniques to further strengthen the assessment's psychometric foundation.

Draw-A-Person Test

The pioneer of using the Draw-A-Person (DAP) Test in a psychodynamic approach is Karen Machover. Since she first introduced the use of this projective assessment tool, DAP has been widely accepted in the area of psychological testing. In fact, it was ranked as the eighth most used tool for clinical diagnosis in the United States. This popularity and appeal may be attributed to its being interesting and highly imaginative. But, in spite of its creativity, it remains to be objective and strongly founded.

In administering the DAP, the examiner always starts by providing the examinee with a blank sheet of paper and a pencil with eraser. The examiner, then, instructs the examinee to "draw a person", thus, the name of the test. After drawing one person, the examinee then proceeds to draw another person of the opposite sex with the first one. The exam ends with

the examinee narrating a story that features the figures he or she has drawn as characters.

House-Tree-Person Test

Another projective personality assessment method is the House-Tree-Person (HTP) Test. It uses freehand drawings of house, tree, and person, quite similar to Draw-A-Person (DAP) Test. Though it was originally devised as a method for measuring intelligence, it is now widely used to measure personality.

The examiner will be requested to draw sketches of a house, tree and person in separate pencil and crayon drawings. Psychologists have produced a form with four pages, including an information portion at the first page. A separate form is also set aside for a post-drawing interrogation.

The post-drawing interrogation is composed of 60 questions aimed at gathering the examinee's feelings about the figures he or she has drawn. Three assumptions are also considered as the basic interpreting guidelines for HTP. The house figure reflects the test-taker's home life and relationships with the family. The tree figure reveals the experiences of the test-taker. The person figure describes the test-taker's relationships with other people, aside from his or her family. In general, the test reveals areas of conflict or concerns that need immediate concerns. A child who draws himself looking out from his or her house signifies feelings of being trapped, abused or imprisoned.

Summary

Psychological assessment is a complete and thorough examination of a person's mental state. Problems or dire situations arise in all vistas of life. These problems can be physical or mental. If the problem is mental then a professional, license holder psychologist can be of help. Psychological evaluation can be performed only by a professional.

Psychological assessment is necessary in certain situations when a confirmed opinion of a professional psychologist is required about a person. This psychological evaluation can have negative or positive effect on the life of the evaluated. So an unbiased, clinical observation is very important.

Such applicants have to undergo a psychological evaluation program for the background checking and also to check the past records of a person. The complicated cases in a courtroom are solved by the help of psychological evaluation. The court may order a complete psychoanalysis of a defendant or a criminal. Some criminals or defendants are not mentally competent to undergo the trials and some fake mental incompetence to avoid the procedures of a trial. In such dicey situations psychological evaluation plays an important role and helps to solve the cases through thorough psychoanalysis.

Psychological evaluation is considered only when behavior imbalance becomes significant. Abnormal behavior which persists seriously requires psychological evaluation. Through psychological evaluation the psychologist can determine the cause of the problem. With proper guidance the patient can be cared and restored to a normal life.

CHAPTER 13 SUMMARY

FREUD'S MODEL OF PERSONALITY

Freud described two different models that describe personality, one being a stage theory of the development of the unconscious. The more basic topographic model organizes the mind into three distinct functional aspects:

- conscious
- preconscious
- unconscious

Each of these are processes that organize our experience of the world. An important feature of this model involves how conflict and ambivalence are handled by the organism, which Freud suggested are everyday aspects of life. That is, resolving conflicts and ambivalence is a necessary aspect of the human condition.

The psychosexual stages describe a developmental process for the basic structures of the unconscious, and how one shows different personality styles later in life. The psychosexual stages are divided into the following sequence:

- oral (0-18 months)
- anal (2-3 years)
- phallic (4-6 years)
- latency (7-11 years)
- genital (12 years and above)

It is worthwhile to emphasize and clarify Freud's original intent in describing each of these stages, and dispel any misconceptions about each developmental stage. For example, students may have heard about Freud's notions of the phallic stage, but be grossly misinformed about the basic theoretical idea behind it.

Each stage is characterized by conflict that must be resolved, usually by a defense mechanism housed within the unconscious. Specifically, in lectures it is worthwhile to describe the conflict, method of adaptive resolution, and the co-occurring development of unconscious structures. These structures are the id, ego, and superego. By doing this, one can also begin to describe the defense mechanisms utilized by the ego in resolving conflicts.

Fixations refer to developmental difficulties encountered at each stage, usually involving an inability to resolve one of the stage related conflicts. Overlaid on the whole model is the drive model, which suggests that all behaviors can be reduced to two basic instinctual drives:

- sex
- aggression

In the structural model (that is, the organization of the unconscious into id, ego, super-ego), there are characteristic processes associated with each structure. Each one can be depicted as follows:
- id → primary process
- ego → secondary process
- superego → ideals

DEFENSE MECHANISMS

Primary process refers to wishful and illogical thinking that typically cannot be manifested in the everyday world. At the other extreme, the superego offers ideals and standards that also may be unreasonably high. In order to counterbalance these forces, the ego works from secondary process, which is goal directed and rational.

Because the ego is under such strain from acting as an intermediary between id and superego, there are a number of defense mechanisms that the ego constructs to alleviate tension. Some of these are
- identification
- repression
- denial
- projection
- reaction formation
- sublimation
- rationalization

Following the theorizing of Freud, several of his followers developed different ideas about how personality is organized, and how it develops.

OBJECT RELATIONS THEORIES

These theoreticians developed from following Freud and his basic ideas about the unconscious and the motivating factors involved in driving behavior, but took different notions and changed them according to differing views, and in order to accommodate shortcomings in the original theory. Each of these theorists developed a special language that served as an outgrowth of the original Freudian model (such as Jung with collective and personal unconscious).

Most contemporary psychodynamic thinking centers upon object relations theory. Unlike previous theories of unconscious behavior, this line of thinking has been empirically examined, with some positive results. At its basis, object relations suggests that there are unconscious representations of relationships that drive our behavior when in the presence of those people, or others that are similar. Representations center on the self, significant others, and relationships in particular.

ASSESSMENT OF UNCONSCIOUS PATTERNS

Typically, students have encountered notions about personality measurement such as projective tests. This is an opportunity to bring to life the ideas that are conveyed by the projective hypothesis—the idea that unconscious responses are borne out by examining ambiguous stimuli. In describing this method of measurement, one can cover popular projective tests such as the Rorschach, TAT, and sentence completion tests.

Throughout the discussion of psychodynamic theories of personality, it is important to highlight the strengths (such as the rich description of personality) and weaknesses (such as the limited empirical support for different parts of these theories) in order to set the tone for examining other theories of personality.

COGNITIVE-SOCIAL THEORIES

A major aspect of cognitive-social theories involves traits, and differential methods of encoding information. These theories suggest that depending on personality styles, one encodes and understands the environment different. Part of the original notion of encoding and traits comes from the theory forwarded by George Kelly, where one has a set of personal constructs that determine how one interprets the world.

Since the early theorizing of traits and encoding, there have been gains in examining more general trends across people that predict behavior. Specifically, expectancies and competencies predict how people behave in later situations. Two particular expectancies deserve special mention: behavior-outcome expectancies and self-efficacy expectancies. The first involves the belief that a behavior will lead to a particular outcome, while the second refers to the sense that one is capable of performing the behavior necessary to attain the desired outcome.

Self-regulation involves the ability to set goals and adjust these goals according to competencies. This ability interacts with both behavior-outcome expectancies and self-efficacy expectancies in predicting behavior. It may be fruitful to consider the strengths and limits of this model as well, now that students have been exposed to two different theoretical frameworks for personality.

TRAIT THEORIES

As noted earlier, at this point students should have been exposed to a psychological definition of traits when discussing the meaning of personality per se. Here is an opportunity to expand upon that definition by couching the terms within a theoretical framework that is not inconsistent with either of the previous theoretical models. That is, trait theories may serve to contribute greatly within each of the other theories, without being contradictory to the basic tenets of each.

Eysenck's theory of traits helped set the foundation for scientific trait research, and specifically, an examination of psychophysiological processes that accompany different traits. There are essentially three major factors associated with Eysenck's model:
- Extroversion
- Neuroticism
- Psychoticism

It is important to emphasize that each of these are on continua, and therefore all students in the class have some levels on each dimension. This sets the occasion to discuss the basic meaning of each construct more fully without individuals in the class remaining stuck on a more stereotyped meaning of particular terms (such as psychoticism).

Another popular, and some have argued more inclusive, trait theory is the Five-Factor Model. This theory posits five basic dimensions that organize personality:
- Openness to experience
- Conscientiousness
- Extroversion
- Agreeableness
- Neuroticism

Although there have been some minor differences depending on the sample used to determine these factors, there has been fairly consistent findings across cultures.

GENETIC FACTORS IN PERSONALITY
It appears that some personality traits are genetically transmitted, although some have greater heritable salience than others. Rather than expect students to commit all of this information to memory, it is instead worthwhile to consider how genetic factors work (such as dominant and recessive genes) and place that discussion in the context of a heritability lecture. Trait theory, and the associated labels, is largely consistent with the language used in genetics.

CONSISTENCY OF PERSONALITY
If traits are to be called traits, then these behaviors should be consistent across situations and time. However, it appears that the picture is more complex than that would suggest. There are situational variables that can produce different behaviors—even contrary to the measured traits in an individual. Interestingly, it also appears that personality patterns can change over time—either in intensity or degree. This is worth pointing out by illustrating how people may 'mellow' with age, or under new situations people may adopt different styles of responding to environmental events.

HUMANISTIC THEORIES

This framework is based largely upon the writings of Carl Rogers. The basic element to convey to students involves a two-pronged idea regarding personality suggested by Rogers—true self and false self. In a related vein, existential approaches involve the idea that one creates their self, often as a means of avoiding anxiety. Anxiety in this case is often existential in nature, typically involving death or a broader life issue. I sometimes describe to students the 'pre-life crisis' that one goes through as part of the college experience of determining life goals and aspirations.

SELF-EFFICACY

Self-efficacy and outcome expectancies are often the source of confusion for students, and may spark considerable interest and discussion. Thoughts can be clearly organized by couching terms in the framework of an example. Some well-known examples currently exist regarding recovery from such as recovery from alcohol use, substance abuse, as well as occupational experiences. The following site helps bring this matter forward clearly.

PSYCHOLOGICAL TREATMENT

INTRODUCTION

According to the most recent Diagnostic and Statistical Manual of Mental Disorders (DSM-IV), there are nearly 400 different psychological disorders. Some of these disorders fit the definition of "disease," a problem that impairs functioning and that mostly stems from biological causes. Common examples include bipolar disorder and schizophrenia. Other "disorders" impair functioning but are determined by a more diverse array of causes, some of which are psychological and social / cultural in nature. In this sense, these conditions are not true "diseases." Examples include anxiety disorders, depression, eating disorders, and substance use disorders.

The distinction between "diseases" and "disorders" helps to suggest appropriate treatments. In general, diseases require biological intervention. Research suggests, for example, that medication is very successful in helping individuals to manage symptoms that accompany bipolar disorder and schizophrenia. Although it may encourage them to take their medication regularly, manage stress effectively, and help with emotional struggles, research shows that psychotherapy generally does not help people overcome the symptoms of these diseases without biological intervention.

Biological treatments also may help people with disorders in some cases. For example, in one of the largest and most rigorous studies ever conducted on the treatment of clinical depression, researchers in the late 1980s found that antidepressant medication helped manage the symptoms of severe depression (which I would define as involving significant suicidal thinking, that often recurs, or that is chronic) more than other treatment options, at least during the time span in which individuals were taking the medicine.

On the other hand, decades of carefully controlled clinical studies have shown that medication often is not the best treatment for many disorders. For instance, a recent meta-analysis found that antidepressants generally perform no better than a sugar pill in the treatment of depression that is mild or moderate in severity. Often times, any symptom relief that medication provides ends when individuals stop taking them.

Approximately 5% of all American men and approximately 10% of all American women are taking an antidepressant medication for some reason. Many of these individuals suffer from significant side effects from the medication. Others believe that they are being helped by the medicine and thus do not work to resolve the underlying issues that are at the "root" of the problem. In fact, much of the therapeutic effect of medicine likely stems from psychological factors such as cathartic release of telling their doctor about their problems, the relationship between them and their doctor, or the faith or hope they experience from the treatment. Of course, there are other ways to treat psychological disorders that may provide these factors without needing to take a pharmacological substance.

The best treatment option for many people who struggle with disorders is psychotherapy. Several forms of psychotherapy – cognitive therapy, behavioral therapy, interpersonal therapy, and psychodynamic therapy – have been found to successfully treat many disorders, including disorders with severe symptoms. Furthermore, compared with the effects of medication, psychotherapy often seems to provide better treatment in the long-term. Perhaps one of the reasons why psychotherapy is so helpful in many cases is that it gets at the "root" causes of people's problems. Furthermore, although psychotherapy seems unrelated to biology, research shows that biological changes happen through this treatment just like it does when medication is helpful.

Available research suggests that there is not necessarily one kind of psychotherapy that is better than the rest (the main exception being that exposure based treatments seem to work better than all other treatments for anxiety disorders). Rather, it seems that there are certain "common factors" involved in good treatment, including a trusting relationship with a treatment provider, individual factors such as motivation to follow suggestions, and the faith and hope that the treatment will help. Based on this, individuals struggling with depression would do well to seek a referral to a good therapist and "try them out" to see how they "click" with them. Usually, someone can tell after the first session whether they like the therapist. If the first therapist one tries doesn't work out, another provider might work better.

There also are other activities that might help people with disorders. Some of these might be encouraged by a therapist, and include working through self-help materials (see David Burns' books "Feeling Good" and "When Panic Attacks" for books shown to work in comparative research), regular aerobic exercise, keeping an emotions journal in which one writes about difficult emotions, keeping a gratitude journal in which one records what one is most thankful for, engaging in pleasurable activities, talking with a trusted friend about one's problems, performing random acts of kindness, getting lost in nature, and managing stress through effective coping techniques. Although these kinds of activities haven't really been established as successful treatments in themselves, they are linked with mood in various ways. In fact, I wouldn't be surprised if many of these lifestyle-based approaches someday are shown to perform at least as well as – if not better than – conventional treatments available today.

In conclusion, people struggling with a mental illness should know that there is hope. Almost all conditions can be managed effectively through the right combination of treatment options. Many disorders can be overcome long-term without the use of medicine. Probably the most difficult step in treatment is acknowledging that you have a problem and taking the first step to seek help. However, with this humility and courage, people can experience relief and improvement.

Early Treatments

In ancient times, mental disturbances were thought to be caused by evil spirits. Any behavior that people find unusual would then prompt others to think that the odd-acting person has been possessed by an evil spirit. Because of this belief, the primary treatment that they practiced was to drive away the evil spirit/s through incantation, spells, or sacrifice. During the Stone Age, skulls of people with unusual behavior were also drilled, believing that these would cast away the evil spirits. This practice is called trephination.

During ancient times, people who shared having unusual experiences were believed to be hallucinating. They also practiced a prehistoric form of brain surgery to cure the hallucination problem. It is quite obvious that the dominant beliefs during the ancient era were supernatural theories. Likewise, the dominant treatment for any abnormalities was exorcism, or casting out of the evil spirits from the sick person's body. Ancient people also rely on the assistance and advice from the shaman or healers. Sometimes, ancient people also resort to extreme harmful measures such as beating, torturing or starving the person just to drive away the evil spirit.

During the Middle Ages, mental disturbances were believed to be signs of witchcraft. Because of this, accused or suspected witches were burned or tortured to prevent the emotional sickness from spreading. The Renaissance became the start of the period of building asylums. In asylums, patients lived in prison-like rooms, confined and isolated from the rest of society. Some of the patients were even chained to the walls. Indeed, the patients lived in extremely harsh conditions that instead of getting better, they even get worse and worse each day.

The first hospital focusing on mental illnesses was established in 1773 in Williamsburg, Virginia. Although clinicians then claimed that the hospital was built to bring back the health and cognitive functioning of the patient, the hospital still turned out to be a bit of a torture chamber. Some patients suffered from electrical shocks, water torture and starvation.

Reality Therapy

William Glasser, the main proponent of reality therapy, believed that individuals are not similar to robots that move and act when controlled by others. Instead, he argued that all individuals possess five biological needs, mainly survival, love and belonging, power, freedom, and fun. These needs direct human behavior and are present in everyone. However, the question of which of these five needs are dominant may vary from one person to another. He also added that our brain has a special place called "quality world" that contains all memories we consider pleasing. This also includes our beliefs, whether personal or convictional.

The choice theory states that behavior is holistic. Behavior is composed of four inseparable components, mainly acting, thinking, feeling and physiology. In the therapy, the freedom of choice is a primary rule.

Therapists are not allowed to use any form of control or manipulation or coercion of the individual's behavior. Through this manner, individuals are encouraged to be creative and to take risks. In reality therapy, the main goal of the therapist is to lead the individual to change of behavior. Take note, leading the individual to change of behavior is different from changing the individual's behavior. Glasser also specified the conditions necessary for the individual to change behavior like ensuring that the individual is convinced that what they are presently doing is unproductive or irrational and convincing the individual that other behaviors can help him or her be more productive.

Reality therapy uses the WDEP system – the discovery and analysis of the individual's wants and needs, directions and doings, evaluation, and planning and commitment. The individual initially shares what he or she really wants in life and what stops him or her from getting what she wants. Then, the individual's behavior and its influence on the individual are further explored by the therapist. An evaluation follows, and the therapy is usually closed with the individual identifying personal action plans and expressing commitment to his or her personal action plans.

The Old Stigma Surrounding Treatment

At one time psychiatrists thought that personality disorders did not respond very well to treatment. This opinion was derived from the notion that human personality is fixed for life once it has been molded in childhood, and from the belief among people with personality disorders that their own views and behaviors are correct, and that others are the ones at fault. More recently, however, doctors have recognized that humans can continue to grow and change throughout life. Most patients with personality disorders are now considered to be treatable, although the degree of improvement may vary. The type of treatment recommended depends on the personality characteristics associated with the specific disorder.

Hospitalization

Inpatient treatment is rarely required for patients with personality disorders, with two major exceptions: borderline patients who are threatening suicide or suffering from drug or alcohol withdrawal; and patients with paranoid personality disorder who are having psychotic symptoms.

Types of Treatment

Cognitive-Behavioral Therapy

Cognitive-behavioral approaches are often recommended for patients with avoidant or dependent personality disorders. Patients in these groups typically have mistaken beliefs about their competence or likableness. These assumptions can be successfully challenged by cognitive-behavioral methods. More recently, Aaron Beck and his coworkers have successfully extended their approach to cognitive therapy to all ten personality disorders as defined by DSM-IV.

There are actually several kinds of Cognitive-Behavioral therapies and they all employ the same general premise: in contrast to the psychodynamic emphasis on insight into unconscious **motivation, the cognitive-behavioral therapies emphasize** the ability of people to make changes in their lives without having to understand why the change occurs. **As such, these therapeutic techniques usually take much less time and are therefore less costly than psychodynamic psychotherapy.**

As a trade-off to the cost, though, the individual usually must do considerable work, such as homework writing assignments and practice of techniques learned in the office. Failure to complete tasks as assigned is taken as a lack of motivation and an unwillingness to change behaviors.

Aaron Beck

The more-or-less pure cognitive therapies—such as Aaron Beck's Cognitive Therapy, focus on changing certain thought patterns. The premise, in Beck's words, is that "the way we perceive situations influences how we feel emotionally," and so by changing thoughts, then behaviors will also change. The pure behavioral therapies, such as classical conditioning or operant conditioning, focus on changing behaviors. And some forms of treatment such as Rational Emotive Behavior Therapy (REBT)—developed by Albert Ellis—mix cognitive and behavioral elements. REBT used to be called Rational Emotive Therapy (RET); the name change reflects the understanding that rational beliefs, emotions, and behaviors are all interdependent and that psychotherapy should work on all these levels. In this regard, it's interesting to note that the psychodynamic forms of psychotherapy focus on understanding experiences, and, as a "side effect," thought processes and behaviors are changed as well.

Albert Ellis

This leads to a simple moral: If you want to get into a house, it doesn't matter whether you get in through the front door or the back door. **Which form of psychotherapy you choose depends only on personal preference, time, and** money. Some therapies that work wonders with one person are a complete flop with another person. You should pay attention to this fact, especially if you have Managed Care.

PSYCHODYNAMIC THERAPIES

Psychodynamic psychotherapy is composed of a variety of different approaches within the broader domains. Traditional psychodynamic psychotherapy is based upon *psychoanalysis*. Psychoanalysis involves a set up with the individual lying upon a couch and describing in detail events and emotional reactions throughout his/her life. This approach is still used in some settings. The more common variety is psychodynamic psychotherapy, which is based on the wide array of related theoretical conceptualizations that have been developed. For example, much of contemporary psychodynamic psychotherapy is based upon *object-relations theory*. In all the other varieties of psychodynamic psychotherapy, therapist and individual sit face-to-face, and discuss difficulties that have been encountered and unresolved, frequently involving repetitive relationship difficulties.

Psychodynamic therapy, also known as insight-oriented therapy, focuses on unconscious processes as they are manifested in a person's present behavior. The goals of psychodynamic therapy are a individual's self-awareness and understanding of the influence of the past on present behavior. In its brief form, a psychodynamic approach enables the individual to examine unresolved conflicts and symptoms that arise from past dysfunctional relationships and manifest themselves in the need and desire to abuse substances.

Several different approaches to brief psychodynamic psychotherapy have evolved from psychoanalytic theory and have been clinically applied to a wide range of psychological disorders. There is a body of research that generally supports the efficacy of these approaches.

Psychodynamic therapy is the oldest of the modern therapies. (Freud's psychoanalysis is a specific form and subset of psychodymanic therapy.) As such, it is based in a highly developed and multifaceted theory of human development and interaction. This chapter demonstrates how rich it is for adaptation and further evolution by contemporary therapists for specific purposes. The material presented in this chapter provides a quick glance at the usefulness and the complex nature of this type of therapy.

PSYCHOTHERAPY

Psychoanalytic psychotherapy is suggested for patients who can benefit from insight-oriented treatment. These patients typically include those with dependent, obsessive-compulsive, and avoidant personality disorders. Doctors usually recommend individual psychotherapy for narcissistic and borderline patients, but often refer these patients to therapists with specialized training in these disorders. Psychotherapeutic treatment for personality disorders may take as long as three to five years.

Insight-oriented approaches are not recommended for patients with paranoid or antisocial personality disorders. These patients are likely to resent the therapist and see him or her as trying to control or dominate them.

Supportive therapy is regarded as the most helpful form of psychotherapy for patients with schizoid personality disorder.

The Adlerian Approach

The Adlerian therapy focuses on spotting concerns or issues revolving around unrealistic ambitions or lack of confidence. The therapist also discovers the successes and failures the individual has gone through and how these experiences have affected him or her. The diagnostic tool of early recollections is also practiced. With this method, the individual narrates early childhood incidents that keep on happening again and again. According to Adler, these recollections describe how an individual sees himself or herself and what he or she envisions for the future. After gathering these information, the therapist then develops a lifestyle assessment, or the main targets of therapy.

It is a guideline for Adlerian therapists to guide the individual in exploring his or her strength, rather than revealing his or her weaknesses. Therapists use an objective interview that inquires about the beginning of the individual's problems, the individual's medical history, the individual's purpose for engaging in therapy, and the person's coping mechanisms. Indeed, based on this approach, therapists or counselors are "lifestyle investigators".

Questions about family environment have likewise been included in the techniques. The family issues include the individual's similarity or dissimilarity with the parents and other siblings, parents' treatment of the children and discipline in the home. Early recollections are also practiced, commonly starting with the line, "Tell me something that happened one time." This narration is further interpreted by the therapist, according to the individual's perception of the event. Personality priorities are also interpreted based on the four behavioral patterns of superiority, control, comfort, and aim to please.

Adler's Therapy

Adler's therapy was simple and direct. There were no strict rules—it was truly tailored to the individual. Adler said the therapist had four general goals:

1. Establish contact (rapport) with the patient.
2. After a thorough diagnosis, disclose errors in the person's lifestyle.
3. Encourage progress toward a better lifestyle.
4. Encourage the patient to turn outward and get involved in helping others (showing what Adler called social interest).

Several techniques were used to accomplish these goals of therapy. First, to establish rapport, one maintained a friendly and accepting attitude while allowing the individual to talk freely about his or her entire life. While doing this, the Adlerian therapist would observe all actions and choices made by the person, verbal and non-verbal. The therapist might notice posture, or gestures, or tone of voice, or choice of clothing. Adler felt that people were consistent in all the details of the person, so it should all add up to a consistent picture.

Karen Horney – Self Analysis

So far we have discussed the therapy techniques of three personality theorists whose theories were discussed in Chapter 11 (Personality Theories): Freud, Jung, and Adler. The next theorist described in that chapter, Karen Horney, also had a distinct approach to therapy. She was the only one in the group who advocated *self-analysis*.

Horney believed that, in some respects, we can understand our inner worlds better than anyone else. Horney disagreed with Freud's belief that self-analysis could be dangerous. . She thought there were some built-in protections that made self-analysis safe. Horney said if a patient had something in the past that was so painful, so traumatic, that it could traumatize the patient if introduced to consciousness, the patient was unlikely to come upon it in self-analysis anyway.

The goals of self-analysis were to

1. To be completely frank and honest with oneself.
2. To become aware of unconscious driving forces and motivations.
3. To develop a capacity for changing, especially in relationships with others.

Horney advocated such techniques as free association and dream analysis. Free association, when self-administered, meant giving totally free range to thoughts. Odd associations could be analyzed for meaning, especially if they evoked emotion.

Another technique was looking for *contradictions* and *exaggerations* in reactions to everyday events. A dramatic overreaction to some event could provide a valuable clue about psychic conflicts. Horney said to pay attention to feelings we *might prefer to ignore*(in dreams, for example). However, people should avoid blame when doing a self-analysis, Horney believed. The effort should be to understand, not to blame.

Summary of Psychodynamic Therapy

Psychodynamic approaches analyze the energies or movements (dynamics) within the individual's mental world or psyche. Such approaches are distinguished by an emphasis on **personal history** and **unconscious motivations.**

Carl Jung's therapy emphasized *complexes*. Jung said every patient has a story. The therapist must discover this story and share it with the patient.

Alfred Adler believed that neurotics were troubled by deficient *styles of life* that were set up in early childhood as ways of coping with felt inferiorities. Adler used early memories, dream interpretation, and observation of a person's way of dealing with social situations to diagnose the style of life. Adler believed human misery involved problems in friendship, work, and love. He encouraged activities oriented toward helping others as a way of turning away from excessive self-interest, a characteristic of neurosis.

Karen Horney was unique among early analysts in recommending self-analysis. She said it was revealing to look for exaggerating reactions to life events, unconscious motivations, or feelings (in dreams, for example) that we might prefer to ignore. She emphasized that the goal of therapy was not just to make a clever analysis but to cultivate the ability for growth and change.

APPROACHES TO COUNSELING

Rogerian Counseling

Several radically different approaches to therapy can be identified in the profession of counseling and clinical psychology. In the early 1980s, Smith (1982) reported that the two most influential figures in counseling and clinical psychology were Carl Rogers and Albert Ellis. Years later, these two approaches are still influential. They also provide a good way to contrast different styles of counseling, because in some ways they are completely opposites. Rogers, often called "the father of counseling psychology, practiced *non-directive* or *person-centered* therapy. In Rogerian therapy, the individual determined his or her own direction of change. Ellis, by contrast, offered a *prescriptive* therapy—one which gave definite, sometimes sharply worded,

advice. We will consider the approach of Rogers first, then Ellis.

ELLIS–RATIONAL EMOTIVE BEHAVIOR THERAPY

Not everybody responds well to non-directive therapy, with its insistence that the direction for change come from the individual. Some people seem to respond better to a direct challenge or specific advice. Such a person might respond well to the therapy of Albert Ellis. Ellis called his technique *rational-emotive behavior therapy* (REBT).

Ellis claimed high success rates using principles and assumptions almost opposite to Rogerian therapy. REBT is a short-term therapy, whereas nondirective counseling can go on for many months. Unlike Rogers, Ellis uses a *directive* or *prescriptive* approach. He did not wait for individuals to arrive at their own solutions to problems. Instead, he pointed out problems immediately and insistently, refusing to let a individual divert attention.

Ellis believed *emotional dysfunctions* are related to *self-talk*. Self-talk was his label for the way a person's inner voice described situations. Self-talk determined a person's *reactions* to situations. Basic psychological dysfunctions are due to *irrational* modes of thinking expressed in irrational statements we make to ourselves, according to Ellis.

RATIONAL EMOTIVE BEHAVIOR THERAPY

One of the more contemporary approaches to counseling or psychological therapy is the rational emotive behavior therapy, proposed by Albert Ellis. This approach focuses on the interplay between cognition, emotion and behaviors. It is grounded on the main principle that people also cause their own psychological problems with their own interpretation or perception of different events and situations. Likewise, a redesign or modification of a person's personal statements can also produce to a redesign or modification of behavior.

This therapeutic approach emphasizes the importance of a warm and collaborative dialogue between the therapist and the individual. It also stresses out that psychological problems are more dominantly caused by discrepancies in one's own thinking. Therefore, this helping method is more specific and identifies specific structured target problems for the therapy sessions. Similar to other cognitive behavioral techniques, this method also includes homework, further encouraging personal responsibility, initiative and commitment from the individual. It also makes the individual feel more active and more in control.

According to the rational emotive behavior therapy, individuals possess both rational and irrational beliefs. These beliefs include the helpful ones such as happiness, optimism, love, aim for growth and development, as well as the unhelpful ones such as self-destruction, self-blames procrastination and repetition of mistakes or failures. Thus, it is considered another significant goal of this therapy to guide the individual to accept that though he or she fails at one point or another, he or she can also end up victorious in other areas.

The main process followed by the rational emotive behavior therapy is the ABC theory of personality. It states that A (the activating event) does not really cause C (the psychological consequence), in the way we expect it does. Instead, a person's B (belief) about the activating event is the factor that causes the consequence.

Group therapy

Group Therapy is frequently useful for patients with schizoid or avoidant personality disorders because it helps them to break out of their social isolation. It has also been recommended for patients with histrionic and antisocial personality disorders. These patients tend to act out, and pressure from peers in group treatment can motivate them to change. Because patients with antisocial personality disorder can destabilize groups that include people with other disorders,

it is usually best if these people meet exclusively with others who have APD (in homogeneous groups).

Family therapy

Family Therapy may be suggested for patients whose personality disorders cause serious problems for members of their families. It is also sometimes recommended for borderline patients from over involved or possessive families.

Summary of Approaches to Counseling

Two of the most influential counseling psychologists were Carl Rogers and Albert Ellis. In many ways they are opposites. Rogers was warm, accepting, and refused to criticize or give advice. He dealt with many problems and said the underlying problem was always the question, "Who am I, really?" Rogers felt people would find their own solutions to their problems, given a supportive social relationship. Self generated solutions were the only solutions that would last, Rogers maintained.

Albert Ellis gave direct advice to his individuals, mostly about getting rid of "irrational ideas" such as "everybody must love me." His A-B-C-D-E mnemonic spells out the basic ingredients of his approach. Ellis was known for challenging his individuals directly (the "D" in his scheme standing for *disputing irrational beliefs*). Ellis advocated taking control of one's life and not dwelling on problems. Ellis was criticized for an "anything you can do, I can do better" attitude. He sometimes alienated individuals, who either "gave in" or "fled" from him. Ellis accepted this as a normal part of therapy.

Sometimes reverse psychology works better than direct advice. Leon Seltzer described *paradoxical strategies in therapy*. A problem is made to disappear by asking a individual to practice it. This surprising technique has a long history, including Frankl's *paradoxical intention* and Dunlop's *negative practice*.

Behavior Therapies

Wolpe's Desensitization Therapy

Desensitization was the first therapy to be called a *behavior therapy*. It was self-consciously designed to use insights from laboratory work on conditioning, and it focused directly on problem behavior rather than trying to treat an underlying mental illness. Desensitization was proposed by Joseph Wolpe (pronounced VOLE-py). Because desensitization was the first widely-adopted therapy based on behavioral principles, Wolpe is often called the father of behavior therapy.

Wolpe devised a procedure for counter-conditioning in humans. First, he taught the patient to relax deeply, using a technique called *Jacobsonian progressive relaxation* which may itself take a few weeks to master. Then he encouraged patients to *visualize* or *imagine* the anxiety-arousing stimulus *while remaining relaxed*. To gradually eliminate the anxiety-arousing characteristics of the feared stimulus, Wolpe had his patients make a *fear hierarchy* from least-fearsome to most-fearsome imagery. For example, if the patient was snake-phobic (terribly afraid of snakes) he or she might produce this list:

1. A tiny snake 50 feet away (the least fearsome image)
2. A larger snake 30 feet away
3. A large snake 10 feet away
4. A large snake on the ground right in front of me
5. A snake bumping against my foot then slithering away
6. A snake being placed in my hands
7. A snake wrapping itself around my arm
8. A snake slithering up my arm toward my neck
9. A snake taking a big bite out of my cheek
10. Falling into a pit of poisonous snakes (the most fearsome image)

The patient started with the least anxiety-arousing image (#1) and moved on to the next *only when able to imagine the first image while staying fully relaxed*. Given enough time, and enough practice with relaxation techniques, a snake-phobic individual could work through the hierarchy. Eventually he or she would be able to imagine the worst, most horrible scene while staying fully relaxed. At this point, the conditioned emotional response (CER) was fully undone or *extinguished*. To use the terminology from the Conditioning chapter, the *conditional stimulus* (sight of the snake) no longer elicited a *conditional response* of anxiety.

Desensitization works, and it is simple to administer, although the classic Wolpe procedure often took months. As noted earlier certain types of phobias seem to be "prepared" by evolution and are more difficult to treat. These include snake, spider, and small animal phobias. However, even these instinctive fears usually yield to desensitization in the long run. Less biologically-based phobias such as test anxiety and fear of flying often can be eliminated quickly.

Wolpe (1958) described a three-part systematic desensitization procedure:

1. The individual is trained in deep relaxation.
2. The individual and therapist construct a list of anxiety-eliciting stimuli, the so-called *fear hierarchy*, ordered from least to most distressing.
3. Starting with the least anxiety-arousing image, the feared stimuli are paired with relaxation, until eventually the most feared stimulus is tolerated calmly.

In the years after Wolpe publicized his original procedure, researchers tried out dozens of variations, looking for more efficient procedures. For example, researchers found that drugs or carbon dioxide/oxygen mixtures could provide rapid relaxation, making time-consuming relaxation training unnecessary.

Exposure Therapy

Exposure therapy is a quick, extreme version of desensitization was tested in the 1970s. It was initially called *flooding* or *immersion therapy*. Now it is simply called *exposure therapy*. In comparison after comparison, it worked as well or better than the Wolpe approach, and it took much less time. Individuals no longer had to learn progressive relaxation or work through a hierarchy. In exposure therapy, a individual is exposed to a safe version of the fearsome stimulus at maximum intensity. The anxiety reaction burns out, and extinction occurs after that.

Eysenck, like many other investigators, found that *time of exposure* was critically important in this type of therapy.

Exposure therapy was the only therapy that worked for obsessive *hand-washing*, in Eysenck's experience. Some people washed their hands hundreds of times a day, until their hands were red and sore. A deeply rooted anxiety about contamination seemed to be involved. Eysenck tried an extinction procedure. He had compulsive hand-washers immerse their hands in a barrel of rubbish, then just stand there with contaminated hands for several hours, without being allowed to wash them.

Modeling and Behavior Change

After the success of desensitization therapy called attention to the new field of behavior therapy in the 1950s and 1960s, behavior therapists began to branch out from desensitization and sensitization to different types of therapy. Albert Bandura's *Principles of Behavior Modification* (1967) introduced the concepts of *vicarious reinforcement, modeling*, and *behavior rehearsal* to behavior therapists.

Bandura was a leading *social learning theorist* of the 1960s and 1970s. He emphasized *observational learning*. Observational learning occurs through *vicarious reinforcement* (being influenced by seeing somebody else get reinforced), *modeling* (learning by watching another person perform a behavior), and *behavior rehearsal* (acting out a behavior to learn it and refine it as a skill).

Behavioral Contract Therapy

Self-modification can also be encouraged through behavioral contracting and through the procedure (briefly described in Chapter 5) called **self-monitoring**.

For example, a person who wishes to diet may make a contract with a behavior therapist to keep track of all calories eaten during the day. The record-keeping activity forces attention to the behavior that the individual wishes to change. Often this—combined with the social pressure of the "contract" with therapist—is enough to encourage self-directed change in individuals.

SUMMARY OF BEHAVIOR THERAPIES

Behavior therapies use the conditioning principles in attempts to change problem behaviors. Almost all therapies can be construed as extinction therapies, in part, because almost all therapies lead a individual to confront previously-avoided emotional issues in a safe therapeutic environment. The result, predictably, is a diminished emotional response. This allows rational thinking and problem-solving.

Desensitization is a therapy aimed at eliminating unwanted emotional responses. Relaxation is used to "counter" the effects of anxiety. In the classic version of desensitization, a individual imagines gradually more fearsome scenes, while fully relaxed, until able to tolerate the most fearsome images.

Researchers explored many variations on the classical desensitization procedure. *Flooding* is direct exposure to a feared stimulus at a high intensity. *In vivo* desensitization uses a real life situation rather than imagined scenes. The two techniques were combined into *exposure therapy*, one of the most commonly used behavior therapies in the 2000s.

Sensitization is the opposite of desensitization. Whereas desensitization *decreases* response to a stimulus, sensitization *increases* it. A classic example is O. Hobart Mowrer's anti-bedwetting apparatus, which sounds a loud alarm when urine hits a bed pad sensitive to moisture. Soon the feeling of a full bladder awakens the child as an anticipatory response. Sensitization is also used in marriage therapies, to rekindle romantic feelings. Couples are encouraged to set up stimulus conditions which become cues predicting positive romantic encounters.

Modeling and *behavior rehearsal* were embraced by behavior therapists when social learning concepts became popular in American psychology. Behavior rehearsal is illustrated by a case history from Wolpe and Lazarus (1966)) in which a man is taught how to present himself in an interview.

Beck's therapy for depression also aims to modify thoughts, as a way of "restructuring experience." Individuals learn to recognize and eliminate destructive patterns of thinking. Realistic appraisals of life situations are encouraged instead. Behavior therapists often use *behavioral contracting* to help individuals achieve change on their own or in family settings.

Cognitive-behavioral therapy

Cognitive-behavioral approaches are often recommended for patients with avoidant or dependent personality disorders. Patients in these groups typically have mistaken beliefs about their competence or likableness. These assumptions can be successfully challenged by cognitive-behavioral methods. More recently, Aaron Beck and his coworkers have successfully extended their approach to cognitive therapy to all ten personality disorders as defined by DSM-IV.

Psychology and Medicine

Many different specialties within psychology relate to health and medicine. Medications may be prescribed for patients with specific personality disorders. The type of medication depends on the disorder. In general, however, patients with personality disorders are helped only moderately by medications.

Anti-psychotic Drugs. Antipsychotic drugs, such as haloperidol (Haldol), may be given to patients with paranoid personality disorder if they are having brief psychotic episodes. Patients with borderline or schizotypal personality disorder are sometimes given antipsychotic drugs in low doses; however, the efficacy of these drugs in treating personality disorder is less clear than in schizophrenia. Some drug treatments include: Clozaril, Haldol, Risperdal, Seroquel.

Mood Stabilizers. Carbamazepine (Tegretol) is a drug that is commonly used to treat seizures, but is also helpful for borderline patients with rage outbursts and similar behavioral problems. Lithium and valproate may also be used as mood stabilizers, especially among people with borderline personality disorder. Other mood stabilizers include: Depakote, Cibalith-S, and Eskalith.

Anti-depressants and Anti-anxiety Medications. Medications in these categories are sometimes prescribed for patients with schizoid personality disorder to help them manage anxiety symptoms while they are in psychotherapy. Antidepressants are also commonly used to treat people with borderline personality disorder.

Treatment with medications is not recommended for patients with avoidant, histrionic, dependent, or narcissistic personality disorders. The use of potentially addictive medications should be avoided in people with borderline or antisocial personality disorders. However, some avoidant patients who also have social phobia may benefit from monoamine oxidase inhibitors (MAO inhibitors), a particular class of antidepressant. Other drug treatments are Anafranil, BuSpar, Effexor, Paxil (SSRI), and Prozac (SSRI).

RELAXATION AND BIOFEEDBACK

One way to avoid uncontrolled tension is to cultivate the ability to relax at will. In the 1930s, Edmund Jacobson developed a simple technique for this called *progressive relaxation*. Jacobson said it was important to *learn to recognize and create the feeling of muscle relaxation by contrasting it with the feeling of muscle tension*. Therefore a person learning Jacobsonian progressive relaxation practices tensing and relaxing various muscle groups of the body, from the feet up. At each level one is supposed to notice the feeling of muscle tension (when muscles are tense) and the contrasting feeling of relaxation (when letting go). Gradually one learns to discriminate the feeling of relaxation, then to bring it under control, so it can be made to happen at will.

Biofeedback

Biofeedback is very helpful in learning muscle relaxation. This type of biofeedback involves the measurement of muscle tension by a device known as an EMG or *electromyograph*. In this type of biofeedback training, electrodes are placed on a muscle such as the forearm or the forehead. The biofeedback machine produces an audible tone which rises when the muscle fibers are more active and falls when they are less active. The goal, in relaxation training, is to lower the tone as far as possible.

EMG biofeedback confronts people with a fact about human muscle physiology. There is nothing a person can «do,» in an active sense, to relax a muscle. There are no commands from the brain which make a muscle relax. Relaxation is the *absence* of commands from the brain to the muscle. The only way to make relaxation happen is to *let go*. This becomes clear when a person is hooked up to a biofeedback machine, because the only way to make the tone drop (indicating lower muscle tension) is to cease all attempts to influence the activity of the muscle and simply let it go limp. Then it becomes relaxed. Once this is learned, relaxation can be accomplished at will, by letting go of the desired muscle group.

Contemporary Therapies

There are several concepts of thought regarding the foundations of music therapy, including philosophies based on education, psychology, neuroscience, and music therapy itself.

Music therapists may work with individuals who have behavioral-emotional disorders. To meet the needs of this population, music therapists have taken current psychological theories and used them as a basis for different types of music therapy. Different models include behavioral therapy, cognitive behavioral therapy, and psychodynamic therapy.

The therapy model based on neuroscience is called "neurological music therapy" (NMT). NMT is "based on a neuroscience model of music perception and production, and the influence of music on functional changes in non-musical brain and behavior functions." In addition, NMT trains motor responses (ie. tapping foot or fingers, head movement, etc.) to better help individuals develop motor skills that help "entrain the timing of muscle activation patterns."

Art Therapy

Art therapy is a form of expressive therapy that uses the creative process of making art to improve a person's physical, mental, and emotional well-being. The creative process involved in expressing one's self artistically can help people to resolve issues as well as develop and manage their behaviors and feelings, reduce stress, and improve self-esteem and awareness. Art therapy can be used for counseling by therapists, healing, treatment, rehabilitation, psychotherapy, and in the broad sense of the term, art therapy can be used to massage one's inner-self in a way that may provide the individual with a deeper understanding of him or herself.

One of the major differences between art therapy and other forms of communication is that most other forms of communication elicit the use of words or language as a means of communication. Often times, humans are incapable of expressing themselves within this limited range. An art therapist may use a variety of art methods including drawing, painting, sculpture and collage with individuals ranging from young children to the elderly. Individuals who have experienced emotional trauma,

physical violence, domestic abuse, anxiety, depression and other psychological issues can benefit from expressing themselves creatively. Hospitals, private mental health offices, schools and community organizations are all possible settings where art therapy services may be available.

15

SOCIAL PSYCHOLOGY: THE NATURE OF GROUPS AND PROCESS

LEARNING OBJECTIVES

After completing Chapter 17, students should be able to:

- Outline the factors leading to interpersonal attraction.
- Sketch the most important taxonomies of love.
- Discuss the role of sexual strategies in ensuring reproductive success.
- Explain why it is said that close relationships have a dark side ("cost").
- Define and provide examples of altruism.
- Contrast the ethical hedonism view of altruism with that of genuine altruism.
- Discuss the connection between diffusion of responsibility and the failure of bystander intervention.
- Define aggression and discuss its biological components.
- Discuss the frustration-aggression hypothesis of aggression.
- Contrast the psychodynamic perspective on aggression with that of the evolutionary perspective.
- Discuss the general aggression model.
- Discuss obedience and conformity as types of social influence.
- Outline the various elements that define groups.
- Contrast social facilitation with social loafing.
- Describe the various approaches that can be taken in the course of influence.
- Discuss the impact of leadership style on group followers.
- Provide three examples of everyday social influence.

Social psychology is a discipline that uses scientific methods "to understand and explain how the thought, feeling and behavior of individuals are influenced by the actual, imagined or implied presence of other human beings"

—Gordon Allport, 1985

INTRODUCTION

Social psychology is about how people interact. Being part of psychology, it focuses on psychological processes that accompany those interactions. The topics in this chapter, such as obedience, conformity, persuasion, and first impressions, all involve how individuals respond to other people and influence other people.

SOCIAL PSYCHOLOGY DEFINED

Social Psychology is a branch of psychology that studies individuals in the social context. This discipline examines a wide range of social topics, including group behavior, social perception, nonverbal behavior, conformity, aggression and prejudices. It is important to note that social psychology does not focus on social influences alone, but considers social perception and social interaction as vital to understanding social behavior.

Social psychology is related to sociology in this regard, but instead of focusing on group factors such as race and socioeconomic class, it focuses on the individual. Also, it relies on the scientific research to generate the theories of social behavior.

Social Psychology is important because it provides a better understanding of how stereotypes are formed, why racism and sexism exist, how a person can seem like an entirely different person in different situations, and even how people fall in love.

HISTORY OF SOCIAL PSYCHOLOGY

Kurt Lewin, the "father of social psychology."

The discipline of social psychology began in the United States after the 20th century. Norman Triplett published the first study on social facilitation. During the 1930s, many Gestalt psychologists, notably Kurt Lewin, fled to the United States from Nazi Germany. They were instrumental in developing the field as being distinctly different from the theoretical perspective of behaviorism and psychoanalysis. Social psychology has always maintained the legacy of their interests in perception and cognition. Attitudes and small group phenomena were the most commonly studied topics in this era.

During WWII, social psychologists studied behaviors such as persuasion and propaganda for U.S. military purposes. After the war, researchers became interested in a variety of social problems, including gender issues and racial prejudice. In the sixties, there was growing interest in new topics, such as cognitive dissonance and aggression. Later, in the 1970s, social psychology engaged in debate over the ethics of laboratory experimentation, whether or not attitudes really predicted behavior, and how much science could be done in a cultural context.

Social psychology reached maturity in both theory and method during the 1980s and 1990s. Modern researchers are interested in a many phenomena, however, attribution, social cognition, and the self-concept are perhaps the greatest areas of growth in recent years. Social psychologists have also maintained their applied interests while making contributions in the health discipline and environmental psychology.

Social Groups

A social group consists of two or more people who interact with one another and who recognize themselves as a distinct social unit. The definition is simple enough, but it has significant implications. Frequent interaction leads people to share values and beliefs. This similarity and the interaction cause them to identify with one another. Identification and attachment, in turn, stimulate more frequent and intense interaction. Each group maintains solidarity with all to other groups and other types of social systems.

Groups are among the most stable and enduring of social units. They are important both to their members and to the society at large. Through encouraging regular and predictable behavior, groups form the foundation upon which society rests. Thus, a family, a village, a political party a trade union is all social groups. These, it should be noted are different from social classes, status groups or crowds, which not only lack structure but whose members are less aware or even unaware of the existence of the group. These have been called quasi-groups or groupings. Nevertheless, the distinction between social groups and quasi-groups is fluid and variable since quasi-groups very often give rise to social groups, as for example, social classes give rise to political parties.

Characteristics of secondary group:

Dominance of secondary relations: Secondary groups are characterized by indirect, impersonal, contractual and non-inclusive relations. Relations are indirect because secondary groups are bigger in size and members may not stay together. Relations are contractual in the sense they are oriented towards certain interests

Largeness of the size: Secondary groups are relatively larger in size. City, nation, political parties, trade unions and corporations, international associations are bigger in size. They may have thousands of members. There may not be any limit to the membership in the case of some secondary groups.

Membership: Membership in the case of secondary groups is mainly voluntary. Individuals are at liberty to join or to go away from the groups. However there are some secondary groups like the state whose membership is almost involuntary.

No physical basis: Secondary groups are not characterized by physical proximity. Many secondary groups are not limited to any definite area. There are some secondary groups like the Rotary Club and Lions Club which are international in character. The members of such groups are scattered over a vast area. Specific ends or interest: Secondary groups are formed for the realization of some specific interests or ends. They are called special interest groups. Members are interested in the groups because they have specific ends to aim at. Indirect communication: Contacts and communications in the case of secondary groups are mostly indirect. Mass media of communication such as radio, telephone, television, newspaper, movies, magazines and post and telegraph are resorted to by the members to have communication. Communication may not be quick and effective even. Impersonal nature of social relationships in secondary groups is both the cause and the effect of indirect communication.

Nature of group control: Informal means of social control are less effective in regulating the relations of members. Moral control is only secondary. Formal means of social control such as law, legislation, police, court etc are made of to control the behavior of members. The behavior of the people is largely influenced and controlled by public opinion, propaganda, rule of law and political ideologies. Group structure: The secondary group has a formal structure. A formal authority is set up with designated powers and a clear-cut division of labor in which the function of each is specified in relation to the function of all. Secondary groups are mostly organized groups. Different statuses and roles that the members assume are specified. Distinctions based on caste, color, religion, class, language etc are less rigid and there is greater tolerance towards other people or groups.

Limited influence on personality: Secondary groups are specialized in character. People involvement in them is also of limited significance. Member's attachment to them is also very much limited. Further people spend most of their time in primary groups than in secondary groups. Hence secondary groups have very limited influence on the personality of the members.

Society

The term society is most fundamental to sociology. It is derived from the Latin word socius which means companionship or friendship. Companionship means sociability. According to George Simmel it is this element of sociability which defines the true essence of society. It indicates that man always lives in the company of other people. Man is a social animal said Aristotle centuries ago. Man needs society for his living, working and enjoying life. Society has become an essential condition for human life to continue. We can define society as a group of people who share a common culture, occupy a particular territorial area and feel themselves to constitute a unified and distinct entity. It is the mutual interactions and interrelations of individuals and groups.

Cultural Relativism

This is a method whereby different societies or cultures are analyzed objectively without using the values of one culture to judge the worth of another. We cannot possibly understand the actions of other groups if we analyze them in terms of our motives and values. We must interpret their behavior in the light of their motives, habits and values if we are to understand them. Cultural relativism means that the function and meaning of a trait are relative to its cultural setting. A trait is neither good nor bad in itself. It is good or bad only with reference to the culture in which it is to function. Fur clothing is good in the Arctic but not in the tropics. In some hunting societies which occasionally face long periods of hunger to be fat is good; it has real survival value and fat people are admired. In our society to be fat is not only unnecessary but is known to be unhealthful and fat people are not admired.

The concept of cultural relativism does not mean that all customs are equally valuable, nor does it imply that no customs are harmful. Some patterns of behavior may be injurious everywhere, but even such patterns serve some purpose in the culture and the society will suffer unless a substitute is provided. The central point in cultural relativism is that in a particular cultural setting certain traits are right because they work well in that setting while other traits are wrong because they would clash painfully with parts of that culture.

Social cognition

Social cognition is a growing area of social psychology that studies how people perceive, think about, and remember information about others. A major research topic in social cognition is *attribution*. Attributions are the explanations we make for people's behavior, either our own behavior or the behavior of others. We can ascribe the locus of a behavior to either internal or external factors. An *internal*, or dispositional, locus of causality involves factors within the person, such as ability or personality. An *external*, or situational, locus involves outside factors, such as the weather. A second element of attribution ascribes the cause of behavior to either stable or unstable factors. Finally, we also attribute causes of behavior to either controllable or uncontrollable factors.

Numerous biases in the attribution process have been discovered. The Fundamental Attribution Error is the tendency to make dispositional attributions for behavior. The Just-World Phenomenon is the tendency to blame victims (a dispositional attribution) for their suffering.

Another key concept in social cognition is the assumption that reality is too complex to easily discern. As a result, we tend to see the world according to simplified schemas or images of reality. Schemas are generalized mental representations that organize knowledge and guide information processing. Schemas often operate automatically and unintentionally, and can lead to biases in social perception and memory. Expectations from schemas may lead us to see something that is not there. One experiment found that people are more likely to misperceive a weapon in the hands of a black man than a white man. This type of schema is referred to as a stereotype, a generalized set of beliefs about a particular group of people. Stereotypes are often related to negative or preferential attitudes and prejudices) and behavior (discrimination).

Perceiving groups through Stereotypes

A *stereotype* is a set of beliefs that associates a whole group of people with a few certain traits. They are formed through 2 different processes: categorization, sorting individual objects or people in groups, and outgroup homogeneity effect, which is a tendency of people to overestimate to similarity of people in the outgroups than people in the ingroup. Although categorization and other short-cut methods of thinking can be very helpful, they also contribute and arise from *racism*, *sexism*, and other forms of *prejudice* and *discrimination*.

Social Influences

Attitudes

In social psychology, attitudes are defined as learned, global evaluations of a person, object, place, or issue that influence thought and action. Social psychologists have studied attitude formation, the structure of attitudes, attitude change, the function of attitudes, and the relationship between attitudes and behavior. Because people are influenced by the situation, general attitudes are not always good predictors of specific behavior. For a variety of reasons, a person may value the environment and not recycle a can on a particular day. Attitudes that are well remembered and central to our self-concept, however, are more likely to lead to behavior, and measures of general attitudes do predict patterns of behavior over time.

Attitudes are also involved in several other areas of the discipline, such as the following; conformity, interpersonal attraction, social perception, and prejudices.

Interpersonal Phenomenon

Social influence

Social influence refers to the way people affect the thoughts, feelings, and behaviors of others. Like the study of attitudes, it is a traditional, core topic in social psychology. In fact, research on social influence overlaps considerably with research on attitudes and persuasion. Social influence is also closely related to the study of group dynamics, as most of the principles of influence are strongest when they take place in social groups.

Persuasion

The topic of persuasion has received a great deal of attention in recent years. Persuasion is an active method of influence that attempts to guide people toward the adoption of an attitude, idea, or behavior by rational or emotive means. Persuasion relies on "appeals" rather than strong pressure or coercion. Numerous variables have been found to influence the persuasion process, and these are normally presented in five major categories: *who* said *what* to *whom* and *how*.

1. The Communicator, including credibility, expertise, trustworthiness, and attractiveness.
2. The Message, including varying degrees of reason, emotion (such as fear), one-sided or two sided arguments, and other types of informational content.
3. The Audience, including a variety of demographics, personality traits, and preferences.
4. The Channel, including the printed word, radio, television, the internet, or face-to-face interactions.
5. The Context, including the environment, group dynamics, pre-amble to the message

Dual process theories of persuasion (such as the elaboration likelihood model) maintain that the persuasive process is mediated by two separate routes. Persuasion can be accomplished by either superficial aspects of the communication or the internal logic and evidence of the message. Whether someone is persuaded by a popular celebrity or factual arguments is largely determined by the ability and motivation of the audience.

Cognitive Dissonance

Leon Festinger

Cognitive dissonance is a feeling of unpleasant arousal caused by noticing an inconsistency among one's cognition.[13] These contradictory cognitions may be attitudes, beliefs, or ones awareness of his or her behavior. The theory of cognitive dissonance proposes that people have a motivational drive to reduce dissonance by changing their attitudes, beliefs, and behaviors, or by justifying or rationalizing their attitudes, beliefs, and behaviors.[13] Cognitive dissonance theory is one of the most influential and extensively studied theories in social psychology.

Cognitive dissonance theory was originally developed as a theory of attitude change, but it is now considered to be a theory of the self-concept by many social psychologists. Dissonance is strongest when a discrepancy has been noticed between one's self-concept and one's behavior, e.g. doing something that makes one ashamed. This can result in self-justification as the individual attempts to deal with the threat. Cognitive dissonance typically leads to a change in attitude, a change in behavior, a self-affirmation, or a rationalization of the behavior.

An example of cognitive dissonance is smoking. Smoking cigarettes increases the risk of cancer, which is threatening to the self-concept of the individual who smokes. Most of us believe ourselves to be intelligent and rational, and the idea of doing something foolish and self-destructive causes dissonance. To reduce this uncomfortable tension, smokers tend to make excuses for themselves, such as "I'm going to die anyway, so it doesn't matter."

The two major motives in conformity are normative influence, the tendency to conform in order to gain social acceptance, and avoid social rejection or conflict, as in peer pressure; and informational influence, which is based on the desire to obtain useful information through conformity, and thereby achieve a correct or appropriate result. Minority influence is the degree to which a smaller faction within the group influences the group during decision making. Note that this refers to a minority position on some issue, not an ethnic minority. Their influence is primarily informational and depends on consistent adherence to a position, degree of defection from the majority, and the status and self-confidence of the minority members. Reactance is a tendency to assert oneself by doing the opposite of what is expected. This phenomenon is also known as anticonformity and it appears to be more common in men than in women.

There are two other major areas of social influence research. Compliance refers to any change in behavior that is due to a request or suggestion from another person. The Foot-in-the-door technique is a compliance method in which the persuader requests a small favor and then follows up with a larger favor, e.g. asking for the time, and then asking for ten dollars. A related trick is the Bait and switch.[14] The third major form of social influence is obedience. This is a change in behavior that is the result of a direct order or command from another person.

Group Dynamics

A group can be defined as two or more individuals that are connected to each another by social relationships.[15] Groups tend to interact, influence each other, and share a common identity. They have a number of emergent qualities that distinguish them from aggregates:

- Norms—implicit rules and expectations for group members to follow, e.g. saying thank you, shaking hands.
- Roles—implicit rules and expectations for specific members within the group, e.g. the oldest sibling, who may have additional responsibilities in the family.
- Relations—patterns of liking within the group, and also differences in prestige or status, e.g. leaders, popular people.

Temporary groups and aggregates share few or none of these features, and do not qualify as true social groups. People waiting in line to get on a bus, for example, do not constitute a group.

Groups are important not only because they offer social support, resources, and a feeling of belonging, but because they supplement an individual's self-concept. To a large extent, humans define themselves by the group memberships which form their social identity. The shared social identity of individuals within a group influences intergroup behavior, the way in which groups behave towards and perceive each other. These perceptions and behaviors in turn define the social identity of individuals within the interacting groups. The tendency to define oneself by membership of a group leads to intergroup discrimination, which involves favorable perceptions and behaviors directed towards the in-group, but negative perceptions and behaviors directed towards the out-group. [16] Intergroup discrimination leads to prejudice and stereotyping, while the processes of social facilitation and group polarization encourage extreme behaviors towards the out-group.

Groups often moderate and improve decision making, and are frequently relied upon for these benefits, such as committees and juries. A number of group biases, however, can interfere with effective decision making. For example, group polarization, formerly known as the "risky shift," occurs when people polarize their views in a more extreme direction after group discussion. More problematic is the phenomenon of groupthink. This is a collective thinking defect that is characterized by a premature

consensus or an incorrect assumption of consensus, caused by members of a group failing to promote views which are not consistent with the views of other members. Groupthink occurs in a variety of situations, including isolation of a group and the presence of a highly directive leader. Janis offered the 1961 Bay of Pigs Invasion as a historical case of groupthink.[17]

Groups also affect performance and productivity. Social facilitation, for example, is a tendency to work harder and faster in the presence of others. Social facilitation increases the likelihood of the dominant response, which tends to improve performance on simple tasks and reduce it on complex tasks. In contrast, social loafing is the tendency of individuals to slack when working in a group.

Social psychologists study group-related (collective) phenomena such as the behavior of crowds. An important concept in this area is deindividuation, a reduced state of self-awareness that can be caused by feelings of anonymity. Deindividuation is associated with uninhibited and sometimes dangerous behavior. It is common in crowds and mobs.

Prosocial Relationships

Social psychologists are interested in the question of why people sometimes act in a prosocial way (helping, liking, or loving others), but at other times act in an antisocial way (hostility, aggression, or prejudice against others). These Dr. Jekyl and Mr. Hide personalities are confusing to most, especially when met with aggression and hostility.

Aggression can be defined as any behavior that is intended to harm another human being. Hostile aggression is accompanied by strong emotions, particularly anger. Harming the other person is the goal. Instrumental aggression is only a means to an end. Harming the person is used to obtain some other goal, such as money. Research indicates that there are many causes of aggression, including biological factors like testosterone and environmental factors, such as social learning. Immediate situational factors such as

Although violence is a fact of life, people are also capable of helping each other, even complete strangers in emergencies. Research indicates that altruism occurs when a person feels empathy for another individual, even in the absence of other motives. However, according to the bystander effect, the probability of receiving help in an emergency situation drops as the number of bystanders increases. This is due to both conformity and diffusion of responsibility, the tendency for people to feel less personally responsible when other people are around.

Interpersonal Attraction

A major area in the study of people's relations to each other is interpersonal attraction. This refers to all of the forces that lead people to like each other, establish relationships, and in some cases, fall in love. Several general principles of attraction have been discovered by social psychologists. For example, physical proximity tends to increase attraction, whereas long distances make relationships difficult to form and maintain. Even very small differences in distance—such as the case of a next door neighbor versus someone who lives down the block—can make a significant difference in friendship patterns. Familiarity, or "mere exposure," also increases attraction, influencing people even if the familiarity is not consciously noticed. One of the most important factors in interpersonal attraction is similarity: the more similar two people are in attitudes, background, and other traits, the more probable it is that they will like each other. Contrary to popular opinion, opposites do not usually attract, only when an alterio motive is consciously or unconsciously present.

Physical attractiveness is an important element of romantic relationships, particularly in the early stages characterized by high levels of passion. Later on, similarity and other compatibility factors become more important, and the type of love people experience shifts from passionate to companionate. Robert Sternberg has suggested that there are actually three components of love: intimacy, passion, and commitment. When two people experience all three, they are said to be in a state of consummate love; this

condition is relatively rare and difficult to maintain for a long period of time.

According to social exchange theory, relationships are based on rational choice and cost-benefit analysis. If one partner's costs begin to outweigh his or her benefits, that person may leave the relationship, especially if there are good alternatives available. This theory is similar to the minimax principle proposed by mathematicians and economists. With time, long term relationships tend to become communal rather than simply based on exchange.

Conformity is likeness or similarity of behavior and appearance. A *conformist* is one who tries to be the same as everyone else. A *non-conformist* tries to be different. Most people feel anxiety if they stand out as different from other people, so most people feel a strong pressure toward conformity to avoid this anxiety and fit into the group.

The Art of Loving

Humans have been concerned with love for centuries, so it should be no wonder that a perfectly up-to-date book on the psychology of love was written before most of today's students were born. This book is *The Art of Loving* (1956) by Erich Fromm. Fromm—who died in 1980—wrote 20 books on different topics, but *The Art of Loving* is his best-known work. It is a slim volume

Fromm made a famous statement in *The Art of Loving* : "Love is the only sane and satisfactory answer to the problem of human existence." To Fromm, our biggest problem as humans comes from our biggest gift: *our awareness that we exist*. We are "life being aware of itself." The degree to which we have developed this awareness is unique. This is part of what makes human experience precious, but it also leads to problems. If you realize you exist as a distinct person, a thing apart, then you can also feel separateness and existential loneliness.

Six Types of Love

In a classic book titled *Colors of Love (1973)*, J. A. Lee defined six varieties of relationship that might be labeled *love*.

Eros is romantic, passionate, love—what Tennov labeled limerence. In this type of relationship, love is life's most important thing. Lee said a search for physical beauty or an ideal type also typifies this type of love.

Ludus is a game-playing or uncommitted love. Lying is part of the game. A person who pursues ludic love may have many conquests but remains uncommitted.

Storge (STORE-gay) is a slow developing, friendship-based loved. People with this type of relationship like to participate in activities together. Often storge results in a long-term relationship in which sex might not be very intense or passionate.

Pragma is a pragmatic, practical, mutually beneficial relationship. It may be somewhat unromantic. A person who leans toward this type of relationship may look for a partner at work or where the person is spending time. Sex is likely to be seen as a technical matter needed for producing children, if they are desired.

Mania is an obsessive or possessive love, jealous and extreme. A person in love this way is likely to do something crazy or silly, such as stalking. The movie *Fatal Attraction* was about this type.

Agape (a-GOP-aye) is a gentle, caring, giving type of love, brotherly love, not concerned with the self. It is relatively rare. Mother Theresa showed this kind of love for impoverished people.

When studying Lee's six types of love Hendrick, Hendrick, Slapion-Foote, and Foote (1985) found that men were more likely to show the ludic type of love, while women were more likely to be storgic or pragmatic. Studies of couples happily married for over 30 years showed that couples who rated their marriages as highly satisfactory described their relationship in terms which resembled erotic love more than the other five types. This might be surprising; in view of the earlier-mentioned finding that limerence type relationships tend to flare out quickly among college students. However, it might be the case that long-term relationships that contain both friendship and a passionate spark are more likely to endure and provide satisfaction to both parties than relationships that are low-key and pragmatic.

The Jealous Male

A common element in many troubled male/female relationships is the jealous male. A male who attempts to dominate a relationship, playing what Fromm called the sadistic role, shows exaggerated jealousy in protecting his "property." White (1981) notes that extreme jealousy in love correlates with low self-esteem, overdependence on the partner, low educational background, and unhappiness.

The typical characteristics of a jealous male is a the *double standard*. They believe it is acceptable for males to cheat on their girlfriends and, later, on their wives. But women must remain faithful.

So the jealous male cheats, and that probably explains why he is jealous. This is a classic example of the Freudian defense mechanism called *projection*. Projection occurs when a person sees his or her own unpleasant qualities in someone else. The jealous male accuses his girlfriend of flirting with other men or giving them subtle "come ons" if she looks in their direction. In reality, such suspicions reveal the male's guilt and his assumption that his girlfriend's mind works the same way his does.

Date Rape

In the late 1980s, a new term entered the vocabulary of college students in the United States: *date rape*. This is what happens when a male forces sex on a female he is dating, usually in the mistaken belief she has "asked for it" or "wants it." Research shows that men who are prone to dating violence and rape are remarkably poor at interpreting a woman's true attitudes and feelings, especially on a first date. They see what they want to see. A friendly conversation or an offer of a ride home may be interpreted as an invitation to have sex.

How can a man not realize he is raping a woman? As one psychologist put it, some males act as if they believe, "Good Girls do not say Yes, and Real Men do not take No for an answer." So a girl is expected to protest, and a man is expected to go ahead anyway. Not all men adopt this attitude, but the ones who think this way are the ones most likely to commit rape.

A study of women at 32 campuses showed that 15% said they had been raped, and 89% of the time it was by somebody they knew. That meant about 13% of all the women had experienced *acquaintance rape*—rape by someone they knew beforehand. Meanwhile, a survey of 1,152 male college students showed that only 1.4% admitted to forcing sex on a woman when she protested or said she did not want to. That meant women are about *ten times as likely as men to say they have participated in a situation they interpreted as rape.* Clearly men are not seeing themselves as rapists on

many occasions when women feel they have been raped. (Goleman, 1989)

Summary: Different Sorts of Relationships

Sex and aggression are tied together by the effects of hormones. Steroids increase both sexual and aggressive impulses. A monkey that wins a fight for dominance secretes more testosterone, adds muscle mass, and mates more often. Erections are a common threat display among primates. Eibl-Eibesfeldt found the same symbolism in religious figurines on the island of Bali.

Dating violence is common on college campuses. Some psychologists argue that a masochistic or teasing role is natural for human females; others find that idea an appalling example of sexism in our culture. The jealous male, often a violent type, is typically a person with low self-esteem and a troubled family background who combats insecurity with a domineering attitude.

Gray Rape

Cosmopolitan magazine created a mini-controversy in 2007 by publishing an article about so-called *gray rape*. This is essentially date rape that occurs when the female participant (typically a college student or similar young female in her 20s) is intoxicated and never intended to have sex, but emerges out of a drug-induced fog (after willingly participating in some kissing or other pre-sexual activity) to find that her male companion is having sex with her. She realizes she does not want this to happen and "is left feeling violated and confused and angry." ("Do you want to share your story?" August 30, 2007)

The concept was greeted immediately with scorn and derision from feminist bloggers who said any sex without consent is rape, whether or not there is a "gray area" caused by intoxication. Other bloggers were suspicious of the concept because the author of the Cosmopolitan article (Laura Sessions Stepp) had previously written a book called *Unhooked* that was critical of the "hooking up" culture of the 2000s, in which young people engage in sex without obligation. Some bloggers saw the article as an extension of (and advertisement for) the author's moralistic criticisms of the hooking-up culture.

Whether or not "gray rape" proves to be a useful concept, the controversy drew attention to a simple fact. In almost every case in which a woman's ability to consent to sex is later called into question, alcohol is involved. Just as alcohol is a leading risk factor for AIDS, it is a leading risk factor for date rape.

SUCCESSFUL LONG-TERM RELATIONSHIPS

The great novelist Tolstoy wrote, in the famous opening line of *Anna Karenina*, "Happy families are all alike; each unhappy family is unhappy in its own way."

Dr. Nicholas Stinette of Oklahoma State University set out to determine the ways in which happy families were alike. He studied 100 families in which both the marriage and the parent-child relationships seemed unusually good. Happy families shared the following qualities:

1. The members frequently and spontaneously show appreciation of each other.

2. They communicate easily and well, facing conflicts openly and trying to solve them—not just settling for the dubious advantage of being the person in the "right."

What were qualities shared by happy families?

3. They have a high degree of spiritual unity, and share common values and goals.

4. They do a lot of things together (Mace, 1977).

Lauer and Lauer (1985) surveyed 351 couples who had been together 15 years or more. Of this group, 300 said they were happily married, 19 said unhappily married but staying together for other reasons, and in 32 cases one member was happy and the other unhappy. The 300 happy couples consistently stressed several themes:

What are common qualities of happy marriages?

1. The spouse was viewed as a best friend, a person who would be chosen as a friend if he or she were not a marriage partner.

2. The couples were committed to the institution of marriage and willing to work hard at maintaining it. They endorsed statements like "Marriage is a long-time commitment" and "Marriage is sacred."

3. There was great agreement and compatibility on major areas of concern, such as philosophy of life, sex life, how often to show affection, and aims or goals of the relationship.

4. There was a willingness to seek out complexities in the spouse. Many respondents said, "My spouse has grown more interesting." Others said, "I confide in my spouse" and "We laugh together" and "We have a stimulating exchange of ideas."

THE FOUR HORSEMEN

Researcher John Gottman of the University of Washington has made a career of studying marital interactions. He claims to be able to predict with 95% accuracy which couples will eventually divorce.

After an earlier study that gathered data from thousands of couples over 13 years, Gottman's research team studied 130 newlyweds intensively over a six-year period. The couples were invited to Gottman's laboratory, where they were hooked to instruments that measured variables such as heart rate, sweating, and muscle tension. The couples were recorded with a video camera while they had a conversation about a disagreement. In a frame-by-frame analysis, their facial expressions, movements, and comments were analyzed.

What sort of research did Gottman do? What were Gottman's "Four Horsemen"?

After correlating the data with marriage outcomes, Gottman found four factors that predicted divorce. He called these the Four Horsemen of the Apocalypse for marriage. They were:

1) **criticism** (telling the other person his or her faults)

2) **defensiveness** (reacting to certain subjects by denying responsibility, or refusing to discuss an issue the spouse regards as important)

3) **contempt** (making sarcastic or cutting remarks about the other person)

4) **withdrawal** (also called "stonewalling": showing no reaction, having a blank look, or ceasing to care)

Perhaps the most "corrosive" of the four, according to Gottman, is *contempt*, which he said should be "banned from marriages."

What did later analysis show?

Later analysis of his data provided a surprise for Gottman. While the Four Horsemen remained important, he found *one* factor that was the best predictor of all. This was a positive predictor, one that predicted long-term success rather than failure in marriage. Gottman found that marriages are likely to thrive when *the man was willing to be influenced by his wife* ("Want a successful marriage? Listen to your wife" CNN, February 20, 1998).

Finding Romance

Maintaining a happy marriage is fine if you are married, but how do you find someone if you are lonely and have no romantic relationship? Neediness or an apparent eagerness to enter into a relationship can backfire; it is a big "turn-off" to many people, so it may perpetuate the problem.

Exploring the Depths

One study followed 200 college-age couples over a two-year period (Hill, Rubin, & Peplau, 1976). All the couples were dating steadily and said they were in love at the beginning of the study. After two years, 45% were no longer together. The leading cause of break-ups, according to both males and females, was *becoming bored with the relationship*. This was cited as a factor by 77% of those who broke up.

Many students know from personal experience that romantic interest can turn into boredom. Some students ask a penetrating question. How do you *avoid* getting bored? Isn't it inevitable? Here the research data is actually encouraging. Boredom is *not* an inevitable outcome of a long relationship. For example, Lauer and Lauer (1985) found that many of their 300 happily married couples were *more* interested in their spouses after a 15-year period. They interacted in complex ways. They felt that they shared humor, philosophy, life goals, and stimulating ideas. Perhaps this is the secret. One avoids boredom by cultivating *complexity* and *depth* in a relationship. This is the factor called *intimacy* by Sternberg.

This does not mean that happily married couples spend all their free time in rapt fascination of each other's conversation. However, they communicate well about the things that matter most, enjoy each other's company, share basic values, and tolerate each other's oddities.

Why would the factor of being willing to listen to your wife be so highly predictive? Here it is tempting to fall into the trap of imposing a cause-effect interpretation on a correlation that *might be due entirely to self-selection*. After all, this is not random-assignment research. Gottman did not tell one randomly chosen group of men to respect their wives' opinions, while another randomly chosen group served as a control. The group is self-selected, so *any variable that correlates with the variable of "willingness to be influenced by wife"* could be the real cause of a more durable marriage. These could include higher income, more education, better social intelligence, more inclination to cooperate rather than compete, a more satisfying approach to sexuality...you name it. We have here a perfect opportunity to apply the critical thinking habits encouraged in Chapter 1. Any of these variables, or any combination of them, could be the real explanation for longer marriages.

Whatever the underlying reasons or combination of reasons for the correlation, the predictive information is still useful and interesting. If Gottman is correct, measuring a male's willingness to take advice or be influenced by his wife provides the most accurate way to make a forecast about the long-term success of a marriage.

Summary: The Art of Loving

Erich Fromm wrote, in *The Art of Loving* (1956), "Love is the only sane and satisfactory answer to the problem of human existence." To Fromm, human consciousness makes it possible for us to know our loneliness and limitations as well as to rejoice in existence. Fromm wrote that humans have a deep need to achieve union with something outside their egos. He identified several strategies or solutions for this but said the best was love.

Research shows a common pattern in happy long-term relationships. People in happy long-term marriages tend to regard each other as best friends as well as lovers. John Gottman of the University of Washington identified "four horsemen" which predicted divorce. Fromm wrote that the attitude of love was not confined to romantic relationships but could be applied to many different situations. He identified brotherly love, motherly love, and self-love (which is distinct from selfishness) as distinct categories. Fromm also believed that different conceptions of God, found in various human civilizations, embodied different kinds of love.

The hedgehog theory of Edward L. Walker is relevant here. Walker pointed out that people prefer stimuli of moderate complexity, neither chaotic nor simple, but moderately challenging. This applies to relationships as well. A chaotic, unpredictable relationship is aversive. So is a boring, predictable, unstimulating relationship. Fortunately, humans are inherently deep. By opening up to each other and exploring these depths, a couple can continually add complexity to their conversations and other interactions. This maintains interest and enthusiasm in the relationship, particularly if there are other good things (such as love, sex, or children) happening as well.

CHAPTER 15 SUMMARY

I. DEFINITION

Attitude = a favorable or unfavorable evaluative reaction toward something or someone, exhibited in ones beliefs, feelings, or intended behavior (Myers, p. 36). It is a social orientation—an underlying inclination to respond to something either favorably or unfavorably.

Components of attitudes.

a. Cognitive—our thoughts, beliefs, and ideas about something. When a human being is the object of an attitude, the cognitive component is frequently a stereotype, e.g. "welfare recipients are lazy"

b. Affective—feelings or emotions that something evokes. e.g. fear, sympathy, hate. May dislike welfare recipients.

c. Conative, or behavioral—tendency or disposition to act in certain ways toward something. Might want to keep welfare recipients out of our neighborhood. Emphasis is on the tendency to act, not the actual acting; what we intend and what we do may be quite different.

II. THEORIES OF ATTITUDE FORMATION AND CHANGE

1. Functionalist theory. Daniel Katz proposed a functionalist theory of attitudes. He takes the view that attitudes are determined by the functions they serve for us. People hold given attitudes because these attitudes help them achieve their basic goals. Katz distinguishes four types of psychological functions that attitudes meet.

A. Instrumental—we develop favorable attitudes towards things that aid or reward us. We want to maximize rewards and minimize penalties. Katz says we develop attitudes that help us meet this goal. We favor political parties that will advance our economic lot—if we are in business, we favor the party that will keep our taxes low, if unemployed we favor one that will increase social welfare benefits. We are more likely to change our attitudes if doing so allows us to fulfill our goals or avoid undesirable consequences.

B. Knowledge—attitudes provide meaningful, structured environment. In life we seek some degree of order, clarity, and stability in our personal frame of reference. Attitudes help supply us with standards of evaluation. Via such attitudes as stereotypes, we can bring order and clarity to the complexities of human life.

C. Value-expressive—Express basic values, reinforce self-image. EX: if you view yourself as a Catholic, you can reinforce that image by adopting Catholic beliefs and values. EX: We may have a self-image of ourselves as an enlightened conservative or a militant radical, and we therefore cultivate attitudes that we believe indicate such a core value.

D. Ego-defensive—Some attitudes serve to protect us from acknowledging basic truths about ourselves or the harsh realities of life. They serve as defense mechanisms. EX: Those with feelings of inferiority may develop attitude of superiority.

Katz's functionalist theory also offers an explanation as to why attitudes change. According to Katz, an attitude changes when it no longer serves its function and the individual feels blocked or frustrated. That is, according to Katz, attitude change is achieved not so much by changing a person's information or perception about an object, but rather by changing the person's underlying motivational and personality needs.

> ex: As your social status increases, your attitudes toward your old car may change—you need something that better reflects your new status. (For that matter, your attitudes toward your old friends may change as well).

2. Learning theory (which stresses attitude formation). There are several means by which we learn attitudes.

A. Classical conditioning. ex: A father angrily denounces the latest increase in income taxes. A mother happily announces the election of a candidate she worked for. These parents are expressing opinions, but they are also displaying nonverbal behavior that expresses their emotions. For a child watching the parents, the association between the topic and the nonverbal behavior will become obvious if repeated often enough. And the nonverbal behavior will trigger emotional responses in the child: the child feels upset and disturbed when listening to the father and happy when listening to the mother.

This is an example of classical conditioning: when two stimuli are repeatedly associated, the child learns to respond to them with a similar emotional reaction. In this case, the stimuli are the attitude topic and the parental emotion. Through repeated association, a formerly neutral stimulus (the attitude topic—taxes or politicians) begins to elicit an emotional reaction (the response) that was previously solicited only by another stimulus (the parental emotion). Whenever tax increases are mentioned, the child feels an unpleasant emotion; when the elected official is mentioned, the child feels a pleasant emotion.

> ex: Pavlov's dogs. Bell was rung when dogs received food. Food made dogs salivate. Then whenever a bell was rung, dogs salivated even when food was not present.
> ex: When you were a child, parents may have cheered for N.D. football. You may not have even known what N.D. football was, but you liked your parents happy attitude. Now N.D. football evokes that same response in you.
> ex: Men with bow ties. Meet a bad man who wears bow ties, and you may come to hate all bow ties.

COMMENT: This explains why behaviors can persist even after reinforcement is withdrawn. Also helps explain self-reinforcement.
B. Instrumental, or operant, conditioning. Behaviors or attitudes that are followed by positive consequences are reinforced and are more likely to be repeated than are behaviors and attitudes that are followed by negative consequences.
   ex: People agree with your opinion.

C. Observational learning. Children watch the behavior of people around them and imitate what they see. EX: If a young girl hears her mother denounce all elected officials as crooks, she may repeat that opinion in class the next day. Whether she continues to repeat that opinion depends on the responses of her classmates, teacher, and parents. That is, observations determine the responses we learn, but reinforcement determines the responses we express.

3. Cognitive dissonance theory—stresses attitude change—and that behaviors can determine attitudes.

A. Defn: Cognition = individuals perception of own attitudes, beliefs, behaviors. Cognitive dissonance = feelings of tension that arise when one is simultaneously aware of two inconsistent cognitions. For example, when we act contrary to our attitudes; or, when we make a decision favoring one alternative despite reasons favoring another.

B. Consistency theories hypothesize that, should inconsistencies develop among cognitions, people are motivated to restore harmony.

C. Key propositions of dissonance theory
1. Dissonance theory says relationships among two cognitions can be either consonant, dissonant, irrelevant
2. Cognitive dissonance is a noxious state. It produces unpleasant physical arousal.
3. Individual will attempt to reduce or eliminate dissonance—and will try to avoid things that increase dissonance.
ex: Selective observation.
4. Cognitive dissonance can be reduced or eliminated only by (a) adding new cognitions, or (b) changing existing ones.
ex: Can change our minds. Decide we were wrong.
ex: Can "make up" information, as in the "When prophesy fails" example.
ex: We may seek new information that can restore consonance.
ex: Try to discredit source of dissonance in some way—either by making up info or seeking counter-evidence.

D. Sources of dissonance
1. Informational inconsistency. Receive information that contradicts what they already know or believe.

ex: Suppose you believe George Bush did not know about Iran-Contra—and then suppose Oliver North testified that he was the mastermind behind it. (Real life example: some Iranians are said to believe George Bush did head up Iran-Contra, since he used to be head of the CIA and they think the CIA runs the country.)

2. <u>Disconfirmed expectations</u>. People prepare themselves for an event that never occurs—or even worse, an event whose opposite occurs. EX: You expect to do well on an exam, and you don't.

> *ex: When prophesy fails. In 1955, Marian Keech predicted that a great flood was going to destroy the Western Hemisphere on Dec. 21. She said she got her information from the planet Clarion. She attracted a band of followers, and received further messages about how the faithful could save themselves. Midnight of the big day came and passed, and nothing happened. At 4:45 a.m., they received a Christmas message informing them that because of their commitment and faithfulness, the earth had been spared.*

Q: How did the followers behave, both before and after the event?

Prior to the big day, they were very secretive, and shunned publicity. After the big day, they called the media, sent out press releases, and recruited new followers. Why?

Many of these people had quit their jobs, and broken up with their spouses and friends, based on a belief that had been disconfirmed. This produced dissonance. They couldn't deny their past beliefs—they couldn't say the flood had occurred—they couldn't deny they had quit their jobs. They could have decided they were mistaken, but that would create dissonance with other cognitions, such as their being intelligent people. hence, they convinced themselves they were right all along, and their faithfulness had saved the world. Further, if they could convince others to adopt their views, this would affirm their sense that their views were correct.

3. <u>Insufficient justification for behavior</u>. People do things which they lack justification for.

> *ex: In a classic Festinger experiment, subjects were given a peg board and told to carefully turn each peg 1/4 turn. Then, after doing all the pegs, they were told to turn them another 1/4 turn. Later they had to carefully remove each peg, and then put them all back. After an hour, they were told they were done. The experimenter then said "We are comparing the performance of subjects who are briefed in advance with those who are not briefed in advance. You did not receive a briefing. The next subject is supposed to be briefed, but my assistance who usually does this couldn't come to work today." Subjects were then asked to tell the next student the task was fun and exciting, and were offered either $1 or $20 for doing so. Those who only got paid a $1 were more likely to report they thought the task was interesting, because they lacked a strong justification for their actions.*

4. <u>Postdecision dissonance</u>—after every decision, you feel dissonance because you have rejected some good things and accepted some bad. We tend to become more certain of decisions afterwards.

ex: Bettors approached after they had placed bets at the racetrack were more sure of their choices than those approached before placing bets.

NOTE: This does not mean we never regret a decision. Disconfirmed expectations, new information, or whatever may cause us feel we made a mistake. However, until these new events/information or whatever comes along, we will tend to feel more confident about our decision. Obviously, in the case of the racetrack example, people may have felt more confident after they placed their bets, but after the race was run a lot of them probably didn't feel so confident anymore!

E. Not all inconsistencies result in cognitive dissonance. How is inconsistency possible?

1. Cognitions may not be important to the individual—hence inconsistency does not produce discomfort.

2. Cognitions may not come in contact with each other—contradictions can go unnoticed. Behavior may be mindless. EX: We might enjoy a national park—without realizing we are overtaxing it.

NOTE: <u>The following relate primarily to counterattitudinal behavior.</u>

3. Aversive consequences are not perceived. In order for cognitive dissonance to occur, a product must result from the counterattitudinal behavior. That product is the bringing about, or possible occurrence, of an aversive event. Aversive event = something that goes against your self interest, or that you would rather not have occur.

> *ex: In a variation of the boring tasks experiment, some subjects were led to believe they had actually deceived their fellow student, while others thought they had not deceived them. Only those who thought they had <u>succeeded</u> experienced dissonance.*

> *ex: In another variation, subjects were led to <u>like or dislike</u> the other student. The only subjects who changed their attitude about the task were those who successfully convinced a student they liked.*

Note that the consequences need not actually occur; it is the subjects <u>perceptions</u> that the consequences will result from their actions that is important.

4. Person must feel <u>personally responsible</u>. If the person feels that environmental forces caused the action, or that the unwanted events were unforeseeable, they won't feel dissonance. How voluntary is the behavior? Were the consequences foreseeable. Note that foreseeable is not the same as foreseen—if you could have foreseen it but didn't, you can feel dissonance.

We close with a commonly proposed alternative to dissonance theory.

4. <u>Bem's Self-perception theory</u>. Says we infer our attitudes from our behavior. There is no tension, rather, behavior just serves an informative purpose. We calmly observe our behavior, and draw reasonable inferences from it, just as we do when observing other people.

> *ex: In the Festinger experiment, those who got $20 would assume their behavior was forced by the environment. Those who only got $1 would assume they did what they did because what they said was true.*
>
> *ex: Bem showed that the results of cognitive dissonance experiments could be replicated quite well by observers. People read descriptions of the procedures, and predicted people's attitudes correctly.*
>
> *ex: "I must have really been tired, I slept a long time."*
>
> *"I must not like him, I was really rude to him."*
>
> *"I must really like this course, I studied really hard for the exam."*

It is hard to choose between self-perception and cognitive dissonance theory since both usually make the same predictions. However, there is evidence that, as c. d. theory predicts, physiological arousal (that is, tension) accompanies dissonance conditions. Further, when arousal is eliminated (through the use of drugs or alcohol), attitude change does not occur.

On the other hand, self-perception can explain some things dissonance can't. For example, when people are suddenly rewarded for doing something they did before just because they liked it, they can come to like it less.

> *ex: (From Myers): Child was reading 6-8 books a week. Library then started a reading club which promised a party to those who read 10 books in three months. Child started checking out only 1 or 2 books a week. Why? "Because you only need to read 10 books."*

Myers suggests dissonance theory successfully explains what happens when we act contrary to our clearly defined attitudes. We feel tension, so we adjust our attitudes to reduce it. Dissonance explains attitude change. When attitudes aren't well-formed, self-perception theory explains attitude formation that occurs as we act and reflect. (I think he may be right about the latter point, but I'm not so sure about the first.) Key thing, then, is how discrepant is the behavior with the attitude.

III. REAL WORLD APPLICATIONS

A. <u>Racism</u>. It has often been said you can't legislate morality. Yet, changes in civil rights laws and policies have been accompanied by changes in attitudes. Since Brown vs. Board of Education in 1954, the percentage of white Americans favoring integrated schools has more than doubled. Since Civil rights act of 1964, the percentage of white Americans who described their neighborhoods, friends, co-workers, or fellow students as all white declined by 20 percent for each of these measures. Possible explanations:
1. Disconfirmed expectations. Predicted calamities did not occur.
2. Information inconsistent with previous beliefs led to attitude change.

3. People were forced to behave in a counter-attitudinal manner. People who said they would not comply with laws did. Ergo, they reasoned blacks must not be so bad.
4. Racist attitudes became non-instrumental, because of the high costs of violating laws. You had to interact with blacks, so you might as well like them.
5. Value-expressive—racism became inconsistent with the images most people like to hold, so they adopted anti-racist attitudes.

B. Suppose you wanted a friend to <u>support a political candidate</u>. What might you do?
1. Get them to do some small task as a favor to you. Counter-attitudinal actions might influence attitudes; exposure to dissonant info might change their minds; classical or instrumental condition could take place—they receive praise for working for the candidate, which leads to positive attitudes.
2. If friend is for another candidate—provide them with dissonant info. Point out candidate is weak in areas friend likes him.
3. What if friend doesn't change his mind? This could occur because (a) friend discredits the source of the info—you (b) instead of liking the candidate, friend could decide he doesn't like you.

IV. ATTITUDES AND BEHAVIORS

1. Is there an attitude-behavior relationship?
A. LaPiere's work apparently said no.

B. Subsequent work over next 35 years did little better. As Abelson (quoted in Myers) said, "we are, apparently, very well trained and very good at finding reasons for what we do, but not very good at doing what we find reasons for."

2. Later work found a relationship
A. <u>Expressed attitudes are not always the same as true attitudes</u>, especially when dealing with sensitive topics. Methods such as the "bogus pipeline" and other methods for dealing with sensitive questions are helpful here.

B. <u>Specificity of measures was found to be important</u>—items used were not specific enough. Should determine attitudes toward the specific behavior, rather than some more general topic. Fishbein and Aizen note that, ideally, measures should correspond in Target, Action, Context, and Time.
    i. <u>Target</u>. Suppose I say I think drugs are bad—yet I smoke marihuana, or drink alcohol. There are different targets here. When you say drugs, I may think more of thinks like cocaine and heroin than I do marihuana or alcohol. I might have favorable attitudes toward the environment, but have negative attitudes toward recycling because I find it inconvenient. In LaPiere's case, subjects may have

viewed the target as a devious oriental, rathern than a nicely dressed oriental couple traveling with a white man.

ii. <u>Action</u>. I can be against selling cocaine, but still willing to use it personally. I might support somebody's right to have an abortion, while being opposed to having an abortion myself. (We see this in public opinion polls today—a lot of people oppose abortion, while still supporting the right of others to have abortions, at least under certain circumstances.)

iii. <u>Context</u>. I might support the right to have an abortion under certain circumstances (save the life of the mother, rape, incest) while being opposed to it in others. Indeed, depending on the question asked, you get widely varying levels of support for abortion. I might think it is ok to drink when I am going to stay at home, but not when I am going to drive.

iv. <u>Time.</u> It is ok to drink at night or on the weekends, but not in the morning.

C. <u>Type of attitude measured is important</u>—cognitive, affective, conative. These are not identical or totally consistent—our minds are not efficient enough to process all information immediately and consistently. The behavioral component of attitudes best determines what we do.

A. Fishbein refers to beliefs, attitudes, and intentions. We have referred to these as the cognitive, affective, and conative (behavioral) components of attitudes.

B. Assumptions of model:
1. <u>Behavioral intentions are the only direct determinant of behavior.</u>
2. <u>Behavioral intentions are determined by affective attitudes and subjective norms</u>.
3. <u>Affective attitudes are a function of beliefs about consequences * subjective evaluation of those consequences.</u>
    ex: I believe that smoking causes cancer. I believe that cancer is very bad. Ergo, I have negative feelings about smoking.
    ex: I believe that studying leads to higher grades. I do not care what my grades are. Ergo, I do not have favorable attitudes toward studying.
4. <u>Subjective norms are a function of beliefs about the expectations of others times my motivation to comply with them.</u>
    ex: My friends expect me to smoke. I want to please my friends. Ergo, I feel I should smoke.
    ex: My parents expect me to study. I want to please my parents. Ergo, I feel I should study.

C. Implications of the model.
1. <u>Only behavioral intentions directly affect behavior</u>. Effects of any other kind of attitude will only be indirect, and relationship with behavior could be weak.

2. <u>Sometimes affective attitudes will determine our intentions, other times subjective norms will</u>. Even if we dislike something, we may do it anyway, because of subjective norms. Further, the relative importance of affective attitudes and subjective norms may differ across people. EX: You might think that somebody who doesn't like to study would not study. But, s/he may do so because of subjective norms.

3. <u>Model shows the importance of considering how valued the consequences are</u>. For example, two people might agree that smoking leads to cancer. But if one person doesn't care that much about cancer ("we're all going to die sometime") their belief about cancer may not keep them from smoking. You shouldn't assume that your evaluation of the consequences is the same as theirs.

4. <u>Shouldn't just measure attitudes toward the object—should measure attitudes toward the behavior</u>.

   ex: You might think that somebody who doesn't like blacks may discriminate against them. But maybe not. Non-discriminatory behavior may be favorably viewed because of its positive consequences (More customers and more money for my business—a bigger pool of laborers I can call upon). Or, subjective norms may force non-discrimination. MORAL: Don't just ask people how they feel about blacks—ask them how they feel about specific behaviors. (At least if you are interested in prediction).

5. <u>Several beliefs may determine your affective attitudes or subjective norms</u>. Affective attitudes are based on the total set of salient beliefs about performing a behavior. <u>Changing one or more beliefs may not be enough to bring about a change in the overall attitude or intention</u>.

   ex: I may believe that studying leads to high grades and that high grades are desirable. I may also believe that studying cuts down on party time, and I love to party. Hence, overall I may have a negative feeling towards studying.

   ex: I believe smoking causes cancer and that cancer is bad. I also believe that quitting smoking will cause me to gain weight. If I fear gaining weight more than I fear cancer, my overall evaluation of smoking may be positive. REMEMBER: Several beliefs can be involved in the determination of your final evaluation and your intention.

   ex: I might change affective attitudes toward smoking—but if normative pressures are the primary determinant of behavior, behavior won't change.

   ex: I might convince you that your friends expect you to study—but if you don't care what your friends think, your behavior won't change.

MORAL: If you want to change behavior, you have to figure out what beliefs are having the strongest impact on behavior.

3. Criticisms and proposed modifications of Fishbein—when, and how strongly, do attitudes affect behavior? When do attitudes not affect behavior? Fishbein said intentions were the only direct influence on Behavior—but many question this.

A. <u>Many have found that feelings (the affective component of attitudes) may be a better predictor of what you will do than your intentions</u>. Often, we don't bother to figure out what we want to do until it is time to do it. When intentions are weak or ill-formed and other beliefs are strong, affective attitudes may be the best predictor of behavior.

> *ex: 1980 elections. Liberal Democrat incumbents showed big leads in the polls, yet one after one they fell. People had not finalized their intention to vote, but they had strong feelings against liberal policies (or at least against the current state of the country.)*

Why is this? The model views attitude formation and change as a product of information processing. Yet, as information processing takes time, changes in attitudes may lag behind changes in beliefs, perhaps by months or even years. Intentions are often not even formed until immediately before behaving. This helps explain why variables besides intentions can be better predictors of behavior.

B. <u>Resources, degree of volitional control may affect A/B consistency</u>. More difficult it is to follow through on intentions, less likely it is you will. Also sometimes need cooperation from others.

> *ex: Suppose a prejudiced person does not intend to hire Hispanics. Suppose it turns out to be extremely difficult to staff his business otherwise. He may give up on his intention, whereas he would not do so under more favorable conditions.*
> *ex: N.D. intends to hire minority scholars. Hopefully, it will do so, but it would be easier to follow through on its intentions if it intended to hire a bunch of white males.*

C. <u>Psychological traits</u>—willingness to take responsibility—Locus of control.
ex: Locus of control. How much control do you feel you have over what happens in your life. If you don't feel you have control, why bother acting consistently?

D. <u>Experience </u>affects how consistent you are. Affects attitude intensity. Also may affect your knowledge of how to achieve your goals.

E. <u>Some would say he has it backwards—</u>behavior influences attitudes, rather than the other way.

4. Application. Few unwed teenagers want to get pregnant—yet many do. How can A/B theory explain this inconsistency?
A. Not wanting to get pregnant is an <u>attitude toward an object</u>; pregnancy is not a behavior in and of itself, it is a result of other behaviors. Attitudes toward premarital sex and use of contraceptive might not show such discrepancies.

B. Attitudes may not be firmly held, because of <u>lack of prior experience</u>. Those who have been pregnant before may act more consistently.

C. <u>Lack of resources</u>. People may not know about, or have access to, effective means of contraception.

D. <u>Subjective norms may be determining behavior,</u> rather than affective attitudes.

E. <u>Beliefs about consequences—may not believe their behavior is likely to produce a pregnancy</u>. There is some rational basis for this—some teenagers have sex at very young ages, when they are subfecund; their failure to get pregnant leads them to think they can't.

F. <u>Other beliefs enter into their evaluation of the behavior</u>. It is very costly to use contraceptives—have to admit that you are "that kind of girl." Those who think of themselves as "good girls" are often the ones who get pregnant, because the so-called "bad girls" don't have the same inhibitions about contraceptives. Also, sacrifice spontaneity, run the risk of behavior.

G. <u>Personality traits</u> might offer some insights.

MAJOR HISTORICAL FIGURES IN PSYCHOLOGY

Harry Harlow
1905—1981

Harry Harlow was born in Fairfield, Iowa and was educated in the field of Ethology, or the study of primates. He spent his entire professional career teaching at the University of Wisconsin from 1930-1974. His focus of research was on the learning abilities in primates and he observed the phenomenon of 'learning to learn.' His work with infant monkeys and their surrogate mothers (terrycloth dummies) demonstrated the importance of bonding between primate mothers and infants for emotional health and growth. He found that although other surrogate mothers provided nourishment, the infants preferred the 'warm and fuzzy' surrogate mother and without this interaction had emotional and physical difficulties later in life.

William James
1842—1910

William James was born in New York City. His family lived in several countries affording James a multicultural education, including schools in the U.S., England, France, Switzerland, and Germany. He became fluent in five languages by the time he earned his M.D. in 1869.

The publication of his first work, The Principles of Psychology, secured his place in the history books. He initiated the move of psychology away from Philosophy and toward a discipline of science. The application of scientific methods to the study of human psychology is perhaps his greatest donation to the field.

Carl Jung
1875—1961

Born in Kesswil, Switzerland, Carl Jung was trained as a psychiatrist after receiving his M.D. from Basel University. He then began research on psychoanalytic techniques and theories such as word association and began correspondence with <u>Sigmund Freud</u> in 1906. The two men met a year later and eventually presented seminars on psychoanalytic theory together in 1909.

Their relationship ended in 1913, when Jung broke away from Freud, resigned his professional positions and began the exploration of his own theories of psychology, religion, and what is known termed the collective unconscious. Although much of his later work is very detailed and intellectual, terms such as introvert and extrovert, parts of his theory, are commonly used expressions today.

Emil Kraepelin
1855-1925

Emil Kraepelin was a psychiatrist who studied the description and classification of mental disorders, leading to what we now call the Diagnostic and Statistical Manual of Mental Disorders, published by the American Psychiatric Association. He believed that if symptom clusters could be identified then research could more easily begin the work of identifying the etiology or causation. He is likely best known for identifying and naming dementia praecox, the precursor to what we now call schizophrenia.

Abraham Maslow
1908-1970

Abraham Maslow was an American psychologist born in Brooklyn, NY. He taught at several universities in the New York area and perhaps best known for his belief in Humanistic Psychology.

His Hierarchy of Needs has been applied to many professional fields outside of psychology, including sociology, business, medicine, and others. The Hierarchy is a set of five stages that each individual passes through in his or her search for Self-Actualization (See Below).

He believed that we are driven to understand and accept ourselves as fully as possible, and are motivated to this end. He also stated that nobody ever reaches the top of the pyramid and the goal should be getting as close as possible rather than achieving the top of the hierarchy. As we progress through life, we are presented with obstacles that cause us to either grow or slip backward. After which we can choose to either learn from the event and continue climbing or give up. Despite the challenges of life, most people choose to continue their climb.

Henry A. Murray
1893—1988

Henry Murray taught at Harvard University for over 30 years and like his psychoanalytic predecessors, Freud and Jung, he believed that personality could be better understood by investigating the unconscious mind. He is most famous for the development of the Thematic Apperception Test (TAT), a widely used projective measure of personality.

Ivan Pavlov
1849-1936

A Physiologist by training, Ivan Pavlov's most famous experiment in psychology began as a study of digestion. Although very concerned with biases and controlling for variables, during his experiment he noticed that his subjects (dogs) would elicit a salivation response prior to being presented with food. He began to explore this phenomenon and eventually developed one of the most applauded behavioral studies on conditioning that won him the Nobel Prize.

Classical conditioning refers to the phenomenon of stimulus pairing that result in similar responses. In other words, when food (referred to as the unconditioned or unlearned stimulus) is paired with the sound of a bell, the sound of the bell (called the conditioned or learned stimulus) eventually results in the same response (salivation).

Jean Piaget
1896—1980

Jean Piaget was born in Switzerland and by age 10 had already begun his professional career as a researcher and writer. He was interested in biology and wrote a paper on the sighting of an albino sparrow that propelled his interest in the scientific study of nature.

He studied natural sciences at the University of Neuchâtel where he obtained a Ph.D. in Zoology. During his tenure as a professor of child psychology, he conducted many research studies on **Genetic Epistemology** (the theory of knowledge on Genetics). He was interested in the role of genetics and child development, and is most well known for his <u>Theory of Cognitive Development</u>.

In this theory, Piaget introduced the stages that a child passes through on his or her way to the development of formal though processes. His theory has been well accepted and included in every developmental text in psychology and education. He died in Geneva at the age of 84.

Carl Rogers
1902—1987

Carl Rogers was a <u>Humanistic</u> Psychologist who is most known for his approach to psychological treatment and his belief in the genuine good in the individual. He received his Master's degree in psychology from Columbia University in 1928 and his doctorate in 1931. In 1942 he served as the president of the American Psychological Society.

His most respected works include <u>Client-Centered Therapy</u>, and <u>On Becoming a Person</u>. In these books he emphasized the power in a non-judgmental attitude and a mutual respect in the treatment of many of life's problems. He believed that the individual has the answers and the therapist's job is to lead the individual in the correct direction. Assessment techniques and the therapist's opinion are not important at all in the treatment of a individual.

B. F. Skinner
1904—1990

Burrhus Frederic Skinner was born in a small Pennsylvania town. His father was an attorney and his mother a housewife. His family life was described as old-fashioned and hard working.

Skinner received his Bachelor's degree in English in hopes of becoming a writer. He wrote for the school paper but saw himself as an outsider, being an atheist in a religious school, and often criticized the school and its beliefs. After graduation, he continued with his hopes of being a writer and worked for a newspaper, eventually moving to Greenwich Village in New York City.

He later returned to his life as a student and completed his Master's degree in 1931 from Harvard, and his Doctorate a year later, both in the field of psychology. He married that same year and had two children, one of whom became famous, or perhaps infamous, as the baby raised in an artificial environment known as an ‹air crib.'

In 1945, he became the chairman of the psychology department at Indiana University and left to teach at Harvard three years later, where he spent the remainder of his career. Although he never became the writer he had dreamt of, he did write several books and hundreds of articles on behavior theory, reinforcement,

and Learning Theory. Today he is known as one of the most published psychologists. His biggest criticism of psychological thought was against the growing following of Sigmund Freud. Skinner believed that examining the unconscious or hidden motives of human beings was a waste of time, for the only thing worth researching was outward behaviors. It was this core belief that led him to reject most of the theories prominent in the field of psychology.

Concepts such as self-actualization and striving to reach one's potential, such as the belief held by humanists was rejected due to the inability to research such an abstract idea. The idea of inner drives such as Freud's Id, Ego, and Superego were seen as preposterous. And the defense mechanisms, archetypes, and drives merely gave theoretical names to ideas that are poorly understood and likely nonexistent.

Instead, Skinner focused on observable behaviors and spent the majority of his professional career refining his theories of reinforcement. He believed that personality develops, that our behavior responds only because of external events. In other words, we are the way we are because we were rewarded for being that way. It is this belief that discounts emotions, thoughts, and even human freedom of choice.

Skinner got most of his criticism due to his belief that through rewards and punishments, we could design the perfect Utopia. His most famous and most controversial books, <u>Walden II</u> and <u>Beyond Freedom and Dignity</u>, described his theory of behavioral determinism despite the protests and criticism from religious leaders and others. In 1990, Skinner died from leukemia but is known worldwide, with the likes of Sigmund Freud, as a forefather in modern day psychology.

Edward Thorndike
1874-1949

Edward Thorndike is best known for his work with animal research, spending the majority of his career at Teacher's College, Columbia University. He is most famous for his 'trial and error learning' theory and advancements in learning theory, behaviorism and educational psychology.

John Watson
1878—1958

John Watson is considered the father of behaviorism due to his opposition to the mainstream psychological view of the unconscious and psychoanalytic thought. To the behaviorist, the outward expression of the self is all that can be measured and therefore the only variable worthy of exploration.

His lecture at Columbia University entitled 'Psychology as the Behaviorist Views It' has become the manifesto for behavioral psychologists such as B.F. Skinner. His opposition to psychoanalytic theory split the field of psychology into two distinct and almost always oppositional schools of thought.

Max Wertheimer
1880-1943

Max Wertheimer is considered the founder of Gestalt Psychology. He studied law for several years before graduating with his degree in philosophy. He served as a professor at several Universities in Germany before leaving the country in 1934 due to the war in Europe. After which, he moved to the United States and began work with the New School for Social Research in New York City.

In 1910, at only 30 years of age, he developed an interest in perception after viewing a stroboscope in a child's toy store. After researching with this toy and the science behind it, he developed, along with his colleagues, theories of perception and perceptual grouping.

Wilhelm Wundt
1832-1920

Considered the father of modern psychology, Wilhelm Wundt studied medicine in his native Germany before his interests began to lean more toward physiology and psychology. His main areas of research included sensory processes. In 1875, he moved to Leipzig where he developed the first psychological laboratory and spent the next 46 years training psychologists and writing more than 54,000 written pages of research and theory.

Kenneth Bancroft Clark

Kenneth Bancroft Clark was one of the most influential and prominent social psychologist of his time. Throughout his life, he and his wife's psychological and educational accomplishments prove to be a big contribution to the change of this great nation. He had a number of first associated with his career. He was the first black Ph. D recipient in Columbia University history. The Brown v. Board of Education was the first time that social science results had been used for a ruling in the Supreme Court. Dr. Clark was a key figure in the participation African Americans in the American Psychological Association, being named the first African American to become president of this respected organization.

Appendix B

Glossary of Terms

AB Design

A single subject research design that contains one baseline (A) and one treatment (B).

ABAB Design

A single subject research design that contains a baseline (A1), treatment (B1), a second baseline (B2) and a second treatment phase (B2)

Alpha (lowercase)

The abbreviation for probability of error in statistical results. See Type I Error. (a)

Alternative Hypothesis

The hypothesis that states there is a difference between two or more sets of data.

Absolute Zero

Characteristic of a scale of measurement that contains a point where the scale has no value.

Accommodation

The creation of new cognitive schemas when objects, experiences, or other information does not fit with existing schemas.

Action Potential

The firing on a neuron. Occurs when the charge inside the neuron becomes more positive than the charge outside.

Acetycholine

A neurotransmitter associated with voluntary movement, sleep and wakefulness.

Aggressive

An interpersonal style where only the immediate needs of the self are considered rather than the needs of others. (As opposed to passive or assertive)

Agoraphobia

An anxiety disorder characterized by an intense fear of leaving one's home.

All or None Law

Either a neuron completely fires or it does not fire at all.

Alpha (lowercase)

The abbreviation for probability of error in statistical results. See Type I Error. (a)

Alternative Hypothesis

The hypothesis that states there is a difference between two or more sets of data.

Altruism

Behavior that is unselfish and may even be detrimental but which benefits others.

Amnesia

Loss of memory. Usually only a partial loss such as for a period of time or biographical information.

Amygdala

A part of the brain's limbic system that attaches emotional significance to information and mediates both defensive and aggressive behavior.

Anal Expulsive Personality

Stemming from the Anal stage, a child who becomes fixated due to over control transfers his or her unresolved anal (or control) issues into characteristics such as cruelty, pushiness, messiness, or disorganization.

Anal Retentive Personality

Stemming from the Anal stage, a child who becomes fixated due to under control transfers his or her unresolved anal (or control) issues into characteristics such as compulsivity, stinginess, cleanliness, organization, and obstinacy.

Anal Stage

Freud's second stage of psychosexual development where the primary sexual focus is on the elimination or holding onto feces. The stage is often thought of as representing a child's ability to control his or her own world.

Analysis

See Psychoanalysis.

Analysis of Variance

An inferential statistical procedure used to test whether or not the means of two or more sets of data are equal to each other.

ANOVA

Analysis of Variance.

Anxiety

The physiological and psychological reaction to an expected danger, whether real or imagined.

Aphasia

The impairment of the ability to communicate either through oral or written discourse as a result of brain damage.

Approach-Approach Conflict

The conflict presented when two opposite but equally appealing choices are available but cannot both be obtained.

Approach-Avoidance Conflict

The conflict presented when the best positive choice will result in a negative outcome as well as positive.

Arousal Theory

The theory stating that we are motivated by our innate desire to maintain an optimal level of arousal.

Assertive

Style of interpersonal interaction where both the needs of the self and others are considered. (As opposed to passive or aggressive)

Assimilation

Incorporating objects, experiences, or information into existing schemas.

Associations

The phenomenon in learning that states we are better able to remember information if it is paired with something we are familiar with or otherwise stands out.

Attachment

The strong bond a child forms with his or her primary caregiver.

Attribution

An idea or belief about the etiology of a certain behavior.

Attribution Theory

The theory that argues people look for explanation of behavior, associating either dispositional (internal) attributes or situational (external) attributes.

Authoritarian [parents]

Parenting style focused on excessive rules, rigid belief systems, and the expectation of unquestioned obedience.

Authoritative [parents]

Parenting style focused on setting reasonable rules and expectations while encouraging communication and independence.

Autonomic Nervous System

Part of the peripheral nervous system that regulates the involuntary actions of the body (e.g., breathing, heart rate, blood pressure, pupil dilation). Also regulates the Fight or Flight Phenomenon.

Availability Heuristic

A rule of thumb stating that information more readily available in our memory is more important than information not as easily accessible.

Aversion Therapy

A type of behavioral treatment where an aversive stimuli is paired with a negative behavior in hopes that the behavior will change in the future to avoid the aversive stimuli.

Avoidance-Avoidance Conflict

The conflict where both possible choices have an equal negative outcome.

Axon

The tail-like part of the neuron through which information exits the cell.

Behavior Modification

The application of behavioral theory to change a specific behavior.

Behavior Therapy

The application of behavioral theory (e.g. conditioning, reinforcement) in the treatment of mental illness.

Behaviorism

The school of psychology founded on the premise that behavior is measurable and can be changed through the application of various behavioral principles.

Bell-Shaped Curve

Also referred to as a normal distribution or normal curve, a bell-shaped curve is a perfect mesokurtic curve where the mean, median, and mode are equal.

Beta (uppercase)

Abbreviation for Power in statistical results. See Type II Error. (β)

Binocular Cues

Visual cues (convergence and retinal disparity) that require both eyes to perceive distance (as opposed to monocular cues)

Bisexuality

Being attracted to or aroused by members of both genders. See Sexual Orientation.

Blind Study

As a way to avoid the placebo effect in research, this type of study is designed without the subject's knowledge of the anticipated results and sometimes even the nature of the study. The subjects are said to be 'blind' to the expected results.

Broca's Aphasia

An aphasia associated with damage to the Broca's area of the brain, demonstrated by the impairment in producing understandable speech.

Burnout

Changes in thoughts, emotions, and behavior as a result of extended job stress and unrewarded repetition of duties. Burnout is seen as extreme dissatisfaction, pessimism, lowered job satisfaction, and a desire to quit.

Canonical Correlation

A correlational technique used when there are two or more X and two or more Y. (Example: The correlation between (age and sex) and (income and life satisfaction)

Castration Anxiety

According to Freud's Stages of Psychosexual Development, the fear a boy in the phallic stage experiences due to a fear that his father will render him powerless if his father finds out about his attraction toward his mother.

Catharsis

The emotional release associated with the expression of unconscious conflicts.

CEEB Score

A standard score that sets the mean to five-hundred and standard deviation to one-hundred. Used on the Scholastic Aptitude Test (SAT)

Cell Body

The main part of a neuron where the information is processed.

Central Nervous System

The brain and the spinal cord.

Central Tendency

A statistical measurement attempting to depict the average score in a distribution (see mean, median, and/or mode)

Centration

A young child's tendency to focus only on his or her own perspective of a specific object and a failure to understand that others may see things differently.

Cerebellum

Part of the brain associated with balance, smooth movement, and posture.

Cerebral Hemispheres

The two halves of the brain (right and left)

Chemical Imbalance

A generic term for the idea that chemical in the brain are either too scarce or too abundant resulting in or contributing to a mental disorder such as schizophrenia or bipolar disorder. Others believe that the disorder precedes the imbalance, suggesting that a change in mood, for example, changes our chemicals rather than the chemical changing our mood.

Chunk

A unit of information used in memory

Chunking

Combining smaller units of measurement or chunks into larger chunks. (e.g., a seven chunk phone number such as 5-5-5-1-2-1-2 becomes a five chunk number such as 5-5-5-12-12)

Classical Conditioning

The behavioral technique of pairing a naturally occurring stimulus and response chain with a different stimulus in order to produce a response which is not naturally occurring.

Client Centered Therapy A humanistic therapy based on Carl Roger's beliefs that an individual has an unlimited capacity for psychological growth and will continue to grow unless barriers are placed in the way.

Coefficient of Determination

The statistic or number determined by squaring the correlation coefficient. Represents the amount of variance accounted for by that correlation.

Coercive Power

Power derived through the ability to punish.

Cognition

The process of receiving, processing, storing, and using information.

Cognitive Behavioral Therapy

Treatment involving the combination of behaviorism (based on the theories of learning) and cognitive therapy (based on the theory that our cognitions or thoughts control a large portion of our behaviors).

Cognitive Dissonance

The realization of contradictions in one's own attitudes and behaviors.

Cognitive Psychology

The sub-field of psychology associated with information processing and the role it plays in emotion, behavior, and physiology.

Cognitive Therapy

The treatment approach based on the theory that our cognitions or thoughts control a large part of our behaviors and emotions. Therefore, changing the way we think can result in positive changes in the way we act and feel.

Cohort Effects

The effects of being born and raised in a particular time or situation where all other members of your group has similar experiences that make your group unique from other groups

Collective Unconscious

According to Jung, the content of the unconscious mind that is passed down from generation to generation in all humans.

Compulsion

The physical act resulting from an obsession. Typically a compulsive act is done in an attempt to alleviate the discomfort created by an obsession.

Concrete Operational Stage

According to Piaget, the stage of cognitive development where a child between the ages of 7 and 12 begins thinking more globally and outside of the self but is still deficient in abstract thought.

Concurrent Validity

A measurements ability to correlate or vary directly with an accepted measure of the same construct

Conditioned Response

The response in a stimulus-response chain that is not naturally occurring, but rather has been learned through its pairing with a naturally occurring chain.

Conditioned Stimulus

The stimulus in a stimulus-response chain that is not naturally occurring, but rather has been learned through its pairing with a naturally occurring chain.

Conditioning

The process of learning new behaviors or responses as a result of their consequences.

Confidence Interval

The level of certainty that the true score falls within a specific range. The smaller the range the less the certainty.

Conformity

Changing your attitudes, beliefs, thoughts, or behaviors in order to be more consistent with others.

Confound

Any variable that is not part of a research study but still has an effect on the research results

Conscience

According to Freud, the restriction demanded by the superego.

Consciousness

Awareness of yourself and the world around you.

Conservation

The understanding, typically achieved in later childhood, that matter remains the same even when the shape changes (i.e., a pound of clay is still a pound of clay

whether it is rolled in a ball or pounded flat).

Consolidation

The physiological changes in the brain associated with memory storage.

Consolidation Failure

The failure to store information in memory.

Constant

Any variable that remains the same throughout a study.

Construct

Any variable that cannot be directly observed but rather is measured through indirect methods. (Examples: intelligence, motivation)

Construct Validity

The general validity of a measuring device. Construct validity answers the question of whether or not the measuring device actually measures the construct under question.

Content Validity

A measurement device's ability to be generalized to the entire content of what is being measured.

Context Dependent Memory

The theory that information learned in a particular situation or place is better remembered when in that same situation or place.

Continuous Reinforcement

The application of reinforcement every time a specific behavior occurs.

Control Group

The group of subjects in an experiment that does not receive the independent variable.

Convergence

The binocular cue to distance referring to the fact that the closer an object, the more inward our eyes need to turn in order to focus

Convergent Thinking

Logical and conventional thought leading to a single answer.

Conversion Disorder

A somatoform disorder where the individual experiences a loss of sensation or function due to a psychological belief (e.g., paralysis, blindness, deafness).

Correlated Sample

Sample data that is related to each other.

Correlation

The degree to which two or more variables a related to each other. A correlation refers to the direction that the variables move and does not necessarily represent cause and effect. (Example: height and weight are correlated. As one increases, the other tends to increase as well)

Correlation Coefficient

The statistic or number representing the degree to which two or more variables are related. Often abbreviated 'r.'

Counterconditioning

The use of conditioning to eliminate a previously conditioned response. The conditioned stimulus (CS) is repaired with a different unconditioned stimulus (UCS) to eventually elicit a new conditioned response (CR)

Critical Period

A time frame deemed highly important in developing in a healthy manner; can be physically, emotionally, behaviorally, or cognitively.

Critical Value

The value of a statistic required in order to consider the results significant.

Cross Sectional Study

A research study that examines the effects of development (maturation) by examining different subjects at various ages

Cross Sequential Study

A research study that examines the effects of development (maturation) by combining longitudinal and cross sectional studies

Crowding

The psychological and psychological response to the belief that there are too many people in a specified area.

Crystallized Intelligence

The part of intelligence which involves the acquisition, as opposed to the use, of information

Decay

Theory which states that memory fades and/or disappears over time if it is not used or accessed.

Declarative Memory

The part of long-term memory where factual information is stored, such as mathematical formulas, vocabulary, and life events.

Deductive Reasoning

Decision making process in which ideas are processed from the general to the specific.

Defenses (Defense Mechanisms)

Psychological forces which prevent undesirable or inappropriate impulses from entering consciousness (e.g., forgetting responsibilities that we really didn't want to do, projecting anger onto a spouse as opposed to your boss). Also called Defense Mechanisms, Defense System, or Ego Defenses.

Degrees of Freedom

The number of individual scores that can vary without changing the sample mean. Statistically written as 'N-1' where N represents the number of subjects.

Delusion

False belief system (e.g., believing you are Napoleon, have magical powers, or the false belief that others are 'out to get you.').

Dendrites

Extensions of the cell body of a neuron responsible for receiving incoming neurotransmitters.

Dependent Variable

The variable in an experiment that is measured; the outcome of an experiment.

Descriptive Statistics

The branch of statistics that focuses on describing in numerical format what is happening now within a population. Descriptive statistics require that all subjects in the population (the entire class, all males in a school, all professors) be tested.

Developmental Psychology

The area of psychology focused on how children grow psychologically to become who they are as adults.

Deviation IQ Score

A standard score used for reporting IQ scores where the mean is set to 100 and standard deviation to 15

Difference Threshold

The smallest change in perception which is noticeable at least 50% of the time.

Discrimination

In behavioral theory, the learned ability to differentiate between two similar objects or situations.

Disorientation

Inability to recognize or be aware of who we are (person), what we are doing (situation), the time and date (time), or where we are in relation to our environment (place). To be considered a problem, it must be consistent, result in difficulty functioning, and not due to forgetting or being lost.

Displacement

The pushing out of older information in short term memory to make room for new information.

Dispositional Attribute

An attribute explained or interpreted as being caused by internal influences.

Dissociation

A separation from the self, with the most severe resulting in Dissociative Identity Disorder. Most of us experience this in very mild forms such as when we are driving long distance and lose time or find ourselves day dreaming longer than we thought.

Distinctiveness

The phenomenon in memory that states we are better able to remember information if it is distinctive or different from other information.

Divergent Thinking

The ability to use previously gained information to debate or discuss issues which have no agreed upon definitive resolution.

Dopamine

A neurotransmitter associated with movement, attention and learning and the brain's pleasure and reward system.

Dopamine Hypothesis

The theory that schizophrenia is caused by an excess amount of dopamine in the brain. Research has found that medication to reduce dopamine can reduce the positive symptoms of schizophrenia.

Double Blind Study

Research method in which both the subjects and the experimenter are unaware or 'blind' to the anticipated results.

Drive

An internal motivation to fulfill a need or reduce the negative aspects of an unpleasant situation.

Drug Therapy

The use of medication to treat a mental illness.

Ego

In Psychoanalytical theory, the part of the personality which maintains a balance between our impulses (id) and our conscience (superego).

Egocentric

The thinking in the preoperational stage of cognitive development where children believe everyone sees the world from the same perspective as he or she does.

Ego Defense Mechanisms

See Defenses

Ego Ideal

In psychoanalytic thought, this is the ideal or desired behavior of the ego according to the superego.

Ellis, Albert

A cognitive Psychologist who developed the concept of Rational-Emotive Therapy.

Emotion

Feelings about a situation, person, or objects that involves changes in physiological arousal and cognitions.

Emotional Intelligence (EQ)

The awareness of and ability to manage one's emotions in a healthy and productive manner.

Encoding

The transformation of information to be stored in memory.

Endorphins

A neurotransmitter involved in pain relief, and feelings of pleasure and contentedness.

Epinephrine

A neurotransmitter involved in energy and glucose metabolism. Too little has been associated with depression.

Episodic Memory

Subcategory of Declarative memory where information regarding life events are stored.

Equal Intervals

Characteristic of a scale of measurement where the individual units possess the qualities of equal intervals. The difference between each unit of measurement is exactly the same.

Equity Theory

The theory that argues a couple must see each other as contributing and benefiting equally to the relationship for them both to feel comfortable in the relationship.

Error

The amount of other variables (aside from what you are measuring) that can impact the observed score

Error Level

The level of accepted error within a given set of data. The greater the error level, the wider the confidence interval.

Escape Conditioning

Operant conditioning based on the idea that a behavior is more likely to be repeated if it results in the cessation of a negative event.

Estimate

An idea about a characteristic of a population based on sample data (e.g., the sample mean IQ was 102 so we estimate that the population mean IQ is also 102)

Eta

A correlational technique used primarily for non-linear relationships. (Example, income and age are positively correlated until older age at which point the correlation reverses itself to some extent.)

Etiology

Causal relationships of diseases; theories regarding how the specific disease or disorder began.

Experimental Group

In research, the group of subjects who receive the independent variable.

Experimental Method

Research method using random assignment of subjects and the manipulation of variables in order to determine cause and effect.

Experimenter Bias

Errors in a research study due to the predisposed notions or beliefs of the experimenter.

Expert Power

Power derived through advanced knowledge or experience in a particular subject.

Ex-Post-Facto (After the Fact) Research

Research method in which the independent variable is administered prior to the study without the researcher's control and its effects are investigated afterward

External Locus of Control

The belief that the environment has more control over life circumstances than the individual does.

External Validity

The extent to which the data collected from a sample can be generalized to the entire population.

Extinction

The reduction and eventual disappearance of a learned or conditioned response after it is no longer paired with the unconditioned stimulus-response chain.

Extrinsic Motivation

The desire or push to perform a certain behavior based on the potential external rewards that may be received as a result.

Extroversion

Personality style where the individual prefers outward and group activity as opposed to inward and individual activity.

Factor Analysis

A statistical technique used to determine the number of components in a set of data. These components are then named according to their characteristics allowing a researcher to break down information into statistical groups.

Factorial ANOVA

An Analysis of Variance used when there are two or more independent variables. When there are two, the ANOVA is called a Two-Way ANOVA, three independent variables would use a Three-Way ANOVA, etc.

Family Therapy

Treatment involving family members which seeks to change the unhealthy familial patterns and interactions.

Fixation

In Freud's theory of psychosexual development, the failure to complete a stage successfully which results in a continuation of that stage into later adulthood.

Fixed Interval Schedule

A schedule in which the reinforcement is presented after a specific period of time.

Fixed Ratio Schedule

A schedule in which the reinforcement is presented after a specific number of responses.

Fetish

A condition in which arousal and/or sexual gratification is attained through inanimate objects (shoes, pantyhose) or non-sexual body parts (feet, hair). Is considered a problem when the object is needed in order to obtain arousal or gratification and the individual cannot complete a sexual act without this object present.

Frequency Distribution

A table showing the number of occurrences for each score

Frequency Effect

The phenomenon in memory which states that we tend to remember information better if it is repeated.

Freud, Sigmund

Dr. Freud is often referred to as the father of clinical psychology. His extensive theory of personality development (psychoanalytical theory) is the cornerstone for modern psychological thought, and consists of (1) the psychosexual stages of development, (2) the structural model of personality (id, ego, superego), and (3) levels of consciousness (conscious, subconscious, and unconscious). See Psychoanalysis.

Flooding

A behavioral technique used to treat phobias in which the individual is presented with the feared stimulus until the associated anxiety disappears.

Fluid Intelligence
According to Cattell, the part of intelligence which involves the use, as opposed to the acquisition, of information.

Formal Operational Stage
Pavlov's fourth and final stage of cognitive development where thinking becomes more abstract.

Framing
Presenting information either positively or negatively in order to change the influence is has on an individual or group.

Free Association
The psychoanalytic technique of allowing a patient to talk without direction or input in order to analyze current issues of the individual.

Frontal Lobe
The lobe at the front of the brain associated with movement, speech, and impulsive behavior.

Frustration
The feelings, thoughts, and behaviors associated with not achieving a particular goal or the belief that a goal has been prematurely interrupted.

Frustration-Aggression Hypothesis
The theory arguing that aggression is the natural reaction to frustration.

Functionalism
The school of thought popular in the 19th century emphasizing conscious experiences as a precursor to behavior

Fundamental Attribution Error
The tendency to overestimate the internal attributes of another person's actions.

General intelligence
Typically compared to s which represents specific intelligences. G is the culmination of all possible s's.

GABA (Gamma-Amino Butyric Acid)
A neurotransmitter involved in the inhibition of anxiety and excitation. Too little GABA has been associated with anxiety disorders.

Gender Identity
The internal sense of being either male or female. Usually congruent with biological gender, but not always as in Gender Identity Disorder.

Gender Role
The accepted behaviors, thoughts, and emotions of a specific gender based upon the views of a particular society or culture.

Gender Typing
The process of developing the behaviors, thoughts, and emotions associated with a particular gender.

Generalization
The tendency to associate stimuli, and therefore respond similarly to, due to their closeness on some variable such as size, shape, color, or meaning.

Genital Stage
Freud's final stage of psychosexual development where healthy sexual development is defined as attraction to a same aged, opposite sexed peer.

Gestalt
German word typically translated as meaning ‹whole' or ‹form.'

Gestalt Therapy

Treatment focusing on the awareness and understanding of one's feelings.

Grouped Frequency Distribution

A table showing the number of occurrences for a grouping of scores. Used a lot in educational settings where a score of 90 to 100 may be grouped as an A, a score of 80 to 90 may be grouped as a B, etc.

Group Polarization

The tendency for members of a cohesive group to make more extreme decisions due to the lack of opposing views.

Group Therapy

Psychotherapy conducted with at least three or four non-related individuals who are similar in some are, such as gender, age, mental illness, or presenting problem.

Group Think

The tendency for members of a cohesive group to reach decisions without weighing all the facts, especially those contradicting the majority opinion.

Gustation

Sense of taste.

Habituation

The decrease in response to a stimulus due to repetition (e.g., not hearing the ticking of a clock after getting used to it)

Hallucination

False perception of reality (e.g., hearing voices that aren't there or seeing people who do not exist) [auditory (hearing); visual (sight); olfactory (smell); tactile (touch); and taste].

Halo Effect

The tendency to assign generally positive or generally negative traits to a person after observing one specific positive or negative trait, respectively.

Hawthorne Effect

The phenomenon that subject behavior changes by the mere fact that they are being observed.

Health Psychology

The specific field in psychology concerned with psychology's impact on health, physical well being, and illness.

Heterosexuality

Being attracted to or aroused by members of the opposite gender. See Sexual Orientation.

Heuristic

A rule of thumb based on experience used to make decisions.

Hierarchy of Needs

Maslow's Theory of Motivation which states that we must achieve lower level needs, such as food, shelter, and safety before we can achieve higher level needs, such as belonging, esteem, and self-actualization.

Higher Order Conditioning

Pairing a second conditioned stimulus with the first conditioned stimulus in order to produce a second conditioned response.

Hippocampus

Part of the limbic system. Involved more in memory, and the transfer of information from short-term to long-term memory.

History

External events that take place during a research study that are not part of the study but have an effect on the outcome

Homeostasis

The tendency of the body (and the mind) to natural gravitate toward a state of equilibrium or balance.

Homophobia

An irrational hostility, hatred, or fear of homosexuals.

Homosexuality

Being attracted to or aroused by members of the same gender. See Sexual Orientation.

Humanistic Psychology

A theoretical view of human nature which stresses a positive view of human nature and the strong belief in psychological homeostasis.

Humanistic Therapy

Treatment focused on increasing awareness of one's self concept.

Hypnosis

A deep state of relaxation where an individual is more susceptible to suggestions.

Hypnotherapist

A trained, and often licensed, therapist who utilizes the therapeutic technique of hypnosis as part of a treatment regimen.

Hypnotist

An individual, most likely unlicensed, who uses hypnosis techniques or variations of these techniques for a variety of reasons, including treatment and/or entertainment.

Hypothalamus

A part of the brain that controls the autonomic nervous system, and therefore maintains the body's homeostasis (controls body temperature, metabolism, and appetite. Also translates extreme emotions into physical responses.

Hypothesis

A prediction about the relationship between two or more variables.

Id

In Psychoanalytical theory, the part of the personality which contains our primitive impulses such as sex, anger, and hunger.

Ideal Self

Humanistic term representing the characteristics, behaviors, emotions, and thoughts to which a person aspires.

Illusion

Misperception of reality (e.g., the illusion of a lake in the middle of a desert).

Imagery

Utilizing the mind to create a mental representation of a sensory experience.

Inappropriate Affect

Expressing contradictory behavior when describing or experiencing an emotion (e.g., smiling when discussing something sad; laughing when talking about the death of a loved one).

Independent Samples

Sample data that is independent or not related to each other.

Independent Variable

The variable in an experiment that is manipulated or compared.

Inductive Reasoning
Decision making process in which ideas are processed from the specific to the general.

Industrial/Organizational Psychology
The area or specialty in psychology focused on the application of psychological principles in the work force.

Inferential Statistics
The branch of statistics that focuses on describing in numerical format what might be happening or what might happen (estimation) in the future (probability). Inferential statistics required the testing of only a sample of the population. (Example: 100 students rather than all students).

Inhalant
Substances such as spray paint, freon, and glue that produce an intoxicating effect when inhaled.

Innate
Occurring without learning, inborn.

Insanity
A legal term representing the inability to know right from wrong or the inability to understand the consequences of one's actions.

Insight
The understanding of a relationship between current thoughts, feelings, and/or behaviors and where these originated or how they are maintained.

Instinct
A behavior we are born with and therefore does not need to be learned.

Intelligence
The degree to which one can adapt to one's environment.

Intelligence Quotient [IQ]
The scores achieved on psychological tests aimed at quantifying intellectual ability.

Interaction Effects
When the effect of one variable on another is contingent on a third variable, this contingency is called an interaction effect.

Internal Consistency
An estimate of how reliable a test is when items on the test are compared to each other. See split-half and odd-even reliability.

Internal Locus of Control
The belief that an individual has more control over life circumstances than the environment does.

Internal Validity
A measure of the trustworthiness of a sample of data. Internal validity looks at the subject, testing, and environment in which the data collection took place.

Interquartile Range
The difference between the scores (or estimated scores) at the 75th percentile and the 25th percentile. Used more than the range because it eliminates extreme scores.

Interval Estimation
Estimating the population statistic based on a range around a sample statistic.

Interval Scale
Any scale of measurement possessing magnitude and equal intervals, but not an absolute zero.

Interview

A subjective personality and mental health assessment typically consisting of questions and answers.

Intrinsic Motivation

The motivation or desire to do something based on the enjoyment of the behavior itself rather than relying on or requiring external reinforcement.

Introspection

The process of examining one's own consciousness.

Introversion

The tendency to focus energy inward resulting in decreased social interaction.

Just Noticeable Difference

The smallest change in a sensory perception that is detectable 50% of the time.

Jung, Carl

A student of Freud who split from the Psychoanalytic Society because of his disagreements with Freud, especially his view of the collective unconscious.

Kurtosis

The shape of a curve or distribution of scores (See Leptokurtic, Mesokurtic, and Platykurtic).

Latency Stage

Freud's fourth stage of psychosexual development where sexuality is repressed in the unconscious and children focus on identifying with their same sex parent and interact with same sex peers.

Latent Content

Freud's term for the underlying or hidden content represented in the symbols of dreams.

Latent Learning

Learning that occurs without apparent reinforcement but is not demonstrated until such time as reinforcement occurs.

Law of Effect

Theory proposed by Thorndike stating that those responses that are followed by a positive consequence will be repeated more frequently than those that are not.

Learned Helplessness

A condition that occurs after a period of negative consequences where the person begins to believe they have no control.

Learning

A relatively permanent change in behavior due to an interaction with the environment.

Learning Theory

Based on the idea that changes in behavior result more from experience and less from our personality or how we think or feel about a situation.

Legitimate Power

Power derived through one's position, such as a police officer or elected official.

Libido

Sigmund Freud's terminology of sexual energy or sexual drive.

Limbic System

A brain system that plays a role in emotional expression, particularly in the emotional component of behavior, memory, and motivation.

Locus of Control

A belief about the amount of control a person has over situations in their life.

Longitudinal Study

A research design that assesses the effects of development (maturation) by using the same subjects over an extended period of time

Long Term Memory

Relatively permanent memory.

Lower Confidence Limit

The lower limit of a confidence interval. If prediction states that the true score falls between 80 and 90, then the lower confidence level is 80.

Lucid Dream

A dream in which you are aware of dreaming and are sometimes able to manipulate the dream.

Magnitude

Characteristic of a scale of measurement where the individual units possess the qualities of greater than, equal to, or less than.

Main Effect

The effect of one variable on another without any other variables or subgroups involvement.

Manifest Content

According to Freud, the story-like superficial content of a dream, often representing only the daily activities and little underlying unconscious material.

Maslow, Abraham

Humanistic Theorist most famous for the development of the Hierarchy of Needs.

Maturation

Changes due to the natural process of aging as determined by your genetics

Mean

A measure of central tendency determined by adding all scores together and dividing by the number of scores. Often referred to as the statistical average.

Measure of Central Tendency

An average (see Mean, Median, and/or Mode)

Measurement, Scales of

Categories of data based on their numerical characteristics (See Ratio, Interval, Ordinal, and Nominal Scales)

Median

A measure of central tendency that uses the middle most occurring score in a distribution (the score that occurs at exactly the 50th percentile).

Medulla Oblongata

Part of the brainstem that controls vital life-sustaining functions such as heartbeat, breathing, blood pressure, and digestion.

Memory Effect

Error in research that results from subjects recalling previous testing and applying that knowledge to current testing.

Mesokurtic

A curve or distribution that has a balanced amount of variance so that is resembles a normal curve.

Meta Analysis

The statistical procedure used to combine numerous   and   independent   research results into one study. Each research study becomes one subject in the meta-analysis.

Minnesota Multiphasic Personality Inventory, 2nd. Edition

An Objective test utilizing 567 items which have been empirically derived to measure a variety of psychological concerns.

MMPI-2

See Minnesota Multiphasic Personality Inventory, 2nd. Edition.

Mode

A measure of central tendency that uses the most frequently occurring score. A distribution with two or more scores that are equal and occur most frequently is called multi-modal.

Modeling

Learning through the imitation or observation of others.

Mortality

Subject drop-out in a research study. Mortality becomes a problem when a disproportionate dropout rate occurs between two or more groups (Example: 30% of males drop out of group one while only 2% of males drop out in group two, resulting in uneven groups).

Motivation

The process that energizes and/or maintains a behavior.

Motive

Internal states that provide direction for one's behaviors.

Multiple Correlation

A correlational technique used when there is one X and two or more Y. (Example: the correlation between age and (math and English ability).

N

Symbol used for the number of subjects or data in a distribution. A study with 10 subjects would have an N equal to 10.

Naturalistic Observation

A research method where the subject(s) is(are) observed without interruption under normal or natural circumstances.

NCE Score

A standard score that sets the mean to fifty and standard deviation to 21.06, allowing the 99th percentile to have a score of 99 and the first percentile a score of 1.

Negative Correlation

A correlation where one two variables tend to move in the opposite direction (example: the number of pages printed and the amount of ink left in your printer are negatively correlated. The more pages printed, the less ink you have left.)

Negative Skew

A curve or distribution of scores that has extreme scores below the mean that are atypical of the majority of scores.

Neuron

A specialized nerve cell.

Neurotransmitter

A chemical found in animals that plays a role in our behavior, cognitions, and emotions.

Nightmare

A frightening dream occurring in REM sleep.

Nominal Scale

Any scale that contains no magnitude. Often nominal is thought of as name only, meaning that the variables of a nominal scale can be identified but not measured.

Nondeclarative Memory

A subsystem within Long term memory which consists of skills we acquire through repetition and practice (e.g., dance, playing the piano, driving a car)

Nonparametric Test

Any statistic that is designed for ordinal or nominal data or data that is not normally distributed

Norepinephrine

A neurotransmitter associated with eating and alertness. Too little has been associated with depression and too much has been associated with schizophrenia.

Norm

An expectation based on multiple observations.

Normal Curve

A graphical interpretation of a population that is 'bell shaped' as it has the highest frequency in the middle and this frequency diminishes the farther you get from the center on either end. The mean, median, and mode are all equal in a perfect normal curve.

Normal Distribution

The scores of a sample or population that, when graphed, fall on or close to a normal curve. A normal distribution is often ideal in research because the data can then be said to have all of the characteristics of a normal curve.

Null Hypothesis

The hypothesis that states there is no difference between two or more sets of data.

Panic Attack

Period of extreme anxiety and physical symptoms such as heart palpitations, shakiness, dizziness, and racing thoughts. Initial attacks are often reported to feel like a heart attack due to the heart palpitations. A medical exam should be conducted to rule out any such condition.

Parallel Form Reliability

The correlation coefficient determined by comparing the scores of the two similar measuring devices (or forms of the same test) administered to the same people at one time.

Parameter

A summary value of a specific population characteristic (e.g., mean age, standard deviation of IQ's, median income)

Parasympathetic Nervous System

A subsystem of the Autonomic Nervous System (ANS) that returns the body to homeostasis.

Parietal Lobe

One of four lobes of the brain. Contains the Somatosensory Cortex d is therefore involved in the processing of touch, pressure, temperature, and pain.

Peak Experience

A life experience considered paramount due to the feeling of unity with the world.

Pearson Product-Moment Correlation

A correlation statistic used primarily for two sets of data that are of the ratio or interval scale. The most commonly used correlational technique.

Penis Envy

In Psychoanalytic Thought, the desire of girls to possess a penis and therefore have the power that being male represents.

Percentile Rank

Percentage of scores falling at or below a specific score. A percentile rank of 95 means that 95% of all of the scores fall at or below this point. In other words, the score is as good as or better than 95% of the scores.

Perception

The process of organizing and using information that is received through the senses.

Perceptual Constancy

The ability to perceive objects as unchanged despite the change noticed by the senses (e.g., the ability to understand and see buildings as remaining the same height even though they appear larger as we get closer to them).

Perfect Correlation

A correlation of either +1.0 or -1.0. A perfect correlation is extremely rare and when it occurs means that predicting one score based on another score is perfect or without error.

Person Centered Therapy

The therapeutic technique based on humanistic theory which is non-directive and empathic.

Personality

The stable set of individual characteristics that make us unique.

Personality Disorder

A maladaptive and stable set of individual characteristics that cluster to form a recognized disorder.

Permissive [parents]

Parenting style consisting of very few rules and allowing children to make most decisions and control their own behavior.

Persuasion

The deliberate attempt to influence the thoughts, feelings or behaviors of another.

Phallic Personality

Stemming from the Phallic stage, a child who becomes fixated may develop a personality characterized by selfishness, impulsivity, and a lack of or reduced ability to feel empathy.

Phallic Stage

Freud's third stage of psychosexual development where the primary sexual focus is on symbolism of the genitals.

Phi Correlation

A correlational technique used when both variables are binary (Example true/false, yes/no, or on/off)

Phi Phenomenon

The perception of motion based on two or more stationary objects (e.g., the perception of chaser lights brought about by different lights blinking at different times).

Phobia

An intense fear of a specific object or situation. Most of us consider ourselves to have phobias, but to be diagnosable, the fear must significantly restrict our way of life.

Placebo

A treatment condition used to control for the placebo effect where the treatment has no real effect on its own.

Placebo Effect

The phenomenon in research where the subject's beliefs about the outcome can significantly affect the outcome without any other intervention.

Plasticity

The ability of the brain, especially in our younger years to compensate for damage.

Platykurtic

A curve or distribution of scores that has a lot of variance

Pleasure Principle

Freud's theory regarding the id's desire to maximize pleasure and minimize pain in order to achieve immediate gratification.

Point Biserial Correlation

A correlational technique used when one variable is numeric and the other is binary (Example age and sex or income and true/false)

Point Estimation

Estimating the population statistic based on a single sample statistic.

Pons

Part of the brain that plays a role in the regulation of states of arousal, including sleep and dreaming.

Population

The entire group to which research is hoping to generalize (e.g., males, adults, U.S. citizens).

Population Mean

The true mean of the entire population often estimated using the sample mean. Abbreviated with the lowercase Greek letter mu. (m)

Population Standard Deviation

The true standard deviation of the population often estimated by using the sample standard deviation. Often abbreviated with the lowercase Greek letter sigma. (s)

Positive Correlation

A correlation where as one variable increases, the other also increases, or as one decreases so does the other. Both variables move in the same direction.

Positive Reinforcement

Something positive provided after a response in order to increase the probability of that response occurring in the future.

Positive Skew

A curve or distribution of scores that has extreme scores above the mean that are atypical of the majority of scores

Power

The strength or the data to find a difference when there truly is a difference. Power is abbreviated with the capital Greek letter beta (b).

Predictive Validity

A measurements ability to predict scores on another measurement that is related or purports to measure the same or similar construct

Prejudice

Negative beliefs, attitudes, or feelings about a person's entire character based on only one characteristic. This belief is often based on faulty information.

Preoperational Stage
Piaget's second stage of cognitive development in which a child develops objects permanency and language.

Pretest-Posttest Method
A method of determining the amount of change that occurred in a set of data by measuring the data prior to treatment and then after treatment and comparing the two measurement outcomes.

Primacy Effect
The tendency to remember the first bit of information in a series due to increased rehearsal.

Primary Reinforcer
A reinforcer that meets our basic needs such as food, water, sleep, or love.

Proactive Interference
Interference in memory due to prior learning.

Probability of Error
The likelihood that error caused the results of data analysis. If the probability of error is greater than the predetermined acceptable level of error then the results are said to be 'not significant.'

Probability Sample
Also called representative samples, a probability sample consists of characteristics that are close to the population that they represent.

Projection
In Psychoanalytic Theory, the defense mechanism whereby we transfer or project our feelings about one person onto another.

Projective Techniques
A generic term for the psychological procedures used to measure personality which rely on ambiguous stimuli.

Psychiatrist
A medical doctor with training in mental illness.

Psychoanalysis
Developed by Sigmund Freud, this type of therapy is known for long term treatment, typically several times per week, where the unresolved issues from the individual's childhood are analyzed and resolved. These issues are considered to be primarily unconscious in nature and are kept from consciousness through a complex defense system.

Psychoanalytic Theory
Theory developed by Freud consisting of the structural model of personality, topographical model of personality, defense mechanisms, drives, and the psychosexual stages of development. The primary driving force behind the theory is the id, ego and superego and the division of consciousness into the conscious mind, the pre/subconscious, and the unconscious.

Psychodynamic Therapy
A modern adaptation of psychoanalytic therapy which has made sometimes minor and sometimes major changes to Freud's original theories.

Psychotherapy
The treatment of mental illness or related issues based on psychological theory.

Psychology

The study of emotion, cognition, and behavior, and their interaction.

Psychosis

Break from reality, usually identified by hallucinations, delusions, and/or disorientation.

Psychotropic Medication

Prescription medication used primarily to treat mental illness.

Punishment

The adding of a negative stimulus in order to decrease a response (e.g., spanking a child to decrease negative behavior).

Quasi-Experimental Research

Any research study that uses specific experimental methods but does not randomize subjects

r

Symbol used for the Pearson-product moment correlation (correlation coefficient)

Random Assignment

Assigning subjects to experimental groups based on chance.

Random Sample

A group of subjects representing the population who are selected through chance.

Range

The difference between the highest and lowest score in a distribution (often 1 is added to the result when computing statistics to allow for the 0.5 on either end lost due to rounding).

Rank-Ordered Array

A table consisting of data in order of highest to lowest or lowest to highest where each data is given a numbered rank depicting it's difference from the highest or lowest score

Ratio Scale

Any scale of measurement possessing magnitude, equal intervals, and an absolute zero

Rational Emotive Therapy

A Cognitive Therapy based on Albert Ellis' theory that cognitions control our emotions and behaviors; therefore, changing the way we think about things will affect the way we feel and the way we behave.

Rationalization

A defense mechanism where one believes or states an acceptable explanation for a behavior as opposed to the real explanation.

Raw Data

The initial data gathered that has not yet been graphed, organized, or analyzed.

Reaction Formation

A defense mechanism where unacceptable impulses are converted to their opposite.

Reality Principle

According the Freud, the attempt by the ego to satisfy both the id and the superego while still considering the reality of the situation.

Recency Effect

The tendency to remember the last bit of information due to the shorter time available for forgetting.

Reconstruction

Tendency to fill in the gaps in our memory and often believe these represent true memories.

Referent Power

Power given to an individual due to respect and/or desire to be similar to that individual.

Reflection

A therapeutic technique in humanistic therapy where the feelings and thoughts of the individual are reflected or reworded back to the individual to assist in understanding them.

Regression Analysis

Used with a correlation to determine a regression equation that predicts or estimates a person's score on one variable if the other is known.

Rehearsal

Repeating information in order to improve our recall of this information.

Reinforcer

Anything that follows a behavior that increases the chances of that behavior occurring again.

Regression

A defense mechanism where one reverts to an earlier stage of development.

Reliability

A statistical measure of a tests consistency, or ability to result in similar scores if given repeatedly.

Reliability Coefficient

The correlation coefficient is called the reliability coefficient when a correlation is used to determine or estimate reliability.

Replication

The strength of a research study is only as good as its ability to be replicated. In other words, if a study has significant results but cannot be done again, it is difficult to assess whether it was a good study or a result of error.

Representative Sample

A sample or subgroup of the population that possesses the same characteristics of the population

Representativeness Heuristic

A rule of thumb where similarity to a prototype or similar situation dictates a decision.

Repression

In Psychoanalytic Theory, the defense mechanism whereby our thoughts are pulled out of our consciousness and into our unconscious.

Resistance

In psychoanalysis, the individual's refusal to participate in a therapeutic intervention due to underlying issues unrelated to the intervention.

Response Prevention

A therapeutic technique where stimuli is presented to the individual but the individual is not permitted to exercise his or her typical response. Used for the treatment of phobias, obsessive compulsive disorder and other anxiety disorders.

Reticular Formation (Reticular Activating System)

Part of the brain stem involved in arousal and attention, sleep and wakefulness, and control of reflexes.

Retinal Disparity

The binocular cue to distance referring to the distance between the two images sent to the brain by our eyes. The farther apart these images, the closer the object.

Retrieval

The process of bringing material out of long term memory and into consciousness.

Retroactive Interference

Interference in memory created by later learning.

Reversal Design

Any single subject design that includes the removal of treatment to determine if the subject reverts to baseline (ex. ABA, ABAB)

Reversibility

A child's ability to reverse operations and therefore recognize that the qualities of an object remain the same despite changes in appearance. Occurs in Piaget's Concrete Operational Stage of Cognitive Development (e.g., 1+2=3 to 3-2=1).

Reward Power

Power derived through an ability to offer rewards.

Rogers, Carl

A humanistic Psychologist who developed Client-Centered Therapy.

Rorschach Inkblot Test

A projective technique utilizing ambiguous inkblots as stimuli.

Sample

Portion of the entire population used to estimate what is likely happening within a population.

Sample Mean

Abbreviated with a lowercase x with a horizontal line over top (called 'x-bar'), the sample mean is the true mean of a sample of data often used to estimate the true mean of the entire population.

Sample Standard Deviation

The standard deviation of a sample of the population. Often used to estimate the true population standard deviation. Often abbreviated 'SD."

Sampling Error

The amount of error associated with a sample due to its deviation from the population

Scatter Plot

A graphical representation of data received in a correlational study.

Schema

The cognitive structure utilized to make sense of the world.

Secondary Reinforcer

A reinforcer other than one which meets our basic needs such as food or water (e.g., intellectual stimulation, money, praise).

Selection Bias

Errors in the selection and placement of subjects into groups that results in differences between groups which could affect the results of an experiment.

Self Actualization
The process of understanding oneself more completely and being aware of issues affecting one's life.

Self-Concept
The subjective perception of the self.

Self Efficacy
One's belief in his or her own ability.

Self Serving Bias
The tendency to assign internal attributes to successes and external factors to failures.

Semantic Memory
The part of declarative memory that stores general information such as names and facts.

Semi-Interquartile Range
One half of the interquartile range

Sensation
Information brought in through the senses.

Sensorimotor Stage
The first stage in Piaget's Stages of Cognitive Development where a child's primary way of learning about the world is through the senses and movement.

Sensory Adaptation
The reduced ability to sense a stimulus after prolonged exposure.

Sensory Memory
The brief storage of information brought in through the senses; typically only lasts up to a few seconds.

Separation Anxiety
Distress caused by the absence of an infant's primary caregiver

Serotonin
A neurotransmitter involved in mood, sleep, appetite, and impulsive and aggressive behavior. Too little has been associated with depression and some anxiety disorders (e.g., obsessive-compulsive disorder). Many antidepressants attempt to reduce the amount of serotonin that is taken back (reuptake) into the sending neuron (e.g., Serotonin Reuptake Inhibitors [SRI]).

Sexual Orientation
A feeling of attractedness or arousal associated with a particular gender. Sexual behavior can be a result of this but does not necessarily define a person's orientation.

Shaping
Gradually molding a specific response by reinforcing responses that come close to the desired response.

Short Term Memory
The stage of memory where information is stored for up to 30 seconds prior to either being forgotten or transferred to long term memory.

Sigma (lowercase)
The abbreviation for the standard deviation of a population. (s)

Sigma (uppercase)
The abbreviation for summation. (S)

Situational Attribute
An attribute explained or interpreted as being caused by external influences.

Skinner, B. F.

Considered the father of behavioral therapy. He once stated that with the ability to control a child's environment, he could raise a child to become anything he wanted.

Skinner Box

A cage designed for animals in operant conditioning experiments.

Skew

The degree to which a curve or distribution of scores has extreme scores atypical of the majority of scores

Social Facilitation

The effect of other's presence on one's performance. Typically we perform simple or well-learned tasks better in front of others and difficult or novel tasks worse.

Social Learning Theory

Developmental theory arguing that personality is learned through the interactions with the environment.

Social Loafing

The tendency for people to work less on a task the greater the number of people are working on that task.

Social Psychology

The branch of psychology which focuses on society and its impact on the individual.

Social Roles

Accepted behaviors associated with a particular position within a group.

Social Skills

Skills or behaviors deemed desirable or necessary to effectively interact with society.

Social Support

Term used to describe the degree of emotional support afforded a individual by friends, family, and other acquaintances.

Somatic Nervous System

Sub system of the Peripheral Nervous System (PNS). Primary function is to regulate the actions of the skeletal muscles.

Spearman's Rho

A correlational technique used primarily for rank ordered data (ordinal scale).

Split-Half Reliability

The correlation coefficient determined by comparing first half of the measurement to the second half. Measure of the internal consistency of a test or measuring device.

Spontaneous Recovery

The tendency for previously learned information to resurface rapidly after a period of extinction. Information that is spontaneously recovered is thought to lay dormant but not forgotten (e.g., riding a bicycle after a long period of not riding).

Stage

A period of development that occurs at about the same time for each person. Developmental and Personality theories are often made up of a series of stages.

Stage Theory

The idea that an individual must pass through one stage of development before he or she can reach the next stage.

Standard Deviation

A measure of spread within a distribution (the square root of the variance). The most popular and most reliable measure of variability but the more skewed a distribution, the more error there will be in the standard deviation because of its reliance on the mean.

Standard Error of Measurement

a statistical procedure used to determine the amount of error of any measurement device

Standard Error of the Mean

An estimation of the unaccounted for error within a mean. If the mean is 10 and the standard error of the mean is 2, then the true score is likely to fall somewhere between 8 and 12 or 10 +/- 2.

Standardization

The process of making a test or procedure the same for everyone so that results can be compared to each other.

Standard Score

A score derived by transforming the data based on the standard deviation. Standard scores can then be compared to one another on face value. (See z-score, T-score, NCE score, stanines, and Wechsler's Deviation IQ Score)

Stanine

A standard score that literally means Standard Nine, stanines have a mean of five and a standard deviation of approximately two. Stanines 2 through 8 are exactly 1/2 standard deviations and stanines one and nine or open ended.

Statistic

An observed characteristic of a sample (e.g., 20% improvement rate, range of IQ's)

State

A temporary internal characteristic (e.g., depressed, angry)

State Dependent Memory

The theory that information learned in a particular state of mind (e.g., depressed, happy, somber) is more easily recalled when in that same state of mind.

Stem and Leaf Display

A multiple column table depicting the individual digits of the scores. A score of 95 would have a stem of 9 and a leaf of 5, a score of 62 would have a stem of 6 and a leaf of 2. If a particular stem has more than one leaf, such as the scores 54, 58, and 51, the stem of 5 has three leaves, in this case 458.

Stimulus

Anything in the environment to which one responds.

Stimulus Discrimination

The ability to tell the difference and therefore not respond to similar stimuli.

Stimulus Generalization

The response to new stimuli due its similarity to the original stimuli.

Storage

The process of saving information in long term memory

Stress

The physical and psychological result of internal or external pressure.

Stressor

Anything, internal or external, which applies psychological pressure on an individual.

Structuralism

School of thought from the 19th century focused on the gathering of psychological information through the examination of the structure of the mind.

Subjective Reality

The perception of reality made by an individual that may be different from the perception made by another person.

Subject Matching

A method of reducing bias in a sample of subjects by matching specific criteria of the sample to the true characteristics of the population. (Example: If the population is 60% female then 60% of the subjects in the sample should also be female)

Sublimation

A defense mechanism where undesired or unacceptable impulses are transformed into behaviors which are accepted by society.

Superego

In Psychoanalytical theory, the part of the personality that represents the conscience.

Supertraits

Hans Eysenck's term for his two distinct categories of personality traits. They include Introversion-Extroversion and Neuroticism. According to Eysenck, each of us fall on a continuum based on the degree of each supertraits.

Suppression

The defense mechanism where we push unacceptable thoughts out of consciousness and into our unconscious.

Survey

A research technique in which subjects respond to a series of questions.

Syllogism

Aristotle's theory of reasoning where two true statements are followed by a single logical conclusion.

Sympathetic Nervous System (SNS)

Part of the Autonomic Nervous System responsible for the fight or flight phenomenon and which plays a role (along with the Parasympathetic Nervous System) in maintaining the body's homeostasis.

Synapse

The space between the axon of one neuron and the dendrites of another through which neurotransmitters travel.

Systematic Desensitization

A treatment technique where the individual is exposed to gradually increasing anxiety provoking stimuli while relaxing; the goal is for the individual to eventually confront a phobia or fear without the previously associated anxiety.

T-Score

A standard score that sets the mean to fifty and standard deviation to ten. Used on a number of tests including the MMPI.

t-Test

A group of statistics used to determine if a significance difference exists between the means of two sets of data.

Tactile

The sense of touch.

TAT

See Thematic Apperception Test

Temperament

A person's typical way of responding to his or her environment.

Temporal Lobe

One of the four lobes of the brain. Contains the auditory cortex and therefore plays a role in receptive language as well as memory and emotion.

Test-Retest Reliability

The correlation coefficient determined by comparing the scores of the same measuring device administered to the same people on two different occasions.

Tetrachoric Correlation

A correlational technique used to estimate the Pearson-Product correlation of two continuous variables that have been dichotomized (Example: age is continuous, but when it is split into two groups, such as over 40 and under 40, it becomes dichotomous).

Thalamus

Considered the central switching station of the brain because all of the body's senses (except the olfactory senses) pass through this before being relayed to the brain.

Thematic Apperception Test (TAT)

A subjective personality test where ambiguous pictures are shown to a subject and they are asked to tell a story related to them.

Theory

A general idea about the relationship of two or more variables.

Time Series Design

A research design where subjects are measured at specific times before and after the treatment has been administered in order to determine the long term effects of the treatment

Trait

A relatively permanent internal characteristic (e.g., friendly, outgoing)

Transference

Intense feelings directed toward the therapist that many individuals experience in the process of therapy.

Trial and Error Learning

Learning that takes place through the application of possible solutions to a problem.

True Experiment

Research design that utilizes the most control over subjects and utilizes randomization

True Score

the amount of the observed score that truly represents what you are intending to measure.

Two-Way ANOVA

An Analysis of Variance used when there are two independent variables.

Type A Personality

A theory used to describe a person with a significant number of traits focused on urgency, impatience, success, and excessive competition.

Type B Personality

A theory used to describe person with a significant number of traits focused on relaxation, lack of urgency, and normal or reduced competition.

Type I Error

The error that is committed when a true null hypothesis is rejected erroneously. The probability of a Type I Error is abbreviated with the lowercase Greek letter alpha.

Unconditional Positive Regard

The nonjudgmental empathy and respect for another person.

Unconditioned Response

The response in a stimulus-response chain that is naturally occurring as opposed to learned.

Unconditioned Stimulus

The stimulus in a stimulus-response chain that is naturally occurring as opposed to learned.

Unconscious

According to Freud, the area of the psyche where unknown wishes and needs are kept that play a significant role in our conscious behavior.

Upper Confidence Level

The upper limit of a confidence interval. If prediction states that the true score falls between 80 and 90, then the upper confidence level is 90.

Validity

Statistical technique used to determine if a test is actually measuring what it is intended to measure.

Variability

The degree to which a distribution of scores vary around the mean. High variability means scores are spread wider apart and low variability means scores are relatively close together. Typical ways of determining variability are the range, interquartile range, semi-interquartile range, variance, and standard deviation.

Variable

Any factor which has the potential to influence another factor in a research study.

Variable Interval Schedule

A schedule in which the reinforcement is presented after a varying amount of time.

Variable Ratio Schedule

A schedule in which the reinforcement is presented after a varying number of responses.

Variance

A measure of spread within a distribution (the square of the standard deviation).

Vicarious Reinforcement

The reinforcement that occurs as a result of watching a model get reinforced for a specific behavior or series of behaviors.

WAIS-III

See Wechsler Adult Intelligence Scale, Third Edition.

Weber's Law

The amount of change necessary to detect a different in a stimuli must be staged in a percentage since recognition of the change is relative to the characteristics of the initial stimulus (e.g., a one pound change in the weight of a pencil would be more easily recognized than a one pound weight added to a 300 pound barbell because it represents a much greater percentage of the total weight).

Wechsler Adult Intelligence Scale, Third Edition

An objective measure of intelligence. The Stanford-Binet test is also used, has very similar validity, but is not as popular.

Wernicke's Aphasia

Aphasia resulting from damage to the Wernicke's area of the frontal lobe. Affects written and spoken language.

Yerkes-Dodson Law

Theory arguing that for performance to be optimal, the amount of arousal required must be opt

Zero Correlation

the absence of a relationship between two or more variables as determined by a correlational statistic. Often abbreviated as 'r=0.'

z-score

a standard score that sets the mean to zero and standard deviation to one.

z-test

The statistical formula to determine the z-score of a particular raw score.

APPENDIX C

PSYCHOLOGICAL ACADEMIES

Academy for Eating Disorders
http://www.aedweb.org/
A multidisciplinary professional organization focused on eating disorders research and treatment. Website offers information on group memberships, annual conferences, and links.

Academy of Counseling Psychology
http://www.aacop.net/
Site provides information about the organization and also provides helpful links to other sites.

American Academy of Child and Adolescent Psychiatry (AACAP)
http://www.aacap.org/
Website has information on AACAP membership, meetings, publications, research and more.

American Academy of Clinical Neuropsychology
http://www.theaacn.org/
Website provides AACN mission statement, news, bylaws and other links.

American Academy of Psychiatry and the Law
http://www.aapl.org/

AAPL is an organization of psychiatrists dedicated to excellence in practice, teaching, and research in forensic psychiatry.

American Academy of Psychoanalysis and Dynamic Psychiatry
http://aapsa.org/
An online journal with articles related to the field of psychoanalysis.

American Association of Community Psychiatrists (AACP)
http://www.communitypsychiatry.org/
Website contains the association's mission statement as well as links to electronic communities, information about conferences, and links related to community psychiatry.

American Association of Geriatric Psychiatry
http://www.aagpgpa.org/
Website provides news, facts, tools, and expert information for adults coping with mental health issues and aging. Also includes materials for the medical community and other professionals with an interest in geriatric mental health, as well as an online catalog of AAGP news, events, and the association's background.

American Psychiatric Association
http://www.psych.org/
 A site that contains information on diagnosis and treatment of mental and emotional illnesses and substance abuse disorders.

American Psychiatric Nurses Association
http://www.apna.org/
 This website contains news on the field of the psychiatric nursing, position papers, resources from APNA News, and graduate programs in Psychiatric Nursing.

American Psychoanalytic Association
http://apsa.org/
 New research in the field, including subjects such as dreaming, homophobia, and recovered memories. Also includes information about membership, new publications, and other news.

American Psychological Association
http://www.apa.org/
 The APA website contains information about APA publications and other news in the field of psychology. Also, it contains links to other psychology sites, as well as opportunities for research.

American Psychological Society (APS)
http://www.psychologicalscience.org/
 Through the web page of APS, you can find job listings and an electronic form for placing employment ads in the Observer. The site also has the latest convention program information as well as links to dozens of psychology organizations and federal agencies. Also, you can find online news and reports on a wide variety of topics in the field.

Association for Advancement of Behavior Therapy
http://www.aabt.org/

In addition to general information about behavior therapy, this website provides access to the publications of the association and convention news.

Association for Behavior Analysis
http://www.wmich.edu/aba/
 The Association for Behavior Analysis is dedicated to promoting the experimental, theoretical, and applied analysis of behavior. It encompasses contemporary scientific and social issues, theoretical advances, and the dissemination of professional and public information.

Association of Black Psychologists
http://www.abpsi.org/
 The Association of Black Psychologists is the leader and international resource for addressing the psychological needs of African people in the Diaspora. Website offers information on the organization's history, as well as information on membership and the association's annual convention.

Anxiety Disorders Association of America
http://www.adaa.org/
 The ADAA promotes the prevention and cure of anxiety disorders and works to improve the lives of all people who suffer from them. The association consists of professionals who conduct research and treat anxiety disorders, and individuals who have a personal or general interest in learning more about such disorders.

B. F. Skinner Foundation
http://www.bfskinner.org/
 The B. F. Skinner Foundation was established in 1987 to publish significant literary and scientific works in the analysis of behavior and to educate both professionals and the public about the science of behavior.

Eating Disorders Association (EDA)

http://www.edauk.com/

This site provides information and help on all aspects of eating disorders including Anorexia Nervosa, Bulimia Nervosa, Binge Eating Disorder and related eating disorders.

Experimental Psychology Society

http://www.eps.ac.uk/

The Experimental Psychology Society is for the promotion of scientific inquiry within the field of psychology and cognate subjects. It holds periodical meetings at which papers are read and discussions held. The Society also disseminates information and educational material made available as a consequence of psychological research, including the Quarterly Journal of Experimental Psychology.

Federation of Behavioral, Psychological and Cognitive Sciences

http://www.thefederationonline.org/

A coalition dedicated to science, advocacy, education, and communication.

International Association for Cross-Cultural Psychology

http://www.fit.edu/CampusLife/clubs-org/iaccp/

Find news related to the association as well as membership information, IACCP publications, and seminars.

International Association of Applied Psychology

http://www.iaapsy.org/

The International Association of Applied Psychology is the oldest international association of psychologists. Its official languages are English and French. Founded in 1920, it now has more than 2,000 members from more than 94 countries. Its aims are to establish contact between those who, in different countries, devote themselves to scientific work in the various fields of applied psychology, and to advance the study and achievement of means likely to contribute to the scientific and social development in these fields.

International Society for Research on Aggression

http://www.israsociety.com/

A society of scholars and scientists interested in the scientific study of aggression and violence. Website provides information about the history of ISRA, the location of previous ISRA World Meetings, information about the upcoming World Meeting, abstracts of papers presented at the XIII and XIV World Meetings, and links to other societies of researchers.

International Society of Political Psychology

http://ispp.org/

Through this web page you can explore the Political Psychology archives, find information on the annual meetings, read the ISPP Newsletter, find examples of political psychology syllabi, view political psychology bibliographies by topics, connect to political psychology resources on the web, and find out about degree programs in Political Psychology.   .

The Higher Education Academy Psychology Network (formerly LTSN Psychology)

http://www.psychology.ltsn.ac.uk/

Find out about LTSN Psychology: its structure and its activities including departmental contacts, specialists, and miniprojects. Also features a searchable database of over 2,000 resources (including software, web pages, videos and textbooks) useful for learning and teaching psychology.

National Alliance for Research on Schizophrenia and Depression (NARSAD)

http://www.narsad.org/

Website contains information about the NARSAD as well as links to information about research grants, publications, and facts on brain disorders.

National Alliance for the Mentally Ill
http://www.nami.org/
A searchable web page that provides information on several subjects such schizophrenia and depression in relation to such issues as youth, family, and sexuality.

National Association of Cognitive-Behavioral Therapists
http://www.nacbt.org/
A website that offers online articles in the field of Cognitive-Behavioral Therapy.

National Center for Post-Traumatic Stress Disorder
http://www.ncptsd.org/
This website offers information on Post-Traumatic Stress Disorder in context of several populations. Offers the ability to search the PTSD Quarterly and the NCP Clinical Quarterly.

National Mental Health Association (NMHA)
http://www.nmha.org/
The NMHA is the country's oldest and largest nonprofit organization addressing all aspects of mental health and mental illness. Website provides links to news, advocacy, and mental health information, as well as an online bookstore and a calendar of events.

Psi Chi-The National Honor Society in Psychology
http://www.psichi.org/
The National Honor Society in Psychology is affiliated with the American Psychological Association and the Association of College Honor Societies.

Society for Human Resource Management
http://www.shrm.org/
The website of SHRM provides the chances for searching the HR Library, as well as the online publications of the society.

Society for Industrial and Organizational Psychology
http://www.siop.org/
Use this website to find information on psychological and behavioral research, ethnic and minority affairs, etc.

Society for Judgment and Decision Making
http://www.sjdm.org/
An interdisciplinary academic organization dedicated to the study of normative, descriptive, and prescriptive theories of decision. Its members include psychologists, economists, organizational researchers, decision analysts, and other decision researchers.

Society for Personality and Social Psychology
http://www.spsp.org/
Information about the society's publications and news is available.

Society for Research in Child Development
http://www.srcd.org/
The purposes of the society are to promote multidisciplinary research in the field of human development, to foster the exchange of information among scientists and other professionals of various disciplines, and to encourage applications of research findings.

Society for the Psychological Study of Social Issues
http://www.spssi.org/
SPSSI is an international group of over 3500 psychologists, allied scientists, students, and others who share a common interest in research on the psychological aspects of important social issues. Website

offers information of conventions and workshops, grants and awards, publications, and teaching resources, including student fellowships.

Substance Abuse and Mental Health Services Administration (SAMHSA)
http://www.samhsa.gov/
Provides information on SAMHSA, grant opportunities, job opportunities, and statistics and data. Affiliated with the U.S. Department of Health and Human Services.

World Psychiatric Association
http://www.wpanet.org/
This web site provides information on psychiatric and mental health education, research, clinical care, and public policy.

APPENDIX D

REFERENCES

Encyclopædia Britannica. Encyclopædia Britannica Online. Encyclopædia Britannica, 2011. Web. 18 Feb. 2011.[2].

"Counseling Psychology Division 17 of the American Psychological Association".

"Distribution of IQ Scores". MSN Encarta. Retrieved 2007-07-08.

"SRMHP: Our Raison d'Être". Retrieved 2008-07-01.

"The mission of the APA [American Psychological Association] is to advance the creation, communication and application of psychological knowledge to benefit society and improve people's lives"; APA (2010). About APA. Retrieved 20 October 2010.

"The Nobel Prize in Physiology or Medicine 1973". Nobel Foundation. Retrieved 2007-07-28.

"Wechsler Adult Intelligence Scale--Revised". Retrieved 2009-03-31.

Adams, H. and Sutker, P. Comprehensive Handbook of Psychopathology, 3rd Ed. Springer. 2001

APA.org

Aristotle Hist. Anim. I.1.488b.25-26.

Aristotle On Memory 450a 15-16.

Arjo Klamer, Robert M. Solow, Donald N. McCloskey (1989). *The Consequences of economic rhetoric.* Cambridge University Press. pp. 173-174. ISBN 978-0521342865.

Association of Black Psychologists, About ABSPi

Banyard, P. (2002). *Psychology in practice: Health.* London, England: Hodder & Stoughton Educational.

Barkow et al. 1992

Barrett, Deirdre. Supernormal Stimuli: How Primal Urges Overran Their Evolutionary Purpose. New York: W.W. Norton, 2010

Barrett, Deirdre. Waistland: The R/Evolutionary Science Behind Our Weight and Fitness Crisis (2007). New York: W.W. Norton. p. 31-51.

Bateman, A. J. (1948). "Intra-sexual selection in Drosophila".*Heredity* **2** (Pt. 3): 349–821. doi:10.1038/hdy.1948.21.PMID 18103134. edit

Beirness, D.J. (1993). Do we really drive as we live? The role of personality factors in road crashes. *Alcohol, Drugs & Driving*, 9, 129–43.

Berman, B.; Singh B.B.; Lao, L.; Langenberg, P.; Li, H.; Hadhazy, V.; Bareta, J. & Hochberg, M. (1999). A randomized trial of acupuncture as an adjunctive therapy in osteoarthritis of the knee. *Rheumatology*, 38, 346–54.

Bowlby, John "Attachment" 1982, P. 57

Boyle, C.M. (1970). Difference between patients' and doctors' interpretation of some common medical terms. *British Medical Journal*, 2, 286–89.

Brune, M. (2006). Evolutionary psychiatry is dead: Long liveth evolutionary psychopathology. Behavioral and Brain Sciences. 29(4), p. 408

Brune, M. (2006). Evolutionary psychiatry is dead: Long liveth evolutionary psychopathology. Behavioral and Brain Sciences. 29(4), p. 408.

Buss, D. M. (1988). "From vigilance to violence: Tactics of mate retention in American undergraduates" (PDF).*Ethology and Sociobiology* **9** (5): 291–317. doi:10.1016/0162-3095(88)90010-6.

Buss, D. M. (2011). Evolutionary psychology.

Buss, D. M.; Larsen, R. J.; Westen, D.; Semmelroth, J. (1992)."Sex differences in jealousy: Evolution, physiology, and psychology". *Psychological Science* **3** (4): 251–255.doi:10.1111/j.1467-9280.1992.tb00038.x.

Buss, D.M. (2011). Evolutionary Psychology: The New Science of the Mind

Buss, David (2004). *Evolutionary Psychology: The New Science of the Mind*. Boston: Pearson Education, Inc. ISBN 978-0205483389.

Cassileth, B.R.; Lusk, E.J.; Strouse, T.B.; Miller, D.S.; Brown, L.L.; Cross, P.A. & Tenaglia, A.N. (1984). Psychosocial status in chronic illness. *New England Journal of Medicine*, 311, 506–11.

Cavalli-Sfornza, L. and M. Feldman. 1981. *Cultural Transmission and Evolution: A Quantitative Approach*. Princeton, New Jersey: Princeton University Press.

CDC pdf

Charles Taylor, *Philosophical Arguments* (Harvard University Press, 1997), 12; 15.

Chomsky, N.A. (1959), A Review of Skinner's Verbal Behavior

Clark, M.; Hampson, S.E.; Avery, L. & Simpson, R. (2004). Effects of a tailored lifestyle self-management intervention in patients with type 2 diabetes. *British Journal Of Health Psychology*, 9 (Pt 3), 365–79.

Confer et al. 2010; Buss, 2005; Durrant & Ellis, 2003; Pinker, 2002; Tooby & Cosmides, 2005

Daly & Wilson 1998

Daly, Matin, and Margo I. Wilson. (1999)

Dawkins, Richard, "The Extended Phenotype", Oxford University Press 1982 (Chapter 9)

Deacon, Terrence W. (1997) The Symbolic Species: The Co-evolution of Language and the Brain. W.W. Norton & Co

Definition and explanation of inclusive fitness from Personality Research.org

Demetriou, A. (1998). *Cognitive development. In A. Demetriou, W. Doise, K. F. M. van Lieshout (Eds.)*, Life-span developmental psychology *(pp. 179-269). London: Wiley.*

Dowsett, S.M.; Saul, J.L.; Butow, P.N.; Dunn, S.M.; Boyer, M.J.; Findlow, R. & Dunsmore, J. (2000). Communication styles in the cancer consultation: Preferences for a patient-centred approach. *Psycho-Oncology*, 9, 147–56.

Duntley, J.D.; Buss, D.M. (2008). "Evolutionary psychology is a metatheory for psychology" (PDF). Psychological Inquiry 19: 30–34.

Dusseldorp, E.; van Elderen, T.; & Maes, S. (1999). A meta-analysis of psychoeducational programs for coronary heart disease patients.*Health Psychology*, 18, 506–19.

Eccles, J. C. (1992). "Evolution of Consciousness". *Proceedings of the National Academy of Sciences of the United States of America* **89** (16): 7320–7324. JSTOR 2360081.PMC 49701. PMID 1502142.

Everly, G.S., Jr. (1986). An introduction to occupational health psychology. In P.A. Keller & L.G. Ritt (Eds.), *Innovations in clinical practice: A source book*, Vol. 5 (pp. 331–38). Sarasota, FL: Professional Resource Exchange.

Ferguson C.J. & Meehan, D.C. (2011). With friends like these...: Peer delinquency influences across age cohorts on smoking, alcohol and illegal substance use. *European Psychiatry*, 26(1), 6–12.

Francisco W.S. Lima; Tarik Hadzibeganovic, and Dietrich Stauffer. (2009). "Evolution of ethnocentrism on undirected and directed Barabási-Albert networks" (PDF). *Physica A: Statistical Mechanics and its Applications* **388**: 4999–5004.doi:10.1016/j.physa.2009.08.029.

Freeman and Herron. *Evolutionary Analysis.* 2007. Pearson Education, NJ.

G.W.F. Hegel *The Philosophy of History*, p. 9, Dover Publications Inc., ISBN 0-486-20112-0; 1st ed. 1899

Gangestad, S. W.; Simpson, J. A.; Cousins, A. J.; Garver-Apgar, C. E.; Christensen, P. N. (2004). "Women's preferences for male behavioral displays change across the menstrual cycle" (PDF). *Psychological Science* **15** (3): 203–207.doi:10.1111/j.0956-7976.2004.01503010.x.PMID 15016293.

George C Williams, *Adaptation and Natural Selection*. p.4.

Geraskov, Emil Asenov The internal contradiction and the unconscious sources of activity. The Journal of Psychology November 1, 1994 Retrieved from [1] April 17, 2007

Gestalt Theory, By Max Wertheimer, Published by Hayes Barton Press, 1944, ISBN 1593776950, 9781593776954

Gray, P.O. (2010). Foundations for the study of psychology.*Psychology* (6th ed.). New York, New York: Worth Publishers.

Green, C.D. & Groff, P.R. (2003). *Early psychological thought: Ancient accounts of mind and soul*. Westport, Connecticut: Praeger.

Hagen, E and Hammerstein, P (2006). "Game theory and human evolution: A critique of some recent interpretations of experimental games". *Theoretical Population Biology* **69** (3): 339. doi:10.1016/j.tpb.2005.09.005. PMID 16458945

Hagen, EH; Hammerstein, P (2006). "Game theory and human evolution: a critique of some recent interpretations of experimental games". *Theoretical population biology* **69** (3): 339–48. doi:10.1016/j.tpb.2005.09.005. PMID 16458945.

Harper, Douglas. "Etymology of Thought". Online Etymology Dictionary. Retrieved 2009-05-22.

Harris, C. R. (2002). "Sexual and romantic jealousy in heterosexual and homosexual adults". *Psychological Science***13** (1): 7–12. doi:10.1111/1467-9280.00402. PMID 11892782.

Haselton, M. G.; Miller, G. F. (2006). "Women's fertility across the cycle increases the short-term attractiveness of creative intelligence" (PDF). *Human Nature* **17** (1): 50–73.doi:10.1007/s12110-006-1020-0.

Hershey, J.C.; Niederdeppe, J. & Evans, W.D. (2005). The theory of 'truth': How counterindustry campaigns affect smoking behavior among teens. *Health Psychology*, 24, 22–31.

Hockenbury & Hockenbury. Psychology. Worth Publishers, 2010.

How weird are you oddball minds of the Western world(registration required)

Jacob Klein *A Commentary on the Meno* p. 112

Jacob Klein *A Commentary on the Meno* p.109

Jensen, Peter S., Mrazek, David, Knapp, Penelope K., Steinberg, Laurence, Pfeffer, Cynthia, Schowalter, John, & Shapiro, Theodore. (Dec 1997) Evolution and revolution in child psychiatry: ADHD as a disorder of adaptation. (attention-deficit hyperactivity syndrome). Journal of the American Academy of Child and Adolescent Psychiatry. 36. p. 1672. (10). July 14, 2007.

Johnson, J.V.; Stewart, W.; Hall, E.M.; Fredlund, P.; & Theorell, T. (1996). Long-term psychosocial work environment and cardiovascular mortality among Swedish men. *American Journal of Public Health*, 86, 324–31

Johnson-Laird, P.N. & Byrne, R.M.J. (1991). *Deduction*. Hillsdale: Erlbaum

Johnson-Laird, P.N. (2006). *How we reason*. Oxford: Oxford University Press

Kasl, S.V. & Cobb, S. (1970). Blood pressure changes in men undergoing job loss: A preliminary report. *Psychosomatic Medicine*, 32, 19–38.

Kaufman, Alan S.; Lichtenberger, Elizabeth (2006). *Assessing Adolescent and Adult Intelligence* (3rd ed.). Hoboken (NJ): Wiley. p. 3. ISBN 978-0-471-73553-3. Lay summary (22 August 2010).

Kaufman, Alan S.; Lichtenberger, Elizabeth (2006). *Assessing Adolescent and Adult Intelligence* (3rd ed.). Hoboken (NJ): Wiley. p. 6. ISBN 978-0-471-73553-3. Lay summary (22 August 2010).

Kaufman, Alan S.; Lichtenberger, Elizabeth (2006). *Assessing Adolescent and Adult Intelligence* (3rd ed.). Hoboken (NJ): Wiley. p. 7. ISBN 978-0-471-73553-3. Lay summary (22 August 2010).

Kirk; Raven; Schofield (1983), *The Presocratic Philosophers*(second ed.), Cambridge University Press. See pages 204 and 235.

Kompier, M.A.J.; Aust, B.; van den Berg, A.-M. & Siegrist, J. (2000). Stress prevention in bus drivers: Evaluation of 13 natural experiments.*Journal of Occupational Health Psychology*, 5, 32–47.

Laland, Kevin N. and Gillian R. Brown. 2002. *Sense & Nonsense: Evolutionary Perspectives on Human Behavior.*Oxford University Press, Oxford. pp. 287-319.

Lander, D.A. & Graham-Pole, J.R. (2008). Love medicine for the dying and their caregivers: The body of evidence. *Journal of Health Psychology*, 13, 201–12.

Li, N. P.; Bailey, J. M.; Kenrick, D. T.; Linsenmeier, J. A. W. (2002). "The necessities and luxuries of mate preferences: Testing the tradeoffs" (PDF). *Journal of Personality and Social Psychology* **6**: 947–955. PMID 12051582.

Manktelow, K.I. 1999. *Reasoning and Thinking (Cognitive Psychology: Modular Course.)*. Hove, Sussex:Psychology Press

Marmot, M.G. & Theorell, T. (1988). Social class and cardiovascular disease: The contribution of work. *International Journal of Health Services*, 18, 659–74.

Martin Heidegger, *What is Called Thinking?*

Maslow's Hierarchy of Needs

Mealey, Linda (2010). "The sociobiology of sociopathy: An integrated evolutionary model". *Behavioral and Brain Sciences***18** (3): 523–541. doi:10.1017/S0140525X00039595.

Melzack, R. (1975). The McGill Pain Questionnaire: Major properties and scoring methods. *Pain*, 1, 277–99.

Miller, G. F. (2000b) *The mating mind: How sexual choice shaped the evolution of human nature.* Anchor Books: New York.

Nichols, S.; Grantham, T. (2000). "Adaptive Complexity and Phenomenal Consciousness". *Philosophy of Science* **67** (4): 648–670. JSTOR 188711.

Nowak, MA; Sigmund, K (1998). "Evolution of indirect reciprocity by image scoring". *Nature* **393** (6685): 573–7.doi:10.1038/31225. PMID 9634232.

O'Connell, H. (2004) Evolutionary theory in psychiatry and psychology. Irish Journal of Psychological Medicine, 21 (1), pp. 37-37.

O'Brien, J.M.; Forrest, L.M. & Austin, A.E. (2002). Death of a partner: Perspectives of heterosexual and gay men. *Journal of Health Psychology*, 7, 317–28.

Ogden, J.; Bavalia, K.; Bull, M.; Frankum, S.; Goldie, C.; Gosslau, M.; et al. (2004) 'I want more time with my doctor': A quantitative study of time and the consultation. *Family Practice*, 21, 479–83.

Ohman, A.; Mineka, S. (2001). "Fears, phobias, and preparedness: Toward an evolved module of fear and fear learning" (PDF). *Psychological Review* **108** (3): 483–522.doi:10.1037/0033-295X.108.3.483. PMID 11488376. Retrieved 2008-06-16.

Omar Tonsi Eldakar; David Sloan Wilson, and Rick O'Gorman. (2006). "Emotions and actions associated with altruistic helping and punishment" (PDF). Evolutionary Psychology 4: 274–286. Retrieved 2010-08-15.

Omar Tonsi Eldakar; David Sloan Wilson. (2008)."Selfishness as second-order altruism" (PDF). *Proceedings of the National Academy of Sciences of the USA* **105** (19): 6982–6986. doi:10.1073/pnas.0712173105.PMC 2383986. PMID 18448681. Retrieved 2010-08-15.

O'Neil HF, cited in Coon D; Mitterer JO (2008). Introduction to psychology: Gateways to mind and behavior (12th ed., pp. 15–16). Stamford, CT: Cengage Learning.

Online Etymology Dictionary. (2001). "Psychology".

Panksepp, J. & Panksepp, J. (2000). The Seven Sins of Evolutionary Psychology. Evolution and Cognition, 6:2, 108-131.

Panskepp J (1998). *Affective neuroscience: The foundations of human and animal emotions.* New York: Oxford University Press, p. 9.

Piaget, J. (1951). *Psychology of Intelligence.* London: Routledge and Kegan Paul

Pierce, J.P.; & Gilpin, E.A. (1995). A historical analysis of tobacco marketing and the uptake of smoking by youth in the United States: 1890–1977. *Health Psychology*, 14, 500–508.

Pinker 2002

Pinker, S. (1999). *How the Mind Works*. WW Norton & Co. New York. pp. 386–389

Pinker, Steven. (1994)The Language Instinct

Politics I.2.1252b15

Psychology. (n.d.). In Merriam-Webster Medical Dictionary. Retrieved from merriam-webster.com

Resnicow, K.; Jackson, A.; Blissett, D.; Wang, T.; McCarty, F.; Rahotep, S.; & Periasamy, S. (2005). Results of the Healthy Body Healthy Spirit Trial. *Health Psychology*, 24, 339–48.

Rousseau (1997), "Preface", in Gourevitch, *Discourse on the Origin and Foundations of Inequality Among Men or Second Discourse*, Cambridge University Press

Rowan, John. (2001). Ordinary Ecstasy: The Dialectics of Humanistic Psychology. London, UK: Brunner-Routledge.ISBN 0-415-23633-9

Ryan, Christopher and Cacilda Jethá. Sex at Dawn: The Prehistoric Origins of Modern Sexuality. Harper. 2010.

Sharman, S.J.; Garry, M.; Jacobsen, J.A.; Loftus, E.F.; & Ditto, P.H. (2008). False memories for end-of-life decisions. *Health Psychology*, 27, 291–96.

Snowden, Ruth (2006). *Teach Yourself Freud*. McGraw-Hill. p. 107. ISBN 9780071472746.

Sterelny, Kim. 2009. In Ruse, Michael & Travis, Joseph (eds) Wilson, Edward O. (Foreword) Evolution: The First Four Billion Years. Harvard University Press, Cambridge, Ma. ISBN 978-0674031753. p. 314.

Strauss, Leo, "Progress or Return", *An Introduction to Political Philosophy*

Sulloway, F. (1996). Born to rebel. NY: Pantheon.

Symons, D. (1979). The evolution of human sexuality. Oxford: Oxford University Press. Chapter 6.

The Cambridge companion to Freud, By Jerome Neu, Published by Cambridge University Press, 1991, pg, 29, ISBN 052137779X, 9780521377799

The Handbook of Evolutionary Psychology (2005), David M. Buss, Chapter 1, pp. 5-67, Conceptual Foundations of Evolutionary Psychology, John Tooby and Leda Cosmides

The Origins of the Modern Mind p.173 see also *A Mind So Rare* p.140-1

The Psychology of the Social, Uwe Flick, Cambridge University Press, 1998. ISBN 0521588510.

Velkley, Richard (2002), "Freedom, Teleology, and Justification of Reason", *Being after Rousseau: Philosophy and Culture in Question*, University of Chicago Press

Velkley, Richard (2002), "Speech. Imagination, Origins: Rousseau and the Political Animal", *Being after Rousseau: Philosophy and Culture in Question*, University of Chicago Press

Vickers, John, "The Problem of Induction", The Stanford Encyclopedia of Philosophy, 2009,http://plato.stanford.edu/entries/induction-problem/

Webster's II New College Dictionary, Webster Staff, Webster, Houghton Mifflin Company, Edition: 2, illustrated, revised Published by Houghton Mifflin Harcourt, 1999, ISBN 0395962145, 9780395962145, pg. 1147

Wechsler, David (1939). The Measurement of Adult Intelligence. Baltimore (MD): Williams & Witkins. p. 229.

Whalen, C.K.; Jamner, L.D.; Henker, B. & Delfino, R.J. (2001). Smoking and moods in adolescents with depressive and aggressive dispositions: Evidence from surveys and electronic diaries. *Health Psychology*, 20, 99–111.

Wilcox, A. J.; Dunson, D. B.; Weinberg, C. R.; Trussell, J.; Baird, D. D. (2001). "Likelihood of conception with a single act of intercourse: Providing benchmark rates for assessment of post-coital contraceptives". *Contraception* **63** (4): 211–215.doi:10.1016/S0010-7824(01)00191-3. PMID 11376648.

Wilson, Edward O. 1975.*Sociobiology: The New Synthesis.*Harvard University Pre ss, Cambridge, Ma. ISBN 0-674-00089-7 p.4.

Wilson, Edward O. 1978. *On Human Nature*. Harvard University Press, Cambridge, Ma. p. x.

Wilson, G.D. Love and Instinct. London: Temple Smith, 1981.

Windholz, G. (1997). "Ivan P. Pavlov: An overview of his life and psychological work". *American Psychologist* **52**: 941–946.doi:10.1037/0003-066X.52.9.941.

Workman & Reader (2008), Evolutionary Psychology, 2nd Ed. Cambridge: Cambridge University Press.

Workman, Lance and Will Reader (2004) Evolutionary psychology: an introduction. Cambridge University Press, Chapter 13.

Wozniak, R.H. (1999). Introduction to memory: Hermann Ebbinghaus (1885/1913). Classics in the history of psychology

Wright 1995

"ABPsi Homepage".

"MFDP / College Programs / HPSP / Associations".

"Nature vs. Nurture: An Unnecessary Debate." A Public Health Perspective. ;July. 2000. 20 Nov. 2001. http://www.cdc.gov/genetics/info/files/text/nvsn.pdf

"Ncabr.Org: About Biomedical Research: Faq". Retrieved 2008-07-01.

"SAGE—the natural home for authors, editors and societies—Journal of Black Psychology".

^ Adams, H. and Sutker, P. Comprehensive Handbook of Psychopathology, 3rd Ed. Springer. 2001. Chapter 3, p 53-84.

^ Hergenhahn BR (2005). An introduction to the history of psychology. Belmont, CA, USA: Thomson Wadsworth. pp. 528–536.

_development_nature_vs.html?page=3.

Abramson, P. R. & Pinkerton, S. D. (1995). *h Pleasure: Thoughts on the Nature of Human Sexuality*. New York, NY: Oxford University press.

AC Content Producer (December 16, 2005). *The Childhood Nature vs. Nurture Debate Continues*. Retrieved January 7, 2008, from the Associated Content Web site: http://www.associatedcontent.com/article/16572/the_childhood

Achterbergh, Jan & Vriens, Dirk (May-June 2002). "Managing viable knowledge." *Systems Research and Behavioral Science*. V19 i3 p223(19).

Adams, H. and Sutker, P. Comprehensive Handbook of Psychopathology, 3rd Ed. Springer. 2001. Chapter 5, p 105-127

Adler, A. (1989). *Individual psychology of Alfred Adler: A systematic presentation in selections from his writings*. New York: HarperCollins.

Aidman, Eugene, Galanis, George, Manton, Jeremy, Vozzo, Armando and Bonner, Michael (2002)

'Evaluating human systems in military training', Australian Journal of Psychology, 54:3, 168–173

Alasdair MacIntyre, *Dependent Rational Animals: Why Human Beings Need the Virtues*, Peru, Illinois: 2002.

Alderfer, C. (1972). *Existence, relatedness, & growth*. New York: Free Press.

Allen, G. (2002). The measure of a Victorian polymath: Pulling together the strands of Francis Galton's legacy to modern biology. *Nature*, 145(3), 19-20.

Allport, G. (1955). *Becoming: Basic considerations for a psychology of personality*. New Haven, CT: Yale Univ Press.

Allport, G. (1960). *Personality and social encounter: Selected essays*. New York: Beacon Press.

Allport, G. (1961). *Pattern and growth in personality*. New York: Holt, Rinehart and Winston.

American Psychiatric Association. Diagnostic and statistical manual of mental disorders (4th ed., text revision). 2000. Culture Bound Syndromes, p 897-903.

Ames, C. (1992). Classroom goals, structures, and student motivation. *Journal of Educational Psychology*, *84*(3), 261-271.

Aristotle, Complete Works (2 volumes), Princeton, 1995,ISBN 0-691-09950-2

Aristotle's Psychology". Stanford Encyclopedia of Philosophy.

Awodola, Orisade (November 17, 2004). "Association of Black Psychologists Aim Towards Certification". Washington Informer. Retrieved 2008-06-15.

Ayres, A. (2005) *Sensory Integration and the Child: Understanding Hidden Sensory Challenges* Los Angeles: WPS.

Baars, Bernard J. *A Cognitive Theory of Consciousness*.1993. Cambridge University Press.

Bailey, J. M., & Pillard, R. C. (1991). A genetic study of male sexual orientation. *Archives of General Psychiatry*, 48:1089-1096.

Bailey, J. M., & Pillard, R. C., Neale, M. C., & Agyei, Y. (1993). Heritable factors influence sexual orientation in women. *Archives of General Psychiatry*, 50:217-223.

Bandura, A. (1973). Aggression: A social learning analysis. Englewood Cliffs, NJ: Prentice-Hall.

Bandura, A. (1986). *Social foundations of thought and action: A social-cognitive theory*. Upper Saddle River, NJ: Prentice-Hall.

Bandura, A. (1997). *Self-efficacy: The exercise of control*. New York: W. H. Freeman.

Bergin, D. A., & Cizek, G. J. (2001). Alfred Binet. In J. A. Palmer (Ed.), *Fifty major thinkers on education: From Confucius to Dewey* (pp. 160-164). London: Routledge.

Bernstein, D. A., Clarke-Stewart, A., Roy, E. J., & Wickens, C. D. (1997). *Psychology*, 4th ed. MA: Houghton Mifflin Company.

Beveridge A (2002). "Time to abandon the subjective—objective divide?". The Psychiatrist 26, pp. 101–103. Retrieved 20 April 2010.

Beyerstein, B.L. (2001). Fringe psychotherapies: The public at risk. The Scientific Re-view of Alternative Medicine, 5, 70–79

Bhagavad Gita, Sarvepalli Radhakrishnan: "Hinduism is not just a faith. It is the union of reason and intuition that can not be defined but is only to be experienced."

Binet, A. (1916). New methods for the diagnosis of the intellectual level of subnormals. In E. S. Kite (Trans.), *The development of intelligence in children*. Vineland, NJ: Publications of the Training School at Vineland. (Originally published 1905 in *L'Année Psychologique, 12*, 191-244.) See related introduction and commentary by Henry L. Minton.

Binet. A., & Simon, T. (1916). *The development of intelligence in children*. Baltimore, Williams & Wilkins. (Reprinted 1973, New York: Arno Press; 1983, Salem, NH: Ayer Company). The 1973 volume includes reprints of many of Binet's articles on testing.

Bloom B. S. (1956). Taxonomy of Educational Objectives, Handbook I: The Cognitive Domain. New York: David McKay Co Inc.

Blum 1994, p. 95, Blum 2002, pp. 218–219. Blum 1994, p. 95: "... the most controversial experiment to come out of the Wisconsin laboratory, a device that Harlow insisted on calling the "pit of despair."

Blum, Deborah. Love at Goon Park: Harry Harlow and the Science of Affection. Perseus Publishing, 2002. ISBN 0-7382-0278-9

Booth, Wayne C. *Modern Dogma and the Rhetoric of Assent*, Volume 5, of University of Notre Dame, Ward-Phillips lectures in English language and literature, University of Chicago Press, 1974, p. 114. Booth is explicitly discussing this experiment. His next sentence is, "His most recent outrage consists of placing monkeys in "solitary" for twenty days—what he calls a "vertical chamber apparatus ... designed on an intuitive basis" to produce "a state of helplessness and hopelessness, sunken in a well of despair."

Boulding, K. (1956). General systems theory--the skeleton of science. Management Science, 2, 197-208. (Reprinted in E:CO, 6(1-2), 127-139, 2004). Retrieved April 2005, from http://emergentpublications.com/eco/ECO_other/Issue_6_1-2_18_CP.pdf

Brain, Christine. (2002). Advanced psychology: applications, issues and perspectives. Cheltenham: Nelson Thornes. ISBN 0-17-490058-9

Breslow, L., & Buell, P. (1960) Mortality form CHD and physical activity of work in California. Journal of Chronic Disease, 11, 615-626.

Bruner, Jerome (1990). *Acts of Meaning*. Harvard University Press. ISBN 0674003608.

Brunstein, J. C., & Maier, G. W. (2005). Implicit and self-attributed motives to achieve: Two separate but interacting needs. *Journal of Personality and Social Psychology, 89*, 205-222.

Bryner, Jeanna (July 19, 2006). *Nature vs. Nurture: Mysteries of Individuality Unraveled*. Retrieved January 7, 2008, from the LiveScience Web site: http://www.livescience.com/health/

BSA (2006) *Is There a Cure for Stammering?* British Stammering Association [WWW] http://www.stammering.org/cure.html Accessed 29.01.2010.

Buller, David J. and Valerie Gray Hardcastle (2005) Chapter 4. "Modularity", in Buller, David J. The Adapted Mind: Evolutionary Psychology. The MIT Press. pp. 127—201

Bureau of Labor Statistics, U.S. Department of Labor, Occupational Outlook Handbook, 2010–11

Edition, Psychologists, on the Internet at bls.gov (visited July 08, 2010).

Bureau of Labor Statistics, U.S. Department of Labor, *Occupational Outlook Handbook, 2006-07 Edition*, Psychologists, on the Internet at http://www.bls.gov/oco/ocos056.htm

Buss, D. M. (1989). "Sex differences in human mate preferences: Evolutionary hypotheses tested in 37 cultures".*Behavioral and Brain Sciences* **12**: 1–49. doi:10.1017/S0140525X00023992.

Buss, D. M. (1994). *The evolution of desire: Strategies of human mating.* New York: Basic Books.

Buss, D. M.; Barnes, M. (1986). "Preferences in human mate selection" (PDF). *Journal of Personality and Social Psychology* **50** (3): 559–570. doi:10.1037/0022-3514.50.3.559.

Buss, D.M. (2011). Evolutionary Psychology. Monterey: Brooks-Cole.

Butler, R. (1999). Information seeking and achievement motivation in middle childhood and adolescence: The role of conceptions of ability.*Developmental Psychology, 35,* 146-163.

Bynum, W. F. (2002). The childless father of eugenics. *Science, 296,* 472.

Byrne, R.M.J. (2005). *The Rational Imagination: How People Create Counterfactual Alternatives to Reality.* Cambridge, MA: MIT Press

Calkins, M. W. (1906) A reconciliation between structural and functional psychology. *Psychological Review,* 13, 61-81*

Carli, L. L., Ganley, R., & Pierce-Otay, A. (1991). Similarity and satisfaction in romantic relationships. *Personality and Social Psychology Bulletin,* 17:419-426.

Carver, C., & Scheier, M. (2004). Perspectives on Personality (5th ed.). Boston: Pearson.

Catherwood, D. (2000) 'New views on the young brain: offerings from developmental psychology to early childhood education' *Contemporary Issues in Early Childhood* 1, 1.

Clark, William R. and Michael Grunstein. Are we Hardwired?. New York, NY: Oxford University Press, 2000.

Clarkson P (1996). The eclectic and integrative paradigm: Between the Scylla of confluence and the Charybdis of

confusion. In Handbook of Counselling Psychology (R Woolfe & WL Dryden, eds.). London: Sage, pp. 258–283. ISBN 0-8039-8991-1

Classics in the History of Psychology—Marko Marulic – The Author of the Term "Psychology"

Clayes, G. (2001). Introducing Francis Galton, 'Kantsaywhere' and 'The Donoghues of Dunno Weir.' *Utopian Studies,* 12(2), 188-190.

Cobb S, Rose RM. (1973) Hypertension, peptic ulcer, and diabetes in air traffic controllers. JAMA 1973; 224: 489–92

Cobb, S. (1976) Social support as a moderator of life stress. Psychosomatic Medicine, 38, 300-314.

Cofer, C. N. (1972). *Motivation and Emotion.* Glenview, IL: Scott, Foresman and Company.

Cohen, J. (1994). [www.ics.uci.edu/~sternh/courses/210/cohen94_pval.pdf The Earth is round, p < .05], *American Psychologist,* 49, 997–1003.

Cohen, L.M.; McChargue, D.E.; & Collins, Jr. F.L. (Eds.). (2003). *The health psychology handbook: Practical issues for the behavioral medicine specialist.* Thousand Oaks, CA: Sage Publications.

Companion to Metaphysics, By Jaegwon Kim, Gary S. Rosenkrantz, Ernest Sosa, Contributor Jaegwon Kim, Edition: 2, Published by Wiley-Blackwell, 2009, ISBN 1405152982, 9781405152983

Confer, J. C.; Easton, J. A.; Fleischman, D. S.; Goetz, C. D.; Lewis, D. M. G.; Perilloux, C.; Buss, D. M. (2010)."Evolutionary psychology: Controversies, questions, prospects, and limitations". *American Psychologist* **65** (2): 110–126.doi:10.1037/a0018413. PMID 20141266. edit

Coon, D. (1997). *Essentials of Psychology: Exploration and Application,* 7th ed. Pacific Grove, CA: Brooks/Cole Publishing Company.

Cooper. C. L. & Marshall, J. (1976) Occupational sources of stress: A review of the literature relating to CHD and mental ill-health. Journal of Occupational Psychology, 49, 11-28.

Cornelius, R. R. (1996). *The Science of Emotion: Research and Tradition in the Psychology of Emotions.* Upper Saddle River, NJ: Prentice Hall

Cosmides, L; Tooby J (1997-01-13). "Evolutionary Psychology: A Primer". Center for Evolutionary Psychology. Retrieved 2008-02-16.

Costantini, Stefania (2002), "Meta-reasoning: A Survey", *Lecture Notes in Computer Science* **2408/2002** (65), doi:10.1007/3-540-45632-5_11

Cox, R. H. (1991) Intervention strategies. Stress and coping. A. Monet & R. S. Lazarus (eds.) New York: Columbia University Press.

Cox, T., & Mackay, C. (1976). *A psychological model of occupational stress.* A paper presented to The Medical Research Council. Mental Health in Industry, London, November.

Csikszentmihihaly, M. (1990). *Flow: The psychology of optimal experience.* New York: Harper & Row.

Dallman MF, Pecoraro NC, la Fleur SE. Chronic stress and comfort foods: self-medication and abdominal obesity. *Brain Behav Immun.* 2005;19:275-280.

Damásio, A. (1994). Descartes' error: Emotion, reason, and the human brain.

Damásio, A. (1996). *The somatic marker hypothesis and the possible functions of the prefrontal cortex.*

Damásio, A. (1999). *The feeling of what happens: Body and emotion in the making of consciousness.*

Damásio, A. (2003). *Looking for Spinoza: Joy, sorrow, and the feeling brain.*

Dave, R. H. (1975). *Developing and Writing Behavioral Objectives.* (R. J. Armstrong, ed.). Tucson, Arizona: Educational Innovators Press.

Davenport T., Prusak L. (1998). Working Knowledge. Harvard Business School Press: Boston, MA.

David F. Marks, Michael Murray, Brian Evans & Emee Vida Estacio (2011) *Health Psychology. Theory-Research-Practice* (3rd Ed.) Sage Publications. ISBN 1848606222 (hbk) 978-1848606227 (pbk).

David F. Marks, Michael Murray, Brian Evans & Emee Vida Estacio (2011) *Health Psychology. Theory-Research-Practice* (3rd Ed.) Sage Publications. ISBN 1848606222 (hbk) 978-1848606227 (pbk).

David G. Myers, McGraw Hill, 1993. *Social Psychology.* ISBN 0070442924.

Davidson, Herbert (1992), *Alfarabi, Avicenna, and Averroes, on Intellect*, Oxford University Press, page 3.

Dawes, Robyn (1994). *House of Cards—Psychology and Psychotherapy Built on Myth.* Free Press. ISBN 978-0029072059.

Dawkins, R. (1982) "Replicators and Vehicles" King's College Sociobiology Group, eds., *Current Problems in Sociobiology*, Cambridge, Cambridge University Press, pp. 45–64. "A replicator may be defined as any entity in the universe of which copies are made."

De Anima III.i-iii; *On Memory and Recollection, On Dreams*

Demetriou, A. (1998). Cognitive development. In A. Demetriou, W. Doise, K.F.M. van Lieshout (Eds.), Life-span developmental psychology (pp. 179-269). London: Wiley.

Descartes, "Second Meditation".

Dion, K., & Berscheid, E. (1988). Physical attractiveness and sociometric choice in nursery school children. *In*: E. Aronson, *The Social Animal*, 5th ed. New York: W. H. Freeman and Company.

Douglas Hofstadter, Gödel, Escher, Bach, Vintage, 1979, ISBN 0-394-74502-7

Douzenis, A. (2010). Evolution and Psychiatry. 196(3), pp. 246-247

Dweck, C. (1986) Motivational processes affecting learning. *American Psychologist. 41*(10), 1040-1048.

Elliot, A. J., & Church, M. A. (1997). A hierarchical model of approach and avoidance achievement motivation. *Journal of Personality and Social Psychology, 72,* 218-232.

Elliot, A. J., & Harackiewicz, J. M. (1996). Approach and avoidance achievement goals and intrinsic motivation: A mediational analysis. *Journal of Personality and Social Psychology, 70,* 461-475.

Elliot, A. J., & McGregor, H. A. (1999). Test anxiety and the hierarchical model of approach and avoidance achievement motivation. *Journal of Personality and Social Psychology, 76,* 628-644.

Elliot, A. J., & Sheldon, K. M. (1997). Avoidance achievement motivation: A personal goals analysis. *Journal of Personality and Social Psychology, 73,* 171-185.

Elliot, Robert. (1998). Editor's Introduction: A Guide to the Empirically Supported Treatments Controversy. *Psychotherapy Research, 8(2),* 115.

Encyclopædia Britannica. Encyclopædia Britannica Online. Encyclopædia Britannica, 2011. Web. 09 Feb. 2011.[4].

Encyclopædia Britannica. Encyclopædia Britannica Online. Encyclopædia Britannica, 2011. Web. 23 Jan. 2011. [1].

Environment of evolutionary adaptation," a variation of the term used in Economics, e.g., in Rubin, Paul H., 2003, *"Folk economics"* Southern Economic Journal, 70:1, July 2003, 157-171.

Erikson, E. (1993). *Childhood and society.* New York: W. W. Norton & Company.

Evolutionary Psychology at the University of Texas

Fancher, R. E. (1985). *The intelligence men: Makers of the IQ controversy.* New York: W. W. Norton & Company.

Fancher, R. E. (1985). *The intelligence men: Makers of the IQ controversy.* New York: W. W. Norton & Company.

Fancher, R. E. (1996) *Pioneers of Psychology.* New York: Norton.

Fanelli, Daniele (2010). ""Positive" Results Increase Down the Hierarchy of the Sciences". *PLoS ONE* **5** (4).doi:10.1371. Retrieved 10 April 2011.

Farber, Susan. Identical Twins Reared Apart. New York: Basic Books, Inc., 1981

Feingold, A. (1988a). Matching for attractiveness in romantic partners and same-sex friends: A metaanalysis and theoretical critique. *Psychological Bulletin,* 104:226-235.

Feldman M., Cavalli-Sforna L. (1976). "Cultural and biological evolutionary processes, selection for a trait under complex transmission". *Theoretical Population Biology* **9** (2): 238–59.doi:10.1016/0040-5809(76)90047-2. PMID 1273802.

Festinger, L. (1957). *A theory of cognitive dissonance.* Evanston, IL: Row, Peterson.

Field T, Hernandez-Reif M, Diego M, et al. Cortisol decreases and serotonin and dopamine increase following massage therapy. *Int J Neuro*sci. 2005;115:1397-1413.

Fisher, H. (1993). Biology: The natural history of monogamy, adultery, and divorce. *Psychology Today,* March/April:40-45, 82.

Fiske, A.; Kitayama, S.; Markus, H.R.; & Nisbett, R.E. (1998). The cultural matrix of social psychology. In D. Gilbert & S. Fiske & G. Lindzey (Eds.), *The Handbook of Social Psychology* (4th ed., pp. 915–981). San Francisco: McGraw-Hill.

Forest, D. (1995). Francis Galton (1822-1911). In R. Fuller (Ed.), *Seven pioneers of psychology: Behavior and mind* (pp.1-19). Routledge: London and New York.

Fowler, James H. (22 September 2005). "Human cooperation: Second-order free-riding problem solved?".*Nature* **437** (7058): E8. doi:10.1038/nature04201.PMID 16177738.

Franken, R. (2006). *Human motivation* (6th ed.). Florence, KY: Wadsworth.

Franken, R.E. (1988). *Human Motivation.* California: Brooks/Cole.

Frankenhaeuser, M. (1975) Sympathetic adreno-medullary activity and the psychosocial environment. In P. H. Venables & M. J. Christie (eds.) Research in psychophysiology. New York: Willey

Frankenhaeuser, M. et al. (1976) Sex differences in sympathetic adrenal medulary reactions induced by different stressors. Psychopharmacology, 47, 1-5.

Frankl VE (1984). *Man's search for meaning (rev. ed.).* New York, NY, USA: Washington Square Press. pp. 86.

Frankl, V. (1998). *Man's search for meaning* (Revised ed.). New York: Washington Square Press.

Fredrickson, B. (2009). *Positivity: Groundbreaking research reveals how to embrace the hidden strength of positive emotions, overcome negativity, and thrive.* New York: Crown Publishers.

French, J. R. P. Jr. (1974) Person role fit. In A. Mclean (ed) Occupational stress. Springfield Ill: Thomas.

Freud S (1900). *The Interpretation of Dreams.* **IV and V** (2nd ed.). Hogarth Press, 1955.

Freud S (1915). *The Unconscious.* **XIV** (2nd ed.). Hogarth Press, 1955.

Freud, S. (1990). *Beyond the pleasure principle.* New York: W. W. Norton & Company.

Gaulin & McBurney (2004), Evolutionary Psychology, 2nd Ed. NY: Prentice Hall

Gaulin and McBurney 2003 Chapter 7.

Gaulin and McBurney 2003 Chapter 8.

Gaulin and McBurney 2003 Chapter 9.

Gaulin and McBurney 2003 p 101-121.

Gaulin and McBurney 2003 p 121-142.

Gaulin and McBurney 2003 p 1-24.

Gaulin and McBurney 2003 p 239-256.

Gaulin and McBurney 2003 p 25-56.

Gaulin and McBurney 2003 p 81-101.

Gaulin, Steven J. C. and Donald H. McBurney. Evolutionary Psychology. Prentice Hall. 2003. ISBN 13: 9780131115293, Chapter 14, p 323-352.

Gaulin, Steven J. C. and Donald H. McBurney. Evolutionary Psychology. Prentice Hall. 2003. ISBN 9780131115293, Chapter 14, p 323-352.

George A. Miller. The cognitive revolution: a historical perspective, Trends in Cognitive Sciences, Vol.7, No.3, March 2003

Ginsburg KR and the Committee on Communications and Committee on Psychosocial Aspects of Child and Family Health. Clinical Report: The Importance of Play in Promoting Healthy Child Development and Maintaining Strong Parent-ChildBonds. Last accessed on 17 October, 2006.

Gintis, H. (2006). "A framework for the integration of the behavioral sciences". *Behavioral and Brain Sciences* **30**: 1–61.

Glaser, B., & Strauss, A. (1967). *The discovery of grounded theory: Strategies for qualitative research*. Chicago: Aldine.

Goldfried MR, Wolfe BE (1998). Toward a more clinically valid approach to therapy research. *Journal of Consulting and Clinical Psychology, 66*(1), pp. 143–150.

Goldiamond I (1965) 'Stuttering and fluency as manipulable operant response classes' in Krasner, L. and Ullman, L. (eds) *Research in Behavior Modification* New York: Holt, Rinehart and Winston.

Gollowitzer, P. (1996). The psychology of action: Linking cognition and motivation to behavior. New York: Guilford.

Hammerfald K, Grau M, et al. Persistent effects of cognitive-behavioral stress management on cortisol responses to acute stress in healthy subjects-A randomized controlled trial. *Psychoneuroendocrinology*. 2005 Sep 22; epub ahead of print.

Hans Selye (2008). Retrieved from http://en.wikipedia.org/wiki/Hans_Selye on 21 July, 2008

Harackiewicz, J. M., Barron, K. E., Carter, S. M., Lehto, A. T., & Elliot, A. J. (1997). Predictors and consequences of achievement goals in the college classroom: Maintaining interest and making the grade. *Journal of Personality and Social Psychology, 73,* 1284-1295.

Harlow (1868), Fig. 2, p. 347 Harlow, John Martyn (1868). "Recovery from the Passage of an Iron Bar through the Head." Publications of the Massachusetts Medical Society 2:327–347 (Republished in Macmillan 2000).

Harrow, A. (1972) A Taxonomy of Psychomotor Domain: A Guide for Developing Behavioral Objectives. New York: David McKay.

Hatfield, E., & Rapson, R. L. (1993). *Love, Sex and Intimacy*. New York: Harper/Collins.

Hatfield, E., Walster, G. W., Piliavin, J., & Schmidt, L. (1988). "Playing hard to get": Understanding an elusive phenomenon. *In*: L. A. Peplau, D. O. Sears, S. E. Taylor, & J. L. Freedman, eds. *Readings in Social Psychology: Classic and Contemporary Contributions*. pp. 123-132.

Heider, F. (1958). *The psychology of interpersonal relations.*. New York: John Wiley & Sons.

Heine, S.J.; Lehman, D.R.; Peng, K.; Greenholtz, J. (2002). "What's wrong with cross-cultural comparisons of subjective Likert scales: The reference-group problem". *Journal of Personality and Social Psychology* **82**: 903–918. doi:10.1037/0022-3514.82.6.903.

Henriques, G.R. (2003). The Tree of Knowledge System and the Theoretical Unification of Psychology. Review of General Psychology, 2, 150–182.

Herdt, G. (1984). *Ritualized Homosexuality in Melanesia*. Berkeley: University of California Press.

Hergenhahn BR (2005). *An introduction to the history of psychology*. Belmont, CA, USA: Thomson Wadsworth. pp. 523–532.

Hergenhahn BR (2005). *An introduction to the history of psychology*. Belmont, CA, USA: Thomson Wadsworth. pp. 546–547.

Hobbes, Thomas, "VII. Of the ends, or resolutions of discourse", *The English Works of Thomas Hobbes*,

3 (Leviathan) and Hobbes, Thomas, "IX. Of the several subjects of knowledge", *The English Works of Thomas Hobbes*, **3 (Leviathan)**

Hokanson, J. E. (1969). *The Physiological Bases of Motivation.* NY: John Wiley & Sons, Inc.

Holder, M.K. What does handedness have to do with Lateralization(and who cares)?

Holland, Maximilian, "Social Bonding and Nurture Kinship: Compatibility between Cultural and Biological Approaches", London School of Economics, PhD Thesis 2004

Howie, P.M., Tanner, S. and Andrews, G. (1981) 'Short and long-term outcome in an intensive treatment program for adult stammerers' *Journal of Speech and Hearing Disorders* 46, 104–9.

http://en.wikipedia.org/wiki/Reason

http://www.abpsi.org/about_abpsi.htm

http://www.chem1.com/acad/sci/pseudosci.html

http://www.chem1.com/acad/sci/pseudosci.html

http://www.nlm.nih.gov/medlineplus/spinalcordinjuries.html

Hubert Dreyfus, Telepistemology: Descartes' Last Stand",[1] Accessed February 23, 2011.

Huitt, W. & Dawson, C. (2011, April). Social development: Why it is important and how to impact it. Educational Psychology Interactive. Valdosta, GA: Valdosta State University. Retrieved from http://www.edpsycinteractive.org/papers/socdev.pdf

Hume, David, "I.III.VII (footnote) Of the Nature of the Idea Or Belief", A Treatise of Human Nature. It followed from this that animals have reason, only much less complex than human reason.

Hume, David, "I.III.XVI. Of the reason of animals", A Treatise of Human Nature. It followed from this that animals have reason, only much less complex than human reason.

Hume, David, "I.IV.VI. Of Personal Identity", A Treatise of Human Nature

Hume, David, "II.III.III. Of the influencing motives of the will.", A Treatise of Human Nature

Immanuel Kant, *Critique of Pure Reason*; *Critique of Practical Reason.*

Intelligence

Introduction" to the translation of *Poetics* by Davis and Seth Benardete p. xvii, xxviii

Irvine, P. (1986). Sir Francis Galton (1822-1911). *Journal of Special Education*, 20(1).

Izard, C. (1990). Facial expressions and the regulation of emotions. *Journal of Personality and Social Psychology*, 58, 487-498.

Jacob Klein *A Commentary on the Meno* p.122

Jacob Klein A Commentary on the Meno Ch.5

James, W. (1892/1962). *Psychology: Briefer course.* New York: Collier.

James, W. (1904) The Chicago school. *Psychological Bulletin. 1*, 1-5.

James, W. (1997). *The varieties of religious experience* (Reprint ed.). New York: Macmillan.

Jarzombek, M. *The psychologizing of modernity: Art, architecture and history* (Cambridge UK: Cambridge University Press, 2000).

Jeffrey, Richard. 1991. *Formal logic: its scope and limits*, (3rd ed.). New York: McGraw-Hill:1.

Jensen JP, Bergin AE, Greaves DW (1990). The meaning of eclecticism: New survey and analysis of components.*Professional Psychology: Research and Practice, 21*(2), pp. 124–130.

Jensen, A. (2002). Galton's legacy to research on intelligence. *Journal of Biosocial Science*, 34, 145-172.

June 2008 study by the American Psychoanalytic Association, as reported in the *New York Times*, "Freud Is Widely Taught at Universities, Except in the Psychology Department" by Patricia Cohen, November 25, 2007.

Jung, C. (1953). *Modern man in search of a soul.* New York: Harcourt Brace.

Jung, C. (1997). *Man and his symbols* (reissue). New York: Laurelleaf.

Jürgen Habermas, *Moral Consciousness and Communicative Action*, Cambridge, MA: MIT Press, 1995.

Jürgen Habermas, *The Philosophical Discourse of Modernity*, Cambridge, MA: MIT Press, 1990.

Jürgen Habermas, *The Theory of Communicative Action: Reason and the Rationalization of Society*, translated by Thomas McCarthy. Boston: Beacon Press, 1984.

Kalat, J. W. (1996). *Introduction to Psychology*, 4th ed. Pacific Grove: CA Brooks/Cole Publishing Company.

Kamin, L. J. (1995). The pioneers of IQ testing. In Ressell Jacoby & Naomi Glauberman (Eds.), *The Bell Curve Debate: History, Documents, Opinions*. New York: Times Books.

Kant, Immanuel; translated by James W. Ellington [1785] (1993). *Grounding for the Metaphysics of Morals 3rd ed.*. Hackett. pp. 30. ISBN 0-87220-166-x.

Kaplan-Solms, K., & Solms, M. (2000). *Clinical studies in neuro-psychoanalysis: Introduction to a depth neuro-psychology*. London: Karnac Books.

Karl Popper, Conjectures and Refutations, London: Routledge and Keagan Paul, 1963, pp. 33–39; from Theodore Schick, ed., Readings in the Philosophy of Science, Mountain View, CA: Mayfield Publishing Company, 2000, pp. 9–13.Faculty.washington.edu

Kim, J. (1995). Honderich, Ted. ed. *Problems in the Philosophy of Mind. Oxford Companion to Philosophy*. Oxford: Oxford University Press.

Kinsey, A. C., Pomeroy, W. B., & Martin, C. E. (1948). *Sexual Behavior in the Human Male*. Philadelphia: Saunders.

Kinsey, A. C., Pomeroy, W. B., Martin, C. E., & Gebhard, P. H. (1953). *Sexual Behavior in the Human Female*. Philadelphia: Saunders.

Kitayama, S. (2002). "Culture and basic psychological processes—Toward a system view of culture: Comment on Oyserman et al.". *Psychological Bulletin* **128** (1): 89–96. doi:10.1037/0033-2909.128.1.89. PMID 11843550.

Kitayama, S.; Duffy, S.; Kawamura, T.; Larsen, J.T. (2003). "Perceiving an object and its context in different cultures: A cultural look at new look". *Psychological Science* **14** (3): 201–206. doi:10.1111/1467-9280.02432. PMID 12741741.

Kitayama, Shinobu, & Cohen, Dov (2007). *Handbook of Cultural Psychology*. Guilford.

Kleinginna, P., Jr., & Kleinginna A. (1981a). A categorized list of motivation definitions, with suggestions for a consensual definition.*Motivation and Emotion, 5*, 263-291.

Kleinginna, P., Jr., & Kleinginna A. (1981b). A categorized list of emotion definitions, with suggestions for a consensual definition.*Motivation and Emotion, 5*, 345-379.

Kohl , J. V. & Francoeur, R. T. (1995). *The Scent of Eros: Mysteries of Odor in Human Sexuality*. New York: Continuum.

Krathwohl, D. R., Bloom, B. S., & Masia, B. B. (1973). Taxonomy of Educational Objectives, the Classification of Educational Goals. Handbook II: Affective Domain. New York: David McKay Co., Inc.

Kreitzer MJ, Gross CR, Ye X, et al. Longitudinal impact of mindfulness meditation on illness burden in solid-organ transplant recipients. *Prog Transplant.* 2005;15:166-172.

Krough G., Ichijo K., Nonaka I. (2000). Enabling Knowledge Creation. New York: Oxford University Press.

Laan, E., Everaerd, W., Van Bellen, G., & Hanewald, G. J. F. P. (1994). Women's sexual and emotional responses to male- and female-produced erotica. *Archives of Sexual Behavior*, 23(2):153-169.

Large-Scale Features of the Brain, a stop on a Brief Tour of the Brain led by Syracuse

Larzelere MM, Jones GN. Stress and Health. *Primary Care: Clinics in Office Practice.* 2008;35(4):839-856.

Laumann, E. O., Gagnon, J. H., Michael, R. T., & Michaels, S. (1994). *The Social Organization of Sexuality: Sexual Practice in the United States*. Chicago: University of Chicago Press.

LeDoux, J.E. (1998). *The emotional brain: The mysterious underpinnings of emotional life (Touchstone ed.)*. Simon & Schuster. Original work published 1996. ISBN 0-684-83659-9.

Leger, D. W. (1992). *Biological Foundations of Behavior: An Integrative Approach*. NY: Harper Collins Publishers Inc.

Lehrer, Jonah (December 13, 2010). "The Truth Wears Off". The New Yorker. Retrieved 10 April 2011.

Leichsenring, Falk & Leibing, Eric. (2003). The effectiveness of psychodynamic therapy and cognitive behavior therapy in the treatment of personality disorders: A meta-analysis. *The American Journal of Psychiatry, 160(7),* 1223–1233.

Leigh, B. C. (1989). Reasons for having and avoiding sex: Gender, sexual orientation, and relationship to sexual behavior. *The Journal of Sex Research*, 26(2):199-209.

Leonard, N., Beauvais, L., & Scholl, R. (1999). Work motivation: The incorporation of self-concept-based processes. *Human Relations, 52*(8), 969-997

Lesnick-Oberstein, M. & Cohen, L. (1984) Cognitive style, sensation seeking and assortative mating. J. of Personality and Social Psychology, 46(1), 112-117.

LeVay, S. (1995). *Queer Science: The Use and Abuse of Research into Homosexuality*. Cambridge, MA: The MIT Press.

Leviathan Chapter IV: "The Greeks have but one word, logos, for both speech and reason; not that they thought there was no speech without reason, but no reasoning without speech"

Lewis, Charlton; Short, Charles, "ratio", A Latin Dictionary

Liddell, Henry George, "logos", *A Greek-English Lexicon*. For etymology of English "logic" see any dictionary such as the Merriam Webster entry for logic.

Lienard, P.; Boyer, P. (2006). "Whence collective rituals? A cultural selection model of ritualized behavior". *American Anthropologist* (108): 824–827.

Locke, John (1824) [1689], "XVII Of Reason", The Works of John Locke in Nine Volumes, 2 (12th ed.), Rivington

Locke, John (1824) [1689], "XVIII Of Faith and Reason, and their distinct Provinces.", The Works of John Locke in Nine Volumes, 2 (12th ed.), Rivington

Locke, John (1824) [1689], "XXVII On Identity and Diversity", The Works of John Locke in Nine Volumes, An Essay Concerning Human Understanding (12th ed.), Rivington

Lonner, W.J. (2000). On the Growth and Continuing Importance of Cross-Cultural Psychology. Eye on Psi Chi, 4(3), 22-26.

Lumsden C., and E. Wilson. 1981. *Genes, Mind and Culture: The Coevolutionary Process*. Cambridge, MA: Harvard University Press.

Mandler, G. (2007). A history of modern experimental psychology: From James and Wundt to cognitive science. Cambridge, MA: MIT Press.

Markus, H.R.; Kitayama, S. (1991). "Culture and the self: Implications for cognition, emotion, and motivation". *Psychological Review* **98**: 224–253. doi:10.1037/0033-295X.98.2.224.

Markus, H.R.; Kitayama, S. (2003). "Culture, Self, and the Reality of the Social". *Psychological Inquiry* **14**: 277–283.doi:10.1207/S15327965PLI1403&4_17.

Martin, G., & Pear, J. (2003). *Behavior modification: What it is and how to do it.* Upper Saddle River, NJ: Prentice Hall.

Maslow, A. (1943). A theory of human motivation. Psychological Review, 50, 370-396. Retrieved June 2001, fromhttp://psychclassics.yorku.ca/Maslow/motivation.htm

Maslow, A. (1954). *Motivation and personality*. New York: Harper.

Maslow, A. (1971). *The farther reaches of human nature*. New York: The Viking Press.

Maslow, A., & Lowery, R. (Ed.). (1998). *Toward a psychology of being* (3rd ed.). New York: Wiley & Sons.

Masters, W. H., & Johnson, V. E. (1966). *Human Sexual Response*. Boston: Little, Brown.

Masuda, T.; Nisbett, R.A. (2001). "Attending holistically versus analytically: Comparing the context sensitivity of Japanese and Americans". *Journal of Personality and Social Psychology* **81** (5): 922–934. doi:10.1037/0022-3514.81.5.922.

Mathes, E. (1981, Fall). Maslow's hierarchy of needs as a guide for living. *Journal of Humanistic Psychology, 21*, 69-72.

Matsumoto, D. R. (2000). *Culture and psychology (2nd ed.)*. Pacific Grove, CA: Brooks/Cole.

McClelland, D. (1985). *Human motivation*. New York: Scott, Foresman.

McGuire, F. (1994). Army alpha and beta tests of intelligence. In R. J. Sternberg (Ed.), *Encyclopedia of intelligence*. New York: Macmillan.

Merriam Webster "rational" and Merriam Webster "reasonable".

Merriam-Webster.com   Merriam-Webster Dictionary definition of reason

Michael Sandel, *Justice: What's the Right Thing to Do?*, New York: Farrar, Straus and Giroux, 2009.

Michel Foucault, "What is Enlightenment?" in The Essential Foucault, eds. Paul Rabinow and Nikolas Rose, New York: The New Press, 2003, 43-57. See also Nikolas Kompridis, "The Idea of a New Beginning: A Romantic Source of Normativity and Freedom," in Philosophical Romanticism, New York: Routledge, 2006, 32-59; "So We Need Something Else for Reason to Mean?", International Journal of Philosophical Studies 8: 3, 271 — 295.

Michel Foucault, "What is Enlightenment?", *The Essential Foucault*, New York: The New Press, 2003, 43-57.

Michie, S.; & Abraham, C. (Eds.). (2004). *Health psychology in practice.* London. BPS Blackwells.

Milgram, Stanley (1963). "Behavioral Study of Obedience".*Journal of Abnormal and Social Psychology* **67**: 371–378.doi:10.1037/h0040525. PMID 14049516. Full-text PDF.

Milgram, Stanley. (1974), Obedience to Authority; An Experimental View. Harpercollins (ISBN 0-06-131983-X).

Mimesis in modern academic writing, starting with Erich Auerbach, is a technical word, which is not necessarily exactly the same in meaning as the original Greek. See Mimesis.

Moore BE, Fine BD (1968), A Glossary of Psychoanalytic Terms and Concepts, Amer Psychoanalytic Assn, p. 78, ISBN 978-0-318-13125-2

Moore, Edward, "Plotinus", Internet Encyclopedia of Philosophy.

Murray, H. (1938, 1943). *Explorations in personality.* New York: Oxford University Press.

Myers (2004). Motivation and work. *Psychology.* New York, NY: Worth Publishers

National Association of School Psychologists. "Who are school psychologists?". Retrieved June 1, 2008.

Nesse, R., & Williams, G. (1996) Why we get sick. NY: Vintage.

Nesse, R.M. (2000). Tingergen's Four Questions Organized.Read online.

Neuberg, S. L., Kenrick, D. T., & Schaller, M. (2010). Evolutionary social psychology. In S. T. Fiske, D. T. Gilbert, & G. Lindzey (Eds.), Handbook of social psychology (5th Edition, Vol. 2, pp. 761-796). New York: John Wiley & Sons.

Neuringer, A.: "Melioration and Self-Experimentation" Journal of the Experimental Analysis of Board in 1966, and in 1974 ad

Nicomachean Ethics Book 1.

Nikolas Kompridis, Critique and Disclosure: Critical Theory between Past and Future, Cambridge, MA: MIT Press, 2006. See also Nikolas Kompridis, "So We Need Something Else for Reason to Mean", International Journal of Philosophical Studies 8:3, 271-295.

Nisbett, R.E. (2003). The Geography of Thought. New York: Free Press.

Nisbett, R.E.; & Cohen, D. (1996). Culture of Honor: The Psychology of Violence in the South. Denver, CO: Westview Press.

Nisbett, R.E.; Peng, K.; Choi, I.; Norenzayan, A. (2001). "Culture and systems of thought: Holistic vs. analytic cognition".*Psychological Review* **108** (2): 291–310. doi:10.1037/0033-295X.108.2.291. PMID 11381831.

Nohria, N., Lawrence, P., & Wilson, E. (2001). *Driven: How human nature shapes our choices.* San Francisco: Jossey-Bass.

Nonaka, Ikujiro & Takeuchi, Hirotaka (1995). The Knowledge Creating Company. New York: Oxford University Press.

Norwood, G. (1999). Maslow's hierarchy of needs. The Truth Vectors (Part I). Retrieved May 2002, from http://www.deepermind.com/20maslow.htm

O'Donohue, W., Plaud, J. J. (1994). The conditioning of human sexual arousal. *Archives of Sexual Behavior*, 23(3):321-344.

Ogden, J. (2007). *Health psychology: A textbook* (4th ed.). Berkshire, England: Open University Press.

Onslow, M., Costa, L., Andrews, C., Harrison, E. and Packman (1996) 'Speech outcomes of a prolonged-speech treatment for stuttering' *Journal of Speech and Hearing Research* 39, 734-749.

Onslow, M., Menzies, R.G. and Packman, A. (2001) 'An operant intervention for early stuttering: the development of the Lidcombe Program' *Behavior Modification* 25, 1, 116-139.

Origins of the Modern Mind p.169

Origins of the Modern Mind p.172

Overmier, J.B. and Seligman, M.E.P. (1967). Effects of inescapable shock upon subsequent escape and avoidance responding. Journal of Comparative and Physiological Psychology, 63, 28–33.

Overskeid, G. (2007). "Looking for Skinner and finding Freud". *American Psychologist 62*(6), 590-595.

Packman, A., Onslow, M. and van Doorn, J. (1994) 'Prolonged speech and modification of stuttering: perceptual, acoustic, and electroglottographic data' *Journal of Speech and Hearing Research* 37, 724-737.

Palace, E. M., Gorzalka, B. B. (1992). Differential patterns of arousal in sexually functional and dysfunctional women: Physiological and subjective components of sexual response. *Archives of Sexual Behavior*, 21(2):135-159.

Palmer S, Woolfe R (eds.) (1999). *Integrative and eclectic counselling and psychotherapy.* London: Sage.

Panksepp, J. (1998). *Affective neuroscience: The foundations of human and animal emotions.* New York and Oxford: Oxford University Press.

Payne, R. (2005). *Relaxation Techniques – A Practical Handbook for the Health Care Professional (3rd ed.).* New York: Churchill Livingstone.

Peng, K.; Nisbett, R.E.; Wong, N. (1997). "Validity problems of cross-cultural value comparison and possible solutions".*Psychological Methods* **2**: 329–341. doi:10.1037/1082-989X.2.4.329.

Peters, Frederic "Consciousness as Recursive, Spatiotemporal Self-Location"

Peterson C (2009, 23 May). "Subjective and objective research in positive psychology: A biological characteristic is linked to well-being". Psychology Today. Retrieved 20 April 2010.

Peterson, C., & Seligman, M. (2004). *Character strengths and virtues: A handbook and classification.* Oxford and New York: Oxford University Press and American Psychological Association.

Piethish, Paul. Splitting the Human Brain. Introduction to the split-brain phenomenon.

Pinel, J. P. J. (2007). Basics of biopsychology. Boston, MA: Allyn and Bacon.

Pinel, John (2010). *Biopsychology*. New York: Prentice Hall.ISBN 0-205-83256-3.

Pink, D. (2009). *Drive: The surprising truth about what motivates us.* New York: Riverhead Books.

Pinker, S. (2003). The blank slate. NY: Penguin

Pinker, S.; Bloom, P. (1990). "Natural language and natural selection". *Behavioral and Brain Sciences* **13** (4): 713–733.

Pintrich, P. (2000). An achievement goal theory perspective on issues in motivation terminology, theory, and research. Contemporary Educational Psychology, 25, 92-104. Retrieved February 2004, fromhttp://www.unco.edu/cebs/psychology/kevinpugh/motivation_project/resources/pintrich00.pdf

Plattner, Marc (1997), "Rousseau and the Origins of Nationalism", *The Legacy of Rousseau*, University of Chicago Press

Plotkin, Henry. 2004 Evolutionary thought in Psychology: A Brief History. Blackwell. p.149.

Plotkin, Henry. 2004 Evolutionary thought in Psychology: A Brief History. Blackwell. p.150.

Pohl, M. (2000). Learning to Think, Thinking to Learn: Models and Strategies to Develop a Classroom Culture of Thinking. Cheltenham, Vic.: Hawker Brownlow.

Prentice Hall.

Proctor, C. (1984, March). Teacher expectations: A model for school improvement. *The Elementary School Journal*, 469-481.

Progress or Return" in An Introduction to Political Philosophy: Ten Essays by Leo Strauss. (Expanded version of Political Philosophy: Six Essays by Leo Strauss, 1975.) Ed. Hilail Gilden. Detroit: Wayne State UP, 1989.

Quick, J.C.; & Tetrick, L.E. (Eds.). (2003). *Handbook of occupational health psychology.* Washington, DC: American Psychological Association.

RCSLT (2005) *Clinical Guidelines* (Royal College of Speech and Language Therapists) Bicester: Speechmark Publishing Ltd.

RCSLT (2005) *Clinical Guidelines* (Royal College of Speech and Language Therapists) Bicester: Speechmark Publishing Ltd.

Reisner, Andrew. (2005). The common factors, empirically validated treatments, and recovery models of therapeutic change. *The Psychological Record, 55(3),* 377–400.

Reschly, D. & Wilson, M. (1995). School psychology practitioners and faculty: 1986 to 1991-92 trends in demographics, roles, satisfaction, and system reform. *School Psychology Review*, 24(1), 62-80.

Reviewed by: Harvey Simon, MD, Editor-in-Chief, Associate Professor of Medicine, Harvard Medical School; Physician, Massachusetts General Hospital. Also reviewed by David Zieve, MD, MHA, Medical Director, A.D.A.M., Inc

Reviewed last on: 2/13/2009

Richard Frankel, Timothy Quill, Susan McDaniel (2003). *The Biopsychosocial Approach: Past, Present, Future.* Boydell & Brewer. ISBN 1580461026, 9781580461023.

Roleff, Tamara L. Genetics and Intelligence. San Diego, CA: Greenhaven Press, Inc, 1996

Ron Sun, (2008). The Cambridge Handbook of Computational Psychology. Cambridge University Press, New York. 2008.

Rose, S. (2001). "Revisiting evolutionary psychology and psychiatry". *The British Journal of Psychiatry* **179**: 558.

Ruth M.J. Byrne (2005). The Rational Imagination: How People Create Counterfactual Alternatives to Reality. Cambridge, MA: MIT Press.

Ryan, R., & Deci, E. (2000). Self-determination theory and the facilitation of intrinsic motivation, social development, and well-being.*American Psychologist,* 55(1), 68-78.

Sacks, O. (1984). *A leg to stand on.* New York: Summit Books/Simon and Schuster.

Santrock, W. John (2005). A Topical Approach to Life-Span Development (3rd ed.). New York, NY: McGraw-Hill. pp.62.

Schacter et al. 2007, pp. 26-27

Schlinger, H.D. (2008). *The long good-bye: why B.F. Skinner's Verbal Behavior is alive and well on the 50th anniversary of its publication.*

Schmitt, D. P.; Buss, D. M. (2001). "Human mate poaching: Tactics and temptations for infiltrating existing relationships" (PDF). *Journal of Personality and Social Psychology* **80** (6): 894–917. doi:10.1037/0022-3514.80.6.894. PMID 11414373.

Schulz KF, Altman DG, Moher D; for the CONSORT Group (2010). "CONSORT 2010 Statement: updated guidelines for reporting parallel group randomised trials". *BMJ* **340**: c332.doi:10.1136/bmj. c332. PMC 2844940. PMID 20332509.

Schumaker, J. The Age of Insanity: Modernity and Mental Health. Praeger. 2001. Chapter 3, p 29-49.

See this Perseus search, and compare English translations. and see LSJ dictionary entry for ⬚⬚⬚⬚⬚, section II.2.b.

Seligman MEP (1995). The effectiveness of psychotherapy: The *Consumer Reports* study. *American Psychologist, 50*(12), pp. 965–974.

Seligman, D. (2002). Good breeding. *National Review*, 54(1), 53-54.

Seligman, M. (2011). *Flourish: A visionary new understanding of happiness and well-being.* New York: Free Press.

Seligman, M.E.P. (2002). *Authentic happiness: Using the new positive psychology to realize your potential for lasting fulfillment.* New York: Free Press.

Seligman, M.E.P. and Maier, S.F. (1967). Failure to escape traumatic shock. Journal of Experimental Psychology, 74, 1–9.

Selye, H. (1974). *Stress without distress.* Philadelphia: J. B. Lippincott Co.

Sewell, W.H. (1989). Some reflections on the golden age of interdisciplinary social psychology. *Annual Review of Sociology*, Vol. 15.

Sherwin, B. B., & Gelfand, M. M. (1987). The role of androgen in the maintenance of sexual functioning in oophorectomized women. *Psychosomatic Medicine*, 49:397-409.

Sherwin, B. B., Gelfand, M. M., & Brender, W. (1985). Androgen enhances sexual motivation in females: A prospective crossover study of sex steroid administration in the surgical menopause. *Psychosomatic Medicine*, 47:339-351.

Sherwin, C.M., Christionsen, S.B., Duncan, I.J., Erhard, H.W., Lay Jr., D.C., Mench, J.A., O'Connor, C.E., & Petherick, J.C. (2003). Guidelines for the Ethical use of animals in the applied ethology studies. Applied animal Behaviour science, 81, 291–205.

Shore, B. (1996). *Culture in mind: Cognition, culture and the problem of meaning*. New York: Oxford University Press.

Shweder, R.A.; & Levine, R.A. (Eds., 1984). *Culture theory: Essays on mind, self, and emotion*. New York: Cambridge University Press.

Shweder, Richard (1991). *Thinking Through Cultures*. Harvard University Press. ISBN 0674884159.

Siegler, R. S. (1992). The other Alfred Binet. *Developmental Psychology, 28*, 179-190.

Siegler, R. S. (1992). The other Alfred Binet. *Developmental Psychology, 28*, 179-190.

Simonton, D. K. (2003). Francis Galton's Hereditary Genius: Its place in the history and psychology of Science. In R. J. Sternberg (Ed.), *The anatomy of impact: What makes the great works of psychology great* (pp. 3-18). American Psychological Association: Washington, D.C.

Simpson E. J. (1972). *The Classification of Educational Objectives in the Psychomotor Domain*. Washington, DC: Gryphon House.

Skinner, B.F. (1974). About Behaviorism. New York: Random House

Sleep and Language, from Washington University's Dept. of Anatomy and Neurobiology

Smith, P. B., Bond, M. H., & Kağıtçıbaşi, Ç. (2006). *Understanding social psychology across cultures: Living and working in a changing world (3rd rev. ed.)*. London, UK: Sage.

social behaviour, animal." Encyclopædia Britannica. Encyclopædia Britannica Online. Encyclopædia Britannica, 2011. Web. 23 Jan. 2011. [3].

Sokejima, S. & Kagamimori, S. (1998) Working hours as a risk for acute myocardial infarction in Japan: Case control study. British Medical Journal, 317, 775-780.

Solms, M., & Turnbull, O. (2002). *The brain and the inner world: An introduction to the neuroscience of subjective experience*. New York: Other Press.

Soper, B., Milford, G., & Rosenthal, G. (1995). Belief when evidence does not support theory. *Psychology & Marketing, 12*(5), 415-422.

Sosis, R.; Alcorta, C. (2003). "Signaling, solidarity, and the sacred: the evolution of religious behavior". *Evolutionary Anthropology* (12): 264–274.

Stanford Encyclopedia of Philosophy. (2006). "Wilhelm Maximilian Wundt".

Sterling, Theodore D. (March 1959). "Publication decisions and their possible effects on inferences drawn from tests of significance—or vice versa.". Journal of the American Statistical Association, Vol 54: 30-34. Retrieved 10 April 2011.

Steven Blankaart, p. 13 as quoted in "psychology n." A Dictionary of Psychology. Edited by Andrew M. Colman. Oxford University Press 2009. Oxford Reference Online. Oxford University Press. oxfordreference.com

Stipek, D. (1988). *Motivation to learn: From theory to practice*. Englewood Cliffs, NJ:

Stone, Arthur A. et al. (1987) Evidence that secretory IgA antibody is associated with daily mood. Journal of Personality and Social Psychology 52, no. 5, pp. 988-993.

Stone, Sherry (August 5, 1994). "Black psychologists here for annual conference". Philadelphia Tribune. Retrieved 2008-06-15.

Stress and Coping

Sullivan, H. S. (1968). *The interpersonal theory of psychiatry*. New York: W. W. Norton & Company.

Symons, Donald (1992). "On the use and misuse of Darwinism in the study of human behavior". *The Adapted Mind: Evolutionary psychology and the generation of culture*. Oxford University Press. pp. 137–159. ISBN 0195101073.

T.S. Kuhn, *The Structure of Scientific Revolutions*, 1st. ed., Chicago: Univ. of Chicago Pr., 1962.

Taylor, S.E. (1990). Health psychology. *American Psychologist*, 45, 40–50.

Terrence Deacon, The Symbolic Species: The Co-Evolution of Language and the Brain, W.W. Norton & Company, 1998,ISBN 0-393-31754-4

Testing ideas about the evolutionary origins of psychological phenomena is indeed a challenging task, but not an impossible one" Buss et al. 1998; Pinker, 1997b).

The American Psychological Society: Responsible Conduct of Research

The Principles of Psychology (1890), with introduction by George A. Miller, Harvard University Press, 1983 paperback,ISBN 0-674-70625-0 (combined edition, 1328 pages)

The Wada Test. A description.

Thompson, M., Grace, C., & Cohen, L. (2001). *Best friends, worst enemies: Understanding the social lives of children.* New York: Ballantine Books.

Thompson, T., Davidson, J. A., & Barber, J. G. (1995). Self-worth protection in achievement motivation: Performance effects and attributional behavior. *Journal of Educational Psychology, 87,* 598-610.

Tiefer, L. (1995). *Sex Is Not A Natural Aact and Other Essays.* Boulder, CO: Westview Press.

Tooby & Cosmides 2005, p. 5

Treatise of Human Nature of David Hume, Book I, Part III, Sect. XVI.

Triandis, H.C. (1989). "The self and social behavior in differing cultural contexts". *Psychological Review* **96**: 506–520.doi:10.1037/0033-295X.96.3.506.

Trivers, R. (1972). Parental investment and sexual selection. In B. Campbell (Ed.), *Sexual Selection and the Descent of Man.* Chicago: Aldine-Atherton.

Trivers, R. L. (1971). "The Evolution of Reciprocal Altruism".*The Quarterly Review of Biology* **46** (1): 35–57.doi:10.1086/406755. JSTOR 2822435.

Trivers, R. L. (1971). "The Evolution of Reciprocal Altruism".*The Quarterly Review of Biology* **46** (1): 35–57.doi:10.1086/406755. JSTOR 2822435.

Urdan, T., & Maehr, M. (1995). Beyond a two-goal theory of motivation and achievement: A case for social goals. *Review of Educational Research, 65*(3), 213-243.

V.E. Stone, L. Nisenson and M.S. Gazzaniga. Processing of emotional information in the Two Cerebral Hemispheres. An abstract from Gazzaniga's lab at UC Davis.

Velkley, Richard (2002), "On Kant's Socratism", Being After Rousseau, University of Chicago Press and

Kant's own first preface to The Critique of Pure Reason.

Vroom, V. (1964). *Work and motivation.* New York: Wiley.

W. Tecumseh Fitch (2010) The Evolution of Language. Cambridge University Press p.65-66

Wade, C. & Tavris, C. (1996). *Psychology,* 4th ed. New York: Harper Collins College Publishers.

Wahba, A., & Bridgewell, L. (1976). Maslow reconsidered: A review of research on the need hierarchy theory. *Organizational Behavior and Human Performance, 15,* 212-240.

Waitley, D. (1996). *The new dynamics of goal setting: Flextactics for a fast-changing world.* New York: William Morrow.

Walster, E., Aronson., V., Abrahams, D., & Rottman, L. (1966). Importance of physical attractiveness in dating behavior. *Journal of Personality and Social Psychology,* 5:508-516.

Walter Cannon (2008). Retrieved from http://en.wikipedia.org/wiki/Walter_Bradford_Cannon on 21 July, 2008.

Wang J. Work stress as a risk factor for major depressive episode(s). *Psychol Med.* 2005;35:865-871.

Weinberg, M. S., Lottes, I. L., & Shaver, F. M. (1995). Swedish or American heterosexual college youth: Who is more permissive? *Archives of Sexual Behavior,* 24(4):409-437.

Weiner, B. (1974). *Achievement motivation and attribution theory.* Morristown, NJ: General Learning Press.

Wellings, K., Field, J., Johnson, A. M., & Wadsworth, J. (1994). *Sexual Behavior in Britain: The National Survey of Sexual Attitudes and Lifestyles.* London: Penguin Books.

White, G. (1980). Physical attractiveness and courtship progress. *Journal of Personality and Social Psychology,* 39:660-668.

White, S. (2000). Conceptual foundations of IQ testing. *Psychology, Public Policy, and Law,* 6(1), 33-43.

Wood, S. E., & Wood, E. G. (1996). *The World of Psychology,* 2nd ed. MA: Allyn and Bacon.

Workman & Reader 2008:277 "There are a number of hypotheses suggesting that language evolved to fulfil a social function such as social grooming (to bind large groups together), the making of social contracts (to enable monogamy and male provisioning) and the use of language to impress potential mates. While each of these hypotheses has its merits, each is still highly speculative and requires more evidence from different areas of research (such as linguistics and anthropology)."

Workman, Lance and Will Reader (2004) Evolutionary psychology: an introduction. Cambridge University Press p. 259

Workman, Lance and Will Reader (2004) Evolutionary psychology: an introduction. Cambridge University Press p. 267

Workman, Lance and Will Reader (2004) Evolutionary psychology: an introduction. Cambridge University Press p. 277

Workman, Lance and Will Reader (2008). Evolutionary psychology: an introduction. 2nd Ed. Cambridge University Press. Chapter 10.

www.4therapy.com/consumer/assessment/taketest.php -- Assess stress levels

www.4therapy.com/consumer/assessment/taketest. php?&uniqueid=19& -- Find a therapist

www.aabt.org -- Association for the Advancement of Behavior Therapy

www.aabt.org -- Association for the Advancement of Behavior Therapy (800-685-AABT)

www.aacap.org -- American Academy of Child and Adolescent Psychiatry

www.aacap.org -- American Academy of Child and Adolescent Psychiatry

www.amtamassage.org -- American Massage Therapy Association

www.amtamassage.org -- American Massage Therapy Association

www.apna.org -- The American Psychiatric Nurses Association

www.cmhc.com -- Mental Health Net (800-528-9025)

www.cognitivetherapynyc.com -- American Institute for Cognitive Therapy

www.cognitivetherapynyc.com -- American Institute for Cognitive Therapy

www.fda.gov

www.healthyminds.org -- The American Psychiatric Association

www.http://allpsych.com/biographies/index. html)

www.meditationcenter.com -- Meditation techniques

www.mentalhealth.com -- Encyclopedia of mental health information

www.nami.org -- National Alliance for the Mentally Ill

www.nami.org -- National Alliance for the Mentally Ill (800-950-6264)

www.naswdc.org -- The National Association of Social Workers

www.naswdc.org -- The National Association of Social Workers

www.nimh.nih.gov -- National Institute of Mental Health

www.nimh.nih.gov -- National Institute of Mental Health

www.nmha.org -- National Mental Health Association

www.nmha.org -- National Mental Health Association

www.psych.org -- The American Psychiatric Association (888-357-7924)

www.psychologicalscience.org -- The American Psychological Society

www.stress.org -- The American Institute of Stress

www.tm.org -- Transcendental Meditation (888-532-7686)

www.wildmind.org -- Meditation techniques

Yerkes, R., & Dodson, J. (1908). The relation of strength of stimulus to rapidity of habit-formation. *Journal of Comparative Neurology and Psychology, 18,* 459-482.

Zellman, G. & Goodchilds, J. (1983). Becoming sexual in adolescence. *In*: E. R. Allgeier & N. B. McCormick, eds., *Changing Boundaries: Gender Roles and Sexual Behaviors.* Palo Alto, CA: Mayfield.

Zuckerman, M. (1979) 'Sensation-seeking: Beyond the optimal level of arousal' Hillside, NJ: Erlbaum

CPSIA information can be obtained
at www.ICGtesting.com
Printed in the USA
LVHW10s2150310818
588410LV00020B/26/P

9 781609 275099